Is Superman
Circumcised?

Is Superman Circumcised?

The Complete Jewish History of the World's Greatest Hero

Roy Schwartz

McFarland & Company, Inc., Publishers
Jefferson, North Carolina

LIBRARY OF CONGRESS CATALOGUING-IN-PUBLICATION DATA

Names: Schwartz, Roy, 1980– author.
Title: Is Superman circumcised? : the complete Jewish history of the
world's greatest hero / Roy Schwartz.
Description: Jefferson, North Carolina : McFarland & Company, Inc.,
Publishers, 2021 | Includes bibliographical references and index.
Identifiers: LCCN 2021018193 | ISBN 9781476662909 (paperback : acid free paper) ∞
ISBN 9781476644417 (ebook)
Subjects: LCSH: Superman (Fictitious character) | Jews in literature. |
Comic books, strips, etc.—United States. | Literature and
society—United States. | BISAC: LITERARY CRITICISM / Comics & Graphic
Novels | SOCIAL SCIENCE / Jewish Studies
Classification: LCC PN6728.S9 S45 2019 | DDC 741.5/973—dc23
LC record available at https://lccn.loc.gov/2021018193

BRITISH LIBRARY CATALOGUING DATA ARE AVAILABLE

ISBN (print) 978-1-4766-6290-9
ISBN (ebook) 978-1-4766-4441-7

Front cover image © 2021 Shutterstock

Printed in the United States of America

McFarland & Company, Inc., Publishers
Box 611, Jefferson, North Carolina 28640
www.mcfarlandpub.com

To Kim,
As a kid I'd ask myself "what would Superman do?"
As an adult I ask myself "what would Kim do?"
You're my hero.

Table of Contents

Acknowledgments

First and foremost, my gratitude and love to my family; my wise and supportive wife Kim, without whom this book would have been a lot less coherent, and my son Ethan and daughter Iris, without whom it would have been finished a lot sooner.

My thanks to Rabbi Yoni Greenwald, a gentleman and a scholar, who helped ensure the book is accurate not just historically and academically but also theologically.

Many thanks to the New York Public Library and the writer-in-residence program, particularly Research Study Liaison Melanie Locay and Research Coordinator Rebecca Federman. Special thanks to Eleanor Yadin from the NYPL Dorot Jewish Division, who spent hours helping me track down elusive sources. And to Karen Green, Curator for Comics and Cartoons for the Columbia University Libraries, for guiding me to rare treasures.

My heartfelt appreciation to Christopher Cappelluti and Tim Duffy, who read drafts of this book with care and intelligence and helped me alchemize manure into potpourri, and to my editor Charlie Perdue.

Thank you also to David Giovanella and Suzanne Collado from the NYU Graduate School of Arts and Science, who helped me realize that if you don't make it entertaining, it doesn't really matter what it is that you're saying.

I'd like to thank Chuck Rozanski from Mile High Comics, a real-life hero; Jerry Siegel and Joe Shuster, who refused to give up on their dream and changed the world; and all the writers, artists and editors that followed whose work has given me joy and inspiration. My sincerest apologies for any names or contributions left out from this book.

Finally, my thank-you to Richard Donner, Tom Mankiewicz and Christopher Reeve, for igniting my love of Superman, providing me with a lifelong role model and making me comfortable saying "swell."

Preface

In a manner, I started writing this book when I was in grade school. I spent the formative years of my education filling out school notebooks in nearly every class with stories and comics and what I would later come to realize were essays. They'd feature my favorite fictional characters—typically superheroes, usually Superman or Captain America—fighting the good fight against ne'er-do-wells like aliens, Nazis, terrorists and, when they'd reach the Boss Level, some variation of my ogreish home-room teacher, Mrs. Yaakobi.

But I was interested in more than just the action and spectacle of it. My heroes' speech balloons and my narrator captions were often large, taking up half the page, filled with deliberations on all kinds of things. For example, neither Superman nor Cap cared much for Rambo and Robocop's eagerness to kill their enemies (it was the '80s, so children's cartoons and toys were naturally based on R-rated movies), and whenever they'd team up to battle villains they'd also debate the use of violence, sanctity of life, and subjectivity of good and evil. As far as I remember no consensus was ever reached, though they all made some good points. Of course, to my teachers all this was just silly doodling I was wasting my time on when I should been paying attention. But I knew better.

I started reading and collecting comic books around the age of nine. I knew of them earlier, mainly through the superhero genre I loved so much on TV and in movies, but as an Israeli, born and raised in Tel Aviv, my English wasn't good enough until then to read them (comics are actually how I learned English, which is why I'm comfortable using words like "swell"). As I delved deeper into comics over the course of my tweens and teens I found that, contrary to popular misconception, they were far from fatuous. The cartoons based on them may have been aimed at young children, and campy movie maladaptations didn't help, but the comics themselves were often sophisticated, pithy, avant-garde and sometimes filled with gravitas. Like the rest of my generation I was an avid consumer of all things pop culture, but my parents also instilled in me a love of fine arts and literature. In comics I found the perfect mix of both.

My interests hadn't changed much by the time I moved to New York to attend college. I spent most of my time as an English major trying to convince my professors that *Uncanny X-Men* had no less depth and was worthy of the same critical examination as *Pride and Prejudice*. My freshman essay was titled "Worlds' Finest: Superman and Batman as Didactic Utopian and Dystopian Figures." My sophomore essay was

"Absolute Power: Ethics and Geopolitics in the *Squadron Supreme* Graphic Novel." In junior year I wrote "Starship Storm Troopers: Themes of Propaganda and Indoctrination in Paul Verhoeven's *Starship Troopers*." And my senior paper was "Identity Crisis: Superman as a Christ Figure." It was this last paper in particular that helped me make a case for academic inquiry into sequential art and that started the line of thinking which culminated in this book.

From grade school to grad school, whatever else held my interest, I kept reading and writing about comics. But while bachelor studies at the freethinking New School University might have accommodated my flights of fancy, the level of academic rigor expected at an NYU master's program was a different story. I had to demonstrate, convincingly, scholarly merit in the examination of the works of Siegel and Shuster, Kane and Finger, Eisner, Lee, Kirby and others.

Superman, as the paradigm for all superheroes, was the logical place to start. I also felt a special kinship with the character. I too was an immigrant, and shared his alienation, loneliness and sense of mission. As luck would have it, around then books about comic books started becoming popular, including several discussing the Jewish background of early creators. It then struck me, like a lightning bolt striking a forensic scientist—Superman isn't a Christ figure at all. He's Jewish!

It was like I had found the decryption key to a nearly century-old secret code. His colorful mythology suddenly revealed obvious threads of Jewish culture and folklore, tracing all the way back to the Bible. And with this revelation came validation and vindication of my crusade. Comics, including superheroes, have much more to them than meets the eye, and it is perfectly within the purview of academia to study them.

My graduate thesis was titled "Is Superman Circumcised? The Jewish Heroic Figure from the Bible to Comics." To my knowledge it's the first grad thesis ever written on this particular subject, and a satisfying culmination of my academic career to that point. What I didn't expect in the least is that it would also win second place in the NYU annual thesis competition. I was even more surprised when it lead to articles and interviews in the press and, after additional research (a lot of it), this book.

Ever since my silly doodling in grade school I've simply been writing about what I love. It's both humbling and uplifting that it's something others want to read. It's really super.

Introduction

Superman is the most famous man in the world.

There's no real way to prove this, of course, but the Man of Steel's image—the muscular body wrapped in skintight primary colors, a cape billowing behind him and a large *S* splayed across his chest—is universally recognized. More than that; it's recognized as iconic. People who've never read an issue of *Action Comics*, or seen *Superman: The Movie*, or have ever given him a second thought, still wear his T-shirts, evoke him in everyday speech ("what am I, Superman?") and tattoo his symbol on their arm. He can be found in every book, clothing, toy and magazine store, every costume party, on the nightly news when a barefoot child in a dusty village somewhere is wearing a Superman T-shirt. From the very young to the very old, from Australia to Algeria to Alaska, it's a pretty safe bet that almost everyone knows Superman.

And yet, surprisingly, the septuagenarian superhero (he turned 80 in 2018, though he doesn't look a day over 30) hasn't been the subject of much academic inquiry. Most notable is "The Myth of Superman,"[1] a little-known essay by the well-known writer, linguist and philosopher Umberto Eco, first published in Italian in 1962 and translated into English a decade later, but its obscurity and datedness speak to the relative lack of scholarly interest in truly exploring the modern mythology of Superman.

In recent years, however, a growing body of work has been dedicated to examining the character, part of a larger trend of serious interest in the comic book medium and the superhero genre. Some of these writings serve as sources for this book to quote from, respond to, expand upon or argue with, sometimes all of the above.

Superman's cultural presence is ubiquitous and his mythology is rich and intricate. There are endless possible approaches to examining him, from the signification of his costume (why spandex? why the trunks?) to the ethical dilemmas that come with his powers (does he have a responsibility to topple dictators? does he have the right?) to the socioeconomics of his debut medium (why a comic magazine? why not a radio program or movie serial?). This book touches upon some of these as they relate to its central thesis—that Superman is a Jewish character.

That's right. Superman, the Man of Steel, the symbol of Americana, is Jewish. And it's not some newly concocted, superimposed meaning. He's secretly been a Member of the Tribe since the very beginning. Christianity has also claimed him as its own, seeing as there are strong Christ parallels, and there's a good argument to be made for shared custody. But when his mythology is examined more closely, what can be found are deeper themes of Jewish theology, folklore, culture and history.

The question is how to glean it. How can critical analysis be applied to a comic book? Even if the ideas behind a comic like Superman are laden with meaning, how much of that can be expressed in the real estate of a few panels and word balloons?

Even today, after decades of growth and maturation, the medium seldom offers extensive, nuanced exploration of complex ideas. Like cinema, it mostly consists of violence, humor and melodrama. But comic books greatly differ from movies in that, while visual in nature, they aren't a principally explicit medium. Whereas a film has 24 frames per second in which to tell its story, a traditional comic book only has a small number of frames, or panels, per page, usually between five and nine, across a total of 22 pages. Comparatively, a comic book is equivalent to about six seconds of film. But obviously, any comic contains more narrative than the time it takes to read this sentence. So where, then, does the content "hide"?

In *Comics and Sequential Art* (named so based on the premise that the defining characteristic of the art form is its visual progression through time), widely regarded as the authoritative text on the subject, legendary writer-artist Will Eisner explains that comic panels are "part of the creative process, rather than the result of the technology ... the framing of a series of images moving through space undertakes the containment of thought, ideas, actions and location or site. The panel thereby attempts to deal with the broadest elements ... cognitive and perceptive ... [and] must take into consideration both the commonality of human experience and the phenomenon of our perception of it."[2] Unlike a movie frame, which literally frames the narrative, a comic book panel is part of the narrative itself, along with the "gutter"—the space between and around panels. Time, space and action can progress within a panel but it's still a frozen moment, a glimpse, with most of the story taking place off-panel, or off-page, requiring the reader to be an active participant in the storytelling. Whatever meaningfulness comics have, by their very nature it's expressed pithily and largely implicitly.

To examine them, then, requires a Gestalt or deconstructionist approach (deconstruction here meaning unraveling perceived simplicity and naturalness to expose underlying workings, a reverse-engineering from concept to conception), supposing that any and all elements carry meaning, whether deliberately or not. This runs the risk of reading too readily into things, but the body of evidence makes for a convincing case that there's more to superheroes than meets the eye. There's a rich, intricate mythology at play, much of it owing to Jewish tradition with roots extending back to the Bible. And no superhero exemplifies this better than Superman.

By virtue of there being no explicit expression in the prime sources and little historical testimony, much of the argumentation here is conjectural, its evidence circumstantial, its conclusions only plausible—but the primary claim is nonetheless substantiable. When looked at together, the different themes and motifs of Superman's mythology form a clear pattern, rife with Jewish signification and consistent in its allegory.

The comic art form has had a direct and meaningful impact on wider culture. Picasso's creation of Cubism, possibly the greatest artistic revolution since the

Renaissance, was influenced by American comic strips, particularly Rudolph Dirks's *The Katzenjammer Kids*.[3] The pop art masters, including Lichtenstein, Warhol, Hamilton and Ruscha, were inspired by and incorporated in their works elements from comic books. John Updike credited the crispness and animation of his writing to comics, which he aspired to draw professionally before settling for being a writer.[4] The list continues, and so does the medium's effect on how the world is seen and expressed.

Its origins, though, are humble. They can be traced to a specific time, place and group of originators: Comic books are an American invention, as uniquely American as baseball and jazz. More specifically, they're New Yorkers, working- to lower-middle class, and Jewish. Superheroes, for all their grandiosity and flamboyance, were created in the Jewish ghetto of the Lower East Side and the Bronx in the 1930s and '40s by a small group of young Eastern European Jews. The economic hardship of the Great Depression, the rising threat of Antisemitism at home and abroad and the Jewish tradition of storytelling all converged to create comic books, the bastard medium of literature and art, and the superhero genre, the pulp progeny of biblical heroes.

Owing to the immense popularity of superhero movies, the last few years have seen a veritable explosion of interest in all things comics, including the history of the medium and its lore. Works like Danny Fingeroth's *Disguised as Clark Kent: Jews, Comics, and the Creation of the Superhero*, Rabbi Simcha Weinstein's *Up, Up, and Oy Vey: How Jewish History, Culture and Values Shaped the Comic Book Superhero* and Arie Kaplan's *From Krakow to Krypton: Jews and Comic Books* have explored Jews' role and offered new and exciting interpretations to familiar characters and tropes. Their discoveries and insights are the foundation upon which this book makes its own.

What new contribution this book brings is threefold: it examines the entirety of Superman's career, from 1938 to date, whereas others have limited themselves to his formative "Golden Age," ending around 1945, with a few ventures up to 1960. It also explores more deeply the Jewish parallels, including their theological, folkloric, historical and sociological meaning. And it's the first to focus exclusively on Superman.

Superman may have been rocketed to Earth from the distant planet Krypton, but the idea of him wasn't. It was conceived in the inexhaustible imagination of two Jewish teenagers, Jerry Siegel and Joe Shuster, who freely borrowed elements from their cultural environment, including the extensive Jewish tradition of heroic stories about men and women given special abilities to defend the helpless, from biblical to rabbinical.

Their Man of Tomorrow reimagined a mythology as old as civilization, capturing the imagination of America and the world. From Krypton's destruction echoing the biblical flood in Genesis, to his origin as a baby rocketed to safety paralleling that of Moses in Exodus, to the Clark Kent persona as a metaphor for Jewish immigrant assimilation, to Kryptonite symbolizing remnants of the Jewish civilization destroyed in the Holocaust, to his role as a modern golem advocating the New Deal, open immigration and interventionism in World War II, Superman's legend is consistent as Jewish allegory.

The question then is, so what? What does it matter if Superman is a Jewish character? The answer is that the world's most famous hero, possibly the most famous character in fiction, gains a new layer of meaning. He's a projection of his creators' innermost desires, a torchbearer of Jewish tradition, and a conduit of the Jewish community to the wider world. His original comics earn their rightful place in the canon of modern Jewish literature, alongside the works of Philip Roth, Saul Bellow, Primo Levi and Sholem Aleichem. And Superman, known around the world as an American icon, is revealed to actually be a Jewish-American icon.

> *That which has been is that which will be.... So there is nothing new under the sun.*
>
> —Ecclesiastes 1:9

Methodology

Comics

- Text in comic books (dialogue, captions, story titles, etc.) is customarily written in capital letters, which makes for uncomfortable reading in prose. Quotes here have been gently altered to lowercase, with bold and italic—indicating phonetic emphasis in comics—remaining unchanged.
- When citing a comic book, pagination follows the original edition. Since comics are often reprinted in collections with different page numbering, this ensures more accurate citation. Similarly, when a comic containing several stories numbers each separately, page citation refers to the relevant story.
- For creator credits, the following system is used, and is particularly important in the notes: (w)=writer, (p)=penciler, (i)=inker, (c)=colorist. Credits may be imprecise in cases where not listed clearly in the comic.
- Publishing dates reference the official cover date of a comic, customarily distributed one to four months earlier.
- Unless otherwise specified, sales figures refer to print sales in the North American direct market. These account for sales by publishers to stores, not stores to customers, since most orders are nonrefundable (sold later as back issues).

Scripture

- Bible quotes are taken from different versions, chosen based on fidelity of translation to the original Hebrew. Cases in which the Hebrew lends itself to different interpretations are noted.

PART I

Scriptural Superheroes

*The Ancient Roots
of the Man of Tomorrow*

Samson, Solomon and Other Supermen

The first story ever told is a superhero story. *The Epic of Gilgamesh*, the Sumerian cuneiform poem dating back to at least 2000 BCE, is the world's first known work of literature. And it's essentially a superhero story. It tells of Gilgamesh, king of Uruk, who's two-thirds god and one-third man, bestowed with superhuman strength and stamina. The hero embarks on a grand quest to fight evil monsters and other gods, gaining everlasting fame.

Even the superhero convention of the "team-up," in which heroes meet, fight—usually as a result of a misunderstanding or conflict of methods—only to realize they're on the same side and join forces to defeat their true adversary, originates in the clash of Gilgamesh and Enkidu the wild man, who's created by the gods to defeat the hero but instead becomes his partner in adventure.

Humanity's earliest stories, our nascent collective culture, are fantasies so compelling that they inspired a form of perpetual sharing—the written story—and they were about noble champions with powers and abilities far beyond those of mortal men. Pictorial narratives of heroic deeds are even older, dating back to Paleolithic cavemen's paintings of great hunts on cave walls. As human expression evolved from pictographic to phonetic writing, stories, especially of historical or religious significance, came to include image alongside prose. The Bayeux Tapestry, created in the 1070s to chronicle the Norman conquest of England, conveys action through illustration and meaning through accompanying text, making it essentially an embroidered comic strip. The *Haggadah* book of the Passover Seder, created some time around 170 to 360 CE, is an illuminated manuscript combining written prayer and song with drawings of characters and scenes. It's the only Jewish religious text to do so, done, according to tradition, so that all, young and old, learned and unlearned, can understand its important story—the account of the Book of Exodus, the greatest epic of Jewish legend, featuring its greatest hero, Moses, who performed miracles to bring freedom and law to the Israelites.

The appeal behind comic books and superheroes as vehicles of grand narratives isn't new. Superman, despite his standing as archetype, is simply one of the latest, perhaps the best, iteration of a long line of superhuman champions, whose stories trace back through civilization to its very beginning.

Acclaimed comic book writer and historian Mark Waid points out that superheroes, "as literary constructs go ... don't need to be terribly complex; in their primary-colored-costumes, fighting gaudy villains and hyper-dramatic menaces that aren't terribly subtle, they're intended to excite the imaginations of children with the same fire and energy as the myths and fairy tales of years past."[1] Superheroes are modern folklore, and folklore is usually hyperbolic. As Waid notes, they share a commonality with fabular characters like King Arthur, who could just as easily be a superhero: a man of pure heart who fights and inspires in the defense of the commonwealth, often robed in a cape, wielding the magical sword Excalibur that grants him invincibility, aided by other supernaturally powered beings like the wizard Merlin and the Lady of the Lake, fighting against the supervillain witch, Morgan le Fay.

But there's a significant difference between most superhero narratives and classical fairy tales. American fantastical literature in general has been firmly rooted in realism, compared to the European tradition, which owes more to its pagan, supernatural heritage. Folkloric characters like Paul Bunyan, John Henry and Johnny Appleseed, along with mythologized historical figures like Daniel Boone and Davy Crockett, are much more earthbound than England's mystical Arthurian legend and dragons, fairies, goblins and wraiths. (A notable exception is the rich and diverse Native American folklore, which has been largely excluded from the popular American ethos. It's also interesting to note that, except for witches, European folklore has for the most part failed to immigrate to the U.S. along with its respective populations, from the Irish banshee to German elves.) Superheroes, being an American cultural phenomenon, are still firmly rooted in the American city life of the 20th century, Superman included. Even the amazing elements of his mythology—planet Krypton, his spaceship, the Fortress of Solitude, Kryptonite, etc.—all fall within the ambit of science fiction, distinguished from fantasy, as a genre, as being based on science and anchored in realism. His superpowers, too, are explained, however implausibly, using scientific rationale like Earth's lower gravity and his evolved physiology, conforming, in principle, to the same laws that govern known reality. His extraterrestrial origins lead straight to a countryside upbringing and his superhuman exploits are in answer to the demands and challenges of modern city living, if exaggerated. Most everything else around him remains familiar, placing him more within magical realism than fantastical fiction.

This convention of American mythmaking, in contrast to the European, interestingly fits more within the Jewish tradition of storytelling than the Christian one. Despite biblical theology and Kabbalistic mysticism, Judaism focuses less on metaphysics, angelology and demonology, all intricately developed in Christianity, and more on the practical application of dogma. Even Jewish fables, like the Golem of Prague and the various miracle-working rabbis, are firmly rooted in the sociohistorical reality of their time, with usually only one fantastical element in each fable. More than anything they're morality tales, like American folk tales and their modern manifestation, superhero comics.

Another commonality between Jewish and American mythical traditions, as opposed to continental and Christian, is the distinction between nobility of spirit and nobility of birthright. King Arthur is son of King Uther, Aragorn is descendant of King Elros, Jesus is son of God, but the Jewish heroes, like Abraham, Moses, David and Samson, are all commoners, chosen by character or circumstance. American heroes, reflecting the nation's antimonarchical rebelliousness, are likewise common folk, often frontiersmen, whose virtue is earned through adversity, not inherited or preordained. Superman, in this regard, is a mix of both. He was born to Kryptonian gentry but raised as a humble laborer, and his great heroics are the result of his alien bloodline, his salvation by chance as an infant and his wholesome rearing.

It's only natural that the Man of Steel would embody the two cultural momentums that combined to create him. His creators, Jerome "Jerry" Siegel and Joseph "Joe" Shuster, were American Jews, and they confected their character from the influences of their youth. In *Superman: The High-Flying History of America's Most Enduring Hero*, the definitive biography of the character, author Larry Tye describes how, in forming their new breed of hero, Siegel and Shuster "started out with the models of the past, then added new twists."[2] Siegel, the writer, and Shuster, the artist, spun a yarn that pulled threads from of a wide range of literary themes and influences, starting with the epic sagas of antiquity and ending with the speculative science of eugenics.

But Superman's brand of heroism can be traced back directly to the Bible. The word "hero" originates in the Greek *heros*, meaning defender. It's somewhat of a misnomer considering the Greek heroes, gods and demigods and kings and warriors, were celebrated for their strength, bravery, cunning, determination, and attainment of glory, elements that are still part and parcel of any heroic lore, but not for selflessness, self-sacrifice, an urge for justice, protection of the weak and a life in the servitude of others, which are seen today as the essence of heroism. (Hercules, Achilles, Odysseus and Jason all vanquished various predatory monsters, but for glory and personal score-setting, not to protect the innocent.) These moral concepts that encapsulate superheroes originate in the Bible, which introduced to the ancient world the idea of divine benevolence and morality. The morals of the Greek gods and champions, like that of other pantheons, differed little from people's; they were given to the same petty jealousy, hatred, treachery and lust as humans, and yet they were superior, and so entitled to them. The monotheistic god of the Hebrew Bible was the first to be purely good and to introduce a codex of worship based in ethical social behavior. His champions—the messengers, prophets and kings of scripture—weren't brave heroes favored by gods possessing "superpowers" but regular, flawed people endowed with amazing abilities by an omnipotent god, chosen to defend the wellbeing of their fellow men and promote the ideals of truth and justice.

Seeing Superman as a religious metaphor is perhaps inevitable. He's come to embody our collective moralistic ideals in their purest, and so he's no longer a hero to identify with but to aspire to. He may not be infallible but he's the hardest to imagine making moral compromises, and he stands for hope, that which requires faith and promises redemption. When he appears we are told to look up in the sky, the traditional place of God, and so it's little wonder that this Man of Might has been associated with the almighty, be it through Moses or Jesus or another messianic figure.

Superhero comics have taken the place of biblical tales as morality plays, but there's also an inherent religion-like quality to them. They rely on a canon unique to each publisher, with its own core narrative, cosmology and metaphysics. Superheroes, and the reality they inhabit, constantly change and at once remain immutable;

the same characters and stories are preserved and retold down the generations, but they're also constantly altered, adapted to the spirit of the times and sensibilities of their audience, which consists of loyal followers, tentative newcomers and disillusioned renouncers. The result is an organized narrative, guarded and expounded by sacerdotalist caretakers—writers, artists and editors—perpetually seeking to give it new context, understanding and validation.

Before superheroes existed, before Superman, biblical heroes still held prominence in the cultural landscape. In the 1920s and 1930s, when Siegel and Shuster were growing up, Hollywood blockbusters included the *Ten Commandments* ('23), *Ben-Hur: A Tale of Christ* ('25), *The King of Kings* ('27), *Noah's Ark* ('28) and *The Sign of the Cross* ('32). For young creators seeking inspiration, the Bible offered an indelible source of archetypal mythic stories—which weren't copyrighted. And while these stories are part of the world's shared cultural heritage, Superman manifests a distinctive Jewish connotation, both in the context of his creation and the content of his mythology. As Tye confirms, while "every faith on this planet thinks Superman is theirs.... Superman is, in fact, one of the chosen people."[3] (It's worth noting here that "chosen people" isn't a claim of superiority; the Hebrew phrase, originating in God's conversation with Moses on mount Sinai [Ex. 19:3–6], doesn't mean chosen in the sense of "finest" [מוּבְחָר] but of "selected" [נִבְחָר], by which the Hebrews, delivered from bondage, are in turn called upon to deliver God's message to the nations of the world. It's an appellation of responsibility, not entitlement, one which fits well with Superman's mission.)

The mythopoetic undercurrent in the Man of Steel's narrative runs surprisingly close to the surface, beginning with the most elemental; his name. As Rabbi Simcha Weinstein, author of the deliciously titled *Up, Up, and Oy Vey: How Jewish History, Culture and Values Shaped the Comic Book Superhero*, elucidates, "Superman's original name on Krypton … reveals biblical underpinnings. Superman is named Kal-El and his father Jor-El. The suffix 'El' is one of the ancient names for God used throughout the Bible. It is also found in the names of great prophets, such as Isra-el, Samu-el, and Dani-el and angels, such as Micha-el and Gavri-el." And while the hero's surname means God in Hebrew, "The prefix of Superman's name, 'Kal,' is the root of several Hebrew words meaning 'with lightness,' 'swiftness,' 'vessel' and 'voice.'" Tye also offers an interpretation of the name as voice or vessel of God, with yet another suggested by Superman and *Mad* magazine writer Arie Kaplan, in his book *From Krakow to Krypton: Jews and Comic Books*, by which it "roughly means 'All that God is.'"[4] Similar claims have been echoed in various articles and books discussing Superman.

These translations aren't consensus, however. Danny Fingeroth, veteran comic book writer and editor and a leading historian of the field, disputes the claims in his book, *Disguised as Clark Kent: Jews, Comics, and the Creation of the Superhero*, noting that "there's no record of them [Siegel and Shuster] ever suggesting there was any religious connection intended." His view is corroborated by Siegel himself, who, in his unpublished memoir, *Creation of a Superhero*, written in 1979, reveals that "Jor-L" is in fact an anagram of his own name, Jerome Siegel.[5] And yet, Superman's birth name does carry an undeniable Hebraic resonance, lending itself to various interpretations, and so the question of its meaning, deliberate or otherwise, remains.

The names Jor-L and Kal-L first appeared in the *Superman* newspaper comic strip, the former in its January 16, 1939, debut and the latter the next day, written by Siegel and illustrated by Shuster. They didn't appear in the comics until January 1945's *More Fun Comics* #101, in the story "The Origin of Superboy," illustrated by Shuster but ghostwritten, likely by Don Cameron, by which point the names were changed to their phonetic spelling, Kal-El and Jor-El.

The word "El" does, in fact, mean God in Hebrew (though usually in the lower case "g," not the proper noun). "Kal-El" does fit, then, etymologically, with the biblical names of various angels, prophets and heroes, as Weinstein describes. Every angel named in the Hebrew Bible and many of the prophets have names that are comprised of an epithetic root, conveying their specific character or mission, conjoined with the theophoric suffix "el," attributing them to God. The name Michael, for example, reads as "who is as God," a rhetorical praise. Similarly, Gabriel means "man of God," which can be understood as either a hero of God, strength derived from God, or a manifestation of God as man. Uriel means "light of God" and Raphael "healing of God."[6]

Casting Superman in the role of an angel isn't difficult. Celebrated Superman writer Grant Morrison, in his autobiographical disquisition, *Supergods: What Masked Vigilantes, Miraculous Mutants, and a Sun God from Smallville Can Teach Us About Being Human*, describes superheroes as "role models whose heroism and transcendent qualities would once have been haloed and clothed in floaty robes." As defenders of humanity and heralds of morality, the caped and cowled characters of comics have inherited the mythological role once held by angels, Superman most so, considering his celestial origins. His creators weren't unaware of this. In yet another unpublished work of Siegel's, a 1945 two-page essay (or possibly memoir outline) titled "The Life and Times of Jerry Siegel," he describes him as "a sort of guardian angel."[7] Even though Siegel likely meant the idiomatic, general concept and not the literal, scriptural one from which it derives, both the angel and the prophet roles are apt for Superman, seeing as how he swoops down from the heavens to work miracles and save people, and how he spreads the gospel of Truth, Justice and the American Way—a man with a message. That "el" also means "toward" in Hebrew, particularly connoting ascent (Israel's largest airline is named El Al), is fitting.

But while "El" means God, and in angelic lore "Kal" would be its epithet, the word has no Hebrew meaning in this context, despite specious claims to the contrary. "Kal" isn't the root of voice or vessel. Voice—kol (קוֹל)—is a rootless noun, and vessel—kli (כְּלִי)—has a different root. "All that God is" would be "Kol-El," sounded and spelled differently (כֹּל אֵל), which, if anything, would actually translate as "any god." What "Kal" does mean in Hebrew is "lightweight" or "easy" (קַל), or, figuratively, something ephemeral in nature, none of which signifies anything when conjoined with "God" (קַל-אֵל). It's possible that Siegel, who originated the names, did mean to imbue them with Jewish meaning but simply didn't know Hebrew well enough, adapting an approximation instead, but it's improbable. At best they're homonymous, and trying to shoehorn extra meaning into things waters them down.

("Kal" does actually have scriptural meaning, though one so obscure that any connotation is more playful than revelatory. In the Book of Daniel 4:31, it's described that "a voice came from heaven" to inform the Babylonian King Nebuchadnezzar of the end of his reign. It's one of many mistranslations found in the English Bible; the original Hebrew verse describes "Kal falling down from the sky" [קָל מִן־שְׁמַיָּא נְפַל], referring to the king's *sar* [שַׂר], a spiritual overseer or minister. Detailed in the Midrash [Ex. Rabbah 21:5], Kal is a flying spirit felled by God to precede the king's fall.[8] The misreading of "Kal" as "kol" in Daniel may explain the claim that "Kal-El" means "Voice of God," though it's unlikely.)

There's no evidence that Siegel and Shuster were aware of the Hebrew translation of "El," and Siegel's original spelling of Jor-L and basing it on his own name point to the contrary. However, the two grew up in Glenville, a neighborhood in Cleveland, Ohio, that was almost exclusively Jewish and where Yiddish was the language on the street, attended Hebrew school, and Siegel's mother, Sarah, was heavily active in Jewish community affairs. Accounts differ regarding their level of observance, but it's safe to say they weren't completely secular by today's standards.[9] The boys grew up in a fairly cloistered Jewish milieu, immersed in their cultural heritage. They would have enough familiarity with the language of the synagogue and high holidays, especially core lexicon like a ubiquitous name of God and the names of the main prophets and angels. It's difficult to imagine that both of them were utterly oblivious to such powerfully evocative meaning, or that the name crept from their unconscious without them ever coming to realize its significance.

Either way, "Kal-El" would eventually be given meaning decades later, as "star child" in ancient Kryptonese.[10]

As for his father Jor-El, only the godly surname has any meaning, though a fanciful manipulation does produce an interesting reading; the letter "J" originated as an alternate spelling of "I," and is still read as a vowel in words with Hebraic roots like hallelujah (הַלְלוּיָהּ), meaning "praise the Lord," with "jah" being an abbreviation of Yahweh, meaning "the eternal," the holiest theonym and the tetragrammaton—an ineffability in the Jewish faith. Likewise, Jehovah has come to be read as a consonant in English, but is pronounced originally as Yehovah (יְהֹוָה), another vocalization of Yahweh. Jor-El, then, read Hebraically as "Yor-El," can be interpreted to mean "God-fearing" (יְרֵא אֵל) or, alternatively, "he who will teach (the ways of) God" or "he who will command (in the name of) God" (יוֹרֶה אֵל). It makes for a nice thematic fit, though more a result of happenstance than Siegel and Shuster's onomastic erudition. Nevertheless, the name does have Jewish meaning in at least one regard; as an anagram for Jerome Siegel it's a variation on the Jewish name and a direct representation of Superman's true, Jewish father.

With respect to Superman's mother, Lara Lor-Van doesn't have Hebrew meaning, except that "La ra" means "bad for her," which is true, considering her fate, but still circumstantial.

Writing for *Biblical Archeology Review* in 1979, a year after *Superman: The Movie* brought the character back into the limelight, archeologist James Brower asserted that "the Superman stories—commonly thought to be of purely American origin— are in fact rooted in ancient Hebrew institutions."[11] It was meant as satire, ridiculing the revisionism and recontextualization sometimes found in modern scholarship, but his example of choice would prove prescient and ultimately ironic, as subsequent generations of scholars from a range of disciplines would come to see Superman as, in fact, a manifestation of his creators' Jewish background.

Biblical heroes are the forebears of superheroes, with religious elements re-codified as superhero tropes. Spandex has replaced sandals, but the premise remains the same; people given supernatural abilities and tasked with an onerous responsibility. The greatest of these—the Hebrew Patriarchs Abraham, Isaac and Jacob, along with Moses, David, Amos and others—come from the humblest origins: shepherds, men who lead an ascetic existence, mostly isolated from larger society, until they are called upon to assume their mantle. Clark Kent isn't a shepherd but he's the next best thing, a farmer, toiling in a remote farm, placing him within both the biblical and Jeffersonian traditions of virtue.

Many of the scriptural heroes also possess superpowers. The prophets are all clairvoyant; Ezekiel raises an army of undead (Ezekiel 37:1–14); Elijah revives the dead (1 Kings 17:21–22), conjures fire and water (1 Kings 18:36–38, 41–45 and 2 Kings 1:10, 2:8) and flies through the sky in a chariot of fire (2 Kings 2:11); Elisha splits a river (2 Kings 2:14) and summons bears (to maul children who taunted him for being bald, making him more of a supervillain [2 Kings 2:23–24]); and Solomon has super-wisdom (1 Kings 3:12, 4:30–31) as well as, apocryphally, a magic ring, known as the Seal of Solomon, allowing him to converse with animals as well as command spirits and the elements.[12]

One champion of the Bible who lacks supernatural abilities but is even more of a direct superhero precursor is King David, and not only because of his Robin-style slingshot. As a little shepherd boy, he wouldn't stand for the Philistine giant Goliath terrorizing his people. When the armies of King Saul fail to defeat the colossus, David the weakling takes it upon himself to stand for justice and, with righteousness on his side, singlehandedly defeats him. (1 Sam. 17:1–54). The prophet Samuel anoints him as the king-to-be, but David continues with his daily life, his "alter ego," as a mild-mannered shepherd (1 Sam. 16:11–13). Once he becomes the warrior king, he fashions a shield shaped like a six-pointed star—the Shield of David, known in English as the Star of David (Mishnah, tractate Pesachim 10:117b)—a symbol to represent his creed, that of the Jewish faith.

About 2,800 years later, in 1941, Hymie "Joseph" Simon and Jacob Kurtzberg, better known as the legendary creative team of Joe Simon and Jack Kirby, refashioned the tale of David into that of Steve Rogers, a scrawny youth from New York's Lower East Side—then the Jewish Ghetto—who volunteers for a military experiment that turns him into a super-soldier. Armed with an indestructible, star-spangled shield, he takes on the giant menace of the Axis forces, singlehandedly turning the tide of war as the champion of his nation, Captain America.

Eisner Award–winning writer-artist Kyle Baker, who in 2002 published his *King David* graphic novel through Vertigo, an imprint of Superman's publisher DC Comics, sees these parallels as more than just coincidence: "The whole comic book genre was created by Jews—it's a Jewish medium … [they] were obviously using the Bible as source material."[13] That isn't to say that the biblical and comic book mythologies overlap perfectly; Captain America isn't King David wrapped in Old Glory, nor is Superman Moses with muscles. Rather, superhero narratives, which, as diverse as they may be, all share their fundamentals with Superman, are a result of the natural cultural process of adaptation and alteration, the same reimagining that turned *The Odyssey* into *Ulysses* and *Romeo and Juliet* into *West Side Story*.

This process is also found within the Bible itself; Superman was inspired by a mythic pattern that begins with Noah, recurs in Moses and culminates after a fashion in Jesus, which sees a boy or man become the last of his kind as he's cast away in a specially-built craft to an unknown fate, the only survivor of a catastrophe befallen his people. Saved, he grows to be a righteous person and fulfill his destiny as a great savior and bringer of moral law.

The Book of Genesis, which contains the narrative of the flood, echoed in Superman's origin story, is effectively the genesis of the superhero genre. Planet Krypton, like antediluvian Earth, is a world condemned for its sinfulness. Its evolved people, dedicated to the pursuit of scientific knowledge, refuse to recognize their looming ruin. They are guilty of the greatest sin, hubris, as well as the Jewish original sin, the unbridled pursuit of knowledge that led Adam and Eve to taste of its fruit. In both accounts the catastrophe is tragically avoidable as it is all-consuming, with only few people surviving it: Noah enters the ark along with his wife, three sons and their wives, as well as two of all living creatures (Gen. 6:18–19). Baby Kal-El is placed in his rocket ship alone, but is later joined by his cousin Supergirl, the Phantom Zone criminals, and in the campy 1960s by a Legion of Super-Pets. Delivered from disaster, like Moses, like Superman, Noah's ultimate duty is to deliver truth and justice; through him God establishes his first covenant with mankind (the Noahic Covenant. Gen. 9:8–17) and stipulates laws for man to live by (the Seven Laws of Noah, aka the Noahide Laws, known in Hebrew as the Seven Commandments of the Sons of Noah. Gen. 9:1–7). By some Midrashic interpretations, Noah was forewarned and saved not because he was worthy but because Moses was destined to descend from him (Gen. Rabbah 26:6–7), giving him the same role in the overall biblical narrative as that of Jor-El in Superman's—a character whose main purpose is to beget and save the great hero.

Even more specifically related to Superman is Samson, the scriptural strongman. Superman is known, first and foremost, for his physical prowess, putting him more in line with Greek gods and heroes such as Hercules and Apollo than with the spiritual prophet-servants of the Judeo-Christian tradition like Moses and Jesus and shrewd leaders like David and Solomon, with the notable expectation being Samson, who's renowned for his strength (though he was also a judge). Siegel acknowledged this heredity, stating that "the Superman theme has been one of the themes ever since Samson and Hercules; and I just sat down and wrote a story of that type."[14] The motif of the super-strong adventuring hero is as old as Gilgamesh, found in virtually all world folklores, from the Anglo-Saxon epic of the Norse Beowulf to the Irish Cú Chulainn to the Chinese Sun Wukong. Samson, as one of the most famous, is a staple of the collective cultural narrative of the world, a nondenominational meme connoting great might—particularly at a time when Superman or the Hulk weren't yet referenceable. And yet, he is a fundamentally religious character. For faithful Jews, Christians and many Muslims he is a historical and holy figure, real and relevant in a way that Hercules hasn't been in nearly 2,000 years. And, despite his nonsectarianism, Samson is an Israelite judge, whose story is found in the Hebrew Bible, making him a product of Jewish culture.

Known in Jewish tradition as "Samson the Hero," he possesses powers similar to those of Superman. He wasn't more powerful than a locomotive, but he was stronger than a roaring lion, which he tore in half with his bare hands (Judges 14:5–6), as well as an army of a thousand Philistines, whom he killed with the jawbone of a donkey (15:15). There were no speeding bullets for him to be faster than, but he outran and caught three hundred foxes (15:4). And he could leap long distances in a single bound, travelling in one stride from Zorah to Eshtaol, a distance of roughly four miles (Lev. Rabbah 8:2)—significantly more than Superman's original ability of an eighth of a mile.

Samson, pronounced "Shimshon" in Hebrew (שִׁמְשׁוֹן), means "man of the sun," also readable as a portmanteau of "shemesh" and "on" (שֶׁמֶשׁ-און), meaning "strength derived from the sun." The name could equally describe Superman, who derives his powers from exposure to Earth's yellow sun.[15] Both fit within the tradition of solar deities—to which the Man of Steel has often been compared, though his comparability to Samson in this regard has so far been overlooked—but they differ in that, while their powers are attributed to the sun, they're not solar in manifestation, they're physical, as strength and invulnerability (the exception being Superman's ability to fly, shared with sun gods like Helios and Horus, but that, too, has evolved from his initial ability to "leap tall building in a single bound," a feat of strength).

Superman also shares Samson's weakness, at least etymologically. His alien cells are supercharged by the sun, like solar panels, and prolonged absence, such as interstellar travel, drains his powers. Samson, the man of the sun, loses his might to the temptress Delilah (דְּלִילָה), whose name is interpretable as "of the night," "lilah" (לְיְלָה) being "night" in Hebrew (it can also be read as "fourth night"; ancient Hebrew uses an alphabetic numeral system, by which the fourth letter, Daled (ד), is also the number 4, foreshadowing her role in the narrative—it was on the fourth night of badgering that Samson finally told her the secret of his strength, bringing about his downfall [Judges 16:4–21]). There are also parallels to be found in their stories, when in 1980's *Superman II* the Man of Steel relinquishes his powers, and with them his responsibility as humanity's protector, to be with the woman he loves, Lois. While she doesn't betray him as Delilah does (though she does fall out of love with him as a human very quickly), she can nonetheless be assigned the role of temptress, bringing about his downfall. In the director's cut of the film Superman regains his powers by imploring the spectral recording of his father, like Samson does by praying to the heavenly father, though Superman manages to vanquish his enemies without sacrificing himself.[16]

More than just a structuralist forebear, the themes and iconography of Samson's mythos are present in several of Superman's early comic books. He's repeatedly referred to as "possessing the strength of a dozen Samsons!" In 1939's *Superman* #2 he pulls down the support pillars of a great hall, threatening to bury the evildoers inside, proclaiming that "a guy named Samson once had the same idea!" He's again compared to Samson on the cover of *Superman* #4, where he topples two central pillars, bringing down the roof atop scurrying crooks. It's a virtually exact depiction of the famous scene of Samson tearing down the Philistine temple (Judges 16:29–30). Siegel acknowledged in his memoir that Samson was a "strong influence" on the creation of Superman, and that the cover of *Superman* #4 was a conscious homage, confirming the superhero's roots in Jewish religion and folklore.[17]

The two strongmen even met, twice: in *Adventure Comics* #257 (February '59), a time-traveling Superboy (as he was known in childhood, expunged since from canon) meets both Samson and Hercules, ending up saving their lives. The story repeatedly points them out to be precursors, "the first two Super-men!" In *Superman's Pal, Jimmy Olsen* #79 (September '64), the Man of Steel and the cub reporter meet the pubescent Samson, "the **Superboy** of his era." Superman topples a pair of columns to stop their adversaries, giving Samson the idea.[18]

Superman reflects more than just biblical characters and storylines. Comic book superheroes and the heroes of the Bible are didactic figures, their moral tales meant to provide readers with uplift and edification. Superman, the origin of the superhero concept and its quintessence, inherently conveys great meaning, which is shared with, if not derived from, central Judaic tenets.

The Man of Steel famously stands for "Truth, Justice and the American Way." Originally the phrasing was simply "Truth and Justice," first appearing in the opening to the 1940 *Adventures of Superman* radio series, followed by the 1941 Fleischer Studios *Superman* animated serials. In mid-1942, with the U.S. embroiled in World War II, "the American Way" was added to both the radio show and cartoons, but by 1944, with the war waning, it was removed. It was revived again in 1952, along with Cold War jingoism, in the opening of the *Adventures of Superman* TV series starring George Reeves, where it became forever engrained in pop culture.[19]

Samson, by Valentin de Boulogne. France, 1631. The Cleveland Museum of Art, Mr. and Mrs. William H. Marlatt Fund. Samson is depicted here with a square jaw, black hair, forelock, and wearing a tight blue shirt and flowing red toga.

The Mishnah is the

Samson's Revenge and Death, by Julius Schnorr von Carolsfeld. Wood engraving from *The Bible in Pictures*. Germany, 1860.

written collation of Jewish oral tradition, primarily concerned with legal exegesis of the Torah (Pentateuch) and the application of its commandments. It's the first major work of rabbinical literature, compiled around the 2nd century CE. Together with the Gemara, it forms the Talmud. As Tye and Weinstein both note,[20] Superman's raison d'être bears a remarkable resemblance to a well-known Jewish proverb from the Mishna; in tractate Pirkei Avot ("Ethics of the Fathers," a treatise dedicated to ethical and moral deliberations) 1:18, famed rabbinic sage Shimon ben Gamliel states, "on three things does the world endure: justice, truth and peace." It's a reiteration of a saying attributed to Shimon the Just, the High Priest of the Second Temple in the early period (roughly 300–200 BCE) and one of the last of the Great Assembly: "the world is based upon three things: on Torah, on service [of God], and on acts of kindness" (Pirkei Avot 1:2). Both maxims in turn echo the biblical verse from Zechariah 8:16, "these are the things which you should do: speak the truth to one another; judge with truth and judgment for peace in your gates."

Superman's creed of "Truth, Justice and the American Way" and the Mishnah's "justice, truth and peace" are virtually identical. Both list, of all options, truth and justice as their supreme values, with "the American Way" ostensibly being the

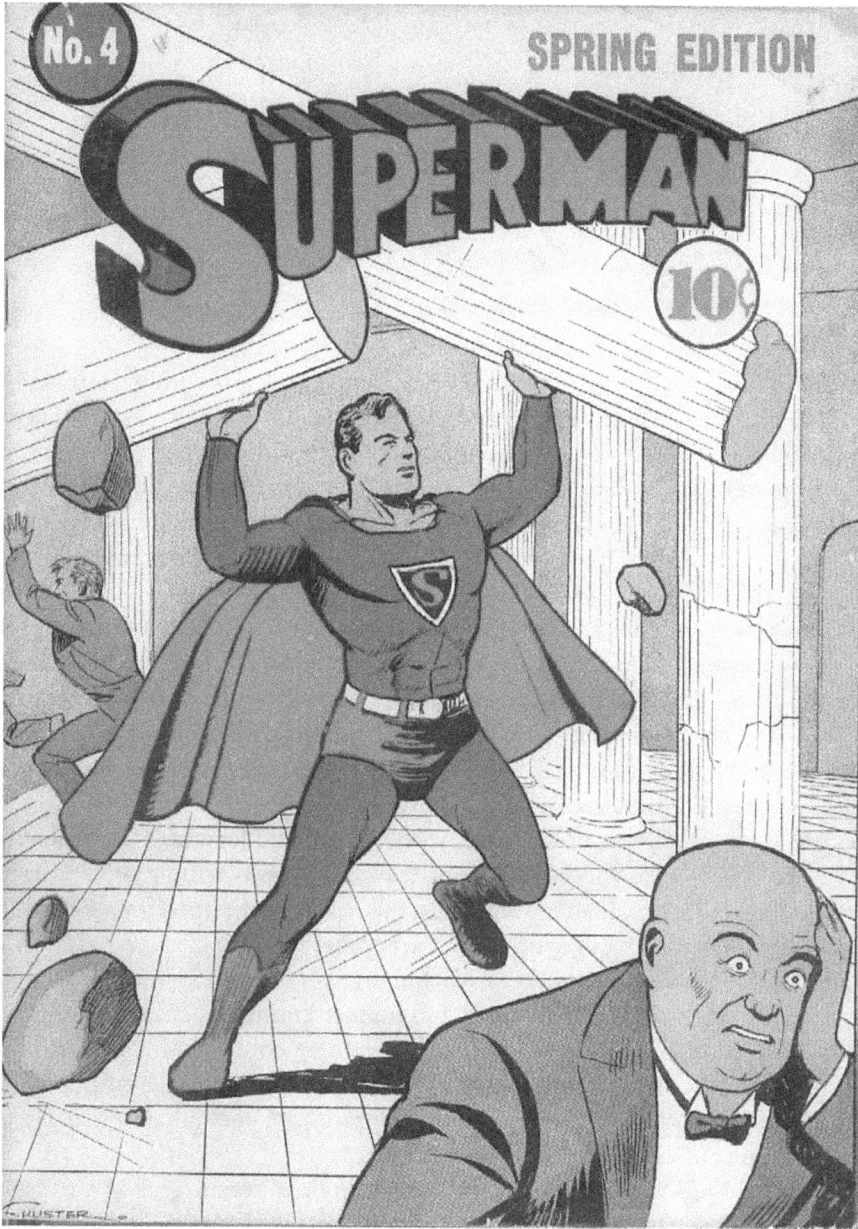

Superman #4, March 1940. Cover by Joe Shuster. DC Comics.

difference. But what is the American way if not democracy, freedom, pluralism and coexistence? It is inherently equal in meaning to peace. Judaism's fundamental precepts, as articulated by the prophet, the priest and the rabbi, are embodied in Superman—the Jewish superhero.

> *I suspect that men have sometimes derived more spiritual sustenance from myths they did not believe than from the religion they professed.*
>
> —C.S. Lewis

Paradigmatic Parallels

Superman as Moses

In *Disguised as Clark Kent*, comic book historian Danny Fingeroth states that "Superman created the template for how bigger-than-life heroes ... should act."[1] The Man of Steel was the first superhero, arguably the first modern mythic hero, establishing the paradigm for the rest to follow. He is the hero all other superheroes aspire to be, both in the macrocosm of the comic book industry and the microcosm of his reality, where he's revered by his superhero colleagues. He is the great patriarch and giver of the superhero law, from moral code to dress code.

But the novelty and excitement of Superman's appearance was a successful *jamais vu*; it felt completely new, though it was a story that had been told before. Undergirding the template he created is an ancient one, a morphology that traces back from the comic book to the Good Book. Specifically, more than any other scriptural champion and miracle worker, comics' greatest hero is a reincarnation of the Bible's greatest prophet. While Superman is Clark Kent's alter ego, Moses is Superman's.

Moses is the paramount figure of Jewish culture and legend. The greatest of the biblical heroes, he saved the Jewish people, fought unwaveringly for truth, justice and freedom, exemplified the responsibility that comes with power, was humble, and dedicated his life to the service of others, an archetype that later recurred in Jesus. Superman is Moses as envisioned in Michelangelo's famous statue; an action hero of rippling muscles, handsome features and intense countenance. In creating Superman, the core elements of Moses's narrative were re-contextualized in contemporary terms, as science fiction and sociopolitical philosophy, and his comics, virtually from the start, have followed the Jewish textual tradition, particularly associated with Moses, of telling and retelling important stories.

The Jewish Encyclopedia notes that "of all Biblical personages Moses has been chosen most frequently as the subject of later legends.... A cycle of legends has been woven around nearly every trait of his character and every event of his life."[2] The beliefs and principles of Jewish faith and culture are rooted in the Mosaic narrative, giving rise to numerous tales that reaffirm his importance and teachings. The most famous of these outside the Bible is the Passover Haggadah, the "comic book" recounting Moses's grand heroics. Its name means "the telling," following the commandment in Exodus 13:8 that each generation must retell the story.

Superman's origin and greatest adventures have likewise been revisited numerous times over the years. The first retelling of his genesis was in 1939's *Superman #1*,[3] only a year after his debut in *Action Comics* #1, and it's been repeated and revised, in full or in anecdote, canonically or apocryphally, countless times since. Superman is unique among superheroes in this regard. Like Moses, despite all the tweaks and updates, his legend remains constant, sacrosanct. Many, if not most, early comic book characters have had substantial changes made to their origin tales over the years (to pick two, Green Lantern went from being an engineer who found a magical Chinese railroad lantern to a test pilot chosen for his fearlessness to become an interstellar policeman. Hawkman, confusingly, started out as an archaeologist who's a reincarnation of an ancient Egyptian prince, then was changed to a winged alien cop, then to a mystical human avatar of hawks, then to an alien fugitive in sentient metal armor working clandestinely for the U.S. government, and at the time of this writing is undergoing yet another reinvention), but Superman's famous beginnings have closely adhered to Siegel and Shuster's original version. From the start, the legend they created enraptured audiences, perhaps because they perfectly reiterated the timeless dreams and aspirations expressed in possibly the most significant story ever told.

They weren't trying to write in cipher. They simply incorporated, like all storytellers, elements of their culture and consciousness. That the legend of Moses occupied both is hardly surprising. For Jews like Siegel and Shuster, especially at an era of relative orthodoxy, the story was as familiar, as much a part of their cultural world, as the story of Jesus is to Christians. More than likely, the parallels between Superman and Moses were entirely unintentional, but they are clear and consistent, the result being a modern secular mythology that's as popular as the ancient religious one—earning its creators a place in *The Jewish 100: A Ranking of the Most Influential Jews of All Time*, alongside Moses himself.[4]

The greatest point of correspondence between Superman and Moses is in their origin stories. This has been commented on often, most notably by Weinstein, Fingeroth, Kaplan and Tye.[5] However, the comparison has always been limited to a paragraph or two, when in truth there is a far more extensive parallel to be explored, not only in the characters' childhood but also in their adolescence and adulthood, and not just anecdotally but, more profoundly, structurally and thematically.

The story of Moses is told in the books of Exodus, Leviticus, Numbers and Deuteronomy—four of the five books that comprise the Torah—and begins at his birth. The Egyptian Pharaoh, fearing that the multiplying Israelite slaves might help his enemies come war, decrees that all their male newborns be killed. Moses is born soon after, the youngest son of Amram and Jochebed (Yocheved). Desperate to save his life, his mother places him in a basket of bulrushes and hides him among the reeds by the bank of the Nile River, whereupon he is found, ironically, by the Pharaoh's daughter Bithiah, who'd come there to bathe and decides to adopt him. Thus it came to be that the future deliverer of Israel was reared as the son of an Egyptian princess (Ex. 1:8–2:10. Pharaoh's daughter isn't actually named until 1 Chronicles 4:17. Similarly, Moses's parents are first named in Exodus 6:20).

Bithiah names the child Moses—Moshe (מֹשֶׁה)—because she drew him out of the water (2:10). The name in Hebrew means "drawn out of" or "delivered," as in from the river and from death, but equally means "deliverer" or "savior," as in from bondage to the Promised Land and from idol worship to God's law. It's also readable as a theophoric name, "mash" (מָשׁ) meaning "extricated" and the letter Hei (ה) being a common biblical name of God, producing Mosh Hei (מש ה); one saved by God, as well as God's chosen savior.[6] (Since Bithiah wouldn't have spoken Hebrew, the name is thought to be epithetic, given to him by the biblical scribes. That the name is believed by some scholars to be Egyptian or even Greek in origin is irrelevant to its common understanding in Jewish tradition.)

Superman's saga, too, begins at his birth, and follows a clear parallel. The only one to foresee the imminent destruction of his planet, scientist Jor-El saves his infant son by placing him in a small rocket and launching him into space. Just as Moses is spared his fate, becoming the last newborn son of Israel, so is Superman, becoming the Last Son of Krypton. Both are castaways, sent adrift in a small craft to risk an unknown fate, a desperate act made by their parents in the face of certain death. Both are refugees fleeing genocide, and both are orphaned by their tragedy (Moses's parents didn't perish as Superman's did, but he nonetheless grew up parentless in Pharaoh's court). Both are also foundlings; Moses is discovered by the papyrus reeds along the Nile bank while baby Kal-El is found amidst the amber waves of grain of a Kansas wheat field. Both are renamed by the women who find them: the Israelite baby is named Moses by Bithiah and the Kryptonian is given the name Clark by Martha Kent.

The origin story is the clearest, but far from only, part of Superman's mythology that corresponds to his biblical cognate. Their chrysalis stage parallels too. Clark and Moses are both raised by people not their own, knowing they are different, and both are awkward teenagers who, in a twist of irony, seeing as how they would later become public leaders and inspirational figures, struggle to communicate with the world around them. Clark Kent in his Metropolis persona is a chronic stammerer,

Bithia (Nina Foch) finds baby Moses. *The Ten Commandments*, 1956. Paramount.

The Kents find baby Kal-El. *From JLA Adventures: Trapped in Time*, 2014. Warner Bros.

just as his antecedent Moses is a heavy stutterer, or "slow of speech and of tongue" (Ex. 4:10).

When Moses has grown up, he goes out to observe his Hebrew brethren's forced labor. Seeing an Egyptian beating a slave, he's overcome with anger and kills him. When word reaches Pharaoh he orders Moses's death, and Moses flees Egypt to the land of Midian, where he meets his wife Zipporah and settles as a shepherd (Ex. 2:11–3:1).

According to a Midrashic fable, Moses was actually caught and brought to the executioner, who chose the sharpest sword with which to kill him. But God made Moses's neck like a marble pillar—granting him invulnerability—allowing him to survive and escape (Ex. Rabbah 1:32).

Though debated, convention holds that Moses is eighteen when he leaves Pharaoh's palace and crosses the Sinai desert to Midian.[7] Years pass, until one day, when Moses leads his flock to Mount Horeb, he comes upon a burning bush, blazing but not consumed. God appears out of the fire and appoints him to return to Egypt and deliver his brethren from their bondage: "I am the God of your father.... I have surely seen the affliction of my people.... I have come down to deliver them ... come now, and I will send you ... that you may bring my people, the sons of Israel" (Ex. 3:1–3:11).

It's one of the most famous scenes in the Bible, and it can be found, with high fidelity, in 1978's *Superman* (aka *Superman: The Movie*), which is as seminal to the superhero genre in cinema as Superman's first issue is in comics. Like Moses, Clark leaves his adoptive home in Smallville at the age of eighteen, to find his destiny across the Arctic wasteland. There, he creates his Fortress of Solitude and encounters the spirit of his father, in the form of a hologram manifested out of the crystalized ice. "I am Jor-El. I'm your father," the apparition tells him, along with his purpose on Earth. "They can be a great people, Kal-El. They wish to be. They only lack the light to show

the way. For this reason above all, their capacity for good, I have sent them you, my only son."[8]

Jor-El's hologram and God's burning bush are analogous in their appearance, function and even speech. Both young heroes journey across a barren, inhospitable land, where each encounters a revelation that takes the form of his father; Clark converses not with Jor-El, long ago dead, but with his interactive recording, just as the burning bush isn't God himself but his manifestation, as "an angel of the Lord" (Ex. 3:2). Jor-El informs Clark that he is his father, as God tells Moses that he is the God of his father. According to the Midrash, God also spoke to Moses in the voice of his father Amram, so as not to frighten him (Ex. Rabbah 45:5), further strengthening the equivalence. There's also an esthetic symmetry between them, in the contrast of God appearing in fire and Jor-El projected out of ice. The two then convey a similar message; God appoints Moses to be his people's savior and leader and Jor-El assigns Superman as humanity's protector. Both men are unsure at first, but eventually answer their calling to become heroes to their people. Moses becomes the greatest prophet in Judaism, bestowing the rule of law (in the form of the Commandments and the Torah) and bringing the message of faith, and Superman becomes the greatest superhero in comics, protecting the rule of law and bringing the message of hope.

These thematic elements—the sojourns, the manifestations, the similar monologues—aren't in fact part of the original comic book narrative. They were first introduced in the film, and can be argued to be apocryphal, though they've since been canonized in the comics and have become immanent parts of the mythology. The original script for the movie, written by bestselling author and Academy Award–winning screenwriter Mario Puzo (*The Godfather*), included Superman's walkabout and Jor-El's hologram, but not the hero's consecration or the strongly evocative language. Those were added by Jewish screenwriter Tom Mankiewicz (credited as "Creative Consultant," following rewrites by David Newman, Leslie Newman and Robert Benton), who placed Superman more within the heraldic tradition of Moses, and not without winking at the audience; he also added Perry White's line, that interviewing Superman would be "the single most important interview since God talked to Moses."[9]

Moses doesn't assume so easily the onerous responsibility God asks of him. He questions his ability and right to become a leader of his people (Ex. 3:11) and asks that someone more capable be sent instead (4:13). There are a number of such instances of self-doubt and humility throughout his story, making Moses a paradoxical leader who inspires faith but shows hesitation, and who reluctantly, but ultimately determinedly, champions a cause far greater than himself. In Judaism Moses is the exemplar of virtuous power, more commonly associated in the larger world with Plato's ideal leader (*Republic* 1.347a–c), who's likewise reluctant to rule but assumes the burden out of necessity because he is the best or only person for the job. Superman

Opposite, top: Moses and the Burning Bush, with Moses Removing His Shoes. Attributed to Dierick Bouts the Elder. Netherlands, c. 1465–1470. John G. Johnson Collection, Philadelphia Museum of Art, cat. 339. Moses is wearing a blue shirt and red toga. *Bottom:* Jor-El's hologram (Marlon Brando) in the Fortress of Solitude. *Superman: The Movie* (extended cut), 1978. Warner Bros.

doesn't show such misgivings in his early comics or in the 1978 film, but he does in 2013's *Man of Steel*, where he wanders the U.S. incognito until his thirties. Only when his destiny is thrust upon him by the plight of humanity, when the conquering alien Zod appears, does he become Superman. It's an arc foreshadowed when, as a young boy, Clark can be spotted reading the *Republic* in school and again when he's bullied by classmates,[10] clearly anchoring him in classical philosophy but equally reflecting his Mosaic roots, as a man born to destiny who, try as he might to shun it, eventually assumes the mantle of hero.

Both men, at this stage of their lives, accept their true heritage, Moses as an Israelite and Superman as a Kryptonian, and both return to their people, though the parallel between them diverges here: Superman dedicates himself to the protection of his adoptive people while Moses returns to save his native people. (In *Moses and Monotheism*, Sigmund Freud makes the argument that Moses was in fact an Egyptian prince, whose father the Pharaoh wished dead and who was sent down the Nile, found and raised by humble Levites, and grew to lead the Israelites who accepted him as their own.[11]) Clark, or Kal-El, assumes the name Superman (in several tellings it's given to him by others, usually Lois Lane), signifying might and heroism, and Moses lives up to his equally heroic name, meaning liberator and savior.

But Superman isn't merely a hero. He's a superhero—*the* superhero—endowed with an array of superpowers, including super-strength and speed, near-invulnerability, heightened hearing and sight, x-ray and heat vision, freeze breath, and of course, flight. These are all genre tropes today but they were novel when he first appeared, setting him apart from the pulp and comic strip heroes that came before. Moses isn't a hero in the physical tradition, but he is super, gifted with signs and abilities far beyond those of mortal men. He performs miracles throughout his biblical narrative, with frequency and on a scale that no other prophet or leader in scripture does before or after, save perhaps Jesus.

When demanding that Pharaoh let his people go (not the same Pharaoh in whose court he grew up, who'd since died [Ex. 2:23], but likely his son, Moses's adoptive brother), he transforms his brother Aaron's staff into a snake, then has it swallow the mystical serpents of Pharaoh's sorcerers (Ex. 7:10–12). And when Pharaoh proves intransigent he calls down on Egypt the Ten Plagues: the Nile, along with all the water in Egypt, turns into blood; an army of frogs; an outbreak of lice; thick swarms of flies; the death of all livestock; an outbreak of festering boils; a lethal storm of hail; a blanketing cloud of locusts; blinding darkness; and the death of all first-borns of Egypt (7:17–12:29).

He then leads the exodus of the Hebrews to freedom after 430 years of slavery, along with a multitude of others (12:38–40), and manifests a pillar of cloud to lead their way during the day and a pillar of fire to guide them at night (13:21). At the Red Sea he parts the water into two walls to allow them passage on dry land, then brings the water back on Pharaoh and his army who're in pursuit (14:21–28). As they cross the Sinai Desert he makes bitter water drinkable (15:23–25), summons manna and quail for food (16:13–15, 35) and draws drinking water out of rocks (17:6, Num. 20:11). At Mount Sinai, Moses delivers to his people the Ten Commandments and the Torah, by one Talmudic account by flying, ascending to the heavens in a cloud (tractate

Yoma 4a. The Talmud is a dense compilation of oral laws annotated with rabbinical discussions, consisting of about two and a half million words comprising two corpora, the Mishnah and the Gemara. Legend has it that God recited the Talmud, the oral law, to Moses on Mount Sinai while simultaneously giving him the Torah, the written law. There are two versions of the Talmud: Babylonian [Bavli], generally regarded as more authoritative, and Jerusalemite [Yerushalmi], both of which were written over a period of 600 years, between the first and seventh centuries CE).

And finally, after a forty-year detour in the desert, he delivers them to the Promised Land. These ancient superpowers aren't innate like Superman's—Moses is merely a conduit for God's omnipotence—but they're no less fantastical and, more importantly, are utilized for the same purpose; to save lives, fight evil and promote freedom and justice.

And just like Superman, the most powerful man on Earth who chooses to live his life as mild-mannered Clark Kent, Moses, the former price of Egypt and God's chosen messenger, is equally modest and humble, until duty calls and God asks "how long wilt thou count thyself so lowly? The hour calls but for thee! Know that you art the man for it, that of all, the calling is but for Moses" (Leviticus Rabbah 1:5), much like the famed call, "this is a job for Superman!"

The two heroes are even depicted similarly; a number of accounts in rabbinical literature describe Moses as an extremely tall, beautiful and immensely strong man,[12] praises reserved for him alone out of all the biblical champions (David, for example, is only beautiful and Samson is only strong), like Superman, who's played by impossibly handsome, tall and muscular actors like Christopher Reeve and Henry Cavill and drawn to put them both to shame.

What places Superman in the heraldic tradition of Moses, however, isn't just the correspondence in their origin stories and supernatural powers. It's his "never-ending battle for Truth, Justice and the American Way." His mission statement, his core values, not only relate to Moses, but in a real sense originate from him.

"Truth," despite its abstractness, is delineated rather definitively in religious doctrine. Much of humanity's understanding of truths—moral, existential, cosmological and historical—is based, directly or genealogically, in the monotheistic religions, which originate in turn in Mosaic Law. Moses, often called Moshe Rabbenu in Hebrew, "Moses our Teacher," is the first exponent of divine truth, in the form of the Decalogue and the Torah, with its additional 613 decrees. These have served as a main template from which modern society's value system evolved, in the name of which Superman fights. Ostensibly, then, Superman's "truth" is the same as Moses's, and with similar fideism; he stands for hope, an unwavering belief in good triumphing regardless, or despite of, the circumstances, requiring, like religiousness, faith.

"Justice," as a value, is the defining characteristic of Moses. All that the Bible tells about him as a man, between his birth and his undertaking of God's mission, are three short stories, told in succession in Exodus 2:11–19, which illustrate his strong sense of justice and compassion.

In the first, despite having grown up as a member of the Egyptian royal court, Moses is still troubled by the plight of the Hebrew slaves. One day, while observing their forced labor, he witnesses a slave driver beating a slave. Coming to the bondman's defense, he strikes the Egyptian dead and, supposing it went unseen, buries him in the sand. The second story takes place the following day, where again Moses walks among the slaves. He sees two Hebrews fighting and intervenes to separate them, when the aggressor taunts him with knowledge of his killing the Egyptian. When Pharaoh hears about this he orders his death, but he flees Egypt to Midian. In the third story, Moses is sitting down by a well when the daughters of Jethro, the priest of Midian, come to draw water for their father's flock. A band of shepherds then arrives and bullies them away, but Moses comes to their rescue and reclaims the well, then waters their sheep for them.

In the first instance, Moses was protecting one of his Hebrew brethren against an Egyptian, and so his actions can be seen as sectarian and personal rather than principled. But in the second case he protected one Israelite against another, and in the third he defended a group of strangers against other strangers, a matter in which he had no personal stake, no connection to, and put him in danger. This trifecta of valiant deeds depict Moses as a man compelled to take action in the name of justice, regardless of circumstances or risk, the innate quality of a hero as well as a leader.

As the main lawgiver of the Jewish faith, and consequently influential in Christianity and Islam, Moses is also an early father of today's legal system. The Commandments and the Torah he delivers to the Israelites in Exodus aren't just a moral code but a legal one, expounded into a complex codex of laws and rules in Leviticus and Deuteronomy and further expanded over millennia of jurisprudence, much of which has evolved into modern law. It makes him, in addition to an embodiment of justice, a definer of its meaning, and to a large extent the originator of the law and justice Superman champions.

"The American Way" would seem to be entirely unelated to Moses; it's hard to imagine that a biblical prophet from the 14th century BCE has anything to do with an 18th-century political revolution or 20th-century nationalistic sentiment. But its ostensible meaning—"life, liberty and the pursuit of happiness," the fundamentals of American democracy, are based on the values of sanctity of life, freedom, equality and self-governance. These principles are firmly rooted in the Judaic tradition established by Moses, as he delivered the Israelites out of bondage and introduced a moral and legal code that was possibly the first to prohibit killing, to establish equality between all people under the law, and to create a government of the people and by the people, answerable only to God.

The inception of the American value system in the Jewish one hasn't gone unrecognized. U.S. President Woodrow Wilson declared that "in applying the Mosaic Code to the order of their internal life ... the pioneer Americans [followed] the Hebrew Commonwealth as a model government. In the spirit and essence of our Constitution, the influence of the Hebrew Commonwealth was paramount ... a divine precedent for a pure democracy, as distinguished from monarchy, aristocracy or any other form of government."[13]

Before Charles Thomson's design for the Great Seal of the United States was approved, Founding Fathers Thomas Jefferson and Benjamin Franklin also sought to recognize Moses as a spiritual father of the fledgling nation. Both submitted their own proposals, with Jefferson's depicting the Israelites' journey to freedom through the wilderness led by the pillar of cloud and Franklin's showing Moses parting the Red Sea in front of the pillar of fire, with Pharaoh and his chariots overwhelmed by the waters.[14] While neither was picked, acknowledgment ultimately found its way to the Liberty Bell. Ushering in the new nation at the first public reading of the Declaration of Independence, the inscription on the bell is God's instruction to Moses in Leviticus 25:10—"And Proclaim Freedom Throughout the Land Unto All the Inhabitants Thereof."

It's not the only American icon to have Mosaic influences: George Washington was frequently compared to him, including in two thirds of his eulogies, and Lady Liberty herself is said to have been inspired by him, the diadem of light rays emanating from her head and the tablet in her arm both referencing Moses's descent from Mount Sinai with the Ten Commandments.[15]

The parallels between Moses and Superman's life mission even extend to those who would oppose it, their archenemies. Superman's nemesis is Lex Luthor, a brilliant but deranged, power-hungry scientist, who in later iterations also became an imperious, Machiavellian plutocrat (beginning in 1986's *The Man of Steel* comics miniseries). The character's origin story and motivation have changed over the years, but most versions, including the first, depict him as a close childhood friend of Clark Kent and Superboy whose animosity toward the Man of Steel stems from feeling betrayed.[16]

Long before Luthor, Pharaoh, the first despotic supervillain, likewise grows up alongside the hero of dual identity, feels betrayed—as his adopted brother defects the royal court to lead the Hebrew slaves in revolt—and hates him with self-destructive compulsion. His father, the first Pharaoh of Exodus, is also a good match: Another of Luthor's motivations is that he sees Superman as an alien threat, like Pharaoh, who mistrusts the Israelites in his midst and therefore tries to destroy them. Intentionally or not, in *Superman* Luthor even adorns his secret lair with small obelisks. Most convincingly, however, may be that all three men are famously bald.

Superman's enemies in general, particularly during his early years, echo a Jewish sensibility of epic storytelling. Seen in mytho-historical context, ancient religions, from Hellenistic to Sumerian to Egyptian, are suffused with inhuman dangers, from Minotaurs to giant scorpion men to Griffins, respectively. Judaism, in contrast, posited no such monsters. There are angels and giants in the Bible, but relatively sparsely and almost never as great adversaries. The real dangers mankind faces are of our own making, either by other evil men or by man's own evil inclinations. Superman's earliest foes were abusive husbands, slumlords, protection racketeers, corrupt politicians and businessmen, Nazis and fascists, and later megalomaniacal scientists like the Ultra-Humanite and Lex Luthor and alien conquerors like Brainiac and General Zod—all manifestations of tyranny and oppression, the same evil Moses fought. In fact, before monikers like "the Man of Steel," Superman was known, beginning in his first appearance, as the "Champion of the Oppressed."[17]

That Superman was created in the Moses mold seems evident. Both are saved from harm, raised by people not their own, and grow, with difficulty, to become great saviors themselves. Both rise from deepest victimhood to highest heroism, becoming questing warrior-prophets who embody humanity's loftiest values. And both exemplify the unlimited power of the individual and the onus to harness it in the service of the community—and in turn the community's benefit of welcoming outsiders, as Moses, a man raised as Egyptian royalty, is the one to free the enslaved Israelites and transform them into the Jewish people, and Superman, a strange visitor from another planet, is Earth's greatest protector and humanity's ultimate role model.

Superman isn't a transfigured Moses. Siegel and Shuster didn't set out to repurpose the biblical character and his narrative with modern trappings. Rather, they drew on him for inspiration, intentionally or not, when they created their hero. Superman is the modern custodian of an ancient mythology that traces back through Jewish tradition to its origins in Moses, making the Hebrew prophet also the first true superhero.

The real hero is always a hero by mistake.—Umberto Eco

Sent by His Father

Superman as Jesus

Despite the strong parallels to Moses, Superman is widely perceived as a Jesus metaphor. Certainly, there are plenty of corresponding elements between them as well, both thematic and anecdotal. It's hard not to see a man whose name means god sending his son, also named god, to Earth, where he becomes humanity's savior, as a Christ allegory.

Superman biographer Larry Tye notes that "like Jesus Christ, he descended from the heavens to help us discover our humanity."[1] Likewise, Super-scribe Grant Morrison writes that "Superman was Christ, an unkillable champion sent down by his father ... to redeem us by example and teach us how to solve our problems without killing one another."[2] Superman isn't just super, he's supernal, God immanent in spandex, who's associated with the notion of saving the whole world like only one other—Jesus, "the Savior of the world" (John 4:42). And like Jesus, who in John 8:23 proclaims, "I am from above; you are of this world, I am not of this world," Superman is an extraterrestrial in human form who walks among humans, dedicated to saving them from their own follies.

Superman is born of the stars and raised in Smallville, just as Jesus is born of the heavens and raised in the small town of Nazareth. Superman's earthly parents are Jonathan and Martha, a humble, godly couple. Jesus' earthly parents are Joseph and Mary, similarly humble and godly. Superman's foster father is a farmer, a modest laborer like Jesus' surrogate father, a carpenter. Both are celestial by nature and human by nurture, Jesus being the human personification of God while Clark is the human persona of Superman. Both also spend their childhood in obscurity, their true identity and amazing powers kept secret. These years of living life as normal people are what allows them to experience, understand and cherish humanity, to see themselves as part of it, resulting in both cases in a simple, egalitarian belief: "we who are strong have an obligation to bear with the failings of the weak" (Romans 15:1).

Superman's birth name is Kal-El. Jesus is first named Immanuel (Immanu-El), Hebrew for "God (is) with us" (mentioned in a prophecy of a virgin birth in Isaiah 7:14, attributed to Jesus in Matt. 1:22–23). Superman is called the Man of Steel. Jesus is called the Man of Sorrows (Isa. 53:3). Superman's adversary is a man named Luthor. Jesus' is named Lucifer. Both villains are characterized by hubris, juxtaposed against the heroes' humility. Superman's supporting cast from the *Daily Planet*, Lois, Jimmy and Perry, as the chroniclers of his exploits and his friends and frequent advocates, can be seen as his apostles, writing the gospels.

Superman is also evocative of Christ in his saintly perfection, at least as he's widely perceived, not found in any of the heroes of the Hebrew Bible. The Jewish heroes, in comic book parlance, are more "Marvel," deeply flawed, sometimes even morally questionable. (Marvel Comics, the biggest competitor of Superman's publisher DC Comics, revolutionized superheroes in the 1960s with greater thematic depth, characterization and realism.) Noah is a drunkard who flashes himself to his son Ham and curses his grandson Canaan (Gen. 9:21–27); Abraham abandons his son Ishmael (Gen. 16:1–6, 21:9–14) and disinherits his other six sons (25:1–5); Jacob favors his son Joseph over his brothers (Gen. 37:1–4); David, the original warrior-poet, seduces and impregnates the married Bathsheba, then orders her husband Uriah the Hittite to his death in the battlefield so he can marry her (2 Sam. 11:2–27); King Solomon intermarries gentile women and is led to worship their gods (1 Kings 11:1–13); Samson blindly loves an enemy woman, the Philistine Delilah (Judges 16:4–21); even Moses, the most righteous of the Hebrew heroes and the closest to Jesus in standing, is notoriously hot-tempered (Ex. 2:11–12, 32:19, Num. 20:10–11) and both doubts and disobeys God (Num. 20:7–12). Christian saints in general, but certainly Jesus, are deified as pure and flawless, a standard Superman, and Superman alone of all superheroes, was held to for much of his career, from the early 1940s to the late 1960s, earning him the nickname Big Blue Boy Scout and an image with which he's had an ambivalent relationship since.

There's even a Trinitarianism built into his mythos, as a character with three consubstantial personas: Kal-El, Clark Kent and Superman. The same can be said metatextually; Jerry Siegel has acknowledged that he based Clark Kent on himself and that "Jor-El" is a wordplay on his own name,[3] making both characters, the son and the father, manifestations of their world's creator.

Beyond the central Jesus equivalence, however, relatively few Christian signifiers can be found in Superman's comic books, at least until recent years. Of note is 1939's *Superman* #1, which tweaked his origin tale so that, instead of being found by a passing motorist and turned over to an orphanage, the star-child is found and adopted by an unnamed man and his wife, Mary. Her name was eventually changed to Martha and her husband given the name Jonathan, making the connotation tenuous but still present; Martha is the sister of Mary and Lazarus of Bethany, pivotal figures in the Jesus narrative. Some have also pointed to Clark Kent's middle name, Joseph, but that's been given interchangeably with Jerome,[4] nods to Superman's creators, and doesn't particularly fit the allegorical structure aside from his real-life father having the same name as Jesus'.

Superman's famous "S" insignia didn't hold any specific meaning beyond his name for the first fifty years of its existence, until in 1978's *Superman* it was shown to be the El family crest. This was adapted and evolved in the 2003 limited series *Superman: Birthright* to also be the Kryptonian symbol for hope,[5] a meaning it's retained since, elevating it from a heraldic emblem to a cross metaphor; a symbol of god (El) representing hope and salvation.

Superman's messianic role and the consequent themes of faith and deliverance are explored head-on in the 1996 miniseries *Kingdom Come* (the name suggesting it wasn't meant to be subtle). Described as "the most spiritual Superman story ever,"[6] it's an eschatological narrative told from the point of view of Norman McCay, a pastor plagued by apocalyptic premonitions that seem to mirror those of the Book of Revelation.

The story opens with "There were voices ... and thunderings, and lightnings ... and an earthquake,"[7] a quote from Revelation 8:5 (KJV), and is framed by more such quotes throughout, equating the Second Coming of Christ to that of Superman's. It takes place in a possible near future, in which the Man of Steel has forsaken the world for a hermetic existence. The general population increasingly doubts the remaining superheroes, and a new generation of young "metahumans," lacking a unifying role model and moral code to follow, indulge in hedonistic hooliganism and infighting. It isn't until the advent of Superman that the moral ambiguity is lifted and the superhumans, young and old, are divided into fairly clear, binary camps of good and evil, with the fate of humanity hanging in the balance.

The comic places Superman squarely in the role of Jesus at the end of days, returning to save, guide and pass judgment, and it can be read as a critique of secularism, as it's concerned with the absence of a god figure to serve as social compass. Visually, it mirrors Revelation's rich symbolism with ample, deftly handled religious imagery by the superstar team of writer Mark Waid and gouache painter Alex Ross: when Superman is first seen in the story he's performing carpentry on his family's barn roof, shirtless, bearded and long-haired, large nails jutting out his pocket and two long wooden beams balanced across his shoulders. One arm hangs over the beams while the other reaches down, with torso slightly turned and one leg bent, successfully evoking the otherwise disparate images of Jesus on the cross and the cover of *Superman* #1.[8]

Superman's comic book apotheosis as a Christ figure, however, is in the 1992–1993 storyline, "The Death and Return of Superman." It features Doomsday, a mindless juggernaut of death and destruction whose very name evokes the biblical end times. Superman manages to defeat him, just barely, saving Metropolis, but in doing so sacrifices his own life. Though he doesn't die for humanity's sins, he dies for the sins of *his* fathers—the monster is a genetically-engineered weapon from Krypton's distant past—his ultimate sacrifice as the world's savior is manifestly reflective of Christ, particularly when, shortly after his burial, his sepulcher is found empty. Superman's death isn't explained away as a mistake or a trick; he enters a state of clinical death and is brought back to life through Kryptonian science, supercharging his cells with solar radiation like a defibrillator, as well as possibly spiritual faith, when Jonathan Kent suffers a heart attack and either hallucinates or actually retrieves his son's soul from the afterlife.[9] Whether through resuscitation or resurrection, Superman eventually returns, but not before four false prophets claim the mantle (Eradicator, a Kryptonian artificial intelligence taken form, who also revives Superman; Superboy, a teenaged clone of Superman; Cyborg Superman, another cloned body of the hero, grafted with cybernetic prosthetics to look like the Terminator; and Steel, a weapons designer in a flying suit of armor). One of them, Cyborg Superman, is revealed to be a genocidal villain, and the real Parousia occurs in the nick of time

Left: Kingdom Come #1, May 1996. Written by Mark Waid and painted by Alex Ross. DC Comics. *Right: Superman* #1, June 1939. Cover by Joe Shuster. DC Comics.

for Superman to save mankind from the deceiver, completing the scriptural thematic arc.

Yet despite these examples, Christian metaphors in Superman's comics are rather scarce, particularly when considering the thousands of issues published over eighty years. What has elevated the character to the status of Jesus analogue in the public imagination is his cinematic oeuvre. His movies have tended to focus on his messianic role, increasingly so, and are laden with Christological themes and symbolism.

The first, and best—both as a film and as a metaphor—is *Superman*, starring Christopher Reeve. Jor-El is played by Marlon Brando, reminiscent of God in Medieval and Renaissance art as a white-haired man dressed in radiant white, carrying himself with perfect poise and gravitas. His eloquent dialogue is evocative of several New Testament passages, particularly the Gospel of John. He tells his wife Lara, "He will not be alone. He will never be alone"[10] while placing his holographic "spirit" in his son's rocket ship, like John 8:16's "I am not alone in it, but I and the Father who sent Me." This binitarian relationship between God and Jesus is expressed clearly when Jor-El says to his son, "you will make my strength your own, see my life through your eyes, as your life will be seen through mine. The son becomes the father and the father the son," likewise suggestive of John 14:10, "I am in the Father and the Father is in me."

Superman, like Jesus, is portrayed here as a manifestation of his astral father on Earth, if more figurative than literal, sent down with a purpose. Later, when Clark activates Jor-El's hologram in his Fortress of Solitude—like a place of worship, a shrine to the past and a hallowed hall of communion—his special calling is revealed. "They can be a great people, Kal-El," his father's ethereal presence proclaims. "They wish to be. They only lack the light to show the way. For this reason above all—their capacity for good—I have sent them you. My only son." It's a pivotal moment in the film, when Clark, assuming his birthright, transforms for the first time into Superman. It's also resonant of a number of Bible quotes, most strongly of John 3:16–19: "For God so loved the world, that he gave his only Son … that the world through him might be saved … the light has come into the world." More than a mere allusion, it marks a thematic shift in Superman's mythology, from a baby sent to Earth as a refugee so he can be saved to a son sent to Earth by his father to become its savior. It forever recast the Last Son of Krypton as a reimagined son of God, a choice that screenwriter Tom Mankiewicz admits was deliberate,[11] and which, while largely disregarded by the comics, has become a central motif in Superman's small and big screen incarnations.

Superman II, the 1980 sequel, was written and in part filmed concurrent to the first, and it expanded the Christian themes of the story. Superman faces three Kryptonian criminals led by the evil General Zod (Terence Stamp), remodeled from his militaristic comic book look: slicked-back widow-peaked hair, a manicured thin beard, and a black and crimson garb, he resembles the popularized image of the devil since Goethe's *Faust*. In an origin story practically exact to that of Lucifer Morningstar in Milton's *Paradise Lost* (borrowing elements, but different, from the comic book origin), Zod is the high general of Krypton's army, entrusted with its protection, but in his hubris and thirst for power he attempts a failed coup, resulting in his downfall. Cast by Jor-El to the Phantom Zone, a hellish prison dimension of "eternal living death," he escapes after Krypton's destruction to destroy the son of his jailer. What role he intends to assume once he does is clear—when the American President, forced to kneel before him, mutters "Oh God," he corrects him: "Zod."[12]

The film also sees Superman relinquish his powers so he can be with Lois, becoming a regular mortal, which leads to a scene of him beaten bloody and humiliated, a Passion of sorts. Its role in the story is different, however, in that it makes him realize he'd made a mistake, a selfish act at the expense of his duties to mankind, the opposite of Christ's redemptive sacrifice. But when Zod and his cronies appear on Earth to enslave it, he returns to the Fortress of Solitude, where in an inexplicable elision he manages to regain his superpowers, just in time for his Second Coming as Superman to save the world.[13]

In *Superman II: The Richard Donner Cut* (director Donner was fired by the producers after filming much of the movie, replaced by Richard Lester who filmed the rest. The result was a rather patchwork theatrical release, largely corrected in Donner's director's cut, released on DVD in 2006), the means by which he recovers his powers are revealed. Jor-El's hologram, powered by the last of Krypton's remaining energy, "sacrifices" himself to repower him. The persona of Superman, for all intents and purposes, was dead, then resurrected at the hands of his father, who reaches out to his him in a manner suggestive of Michelangelo's *Creation of Adam* fresco. (Producer Ilya Salkind felt it was "over the top," given the already "many messianic tones that were absolutely clear and intended since the beginning.") Superman's revivification also mirrors Jesus' Transfiguration (Matt. 17:1–9, Mark 9:2–8, Luke 9:28–36, 2 Pet. 1:16–18), taking place in a blinding halo of light as the disembodied voice of his father calls out "son." And like the Transfiguration, considered a singular miracle of Jesus in that he is not its performer but its recipient, Superman is the one saved rather than the one saving.[14]

The movie was accompanied by a tie-in novel, *Miracle Monday*, written by Elliot S. Maggin, the principal writer of Superman's comics from 1971 to 1986. The plot involves the Metropolis Marvel saving humanity from no less than Samael, the ruler of hell, who seeks to destroy Superman by morally corrupting him. Superman manages to outsmart Samael and win through his unwavering virtue, exactly like the atonement of Jesus, who outwits the devil to redeem mankind through his self-sacrifice. Samael is banished back to hell and the events are expunged from collective memory, but a lingering echo remains within the souls of humanity, manifesting in the future as a festive holiday, giving the book its name.[15]

Twenty years later, in October 2001, *Smallville* premiered, a TV show about an adolescent, pre–Superman Clark Kent. Post-9/11, in a new century defined by a religious act, religion in popular culture moved from subtle allegory to center stage, and *Smallville* led the trend. As Gustav Peebles, New School University Associate Professor of Anthropology, notes, "the show, quite simply, is suffused with Christian propaganda … almost every episode has some vaguely apt Biblical citation, such as a throwaway reference to the Holy Grail, three wise men, or Roman barbarism." Its biblical allusions, particularly to Jesus, are recurrent and obvious, just short of explicit, beginning with the pilot episode, in which a shirtless Clark is strapped and hoisted on a crucifix (contrived as a school hazing), an image also used in the promotional material for the show under the suggestive tagline "Every story has a beginning."[16]

Throughout its ten seasons (making Tom Welling the actor to play Superman the longest, ironically without ever actually playing Superman), *Smallville* regularly finds ways to portray Clark with halos (a streetlight above him) and angel wings (a statue behind him), stock symbolism but nonetheless distinctly Christian imagery, reaching its overwrought apex in the ninth season finale, titled "Salvation." The episode begins with Clark dreaming of his destiny as savior and ends with him battling Zod, who brandishes a Kryptonite dagger as he exclaims, repeating Satan's famous deceleration in *Paradise Lost*, "better to rule in Hell than to serve in Heaven!" To save humanity, Clark allows himself to be impaled by the dagger, plummeting off the rooftop in a crucifixion pose.[17]

This shift from undertone to overtone continues in 2006's *Superman Returns*, a cinematic paean to both *Superman* and the gospels. The film focuses not on Superman's humanity but on his celestial nature, his otherness and alienation, centering around the question of whether or not the world needs a savior. As the title conveys, the hero, played by Brandon Routh, returns to Earth after a prolonged absence—a five-year expedition to Krypton's remains—only to discover that the world has moved on. Even Lois, his greatest advocate, is receiving a Pulitzer for her editorial, "Why the World Doesn't Need Superman." Ultimately, the movie explores the Man of Steel's relevance and place in today's world, both in and out of the film. To its credit, it

Smallville promotional poster and ad featuring Tom Welling as Clark Kent, 2001. The WB/ Warner Bros.

embraces the mythology unabashedly and answers the question of whether the world still needs the archetypal superhero resolutely. What works less well is the argument it makes.

Superman, upon his return, tells Lois, "You wrote that the world doesn't need a savior, but every day I hear people crying for one."[18] With his super-senses, his awareness of the human condition is virtually omniscient, a god in the sky who can hear every prayer and cry and see every plight, but what he dedicates his time to are individual acts of good, from stopping bank robbers to catching a plane falling out the sky, few of which require any real effort on his part, and yet that is enough to turn

Lois from apostate to disciple. It fails to convince—that she would believe again the world depends on him, that the character is unique and perennial, that he is Christ reimagined—because, first, it implies the smallest scope of solution. To save people one by one, or even by multitude when disaster strikes, is a far cry from Jesus saving the entirety of the human race, past, present and future. Superman's heroism, in comparison, is paltry, almost meaningless, and yet the movie places him in the same standing.

Second, he isn't particularly inspiring in the film. Jesus' true success isn't in healing lepers or feeding the hungry, it's in his teachings. For either the story or the metaphor to work, Superman's impact must extend beyond his immediate actions. He needs to inspire hopefulness and betterment in others through example. It's as a symbol, a source of afflatus, not as an action hero, that he's both exceptional and Christlike.

There's also a virgin birth allegory hidden somewhere between *Superman II*, in which Lois and a depowered Man of Steel consummate their love, only for him to later (disconcertingly) erase her memory, and *Superman Returns*, a "loose continuity" sequel, in which Lois has given birth to his son. Alternatively, it's reminiscent of the Jesus bloodline hypotheticals, by which he sired a child with Mary Magdalene.

The film, directed by Brian Singer, is rich in Christian imagery, beginning with Ma Kent cradling her crash-landed son upon his return in a pose suggestive of Michelangelo's *Pietà*, and reaching its Christological peak is Superman's final battle with Lex Luthor. Suffering from acute Kryptonite poisoning, Superman is viciously beaten by Luthor's goons and eventually stabbed with a shard of Kryptonite, piercing his right side just as the Holy Lance (aka the Spear of Destiny) pierced Jesus'. John 19:34 adds that "forthwith came there out blood and water," reflected esthetically in the film when Superman is stabbed in a pool of water, then falls into the ocean. Following, in a final heroic act, he sacrifices his life to thwart Luthor and save the world, dying as he heavy-handedly assumes the exact pose of Christ on the cross. Unaccountably, however, he survives his death, perhaps more of a coma, awakening after the good people of Metropolis, having realized their folly in abandoning faith in him, congregate around the hospital he's brought to, wishing for his return. It's allegorically consistent, but his sacrifice is underwhelming; he manages to save the day by doing the impossible, but then simply faints for a while, wakes up and flies away. It's a disappointing dénouement, ending on a note of bathos.

What's most puzzling about the movie, an altogether enjoyable, if stolid, rendition of the legend, is, considering how hard it works to convey a Jesus parable, just how unlike Jesus Superman is in it. Simply put, he's a craven cad. For one, he leaves Earth unprotected for five years, notifying no one, even Lois, with whom he was clearly involved, because "to say goodbye … was too difficult." When he learns that she's engaged and has a five-year-old son with her fiancé (paradoxically, he was gone five years, the child Jason is his and is five, Lois has been with her fiancé Richard for five years, and Richard believes Jason is his. It's unclear whether Lois knows otherwise), he spies on them at home like a peeping Tom, using his x-ray vision and super hearing. He later flirts with her unabashedly, inviting her to fly with him (Lois: "Richard, he's a pilot. Takes me up all the time." Superman: "Not like this"), then tries

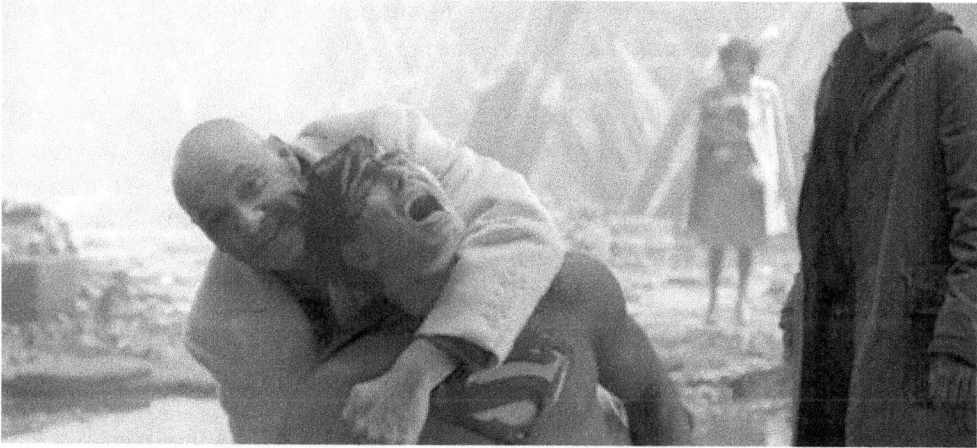

Superman (Brandon Routh) stabbed in the side by Lex Luthor (Kevin Spacey). *Superman Returns*, 2006. Warner Bros.

to kiss her. And at the end, when he knows the child is his, he simply tells Lois, "I'm always around" and flies away.

None of these are treated as moral failings, which only highlights how out of character they are for such a paragon of virtue, let alone for a Christ figure. And they stand in contrast to an otherwise convincing portrayal of the hero as gentle, quiet, and all-powerful, with an unwavering sense of right and wrong, traits worthy of Jesus.

If *Superman Returns*' Christ allegory is clumsy, 2013's *Man of Steel*'s is blatant. The movie makes no qualms about being a retelling of the gospels. Its messianic imagery is copious and clear, as is its Bible-based structure, crossing from evocative to evangelizing and giving Superman a true messiah complex.

The Christian faith–based demographic has grown in size and prominence in the 21st century, and so it's unsurprising that Warner Bros., parent company of DC Comics and the studio producing Superman films, has been increasingly catering to its sensibilities, culminating in the unambiguousness of *Man of Steel*. The film's aggressive marketing campaign included explicit promotions as a vehicle for gospel and edification. Religious figures around the U.S. were invited to attend early screenings and special trailers were prepared, highlighting the "faith-friendly angles" of the movie for ministers to incorporate into their services. The studio also launched a "Pastor Resource Site," providing "everything you need to educate and uplift your congregation," including images, videos and even sermons, with portions like "Superman's mythical origins are rooted in the timeless reality of a spiritual superhero … the story of Superman awaken[s] our passion for the greatest hero who ever lived and died and rose again … [his] humble origins, his high calling and his transforming sacrifice point us towards Jesus, the original superhero."[19]

This particular sermon was authored by theologian and associate professor of communications at Pepperdine University Craig Detweiler, who added that Christian audiences "are finally getting the stories we've been clamoring for."[20] It's a telling statement, illuminating how these aren't intrinsic elements of Superman as much as later additions, designed to engage devout audiences and provide a thematic framework for the general, largely Christian audience to recognize and connect with.

Some, though, found the equivalence of Superman and Jesus in a movie saturated with violence disconcerting. Its controversial ending, which sees thousands, if not hundreds of thousands, of people killed in the devastation of Metropolis and Superman snapping Zod's neck to stop him, has angered some Christian moviegoers to the point of declaring the new Superman the anti–Christ.[21]

The film is a reboot, a retelling of the origin story, and so able to thread new Christological themes into the narrative. It opens on Krypton, where Superman is the first baby in centuries to be born naturally rather than by means of genetic engineering, a reverse Nativity miracle as the only non-virgin birth. When Jor-El prepares to send his son to Earth he tells Lara (Israeli actress Ayelet Zurer), "He'll be a god to them," bookended when, a moment later, she announces, "His name is Kal, son of El."[22]

On Earth, Clark, played by Henry Cavill, grows to be a bearded wanderer, performing miracles and good deeds throughout the land. He's also something of a pacifist, choosing to turn the other cheek in childhood when he's attacked by bullies and as an adult when he's assaulted by a truculent trucker (though to be fair, the man later finds his truck impaled on tree logs).

When Zod (Michael Shannon) appears on Earth to demand that he reveal himself, conflicted, he consults a pastor. Sitting in the church pew, the background is filled by a stained glass window of Jesus, wearing a flowing red sash. Willing to sacrifice himself to save mankind, he surrenders to authorities to decide his fate, bothering to note that he's 33 years old—the same age as Jesus when he did exactly the same (Luke 3:23, John 11:55).

Jor-El's hologram (Russell Crowe), no longer confined to sentimental instructive recordings in the Fortress of Solitude, is a figurative and literal *deus ex machina*, guiding Lois to save Superman from Zod's spaceship and Superman to save the world. An omnipotent (at least when it comes to controlling Kryptonian technology)

Superman (Henry Cavill) and Jesus. *Man of Steel*, 2013. Warner Bros.

Smallville, season 9 episode 21, "Salvation," 2010. The CW/Warner Bros.

Superman Returns, 2006. Warner Bros.

Man of Steel, 2013. Warner Bros.

ghost-father, he's more Godlike than ever, dispensing edifications such as "You will give the people of Earth an ideal to strive towards," implying a covenant-like imparted morality from beyond, and as he looks down on Earth with his son, "You can save all of them," at which point Superman floats into space, arms outstretched, assuming the pose of Jesus Christ.

Composer Hans Zimmer, who, appropriately enough, scored *Man of Steel* right after the History Channel miniseries *The Bible*, affirms that "both stories are passions," as does director Zack Snyder, who told CNN: "The Christ-like parallels, I didn't make that stuff up.... That stuff is there, in the mythology. That is the tried-and-true Superman metaphor. So rather than be snarky and say that doesn't exist, we thought it would be fun to allow that mythology to be woven through."[23] Still, the Christian references in the film are about as subtle as the action, and some of them—like Superman's age or the church visit—come across as story in service of symbolism rather than the other way around. The tone of the film is also a strange choice for an evangelical vehicle. Though impressively mythical and operatic, and a clever updating of the mythology, the movie is largely bleak and joyless, more reminiscent of Medieval orthodoxy than the uplifting celebration of faith one would expect from a Superman movie, which 1978's *Superman* is.

Batman v Superman: Dawn of Justice, the cacophonous 2016 semi-sequel to *Man of Steel*, also directed by Snyder, likewise contains Christian iconography and Jesus metaphors, though they aren't as much at the forefront of the story. The first act is rich in salvific imagery, like a slow-motion montage in which Superman hovers above people reaching for the sky to be saved, with the sun behind his head engulfing him in halo.

There's also a moment of enlightenment atop a mountain, which he ascends humbly—on foot and in warm clothing, neither necessary for him—where he receives moral guidance from a vision of his father (though Jonathan Kent, not Jor-El), a scene that repeats several times in the synoptic gospels (Matt. 14:23, 17:1–5, Luke 6:12, 9:28–35, Mark 6:46, 9:2–7).

The most thematically resonant element of the film is that, despite the altruistic miracles he performs daily, not everyone trusts Superman. Many even fear him and his implications to the social order, just as Jesus was feared. Congress holds a hearing, calling him to capitulate to the law of the land, which he does, answering the summons to appear, echoing the Sanhedrin (judicial council) trial of Jesus, and with fairly similar results; leading, though indirectly, to his sacrificial death.

Lex Luthor (a spasmodic Jesse Eisenberg) spends the film repeatedly calling Superman a god, and his motivation, while incoherent on specifics, is nonetheless clearly iconoclastic in nature. The movie also features Doomsday, created here by Luthor who, before unleashing him, declares not too subtly, "If man won't kill god, the devil will do it!"[24]

Batman, as the title implies, is the film's co-star, portrayed with intense singlemindedness by Ben Affleck. Alarmingly homicidal, he seeks to impale Superman using a Kryptonite spear, an odd choice considering anything from bullets to

Top and above: The spear of Kryptonite and Superman's death scene with crosses in the background. *Batman v Superman: Dawn of Justice,* 2016. Warner Bros.

shrapnel could be fashioned out of Kryptonite. It's mainly a contrived stand-in for the Spear of Destiny, and it similarly plays a role in Superman's self-sacrifice, although it's put to clever use as the tool with which he also saves the world.

When Superman does die at the end of the film, the circumstances reflect those of Jesus' death. Batman is a nonbeliever, rejecting his role in human affairs. He persecutes him, unknowingly manipulated the whole time by the devilish Luthor. In what is the most ham-fisted iconography of the film, Superman falls to the ground in a crucifix pose, then is brought down from the hill upon which he died wrapped in his cape, with large cross-shaped metal debris in the background. It's a Descent from the Cross scene, Jesus being brought down from Golgotha.

Superman obviously can't stay dead, and the movie, like the gospels, ends with the promise of his resurrection and return (which he does in 2017's *Justice League*). After all, it was released on Good Friday.

The Man of Steel's legend—an almighty superhuman who comes to Earth from beyond to save humanity and inspire it to follow his example—bears a clear resemblance to the story of Christ. His movie career, which is where most people know him from, is steeped in Christian themes and signifiers, cementing his status as a Jesus metaphor. He's the other ultimate good guy, a powerful and kind hero, and he, too, loves humanity in a way that maybe only someone who could never be hurt by it can.

All men are Jews, though few men know it.—Bernard Malamud

World's Finest

Settling the Denominational Debate

The idea of a celestial savior is as old as civilization. The idea of one disguised as a mere mortal is Judeo-Christian, starting with the three angels presenting themselves as wayfarers to Abraham in Genesis 18 and culminating in Jesus, the son of God who lived as the son of a carpenter (other mythologies, like Greek, also feature this motif, but the gods disguise themselves as men temporarily and ad hoc, and rarely altruistically, like Zeus in his philandering). The god-man, powerful and protective, is one of the most resonant concepts in cultural history, capturing the essence of human hopes and fears. Superman is the custodian of this tradition, a "perfectly designed emblem of our highest, kindest, wisest, toughest selves," in the words of Grant Morrison.[1] At once a god who would be man and a man born of the gods, Superman has come to embody the noblest aspirations of mankind, a culmination of what was once the purview of divine creed in a modern form of superhumanism.

The debate over Superman's true origins and meaning can be construed as an argument of cultural appropriation, either as an act of supersessionism, a Jewish creation subsumed under mainstream Christian culture, or, alternatively, a creation of mainstream culture claimed by Jews in eisegetical revisionism. Whatever his metaphorical foundation, the Man of Tomorrow is, and was always intended to be, a symbol of cultural collaboration, exemplified by his origin story as an alien refugee taken in by loving Americans and his life's mission of bringing to bear the gifts of his heritage for the benefit of all.

Danny Fingeroth has recognized these dueling pedigrees, writing that "the main metaphor systems at war for credit for the inspiration for Superman are Moses and Jesus."[2] Undoubtedly, the parallels run both ways, and Superman is at the least a Judeo-Christian figure. But many of the thematic and iconographic similarities to Jesus were added years after Superman's debut by subsequent, often gentile writers and artists, who introduced their own cultural connotations to the mythology. Superman's provenance, along with many tropes of the superhero genre, is in Judaism.

None of this is to prove a point of ownership. Exclusivity means exclusion, and Superman was created to be the exact opposite, a bridge between the Jewish world and the larger world, a secular messiah of goodwill and brotherly love. It's to note contribution, the cultural and historical elements from which he was first fashioned and which continue to inform his ethos and adventures today.

Fingeroth notes, "although these two iconic figures are often poised as avatars of conflicting belief systems.... Moses is viewed by some theological thinkers as a precursor to Jesus."[3] Religiously, Moses is the deliverer of the first covenant between God and his chosen people and Jesus is the deliverer of the second, its emendation, creating the first two monotheistic faiths. Typologically, numerous elements in the New Testament are prefigured in the Old Testament and its apocrypha, unsurprising considering Jesus was a Jewish rabbi (John 1:38, Mark 9:5, Matt. 26:25), making Christianity itself a Jewish invention. For historical scale, in the Hebrew calendar, used today for religious observances, the year is 5780, meaning that when Jesus was born Judaism was already older than Christianity is today.

From a literary and folkloric standpoint, Moses can be seen as the foundational myth from which Jesus derives—from which all stories of a child who is the chosen one, who assumes the mantle of hero upon adulthood and undertakes a quest fraught with adversity in the name of grand ideals originate, for that matter. Much of the Jesus narrative echoes that of Moses, beginning with their special birth and the horror that accompanied it. Just as Pharaoh did, Herod, having been foretold by the magi that a newborn king of the Jews would dethrone him, orders the murder of all the male infants of Bethlehem. And like Moses, baby Jesus is snuck to safety in Egypt (Matt. 2:13–18). Both grow to become compassionate men who care greatly for the downtrodden and who are exalted for their humility (Num. 12:3, Matt. 11:29). Both are Jewish preachers advocating religious-moral devotion, are mediators of covenants and founders of religious movements. Both give their famous sermons on a mountain (Ex. 19–24, Matt. 5–7) and both are abandoned by ungrateful followers (Ex. 32:1–6, Mark 14:50). Moses, along with the rest of the Israelites, wanders the wilderness for forty years, and Jesus wanders the wilderness for forty days (Num. 14:34, Matt. 4:1–2). Both perform miracles, including feeding a multitude (Ex. 16:2–16, Mark 8:1–10) and walking through or on water (Ex. 14:21–22, John 6:16–21). Jesus' Last Supper can even be seen as an homage, given that it was a Passover Seder, a celebration of Moses's legacy (Matt. 26:17, Mark 14:1–2, Luke 22:1–15).

A number of these themes are present in Superman's lore, giving him much in common with both prophets. There are other, similar mythological sources, like the Osiris myth, in which the Egyptian goddess Isis, impregnated by Osiris posthumously after he'd been murdered by his brother Set, hides in a thicket of papyrus in the Nile Delta to save her newborn son Horus from his evil uncle. In the ancient Indian epic the *Mahabharata* (Drona Parva), Vasusena (aka Karna) is the son of a sun god and an earthly virgin who's placed in a basket and set afloat down a river to be found and raised by a delegate of a king. The Assyrian king Sargon of Akkad is said to have been the son of a high priestess and unknown father, born in secret and sent down a river in a basket of rushes, found by a commoner and raised as a gardener. The mythical Greek king Oedipus was prophesized to kill his father and so was left to die on a mountainside, where he was found and raised as a prince. Similar elements can be found in later legends, from King Arthur to Luke Skywalker.

These striking similarities suggest that the tales travelled the ancient world and informed one another, though it's also possible that their shared paradigms originate in humanity's collective unconscious, a panhuman fantasy of predestined greatness. Either way, Superman is their modern culmination. And since he was created and developed within the Western tradition, mostly by Jews, and the story of Moses is antecedent to the story of Jesus, Moses can lay claim to being Superman's origin point.

Beyond the inherently Christian motif of an almighty celestial disguised as a mere mortal, there's little throughout most of Superman's comic book narrative to signify Christ, and it's doubtful that Siegel and Shuster, two Jews in the 1930s, intended their hero to be Jesus. But along the way the Jewish Kal-El converted to Christianity, proselytized by later writers, particularly screenwriters, who imbued him with Christological resonance. When director Zack Snyder said that the Christ parallels are all built into the mythology, he was, for the most part, wrong. That thematic structure was introduced in 1978 in *Superman*, and expanded upon in the cinematic corpus by Donner, Singer and Snyder (ironically, all Jewish). Though it proved a good fit, none of its elements, especially the iconography, are anywhere to be found in the source material.

In his earlier comics Superman is never conferred upon the mantle of savior by his father, never hovers in a crucifixion pose, is never identified as 33 years old (his age has changed over the years, originally looking mid–30s and gradually younger later on, usually cited as 29 or a vague thereabouts. The 1986 *The Man of Steel* and 2003 *Superman: Birthright* miniseries both put him at 25, and in the 2011 relaunched *Action Comics* he seems to be about 22. More recently, he looks to be in his mid–30s again. The closest he comes to 33 is in the 1993 *Superman* Vol. 2 #75 collector's edition, which includes a mock *Daily Planet* obituary that states, "he is believed to have been in his early thirties"), is never shown next to Jesus, and seeking the counsel of clergymen is a recent and rare addition to the canon (seen only in 1998's *Superman for All Seasons* #1 and several times in 2004–2005's *Superman* Vol. 2 #209–215).[4]

Snyder did also acknowledge, however, the character's multivalent nature. "When you talk about mythology, you want to … be able to draw from peoples' collective experiences. What is personal to you or to someone who sees a Christ story or someone who doesn't, it might affect the way they see the movie…. But by no means is it for one idea to cancel out the other, or for it to be mutually exclusive to one single idea." Adding to this, Snyder's writer on both his Superman films, David Goyer (despite the surname, also Jewish), noted that the story reflects "also the legend of Moses, clearly the whole way his parents give him up and send him."[5] Superman is a Moses metaphor in print turned Jesus metaphor on screen, which in turn has influenced his comics. These ecclesiastical additions to his mythology don't detract from it. They enrich it, as thematic source material and as points of reference for many readers and viewers. They do compromise it, though, when they're so blatant as to call attention to themselves at the expense of Superman's own story.

Allowing for historicity, Moses and Jesus are arguably the two most influential figures in human history. It's fitting that Superman, the most influential superhero and one of the most important characters in fiction, be modeled after them. But despite their many correspondences, there is an essential difference between them; Moses is a hero, an exceptional man but just a man, who continually champions the cause of others at great personal sacrifice. Jesus is God, an external benevolent force. His corporeal martyrdom, ultimately, is a calculated means to achieve empyrean victory. Which is more apposite is a matter of perspective. If Superman is an alien first, a godly creature who only shares man's image, than he is better matched with Christ. But if, for all his vaunted powers and exobiology, he's a red-blooded American gifted with great powers by his heritage, a man who simply helps his fellow man because he's in a unique position to do so, then he's a better fit with Moses. This duality of divinity and humanity, nature and nurture, Superman and Clark, and the struggle to reconcile them is a question both fans and the hero himself have been wrestling with over the years, with no definitive answer.

From either perspective, however, Superman is a messianic figure. The concept of a messiah is originally a Jewish one: the word comes from Hebrew (מָשִׁיחַ), meaning "anointed one," and is used to refer to a number of rescuers and emancipators throughout Jewish religious and folkloric tradition. Moses, the greatest of these, is even named using the same root (משׁ). The notion branched off into Christianity, clearly, but Jewish and Christian messianism are categorically different. As Rabbi Geoff Dennis, lecturer in the Jewish Studies Program at the University of North Texas, explains, "the uniquely Christian vision of the messiah is the supernal empowered 'chosen one' who surrenders and sacrifices himself and dies for the good of humanity, his death bringing salvation in a way his life could not. The Jewish messiah, by contrast, is the empowered 'chosen one' who strives and struggles, who to the very end lives for the good of humanity, ultimately to triumph over adversity and evil, but without losing himself."[6]

It's a meaningful distinction, one that comic book luminaries Mark Waid, Mark Millar, Grant Morrison and Tom Peyer made note of in their "Superman 2000" proposal: Aiming to revitalize the character for the new millennium, they described the Man of Steel as "a god sent to Earth not to suffer and die but to live and inspire and change."[7] Despite his superpowers Superman isn't omnipotent, and he risks his life daily to protect others from harm. He did sacrifice himself in the "Death of Superman" storyline, but that is a milestone, not the culmination, of his "never-ending battle" and narrative.

Yet, the authors also call him a god, which is a Christian view—Jesus is God himself, whereas the Jewish messiah is an empowered messenger of God. The idea of an otherwise common man given exceptional abilities with which to help and defend others is at the heart of the superhero concept, though Superman, despite being its progenitor, is also its exception. He's an extraterrestrial, his powers innate, analogous to Christ.

In terms of his message, Superman likewise lends himself to interpretation. He can be seen as a champion of truth and justice, abstract ideals greater than himself, and he can also be seen as their embodiment, the ideal to strive toward. He works equally well as either or both, which is part of his syncretic appeal.

As a god figure, however, Superman fits squarely within the Christian tradition. Jewish thought is largely pantheistic, seeing God as more transcendent than immanent, despite also allowing for an anthropomorphized God as allegory (more like a sentient Force from *Star Wars* than Morgan Freeman from *Bruce Almighty*). He's too abstract to father a corporeal child, which is at the root of the religious divide. Superman came to Earth with powers and abilities far beyond those of mortal men, but not as an ethereal spirit, as flesh and bone, just as Jesus did.

Like his mythology, Superman's personality also started out more like that of

Moses and gradually became more Christlike. Superman is largely seen as amiable, gentle and chaste, characteristics associated with Jesus. Moses is humble but more passionate, irritable, certainly not abashed of violence. In his earlier days, in his urtexts, the Big Blue Boy Scout was actually a temperamental vigilante fueled by righteous anger. Before he started fighting for the American Way he fought against those who corrupted the American reality, frequently defying the most hallowed of American tenets—authority, law enforcement, the courts, government—a counterculture rebelliousness that evokes Moses, who challenges Pharaoh's absolute rule as well as the dogma of paganism. Granted, Jesus confronts the money changers in the Temple, overturning their tables and throwing them out (Matt. 21:12–17, Mark 11:15–19, Luke 19:45–48, John 2:13–16), but this act is singular, standing in stark contrast to his otherwise placid, dovish nature. Even when he defies the social order by announcing himself to be the son of God and the king of the Jews, he does so peacefully and passively, attempting no insurgence nor offering resistance when arrested. It's a far cry from Superman circa 1938–1941, who regularly bashed skulls and tossed people out windows. Interestingly, all three figures have morphed over time in the general conception from insurrectionists to symbols of authority and lawgiving.

It's evident that Superman was created from the templates of both Moses and Jesus, whether directly or by virtue of them being cultural paradigms. While the Moses parallels are more pronounced in his comic book oeuvre, his films, as well as later versions in comics, have added Christ correspondences to his lore. And since relatively few people read his comics and Western movie audiences are largely Christian, Superman has come to be seen as a Christ figure. In part, this may explain the emergence of books and articles in recent years about the Man of Steel's and other superheroes' Jewish roots, as acts of reclamation. But as Fingeroth aptly sums it, "the character is a mixed metaphor and works fine that way."[8]

Still, Superman, at his core, as he was originally conceived and in his most profound, not merely allusive, themes, is based on Moses. His origin is a direct adaptation of Moses's. Both are steeped in tragedy, one that later defines their identity and life's mission. Superman is the sole survivor of his entire race, and it's because of this that he is Superman; he's sent to Earth because of Krypton's doom, and it's on Earth that he develops superpowers. Gradually, his motivation for crusading came to include wishing to prevent Earth from meeting Krypton's fate.

(The explanation for Superman's powers has changed over the years, but it's retained the premise that Earth makes him exceptional. The first telling, in 1938's *Action Comics* #1, attributes his abilities to a physical structure millions of years more evolved than humans'. When it was revisited in 1939's *Superman* #1, his strength was also explained by Earth's lower gravity. 1960's *Action Comics* #262 offered the explanation still used today, by which his powers result from Earth's yellow sunlight [unlike Krypton's red giant], fueling his alien physiology like a living solar battery.[9] In all three cases he's ordinary as a Kryptonian and exceptional on Earth.)

Moses's origin is likewise tragic, and equally necessary for him to become the hero. A generation of his people, the firstborn sons of Israel, is massacred by Pharaoh, and it's this catastrophe that sends him down the Nile and into Pharaoh's palace (ironically, bringing about the very fall that Pharaoh was trying to prevent). This

Charlton Heston as Moses. Publicity photograph for *The Ten Commandments*, 1956. Paramount.

ostensibly is what allows him later to gain audience with Pharaoh as emissary of the Israelites, and where perhaps he learns the statecraft to then lead them. It also manifestly serves as powerful motivation, when Moses unleashes the tenth and harshest plague—the death of firstborns—as divine retribution to Pharaoh's infanticide.

The birth of Jesus is also mired in tragedy, but of no real significance to his

Christopher Reeve as Superman. Publicity photograph for *Superman*, 1978. Warner Bros.

character or narrative. The murder of the infants of Bethlehem is of a relatively small scale, its architect Herod is never punished, and while Jesus and his parents flee to Egypt for a while, that period has no lasting effect or importance. Jesus is the son of God, a prophet of peace and love gifted with miraculous abilities, irrespective of these circumstances.

Superman doesn't come to Earth to call its people to repent. He doesn't seek followers, and in his early version he doesn't wish to inspire anyone. He simply does what he thinks is right, and he does so in the name of grand ideals, not in his own. This makes him more like Moses, whose mission is to save his people from immediate harm, in the name of God and his codices of law. And it's a mission that continues throughout his life, heroism through dedication and servitude, not self-sacrifice. Jenette Kahn, president and editor in chief of DC comics from 1976 to 2002 and the daughter of a rabbi, acknowledges that "at DC Comics we were always true to the core of Superman, his Midwestern upbringing, his Moses story. He is very much like the sage Hillel's saying: 'If I am not for myself, who am I? If I am for myself only, who am I? If not now—when?' That is really the core of Superman."[10]

And as someone who is always for others, the Man of Steel is no Prince of Peace. He's a man of action (as suggested by "*Action Comics*"), or more specifically, violence. Like all the superheroes that followed, while his stories may contain rich symbolism, thematic complexity and ethical reflection, they inevitably come down to slugfests with bad guys that have all the nuance of Rock 'Em Sock 'Em Robots. He does sometimes manage to solve things peacefully and rationally, but not often. That's not what sells comic books and movie tickets. In that he's akin to Moses, who doesn't hesitate to employ violence in order to protect his people and enforce justice. Jesus may be of a more evolved nature, but it's Moses that Superman takes after.

Superman's parentage is also more like that of Moses than Jesus. Jor-El is from a different planet, but he isn't deific. Even in versions where Kryptonians are all superpowered, he's like everyone else. And while Superman's lineage, the House of El, has come to be portrayed as Kryptonian nobility, it's neither royalty nor divinity. As scientists (Jor-El has always been a scientist, whereas Lara's profession wasn't given until 1971, where she was an astronaut cadet. This was changed in 1988 to a librarian and historian, a highly esteemed position on Krypton, and then again in 2014 to a military academy cadet[11]), Jor-El and Lara are reflective of Amram and Jochebed, who are both Levites (Ex. 2:1), the Jewish priestly class, keepers of truth and wisdom— the ancient equivalent of scientists, both in function and, at least on Krypton, social standing.

Most significantly, the son of Jor-El isn't sent to Earth by his father to save humanity from itself: he's snuck to safety by parents desperate to save him from inevitable doom (it isn't until 1945's *More Fun Comics* #101—the first Superboy story and an update of the origin—that Jor-El is even aware that his son would develop powers on Earth[12]). He's not predestined for greatness by birthright, but by the circumstance of his escape. It's this overcoming of tragedy and rise to greatness by will, not by providence, which Superman echoes Moses in, and which makes him a true *Mensch* of Steel.

The things that are said in literature are always the same. What is important is the way they are said.

—Jorge Luis Borges

PART II

Shticks from the Shtetl

How Jews Created Comics and Caped Crusaders

Hitler, Hollywood and Houdini

From Eastern Europe to the Lower East Side, Jews came in droves. There had always been a Jewish presence in America, Sephardic Jews since New Amsterdam and German Jews since the early 1800s, but this was an immigration wave of unprecedented proportions. Between 1881 and 1924, hundreds of thousands of Jewish families fled the European and Russian upheaval that preceded and followed the Bolshevik Revolution and the Great War.

It was a modern exodus that changed the face of America as well as Judaism. For nearly a hundred generations of Diaspora, Jews had been subjugated, disenfranchised, ghettoized ("ghetto" was originally coined in reference to Jews; it comes from the Italian *ghèto*, meaning "foundry," a diminutive for the Cannaregio section of Venice to which Jews were confined during the Venetian Republic [697–1797]), pogromed and expelled, the outsiders and victims in virtually every society they'd been part of. In none were they citizens of equal rights and standing. Except for the United States. They still faced suspicion, exclusion and even animosity in America, but nothing compared to what they endured in Europe and, in the eyes of the law at least, they were equals. For the first time in two millennia, Jews were free people.

Between the establishment of the United States in 1776 and 1880, the American Jewish population grew, by rough estimates, from 1,750 to 255,000. By the beginning of the 20th century it had grown to about one million. Another 1.75 million immigrated by 1924, mostly from Eastern Europe. About half of all American Jews lived in New York City, making it the largest Jewish community in the world—over twice the size of the second largest, Warsaw.[1] Most lived and worked in the crowded tenements of the Lower East Side, only five miles, but a world away, from the townhouses and mansions uptown.

In *How the Other Half Lives: Studies Among the Tenements of New York* (1890), renowned photojournalist and social reformer Jacob Riis documented the living conditions in New York's ethnic slums. He describes life in "Jewtown":

> Nowhere in the world are so many people crowded together on a square mile as here…. In Essex Street two small rooms in a six-story tenement were made to hold a "family" of father and mother, twelve children and six boarders … packing of the population that has run up the record here to the rate of three hundred and thirty thousand per square mile…. Life here means the hardest kind of work almost from the cradle … these people who come here in droves from Eastern Europe to escape persecution … working night and day at a tremendous pressure to save a little money…. You are made fully aware of it before you have travelled the length of a single block … by the whir of a thousand sewing-machines, worked at high pressure

from earliest dawn till mind and muscle give out together. Every member of the family, from the youngest to the oldest, bears a hand, shut in the qualmy rooms, where meals are cooked and clothing washed and dried besides ... half of the ready-made clothes that are sold in the big stores, if not a good deal more than half, are made in these tenement rooms.[2]

Six years later, he expanded in an essay for the *Review of Reviews* journal:

As to the poverty, they brought us boundless energy and industry to overcome it.... Nothing stagnates where the Jews are.... Their slums on the East Side are dark mainly because of the constant influx of a new population ever beginning the old struggle over. The second generation is the last found in those tenements, if indeed it is not already on its way uptown to the Avenue.... With still its strong backing of the old faith morality, it runs uptown to philanthropy, to humanitarianism ... our city has to-day no better and more loyal citizen than the Jew, be he poor or rich.[3]

In America, Jews found a society that accepted them with one open arm while keeping them at another's length. It was rife with Antisemitic attitudes and segregative norms, but what was marginalization compared to the horrific waves of violence visited upon their communities across the Pale of Settlement (a region along the borders of Russia, Prussia [Germany] and Austria-Hungary in which Jews were allowed to have permanent residency)? It was all the opportunity they needed, to recreate themselves in an image of their own choosing, to master their own fate, and to have a country to truly, finally, call home.

It's in this period that almost all the creators of the comic book industry and the superhero genre or their parents immigrated to the States, including Michel and Sore Sigalowitz, who came to New York from Kovno, Lithuania, in 1902, and became Michael and Sarah Siegel. They moved to the Midwest, like many Jews did, to try their luck at the less crowded, less competitive, perhaps less stressfully urban Glenville, then a Jewish working class neighborhood of Cleveland, Ohio, where almost half of the city's Jewish population of 85,000 lived, and where in 1914 they had their sixth child, Jerome.[4]

Similarly, Julius Shusterowich, from Rotterdam, Holland, and his wife Ida, originally from Kiev, Ukraine, immigrated first to Toronto, Canada, where they became the Shusters, then in 1924 to Glenville, with their ten-year-old son, Joseph.[5]

For these émigrés and others like them, safety, autonomy, and a chance at success created a newfound need for self-definition, personal and cultural, and for edifying figures to inspire them. The heroes of the past, like Moses, had helped preserve their ancient culture and provide moral guidance, but it was now a brave new world, and their eyes were set to the future. Their new heroes would be men of tomorrow. Superman wouldn't debut until 1938, but it's in this milieu that his prologue begins.

Despite the great rise in economic prosperity and cultural vitality during the Roaring Twenties, most new immigrants, whether Jewish, Irish, Italian or other, eked out a meager or modest living. Some, particularly in New York, did manage to achieve a measure of upward mobility, in some cases considerable, but then came Black Tuesday—the stock market crash of October 29, 1929—and the beginning of the decade-long Great Depression.

By 1933, the nadir of the Depression, 25 percent of the American labor force was unemployed, with millions more finding only part-time or low-paying work.

Between 1934 and 1940 severe drought afflicted most of the 48 states and "Dust Bowl" storms wiped out farms and entire towns across the Great Plains, causing nationwide hunger. Millions of Americans lost their homes. Hundreds of thousands lived on the streets, became vagrants or squatted in "Hooverville" shantytowns. Most local governments were deplete of resources.[6]

Immigration to the U.S., historically motivated by economic opportunity, all but stopped. The exception was Jews, who continued to come as much as immigration caps would allow. They came not only to improve their lives but to save them. Unfortunately, the same sociopolitical trends that afflicted Europe were also manifesting in America. The political tumult, poor economy, rising crime, and fear of an uncertain future gave rise to atavistic tribalism, particularly Antisemitism, like they did in Germany. American Jews were alarmed to see that the ugly specters of old had followed them to the New World.

Prejudice against Jews was blatant and quotidian, even among respected personages and institutions. Jews were not classified as people of color, but they also weren't considered white. Mainstream WASP culture would eventually come to regard them as "honorary whites," but in antebellum America they were still regarded by many as ethnic undesirables. European attitudes were far more severe, and getting worse, exemplified by Hitler's 1923 speech in Munich's Circus Krone, where he stated, "The Jews are undoubtedly a race, but they are not human."[7]

Jewish Americans, both "fresh off the boat" and native-born, faced closed gates to neighborhoods, social organizations and country clubs, and the tacit understanding in many "respectable" business establishments that Jews needn't apply. Many institutions of higher learning, particularly elite schools, established the infamous *Numerus Clausus*, quotas for the number of Jews they admitted, using euphemistic parameters like "character" and "physical characteristics" as well as "legacy preference" of alumni's children. Some of these policies lasted into the 1960s.[8] Cultural tone-setters like Earnest Hemingway and Howard Hughes were openly and casually Antisemitic, helping perpetuate and promote the Medieval stereotype of Jews as greedy and treacherous (presumably because of Judas) which, combined with its updated version as subversive Bolsheviks, fomented mistrust and hatred.

For Jews, Antisemitism was simply the ineluctable way of the world. Part of being Jewish meant always being the Other—godless to the devout and zealous to the reformists, clannish to the assimilationists and impudent to the elitists, communists to the capitalists and financiers to the socialists, separatists to the cosmopolitans and, to nationalists, the International Jews.

But to Jewish immigrants, Franklin Roosevelt's policies and practices offered unprecedented opportunity and social mobility. His New Deal was designed to help the poor, which most of them were. He himself hired several Jews for prominent government positions like Secretary of the Treasury (Henry Morgenthau, Jr.) and Associate Justice of the Supreme Court (Felix Frankfurter). He also advocated for the rearmament of England against Hitler, opposed anti-immigration and anti–Jewish legislative attempts in Congress and supported the Zionist project. As a result, 82 percent of Jews voted for him in 1932, 85 percent in 1936, and 90 percent in both 1940 and 1944. For comparison, his overall support in those elections was 57 percent, 61 percent, 55 percent and 53 percent, respectively. Detractors snidely called his programs the "Jew Deal" and Nazi propaganda in the U.S. accused him of secretly being a Jew named Rosenfeld, but as far as the Jewish community was concerned, he was their "modern Moses."[9]

Yet, despite FDR's unprecedented inclusiveness, Jews found themselves increasingly rather than decreasingly marginalized in America. The interwar period saw a severe escalation in Antisemitism, between the rising popularity of the KKK in the south and the ascent of Nazi Germany bestirring matching sentiments domestically. Hitler's sympathizers were raising "the Jewish question" in the U.S. while he was concocting its Final Solution in Europe. Conspiratorial blood libels like "the Franklin Prophecy" and "the Protocols of the Elders of Zion" (a notorious forged Russian text from 1903 purporting a Jewish conspiracy for global domination) were widely circulated, as was *Mein Kampf*. First published in the U.S. in 1933, by 1939 it had become a best-seller, with three editions in circulation.[10] As a result, a substantial portion of the American public was exposed to hate speech against Jews on a regular basis. "The Jews" were blamed for everything from the death of Jesus to the Great War to the Depression to organized crime to the Bolshevik Revolution to the growing upheaval in Europe. "Jew" was made synonymous with "antagonist."

Jew-bashing wasn't limited to speech and print. Gangs in major cities regularly vandalized Jewish cemeteries and synagogues. Swastikas were increasingly common, as were news reports about attacks on Jewish youngsters.[11]

Several prominent figures spearheaded the campaign against Jews, like the Rev. Charles Edward Coughlin, known as Father Coughlin, a Roman Catholic priest and popular radio preacher from Detroit who, from 1926 to 1941, regularly vilified Jews on 45 radio stations, reaching 15 million listeners—almost one in ten Americans. Secretly connected to the Nazi party in Germany, he served as an unofficial PR consultant in the U.S. and in 1934 began publishing a weekly newspaper, *Social Justice*, rife with pro-fascist, Antisemitic diatribes. It serialized *The Protocols*, echoed Nazi Minister of Propaganda Joseph Goebbels' rhetoric, blamed Jews for their own persecution and justified the violence against them.[12]

One of the biggest celebrities in the world, handsome and daring pilot Charles Lindbergh was a Medal of Honor recipient and all–American hero admired by youths like Siegel and Shuster. He was also an Antisemite, using his pulpit as the spokesman of the America First Committee, an isolationist organization 850,000 members strong, to repeatedly accuse Jews of being "war agitators," who "for reasons which are not American, wish to involve us in the war."[13]

Another American icon, industrialist Henry Ford was also a member of the America First Committee, and likewise promoted the vilification of Jews as warmongers and profiteers. His privately-owned newspaper, *The Dearborn Independent* (aka *The Ford International Weekly*), had the second largest circulation in the U.S. It regularly depicted American Jews as fifth columnists, featuring headlines like "The International Jew: The World's Foremost Problem" and publishing sections from *The Protocols* as fact, along with matching claims that Jews invented the stock market and gold standard as part of a conspiracy to corrupt the world. He republished the baleful articles in four paperbound collections that became immensely influential bestsellers in Weimar Republic Germany. Hitler quoted them in *Mein Kampf*, later displaying Ford's portrait at his Munich office.[14]

In July 1938 Ford received the Grand Cross of the German Eagle, the highest Nazi honor for a non–German, three months before his close friend Lindbergh did. Dressed in an all-white three-piece suit, he proudly displayed for the news cameras his Swastika medal, representing "Hitler's personal admiration and indebtedness." It was presented to him by the German consul in Cleveland, Siegel and Shuster's hometown.[15] Ford's beliefs, his agenda, even the way he was dressed, made him a real-life supervillain. It was a month after Superman debuted, not a moment too soon.

The three Nazi collaborators would later attempt to recant some of their rhetoric, but they'd already done their damage. According to a 1938 survey, 60 percent of Americans disliked Jews, viewing them as greedy, dishonest and pushy.[16]

Worse than the animus toward Jews in commerce and culture was that on Capitol Hill. It was more harmful, and the American Jewish community, through its members in government, NGOs and the press, was fully aware of its prevalence.

The Immigration Act of 1924, aka the Johnson-Reed Act, pegged the admittance of immigrants from any country to 2 percent of their existing number in the U.S. based on the 1890 census, to "preserve the ideal of U.S. homogeneity." Migration from Western European countries like Germany and Britain wasn't significantly affected since they already constituted a sizable population, but it severely restricted the flow of the less desirable Southern and Eastern Europeans, effectively ending the wave of Jewish immigration.[17] Congress would not revise the Act until 1952, seven years after the majority of European Jews had been exterminated.

Joseph Kennedy, Sr., U.S. ambassador to the UK and the most prominent American diplomat at the time (and John F. Kennedy' father), was a friend of Lindbergh's who shared his appeasement and Antisemitic politics. He likewise described Jews as warmongering and ruinous, expressing sympathy for Germany's persecution and violence against them.[18]

But Kennedy often locked horns with Roosevelt, which limited his influence, while Assistant Secretary of State Breckinridge Long leveraged his personal friendship with the president and relative anonymity to lead a genocidal campaign against Jews. A rabid Antisemite and nativist, in January 1940 he was put in charge of the Visa Division at the State Department, and so all matters concerning European refugees. He promptly established an impossibly strict immigration policy that reduced admission from countries under Axis control by 90 percent, upholding it even as thousands of Jews were being slaughtered daily. He also repeatedly obstructed rescue efforts throughout the war, as part of an "underground movement ... to let the Jews be killed." By the time Roosevelt established the War Refugee Board in January 1944, relieving the State Department of responsibility (following the Treasury Department's "Report to the Secretary on the Acquiescence of This Government in the Murder of the Jews"), Long's conspiracy had cost 190,000 Jews their lives. He was allowed to quietly retire, avoiding prosecution and scandal.[19]

By 1939 Antisemitism in America was at a fever pitch. On February 20, seven months before the war began, the *Amerikadeutscher Volksbund*, or German-American Bund, paraded through New York City's Upper East Side down to Madison Square

Garden, where they held a rally. At the heart of the most Jewish-populated city in the world, 22,000 American Nazis packed the arena under a massive portrait of George Washington flanked by swastikas, where they branded FDR a Jewish stooge and called on all "true Americans" to protect themselves against "the slimy conspirators and the parasite hand" of Jews.[20] The Nazi menace didn't just loom beyond the horizon. It had come to besiege American Jews at home.

It was this growing hate that was the impetus for the creation of Superman. As Jerry Siegel recounts in his unpublished memoir, his invincible champion of the oppressed was conceived in large part in response to the threat Jews faced in the U.S. and to their murder at the hands of the Nazis, which, even as a youth in the Midwest, he was well aware of.[21]

The news that came back from the old countries—via letters, telegrams, relatives who made it stateside, rumors in the community and what was reported in the radio and newspapers—was bad and getting worse.

In January 1933 Hitler was appointed Chancellor of Germany, his Nazi Party the largest in the Reichstag parliament. The same month, Siegel and Shuster, then eighteen, introduced in their mimeographed mail-order magazine, *Science Fiction: The Advance Guard of Future Civilization*, a story titled "The Reign of the Super-man," about a megalomaniac with aspirations of world conquest who exploits the down-and-out.

In March one of the first concentration camps opened in Oranienburg, outside Berlin. In April began the Nazi boycott of all Jewish-owned businesses and Jewish children were restricted or expelled from schools. In May German students started burning books written by Jews in giant pyres. Around then Siegel and Shuster decided to turn "The Superman" into a hero, a comic strip character in the vein of Tarzan.[22] The world had enough villains.

Their nascent idea would evolve into the familiar Superman sometime in late 1934,[23] though it would be four more years before it saw light. It was a timely birth for the world's first superhero: in August Hitler became Führer.

The Nuremberg Laws were passed in September 1935, revoking German Jews' citizenship and stripping them of legal rights. "*Juden unerwünscht*" signs—*Jews Not Welcome*—were commonplace. The following three years saw increasing persecution of Jews in Germany and elsewhere largely ignored by an indifferent world, while Siegel and Shuster's defender of the weak continued to be rejected by disinterested publishers.

In March 1938 Germany invaded and annexed Austria in the *Anschluss*. The following week it seized the Sudetenland region from Czechoslovakia. Six tense months of global diplomacy followed, steered by Neville Chamberlain's appeasement policy, resulting, to the horror of most Jews, in the Munich Pact, legitimizing the Nazi takeover in the name of "Peace for Our Time."[24] Soon after, the Évian Conference took place, meant to address the issue of Jewish refugees fleeing Nazi-controlled territories; 32 countries participated, all offering sympathy but few safe haven. The world's great powers didn't care, and Jews were left powerless and desperate. In June 1938 Superman made his debut in the pages of *Action Comics* #1.

Six weeks after Chamberlain boasted of securing "peace with honor," telling

Britons to "go home and get a nice quiet sleep," on the night of November 9–10, 1938, Goebbels instigated *Kristallnacht*, the Night of Broken Glass. Jews throughout Germany and Nazi territories were attacked in a massive, coordinated pogrom. Over 7,500 Jewish storefronts were smashed, littering the streets with broken glass, giving the event its name. Nearly 300 synagogues were burned down. Several hundred men, women and children were dragged out of their homes and brutalized, at least 91 murdered. Up to 30,000 men were arrested and sent to concentration camps.[25] Many European and American Jews understood it was an augur of things to come.

Two months later, in January 1939, Hitler gave a speech at the Reichstag threatening "the annihilation of the Jewish race in Europe."[26] International response was again apathetic, but following *Kristallnacht* and the escalation in state-sponsored persecution, Jews from all over Europe, whether expelled from Nazi lands or fleeing the Nazis' oncoming, sought refuge in the U.S. Most were denied entry, to the great frustration of their American brethren, who lobbied on their behalf. Things came to a head in June, in the "Voyage of the Damned"; the *St. Louis*, carrying 937 Jewish refugees, was refused permission to unload in Florida and sent back to the charnel houses of Europe. The same month also saw the release of *Superman* #1, detailing for the first time in full his origin—a refugee from a destroyed homeland, travelling to safe harbor in a vessel, granted asylum by kindly Americans.

On September 1, 1939, the Nazis invaded Poland, leading Britain, France, Australia and New Zealand to declare war on the Third Reich, and World War II officially began. Four days later the United States proclaimed neutrality, which it would maintain until the attack on Pearl Harbor on December 7, 1941. In those two years most of Europe and large parts of the Mediterranean and Africa fell to the Axis powers, and Britain's chances of winning the war appeared slim. Jews throughout Fortress Europe were quarantined in ghettos, enslaved in labor camps and gassed in concentration camps. While the scale of the horror was unfathomable, news reports and testimonies of escapees made the ongoing Holocaust public knowledge, generating fear, frustration and fury among U.S. Jews.

Things outside Europe were also bleak. Since even before the war, news accounts of Arab riots and massacres of Jews in the British Mandate of Palestine, the Jewish homeland and the primary destination of Jewish refugees after the U.S., arrived on a monthly, sometimes weekly, basis. The Jews of the Holy Land were beleaguered by Hitler ally Haj Amin al-Husseini, the Grand Mufti of Jerusalem, who led the riots, and by Erwin Rommel's forces in North Africa approaching their doorstep. To make things worse, the British White Papers drastically limited Jewish immigration to Mandatory Palestine and illegal Jewish immigrants, virtually all refugees from Europe, were interned in camps.

On the afternoon of June 1, 1941, during the holiday of Shavuot, the *Farhud*—"the Arab Kristallnacht"—erupted across Iraq, primarily in Baghdad. Over the course of two days, Iraqi soldiers and policemen led rioting mobs, murdering as many as 180 Jews, injuring 600, raping an undetermined number of women, and looting some 1,500 stores and homes.[27]

Leading up to the war, Jews, by virtue of being the main targets of Hitler's vitriol, recognized the danger he and his cronies posed, even if they couldn't imagine its extent. And once the war erupted they were forced to stand helplessly by, aware of the carnage, as the world expressed little interest. Early on, American media coverage tended to favor the charismatic, job-creating, anti–Bolshevik German leader. Newspapers like the *New York Times, Christian Science Monitor* and *Philadelphia Evening Bulletin* portrayed Hitler as a misunderstood moderate, dismissing the persecution of Jews as exaggerated. Others, like *The Columbus Dispatch* and *The Christian Century*, justified it.[28]

The Cleveland Press, Siegel and Shuster's hometown newspaper and one of the most influential in the U.S. at the time, claimed the "appointment of Hitler as German chancellor may not be such a threat to world peace as it appears." Even after Jews had been stripped of legal rights, lynched and were being sent to concentration camps, all of which was reported in the news, the *New York Herald Tribune* dismissed the reports as "unfounded," while the *Times* insisted that "German violence had been spent," soon to be replaced with "prosperity and happiness" for Jews. Hitler's Antisemitism, they claimed, wasn't genuine or violent. *Time* magazine didn't bother mentioning Jews or violence at all when they made Hitler their 1938 Man of the Year.[29]

Indifference to Jewish suffering continued even as the war escalated. In June 1942, two years before Allied forces liberated the camps, the *Times* reported on "1,000,000 Jews slain by Nazis," in a small column on page seven. The front page reported a British defeat in a battle in Egypt. By November, national headlines reported the murder of two million Jews (the real number was closer to four) and Americans learned about the Final Solution, including the gas chambers and mass shootings.[30] There was little public or political reaction.

Roosevelt, which was the only hope in the eyes of many Jews of stopping Hitler, seemed equally insouciant. In 430 press conferences held between 1933, when Hitler rose to power, and 1938, the eve of World War II, he mentioned the Jewish plight twice.[31] American Jewish leaders and organizations advocated their cause as best they could, but with scant resources or influence they had no lobbying power. There was no one to defend the Jews, no one to champion their cause, no one to give them voice.

Ironic, considering it was Jewish immigrants who gave America its voice.

In *Disguised as Clark Kent*, Fingeroth points out that "Jews were prominent in the creation and development of most of the important American pop culture movements of the 20th century, including the Broadway musical, popular music, the movies, and of course, comics." Ever since Emma Lazarus's "The New Colossus" sonnet was inscribed on the pedestal of the Statue of Liberty in 1903—inspired by the poet's Jewish heritage and the plight of Jewish refugees from Russia[32]—American Jews have helped frame the nation's ethos and tell its stories. With the advent of radio, silent films and eventually talkies, America was telling stories and creating shared cultural icons more than ever before, particularly those produced in the dream factory of Hollywood.

The movies were where America turned to for idealized reflections of itself, for escapism and for larger than life thrills. It's also an industry that grew into glitz and glamor from seediness and disrepute, not so much staffed as invented by Jews, businessmen and artists who had few other opportunities (mostly behind the camera, as studio heads, executives, producers, directors and writers, leaving stardom to palatably gentile actors). And since American identity was heavily influenced, even coalesced around the entertainment industry's portrayal of it, the American ethos is, in many ways, a Jewish-American one.

What these filmmakers had in mind wasn't the auteurship of Orson Welles. Movies were *luft gesheft*—"air business"—meant to entertain the masses and make a quick buck. But, whatever level of cognizance involved, they also cannily inserted Jewish cultural memes into their films. Though it would be decades before Yiddishisms like "schmuck" became American vernacular, movies of the era were peppered with them and other elements of Yiddishkeit (Ashkenazi Jewish culture), particularly the rapid-fire, self-deprecating humor brought over from the Borscht Belt comedy routines (summer resorts in the Catskill Mountains immensely popular with New York Jews in the 1920s through the 1970s, named after Eastern European beetroot soup).

More so, a great many of these films are marked by a thematic preoccupation with downtrodden protagonists, at conflict with both society and themselves, who overcome impossible odds to earn their happy ending. It was the id of the Yid, a need for Jews to express themselves, at the crossroads of religion, culture, art and schlock. As Jill Robinson, Hollywood historian and daughter of former MGM president Dore Schary, put it, "Hollywood—the American Dream—is a Jewish idea. In a sense, it's a Jewish revenge on America. It combines the Puritan ethic … with baroque magnificence. The happy ending was the invention of Russian Jews, designed to drive Americans crazy."[33]

These were their celluloid manifestos, attempts to universalize the marginal, from the very first talkie, *The Jazz Singer* (1927), featuring a Jewish lead, Al Jolson (Asa Yoelson), playing a Jewish character, the son of a cantor from the Lower East Side who's torn between his success as a singer under an Anglicized name and his place with his family and community.

Many Warner Bros. films depicted the struggle of "the little guy" and the fight for freedom against oppression, like *The Life of Emile Zola* (1937), about the Dreyfus affair, and *Juarez* (1939), about Mexico's struggle for democratic self-rule, both starring Paul Muni (Meshilem Meier Weisenfreund). *The Adventures of Robin Hood* (1938), starring Errol Flynn, was a rousing call for action against dictatorship, racial oppression and effete politics (featuring a codenamed hero in bright tights with an exceptional ability). Leading man John Garfield (Jacob Garfinkle) was famous for his defiant, gruff working class roles, an attitude he brought over from the Lower East Side.

The Marx Brothers, who in many ways defined American comedy, were quintessentially Jewish in their irreverent, deadpan humor ("I don't want to belong to any club that will accept me as a member!"). The movies and shorts of Chico, Harpo and Groucho (Leonard, Adolph and Julius) conveyed pathos through parody, social incisiveness coated with clever wordplay and slapstick *mishegas*.

It's hard to say where economic opportunity, pioneering spirit, artistic aspiration and the need to communicate each begin and end, but the result was the modern American entertainment industry. And through it, particularly Hollywood, this small group of marginalized immigrants and their children effectively reimagined mainstream culture. Along the way they also reinvented themselves, partly because the unprecedented freedom the U.S. offered allowed them to, and partly, as film historian Lester D. Friedman writes in *The Jewish Image in American Film*, because "for many Jews, the entry price into American life required a casting off of 'foreignisms': their religious observances, their names, and their traditions."[34] Almost to a man, Jews in show business Anglicized their names, producing parables of assimilation exalting the nation that took them in. They wanted to be considered real Americans so badly that they ended up defining what America was.

When the Nazis assumed power and the persecution of Jews intensified while the world, including the U.S., remained unmoved, Jack and Harry Warner (Jacob and Hirsz Wonsal or Werner), together with future *Looney Toons* producer Leon Schlesinger, responded within their power. They went after Hitler in September 1933, shortly after he became Chancellor, depicting him as a violent buffoon in lederhosen in their animated short, *Bosko's Picture Show*. But this was an exception to the rule, flying under the radar by virtue of being a cartoon.

The studios were reluctant to address the Nazi menace, fearful of losing the European market as well as the domestic isolationist one, of galvanizing the growing Antisemitism at home and of playing into the Nazi narrative that the Jews were trying to instigate war between the nations. Joseph Kennedy, Sr., pressured them to "stop making anti–Nazi pictures" and "get those Jewish names off the screen." As a result, they cancelled several productions and cut from several films anything that might be construed as critical of the Nazis or favorable to Jews. *The Life of Emile Zola*, for example, about the infamous Antisemitic conspiracy against French Colonel Alfred Dreyfus, doesn't mention Jews once.[35]

But things changed when they learned of Leni Riefenstahl's remarkably effective 1935 propaganda film *Triumph of the Will* and Goebbels's 1940 hate films *The Eternal Jew* and *Süss the Jew*, among others. They banded to produce their own films in response, setting out to convince Americans of the need to get involved. Almost two years before the attack on Pearl Harbor and director Frank Capra's government-commissioned *Why We Fight* series, Hollywood took on Hitler—through humor.

The first to lampoon the Nazis onscreen were the Three Stooges, in their Columbia Pictures shorts *You Nazty Spy!* (January '40) and its sequel *I'll Never Heil Again* (July '41). For Larry, Curly and Moe (Louis Feinberg, Jerome Horwitz and Moses Horwitz), turning Hitler into a laughingstock was a point of pride. In true Stooges fashion they portrayed the Nazi high command as a group of conceited, bumbling idiots and peppered their dialogue with a constant stream of Yiddishisms ("*Beblach!*" [beans], "*Shalom aleichem!*" [peace unto you], "*In pupik gehabt haben*" [I've had it in the bellybutton], etc.), something general audiences then wouldn't have picked up on as anything but gibberish. They also made sure that, amidst the hilarity, moviegoers learned about book burnings and concentration camps.

An interesting side note, the three are spied on by the femme fatale Mattie Herring (a pickled fish of Jewish cuisine), who hides her secret identity in plain sight as their mild-mannered secretary by wearing a pair of large horn-rimmed glasses and changing her hairdo.

The Stooges fired the opening salvo of Jewish counter-propaganda, joined by the mainstream the following October by the greatest of American anti–Nazi films, Charlie Chaplin's *The Great Dictator*.

American Jews fought back in reality through their fiction, but they were still hampered by their image in America, which the Stooges, Marx Brothers and many others largely fit; smart, snarky, funny, and diminutive. At an age of eugenics and the Aryan ideal, equally the all–American ideal—tall, broad, muscular, square-jawed, light-eyed, thick blond-haired—the image of the physique of Jews was scrawny or pudgy, hunched, atrophied, weak. To a large extent this stereotype persists today, associating Jews with Woody Allen and Seth Rogan but not Harrison Ford and Zac Efron.

In fairness, it wasn't completely divorced from reality: Jews were largely sedentary people, accountants, bankers, shopkeepers, merchants and yeshiva students, not farmers, factory workers, firemen and other vocations that involve manual labor. These simply weren't part of their tradition, after centuries of disenfranchisement in Europe where they were forbidden to own and cultivate land and excluded from most forms of industry and public service. That, combined with the Jewish cultural emphasis on study, contributed to Jews being typecast in the American consciousness as intellectuals and savvy businessmen but also unmanly weaklings.

There were plenty of examples to undercut this notion, however, long before Siegel and Shuster originated the superhero physique by enwrapping Greco-Roman esthetic and machismo in bright spandex, giving the world the first musclebound Jewish character since Samson. "There was always an element of the working class that was tough and street smart and worked with their hands and fought with their hands," explains Eddy Portnoy, adjunct professor of Jewish studies at Rutgers and creator of the exhibit "Yiddish Fight Club" at the Center for Jewish History in Manhattan.[36]

These weren't the stereotypical middle- and upper-class doctors and lawyers of today or the well-heeled German Jews that came to the U.S. before the outbreak of World War I. These were lunchbox workers, shtetl folk and their children, and they produced, and fervently followed, warrior tribesmen like eight-time world lightweight boxing champion Benny Leonard, born on the Lower East Side as Benjamin Leiner. A recognizable name to this day, Leonard parlayed his athletic fame—boxing was second only to baseball in popularity in the U.S.—into a film career, long before Arnold Schwarzenegger and Dwayne Johnson thought to do the same, starring in action serials like *The Evil Eye* ('20) and *Flying Fists* ('24–5). "He has done more to conquer Antisemitism than a thousand textbooks," famed newsman Arthur Brisbane said of him.[37]

Another famous New York (later Chicago) Jewish boxer was Barney Ross (Dov-Ber Rasofsky), a mild-mannered Talmudic scholar until his father was murdered in a robbery and he became a boxer, winning the title in three lightweight divisions in the 1930s and personifying an early, real-life version of a superhero origin story.[38]

In fact, Jews were the dominant nationality in professional prizefighting in the interwar era. Nearly a third of all fighters were Jewish, including 26 world champions. For many boxing was a way to assimilate, but it was also a way to overcome stereotypes and represent Jewishness with pride. Most wore a Star of David on their robes and trunks.[39]

Wrestling was also immensely popular, and there, too, Jews had a presence—a particularly big one, in the form of Bostonian Martin "Blimp" Levy, a 600-lbs. wrestler of surprising agility, and after the war, Rafael Halperin, the son of a Viennese ultra-orthodox rabbi who fled with his family to Mandatory Palestine, where he picked up weightlifting and karate in addition to his Talmudic studies, then moved to the U.S., where he became a famous wrestler who wouldn't wrestle on the Sabbath, eventually returning to Israel to become a rabbi himself.[40]

It wasn't just the idea of the street-tough fighting Jew that found its way into comic books. The Yiddish nomenclature of violence, derived from boxing and wrestling, was, like much else in Yiddish, onomatopoeic, ready-made for the comics. Many of the sound effects comics are famous for—*Zap! Bam! Argh! Bonk!*—are reminiscent of the Yiddish *bukh, zbokh, zbeng, tunk, knak, zets, shturkh, flick* and others, all names of particular punches, smacks or kicks.[41]

A generation before toughs like Leonard and Ross exemplified Jewish body culture, the world was enthralled by the fantastic physical feats of the Great Houdini, a magician and escape artist who remains a household name more than a century later. Born Ehrich Weisz in Budapest, Hungary, the son of a rabbi grew up in Milwaukee but found fame and fortune in New York's vaudeville, becoming an "escapologist" and one of the world's most famous performers, touring across Europe and appearing before gentry and royalty.[42]

In the Pulitzer-winning *The Amazing Adventures of Kavalier & Clay*, Jewish author (and grandson of a comic book printing typographer) Michael Chabon posits Houdini as an overlooked source of the superhero idea, a proto–Superman who personified in the flesh much of what would later be expressed in fantasy by the Man of Steel. The book opens with coprotagonist Sam Clay, loosely modeled after Jerry Siegel, telling, "To me, Clark Kent in a phone booth and Houdini in a packing create, they were one and the same thing.... You weren't the same person when you came out as when you went in.... It was never just a question of escape. It was also a question of *transformation*."[43] He speaks of the fantasy to metamorphose from what is to what should be, an inverse of Franz Kafka's Gregor Samsa, transformed not by cruel fate into an insect but by personal strength and virtue into something greater than man. Harry Houdini was the ultimate Jewish wish fulfillment, a poor boy from the Jewish quarter who'd remade himself into a rich and internationally popular man.

Clay's own creation, the Escapist, is a Nazi-fighting superhero who's able to escape any deathtrap, echoing Houdini. He symbolizes the desire of boys, of the poor during the Depression, but most of all of marginalized and persecuted Jews, to be able to escape, outsmart, trick and disappear, to transcend. This allure of the superhero idea is the same as Houdini's, whether it traces back to him or not. The Escapist's co-creator, Joe (Josef) Kavalier, based partly on Joe Shuster, is an apprentice magician and escape artist in Prague who manages to flee the Nazis hidden in a coffin, a story not uncommon for the period, embodying the urgent and all too real need of Jews to escape fate. Clay, his cousin and collaborator, is a first-generation American Jew, born Samuel Klayman in Brooklyn, who, like many of his peers, seeks to escape the shackles of his ethnoreligious identity. Both see a hero in Houdini, the man who with a scoff regularly escaped death and in many ways escaped being Jewish. The fantasy that inspires the creation of the Escapist is the same one that inspired Superman; to be able to leave the mundane and oppressive behind at will.

Houdini is a superhero prototype in other ways. His impossible feats of death-defying escape—from chains, police handcuffs and jail cells, straitjackets, coffins, trunks and all manner of deathtraps, often at once, often while submerged (or appearing to be) longer than humanly possible—gave him an almost supernatural lore. His well-developed musculature wasn't far behind that of a strongman, a sex appeal he promoted in his posters and press photos. He was a mystery man, intentionally enigmatic, and he was close friends with another famous man of mystery, Sherlock Holmes author Sir Arthur Conan Doyle. Houdini's 1906 book, *The Right Way to Do Wrong: An Expose of Successful Criminals*, added the image of a crime fighter. Legends abounded: He had true supernatural powers. He was secretly a spy. He helped the police when they were stumped.

With the rise of spiritualism in the 1920s Houdini became an occult detective, using his training in magic to debunk mediums and psychics, especially those that scientists and academics failed to expose. He chronicled his "supernatural" crime-fighting adventures in his 1924 book, *A Magician Among the Spirits*, which only added to the mystique, danger and otherworldliness of his legend.[44]

Who may have actually been a direct influence on the creation of Superman, though, is Siegmund "Zishe" Breitbart, a musclebound, blue-eyed, Yiddish-speaking Jewish circus performer from Lodz, Poland. Discussed in Thomas Andrae and Mel Gordon's *Siegel and Shuster's Funnyman: The First Jewish Superhero, from the Creators of Superman*, Breitbart was nicknamed the "Iron King" and dubbed the "Strongest Man in the World," performing all over the globe in the 1920s to great fame. His posters touted him as a man able to stop speeding locomotives and the press dubbed him "a being of supernatural powers" who "bends steel as if it were soft rubber." He'd occasionally dress up for his shows like a Roman centurion, replete with flowing cape, or Jewish machismo heroes like Samson and Simon Bar-Kokhba, the famed leader of the revolt against the Roman Empire in 132 CE.

Breitbart's feats of strength included bending iron rods with his bare hands, wrestling bears, absorbing anvil blows, supporting the weight of automobiles driving over his chest and laying on a bed of nails while supporting a spinning carousel of children. Making front page news throughout the U.S., he was dubbed by *The New York Times* the "phenomenon of the ages" and by others as the "World's Mightiest Human," the "Superman of the Ages," the "Jewish Superman," "Superman of Strength" and, eventually, when he parlayed his fame into a mail-order bodybuilding correspondence course (almost twenty years before Charles Atlas's famous "The Insult that Made a Man out of Mac" ads in the backs of comic books), simply "Superman."[45]

Though Siegel and Shuster never made mention of him, Breitbart was famous enough at the time, certainly among Jews, that it's unlikely for them to have not heard of him. He toured across the U.S. to great acclaim, performing in December 1923 in New York's Hippodrome Theatre before an audience of over 85,000 people, setting a world record. He appeared in Cleveland in 1923 and Toronto in 1924, Siegel and Shuster's respective hometowns, a few years before they created Superman.[46] He died shortly thereafter, in 1925, the result of an injury sustained during a performance. But his fame lived on, even experiencing a resurgence in the 21st century in the form of the 2001 movie *Invincible*, loosely based on his life, starring Tim Roth and directed by Werner Herzog, and *Zishe the Strongman*, a 2010 children's picture book by Robert Rubinstein and Woody Miller.

The cultural ingredients for the creation of Superman were in place, from the foundational story of Moses to the politicking of Hollywood movies, from the real villainy of Ford to the fantasy valor of Flynn, from the threat of the Nazis to the promise of the New Deal. All that was missing was the right medium.

Harry Houdini. Publicity photograph, c. 1899. Library of Congress.

We are all in the gutter, but some of us are looking at the stars.—Oscar Wilde

Famous Funnies and Other Firsts
The Birth of Comic Books

New York City has been the *axis mundi* of the comic book world from the dawn of its creation. (Though decreasingly so, particularly with DC Comics' relocation from Midtown Manhattan to Burbank, California, in 2011.) Its creators came from the same background as the men who made Hollywood, motivated by the same lack of opportunity and drive to succeed. They were Eastern European and Russian Jews, either immigrants or children of immigrants, who mostly came from impoverished backgrounds (few were from prosperous families ruined in the Crash), landing firmly in the New York urban working class during a time of great economic hardship. They lived in the hardscrabble Lower East Side tenements and the slightly more upscale South Bronx (largely Jewish in the 1930s[1]), most with only a high school education, most in or barely out of their teens. It isn't hard to imagine how, for these young men, comic books were a way to escape the dead-end world of the ghetto, both as escapist fantasy and as means of socioeconomic mobility.

Like for all Americans, finding work was a challenge, but Jews in particular faced greater odds. "There was a tremendous amount of anti–Semitic bigotry" celebrated *Mad* magazine artist Al (Abraham) Jaffee remembers. "Newspapers strips … and advertising agencies and slick magazines had … an unwritten policy that no Jews need apply."[2] Many industries shunned Jews, limiting or entirely barring their employ, one being publishing. Reputable publishers of books, journals and newspapers were WASP strongholds, all but closed off to Jews, but some which occupied the bottom rung of the industry—cheap periodicals, pulp fiction magazines, romance novellas, etc.—were deemed lowly enough to allow them in. And in they went, through the proverbial back door, occupying what positions they could at the periphery of prose.

Many were writers, artists and businessman manqués, like comics giant William Erwin "Will" Eisner (after whom the industry's most prestigious award, the Eisner, is named), who studied to become a theatrical set designer but couldn't find work,[3] becoming instead a pulp magazine illustrator, before going on to become a pioneering comic book writer and artist.

Comic books' predecessors, the newspaper comic strips, were predominantly populated by Irish-American talent, though notable exceptions include Milt Gross, creator of various nationally syndicated, Yiddish-inflected strips like *Nize Baby*, and Reuben "Rube" Goldberg, whose name has become an adjective for unnecessarily complicated things and whose work greatly influenced Charlie Chaplin's *Modern Times* (1936).[4] For the most part, however, Jews were not welcome in American media, even as cartoonists.

"Newspaper strips back then had a lot of clout. They were a big, big deal, not at all like today," explains Pulitzer Prize-winning *Village Voice* cartoonist Jules Feiffer. "Back then, from the 1920s on, comic strips were a major part of American entertainment, along with movies and network radio." The market was vastly different then—New York alone had over fifty different newspapers, a large number of which boasted Sunday comic pages, or "funny pages"[5]—and cartoonists enjoyed the status of satirists, credited with gravitas and cultured value. The field appealed to many talented Jewish artists, who instead found themselves working in the medium's bastard child, writing and illustrating what were perceived as simple *bubbe meises* for children.

Unlike the respectable magazines or even the sordid pulps, the comic book business was almost entirely created and run by Jews, and so one Jewish artist brought his fellow Jewish artist until they populated the industry. With little formal training but bravura to spare, these young boisterous artists and adroit entrepreneurs built something that, at the time, seemed little more than a way out of poverty and hopefully a springboard into a legitimate, lucrative career later on. It was an industry born out of inopportunity.

"There were Jews in this medium because it was a crap medium," Eisner put it succinctly. "Most cartoonists did not regard comics as a literary form, as I did," he recalls. "Comics were junk food, and the comic artists were *untermenschen* ['Under-men,' a laden term used by the Nazis in reference to inferior races]—even the daily strip artists looked down on us."[6] Comic books were to the art world what Jews were to the world. It was a good fit.

Many of the people involved in comics in those early days were talented, some enormously so, many were not, but they were nearly all poor and willing to work in the louche business. They weren't all self-taught dilettantes and uneducated paupers; some came from more prosperous backgrounds, and they brought with them a more educated, intellectual bend to their work. They had nowhere else to bring it to. Longtime Batman artist and co-creator of Robin and the Joker, Jerry Robinson, for example, was a Columbia University student—a rarity for a Jew at the time—and personal friends with the likes of Kurt Vonnegut and Mike Wallace, who was forced to drop out in order to support his family.[7] They weren't entering a profession. It was an otiose job in an ephemeral business, a gig, a shtick. The last thing that would've occurred to them is that their work would be studied and discussed generations later.

The business model was high-volume, low-yield product, selling hundreds of thousands of units at the low price of 10¢ each. The art was minimal because of tight production schedules more than style choices, the magazines were printed on cheap wood pulp paper, and work paid little, unsteadily and without job security. But it did pay, drawing Jews with few other prospects. They were underpaid, replaceable freelancers working in sweatshop-like production lines, a *schmatte* trade like the garment industry many of their parents worked in. The content they produced was worthless fodder, though by that virtue it also offered unfettered artistic freedom, limited only by their imaginations and deadlines.

It was also an industry of kith and kin. The publishers, editors, writers and artists often knew each other, coming from the same neighborhood, clique or *mischpocha*, immediate or extended. The owners of DC Comics, Harry Donenfeld and Jack Liebowitz (Yakov Lebovitz), favored hiring people from their culture and social circle—not only customary at the time but effectively a requisite, considering the exclusion they faced outside—and so, with the exception of a few Italian-American artists, the roster at DC, especially on Superman, was predominantly Jewish. Martin (Moe) Goodman, a pulp magazine publisher who started Marvel Comics (Marvel didn't have an official company name back then, mostly using Timely Publications from its founding in 1939 until 1951, when it became known as Atlas Comics, before officially adopting the name Marvel Comics in 1961, taken from their inaugural series of the same name. Hereafter referred to as Marvel Comics) as one of his imprints, staffed the company mainly with family members, including his wife's seventeen-year-old cousin, Stan Lee (Stanley Martin Lieber), as an assistant to editor in chief Joe Simon and art director Jack Kirby.[8]

But just as the Hollywood studios didn't invent film, but turned it into an industry, comic book publishers didn't originate the medium, only its mass commercialization. Success having many fathers, the first comic and its ideation are a matter of debate, largely depending on the definition of "comics."

Cave paintings, hieroglyphics, medieval tapestries, illuminated manuscripts, illustrated fairytales, woodcut novels and other examples from throughout history may qualify. But comics as we know them today—not a tableau but a narrative, synergizing words and images, set in successive panels, utilizing unique expressive devices like word balloons, thought bubbles, motion lines and grawlixes (the string of typographical symbols denoting expletives: "$#!*." Also known as obscenicons, they evolved from the dash used beginning in the 1680s in reverence words like God ["G—d"] and damn ["d—"]. Their first recorded use is in a 1902 strip of Rudolph Dirks' *Katzenjammer Kids*.[9] Interesting to note, it included a Star of David alongside an anchor, perhaps implying the swearing of sailors and lower-class Jews) and serialized in print—evolved into their familiar form in early 20th century America.

Political cartoons, usually a single panel, were common in 19th century British and American newspapers, but the first modern comic strip was Richard F. Outcault's 1895 *Yellow Kid*, a New York slum urchin and ostensibly new immigrant, appearing in Joseph Pulitzer's *New York World* and later William Randolph Hearst's *New York Journal*. Both published Yellow Kid strips simultaneously as part of their infamous "Newspaper Wars," giving lowbrow, sensationalistic reporting its name—Yellow Journalism.[10]

Comic strips became immensely popular, and the Kid was soon followed by Rudolph Dirks's *The Katzenjammer Kids* (1897)—which helped inspire Picasso's creation of Cubism[11]—Winsor McCay's *Little Nemo in Slumberland* (1905), George Herriman's *Krazy Kat* (1913) and others. Much of the visual language of comics was developed during this period and when they got their name, funnies, or comics, from their humorous content.

Most featured loud, garish characters, with a heavy emphasis on ethnic jokes and accent-based puns, as well as stylized, hyper-violent slapstick, adapted by

Looney Tunes and Tom and Jerry cartoons years later. "It was lowbrow art, devised by immigrants, or the sons of immigrants, for the entertainment of immigrants," Feiffer notes.[12] Americans from different cultures and languages could enjoy the simple, concise texts and accompanying illustrations, and for many comics were the only familiar depiction of their life and concerns in the paper. Once Hearst established the King Features Syndicate in 1915 (named after its Jewish manager Moses Koenigsberg, "King's Mountain") they went national, spreading the New York, ethnic immigrant sensibility many of them had across America.

Their success led to reprint collections, usually large, bound hardcovers. In October 1929, Dell Publishing launched a sixteen-page, tabloid-size magazine of color strips, selling for 10¢ on newsstands, titled *The Funnies*. A missing link between comic strips and comic books, it was the first to consist of original material in periodical format. The series lasted 36 issues but ultimately proved a failure.[13]

The invention of the modern comic book is generally credited to Jewish New Yorker Maxwell "Max" Gaines (aka M.C. Gaines, né Ginzberg). By the more romantic account of events, Gaines was a 39-year-old unemployed teacher and novelty salesman, forced during the Depression to live at his mother's house in the Bronx with his wife and two children. One day, while cleaning out the attic, he came across some old Sunday funnies. He found himself enjoying them, and it occurred to him that others might also enjoy them independently of the newspapers they came in.

He shared the idea with close friend Harry Wildenberg, a sales manager at Eastern Color Printing, which produced funnies inserts for newspapers, and they persuaded the company to take a chance. The result was *Funnies on Parade*, published in May 1933, regarded by some as the first comic book (largely because, though a reprint of strips, it established the 8" × 11" standard comic book size, changed since to 6⅝" × 10⅛"). Produced not for sale but as a promotional giveaway for Proctor & Gamble, a staggering one million copies were commissioned.

Gaines then conceived of selling comics on newsstands as well. To prove the idea to the incredulous Wildenberg (why would kids pay good money for something they could get for free in their father's newspaper?) he added 10¢ stickers to a handful of copies and delivered them personally to local newsstands, to test how they'd do over the weekend. By Monday they'd sold out and the vendors were clamoring for more.[14]

By the more mundane account, Gaines was already an employee of Eastern, when he or Wildenberg suggested folding the tabloid sheets in quarters to create smaller, more economical book-size pamphlets.[15] Whichever the case, the consensus is that at least the publishing and distribution format of comic books originated with Gaines.

A few more evolutionary steps followed, but July 1934's *Famous Funnies* #1 is widely regarded as the first modern comic book. An ongoing series of 64-page issues sold on newsstands for 10¢ and by the second issue including original material, it was a smash hit. It continued for 218 issues, until July 1955, featuring famed properties like *Buck Rogers* (by Philip Nowlan and Rick Yager) while rejecting other submissions from aspirants like teenager Jerry Siegel.[16]

Funnies' popularity led to other publishers trying their hand at comic books. Harry Donenfeld and Jack Liebowitz founded Detective Comics, named after its inaugural series (launched in March 1937 and the first to feature all-new material devoted to a single theme), later initialized to DC. Like other publishers, they soon started running out of reprint material and by early 1938 were searching for content for a planned new series, *Action Comics*.

As a medium and art form, comic books developed from newspaper strips. In terms of distribution, thematic content and narrative style, they're descended more from the pulps.

Books and magazines named after the cheap, low quality pulpwood paper they were printed on, American pulps appeared in the late 1800s, peaking in popularity in the 1920s and 30s with about 250 titles on newsstands, some reaching a circulation of 600,000.[17]

Most contained adventure fiction, including action, suspense, fantasy and horror, and targeted working class, mainly young men, earning them the stigma of raffish fare. It's in the pulps, not the strips, that the superhero genre has its roots, with their hardboiled detectives, noble gunslingers and valiant swashbucklers (hence "pulp fiction"), but particularly in the trend of fantasy fiction starring extraordinary protagonists that followed Edgar Rice Burroughs's *Tarzan of the Apes*, first appearing in the October 1912 issue of *All-Story*.[18]

The same pulp also introduced Johnston McCulley's Zorro in August 1919,[19] inspired by Baroness Emma Orczy's 1903 British play and following novel series, *The Scarlet Pimpernel*. The Pimpernel is considered the first hero with a secret identity, a patrician by day and vigilante by night, but it was Zorro that added the theatrical flair of a special costume, mask and exciting moniker—"the Fox."

The Shadow debuted on radio in 1930 and his own pulp magazine in 1931, a masked crime fighter with the vague supernatural ability to "cloud men's minds," marking another step toward the idea of the superhero. Other pulp heroes followed, like Conan the Barbarian in 1932, Doc Savage in 1933 and Flash Gordon in 1936, along with pulpy radio characters like the Lone Ranger in 1933 and the Green Hornet in 1936, each contributing elements to what would soon become a new genre of fiction.

Genres that originated in the pulps, like noir and science fiction, went on to gain wider acceptance through the likes of Dashiell Hammett and Isaac Asimov, while pulp heroes mostly transitioned to comics, film and later television. The *Tarzan* and *Buck Rogers* newspaper strips, both starting in January 1929, were the first to feature action rather than comedy.[20]

Regrettably, pulps have received relatively little academic attention as literary, cultural and historical documents. Considering they were created in the wake of the Industrial Revolution and peaked in popularity following World War I, it's hard not to view them as a response of, among other things, traditional masculinity to an increasingly emasculating world. The shift from agrarian to industrial society, urbanization, a Great War of mass death produced by machines and chemicals, socioeconomic collapse, hunger, the rise of organized crime, and authoritarianism and violence in Europe and Russia gave rise to stories and characters that reflected anxieties and offered catharsis.

It can be argued that the same impetus gave rise to Universal Studios' menagerie of monsters, starting with 1923's *The Hunchback of Notre Dame*, followed by *The*

Phantom of the Opera ('25), *Dracula* ('31), *Frankenstein* ('31), *The Mummy* ('32), *The Invisible Man* ('33), the *Bride of Frankenstein* ('35) and *The Wolf Man* ('41). But as World War II raged on, the world outside the movie theater had grown frightening enough. People didn't want stories that made them look over their shoulder. They needed something to make them look up in the sky.

Before Superman lent his name to coin the term "superheroes," they were called "adventurers," "mystery men" or "masked avengers." Any superhuman abilities were the result of either Oriental mysticism, like the Shadow's hypnotism, or advanced science, like Flash Gordon's alien gadgetry, though a case could be made for even earlier forerunners. Sherlock Holmes, created in 1887, possessed impossibly keen detection and deduction skills, and Jean de La Hire's Le Nyctalope ("Night-Seer"), created in 1911, was a crime fighter with artificial heart and eyes that gave him night vision.[21]

Superman is widely recognized as the first superpowered costumed hero and the forefather of all superheroes. As a cultural phenomenon that's certainly the case, but there's actually an entire superhero genre that predates him, and its inceptive medium wasn't comic books, nor was it American, or Jewish.

Kamishibai—"paper theater"—is an ancient form of Japanese street performance that waned in popularity with the advent of television in the 1950s. Traveling entertainers narrated stories illustrated on boards for gathered audiences of children, acting out the characters, much like storytime events today. In its prewar heyday the medium attracted audiences of up to five million people daily across Japan, supplied by forty production houses with 50,000 writers and artists in Tokyo and Kansai alone. The most popular of these featured the fantastic adventures of superhuman costumed heroes.[22]

In 1931, three years before Superman was conceived and seven years before he made his public debut, Japanese children were introduced to Golden Bat (*Ōgon Batto*), created, like Superman, by two youths, 25-year-old writer Ichiro Suzuki and 16-year-old artist Takeo Nagamatsu. They based him on mythological characters of the past, reinventing instead of rehashing them by grounding his powers in science instead of the numinous. A time traveler from the lost continent of Atlantis, Golden Bat (named after a cheap brand of cigarettes, of all things) was invulnerable and could fly, wore a red cape (part of a swashbuckler outfit, with a golden or black skull for a head), lived in a hidden fortress in the Japanese Alps and fought supervillains like galactic despot Dr. Nazō, evil counterpart Dark Bat and generic giant robots.[23] He went on to appear in manga (Japanese comics) in 1948, three live-action movies between 1950 and 1972 and an anime (Japanese animation) series in 1967, attaining widespread recognition in Japan.

Another popular *Kamishibai* character was the Prince of Gamma (*Gamma no Ōji*), an orphaned prince from another planet. Disguised as a poor Tokyo guttersnipe, when duty called he donned a blue bodysuit with chest insignia, yellow cape and bird-shaped headdress. Like Golden Bat he possessed the powers of flight, invulnerability and prodigious strength, and likewise battled dramatic evildoers, including a blue, baldheaded evil scientist and an alien with visible brains.[24]

It's hard to ignore the similarities of these characters and tropes to those of Superman. But despite their popularity in Japan, the characters were and remain obscure in the West, and it's extremely unlikely that Siegel or Shuster would have heard of them in 1934 Cleveland. Siegel also details his influences in his unpublished memoir, and these are not mentioned. Conversely, the story of Moses would, in all likelihood, not have been familiar in detail to most people in Japan then.

One possibility is that these parallels are simply coincidental. Another is that they originate in universal, Jungian archetypes, developed separately by each culture but inevitably culminating in similar concepts. This would also be supported by comparative mythologist Joseph Campbell's theory of the monomyth, or "the hero's journey," by which most world mythologies and most heroic narratives share a common pattern (discussed in 1949's *The Hero with a Thousand Faces* and other of his books, following the works of Otto Rank [*The Myth of the Birth of the Hero*, 1909], Sigmund Freud [*Totem and Taboo*, 1913], Vladimir Propp [*Morphology of the Folktale*, 1928] and folklorism indexes like Aarne-Thompson-Uther and Thompson's motif-index).

This might seem to subvert the argument that Superman is a Jewish creation, informed by the culture and history of his creators. But even if he and Golden Bat—and Jesus and Moses, for that matter—stem from the same psychosocial monomyth, his unique version of it was conceived by two Jews drawing upon their tradition, which developed the universal archetype through its own folklore and philosophy over millennia. Whatever the commonalities, the idea of Superman was born in a Jewish context and imbued with Jewish content, making him a Jewish character.

While Moses and Samson were foundational inspirations for the Man of Steel, they weren't the only ones. Siegel and Shuster confected elements from their cultural orbit, the stories they read at synagogue, in the pulps, in comic strips, novels and newspapers, into an amalgam, yet completely original, creation.

One influence is E.C. Segar's Popeye, whose theatrical cartoons, beginning in 1933, were favorites of the nineteen-year-old duo, who felt the sailor's feats of superhuman strength would best be used in straight action, not comedy.[25]

Later in 1933, Humor Publishers' *Detective Dan, Secret Op. 48* (a pastiche of Dick Tracy and the first action comic book) inspired them to turn the villainous superman from their self-published short illustrated story "The Reign of the Superman" into a heroic Superman, as well as formatting it as a comic book, titled "The Superman." They kept the concept of a normal man unwittingly gaining superpowers at the hands of a mad scientist, but now those were physical rather than mental, turning him into "an outraged avenger."[26]

Lee Falk's (Leon Gross) the Phantom, debuting in a February 1936 comic strip, is the first hero to wear a skintight costume and possess superpowers (though only in pretense, claiming to be immortal), and so has been credited as an influence on Superman, but Siegel and Shuster formed Superman's final version in late 1934, predating the Phantom by two years in inception even if postdating him by two years in print.[27]

Who they do acknowledge as an influence is Tarzan, whom they called "the greatest action hero of the time," and particularly Burroughs's other creation, John Carter of Mars (aka Warlord of Mars), who appeared in February 1912's *All-Story*, eight months before Tarzan, but failed to achieve the same success. Carter, a Civil War veteran transported to an inhabited, warring planet Mars, finds that due to the red planet's weaker gravity he's able to leap great distances and heights and possesses great strength. Siegel used the idea for planet Krypton, making it much larger and so with greater gravity than Earth, explaining Superman's ability to leap tall buildings in a single bound and be more powerful than a locomotive.[28]

Another widely accepted source is the 1930 science fiction novel *Gladiator*, written by *New Yorker* editor Philip Wylie. It features Hugo Danner, whose scientist father injects him *in utero* with an experimental serum that grants him the proportionate strength of an insect; being able to leap great heights and lift objects several times his weight. Accordingly, he outruns trains, jumps over buildings and deflects bullets. He also spends his childhood in bucolic Colorado, pretending to be meek in order to avoid frightening others, on the advice of his father. As Tye notes, the explanation of Superman's powers in the first page of *Action Comics* #1 is even identical to Danner's, using the proportionate strength of an ant and the leaping ability of a grasshopper.[29]

That *Gladiator* was a direct source for some of the ideas used in Superman seems clear, but Siegel flatly denied any influence, signing an affidavit to that effect when Wylie threatened to sue DC for plagiarism. It would seem honest enough, considering he did freely admit to borrowing elements from other sources, like the workings of Superman's strength and leaping from John Carter (who predates Gladiator) and the claim of appropriation has since been called into question by several historians, suggesting that, if he did reuse these ideas, he likely wasn't cognizant. However, Siegel does acknowledge *Gladiator* as an influence in his unpublished memoir.[30] At any rate, Wylie got payback when the cover of the 1949 edition showed a musclebound, dark-haired, square-jawed hero standing with arms crossed under the tagline "an uninhibited superman."

Curiously, Wylie's other work hasn't been pointed to, though it seems to have been just as influential. Coauthored with Edwin Balmer, his serialized story in *Blue Book* magazine (September '32–February '33), novelized in 1933 as *When Worlds Collide*, tells of a prescient scientist who, realizing the Earth's pending doom, builds a rocket ship to carry survivors to another, possibly inhabited, world.

Last but not least of Superman's secular influences is Doc Savage, the Man of Bronze. Created by Henry W. Ralston, John L. Nanovic and Lester Dent, the scientist adventurer debuted in the pulp *Doc Savage Magazine* in March 1933. He possessed no superhuman powers, but was trained from birth to the pinnacle of human perfection in strength, intellect and morality—a concept of self-actualization that, while it may have influenced the early notion of Superman's powers being the result of Kryptonians' advanced evolution, has more in common with Batman and Captain America. His first name, however, is Clark, and he owns a hidden arctic retreat, replete with an advanced science lab, named the Fortress of Solitude. In the third issue, "Quest of the Spider" (May '33), he's even referred to as "a superman!"[31]

These similarities have been spotlighted often, notably by Fingeroth and Tye, but in fact aren't likely influences on Siegel and Shuster. They named Clark Kent after Hollywood stars Clark Gable and Kent Taylor, the reference to Doc Savage as "a superman" was made nearly five months after "The Reign of the Superman," and the Fortress of Solitude, while clearly appropriated, didn't appear until May 1949's *Superman* #58, created by writer William Woolfolk.[32]

That Superman is such a bricolage isn't surprising, nor does it diminish from his originality and brilliance. Seldom does artistic inspiration happen in a vacuum (well into the 1960s, the norm in the comic book field was that everyone "swiped" from everyone. Poses, characters, thematic elements, even entire plotlines were purloined and reused, sometimes by their own creators). The First Lady of comics, Lois Lane, for example, is likewise a collage of influences: her original looks are based on the model Siegel and Shuster used, Joanne Carter (Jolan Kovacs, who later became Joanne Siegel, Jerry's wife); her plucky, fast-talking, no-nonsense, headline-hunting personality comes from actress Glenda Farrell's portrayal of Torchy Blane, a reporter in a series of B-movies in the 1930s; and her last name from another actress to play the role, Lola Lane. Her first name was possibly inspired by Siegel and Shuster's mutual high school crush, Lois Amster.[33]

Siegel and Shuster first met in 1930, at the age of fifteen, while attending Glenville High. Jerome and Joseph, known as Jerry and Joe, were cut from the same cloth. Both were nebbishy and socially awkward. Both were first-generation American Jews (in Joe's case, Canadian-American) born to Eastern European immigrants. Both were sons of haberdasher-tailor fathers, and both were poor. They lived a few blocks from each other. Neither of them was a *wunderkind* at school, but they were both artistically talented, and ardent aficionados of the still-new genre of science fiction. They hit it off from the get-go. The day they met, they went over to Joe's place to work on their first project.[34]

Siegel was already a published writer, of sorts. His first works appeared in the *Sunday Buffalo Times'* kids' section, which invited young readers to submit stories. One, titled "Monsters of the Moon," even got him fan mail. He also wrote for the school's student newspaper, the *Glenville Torch* (after which the *Smallville Torch* is named, the high school newspaper a young Clark Kent cuts his teeth on in the *Smallville* TV show). In 1929, a year before he met Shuster, Siegel self-published what is often regarded as the first science fiction fan magazine, or "fanzine," called *Cosmic Stories*, typewritten under a variety of pennames, hectographed and sold through the mail. When he showed it to his English teacher, she lectured him on wasting his time writing trash when there were so many wonderful types of literature he could be writing instead.[35] He and Shuster were *luftmenschen*—impractical dreamers—their heads perpetually in the clouds. The difference was that they would eventually take the world up there with them.

In 1932, Siegel and Shuster started a new fanzine, bombastically titled *Science Fiction: The Advance Guard of Future Civilization*. It lasted five issues. Copies were made using the school's mimeograph machine and sold via mail, 15¢ apiece. Siegel wrote most of the stories, though he also published submissions from fellow fans like Forrest J. Ackerman and Ray Bradbury, marking their first works in print. Shuster was responsible for illustration and design.[36] In the third issue, dated January 1933, Siegel, under the pseudonym Herbert S. Fine, with artwork by Shuster, included an eight-page story he'd written the year prior, titled "The Reign of the Superman."

The story features William "Bill" Dunn, a homeless man picked from the breadline by the nefarious scientist Professor Ernest Smalley, who coaxes him with the

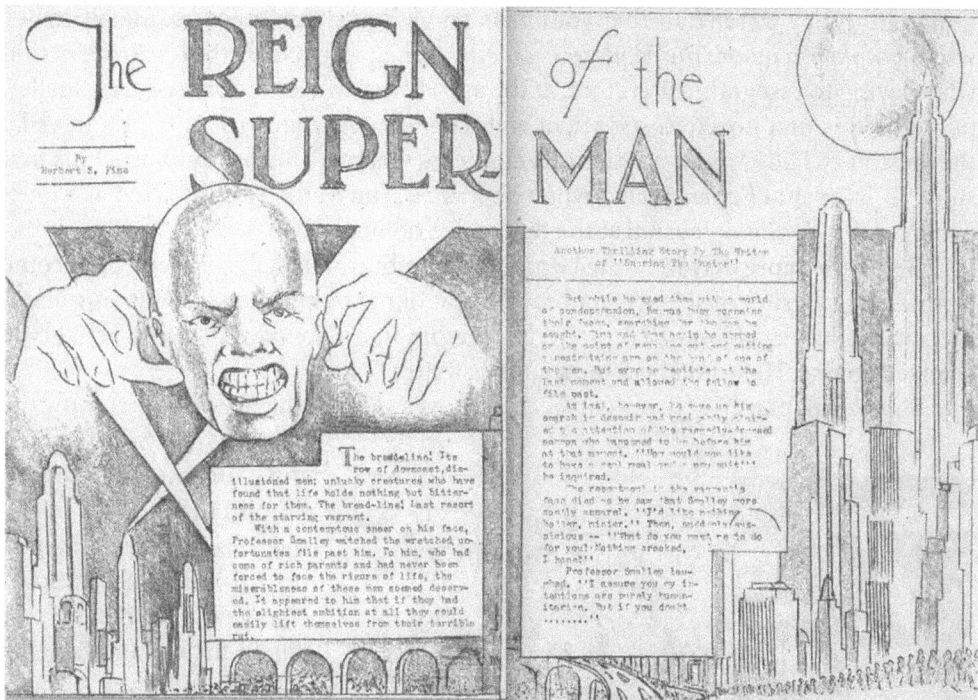

Opening pages of "Reign of the Superman" in *Science Fiction: The Advance Guard of Future Civilization* no. 3, January 1933. Written by Jerry Siegel (as Herbert S. Fine) and illustrated by Joe Shuster.

promise of a warm meal and new suit into becoming the unwitting subject of his experiment; digesting a drug containing a new element derived from a meteor. Dunn escapes, soon finding that he has enhanced hearing, telescopic vision, is able to read and control minds, and can see the near future—becoming the Superman. But with his powers he also gains newfound conceit and aggression, manifesting first in petty fraud and quickly growing into ambitions of world domination. Smalley, consumed with envy and rage, recreates the drug for himself, but the telepathic Superman, wise to his plan, returns to kill him first. They struggle, Dunn emerging the victor. He sets his plan in motion, causing an international peace conference to end in hostility and pitting the world's armies against each other, planning to reign over the winner, but at the very last minute the drug wears off and his powers disappear. Realizing the folly of his ways, Dunn laments not having used his powers for the good of mankind and returns, despondent, to the breadline.[37]

There are several well-known elements of Superman's lore that can be traced back to the short story. Shuster drew the Superman (spelled Super-Man in the title) as bald, a visual motif that would recur in his work, culminating in archenemy Lex Luthor, a composite of the bald Dunn and mad scientist Smalley. The meteor containing an unknown element that gives Dunn his powers is a precursor to Kryptonite, the meteorite remnants of planet Krypton that depower and can kill the Man of Steel. And of course the Superman concept itself, including super-senses but mental rather than physical powers, which the two *boychicks* created when only eighteen years old. (They weren't all that young, as far as literary creators go. Mary Shelley wrote *Frankenstein; or, The Modern Prometheus*, helping give birth to science fiction while laying to rest gothic literature, at the age of twenty. Her husband, Percy Shelley, published his first novel, *Zastrozzi*, at eighteen. Jane Austen wrote her first novella, the epistolary *Lady Susan*, as young as eighteen. Charles Dickens submitted his first story, "A Dinner at Poplar Walk," when he was 21. And Mark Twain started as a journalist for the *Hannibal Journal* at the tender age of fifteen.)

Being the more driven of the two, Siegel's ambition had always been to become a professional writer of science fiction, like that of the pulps. But upon reading about the success and acclaim of comic strip creators in a *Fortune Magazine* article, he changed course. He would become a comics writer.[38]

Superman, like most overnight successes, was years in the making. First came the Superman of Siegel's short story, an anti–Nietzschean morality tale. Then *Detective Dan* came out, inspiring him and Shuster to change the character from villain to hero and to make it a comic book. Around March or April 1933 he and Shuster created "The Superman," an urban Tarzan with no superpowers, dressed simply in T-shirt and pants (in his memoir, Siegel also recalls a version with fantastic strength and imperviousness to bullets who may have also worn a costume and cape in some draft). The cover described it as "A science fiction story in cartoons" and its hero as "The most astounding fiction character of all time." The title was set in familiar-looking, arcing block letters. The teens submitted their idea to different publishers, and in August Consolidated Book Publishers in Chicago, who published *Detective*

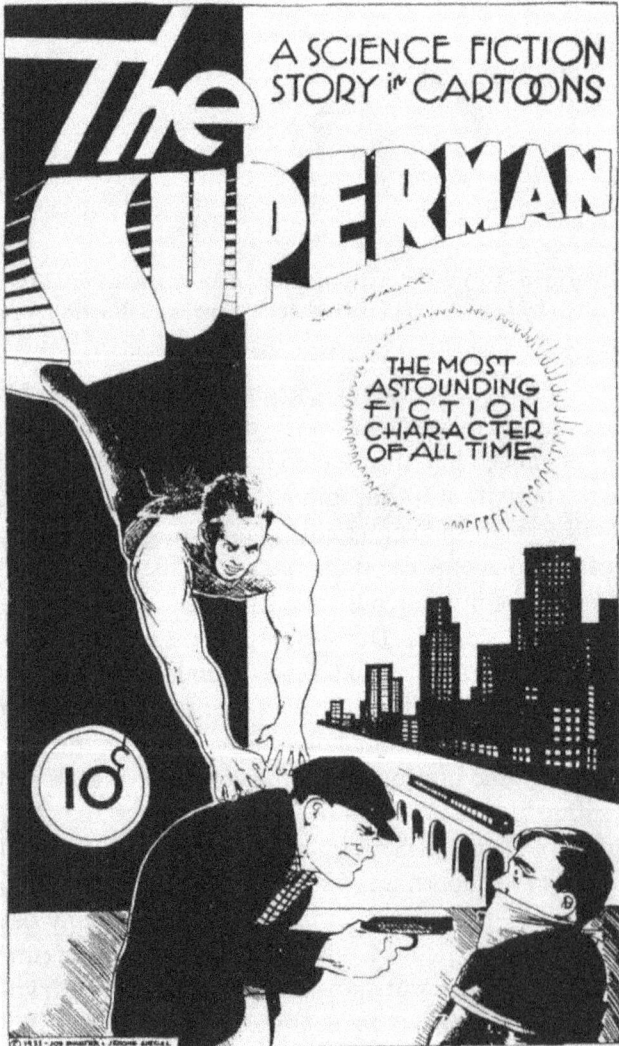

The Superman, 1933. Cover by Joe Shuster.

Dan, seemed interested, but ultimately decided that comic books were an "unprofitable venture."[39]

They soon graduated high school and, with the idea of Superman in their back pocket and no one interested, took odd jobs to help pay the bills. It was more than many other young men could find during the peak of the Depression. They sold empty milk bottles to storekeepers. Shuster sold ice cream bars on the street and delivered groceries. Siegel worked at a printing plant, also managing to sell some funny Valentine's verses to a card company. He remembers being so penniless that he'd cross town on foot instead of taking the bus because he couldn't afford the fare.[40]

They continued pursuing their passion, but nothing came of it—until 1934. In an essay titled "Happy 45th Anniversary, Superman!" in *Action Comics* #544 (June '83), Siegel recounts the fateful summer night that gave birth to the Man of Steel (a 1941 *Saturday Evening Post* article erroneously put it at 1932, leading some future accounts to conflate the 1933 urban Tarzan version with the 1934 superhero. In an August 1983 interview Siegel dates it as late 1934, which would have made it winter. His memoir likewise shows it was mid- to late November). It was hot, and he lay awake late, unable to fall asleep. He passed the time thinking up dramatic story elements for his comic strips. One concept in particular kept coming into sharp focus. This time, he decided, it would be a syndicated comic strip, not a newsstand comic book, and it would be named, simply, *Superman*.[41] In his unpublished memoir, he describes it:

> I thought more and more about the project, ideas coming to me while I was in a state of semi-slumber.... I myself had ambitions about becoming a reporter. And so it occurred to me that it would be very interesting if Superman kept his super-identity a secret and pretended to be just an ordinary reporter. As a reporter, he would uncover crises and people needing the aid of a Superman....
>
> Since Superman is all I would like to have been, though I was meek and mild.... I thought it would be amusing to have Superman, in his dual-identity of reporter Clark Kent, pretend to be meek-and-mild. What fun Superman would have inwardly in that disguise when people sneered at Clark—when he knew that anytime he wished, he could astound one and all as the fantastic, greatly admired Superman!
>
> Girls had not flipped over me ... girls I admired not only seemed turned-off toward me, but almost hostile.... Wouldn't it be really something if a scornful girl I idolized was in love with me, and didn't even know it? Not with the obvious, uninteresting outer me.... But with the inner me, who at least in my imagination could accomplish all things.
>
> And so, in an exercise of wish-fulfillment.... I created attractive girl reporter Lois Lane, who had an antipathy toward meek, mild Clark Kent ... yet she was ga-ga over super-powered Superman....
>
> I kept dozing off, then awakening ... and as I awakened and got more inspirations I would jot down additional script in daily strip form.... This went on until the wee hours of the morning.
>
> At dawn, I enthusiastically raced about a dozen blocks to Joe's apartment. I showed Joe the script and asked him if he would be interested in collaborating with me on this newest version of my Superman.... He enthusiastically agreed, and got to work at once.[42]

Shuster recalls, "I was caught up in Jerry's enthusiasm, and I started drawing as fast as I could use my pencil. My imagination just picked the concept right up from Jerry." They spent the day working on the new strip. Siegel suggested the character have a chest emblem and a cape, Shuster added the trunks, belt and boots (biblically resonant closed-toe sandals that laced up the shins).[43] By evening they had several weeks' worth of strips, telling the story of a prescient scientist on a doomed planet who sends his infant son to Earth, where he grows to possess amazing powers, devoting himself to helping those in need. Superman.

Rejuvenated, they doubled their efforts. They could barely afford the paper, ink and postage for their submission strips,[44] but they believed in their creation. Editors, however, were unimpressed, and they kept getting rejected.

Max Gaines, now a senior executive at the McClure Newspaper Syndicate, reviewed their submission. By one account he wasn't interested. By another, the same instincts that helped him recognize the potential of the medium also helped him recognize the potential of the character, but he failed to interest his bosses.[45]

One magazine publisher turned down the strip because he felt "the field was very crowded."[46]

The big-name United Features Syndicate, home of *Tarzan* and *Li'l Abner*, among 150 comics and editorial columns, called Superman "a rather immature piece of work ... likely to wear off after the feature runs for a while."[47]

Another, Bell Syndicate, owners of popular strips like *Mutt and Jeff* and *Fu Manchu*, rejected the strip because, they wrote, "we are in the market only for strips likely to have the most extraordinary appeal and we do not feel Superman gets into that category."[48]

An editor who rejected the earlier version of Superman for not being sensational enough rejected this new version for the opposite. "The trouble with this, kid," he told Siegel, "is that it's too sensational. Nobody would believe it."[49]

The concept of Superman was so unique, so unprecedented, that the strip had been rejected by every single newspaper in New York for being "too fantastic for even juvenile audiences."[50]

How utterly ridiculous Superman must have seemed to editors then. A strongman from outer space, dressed in long johns, wellingtons and a cape. What a *mashugana* idea.

Daunted but persistent, Siegel and Shuster kept sending out their Superman strip, along with others. In 1935 they finally got, though not quite their big break, a foot in the door. *New Fun: The Big Comic Magazine*, published by National Allied Publications, was looking for original (i.e., royalty-free) material. They rejected *Superman* but bought two of the boys' other strips—their first real published work— both single-page features debuting in October's *New Fun Comics #6*. The first was a hackneyed action-adventure strip called *Henri Duval of France, Famed Soldier of Fortune*, about a 17th-century swordsman. The second was a supernatural sleuth named *Doc Occult* (later *Dr. Occult, the Ghost Detective*), which they created under "Leger & Reuths." While usually attired in the customary trench coat and fedora, in more than one issue he wore Superman's cape as well as face. He remains DC Comics' longest-running character.

(DC Comics started out as two separate companies: National Allied Publications, formed in 1934, and Detective Comics, in 1937. Detective bought National in 1938, and the two merged in 1946 to become National Comics Publications. It soon absorbed a third publisher, All-American Publications, as well as distributor

Independent News and other affiliates, renaming itself National Periodical Publications in 1961. In 1977, after having been known colloquially as DC since 1940, the company officially adopted the name, taken from its longest-running title, *Detective Comics*. Referred to as DC Comics hereafter.)

Paying work couldn't have come soon enough. Shuster in particular was so penurious that paper to draw on was considered a luxury purchase in his household. He used whatever discarded scraps he could find. The *Henry Duval* and *Doc Occult* pitches were drawn on either wrapping paper or the back of wallpaper he'd found, causing them to almost get lost in the shuffle at National's offices. For a drawing board he used his mother's bread board, which she'd take back on Fridays to make challah for Shabbat (making Judaism quite literally baked into Superman). With unemployment and homelessness all around he was happy to be making a living, even if his apartment didn't have heat. He often worked wearing gloves and layers of sweaters.[51]

Time passed. In January 1936 their third strip was published, *Federal Men*, beginning in *New Comics* #2, featuring their unorthodox ideas of law enforcement challenges, like hundred-foot, laser-shooting robots. July's *More Fun Comics* #11 debuted their fourth, *Radio Squad*, about a spirited patrolman equipped with real-life state-of-the-art crime-fighting technology; a police car radio. In March 1937 they helped launch a new series, *Detective Comics* #1, with two more strips: *Spy*, starring Bart Regan, a dashing secret agent (sixteen years before James Bond) and *Slam Bradley*, a tough-guy private eye who originally operated out of Cleveland, then New York, which soon became their most popular strip. It was formulaic, at first glance like dozens, if not hundreds, of similar characters in comics, pulps and the radio. But there was something different about it. Bradley was exceptionally musclebound, and he routinely used his great strength to crash through doors and send criminals flipping through the air, often beating entire gangs singlehandedly.

"*Slam Bradley* was a dry run for Superman," Siegel described. "*Superman* had already been created, and we didn't want to give away the Superman idea; but we just couldn't resist putting into *Slam Bradley* some of the slambang stuff which we knew would be in Superman if and when we got *Superman* launched."[52]

They were splitting $174 a month from their various strips (roughly $3,000 adjusted), not nearly enough to live on, but a promising start. They continued to submit Superman, now as working professionals, eventually reaching the desk of every newspaper syndicate in the U.S. They all said no.[53]

The Ledger Syndicate, interestingly, rejected the idea on the grounds that "editors and the public have had their fill for the time being of interplanetary and superhuman subjects. It would not therefore be worth our while to produce a strip in this already overburdened field."[54] But before Superman there were no superheroes, no gallant demigods. What Ledger were referring to were urban crusaders like the Shadow and Doc Savage, "historical" adventurers like Tarzan and Zorro and spacefaring explorers like Buck Rogers and John Carter, along with their myriad knockoffs. What they failed to recognize was that Siegel and Shuster had reversed the formula; the heroes of the day were all intrepid Earthmen, ordinary humans, more or less, who ventured into fantastical locales like other planets, hidden subterranean cities and mysterious jungles. But for Siegel, as rich as his imagination was, the direness of the reality around kept beckoning. It was stranger and more menacing than fiction, and it was more than any mere mortal could hope to handle. And so he made his hero fantastical, from elsewhere, somewhere better, who came equipped to right the familiar wrongs of the real world. There were costumed, even superhuman heroes before Superman, but only insomuch as there were American leaders before George Washington.

Then, sometime between late 1937 and early 1938, things changed. National Allied Publications, which published *Henry Duval, Dr. Occult, Federal Men* and *Radio Squad*, was owned by ex-cavalry officer and comics pioneer Major Malcolm Wheeler-Nicholson, who also co-owned Detective Comics, Inc., which published *Spy* and *Slam Bradley*. His partners in Detective were duo Harry Donenfeld, a Rumanian-born Jew from the Lower East Side, and his right-hand man, Jack Liebowitz, a Ukrainian Jew and fellow resident of the ghetto.

Donenfeld was a shrewd salesman and entrepreneur, having made his early living as a moonshine bootlegger during Prohibition, where he also became close friends with Frank Costello, head of the Luciano crime family. He later became a producer of what was considered then "porno mags" like *La Paree Stories, Spicy Detective, Spicy Adventure, Spicy Mystery* and *Spicy Western*. Liebowitz worked as a magazine distributor before teaming up with Donenfeld to publish prurient pulps, a business they continued while also publishing Superman. Broadly, Liebowitz headed both the creative and accounting aspects of DC while Donenfeld handled sales and distribution though his other company, Independent News Co.[55]

How Superman came to be discovered and who discovered him is a hotly contested matter, as most everyone involved has taken credit. The first is Wheeler-Nicholson, who claimed to have received the submission in October 1935, thought it had potential, and offered to publish it (according to his son, it was he who first developed *Action Comics*, specifically as a vehicle for Superman, though the claim is unsubstantiated). But his financial difficulties and resultant late payments to Siegel and Shuster for their work made them turn him down, and it remained in the company's "slush pile" of rejected strips until its rediscovery. In 1938 Donenfeld sued Nicholson into bankruptcy, obtaining full ownership of both National Allied Publications and Detective Comics, effectively forming DC.[56]

The second is Max Gaines, who reviewed the Superman submission in 1934 for the McClure Syndicate and liked it, but failed to convince his employers. Still, he remembered it, and in early 1938, when his friend Jack Liebowitz called to ask if he had "any material laying around" for a forthcoming anthology series titled *Action Comics,* he pitched it to him. Liebowitz and Donenfeld liked the idea, and commissioned a thirteen-page story.[57]

Another claimant is Sheldon Mayer, then a twenty-year-old assistant to Gaines, DC's print broker. He remembers, "I went nuts over the thing. It was the thing we were all looking for. It struck me as having the elements that were popular in the movies, all the elements that were popular in novels, and all the elements that I loved." He nagged Gaines, who'd previously ignored the strip, to reconsider, insisting that the colorful hero would be "the next big thing" in comics. Gaines eventually came around and suggested the strip to Donenfeld, who was skeptical but trusted Gaines' proven instincts. Siegel's own recollections support this version of events.[58]

By another account it was Vincent "Vin" Sullivan, the 26-year-old editor of *Action Comics* (and the only gentile in the group), who approached Mayer looking for new content. "Donenfeld had little or nothing to do with the selection of features and things of that nature," he remembers. "When they showed this thing to me that they'd been trying to sell, it looked good to me, and I started it. That's how Superman got going."[59]

Whichever the case, they all played a pivotal role, and Gaines, the man who started the comic book industry in May 1933 with *Funnies on Parade*, also started its main genre, superheroes, when he sent the *Superman* strip to DC in January 1938.[60]

Action Comics was already slated for publication that April (cover dated June), and DC didn't have enough new material to fill it with. Liebowitz later confessed that the decision to put Superman in issue #1 was "a pure accident" based on deadline pressure. "When Harry Donenfeld first saw that cover of Superman holding that car in the air, he really got worried," Mayer remembers. "He felt that nobody would believe it, that it was ridiculous—crazy."[61]

After all their trials and tribulations, even the publisher that finally bought Siegel and Shuster's favorite creation didn't believe in it. Likely because of this, Superman wasn't seen or mentioned on the cover until issue #7, seven months later. But from issue #12, May 1939, he'd almost never leave the cover again, to this day.

Six years since his inception and four since reaching final form, Superman finally took the stage. On March 1, 1938, the boys sold their Superman story to DC for $10 a page, totaling $130 ($2,300 adjusted), and with it signed over ownership of the character.[62]

Donenfeld and Liebowitz, who thought little of it at the time, would prove to be the entertainment industry's Peter Minuit. That $130 investment started a gargantuan multibillion-dollar industry. DC- and Marvel-based movies alone have generated well over $50 billion as of this writing,[63] with comics, TV shows, video games, toys, clothes and other merchandise several times that.

It's unclear whether Siegel and Shuster sought legal counsel prior to signing the Faustian contract, which eminent comic book writer Alan Moore calls unequivocally a "shameful act of theft upon which the vast business ... seems to have been founded."[64] According to the prevailing narrative of events, they got bamboozled out of a bonanza and got *bupkis*. They were hapless, duped victims whose only fault was over-eagerness for their passion project and lack of foresight. But reality, as ever, is a little more complicated.

It's hard to say why they agreed to sell the rights to what they believed in so strongly and worked so hard for so many years to achieve. Perhaps they were strapped for cash, willing to sell their firstborn to Rumpelstiltskin if that's what it took to turn the heat back on at home. Possibly they saw Superman as their big break but not more than that, expecting to follow with equally successful properties. Perhaps, being young and naïve, they just didn't think it through. It was a handsome rate; it could be that they simply thought it was a fair deal. Or they truly were tricked by rapacious *farbrechers* into signing away ownership without realizing it. There are as many versions to the story as there are to Superman's, with one constant. They lived to regret it.

Siegel would later reflect: "Joe and I talked it over, decided we were tired of see-ing the strip rejected everywhere, and would at least like to see it in print." But, he laments, "we concentrated so much on what we were creating that we gave little thought about protecting ourselves." Shuster remembers that "everything happened very fast: they made the decision to publish it and said to us, 'Just go out and turn out 13 pages based on your strip.'"[65]

Ultimately, it seems, selling the character along with the story was an oversight. After years of continuous rejection, they were desperate to have him see the light of day. But the story of two nice Jewish boys who came to the big city with a golden idea and big dreams and got swindled by unscrupulous businessmen, while true in essence, is a romanticized telling.

For one, as timid as Siegel may have been socially, professionally, even as a tyro, he was cocky and full of *chutzpah*. In November 1937, when Gaines had written to him about doing one or more weekly eight-page features for a potential new series, the 23 year old responded to his prospective employer: "what price per page are you offering? Please mention a definite price in your answering letter so that valuable time will not be wasted in negotiating prices. And please make your price per page attractive enough so that such negotiations will be unnecessary."[66]

They also weren't exactly naïfs. At 24 they were young but not children, cer-tainly not in that era, and they'd been working for DC for two years. They knew how things worked and what the going rates were, and they had already sold strips, and with them ownership, to the company. What's more, the contract language for Super-man wasn't ambiguous; "I hereby sell and transfer such work and strip, all good will attached thereto and exclusive right to the use of the characters and story, conti-nuity and title of strip contained therein, to you and your assigs to have and hold forever and to be your exclusive property ... to give you exclusive right to use and acknowledge that you own said characters or story and the use thereof, exclusively."[67] Whether they fully realized it or not, they willingly signed away not just the publish-ing rights to the specific strip but exclusive rights to the characters and his story, in perpetuity.

Donenfeld, for his part, was a glad-handing hustler, and Liebowitz, as Tye describes him, a hardnosed bean counter, but they weren't *gonifs* any more than Sie-gel and Shuster were *schnooks* (thieves and dupes, respectively). Donenfeld in partic-ular was a tough man in a tough industry in a tough town in a tough time, and when it came to business he was all shark, but there's nothing to support the argument that he and Liebowitz set out to connive Siegel and Shuster out of their treasured posses-sion. On the contrary, by most accounts they were dubious of the idea and consid-ered it "a long shot."[68]

Comic book creators then weren't thought of as artists. They were hired hands, producing filler for throwaway magazines. They almost all signed away rights to what they turned in, because none of it was thought of as valued intellectual property. It proved exploitive later on, but in the early days it was a barely lucrative, inconsequen-tial business operating on a shoestring budget. Siegel and Shuster's page rate of $10 was actually 40 percent higher than anyone else DC employed,[69] and they received a byline when almost no one else did.

All that said, there's no question that they suffered iniquitous treatment at the hands of DC. Donenfeld and Liebowitz became Superman's impresarios, raking in millions from sales and royalties while his originators toiled for page rates and bonuses, generous as they may have been. Their relationship, particularly between Siegel and Liebowitz, soured very quickly. Superman's new owners became martinet, derogatory and ultimately dishonest when it came to paying the duo their due, leading them along through a series of excuses that first claimed Superman wasn't all that successful, and when that was no longer possible that expenses outreached revenue,[70] which eventually led to an acrimonious parting of ways and years of litigation.

But all that would come later.

In 1938, the comic book medium was still formless and void, a fledgling, possibly ephemeral industry. Like the formation of the universe, all the matter, all the energy from which everything else would forever be made of, were contained in one single origin point. It all started with a big bang—the explosion of planet Krypton.

Dreams are often most profound when they seem the most crazy.—Sigmund Freud

The Big Bang

In 2003, *Time* magazine dubbed April 15, 1938, one of "80 Days That Changed the World." It was the day *Action Comics* #1 arrived on newsstands (cover dated June), introducing Superman to the world and giving birth to the superhero genre. It was counted alongside the discovery of penicillin, the Nazi invasion of Poland, the *Apollo 11* moon landing and the creation of the internet.[1]

The magazine stood out immediately, its cover boldly declaring … nothing. There was none of the customary ringmaster-style hyperbole. No sound effects. No jutting banner proclaiming an exciting adventure starring a sensational new character. There was no need. It was a simple, powerful image of a man lifting a car over his head as if it were a mattress, smashing it into rocks while frightened men scatter about, set in blue, red and green against a bright yellow background. It was something completely new, pure shock and awe, and it worked. The issue had a print run of 200,000 copies, but soon children were clamoring, not for *Action Comics*, a 64-page anthology featuring ten other strips, but for "that magazine with Superman in it," and sales reached a million copies a month.[2]

Superman's entire origin is told in the span of ten panels on one page, and with that out of the way, he's introduced in medias res, hurtling high over rooftops with a woman, bound and gagged, under his arm, his muscles bulging and cape fluttering in the night wind. The image radiates power and urgency, accompanied by equally dramatic captioning: "A tireless figure races thru the night. Seconds count .. delay means forfeit of an innocent life."[3] After years of inertia, Siegel and Shuster wasted no time putting their hero into action.

They paced the story in staccato, partly due to Shuster's style but mostly because, in a rush to meet the deadline, they cut and pasted four weeks of newspaper strips onto thirteen comic book pages of six to eight panels each,[4] creating an adventure of vignettes. The comic barely has any detail to it. Too static—it's all movement, all action, the shapes of buildings, streets and cars rendered in shorthand, the focus kept squarely on Superman. It's rough-and-ready storytelling, raw and visceral.

Aside from Superman and alter ego Clark Kent, the story also introduced intrepid reporter Lois Lane, arguably the first damsel in heroic fiction to play a greater role than just being in distress. "The first great feminist," longtime Superman writer-artist Dan Jurgens calls her. "Female careers ended up being shaped by Lois Lane."[5]

The rest of Superman's supporting cast and rogues' gallery would come later.

But for his debut adventure, the hero who can toss around cars and shrug off gunfire faced off not against one of Siegel and Shuster's giant robots, or mad scientists, or space warlords. The Man of Steel's first villains were a murderess, a man belting his wife, a gang of hoodlums who kidnap Lois, and a senator and munitions lobbyist conspiring to embroil the U.S. in war— common criminals and malfeasant public officials. From the start, Superman wasn't simply an adventurer or a grim avenger. He was a hero of the people, righting the wrongs that plague the common man, a "champion of the oppressed."[6]

He looked different from any other adventure hero of the time. He was stocky, barrel-chested and musclebound, dressed in a now-famous blue, red and

Action Comics #1, June 1938. Cover by Joe Shuster. DC Comics.

yellow costume of skintight unitard (thirty years before spandex was invented), briefs on top (a look associated with circus strongmen since the Victorian era, signifying masculinity) and billowing cape (a majestic touch owing to medieval royalty). He was of average height, quite a few inches shorter than his current stature, and sported some biblically-evocative trappings, remnants of his earlier strip version, colored over but still visible, of lace-up sandals and wrist cuffs.

In the last panel of their thirteen-page story, Siegel and Shuster declared that "Superman is destined to reshape the destiny of a world!" Little did they know, engaging in the customary boastfulness of the time, how prophetic they were. What Donenfeld and Liebowitz had misgivings about, children responded to with fervent enthusiasm. Superman was like nothing seen before and everything seen thereafter. Jack Kirby, comics' most influential artist save perhaps Will Eisner, remembers that when he first saw Superman in *Action Comics* #1 is when he knew that comic books had truly "arrived." He was right; Superman's arrival on the scene was the missing

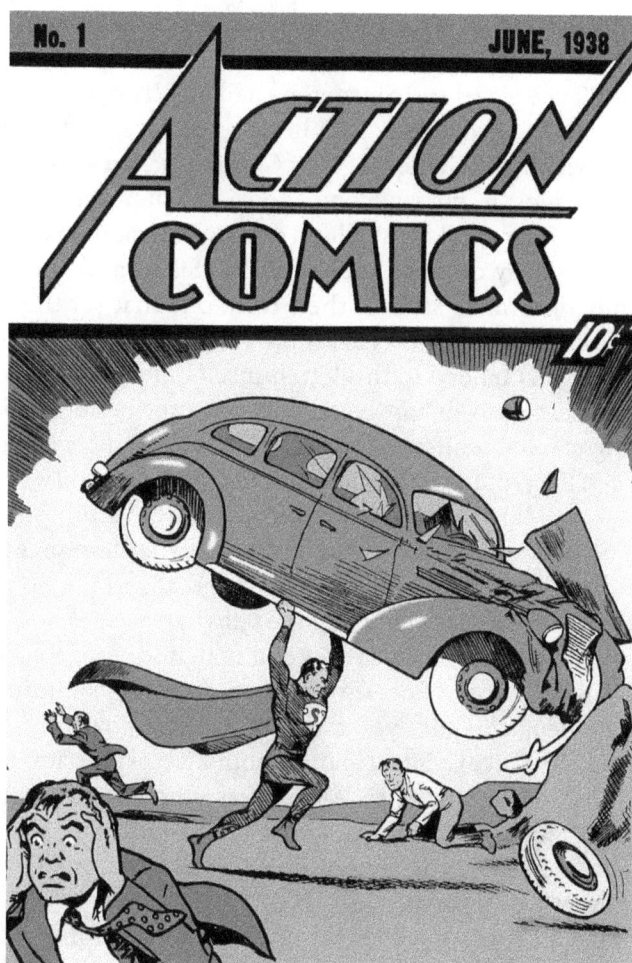

element that turned a nascent industry into an entertainment powerhouse that would captivate the imagination of children and adults the world over. In their roughhewn brilliance Siegel and Shuster created an ideogram—a symbol representing an idea— that would prove universal in its resonance, and heralded what would come to be known as "the Golden Age" of Comics. *Action Comics* #1 would go on to become the single most important comic book ever published, as well as the most expensive. In 2014, a near-mint copy sold in a special auction on eBay for $3.2 million.[7]

As they did with their concept, Siegel and Shuster combined their influences into a narrative style of their own, one that set the standard for others to follow. Siegel's writing, from narration to dialogue to monologue (which was frequent, as Superman tended to think to himself out loud, in word balloons) carried a charge, an eclectic mix of hardboiled pulp noir, the rapid-fire banter and sardonic whimsy of movies, and biblical bombast, which gave Superman, and through him all superheroes, the reputation for larger-than-life theatricality.

Reading Superman was a thrill ride, the action so fast and furious there was nary a panel where he wasn't launching into the air, punching criminals, smashing walls, hurling machinery, deflecting gunfire, absorbing bomb blasts or racing to save the day. Readers got swept up in the tailwind.

Shuster's lines made a good match for Siegel's—simple and blunt, sometimes clumsy, but full of energy and excitement. His minimalistic rendering of the hero, with deep slits for eyes, a narrow line for a mouth and two quick marks for chiseled cheeks gave Superman a sphinxlike expression that lacked expressiveness but added to his stoic allure. And he was simple enough for anyone to project themselves onto. Shuster's characters were a burlesque: thugs looked like troglodytes, evil masterminds like birds of prey, Lois like a glamorous movie star and Superman always perfectly handsome.

Luminary Jules Feiffer called Shuster "a marvel at a sense of immediacy, of action … a true … purveyor of the cartoon arts."[8] His work wasn't as detailed and nuanced as that of other artists like Will Eisner (*Hawks of the Seas*) or Hal Foster (*Prince Valiant*), but what need was there for subtlety with a man who tosses around Oldsmobiles? Shuster was an impressionistic dynamo, seamlessly combining the familiar with the monumental. Nothing looked real; everything felt hyperreal.

Siegel and Shuster's experimentations with form were ahead of their time, incorporating elements like the heavy use of narrator captions, which read like a film noir voiceover (predating the film genre by several years), or depicting background shapes in streaks, conveying a world blurred at tremendous speed. They were masters of the page-turner; the first time Superman is shot at is in the last panel of one page, and only on the next is it revealed that the bullet ricochets harmlessly off his skin. In another instance Lois walks in on him as he's changing back into Clark Kent, only to show the following page that she's in a drug-induced haze.[9]

By November's *Action Comics* #6 Superman was clearly a success. Shuster's art improved, less hurried but equally vibrant, and the story is playfully metatextual, involving crooks trying to capitalize on the hero's burgeoning fame and commercial success. By issue #7 the title outsold the market average by more than double.

Jerry Siegel, left, and Joe Shuster. Publicity photos from *Superman* #1, June 1939.

In January 1939, the McClure Syndicate, which had rejected the strip, now came hat in hand bidding for the newspaper rights.[10] McClure ended up syndicating the strip until 1983. In June, a year after his debut, the Man of Steel's second series launched, simply titled *Superman*—the first comic book series to feature a single character. The cover shows Superman hovering above skyscrapers, framed in a movie marquee design. It was fitting. He was a star.

Siegel and Shuster were remarkably fecund, serving as the full-time creative team on *Action Comics*, *Superman* and the newspaper strip. Their hard work paid off: bestselling comics until then sold 200,000–400,000 copies a month. *Superman* sold 1.3 million. In September 1939, fifteen months into his existence, *Time* magazine reported that "Superman is rapidly becoming the No. 1 juvenile vogue in the U.S." Less than a year later, on July 3, 1940, the famed New York World's Fair held a "Superman Day." It broke attendance records for any single children's event, drawing 36,000 excited fans.[11] Superman was officially a national sensation.

The superhero's dominance of the newsstands also helped affect, or at least mark, the beginning of a paradigm shift in American entertainment. While the early comic books were aimed at the same general readership as the pulps and the strips, mostly young men and adults, publishers soon realized the potential of a new demographic—children and adolescents. "That was the beginning of the comic industry," Liebowitz would later remember.[12]

It's ironic that today Superman is often perceived as old-fashioned when he started out as a maverick who challenged authority and sought to disrupt the unfair order of things. Siegel and Shuster's Superman was a working class crusader, concerned more with corrupt plutocrats, crooked officials and racketeers than mad scientists and mechanical monsters. His plebeian values often put him at odds with authorities, who regarded him as an outlaw and a menace. He was a modern-day Robin Hood, noble but not regal, a feisty scrapper with a fed-up attitude toward bullies.

The ultimate macho man, Superman was tougher than anyone, knew better than anyone, did what no one else would or could. He meted out justice with absolute confidence, unburdened by dilemma. But, at the same time, he wasn't capricious. He followed a strict moral code, by which—though he routinely threatened crooks that he'd kill or maim them, and several ended up hoisted with their own petards—he firmly upheld the Sixth Commandment. The pulp heroes like Tarzan or Sam Spade typically dispensed with their enemies, but virtually all superheroes that came after Superman, well into the 1980s, followed his moral example.

His attitude changed gradually over the course of the next few years. After it was pointed out to Siegel in 1939 that his hero acted as a vigilante he modified him to be more law-abiding, though he still remained a rebellious reformist. According to Siegel, the more Superman became popular and a meaningful source of revenue for DC, the more editorial interference there was in his and Shuster's work, and they were forced to tame him down.[13] It wasn't until 1942, however, when the U.S. was at war, that the Man of Tomorrow went from recalcitrant to respectable.

Even so, he remained trenchant. Despite his origin story and the intermittent robot or ray gun, he was still predominantly a crime noir character, then also a war action hero. It wasn't until the 1950s, when his comics were written and edited by a group of sci-fi magazine veterans, that his main genre became science fiction and he developed a softer edge.

Originally he wasn't even all that powerful. His only superpower was inhuman strength, and even that at a fraction of today's. From this he was also impervious to most harm and could propel himself over distances and heights. His more exotic staples—super-hearing, x-ray, telescopic and heat vision, and freeze-breath—came later. He didn't officially take flight in print, his most famous ability, until *Action Comics* #65, in October 1943. But his powers increased quickly as the world around him grew more menacing. When he first appeared in June 1938, "nothing less than a bursting shell could penetrate his skin." By March 1941, shells were bursting harmlessly on his chest.[14]

The world was fast becoming outsized, and it required a larger than life man to give it a sense of order and control. If Kafka cast man as an insect, reflecting an increasingly inhospitable, dehumanizing world, then Siegel and Shuster, in the opening page of *Action Comics* #1, gave man the proportionate great strength of an insect. The modern world may overwhelm the everyman, but not the superman.

The growing urbanization of America and the rise of skyscrapers, especially the bristling skyline of New York City, hallmarked by art deco and streamline moderne, venerating, grandiosely, speed, flight and power, likewise inspired the idea of the superhero, a man-god befitting an Olympus of giant gleaming spires, humming with electrical power and human excitement. The age of the metropolis begat the age of the superman.

Siegel and Shuster's brilliance was in creating a fantasy not of a great champion descended from above to save the common man but of the common man as mighty, powerful enough to save himself as well as others. The concept had immediate universal appeal; the weakness, insecurity and awkwardness that the world sees are deceptive. Secretly, hidden not too deep, is an invulnerable, omnipotent, super-confident, Superman. It's a fantasy fundamental to human experience, made all the more pertinent by the dehumanizing trends of the 20th century—industrialization, exponential population growth, mass migrations, political turmoil, wars of mass casualties and growing awareness of global affairs—all of which contributed to the individual's sense of unimportance and impotence. At a time when the concept of the atomic bomb was first introduced to the public, the idea that a man can be even more powerful was too good to pass.

Superhero comics, starting with Superman, aren't stories about gods (Thor and a few others being the exception), they're about regular people with the powers of gods. About what humanity aspires to be, and what we dare suspect we might already be. Superman is often talked about as a wish-fulfillment fantasy, but more accurately he's a fulfillment wish.

He is the Adam of superheroes, the *avant-coureur* who heralded the tidal wave of costumed crimefighters that would come to monopolize the comic book medium. More than simply the first, he's the mold from which all other superheroes were produced, where they got their "super" from. As Michael Chabon writes, "Superman invented and exhausted his genre in a single bound. All the tropes, all the clichés and conventions, all the possibilities, all the longings and wishes and neuroses that have driven and fed and burdened the superhero comic during the past seventy years were implied by and contained within."[15]

Renowned Italian writer, philosopher and semiotician Umberto Eco dedicated his 1962 essay, "The Myth of Superman," to the exploration of his unique status as both mythic and literary figure, also positing him, in Hegelian dialectic, as the superhero thesis—the source idea from which all other ideas spring.[16] Everything in the genre that's come after Superman has been affected by his example, whether directly or indirectly, as imitation, commentary or antithesis. Every superhero, even every superhuman character, are inexorably defined by the paradigm he set.

Following the character's success, men and women with impossible abilities populated the comic magazines, almost all following the *sine quibus non* he established; heroes do not kill; heroes are tough but gallant; heroes keep a secret identity; and, paramount, heroes wear the nonsensical ensemble of cape, tights and briefs worn as outer layer.

The second superhero was Batman, first appearing in May 1939's *Detective Comics* #27. Though lacking any superpowers and arguably more a pulp avenger than superhero, "the Bat-Man" helped cement the superhero fad. The yin to Superman's yang, Batman is a dark and brooding revenge fantasy against the crime and violence born of urban decay. (Actor Michael Caine, who played Batman's butler and confidant Alfred Pennyworth in the Christian Bale films, quipped in 2008 that "Superman is the way America sees itself, but Batman is the way the world sees America."[17])

Like Superman before him and most others that followed, the Dark Knight was created by two young impoverished Jews, Bob Kane (Robert Kahn) and Bill (Milton) Finger. Whereas the Man of Steel operated in "Metropolis," a generic term for a big city, the Caped Crusader fought crime in "Gotham City," a nickname for New York, coined by Washington Irving in 1807.[18] Kane and Finger were both New Yorkers, as were the vast majority of their comic book colleagues. Their creations protected thinly veiled proxies like Empire City and Central City, replete with the Statue of Liberty and other landmarks. They wrote what they knew, and New York—with the largest Jewish community in the world—became the backdrop for superhero adventure.

In short order came the Human Torch (October '39), the Flash (January '40), Green Lantern (July '40), Captain America (March '41), Captain Marvel (aka Shazam, March '41), Wonder Woman (January '42), and countless others, the latter two being notable exceptions as purely gentile creations.

Then there was Will Eisner's *The Spirit* (June '40), a genre-bending vigilante detective character who was a superhero only because Eisner put gloves and a domino mask on him to sell him as one. Appearing not in a newsstand magazine but in a sixteen-page insert in the Sunday papers of the Register and Tribune syndicates, it was the most ambitious superhero comic, drawing heavily on German Expressionism and projecting a sense of dark absurdism. Many future writers and artists, like John Updike, have credited the comic as a meaningful influence.[19]

After Superman, the Spirit was also the most laden with Jewish signification. A slovenly, scrappy underdog, his adventures took place in settings strongly suggestive of the Lower East Side, like tenement rooftops, clothesline-strewn alleyways and dilapidated waterfront facades, frequently incorporating, as Fingeroth describes, "a Jewish sensibility, including.... Yiddishisms and Jewish immigrant ghetto-speak."[20] If Superman was straight-laced, sincere and solemn, the Spirit was his caustic, self-deprecating cousin. He was the wisecracking Jew who was often also the butt of the joke, the Oscar Madison to Superman's Felix Unger without the two ever meeting on page.

In 1939 there were eight publishers of comic books. By 1940 there were sixteen, producing 150 different series.[21] Many featured the goofy oddballs and anthropomorphic animals of the early funnies, like Dell Comics' licensed Walt Disney properties, but most featured superheroes, the proprietary genre of the medium and now a neologism. It was a superhero gold rush, with prospectors rushing out half-baked *fakakta* ideas, usually insipid musclemen in capes whose backstories began and ended with the scientific mishap that gave them powers. It spawned a passel of Superman pastiches, though most lacked the original's substance, and so his appeal and staying power.

Despite their meteoric success superheroes were seen as a passing trend, and most publishers outsourced their production to independent studios, which were run by the same garment sweatshop model the owners knew either from their parents or their own experience. The romantic image of the solitary genius at work in his garret in reality was rows of artists and craftsmen churning out comics like a factory production line, working on an endless rotation of pages. In 1965's *The Great Comic Book Heroes*, the first history book on the subject, Jules Feiffer described the nature of the business: "Artists sat lumped in crowded rooms, knocking it out for the page rate.

Penciling, inking, lettering in the balloons for $10 a page, sometime less…. Working blind but furiously, working from swipes, working from the advice of others who drew better because they were in the business two weeks longer."[22]

In truth, Golden Age comics were largely juvenilia, produced by teens and young men, only some of whom had any real talent. "We were kids ourselves," Batman artist Jerry Robinson remembers, "so we were writing what excited us, which our audience then related to." It was, for the most part, expeditiously-produced *dreck*, but what the stories and art lacked in polish they made up for in conviction. They were raw and they roared with energy and action. They were still, as comic book legend Stan Lee, then an office assistant at Marvel, noted, "not held in high regard … and that's putting it mildly,"[23] but they allowed their young creators to bring in much-needed *gelt* for their families, even if not *naches*.

The comic book medium and the superhero genre were created at the lowest level of culture but captured its highest ideals and aspirations. Pulitzer Prize-winning comic book creator Art Spiegelman (Itzhak Avraham ben Zeev) of *Maus* fame theorizes that, precisely because "it was a time when comics always travelled below critical radar," they "offered a direct gateway into the unrestrained dream life of their creators."[24] For all their glory and symbolism of American might and rectitude, superheroes were created by a band of Jewish kids from the ghetto, and they reflected their fears, fantasies and faith—if not religious, then in the promise of the nation that took them or their parents in.

The year of 1940 saw the number of comic book series being published explode from 150 to as many as 700.[25] Superheroes were everywhere, up on every rooftop and down every alley, flying, punching, shooting, blowing things up, like an invasion of Huns in leotards.

Comic books were an unqualified success, all the more so against the backdrop of the Depression. By 1941 the number of publishers had doubled again, to thirty, collectively selling fifteen million copies a month and reaching an estimated readership of sixty million (kids often collected their pennies and bought comics together or traded among themselves, and so each copy sold had multiple readers).[26] This means that at the time, almost one in two Americans was reading comic books regularly. With no television and not many movies and radio series, comics offered a captivating pastime that was relatively cheap and accessible to readers at the time and place of their choosing.

Unrivaled, Superman outsold all others by a factor of five, his daily newspaper strip read by five times that. He was powerful enough to also leap into other media in a single bound, another first for the genre. On February 12, 1940, *The Adventures of Superman* radio series first aired, starring Clayton "Bud" Collyer, the first actor to distinguish Clark Kent from Superman by using tenor for the former and basso profundo for the latter, and who'd go on to voice him in the Fleischer studios cartoon serial. With a Crossley rating of 5.6 it was the most popular children's program on the air, with an audience of 4.5 million—more than a third of which were actually adults.[27] The show ran for eleven years, until March 1951, airing a staggering 2,088 episodes. It introduced virtually every American to the Man of Steel, adding to the mythology (Perry White, Jimmy Olsen), coining idioms ("Look! Up in the sky! It's a bird! It's a plane! It's Superman!") and catchphrasing Superman's raison d'être, as simple as it is famous, "fighting a never-ending battle for Truth, Justice and the American Way."

Supermania was in full swing. Not even two years since his debut, Superman appeared as a giant balloon at the Macy's Thanksgiving Day Parade, as well as in his own special exhibit at the famed department store. *Action Comics*, still featuring only one thirteen-page Superman story per issue, sold 900,000 copies a month and *Superman* sold 1.3 million, the latter alone grossing $950,000 annually (over $17 million adj.). In June 1941 a third Superman title was added, *World's Finest*, costarring DC's other popular property, Batman and Robin, and combined readership, along with the strip appearing in 230 newspapers, reached 25 million, earning DC $1.5 million annually ($26 million).[28]

On June 21, 1941, *The Saturday Evening Post*, the most widely read magazine in America, dedicated seven pages to Superman and his creators. "That boy is growing rare who has no Superman dungarees in his wardrobe or no Superman Krypto-Raygun in his play chest," the article extolled. "No other cartoon character ever has been such an all-around success at the age of three. No other cartoon character ever has carried his creators to such an accomplishment as Siegel and Shuster enjoy at the age of twenty-six."[29]

After years of toiling in anonymity, Siegel and Shuster finally saw their brainchild take off, figuratively and literally. The article describes how Shuster became a "bountiful provider" for his parents and siblings, moving them all into a ten-room house in a better neighborhood of Cleveland. Siegel moved with his first wife, Bella, whom he married in 1939, to a large house filled with expensive furniture, gadgets and toys, including a playroom basement with a bar, though neither drank. Aside from his long hours of hard work at the typewriter, the two lived leisurely, spending their money on fine clothing and outings. No mention is made of his widowed mother and five siblings.[30]

Siegel and Shuster also opened their own artist studio, a small room in a remote office building where they crammed in with five assistants to produce Superman comics at the breakneck rate of a thirteen-page story, a Sunday page and six daily strips each week. But despite the work conditions, they never treated their hires the way they'd been treated. They paid them handsomely, more than they got during Superman's first couple of years.[31]

They were now, however, getting paid very well. Accounts vary: the *Post* reported a combined annual income of $75,000 ($1.3 million), of which over 20 percent went to staff salaries and overhead, but in his unpublished memoir Siegel later argues that the sum was highly inflated, closer to $38,000 ($650,000).[32] Either way, it was more than any Depression-era high school–educated Jews dared dream of. Of course, Donenfeld and Liebowitz were making over $1.5 million ($26 million).

In September 1941, and continuing until July 1943, Fleischer Studios, headed by Austrian-Jewish brothers Max and Dave Fleischer, produced a seventeen-episode Superman cartoon serial in full color, ten minutes each, shown in theaters before feature films. Groundbreaking in quality and popularity, it was the first-ever action cartoon, prefigured film noir in its atmospheric style, and was watched by twenty million Americans.[33]

The Fleischers were the first significant competitors to Walt Disney's monopoly in the market of cartoon serials. They differed themselves from Disney by specializing in cartoons featuring, instead of cuddly and comical creatures, exaggerated humans like *Betty Boop*, *Koko the Clown* and another comic strip strongman, *Popeye the Sailor*. It was the Fleischers who gave Popeye super-strength derived from spinach and Superman the power of flight,[34] making him even more thrilling. For the first time, Superman fans didn't need to imagine his amazing feats based on static images or sound effects. They could see them, in full glory, on a giant screen.

There was even a Supermen of America Club, which could be joined with the purchase of certificates, code cards and buttons. About a quarter of a million youngsters were official members, including child star Mickey Rooney and New York Mayor Fiorello La Guardia's two children.[35]

Superman clearly struck a chord. With economic despair casting doubt on the American dream and the clouds of war gathering over the eastern horizon, he was the right idea at the right time. Superman was the most successful Jewish invention since the Bible.

In 1942, with the U.S. at war, demand for comic books sharply increased, and publishers were scrambling to keep up. A variegated pantheon of super-simulacra proliferated and prospered, with increasingly outlandish powers and personas, like the Fiery Mask, empowered by an overdose of Zombie-ray, or the Red Bee, who fought criminals and Nazis with a trained swarm of bees, including one named Michael that lived in his belt pouch.

Superman remained the superhero par excellence, enjoying during the war years unprecedented, unparalleled and ultimately unsurpassed popularity. An April 1942 article in *Time* reported that his three comic book series—*Action Comics*, *Superman* and *World's Finest*—had a combined readership of twelve million. Daily and Sunday strips were now being published in 285 papers, adding another 25 million readers. The *Adventures of Superman* radio program was broadcast by 85 stations, topping ratings in each, and the Fleischer cartoons were playing in 17,000 movie houses. Siegel and Shuster's income reportedly doubled, to $150,000 ($2.3 million), and comic books in general—the industry they helped launch—sold 25 million copies a month.[36]

There's some debate regarding Siegel and Shuster's Superman corpus, particularly how much of his wartime comics they're responsible for. According to Siegel, with a few exceptions he wrote every *Action Comics*, *Superman* and newspaper strip story from June 1938 to July 1943, when he was drafted into the army, while Shuster handled all the art, aided by assistants (though the art varies enough in style to evince significant contribution by the assistants). During his service Siegel continued to appear in the byline alongside Shuster despite almost all his stories being ghostwritten until his discharge in early 1946, with the exception of the few he managed to send in.[37]

While Siegel served in the 39th Special Service Company, an entertainment outfit, as a staff reporter—just like Clark Kent—for *Stars and Stripes*, Shuster had

Top and above: **Clark Kent and Superman. Fleischer Studios'** *Superman,* **1941. Warner Bros.**

been classified 4-F, unfit for duty, due to severe, and worsening, myopia. As his eyesight deteriorated so did his direct involvement in the comics. He went from creating complete art to inking over his assistants' pencils to eventually just supervising the work. DC took over the process, producing the comics in-house using writers and artists it employed directly, and Shuster dissolved the Siegel and Shuster studio.

He would never return to his character. Upon his discharge, Siegel resumed irregular writing duties, sharing bylines with Alvin Schwartz, Don Cameron and others, until he was fired in 1948.[38]

Of their other joint creations, only Dr. Occult and Slam Bradley remain today, both as minor characters. After Superman they created only one more together, the comedy-based Funnyman in 1948, who lasted all of six issues. Siegel had a few more creations to his name, having occasionally collaborated with other artists on various DC strips. Most noteworthy is the Spectre, co-created with fellow *Action Comics* contributor Bernard Baily (*More Fun Comics* #52, February '40). Interestingly, the Spectre is an inherently religious,

Jerry Siegel and Joe Shuster. Publicity photograph, 1942. Held up is an ad using the cover art from *Superman* #17 with a caption reading "Superman says: will get the Japanazis off the Earth!"

arguably Jewish, character, being not a flesh-and-blood hero but the spirit of vengeance of "The Voice," later explicitly identified as God. Following came the Star-Spangled Kid with Hal Sherman (*Action Comics* #40, September '41) and Robotman, with former studio assistant Leo Nowak (*Star Spangled Comics* #7, April '42). All but Funnyman are owned by DC. Superman was Siegel and Shuster's flash in the pan, but it was a flash so bright that almost a century later it still hasn't dimmed.

As the war continued so did comics' rise in popularity. Tye estimates that by the mid–1940s, 95 percent of boys and 91 percent of girls ages 6 to 11 were reading them regularly, and about 50 percent of men and 40 percent of women at age 30 were reading them occasionally, accounting for forty million copies sold monthly[39]—not including the various comic strips appearing in virtually all newspapers in the country. Everyone read comics, refuting their stigma as kiddie fare. Just like superhero movies today appeal primarily to young audiences but draw substantial viewership from older demographics, comic books were enjoyed by Americans of all ages and backgrounds.

What had started out as a fly-by-night enterprise by a handful of Jewish immigrants and their children, born out of necessity and discrimination, had become an immensely successful industry, all the more remarkable during a time when many

others were collapsing. Jack Liebowitz would later claim to have foreseen it all. "Some people viewed comics as just a passing fad," he said in a 1985 interview. "Not me. From the beginning, I felt that comics could be a vital part of the publishing field. They had a broad appeal and a great potential for telling stories."[40]

Whether aware at the time of its greater implications or not, it was Liebowitz and Donenfeld's mercantile savviness that helped catapult Superman from lowly comic magazine character to an American household name, with the entire industry on his broad shoulders. Siegel and Shuster's brilliant invention would have probably received wide attention even in other hands, but his meteoric media and merchandise dominance were the result of Donenfeld and Liebowitz aggressively and cannily pursuing the expansion of the brand, using their wheeling-dealing ways to secure the character a ubiquitous presence in numerous modes of entertainment and on countless products. Siegel acknowledged, years later, that their foresight and acumen were instrumental in rocketing Superman into the limelight, after years of languishing in obscurity.[41]

Superman's image adorned a host of merchandise, including, but not limited to, bubblegum, dolls and figurines, puzzles, coloring books, birthday, Valentine's and picture cards, costumes, badges and pins, crusader rings, piggy banks, tin vehicles, decals, windup toys, hood ornaments, squirt and ray guns, lunchboxes, pajamas, marionettes, alarm clocks, envelopes and letterheads, handkerchiefs, shirts, sweaters, underwear, oats and cereal boxes, wristwatches, safety matches and even ashtrays, as well as government-issued war bonds. Superman was everywhere. And he was no longer simply a cartoon character; he'd become an indispensable part of Americana. The iconoclast had become an icon, perhaps the ultimate nonreligious icon.

A crusading warrior, Superman was especially popular among servicemen. He was a natural fit for the Air Force, which adopted him as the official insignia of the Air Corps Reserve 33rd Bombardment Squadron. Army jeeps, planes, tanks and tugboats were named after him. The Navy went one step further, including his comics among essential supplies sent to the Midway Islands. Comic books could be found in any exchange on any military base in the U.S. or overseas, outselling the next three most popular magazines combined by a ratio of nearly ten to one, and Superman lead the charge.[42]

The industry reached its zenith as comics became practically regulation equipment among American soldiers. There were more than sixteen million of them, and about half read comics regularly. They were easier to carry around and crumple into pockets than books, provided quick, much-needed escapism from the unforgiving reality around, gave soldiers something to discuss and trade with one another, were cheap for the military to buy—and perhaps most importantly, through their fantastical tales of values and valor reminded soldiers what it was that they were fighting for. With the U.S. government buying them *en masse*, the Golden Age of comics saw sales nearing a billion books a year.[43]

Superman and his costumed cohorts had reached foreign shores as early as 1939, but spread through Europe and Asia with the American invasion. They became favored reading material among British troops, who got them from American GIs, then sent or brought them back to England. Children in London's underground bomb shelters could be found reading and finding courage in Superman while German blitzkrieg shells exploded above.[44]

Arguably the main reason superheroes became so immensely popular with the onset of the war is that it finally provided them with worthwhile opponents. Before the Nazis there weren't any supervillains per se. Pulp and comics heroes battled a revolving repertoire of gangsters, yellow perils, femme fatales, rustlers, anarchists, sorcerers, monsters of folklore, jungle savages and mad scientists. Superman, aside

New York, N.Y. Children's Colony, a school for refugee children administered by a Viennese. German refugee child, a devotee of Superman. Marjory Collins, October 1942. Library of Congress.

from kleptocrats and browbeaters, mostly fought fedora-wearing mobsters (several, curiously, named "Butch").

G.I.s reading comic books. Battle of the Bulge, Belgium, January 1945. U.S. Army Photograph.

Joe Simon, co-creator of Captain America and his nemesis the Red Skull, was responding directly to the rise of Nazism:

> Here was the arch villain of all time. Adolf Hitler and his Gestapo bully-boys were real. There had never been a truly believable villain in comics. But Adolf was live, hated by more than half of the world. What a natural foil he was, with his comical moustache, the ridiculous cowlick, his swaggering, goose-stepping minions eager to jump out of a plane if their mad little leader ordered it.... I could smell a winner. All that was left to do was to devise a long underwear hero to stand up to him.[45]

There were also Mussolini, Hirohito and Stalin, each with his own distinctive, dramatic look and personality, each with his own compulsions, and all unmistakably evil. No fictional villain could rival them in either absurdity or realism.

The Nazi high command was a ready-made team of supervillains, archetypes like the mastermind manipulator Joseph Goebbels, the vicious fighter Erwin Rommel and the mad scientists Josef Mengele and Wernher von Braun. They even had sobriquets; Hitler was known as the Leader or the Wolf, Mengele the Angel of Death, Rommel the Desert Fox, Klaus Barbie the Butcher, Reinhard Heydrich the Hangman, Rudolf Höss the Death Dealer, and so on. And under their command were the SS, black-clad henchmen emblazoned with the symbols of skull and crossbones and twin lightning bolts.

True to trope, the Nazis even developed diabolical "super weapons" to use against the Allies in their mad quest for world domination, from the V-series rockets that blitzed London, the first long-range guided ballistic missiles, to the U-boats, the world's most advanced submarines, to the Messerschmitt Me 262, the first operational jet fighter, to the Zyklon B, the deadly gas used to kill millions.

More than sixteen million Americans left their homes and families and went to foreign lands to kill and die for the cause of freedom. There was no room nor need for moral relativism: Nazis were as evil, as inhuman, as any invading horde of aliens, monsters who couldn't be reasoned with that threatened to destroy everything. And they were real. They provided superheroes with a limitless fodder of foes that elicited no sympathy and served as perfect opposites to their virtue.

It was a war of ideas, of symbols, of mythologies, of Uncle Sam and his bald eagle taking on the Swastika, the Fasces and the Rising Sun. It was a time of high drama and theatrics. Superman fit perfectly.

It's only fitting that America's brightest symbol was born during its darkest hour. He was American ideals given form, an inspirational figure of uplift and edification, a superhuman superhumanist. And he was Siegel and Shuster's answer to the propaganda of Goebbels and Riefenstahl, for what was the might of scores of goose-stepping National Socialists against a man who could scatter them all with a gust of his breath?

On February 27, 1940—almost two years before Pearl Harbor and America's involvement in the war—Siegel and Shuster created a two-page "imaginary story" for *Look* magazine titled "How Superman Would End the War," in which they sent the Action Ace through the impenetrable Westwall to grab Hitler and Stalin and bring them before the World Court in Geneva.

Although he wouldn't fight explicit Nazis in his own comics until the cover of *Action Comics* #40 (September '41), where he punches a Panzer bearing the *Balkenkreuz*, and the first Swastika wouldn't appear until issue #43, he soon after dedicated himself to the war effort, capsizing battleships (*Superman* #13), twisting cannon barrels into knots (*Action Comics* #44), punching planes out of the sky (#48), plucking U-boats out of the water (#54), tearing open tanks (#59), riding American bombs like a cowboy (*Superman* #18) and hawking war bonds (*World's Finest Comics* #8). Most importantly, the Axis always looked appropriately terrified. Perhaps the most iconic cover of the era is *Superman* #14 (January '42), showing a dramatically-lit Superman, cape fluttering, one arm akimbo while the other props up an American bald eagle spreading its majestic wings, standing in front of a giant shield adorned with the stars and stripes and America's tanks, artillery and aircraft charging out behind it. (World War II was the first and last war Superman would be directly involved in. American superheroes have largely been kept out of real wars and global crises since, save for intermittent Cold War spy-bashing.)

Superman's popularity as a propaganda figure rivaled that of Uncle Sam. The erstwhile proletarian dissident was now a boosting government agent, calling for enlistment, blood donations and scrap metal drives. When he asked his young radio listeners to buy war stamps, over 250,000 complied. But Superman didn't come to embody American values because he was all-powerful. It was because of how he used his powers—for the good of others. Clark turning into Superman was the little guy becoming the big guy but sticking around to help the other little guys, an ethos that stood in direct opposition to that of the Axis. "'Truth, justice and the American way' is just a childish slogan to a lot of people," Jack Kirby said,

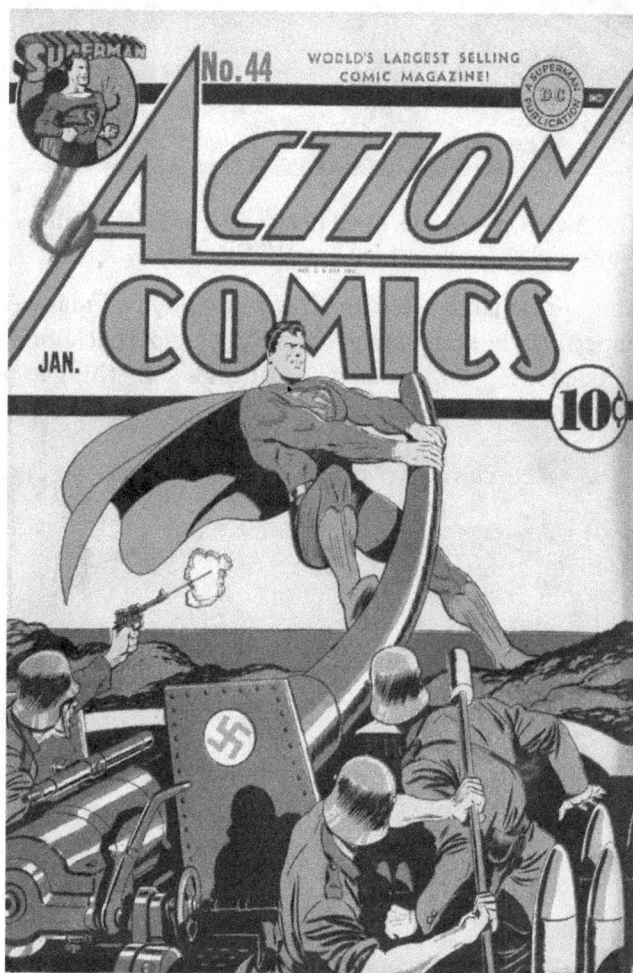

Action Comics #44, January 1942. Cover by Fred Ray. DC Comics.

Left: Action Comics #59, April 1943. Cover by Jack Burnley. DC Comics. *Right: Superman* #14, January 1942. Cover by Fred Ray. DC Comics.

but "Superman created an attitude that helped many Americans in a very bad spot." Superman, he added, was "the psychological backbone for a lot of fellows … [he] galvanized me."[46] Superman gave America something to believe in, to fight for. He gave it hope.

This Nation asks for action, and action now.—Franklin D. Roosevelt

PART III

Mensch of Steel

Fulfilling Jewish Fantasy and Faith

The Jewish Experience

Context Is Content

In *Superheroes and Philosophy: Truth, Justice, and the Socratic Way*, editors Tom Morris and Matt Morris write that, beyond the entertainment value inherent in superhero comics, "what too few people realize is that they also deserve serious intellectual attention for their fascinating presentations of deep philosophical themes and ideas."[1] It is part of a small but growing recognition in recent years, among scholars as well as the general public, that comics' bombastic characters and action belie a world of rich, expressive subtext.

This isn't to say that comic books, whether those of the 1940s or those of today, contain the same complexity, depth and meaning as literary masterworks. "Most comic books really are junk," *Maus* creator Art Spiegelman argues. "But so is most painting and literature."[2] Comics are predominantly a commercial venture, geared toward wide appeal, but the medium still offers sophisticated, eloquent works of gravity, as Spiegelman's Pulitzer attests. And, contrary to common prejudice, sometimes even within the industry, these can include superhero comics.

The point, however, is that it's entirely beside the point. Exceptional or trivial, all art is a reflection of the culture that produced it. It doesn't have to be good to be important. The men who early on defined comic books and superheroes were themselves defined, as all men are, by the time and place they were born into, and their characters and stories are repositories of their worries and wishes. And they were, almost all, young, poor and Jewish.

Luminary artist Gil Kane (Eli Katz), who started out at the age of sixteen in 1942 and co-created the Atom, Iron Fist, and the second Green Lantern, along with seminal work on Superman in the early 1980s, recalls, "it seemed like almost every guy I knew in the field back then was Jewish. The few exceptions were all Italian." Perhaps the tradition of aniconism and the prohibition of graven images in Judaism have made it a textual rather than visual culture, while the Italian tradition of representational art, from Roman to Renaissance to Futurism, is why the few gentiles working in comics in those days were Italian-American artists. It was a preponderantly Jewish industry, however, because it occupied the basement level of publishing, a motley enterprise of syndication leftovers and low production value. It "was essentially part of the rag trade," Spiegelman explains. "Given the chance, Jews would have become painters or written novels, but here was a way for kids with an intellectual bent to express themselves."[3]

A great many of them were, in fact, the children of garment workers, particularly tailors, including both Siegel and Shuster, the Fleischer brothers, Joe Simon, Jack Kirby, Bill Finger and Stan Lee. The *schmatte* business was mainly Jewish; Jews brought the skill and experience with them from the old countries, where for generations it was one of the few occupations allowed to them. By the turn of the 19th century, rapid population growth in the U.S. created demand for an industry that, reliant on international trade, was based in New York. Requiring skills of both craft and commerce and affording a modest but steady living, it employed approximately 60 percent of the city's working Jews, who made up 75 percent of the industry workforce.[4] From wholesale fabric merchants to secondhand suit retailers to bespoke tailors, Lower East Side and Bronx Jews set up shop in Midtown Manhattan just south of Times Square, which came to be known as the Garment District (now Fashion District). A commemorative statue, *The Garment Worker* by Judith Weller, of an old man in a yarmulke hunched over a sowing machine, can today be found on 7th Avenue between 39th and 40th Streets, across the road from the legendary Midtown Comics store, coincidentally but perfectly symbolizing the two industries, created by two generations of New York Jews.

"Jews couldn't go to college except in rare instances, and they had to have money to do so. I didn't come from that kind of background, so I ended up going into comics instead," Will Eisner remembers. "I was like a lot of Jewish kids in the business. We had greater ambitions. As a result, we ended up expressing them in our work—and expanding the limits of the genre in the process." Eisner would receive in 2002 a Lifetime Achievement Award from the National Foundation for Jewish Culture, previously given to the likes of Elie Wiesel and Arthur Miller, in "recognition that in many ways the [comic book] genre is a Jewish-created genre."[5]

Of course, Siegel and Shuster being Jewish doesn't automatically make Superman Jewish, and the same goes for other comics created by Jews. But the expectation that a cadre of writers and artists from a shared background would produce such a body of work in a medium and genre of their creation, bereft of any trace of their culture, is unreasonable. With any story, let alone an entire mythology, the context in which it's created inevitably finds its way, consciously or not, into the telling. Superhero adventures, being a perfect vehicle for wish-fulfillment, were imbued with their creators' culture, folklore and politics. Quite literally, they drew upon what they knew. Their influences, obvious and obscure, had less to do with Homer, Shakespeare and Joyce (though those can be found as well) and more with the Bible, Yiddishkeit and Warner Bros. films.

Jack "King" Kirby, for example, brought to his work "an imagination and range that sat comfortably inside a visionary tradition running all the way from Hebrew Scriptures … [to] Allen Ginsberg." At the same time, the rooftop chases and battles he frequently drew, helping make them a genre trope, were inspired by his real-life experiences in a Jewish youth gang, hurtling across the Lower East Side's huddled tenements.[6]

All this begs the question, why did Jews invent comic book and superheroes? Why in the 1930s and 1940s, and why in New York? Could Superman have been invented by someone else, someplace and sometime else? Is it all a matter of happenstance, a historical syzygy of opportunities, or is there more to it?

As only 3.5 percent of the population at the time,[7] Jews undeniably played an outsized role in many if not most entertainment forms in America, including comics. In part this was a result of their circumstances, with many respectable forms of employment closed off to them or requiring education that was closed off to them. In part it can be attributed to the Jewish spirit of entrepreneurship, fostered over centuries as pariahs in Europe. But this goes little in the way of explaining why so many from a famously pragmatic culture would opt for nonviable careers like composing songs or writing kids' magazines, especially during the Depression when there was no room for these kinds of fanciful *foileshticks*. Why not do what many others did and become haberdashers, bakers, diamond traders?

"My mother worried that I, her impractical son who wanted to be a writer, might not survive in this dog-eat-dog world," Siegel wrote in later years. "Joe's mother worried, too, about the future of Joe who as a child had drawn pictures on the bedroom wall and wanted to be an artist."[8] And yet, like the rest of their colleagues, they chose to pursue their dreams and make comics. Not only that, but despite years of rejection and penurious living they continued undeterred.

Stan Lee, Siegel and Shuster's contemporary who'd go on to become the Walt Disney of comics, allows that "there was something in our background, in our culture, that brought us together in the comicbook field" (Lee made a point to spell it "comicbook," distinguishing it from a comical book). That something, according to Jewish historian and underground "comix" pioneer Trina Robbins, is storytelling. "I don't know if it's in the genes, I don't know if it's the heritage, but there's a thing about Jews and communication," she said.[9] The drive to communicate through stories, the longest and most venerated of Jewish traditions, was perhaps the creative engine behind Jews congregating in comics, the burning passion in their *kishkes* to write, to draw, to express. And that they did, creating comics that frequently revisited themes and even scenarios, repeating but also reexamining, fitting within the Jewish praxis of telling and retelling important stories, from those of Moses to those of Superman.

Underlying virtually all these stories, to one extent or another, is what Simcha Weinstein calls "the particularly Jewish theme of the misunderstood outcast, the rootless wanderer."[10] Certainly Superman, a castaway from an alien culture who can only interact freely with human society through a disguise, fits, but there's also no other Jewish-created superhero of the time that comes to mind who lived comfortably and enjoyed a wholesome social life. They all struggled for acceptance in either or both of their identities and, one and all, were motivated by some tragic, unjust loss in their past, one which usually left them orphans. It isn't particularly hard to see how Jews' history and desire for vindication and justice would take shape in this form.

Alienation isn't a proprietary Jewish experience, obviously. Almost everyone, particularly the young, feels more an outsider than an insider. It's ironically a common bond of the human experience. And Jews were by no means the only immigrant group to suffer from discrimination when arriving in America. New York was home to many Italian, Irish and other émigrés who, similar to Jews, came from impoverished backgrounds, occupied the working class (when there was work to be had) and were not considered truly white by Anglos.

Even so, Jews didn't escape Europe because of poverty or famine alone. To this were added pervasive discrimination, oppression and violence. Itinerancy and rebelliousness in the face of tyranny were much deeper rooted in Diasporic Jewish culture, a tradition over two thousand years long of nomadic wandering across the globe. The Irish came from Ireland, the Italians from Italy, but the Jews came from Poland or Russia, and before then were exiled from Spain or England and before then from somewhere else, a pattern dating as far back as their expulsion from the kingdom of Judea around the 6th century BCE. It's this legacy of immigration and marginality that underpins the unique perspective they brought to their stories.

Their comics, while *schlock*, were far from fatuous. They were a popular bugle for otherwise marginalized voices, and Superman's early comics in particular had a world-weary cynicism to them that was decidedly un–WASPy and discordant with the bright-eyed Superman of most people's idea. Long before he fought supervillains and meteor showers he crusaded against real, everyday social ills. Superman editor Mortimer "Mort" Weisinger, who helped steer the character during and after the war, described his mission as an "incessant war against injustice, intolerance, bigotry and other down-to-earth villains of modern society."[11]

From his first appearance he was Champion of the Oppressed, before going by the Man of Tomorrow and later Man of Steel, a defender not of society as a whole but specifically its weakest members, the downtrodden and the victimized, none more fitting the description then than Jews. His cause was theirs—tolerance, acceptance, fair treatment.

More broadly, Superman espoused a morality that, while contemporary and universal, is in large part religious in provenance, rooted in concepts of equality, goodwill and sanctity of life that were first made law in the Hebrew Bible. Paul Levitz, prolific writer, editor and former president and publisher of DC Comics, sees Superman, and the rest who followed his example, as "the most powerful source of having taken the precepts of social justice that we learned as a community and sending it out to the broad American community and putting it into the American ethos."[12]

In 1996, following Siegel's death, the *Jerusalem Post* described Superman as "perhaps the best known symbol of *tikkun aolam*"[13]—the central Jewish tenet of repairing the world, a Mishnaic term laden with Kabbalistic, metaphysical meaning, but at its simplest taken to mean the betterment of the world through acts of kindness.

Motivated by Jewish values to fight for a Jewish cause, Superman was also heavily influenced by the other great Jewish medium; cinema. "I was especially strongly impressed by the Warner Brothers movies with their social injustice messages," Siegel recalls, and like those films, he and Shuster imbued their stories with a thematic preoccupation, obsession even, with the ostracized, the victimized and the dejected. And, like the heroes of those films, their early Superman wasn't yet the noble and kindly figure he would later become. He was hard-edged and hotheaded, angry, fed up, intolerant toward the intolerant. A hero, as Siegel describes, "whose mission in life is to smack down the bullies of the world."[14]

Siegel was also inspired by a more intimate motivation. In his memoir, he describes being bullied by his schoolmates as well as his teachers, always patronized and scorned.[15] Then, at the end of his junior year, his father was killed.

Michael Siegel owned a secondhand clothing shop at Cedar-Central, a crime-ridden black ghetto of Cleveland. On June 2, 1932, three men entered his shop just before closing and robbed him. They didn't steal money. They didn't hold him at gunpoint. They just took a suit and walked out. The threat of violence was enough. It was also enough to instigate the heart attack that killed him.[16] They were bullies, taking what they wanted, a grownup, felonious version of Jerry's schoolyard tormentors.

Curiously, Siegel has never mentioned his father's death in any interview. Even in his unpublished 99-page memoir he dedicates only a single line to his passing.[17] It could be that he attributed little to it, though silence can speak volumes. It's difficult to deny a causal relation between a boy who lost his father to crime and his creation not long after of the world's greatest crime fighter.

As for Superman's publishers, while scoundrels, it seems they also cared for social causes, particularly Jewish ones, though they were possibly hoping to exonerate themselves from the original sin that made them rich men. Donenfeld spent much of his money to help found the Albert Einstein College of Medicine in the Bronx, along with a variety of other charities. Liebowitz was a trustee of the Federation of Jewish Philanthropies of New York and a founding trustee of Long Island Jewish Hospital, a member of its board and even president of the hospital from 1956 to 1968, all while serving as president of DC Comics.[18] Whatever their motivation, the money Superman earned by saving lives in fiction helped save lives in reality, and still does.

There was one sociopolitical cause in particular that the comics creators advocated in their work. Bradford Wright, author of *Comic Book Nation: The Transformation of Youth Culture in America*, describes the early superheroes as "super New Dealers, like costumed versions of Franklin Roosevelt." Superman in particular was "a butt-kicking New Deal Liberal," Tye agrees. "There was no question who he was voting for, what his politics were."[19]

That Siegel and Shuster were avid supporters of the New Deal isn't surprising, considering the virtually unanimous support for it among American Jews. Most embraced social-democratic values as a balance of liberty and equality, a way to finally be accepted and a worldview commensurate with the teachings of the faith. (Israel, a modern state founded on ancient Jewish values, is a social democracy.) In many ways the New Deal embodied the Jewish doctrine of egalitarianism and collectivism, from "He who oppresses the poor taunts his Maker, But he who is gracious to the needy honors Him" (Prov. 14:31) to "love your neighbor as yourself" (Lev. 19:18), and Superman championed both.

This wasn't vaguely implied. It was self-evident and at times explicit, in the comics and in interviews. Siegel acknowledged, "into the Superman strip I placed a number of elements including fast action, and a liberal outlook favoring 'the little man.' Superman was a sort of guardian angel who saw that justice and tolerance triumphed." He also listed Roosevelt's radio "fireside chats" as an inspiration.[20]

Superman's Golden Age comics were tales full of sound and fury, signifying everything. Metropolis's favorite son was in truth a displaced alien, like the family and people of his creators. He showed that refugees weren't, as some insisted, dangerous strangers from the hinterlands, ungrateful, clannish and treacherous. They were thankful and faithful contributors to the American collective. He repeatedly not only helped the poor but exposed the corrupt rich, espousing social welfare; opposed bigots and supremacists, foreign and homegrown, promoting tolerance and unity; and fought spies, saboteurs and traitors working for barely-veiled substitute Nazis, supporting British rearmament and European intervention.

These complex and profound issues of the day, filtered through the consciousness of two young men, manifested as simplistic yet powerful notions. The superhero concept Siegel and Shuster created wasn't merely about escapism. Like all fantasy fiction, it was a form of engagement, an allegorical reflection of and about the world and the self. It was also, like all fiction, a tool of empathy, a way for left-leaning urban Jews to reach white provincials nationwide, telling stories full of increasingly explicit portents of fascistic power and the persecution of the downtrodden while horrific news from Europe largely went ignored. It was a desperate manifesto through stirring parable, a rabbi's sermon as fable.

While Superman's liberalism in his early comics has been widely noted, it can be traced back even further, to the very beginning, "The Reign of the Superman." Siegel describes the story's genesis; it "was written by me during the agony of the 1930s depression, when I was … unemployed, living in an area chocked by great economic difficulties." It opens with the villain, Professor Smalley, observing men standing in a breadline with contempt. "To him, who had come of rich parents and had never been forced to face the rigors of life," the story reads, "the miserableness of these men seemed deserved. It appeared to him that if they had the slightest ambition at all they could easily lift themselves from their terrible rut."[21] Smalley is an embodiment of conservative elitism, as seen from the perspective of liberal equitability. His meritocratic ideology is born of privilege and entitlement, which he uses to justify his cruel indifference toward those less fortunate. Worse, he seeks to take advantage of them in his pursuit of power.

Siegel has acknowledged that Smalley, a genius megalomaniac, is the forbearer of Lex Luthor,[22] adding a political dimension to the supervillain's yin-yang struggle with Superman. The era's popular concept of mad scientists, always practicing science fiction, not fact, beyond the ken of man, represents both the biblical fear of forbidden knowledge and the modern fear of the specialized elite's control over the common man. The Dunn/Smalley and later Superman/Luthor dynamic is thus the everyman reclaiming supremacy over the intelligentsia, as well as the proletariat wresting power from the bourgeoisie.

Superman, for all the richness and empowerment of his heritage, is a plebeian hero, going against the prevailing pulp archetype of the time of a wealthy industrialist or socialite (like Doc Savage, the Shadow, Phantom Detective, Spider, Avenger, Black Star, Crimson Clown, Man in Purple, Thunderbolt, Green Hornet, Zorro and Batman, to name a few). As Clark Kent, he's raised as a blue-collar farmer, then becomes a reporter, a struggling working man of the Depression. And as Superman, he was mostly known then as the Man of Tomorrow, not of Steel, emphasizing not his strength but his progressiveness.

Action Comics #1 debuted both the hero and his mission statement. He first stops the execution of an innocent woman, having caught the true culprit. He then gives a wife-beater a taste of his own medicine. Next come overbearing gangsters, whom he

sends scurrying away. Finally, in a cliffhanger story, he shakes down a corrupt senator and his lobbyist. They're variations of bullies and brutes, people who abuse their
power over others, until Superman puts them in place. And, though a cheeky insur-
rectionist, he's a reformist, not an insurgent; he doesn't simply burst in to stop the
execution himself, he has the governor stop it,[23] seeking not to usurp law and order
but to align it with the cause of justice.

From the get-go, he seeks justice not just for Americans but also for those
oppressed in other lands. In the two-part story in issues #1 and #2 he stops the
crooked senator and the munitions magnate backing him from passing a bill that
would embroil the U.S. in the war in "San Monte," a proxy for the Spanish Civil War.
But he doesn't simply hand the war profiteer over to authorities, nor does he punish
him himself—the two common solutions of pulp heroes—he first forces him to experience the suffering he'd brought upon others by flopping him in the middle of the
war.[24]

In *Action Comics* #3, poor Eastern European immigrants working as miners are
trapped in a cave-in as a result of unsafe work conditions. The greedy, carousing mine
owner cares little until Superman, having rescued the miners, returns to teach him a
lesson. He traps the owner in his own collapsed mine, forcing him to try and dig his
way out. Having experienced it firsthand he reforms, vowing to make his mine the
safest in the country and his workers the best treated.[25]

Action Comics #8 sees Superman helping a gang of tenement urchins, who at
first impression appear inveterate delinquents. He understands, however, that their
antisocial behavior is the result of their disadvantage, not character. "It's not entirely
your fault," he tells them, "it's these slums," showing a clear liberal bent, especially at
a time when societal responsibility for the actions of its members wasn't the accepted
notion it is today. His solution is to use the government's rehousing initiative by raz-
ing the ghetto, and within weeks in its stead are built "huge apartment-projects …
[of] splendid housing conditions."[26] The story reads like an ad for the New Deal's
"slum clearance" subsidy policies (part of the 1933 National Industrial Recovery Act),
made all the more poignant coming from Jews, a group of people who largely lived in
tenements and were snarled at by society.

The same liberal outlook is found in *Action Comics* #10, in which Superman
doesn't just put criminals behind bars, he makes sure their prison conditions are
humane. When he learns of an abusive superintendent and his guards he comes to
the inmates' rescue, bringing about correctional reform.[27]

Superman #1 is a reprint collection of *Action Comics* #1–4 with an added prelude
story. In it, Superman fights off a lynch mob, making it canonically his first heroic act,
a scene all too familiar to Jews that escaped the pogroms of Eastern Europe and only
eight months after *Kristallnacht*. The story also reveals that the unnamed murder victim in *Action Comics* #1 is Jack Kennedy, an evocative name at the time and possibly a small revenge fantasy against the Antisemitic statesman. Another public official
named Kennedy appears in *Action Comics* #37, this time fired for ineptitude and corruption and later revealed to be the leader of a criminal gang.[28]

In *Action Comics* #15 Superman raises $2 million for Kidtown, an indebted group
home for children, and in *Superman* #3 he stops a child labor operation posing as an

orphanage,[29] shedding light on the deplorable living and often working conditions of poor children, particularly orphans, a common social ill targeted by the New Deal.

By March 1940's *Superman* #4 the Depression had officially ended, while the war in Europe was escalating. Superman faces off against gangsters hired by an unnamed foreign power to act as saboteurs, aiming to "retard the nation's return to prosperity."[30] Siegel and Shuster cleverly tie here domestic and foreign policy, supporting in one fell swoop Roosevelt's economic reform, war on organized crime and interventionist leanings, and linking the fate of America to the war.

Superman #5 dispels any remaining doubt about the hero's politics. Lois and Clark are called reformers, several times, and the following month in *Action Comics* #26 both Superman and his creators as narrators directly promote Roosevelt's Infantile Paralysis Fund.[31]

By this point superheroes had become *de rigueur* in comics, and they almost exclusively fought against local crime and the supernatural in the tradition of their pulp predecessors. Superman, meanwhile, continued in his mission to foster sympathy for fellow men suffering elsewhere. In *Superman* #6, the fictional South American nation of San Caluma is ravaged by disastrous earthquakes, followed by hunger and disease. Superman ensures they receive aid from the U.S. and stops the devious Mumsen (*Mamzer*?) from exploiting it for political gain.[32]

What can also be found throughout these early stories is an emphasis on socio-economic disparity, sometimes subtle, like describing the effete mayor's office as "sumptuous" in *Action Comics* #32, or when, in issue #33 a wealthy philanthropist helps underprivileged children, Lois remarks, "This fellow Hall is all right! I didn't know millionaires were built that way!" to which Clark responds, "A man can have a million and still have a heart!" In *Superman* #11, the unscrupulous board of directors of a large department store chain scheme to enrich themselves at the expense of their employees, until Superman intervenes. And in *Action Comics* #40, the Man of Steel makes note that "usually people who ask for my assistance are hard-pressed for cash."[33]

As Superman became DC's golden goose, however, Siegel's plots had to be vetted by the higher-ups, and they had him curtail Superman's social crusading. They also warned Shuster against making Superman's forelocks too curly—perhaps it was too ethnic a look.[34]

Still, Superman's sine qua non was fighting Nazis. At first they were stand-ins, from "Dukalia" or "Toran" or "Oxnalia," but as soon as the war started and Siegel and Shuster were given the green light, the real thing. Along with Superman, the entire superhero genre was retooled from crime-fighting to warfare, especially following December 20, 1940's *Captain America Comics* #1 (cover dated March '41), the cover of which, despite predating America's involvement in the war by a year, showed the hero punching Hitler. "We were fighting Hitler before our government was," Stan Lee, who assisted Simon and Kirby on the series, said in regard to their Jewishness. "We just could all see what a menace Hitler was."[35]

The affront to the Führer, as well as the Captain's Jewish background, didn't go unnoticed. The Bund, which just a year prior paraded through New York and had set up a militia training camp on Long Island, took umbrage at the depiction of Nazis as murderous villains. Naturally, they protested by inundating Marvel Comics with "death to the Jews" mail and telephone calls. Once menacing-looking groups of men started loitering outside the office building the police were contacted. Soon after, Simon, Captain America's writer as well as Marvel's editor in chief, received a call. It was avid comics fan (and, unbeknownst to most, Jewish) Mayor Fiorello La Guardia, who told him, "You boys over there are doing a good job. The City of New York will see that no harm will come to you." Thereafter a police guard regularly patrolled the offices.

There's a curious dichotomy between the rampant physical violence of superhero comics and their Jewish creators, a people traditionally considered cerebral problem solvers. Partly it was the demands of the medium; it's virtually impossible to depict a long, composed conversation in a series of panels in any engaging way, let alone in ongoing serialization. Its visual nature demands physical action, and gesticulations only go so far.

In part it was just good business; violence sells. The inchoate industry sought to capitalize on the war and its pervasiveness in the zeitgeist, and it provided a simple and easy formula of Allied heroes versus Axis villains, American patriots versus Nazi fascists. But opportunism does little to explain why so many heroes, particularly Superman, fought Nazis or their doppelgängers long before the U.S. entered the war and before most Americans cared to, and even after their creators received death threats.

The Jews behind superheroes weren't looking for a platform in which to deliberate. They needed an outlet for their unimaginable fear and anger, a way to transform their helplessness into strength. For them as well as their readers, the thrill of the comics came from an unstoppable punch to a Nazi's face. "Fighting Hitler was what comics were all about,"[36] Chabon notes. He's right. People with real power don't need to imagine superpowers.

In the 1981 BBC documentary *The Comic Strip Hero*, Siegel relates the influences on his Superman stories: "The world was in pretty bad shape…. Nazism was rising up and millions of innocent people were being killed and countries were being invaded, a lot of innocents slaughtered, and I felt that the world desperately needed a crusader, if only a fictional one." He also wrote in his memoir, "Jews and others were being persecuted and murdered by Nazi Germany … [so] I had Superman use his mighty super-powers to … aid the helpless and the downtrodden."[37]

While the character's inception is in the early 1930s, with themes that trace back to scripture, it's in the crucible of World War II and the Holocaust that he took shape. It was the greatest real-life supervillain that gave rise to the greatest fictional superhero, the gravest threat the Jews had ever known inspiring their loftiest figure. Ultimately, the idea of Superman, the ideology he embodies, proved more powerful, and lasting, than the Thousand-Year Reich.

Siegel and Shuster's fantasy fight against the Nazis manifested gradually. The cover of October 1939's *Action Comics* #17—a month after the war started and the U.S. proclaimed neutrality—features Superman flipping a tank while shrugging off gunfire to the horror of enemy soldiers. On the cover of issue #19 he rips apart an artillery cannon amidst battlefield explosions. In both cases there are no German markings, but the identity is clear.

Then, in the February 1940 issue of *Look* magazine, Superman openly declared war on Hitler and Stalin (Stalin at the time still being an ally of Hitler, following the August 1939 Molotov–Ribbentrop Pact. Hitler would break it less than two months later). In the specially commissioned two-page story, "How Superman Would End the War," the Man of Steel strolls through the Siegfried Line, twists its canons into pretzels and pops open its concrete barricades, then punches the Luftwaffe out of the sky. Having made short order of the German forces he swoops down to Hitler's retreat, lifts him by the throat, declaring, "I'd like to land a strictly non–Aryan sock on your jaw, but there's no time for that! You're coming with me while I visit a certain pal of yours." He then flies over to Russia, plucks Stalin from his balcony, and drags the two dictators by the scruff of their necks to Geneva, to stand trial for war crimes before the League of Nations.[38] The story was produced in shades of red and gray, making Superman appear barelegged. Somehow it added to Hitler's ignominy, being slapped around by a man in his briefs.

Superman's choice of words here is curious. He describes himself as "strictly non–Aryan" even though his frame and features, with his square jaw, cleft chin, sharp small nose and deep blue eyes, are the very definition of Aryan physiognomy. And yet the Man of Steel can be taken at his word, particularly when written by Siegel; he's most definitely not one of "them." He's the Aryan ideal married to the Jewish idea, a eugenic joke at the Nazis' expense.

The Nazis, on their part, recognized Superman as a Jew. As always, while Jews may argue over who counts as one, Antisemites quickly resolve the debate. Following the story, *Das Schwarze Korps* (*The Black Corps*), the official newspaper of the SS, ran a full-page tirade in the April 25, 1940, issue, titled "Jerry Siegel Attacks!":

Jerry Siegel, an intellectually and physically circumcised chap who has his headquarters in New York, is the inventor of a colorful figure with an impressive appearance, a powerful body, and a red swim suit who enjoys the ability to fly through the ether.

The inventive Israelite named this pleasant guy with an overdeveloped body and underdeveloped mind "Superman." He advertised widely Superman's sense of justice, well-suited for imitation by the American youth.

As you can see, there is nothing the Sadducees [a Jewish priestly caste until the Second Temple era who interpreted the written Law of Moses (Torah) literally and wholly rejected the Oral Law (Talmud and Mishnah), as well as the gospel of Christ] won't do for money!

Jerry looked about the world and saw things happening in the distance, some of which alarmed him. He heard of Germany's reawakening, of Italy's revival, in short of a resurgence of the manly virtues of Rome and Greece. "That's fine," thought Jerry, and decided to import the idea of manly virtue and spread them among young Americans. Thus was born this "Superman." On this page we present you with several particularly unusual examples of his activities. We see Superman, lacking all strategic sense and tactical ability, storming the West Wall in shorts. We see several German soldiers in a bunker, who in order to receive the American guest have borrowed old uniforms from a military museum. Their faces express at once both desperation and cheerfulness. We see this bicepped wonder in a rather odd pose, bending the barrels of Krupp guns like spaghetti. "Concrete can't stop me," he shouts in another picture as he knocks the tops off pill boxes like overripe tomatoes. His true strength only shows itself in flight, however. He leaps into the air to tear the propeller from a passing German airplane. As we can see from the next frame, however, Superman has apparently made a mistake, since he seems to have encountered a Yid pilot. No German would say what the pilot says: "Himmel! Vos is diss?" The American answer "Well, here it is" seems to us not quite right. The right response would be something like "Laff if ya likes, I'm Simple Simon!"

Above and next two following pages: "How Superman Would End the War." *Look*, February 27, 1940. By Jerry Siegel and Joe Shuster.

SIEGEL AND SHUSTER GAVE SUPERMAN A BIG JOB in this episode, when they assigned him to solve the international situation just for Look, but such tasks are nothing new for him. He once stopped a war "somewhere in South America" by dumping a munitions profiteer into the trenches for a dose of his own medicine. On another occasion he plucked two opposing generals from their tents and told them to settle their differences with bare fists. They knew no "differences," shook hands and made peace.

A triumphant final frame shows Superman, the conqueror of death, dropping in at the headquarters of the chatterboxes at the League of Nations in Geneva. Although the rules of the establishment probably prohibit people in bathing suits from participating in their deliberations, Superman ignores them as well as the other laws of physics, logic, and life in general. He brings with him the evil German enemy along with Soviet Russia.

I'D LIKE TO LAND A STRICTLY NON-ARYAN SOCK ON YOUR JAW, BUT THERE'S NO TIME FOR THAT! YOU'RE COMING WITH ME WHILE I VISIT A CERTAIN PAL OF YOURS.

PUT ME DOWN! YOU'RE HURTING ME!

Well, we really ought to ignore these fantasies of Jerry Israel Siegel, but there is a catch. The daring deeds of Superman are those of a Colorado beetle. He works in the dark, in incomprehensible ways. He cries "Strength! Courage! Justice!" to the noble yearnings of American children. Instead of using the chance to encourage really useful virtues, he sows hate, suspicion, evil, laziness, and criminality in their young hearts.

Jerry Siegellack stinks. Woe to the American youth, who must live in such a poisoned atmosphere and don't even notice the poison they swallow daily.[39]

Several accounts attribute the article directly to Josef Goebbels, while others, most notably Kaplan and Tye, recount a popular story of Goebbels having a conniption about Superman in the middle of a Reichstag meeting, though Tye ascribes it to overeager reporters. Either way, the article was widely reported on in the States.[40] There's no record of Siegel and Shuster's response, though they must have been unsettled, being the direct targets of Nazi fulmination, as well as immensely proud at having poked their finger in the Führer's eye.

It's worth noting that the article makes no mention of Shuster. Always the mum Teller to Siegel's verbose Penn, Shuster has often been unfairly cast as merely the artist rather than equal co-creator of the character. Superman is Siegel's idea but Shuster's execution. And while it was Siegel's script that had Hitler brought to justice, it was Shuster's art that made him look appropriately pathetic.

Who did give Shuster due credit was the Bund, which sent him hate mail and picketed DC's offices.[41] The threat they posed was more real and immediate than the SS's, but all it succeeded in doing was galvanize him and Siegel even more.

Their personal war with the Nazis, which started in comics and grew into reality, found its way back into the comics. *Superman* #25 features Superman-spoof Geezer, "the strongest man on earth" and the "king of the comic books." Fully adopting *Das Schwarze Korps*'s description of a "pleasant guy with an overdeveloped body and underdeveloped mind," Geezer is a do-gooding musclebound simpleton, dressed in an orange barelegged one-piece swimsuit and a little cape—more than just a silly look, a reference to his discoloration in *Look* and the SS article's comment on it.

Geezer isn't the subject of the story, but "a comic book character who has taken the public by storm." When Clark Kent reads a copy, the cover is a replica of *Superman* #18's, with Geezer straddling a bomb dropped on the Axis. The strip's artist (interestingly, the writing is handled by a bullpen of hires) is named Carson Steele, evoking, of course, the Man of Steel. There's even a little dig at DC, as the publisher sits in a "super-luxurious office." But Steele is a sham, a persona played by a burley actor, to hide the fact that "the real creator of **Geezer** is a timid, anemic little shrimp named Henry Jones. And if the truth came out, it would spell disaster for **Geezer, inc.!**" Jones is shy, short, gaunt, sharp-nosed, and wears heavy spectacles, bearing a strong, if exaggerated, resemblance to Shuster (and to the Jewish stereotype in general).

Enraged at the lampooning of their leaders in his comics, the Nazis try to kill Jones with a letter bomb, which Superman intercepts. Jones is then ambushed at home by a Nazi agent, sent to avenge Hitler's honor for being made "the laughing stock of the world." Superman again saves him, but when Jones is later kidnapped, instead of swooping in as himself, Superman assumes the guise of Geezer—a delightful layering of mimesis, with Superman representing his creators' wishful selves, Jones standing in for Shuster and perhaps Siegel, and Superman taking the place of his own in-comic takeoff: the fantasy pretending to be the reality, in fantasy, created in reality.

A particularly fertile issue, *Superman* #25 also contains a story in which the Action Ace takes on the "101% Americanism Society," a parody of the America First Committee, exposing them as fifth columnists and a front for Nazi espionage.[42]

A month later, on the cover of *Superman* #26, he manhandles the rodent-like Goebbels while ringing the Liberty Bell into a Radio Berlin microphone.

The SS were perhaps the first, but by no means last, Antisemites to spot Superman's Jewish undertones. Others over the years have noted them too, usually in a conspiratorial context, the latest being *Al-Manar*, a Lebanese TV station affiliated with terrorist organization Hezbollah. In a 2014 segment titled "Jews, Movies, Hollywoodism, and the American Dream," they explained that Jews "tried to change society's opinion of them by inventing cinematic characters that would serve as role models," like Superman, "a movie about a Jewish person who was the best, who was a savior, or a hero," the goal of which, of course, was "to take over the greatest superpower in the world, to control all aspects of its daily life, and to harness it in the service of Jewish goals worldwide. Whenever someone challenges this, Superman is ready to deal with him." The segment concluded, "They want to conquer all the world. As we want. But they know how to do it, and we don't."[43]

Following the *Look* strip, the Kryptonian took on the Krauts not just on the covers of his comics but within their pages, if still by proxy. In *Action Comics* #22–23 he fights the Bavarian Toran, a warring nation identified by their Nazi-like uniforms, replete with iron crosses, which invaded its peaceful neighbor Galonia. He smashes their bombers out of the sky, detonates their sea mines and sinks their submarines.[44]

In *Superman* #9 and #10 he busts spy rings stateside, though the latter contains a more important story. Lois and Clark are sent to cover the Dukalia-American Sports Festival, modeled after the 1936 Berlin Olympics. The Dukalians wear more accurate Nazi uniforms (with Teutonic crosses in place of swastikas), goose step around the arena and salute *Sieg Heil*–style their speechifying mustached leader, Karl Wolff. (The SS Liaison Officer to Hitler at the time was named Karl Wolff, though he wasn't particularly known and the story's Wolff is clearly meant to be Hitler himself. More likely, and demonstrative of Siegel's awareness and cleverness, it's a reference to Hitler's nickname, "Herr Wolf," derived from the meaning of Adolf—Adalwolf, or noble wolf.[45])

Despite the pretense of friendly sportsmanship, Kent isn't fooled. He understands the Dukalian regime is subversively "fomenting un-American activities." When at the opening ceremony Wolff declares, "we Dukalians are superior to ny other race or nation! Proof that we are entitled to be the masters of America!" he decides to enter the games as Superman, easily winning all events and humiliating the self-styled master race. He then confronts Wolff, exposing him as a sniveling coward for the world to see.[46]

In reality it was black American athletes like track & field star (and fellow Clevelander) Jesse Owens who humiliated Hitler, winning four gold medals and breaking two world records after the dictator proclaimed the Olympics would demonstrate Aryan physical supremacy. But Siegel and Shuster placed their own avatar in the role, making it a more intimate victory. At this point in time

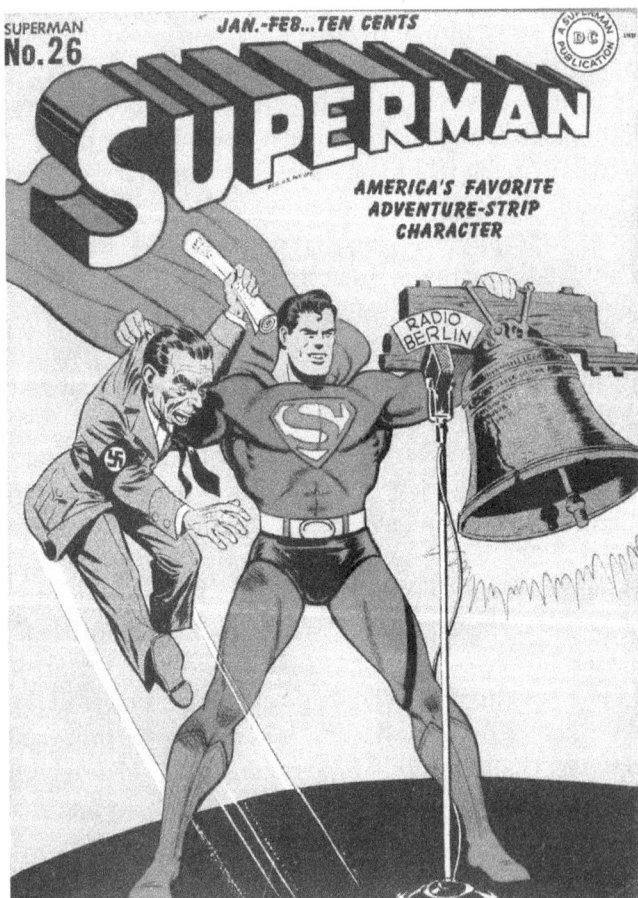

Superman #26, January 1944. Cover by Jack Burnley.

Superman #10, June 1941. Written by Jerry Siegel and illustrated by Wayne Boring. DC Comics.

Hitler was careful not to directly target the U.S. in rhetoric or action, and so the duo skillfully tied together the Dukalian racist ideology with their plans to conquer the U.S., again conjoining Jewish and American interests by making the point of a common enemy and warning Americans not to trust a Wolff in sheep's clothing.

The same month, in *Action Comics* #36, Siegel and Shuster's polemic became more complex. Again Superman faces isolationists, and again they jeopardize American security, but this time rather than malevolent subversives they're Useful Idiots—unwitting stooges manipulated by self-serving interests. Hoodwinked by agents of "Nation X" into believing America isn't menaced by their country while it prepares to invade, the "Volunteers for Peace" blame rearmament efforts on war profiteers who control the media, echoing real claims made at the time against Jews, claims rooted in the Protocols of the Elders of Zion that persist in different forms to this day. *The Daily Planet*, Lois and Superman unequivocally support rearmament, and are proven right when Nation X launches its blitzkrieg against Metropolis. A job for Superman, he stops the invasion by punching their planes out of the sky until the rest turn tail.[47]

Even though it would be another three months before the U.S. entered the war, *Superman* #12's cover shows the superhero marching arm in arm with a sailor and a soldier, a reference to James Montgomery Flagg's *Together We Win* World War I propaganda poster (creator of the famous Uncle Sam *I Want You for the U.S. Army* poster. Likewise, *Superman* #18's cover of him riding a bomb was likely inspired by Richard Fayerweather Babcock's *Join the Navy, the Service for Fighting Men* poster). The story inside involves the Grotak Bund, a pastiche of the German-American Bund, sabotaging munitions factories, yet again portraying Nazi sympathizers as treason-ous fifth columnists.[48]

Following the attack on Pearl Harbor and America's entrance into the war on December 7, 1941, DC decreed that Superman would fight the Axis only on his cov-ers. Ostensibly, it was to not cheapen the heroism and sacrifice of real GIs, though a more likely explanation is that DC, like the Hollywood studios, were reluctant to get too politically involved in fear of alienating readers or calling undue attention to themselves as a Jewish business. Siegel and Shuster didn't share the same reticence. They were, after all, the two youngsters who riled up the vaunted SS. Though they did curtail their hero's crusade against the Nazis and their minions, they continued unleashing him on their facsimiles. By March's *Superman* #15 he reentered the fray, defending the peaceful European democracy of Numark against the invading army of Oxnalia, led by Hitler lookalike Razkal.[49]

Two issues later they put the Führer himself on the cover, for the first and last time, showing the Champion of the Oppressed bestriding the globe, holding up a writhing, terrified Hitler and Hirohito.

Superman's febrile war on the Nazis wasn't limited to his comic books. Beginning in 1940, the *Adventures of Superman* radio show, helmed by Jewish writer-director-producer Robert "Bob" Maxwell (Joffe), sent him after Axis agents, sabotage rings and white supremacists. Strict radio rules for children's programming prevented him from direct involvement in the war,[50] and so he did his bit by defend-ing American citizens.

One memorable storyline addressed Antisemitism head-on, in which Superman comes to the aid of a rabbi who's attacked and his synagogue vandalized. Another running theme of the show, like the comics, was the corruption of public officials. In Germany the entire apparatus of the state had been subordinated to the purposes of conquest and genocide, and Superman constantly reminded Americans that the government's purpose was to work for them. Like Siegel and Shuster and Kirby and Simon, Maxwell received death threats, and he used his to drum up more publicity for the show.[51]

Contrary to American priorities, Superman throughout the war largely ignored the Japanese, focusing his attention on the European theater. *Action Comics* #30 marks a noteworthy exception, though still aligned with Jewish preoccupations; he faces Arab marauders in the Sahara, led by Zolar, a madman commanding suicidal zealots.[52]

An explanation for Superman never officially entering the war (the *Look* story being an uncanonical "imaginary" tale) was offered in 1942, in the *Superman* news-paper strip. He tries to enlist as Clark Kent, but in an uncharacteristic, if convenient, moment of distraction he accidentally reads the eye chart in the next room with his x-ray vision, making him fail his physical and declared 4-F for poor eyesight—just as Shuster was. Instead, he vows to battle saboteurs and collaborators domes-tically, which were ubiquitous in most wartime comics and imaginations.[53] The contrivance made little sense, but it was enough of an answer to solve Superman's dilemma.

Eventually Siegel offered a more sincere, and encomiastic, explanation. As part

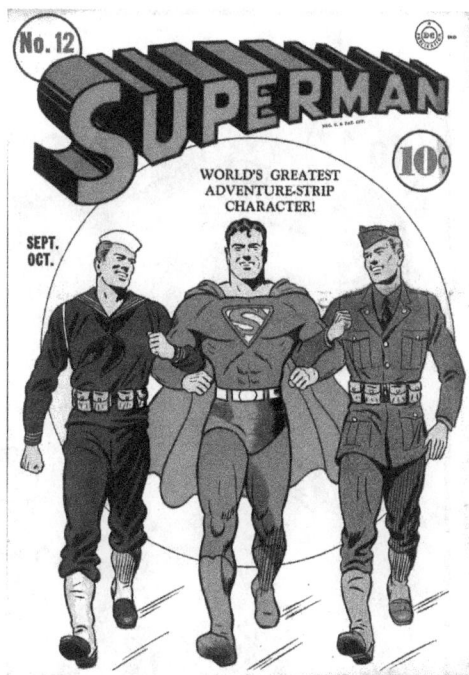

Left: Together We Win, by James Montgomery Flagg. U.S., 1917–1918. Library of Congress. *Right: Superman* #12, September 1941. Cover by Fred Ray. DC Comics.

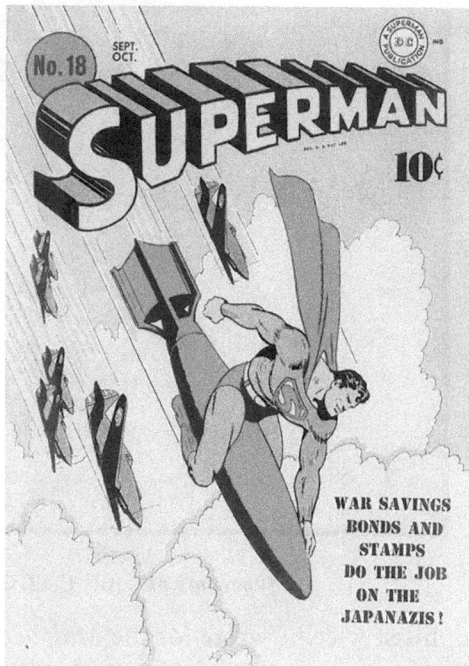

Left: Join the Navy, the Service for Fighting Men, by Richard Fayerweather Babcock. U.S., 1917. Library of Congress. *Right: Superman* #18, September 1942. Cover by Fred Ray. DC Comics.

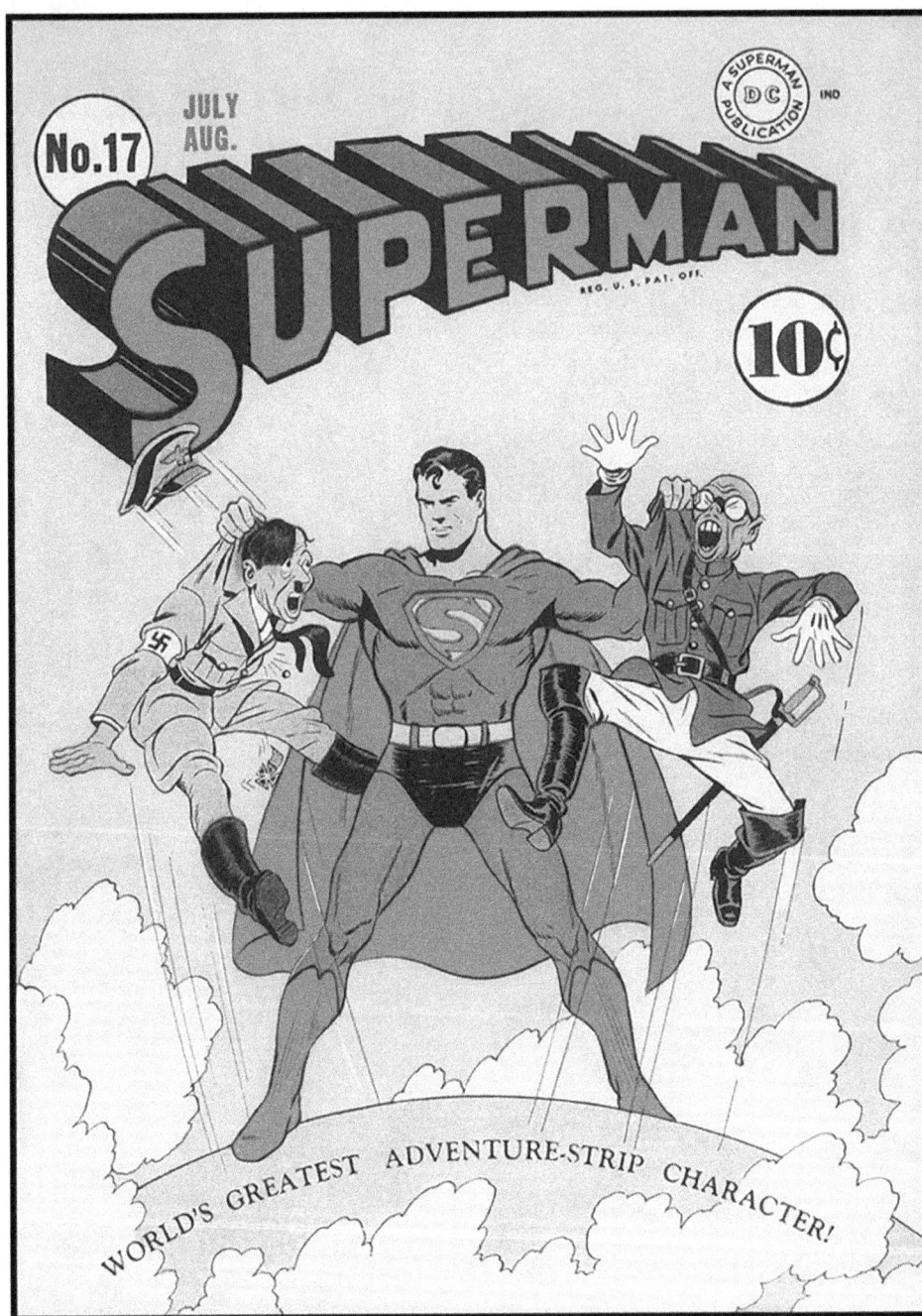

Superman #17, July 1942. Cover by Fred Ray. DC Comics.

of his service he wrote for the *Midpacifican*, the Armed Forces' newspaper in the Pacific Ocean areas. On August 26, 1944, Siegel explained in a front-page column— boasting "*Superman's Old Man Here*" above the banner—why Superman doesn't simply win the war: "real life drama dwarfs fiction's wildest improvisations … no comic strip heroics can hope to compete with the everyday feats of plain, ordinary GI Joe.…

Superman … understands that freedom is a precious commodity: that both individuals and nations should have the right to earn their own salvation … he has the utmost confidence in … our eventual victory."[54]

Superman's mission wasn't just to carry out his creators' fantasies; it was to carry them over into the real world. It was politicking through punching, a dramatized appeal to the American public through a symbol of its best self. At a time of horrifying violence inflicted upon Jews he was a man impervious to harm, and as Jewish refugees were being refused around the world, including the U.S., he was a foreigner who was also America's most celebrated hero. Superman was an emotional answer to an existential question.

The hero symbolizes a man's unconscious self.—Carl Jung

Birthright

Superman's true superpower isn't his strength or speed, it's his iconicity. He's so archetypal that, within the framework of his lore, he's essentially a tabula rasa. Different people project different things onto him, whether their personal fantasy of empowerment or their own interpretation of America. It's only natural that different groups have claimed him as their own, from Christians, in books like *The Gospel According to Superman*, to the LGBTQ community, in articles like "How Gay Is Superman?" in *The Advocate*.[1]

He was, however, created in a decidedly Jewish setting, which raises the question of his affiliation more pointedly. He's not explicitly Jewish in any way—an overtly Jewish hero, or even an implied one, would have been a nonstarter—though Siegel and Shuster's Jewishness was noted in the American press as early as 1941.[2] Of course, Superman's Jewishness isn't corollary to his creators.' *White Christmas* was written by Irving Berlin (Israel Beilin) but certainly isn't a Jewish song. Al Jolson's *The Jazz Singer*, on the other hand, heavily imbued with Jewish themes, is very much a Jewish film. So is Siegel and Shuster's Superman, and so are many of the comics created by their kinfolk. Still, it's hard to say how deliberate or even conscious the use of Jewish signifiers really was, seeing as it's a hotly contested matter even among the creators themselves.

"There are some artists who happen to be Jewish and eventually can somehow make a case that they've made a Jewish contribution to the arts by being born in the right tribe," Spiegelman argues, though he clarifies that's not always the case. Eisner's hero the Spirit, for example, "was clearly circumcised." Joe Simon dismissed the notion, asserting that the collective Jewish background of those in the trade "had absolutely nothing to do with comics. Jack [Kirby] and I never sat around and discussed Jewishness in comics.... We all knew who we were. We were proud of our heritage." But Kirby differs. In his view, "a belief in moral values ... [that] good triumphs over evil.... Those are the things I learned from my parents and from the Bible. It's part of my Jewish heritage."[3]

As with any art form, metacognition isn't a prerequisite for deeper meaning. Not every Jazz song of the Harlem Renaissance was meant to reflect the black experience, yet jazz is firmly rooted in the racial and historical context of its creation and evolution and as such is a distinctly black-American art form. Much the same, American Judaism is the force that shaped the idea of the superhero.

As Lee saw it, his background was germane to his work insomuch that "you can wrap all of Judaism up in one sentence, and that is 'Do not do unto others....' All I tried to do in my stories was show that there's some innate goodness in the human condition. And there's always going to be evil; we should always be fighting evil."[4] What Lee seems to mean is that, though it's a precept of Jewish faith, it's not unique to it; it's a universal sentiment, found in virtually all religions and cultures.

Nevertheless, its common phrasing, the same one Lee uses, is of Jewish origin. It's the most famous aphorism of Hebrew sage Hillel the Elder, one of the most important figures in Judaic history. Hillel was a prominent religious leader, exegete and philosopher who lived in Jerusalem during the time of King Herod (est. 74 BCE–10 CE). His teachings were renowned during the time of Jesus, and his influence is thought to be seen in several of his gospels,[5] including "love thy neighbor," which the rabbi of Nazareth restated in Mark 12:31 and rephrased in the positive in Matthew 7:12 as "Whatever you would that men should do to you, do you even to them, for this is the Torah and the Prophets," commonly known today as the Golden Rule. Hillel's adage is found in the Talmud (Shabbat 31a); when a skeptical heathen challenges Hillel, claiming he'd convert to Judaism if Hillel can sum it up concisely enough that it can be explained while standing on one foot, Hillel obliges, "What is hateful to thee, do not unto thy fellow man: this is the whole Torah; the rest is commentary; now go and learn it." The maxim is based in brotherly love being the fundamental principle of Jewish moral law, as expressed in Leviticus 19:18's "love your neighbor as yourself."

Other early creators fully acknowledge the Jewish subtext of their comics. As Eisner remembers it, "I'm part of a generation that was very conscious of our Jewishness.... If you scratch through the surface, everything I do, write or draw has a Jewish side to it." Feiffer was the first to "out" a character, writing in 1965 that "the Spirit reeked of lower middle-class: his nose may have turned up, but we all knew he was Jewish."[6] Eisner and Feiffer both attest that there was recognition within the industry, even if perhaps unspoken, that some characters were Jewish, representing their authors and artists. Eisner theorizes

> I think that there's a cultural thread underlying the superhero concept. The superhero has his origins in the folk hero. He represents an attempt to deal with forces that are considered otherwise undefeatable, and that ties in somehow with the n'shama (soul) of the Jewish people. Although we may have thought we were creating Aryan characters, with non–Jewish names like Bruce Wayne, Clark Kent and my own Denny Colt [the Spirit], I think we were responding to an inner n'shama that responds to forces around us—just like the story of the golem in Jewish lore.
>
> If you think about it, all of Jewish cultural history has been based around Jewish cultural fighters, like Samson and David. Now, in the 40s, we were facing the Nazis, an apparently unstoppable force. And what better ways to deal with an anti–Jewish supervillain like Hitler than with a superhero?[7]

While it may have been undeliberate, Lee conceded that their comics were nonetheless instilled with "attitudes and emotions that could be called Jewish that may have been in the back of our minds as we were making superhero and all the other kinds of comics."[8] The distinction between conscious and subconscious motivation is fiddly, as is the question of recognition after the fact. What is safe to say is that for some of the comic book creators the presence of Jewish themes in their work was merely coincidental, whereas for others it was the very essence of their work. Either way, who they were manifested in what they did.

This inevitably broaches the subject of what being Jewish means, exactly. The perennially debated question of the Jewish peoplehood continues to elude even Jews themselves, seeing as their definition of identity is in constant flux between racial, ethnic, religious, cultural and national facets. (The concept of the Jewish people predates that of the Jewish religion in the Bible. They're referred to as "a nation" [Gen. 12:2 et seq.], "Hebrews" [Gen. 14:13, 39:14 et seq.] and "Israelites" [Gen. 32:32 et seq.] long before they form Judaism with the receipt of the Ten Commandments and the Torah at Mount Sinai [Ex. 19:3–Lev. 27:34]. This understanding of peoplehood and nationhood pre-exists modern notions of race and political territory by millennia, and continues to inform Jewish thought.)

Scientifically, all of humanity is a single race, skin colors and features being matters of sunlight, latitude and climate. But race is irrefutable as a social construct, and Jews weren't considered white then, certainly not in Europe. (Genetic studies have shown, however, that Jews around the world do share some distinct genetic traits, which trace back to the ancient Middle East.[9])

That Superman, who's of a different species than human but is largely accepted by the population, illustrates just how superficial racial identity and group affiliation are. Biologically he might as well be a dolphin, but as long as he resembles a Caucasian male the denizen of his world, and of the real one, mostly don't mind.

Throughout most of its history, Jewish identity has largely been formed in exile, in the Diaspora, and so has always been defined, in part, by others. By institutionalized Antisemitism, by ostracism and persecution, Jews could tell who they were by those who targeted them, regardless of how they defined themselves. In this regard the Nazis were the de facto authority on who's Jewish, and to them the Man of Steel fit the bill.

There are, undeniably, some clichés, mostly attributed to Ashkenazi (European) Jews, but there's nothing about Judaism that is mutually exclusive from other cultures, nor is there anything which it has a monopoly over. Attribution of one trait or another, as with any group, is artificial, and stigmatizing in such a way is a dangerous slippery slope that can lead to bigotry. Ironically, if there is one trait that can be singled out about the Jewish people it's that throughout history they've been constantly singled out. But scientific taxonomy and political correctness aside, there are certain qualities, a certain sensibility, which even if difficult to peg down is inescapably "Jewish." For better or worse, no one will confuse Billy Crystal or Ben Stiller as anything but New York Jews. In this context, Clark Kent, particularly in his early incarnation as a nebbish yet wisecracking intellectual, personifies the Jewish typecast.

Some, though not many, have recognized the character's Jewish echoes. The satirical website Jew or Not Jew declared Superman a "borderline Jew." The *Jerusalem Post*, the premier Jewish-interest newspaper in English, noted that "the Superman legend seems to resonate with Jewish themes." Eminent British journalist and novelist Howard Jacobson likened Kryptonian culture to Jewish culture, because "all the men are highly scientific and cerebral." The Center for Jewish History in New York even threw Superman a 75th birthday celebration in 2016, cake included.[10]

Most famously, in *The Amazing Adventures of Kavalier & Clay* Chabon writes, "They're all Jewish, superheroes. Superman, you don't think he's Jewish? Coming over from the old country, changing his name like that. Clark Kent, only a Jew would pick a name like that for himself."[11]

Several comic book industry insiders, past and present, have also recognized the Man of Steel as a fellow tribesman. Feiffer, one of the first to propound the idea outside the trade, claimed that "Superman really came not from Krypton, but from the planet Poland" while speaking at the Library of Congress in November 1996. He followed up a month later with a piece in the *New York Times Magazine* titled "Jerry Siegel: the Minsk theory of Krypton," in which he discussed in detail the hero's Jewish patrimony.[12]

Earlier but less prominently, renowned comix writer and *farbissiner* Harvey Pekar, best known for his autobiographical *American Splendor* series, much of which dealt with his Jewish identity (adapted into an eponymous 2003 Academy Award–nominated film), wrote the short story "What Superman Means to Me," illustrated by Gary Dumm with Robert Crumb, in the comics anthology *Snarf* #12. In it, Pekar finds common ground with Siegel and Shuster as a fellow working class Jew from Cleveland, but also bitterly resents their creation, a "rich Jewish superhero" who "hogs the whole comic book field."[13]

Elliot S. Maggin (often spelled "Elliot S! Maggin"), Superman's primary writer for fifteen years and author of three Superman novels—*Miracle Monday* (1978), *Last Son of Krypton* (1981), *Kingdom Come* (1998)—has been as much of an influence on the character as anyone following Siegel. As a Jew and student of Kabbalah and Martin Buber, his religion and culture have played an important role in his approach to writing Superman. "I give all my characters religions, so I've thought this through—really," he tells. "The Kents are Methodist (as is Clark), Lois is Catholic, Perry is Baptist, Jimmy is Lutheran.... And Superman (like the Siegels, the Shusters, the Weisingers, the Schwartzes, the Maggins and the Luthors) is Jewish. This is so self-evident that it may as well be canon."[14] What he presumably means by this is that Superman, as well as his diametric opposite Luthor, created and stewarded by Jews, are expressions of Jewish sociopsychology. After all, Superman wasn't actually born in a crystalline hall on a distant planet, he was born in the bedroom of a Jewish teenager in Ohio. His Jewish attributes, according to Maggin, are obvious. And these are qualities Maggin assigns to Superman only: Clark Kent is a Methodist (apt, considering his upbringing). He's the assimilationist costume, the consensus gentile, whereas Superman, the true persona, hails from a different culture.

That culture is Jewish in essence, if not in fact: "While they are not direct descendants of the Judeans of the Middle East from whom the term 'Jewish' comes, I always ascribed effectively Jewish doctrine and ritual to the Kryptonian tradition,"[15] Maggin reveals. Krypton's value system, hinted at from the beginning and explored over decades of stories, is much like Jewish society's; erudition and rationality are held in the highest regard, at times to a fault, and those dedicated to the exploration of truths awarded the highest status. At the same time, it's also an ancient culture, devoted to upholding venerable age-old traditions.

Other Superman writers, artists and editors over the years have noted his Jewish signification, some adding to it, but Siegel and Shuster's original intent remains conjecture. They never discussed their Jewishness publically, certainly not that of their universally beloved brainchild, leaving no definitive answer.

But Superman was their cherished creation, their personal avatar, into which they funneled all their imagination, enthusiasm, and dreams. They built him from the cultural materials at their disposal, including the traditions of their household, the politics of their people and the fictions of their generation. Such an intimate creation, developed over twelve years by Shuster and nearly twenty by Siegel, would only naturally incorporate their Jewish makeup.

There's nothing to indicate they were deliberate or even aware of it, though these elements are nonetheless there. In his memoir, Siegel describes the ideation as subliminal, writing: "I would look at my hands in a very detached way, watching the fingers flash across the typewriter keys … wondering…. Has my subconscious mind taken over? At times it seemed like the stories were writing themselves."[16]

It seems clear that Siegel and Shuster didn't intend for their Superman to be a Super-Jew, they meant for him to be a Super-American. But they also made him an immigrant, born elsewhere, with a different name in a different language and a different racial heritage.

Siegel acknowledged on various occasions that the rise of Antisemitism and the persecution of Jews were a large part of the inspiration for creating Superman, and that he partly based him on Samson, but never did he confirm that Superman himself had any Jewish underpinnings. He never mentioned it to his wife Joanne, though she was aware of the Jewish connotations and considered that they came from his subconscious.[17]

Ultimately, though, under all the influences, Siegel and Shuster based Superman on themselves. Or rather, Superman was their wish fulfillment, while Clark Kent was their reality. "Clark Kent grew not only out of my private life, but also out of Joe's," Siegel recounts. "So in the artwork, he was able to translate it … he wasn't just drawing it, he was feeling it."[18]

Shuster based much of Superman's physicality on that of Douglas Fairbanks, the lead action hero of the day (and secretly paternally Jewish, born Ullman), including his famous akimbo stance and early devil-may-care attitude, while Clark Kent is an amalgam of comedy star Harold Lloyd and himself, self-described as "mild-mannered, wore glasses, was very shy with women." Though he was gangly and narrow-featured and Siegel portly and round-faced, as well as a few inches taller, they shared the same mien to the point of seeing themselves as carbon copies of each other. Shuster often had Siegel pose for Kent when he drew.[19]

In addition to their mild mannerism, the two also imbued Kent with their social awkwardness. Siegel in particular was unpopular in school, describing himself as a loner and a pariah, which led him to develop "a giant sized inferiority complex." It didn't help that, even at the peak of their success, they were still the subject of ridicule. The 1941 *Saturday Evening Post* article, their moment of fame, repeatedly referred to Siegel as "the plump youth" and implied that he was rather dimwitted. It described Shuster as an "undernourished, bewildered schoolboy of sixteen" (he was 28) and the both of them as "small, shy, nervous, myopic lads."[20]

Clark Kent was more than just their mundane reality. He was their super-neurosis personified, based on their angsts and insecurities as much as Superman was on their fantasies. "Superman was our wish fulfillment. He was everything we weren't and wanted to be," Shuster told the *Los Angeles Times* in 1975. "Superman had the mighty muscles I didn't have," Siegel also wrote in his memoir. "He could amazingly deal out justice to bad guys and correct evil wrongs, which I couldn't do, though I felt indignant.... Superman is what he is because of my life experiences."[21]

In part, he was also Siegel's revenge fantasy against the fairer sex, which scorned him throughout high school. Clark Kent, after all, is merely a pretense, and can change anytime he wants into the world's most powerful, and popular, man. The smart and beautiful Lois Lane may sneer at mousy coworker Clark but she swoons over Superman, clueless that they're one and the same. And in Siegel's early stories, Superman is indifferent to her charms. "I figured that the character would be so advanced that he would be invulnerable in other ways than physically," he explains. "Secretly, I kind of enjoyed ... the fact that he wasn't that affected by ... [her] admiration."[22] There was a bit of misogyny to Superman's curt treatment of Lois, vindication in fiction for Siegel. But ultimately Siegel was a romantic, and his hero softened with time. One of the most beautiful aspects of Superman is that he's been in love with the same woman for eighty years.

Interestingly, from the very first issue, while Superman snubbed Lois he wooed her as Clark—which is puzzling, considering Kent is a sham persona, created to divert attention from Superman. But he's Siegel and Shuster's real self, and that they chose him and not the hero to pursue Lois is telling. It's also revealing of the character's complexity. Clark Kent is more than just an act; he's a facet of Superman's personality through which he interacts with the world.

Lois, too, is a reflection of the real woman she was based on. While she was originally inspired by film character Torchy Blane, she was ultimately based on the model Siegel and Shuster used, Joanne Kovacs, whose "irrepressibility, ambition and spunk" came to inform the character.[23]

Though Superman's mythos is mimetic, reflecting his creators, their culture and the historical moment of his creation, the Lois-Clark-Superman love triangle at the heart of it proved to be equally anti-mimetic, with life imitating art. Kovacs started modeling for Lois around 1935, at the age of eighteen, but it wasn't until 1948, after she'd married and divorced, when she met Siegel again at the New York Cartoonist Society costume ball, that the two became smitten, marrying only a few months later.[24] Finally, Clark got his Lois.

Superman's world mirrors Siegel and Shuster's in more than just theme. They regularly based elements in the comics on their own lives. There was Superman's Midwestern upbringing, for one. "There he was, a first generation Jewish boy of Russian stock, planted in the Midwest." Feiffer wrote of Siegel. "He sensed the difference, his otherness. We were aliens."[25] Siegel and Shuster weren't farmers like Kent, not many American Jews are, but they were an immigrant and a child of immigrants, both decedents of an ancient, faraway culture, growing up in Ohio.

Siegel had aspirations of becoming a reporter and wrote for his high school newspaper, *The Glenville Torch*, which inspired Clark Kent's career. Shuster had actually worked for a great metropolitan newspaper, the *Toronto Daily Star*, as a newsboy before moving to the U.S. Thus, in *Action Comics* #1 Kent writes for the *Daily Star*. By issue #2 his newspaper becomes the *Cleveland Evening News*, a fictional newspaper situated in their hometown. (Likely an oversight in their reuse of the strip they'd originally intended to sell to local papers and situated their character's adventures there.) The paper wouldn't become the *Daily Planet* in the comics until issue #23.[26]

Superman's stomping ground Metropolis is usually associated with New York City, but it was originally modeled after Shuster's birthplace, Toronto. "Cleveland was not nearly as metropolitan as Toronto was, and it was not as big or as beautiful. Whatever buildings I saw in Toronto remained in my mind and came out in the form of Metropolis," Shuster recalls. Still, "The Big Apricot" is based on New York, in a roundabout way; it takes its name from the famous 1927 film by Jewish-German director Fritz Lang, which in turn was inspired by his visit to New York, making the most famous fictional city in the world based on the most Jewish city in the world.[27]

While Siegel and Shuster based Clark Kent on themselves, his "signature attributes—bespectacled, bookish, mild-mannered—could be a burlesque of Jewish stereotypes," Kaplan observes.[28] He fits the typecast, making him not just an expression of how they saw themselves but also of how Jews were seen (and often still are) by American society. Their feelings of social inadequacy, their insecurities about success, recognition and acceptance, are all characteristic of Diasporic Jewish identity, certainly at the time.

Kent is also a writer by trade, like Siegel, like many of the Jews who populated journalism, literature, film, television and comics in significant disproportion to their share of the population. Jews as men of letters is an equally prevalent stereotype, befitting the People of the Book and Jewish culture's promotion of scholarship, particularly, traditionally, the rigorous study of intricately complex texts like the Talmud and Gemara. (Jews are in fact demographically overrepresented to a substantial degree not only in the literary arts but in fields and occupations with the highest cognitive demands in general, like medicine, law and science.) British journalist David Herman observed in the *Guardian* that this prevalence of Jewish writers has resulted in a "strange kind of cultural ventriloquism, with non–Jewish characters … created by Jewish writers who wanted to write about their own experiences but couldn't. As a result, many of the achievements of mid–20th-century American popular culture now look as if they were written in code."[29]

But Gregor Samsa, Willy Loman, Holden Caulfield, Rob Petrie and other mouthpiece characters, while successfully recasting the parochial as universal, could only embody so much the wild hopes and power fantasies of their Jewish creators. That was uniquely a job for Superman.

In *Symbols of Transformation*, Carl Jung describes the extraordinarily potent hero as the archetypal symbol of man's unconscious self. "What we seek in visible human form," he posits, "is not man, but the superman, the hero or god, the *quasi-human* being who symbolizes the ideas, forms, and forces which grip and mould the soul."[30] It's in man's nature to personify his highest ideals in a figure superior to himself since he himself can never actuate them. By giving expression to his deepest desires, the hero or deity serve as a therapeutic tool for his neuroses and an aspirational figure for his drives. It's not difficult to imagine how Siegel and Shuster's mind spawned a mighty hero to address their personal and collective Jewish wishes, or how, in a poverty-stricken nation of immigrants on the eve of war, he became the modern archetype of the superhuman protector.

Of course, archetypes in their Jungian sense are part of the collective unconscious, a universal, preexisting consciousness. In Jung's conception, Superman's Jewish trappings are circumstantial. He isn't based on Moses, nor on Jesus, but rather all three are molded from the same archetype originating in the "archaic heritage of humanity." Siegel even contemplates this possibility in his memoir.[31] Even so, this doesn't contradict Superman's Jewish roots, since all mythology is accumulative. That Superman draws from Moses doesn't change even if the latter is a revision of a primal idea.

Superman wasn't meant to be a hyperbolized autobiography. He's a metaphor, formed at least in part unconsciously, for his creators' experiences, their hopes and worries. And while those are manifestly Jewish, the dream-symbol they conjured resonated with the rest of America, a nation of dreamers.

The metaphor practically wrote itself. All Siegel and Shuster had to do was take the Nazi creed that "the Jews are undoubtedly a race, but they are not human" and turn it on its ear. If the Jews were to be a race of non-humans, they would be Kryptonian—a race so advanced that its people are impervious to harm (originally they were all superpowered), dedicated to scientific pursuit and form a unified, global society. It was a utopian fantasy that was the only sane response to a world gone mad.

Are Kryptonians meant to be space Jews? Maggin openly approached them as such. Seemingly so did his colleagues Paul Kupperberg and Howard Chaykin, both Jewish, who in 1979's *World of Krypton* #1 canonically established education and the pursuit of knowledge as the prime values of Kryptonian culture, making it, ostensibly, the Jewish idea of utopia.[32] (With Jews constituting 0.2 percent of the world's population but 22 percent of Nobel laureates [30 percent since World War II], it's hard to argue with the cliché.)

But Krypton was also insular, forbidding space travel (which is why Kal-El is its sole survivor), making it something of a space shtetl. Ashkenazi Jews came from communities that were isolated from the Christian world, usually confined by decree, and Jewish life was all they'd ever known. Their communities were destroyed by pogroms, wars and eventually the Holocaust, and they found themselves, like Superman, homeless refugees in a world of people not their own. The home that was destroyed and the grand civilization that was lost can also be seen as an expression of the Jewish cultural trauma, ever present in its prayers, blessings, poetry and literature, of the fall of the Second Temple and the scattering of Jews from the Holy Land.

Though an advanced civilization, depictions of Krypton have often included biblical signifiers, like Shuster's frontispiece in the 1942 novel *The Adventures of Superman*, showing them in robed garbs amidst stone pillars. More suggestive, Kryptonians wore tunics and headbands until Superman's revamping in the 1980s and intermittently since. In the first detailed depiction of Krypton in the comics they even wore skullcaps. These kind of uniforms were a common portrayal at the time of futuristic

Superman #264, June 1973. Written by Elliot S. Maggin and illustrated by Dave Cockrum. DC Comics.

or alien apparel, but a specific explanation is given for the headbands by Maggin in *Superman* #264 (June '73): they're symbols of emancipation hailing back to the ancient past, when Kryptonians were enslaved by the pharaonic-sounding Taka-Ne and forced under the yoke of whips to build his ziggurat fortress. They eventually rebelled and gained freedom, using the subterfuge of a plague of hives.[33] The story is an obvious nod to Exodus, which likewise ends with the establishment of a priestly class that's thereafter described wearing headbands (Ex. 28:40, 29:9, 39:28, Lev. 8:13, Isa. 3:20. The HCSB consistently refers to them as headbands, though other Bibles also use caps or bonnets. The original Hebrew, "migba'at" [מִגְבָּעַת], is more accurately translated as a nonspecific headdress).

Jor-El, intermittently an esteemed or the foremost scientist on Krypton, also wears a headband in most of his appearances, denoting his learnedness. A scholar whose son goes on to become a heroic figure, he fits within the tradition of Moses's priestly parents, as well as the rabbi fathers of Harry Houdini, Barney Ross and Rafael Halperin.

As Kaplan and Tye both note, that he sent his son away to spare him the violent death that he could not escape, as well as the annihilation of their people, also reflects the *Kindertransport*—the rescue of about 7,500 Jewish children, infants to teens, from Germany, Austria, Czechoslovakia and Poland, sent on their own to safety in England between 1938 and 1940. Many, like Kal-El, escaped doom at the very last minute, just as German forces were overtaking the countries and cities their trains and ships were leaving from.[34] (As with many other tropes Superman established, virtually all superheroes following are orphaned of at least one, though usually both, of their parents, often by violence. Batman, Flash, Aquaman, Green Lantern, Captain America, Spider-Man, the Hulk, Iron Man, Daredevil and Wolverine, to name a few. Superman, however, remains the only one whose life is shaped not just by personal tragedy but cultural catastrophe.)

This adds a layer of meaning to Jor-El and Lara's farewell to their son. "You will travel far, my little Kal-El," Jor-El tells him in the *Superman* film. "But we will never leave you, even in the face of our death. The richness of our lives shall be yours. All that I have, all that I've learned, everything I feel…. This is all I can send you."[35] It's a poignant moment, made all the more so by its parallel to thousands of such final goodbyes by Jewish parents across besieged Europe. Siegel conceived of Krypton in 1934, several years before the Kindertransport (at least the large-scale organized effort), and so clearly didn't intend the equivalence. Superman's origin story as an infant whisked to safety is based on that of Moses. But history, even mythic, repeats itself.

Before he created and promptly destroyed Krypton, however, Siegel imagined the cataclysm befalling Earth. As he tells it, by the summer of 1933 his earlier version of "The Superman" had been repeatedly rejected and Shuster became despondent, even burning the original artwork. Hoping an established artist would help change things, he wrote to several. One bore out: Russell Keaton, the artist of the popular *Skyroads* strip and an uncredited ghost artist on the *Buck Rogers* Sunday strip, whose style was similar to yet more developed than Shuster's.

Their collaboration was done via correspondence, and between June and November 1934 they produced two weeks' worth of strips, with some tentative interest from Publishers Syndicate. Keaton then withdrew without explanation, likely because he either discovered that Siegel was only twenty years old or he decided not to take a risk on the young dilettante and pursue his own comic. Siegel recounts in his memoir that the day he received Keaton's abrupt rejection letter became the fateful night he dreamt up Superman, likely in late November.[36] (Keaton launched his own strip in 1939, *Flyin' Jenny*, about a daring aviatrix, which achieved some success but was discontinued in 1946.)

Siegel and Keaton's Superman was literally the Man of Tomorrow, a toddler sent from millions of years in the future, when humans have evolved to gain "infinite strength," in a time machine built by his father, the last man on Earth. He's found by Sam and Molly Kent, red-blooded Americans who can't understand the strange language he speaks, leading them to assume that "his people came from a foreign country." Also found in his capsule is a hidden note detailing his advanced cultural heritage, but, alas, the adult Clark Kent finds that he can no longer read it.[37]

This embryonic version includes themes absent in classic Superman lore that further reflect the immigrant experience. Speaking in a different language was the first challenge of assimilation, and forgetting the ancestral tongue over time its cost. The children of the Kindertransport were also sent with letters from their parents to remember them by, and some, along with many hidden Jewish children across Europe, were raised as Christians, sometimes unaware of the community and culture they were uprooted from.

Escaping humanity's extinction at Earth's end was haunting, though not as engaging as the destruction of faraway Krypton. It was also morose and pessimistic, incongruous to Superman's character, and he could still be regarded as a native, losing much of his uniqueness as an alien outsider struggling to do good and be accepted. It did, however, make him more like Moses, a hero returning to his own people with amazing abilities to save them.

Eventually, though, Siegel and Shuster created the familiar Superman who's sent from doomed planet Krypton to Earth, where he's found and raised as Clark Kent in the Rockwellian town of Smallville. Except that Superman's idyllic childhood in the American heartland wasn't part of his original legend. In the first nine years of his comics he's depicted as having grown up in Metropolis—leaping as a child over cityscape, not farmland, in origin stories like *Superman* #1 and attending Metropolis High School in *Superman* #46[38]—an urbanite through and through, like most American Jews.

The first mention of a different hometown, along with the first reference to a family farm, was in 1947, in the radio show, which located Eben (later Jonathan) Kent's farm in Iowa. The town was named Smallville two years later in *Superboy* #2. It was shown to be near the border of Delaware and Maryland in *The New Adventures of Superboy* #22, but it tended to move around the U.S. in following continuity. It wasn't until the 1978 movie that Smallville finally landed in Kansas,[39] ringing true enough to be folded into canon in the 1986 *The Man of Steel* miniseries, where it's stayed since.

While not his doing, placing Superman's childhood in a Heartland rural community enhanced Siegel's message greatly. Drawing on the Jeffersonian ideal of agrarian life as a cultivator of individualism, moral decency and strength of character, the heretofore metropolitan hero was rephrased as a farm boy who grew to be the great city's greatest resident, making Superman a parabolic promise to not only succeed in but tame the urban chaos. At a time when cities were changing rapidly by industrialization and immigration, each fueling the other, many feared that America would become a nation of citizens without citizenry, strangers with no mutual accountability or allegiance to the nation and its ethos. By enlisting the values of the countryside, implying also the continued cultural dominance of homegrown (and white) Americans, Superman was a reassurance that immigrants posed no threat and were in fact the most loyal and grateful of citizens. Like baby Kal-El, they were only to be shown, and they would champion, the American way. It likewise served as a rebuttal of the Antisemitic stereotype of Jews as hopelessly cerebral and urbanized, lacking in old-fashioned, rustic virility.

Israel may have been the Promised Land, but America was the land of promise. Jews were safe and free to succeed, flocking to cities, particularly New York, that inspired in the former villagers and townsfolk both a sense of humble impotence and a fantasy of omnipotence. When Clark first arrives in Metropolis he is the Wandering Jew finding his home in the City upon a Hill, the place where his talents are needed and welcome and where he can finally become super. His journey from Krypton to Smallville to Metropolis is thus also from the ancient kingdom to the Diaspora to the new homeland.

At the same time, to assimilate in the big city Superman must keep his true self hidden. Other heroes before him wore costumes, like Zorro and the Phantom, but they weren't kept under their regular clothes any more than doctors wear scrubs under theirs. The idea of the hero's outfit as undergarment is uniquely Siegel and Shuster's. What's more, these were costumes in the theatrical sense, whereas Superman's is his traditional ethnic garb, a declaration of identity and purpose (that it's impossibly tight, like a nude body painted over, makes it all the more expressive of his true self laid bare). He could just as easily have worn a nondescript acrobat's leotard like the Phantom or all-black ensemble like Zorro or, as he did in the 1933 version, just pants and a T-shirt, but it was important that his attire convey greater meaning.

Clergy aside, most streams of Christianity don't attribute particular significance to clothing. Judaism does, from the yarmulke (skullcap) to the *tallit* (prayer shawl) to the *tzitzit* (ritual tassels) to the *shtreimel* (round fur hat worn by ultra-orthodox Haredim) to the *bekishe* (long coat worn by ultra-orthodox Hasidim). By both biblical and rabbinical decrees, attire has always carried spiritual meaning for Jews and has served in public as a declaration of faith and affiliation. Just like Superman's costume.

His cape lends him grandeur, adding to his mass and emphasizing his strength and speed as it flutters behind him, but in truth it's his baby blanket; it's the garment his mother wrapped him in when she placed him in the rocket ship.[40] It even bears his family crest. The Freudian question of a grown man schlepping around his baby blanket aside, it's really a physical piece of his heritage. Wearing a suit and tie to work at the *Planet* follows the fashion norms of his adoptive society, but his primary colored outfit is his ethnic vestment, connecting him to his lineage as a remnant and an identifier. Clark Kent's horned-rimmed glasses are the costume. He wears his real clothes underneath, displaying them only when he wishes to assert his true identity as a Kryptonian. Like the super-suit, the *tallit* is a mainstay worn under regular clothing, which are subject to the style dictums of a given place and time. It's worn atop clothes on special occasions, like the Shabbat or high holidays, proclaiming then the Jewish identity of its wearer (referring both to the *tallit katan*, a poncho-like undershirt worn continuously by observant Jews, and the *tallit gadol*, a prayer shawl draped over the shoulders like a cape during synagogue services and *tefillin* [phylacteries] prayers). And it, too, is an item of heritage, whether physically bequeathed down generations, as it often is, or as a symbol of succession and faith.

Even Superman's "S" glyph, possibly the most recognized symbol in the world after the Christian cross, can be seen as a Jewish signifier. Chabon posits that the Nazi swastika was the first super-symbol, a dynamic, simple design exuding power and purpose, and Superman's S-shield was Siegel and Shuster's response to it.[41]

Superman's nemesis Lex Luthor (depending on the version, short for Alexei, Alexis or Alexander) also fits within Jewish context. One possible inspiration for the character is personal to Siegel, originating in his childhood. The day after his father died violently, the *Cleveland Plain Dealer* published a letter denouncing vigilantism, written by one A.L. Luther.[42]

The supervillain's name calls to mind, and is often mispronounced like, German Reformation leader Martin Luther, a vehement Antisemite whose repeated calls for violence against Jews in treatises like *On the Jews and Their Lies* (1543) inspired widespread riots, murders and expulsions. His teachings were revived as part of Nazi ideology and found a new audience among American Bund supporters and many Lutherans, renewing his infamy among Jews. It's entirely possible that Luther, a hateful revolutionary priest, inspired Luthor, a hateful power-hungry scientist.

Luthor has changed substantially over the years, from a warmongering profiteer to a mad scientist to a corrupt tycoon, but he's always remained the one man who could best Superman, the enemy whose machinations he can't stop with his fists, who always has a sliver of Kryptonite at the ready. And it's the xenophobic Luthor who always points Superman out, no matter how popular he is, as the alien, the Other. If Superman is a power fantasy then Luthor embodies powerlessness, representing any one of myriad persecutors throughout Jewish history who were in a position of power and sought to oppress or destroy the Jews (a famous Jewish joke is that every Jewish holiday can be summed up as "they tried to kill us, we survived, let's eat"), often given in Jewish lore the same motivation as Luthor; jealousy, of Judaism's inherent moral and spiritual power.

Ostensibly, it's why Harvey Pekar declared Luthor "a big goyische villain,"[43] though Maggin, interestingly, sees him as Jewish, just like Superman. (And Jimmy Olsen as Lutheran, supposedly because of his commonly Lutheran surname. In a way, he's how cynical, urban, historically weary Jews saw their gentile, all-American countrymen; well-meaning but young, full of wide-eyed naïveté, warm and welcoming to the bumbling Kent but in need of guidance and protection by Superman.)

For a villain with no superpowers to be the greatest enemy of the world's most powerful hero seems mismatched, but Luthor is in fact the perfect counterpart precisely because he is a super-man; he's what Superman hopes to inspire humanity to be, its fullest potential, perverted. And considering the Jewish veneration of intellect, what's more offensive to a Jew, more anathema, than intellect in the service of evil? His scientific brilliance makes him an earthly Kryptonian, but his hubris and egotism prevent him from truly helping advance humanity and blind him to Superman, with the scientific and cultural knowledge at his disposal, being potentially his greatest ally. It's the great tragedy that's at the heart of their relationship, and the moral of the tale; that intelligence must be guided by virtue.

Luthor's age has varied through the years, though he's almost always portrayed as older than Superman, often middle-aged to Superman's about-thirty. He represents something of a father figure, a distortion of Jor-El—a rebellious science prodigy who uses his talents to bring death and destruction rather than protect life in the face of it. Superman's ongoing feud with Luthor can thus be framed as a surrogate Oedipus complex, which Freud likewise ascribes to Moses and Pharaoh.[44] In that relationship, too, the villain is a paranoid tyrant whose attempts to kill the hero would also mark the final stage of an extinction event, linking the personal and the collective.

Superman's saga is a "Moses-like story about the last survivor of a dying civilisation sent to Earth so that he might have a decent chance in life," Mark Millar, writer of *Superman Adventures* and the *Superman: Red Son* miniseries, wrote in the *Sunday Times*. It had "a particular poignancy for the Jews, and the idea of a lone immigrant trying to make it in a strange land also resonated with every culture."[45] It was a common experience to many Americans, but it was Jews who told this particular story and it was Jews who based the character on themselves. Even the idiom is Jewish; it's Moses who was "a stranger in a strange land" (Ex. 2:22).

Superman also borrowed the description for the opening sequence of his 1940–1951 radio show, made world-famous when it was reused in the 1952–1958 TV series, calling him a "strange visitor from another world," later changed to "strange visitor from another planet." Despite having grown up on Earth, Superman is forever strange—meaning both foreign and unusual—and a visitor, not fully at home. Like Diasporic Jews, who were strange visitors in whatever country they lived in, even for generations, he came to the U.S. from another world, the Old World, to fight "a never-ending battle for truth, justice and the American way." The "American way" meaning, presumably, peace and pluralism (perhaps more accurately, peace through pluralism), and for immigrants it also meant prosperity. The promise—which no other country in the world could make to Jews at the time—that it was a safe place to live, work and partake in society, where success was possible and predicated on merit, and where life was not spent in service of ideology but rather the other way around; a citizen's calling was to life, liberty and the pursuit of happiness.

Superman is an alien in all senses of the word—extraterrestrial, foreigner, outsider—who not only personifies the best immigrant but also the best in America. (Technically an illegal alien, having jumped the interplanetary fence. For that matter, his Fortress of Solitude in the Arctic likely makes him an illegal resident of Canada.) A hero who is, at once, from elsewhere and "all-American," a reminder that being an immigrant or the child of immigrants *is* all-American. The metaphor could stand for anyone, any minority, any outsider. But Superman can pass for an insider. He looks the part, with just some minor adjustments, which was something few ethnicities besides Jews could do.

Alvin Schwartz was the writer of the *Superman* newspaper strip from 1942 to 1952. In 1976 he published a twelve-page essay in *Children's Literature* journal titled "The Real Secret of Superman's Identity," discussing, among other things, his theory for the Man of Steel's great success: "consciousness and rationality were shattered by World War II. This produced … one of the most persuasive pieces of evidence that Superman had a certain healing quality for those who had no external choices. For during the war, fifty percent of the circulation of Superman went to the armed forces. And no one, regardless of his pre-war status was more lacking in choice than a conscript soldier in the midst of a war."[46] The appeal of a bulletproof, bomb-proof man who can punch out Panzers to a young man, sometimes a teenager, in combat, is clear. But Schwartz's argument that Superman is a healing figure for those with no choices overlooks the obvious. Not only was he created before the war, but his creators belonged to a people that were being hounded and butchered across the world, from Russia to Iraq to Palestine to Germany to, increasingly looking possible, the U.S. There was little young American Jews could do about it, and Superman was the healing catharsis through which they could, if only in fantasy, fight back.

Between the Depression, joblessness, homelessness, famine, dust storms, rampant crime, the rise of Antisemitism and the inevitability of a war even greater than the "war to end all wars," it must have felt like the end of times. How could it not give birth to a messianic hero? This was Superman's true healing power. People have always yearned for a mighty guardian, but never so desperately as Jews then. The Hebrew heroes of antiquity weren't enough. They overcame lions (Samson, Daniel) and giants (David), but the hero of modernity needed to defeat tanks and bombers, and existing heroes like Tarzan or the Lone Ranger, for all their grit, offered little solace. Siegel and Shuster's champion had to possess powers and abilities far beyond those of mortal men, and so he wasn't a man at all. Not just an alien, he was an alien concept—a Jew who couldn't be harmed, who had the power to do anything he wished, who protected and inspired others, and who was loved by all. The International Jew: The World's Foremost Problem became the interplanetary Jew, the world's greatest hero.

Stories like *Don Quixote* or *Frankenstein* or *The Great Gatsby* are cultural constants, used regularly as reference or simile regardless of whether people have actually read the source texts. They're like internet memes, separated from their origins, always altered but always identifiable. So is Superman. (In "The Myth of Superman," Eco explores the character's unique status as both mythic and literary figure, the former requiring his narrative to remain constant while the latter requiring it to progress. The conflict is reconciled by his existence in a perpetual second act, his beginning frequently revisited and end occasionally speculated, as well as uncanonical "imaginary stories" [common in the 1960s and revived in the 1990s as "Elseworlds"], which allow simultaneously for narrative progression and constancy.[47]) Virtually everyone knows who he is and what he does and is broadly familiar with key elements of his lore. His exploits have appeared in every media imaginable for the better part of a century now. But relatively few have actually read his comics, and fewer still have read the originals. And just as the classic fables and fairy tales of yore tend to be more complex and telling of their time and place when read in their authentic versions, so do Superman's early comics reveal a layered work of folklore and tradition.

They reflect Jewish precepts and values filtered through trappings of science fiction and action, a theme established by Siegel and Shuster and explored over decades by successive creative teams. "Superman stories are not about power," Maggin explains. "They're about moral and ethical choices. Each one asks the question: *What does a good person do in a given situation if he's got all the power in the world?*"[48] It's the same type of edification stories found in the Bible, where men appointed by God, with great power at their disposal, are faced with ethical questions of its use. Like Samson, who must choose between his love for a woman and his duty to his people, or Moses, who repeatedly tries to appeal to Pharaoh's reason instead of bringing to bear his overwhelming might, both dilemmas Superman can relate to.

Ethics aren't the intellectual property of Judaism, obviously, though many of today's universal moralistic conventions can either be traced back to the Hebrew Bible or owe their common phrasing to it. Still, as Fingeroth points out, "if there was any Jewish mythological basis for the superheroes that emerged from comics, it was fueled by the same Bible tales to which every child in Western society is exposed, as often as not in a nonreligious, nonethnic context. Samson has become synonymous with great strength as Hercules or John Henry."[49]

It becomes then a question of whether drawing inspiration from the Bible, be it tenets, themes or stories, makes a creation Jewish. Ostensibly no, given the text's foundational place in Christianity and Islam and ubiquity in Western culture. But it's still a Jewish text, written by, about and for Jews. Its DNA is inherently Jewish, even when used to clone modern stories. Adding to this the social and political motifs of early 20th century American Jewish life, Superman's mythology is an entire dictionary of Jewish legend and wishfulness. After all, if Doc Savage was intended by his co-creator to reflect "Christliness,"[50] why not Superman Jewishness?

In his essay, Schwartz writes, "working on Superman, we thought we were, in effect, manufacturing the character. In actuality, we did no more than 'discover' Superman."[51] The character's core elements were always there, ever-present in Jewish culture, waiting to be revisited in a new context—which raises the question of why is it that only fairly recently readers and academics have started noticing them.

One possible answer is that comic books had not been taken seriously enough, and only relatively recently have people bothered to examine them more closely. Another possibility is that the increase in religiosity in America and the world have made people better able or more willing to notice them. Another is that the field and its practitioners have simply been around long enough for a momentum of thought and research to build up, including into this particular topic. Yet another is that the cinematic renaissance of superheroes in recent years, including Superman's, as well as his repetitive overhauls in the comics (five in thirty years), have prompted greater scrutiny into the fundamental building blocks of his lore, which had long been taken for granted. Whatever the case, Superman's Jewish signification has come to be recognized by a growing body of work, though this is the first book to focus solely on him.

The debate over the world's first and greatest superhero being Jewish falls along the obvious fault lines of historical cipher versus postmodern revisionism. An attempt to uncover meaning or to impose it. Of course, whether or not Superman is Jewish is epistemological nonsense; he doesn't exist. He's a cartoon. But so are all symbols, and symbols can have a very powerful effect on the real world. The Star of David, Cross, Old Glory, Swastika, even the Nike Swoosh, are all two-dimensional representations of abstract notions that stir both emotion and action, sometimes to momentous consequences. What makes Superman Jewish is his embodiment of his creators' personal and cultural fears, aspirations and values. A symbol of their hope.

Our truest life is when we are in dreams awake.—Henry David Thoreau

The Secret Identities
of Heroes and Hebrews

Jewish Americans are not as synonymous with comics and superheroes as African Americans and Jazz. The reason is that they did what black people could not; pass for white. They created characters and stories under Anglicized noms de plume, interacting with the world through secret identities.

Changing one's name to reflect a new identity and purpose was nothing new in Jewish tradition. The very first Jew, Avram, became Avraham (Abraham), adding the theophoric Hei (ה) following his covenant with God, as did his wife Sarai, becoming Sarah. The patriarch Ya'akov (Jacob) became Yisrael (Israel), a polysemic name related to God, after he had wrestled an angel. Joseph became Zaphnath-Paaneah when he joined the Egyptian Pharaoh's court. Hadassah became Esther in Xerxes's court. Yosef ben Matityahu became Titus Flavius Josephus when he became a Roman citizen. Just like Kal-El of Krypton became Clark Kent when he arrived on Earth, then Superman when he became a hero.

For showbiz Jews in early 20th-century America adopting stage names was the norm, even backstage. A simple change allowed them to avoid much of the prejudice and conflict they otherwise would have had to contend with, serving as a way to dissimulate and assimilate. And so Ehrich Weisz became Harry Houdini. Asa Yoelson became Al Jolson. Douglas Ullman turned into Douglas Fairbanks, Israel Baline into Irving Berlin, Jacob Gershwine into George Gershwin. Louis Feinberg and Jerome and Moses Horwitz became Larry, Curly and Moe. Benjamin Leiner became Benny Leonard. David Kaminsky was hardly a household name, but Danny Kaye certainly was. Same for Joseph Levitch, better known as Jerry Lewis, Benny Kubelsky, who became Jack Benny and Issur Danielovitch, who became Kirk Douglas.

"Most of us, at the time, were trying to 'pass.' That was the thing to do." Eisner explains.[1] Diversion from the ethnocentric norm was something to obscure, not broadcast. And while comic book creators might not have been in the public eye like their screen and stage counterparts, their work was still subject to mass-market scrutiny. Stan Lee, long before he became the doyen of superhero comics, was Stanley Martin Lieber. Joe Simon's real name was Hymie. Bob Kane's was Robert Kahn and Gil Kane's was Eli Katz. Charles Wojtkowski created the Blue Beetle as Charles Nicholas, a house name he shared with Eisner and Kirby at Fox Publications. Eisner produced work under several goyishe pseudonyms like William Morgan Thomas and William Erwin Maxwell.

Jacob Kurtzberg, by all accounts an out-and-proud Jew, used numerous pennames but not one that sounded even remotely Semitic. He signed his art as Curt Davis, Jack Curtiss, Bob Dart, Bob Brown, Fred Sande, Ted Grey and Lance Kirby, just to name a few, before finally adopting the Irish-sounding Jack Kirby. His parents were none too happy at his choice of exclusively Anglo names, but he wanted to sound "all-American."[2]

Siegel and Shuster were an exception, both by using their real names in their byline and by having a byline. Perhaps it was because they were among the first, or because they were just too proud of their favorite creation. But Shuster was still short for Shusterowich and Siegel for Sigalowitz, and Jerome was an inconspicuous gentile name of Greek origin with a Christian saint connotation. Prior to and following Superman Siegel published work mostly under aliases, all WASPy, including Charles McEvoy, Hugh Langley, Herbert S. Fine, Leger (with Siegel as Reuths), Joe Carter and Jerry Ess.[3]

There were practical reasons for comic book Jews to change their names. The use of pennames allowed the publisher or art studio to seem larger than it was, not an uncommon practice at the time. Some artists, like Kirby, even drew in a different style under each name.[4] Creators were also sometimes assigned pseudonyms by the publisher, possibly as a way of preventing ownership claims.

Moreover, for all their popularity, comics were looked down upon. "I realized that people had no respect for comic books at all. Most parents didn't want their children to read comics," Lee explained. "And I was a little embarrassed to be doing the work I did, and I figured someday I'll write the Great American Novel and I don't want to ruin my possibilities by having my name disliked this way. And [so] I became Stan Lee."[5] For Jews, already marginalized, writing and drawing comics was an added source of ignominy, and so many tried to sublimate their Jewishness.

They were also already a target, and Jews that had Hitler smacked around in their comics put themselves and their families in danger. The Bund could have found them at home instead of the office. And so, like the heroes they created, to protect themselves and their loved ones, to avoid unwanted attention, to appear grander than they were, they took on secret identities.

Another motivation was the cultural and generational gap they experienced. Most were the young children of immigrants, born or raised from an early age in the U.S. Unlike their parents at home they spoke perfect English, were secular, felt relatively safe and were fully assimilated into the norms of the culture around. They defined themselves as Americans first and Jews second, and they felt their ethnic names were pigeonholes they needed to rid themselves of. Like their peers out in Hollywood, they had two ways to go about this: they could change their names or they could create nondenominational characters to act as their mouthpieces. Most did both.

That at least for some their creations were their avatars isn't conjecture. Kirby plainly stated that "Captain America was me, and I was Captain America." Though the character was conceived and designed by Joe Simon, Kirby soon, and for many years following, injected much of himself into him. When he drew the good Captain punching Hitler on the cover of the first issue, it was his "own anger coming to the surface."[6] The hero's alter ego, Steve Rogers, was an undersized young artist from the Lower East Side, just like Kirby.

Likewise, Siegel and Shuster based Clark Kent on themselves and Superman on who they wished to be. Both personas were manifestations of themselves in fiction—the mighty "S," they pointed out in an interview, also stands for Siegel and Shuster.[7]

Eager to prove themselves in America, young talented Jews were told that Clark Kents needn't apply. So they created a new industry and filled it with idealized supermen that America embraced, and through them assimilated into the mainstream. Superman, the first, also proved the most popular, in large part because of his secret identity. Many superheroes had amazing powers and everyman alter egos, but not like Clark Kent. He was as much a victim as Superman was the hero, derided, rejected, painfully mundane and hopelessly lacking. In short, someone almost everyone can identify with, especially the young. The Man of Steel is the aspiration figure; the mild-mannered reporter is the identification figure. And for readers across the country to identify with a character representing his Jewish creators was no small feat.

"In those days, you just didn't go around writing about Jewish heroes," Simon explains.[8] Leading men in entertainment were white and Christian by default (with the notable exception of Zorro, who's Californio nobleman Don Diego de la Vega), and better that their creators' ethnicity didn't intrude. So creators and creations both assumed secret identities with whitewashed names and mannerisms. But here, too, Superman stood apart; he simultaneously played to type and subverted it, by "looking right" but also being an alien. He attained mass appeal while still retaining his otherness, belonging without belonging. It made him the perfect ambassador—there's little a child cares, then or now, about the plight of a refugee arriving in America in pursuit of safety and actualization. But an alien escaping the destruction of his planet and coming to America to become a superpowered crusader of justice is a different story.

Superman's secret identity is unique in its metaphoric and thematic profundity, but he isn't the first to have one. Usually credited is 1903's Scarlet Pimpernel, a heroic swordsman and escape artist named after the flower he drew on his messages, who's secretly aristocrat Sir Percy Blakeney (fittingly, he inspired Swedish diplomat Raoul Wallenberg to save tens of thousands of Hungarian Jews from the Nazis by issuing them Swedish papers in 1944–1945[9]). He was soon followed by Gaston Leroux's 1909 Phantom of the Opera, a cloaked and masked man of action, both of which provided heavy inspiration for Zorro and the Shadow and, in turn, Batman. But even before the Pimpernel, Robert Louis Stevenson's 1886 Dr. Jekyll transformed into the alternate persona of Mr. Hyde and Alexandre Dumas's 1844 Count of Monte Cristo assumed several guises in his quest for revenge. Two centuries prior, practically every other character in a Shakespeare play, whether by mistake or deception, adopted a false identity. Late-medieval folk hero Sir Robert of Loxley (the most known of the versions) may not have gone to great lengths to keep his true self hidden, but as a cowled archer defending commoners came to be known as Robin Hood. In the 6th-century Chinese ballad, Mulan served twelve years in the army disguised as her own father. Even the Greek gods took on disguises, including Zeus, who would descend disguised from Olympus in search of dalliances.

What exactly constitutes a secret identity is a taxonomic question, but possibly the earliest case in literature of the heroic kind—a selfless champion disguised with an alternate persona to save others—is a woman, the titular heroine of the Bible's Book of Esther.

Hadassah hides her Jewish identity, taking the name Esther and marrying the Persian king Ahasuerus (Xerxes). She becomes his favored wife and manages to dissuade him from heeding his evil vizier Haman (he of the taschen), who urges him to kill all the Jews. Her chosen *nom de guerre* signifies her role; its Hebrew root, str, read "seter" (סֵתֶר), means hidden or secret. It's her secret identity as a gentile that allows her to champion her people's cause and save them. Aptly, the Book of Esther is one of two books in the Bible that don't mention God at all (Song of Songs being the other). The Jews don't hinge their fate on deliverance by a higher power, they save themselves through wit and subterfuge. It's a victory commemorated in the Jewish holiday of Purim, a Mardi Gras–like festival involving, appropriately, masks.

There's also Moses, the greatest hero of the Hebrew Bible, who famously has a dual identity as a Hebrew slave and an Egyptian prince, converging eventually at his moment of truth when he becomes a rebel to the rule of Pharaoh and a leader to his people. Contrary to common misconception, however, his true identity is never a secret. Bithiah knows she's fostered a Hebrew child (Ex. 2:6), Moses is raised knowing this too (2:11) and so do the rest of the Israelites (2:14).

Yet tracing the origins of the secret identity convention does little to explain, in narrative logic, why Superman, who's all but invulnerable, needs to keep his identity a secret. In practical terms this has been explained as necessary to protect his loved ones, like his adoptive parents and Lois, as well as to avoid becoming depended on relentlessly for any menial task. But the Superman who debuted in 1938 was orphaned of the Kents, adopted a secret identity before meeting Lane and even then only casually flirted with her, and was more a roughhouse vigilante than the revered figure he is today. He had no real need to lead a double life.

In the Quentin Tarantino film *Kill Bill: Vol. 2*, the title character offers an interpretation of what Superman's secret identity means:

> A staple of the mythology is, there's the superhero and there's the alter ego. Batman is actually Bruce Wayne. Spider-Man is actually Peter Parker. When that character wakes up in the morning, he's Peter Parker. He has to put on a costume to become Spider-Man. And it is in that characteristic that Superman stands alone. Superman didn't become Superman—Superman was born Superman. When Superman wakes up in the morning, he's Superman. His alter ego is Clark Kent. His outfit with the big red "S," that's the blanket he was wrapped in as a baby when the Kents found him. Those are his clothes. What Kent wears—the glasses, the business suit— that's the costume. That's the costume Superman wears to blend in with us. Clark Kent is how Superman views us. And what are the characteristics of Clark Kent? He's weak. He's unsure of himself. He's a coward. Clark Kent is Superman's critique on the whole human race.[10]

The monologue is borrowed almost verbatim from Jules Feiffer's introduction in *The Great Comic Book Heroes*,[11] though that suggests it was likely meant as an homage for the initiated. But Feiffer and Tarantino are wrong. For one, we're in on the joke, not the butt of it. We know he's just pretending. We can identify with the bumbling Kent but we also feel superior to him, allowing us to identify with Superman, our true self. That's why his stories, in print and on screen, used to end with him winking at us.

And while Kent may be a milksop, he's also intelligent, conscientious, kind and loyal. His faults are mostly endearing, not malicious. He isn't a critique of humanity—he's a loving exaggeration of it. Most tellingly, from the day he premiered to date, it's as Clark that he's sought to win Lois's heart, not as Superman. He wants to be accepted, loved, as a human. Humanity aspires to be like Superman, but Superman aspires to be human.

"He sees everything from a slightly off-center position," Mario Puzo wrote in his *Superman* script. "When he becomes Clark Kent, the disguise takes on almost schizoid dimensions: a great personality change, exaggerating all these 'everyday, normal' qualities that are so inherently foreign to his true personality, and yet … there is a part of him that yearns and longs to be Clark Kent, free from the overwhelming responsibilities that come … from being who he is: SUPERMAN."[12] Puzo understood that Kent is more than mere pretense. Here is an alien raised as a human, the ultimate embedded outsider. His perspective will always be different than those around him, and to connect to them he has to walk through the world in their shoes, not fly above it. It's a dissonance familiar to all immigrants, not the least Jews, who, as members of a law-based religion, with its prohibitions on foods and activities on the Sabbath and mandates of prayer and ceremony, struggled to find commonalities with the predominantly Christian culture in the U.S.

Clark Kent's characterization has also fluctuated over the years. Siegel and Shuster's was Superman's diametric opposite, bashful, submissive and cowardly, and a source of comic relief. George Reeves's was a denatured sharp and assertive reporter, indistinguishable from his Superman. He even wore the same muscle padding under both outfits. Elliot Maggin and super-artist Curt Swan's was a slouching introvert but not quite as meek. Christopher Reeve returned him to his roots, making him even more of a blundering klutz. When writer-artist John Byrne rebooted him in the mid–1980s he became the real persona rather than Superman, and with that gained a confident, gentle disposition. Dean Cain followed Byrne's take in the 1990s TV show *Lois & Clark: The New Adventures of Superman*, adding his own wily charm to the mix. Tom Welling's was a kindhearted, pensive Millennial. Brandon Routh echoed Christopher Reeve, though he emphasized awkwardness over clumsiness and gave Superman some of Clark's insecurity. Grant Morrison and Rags Morales revamped him again in 2011, making him younger, pluckier and a little irascible. Henry Cavill has portrayed him with a quiet reticence and permanently furrowed brow. Most recently, since DC's 2016 "Rebirth" overhaul, he's been portrayed as staid but not skittish.

Irrespective of the different iterations, who he really is isn't so cut and dry. As Kent he pretends to be mild-mannered and wears the absurd disguise of horn-rimmed glasses and neatly-combed hair (though perhaps it's not that surprising it's enough to fool the people of Metropolis, considering they regularly mistake him for a bird or a plane), but he doesn't pretend to be someone else entirely. He's a genuine crusading journalist, a man of intelligence and morality (ethical questions of reporting about himself aside), and his job has always been an extension of his mission as Superman, not just as a means to quickly identify crises but a battle for truth and justice in its own right.

Which is the real man is the perennial question of the Superman myth, deliberated even among his writers. Robert Benton, who co-wrote the mercifully short-lived 1966 Broadway musical *It's a Bird.... It's a Plane.... It's Superman*, the redraft of Puzo's script and *Superman III*, couldn't decide the answer, but was fascinated by the question, "is he Clark Kent until that emergency call happens, or is he Superman?" "He's an alien, but he was raised in Kansas," Dennis O'Neil, who wrote his comics in the 1970s, points out. "Where would his values come from?" Even the man who created him seems to have been uncertain. In the early comics Siegel's narration occasionally refers to him as Clark while in Superman costume, and vice versa. And even though Siegel defined the character on various occasions as Superman pretending to be Clark Kent, including in his memoir, in the very same he also describes him as "simply a human with powers ordinary humans do not possess."[13]

Possibly the more interesting question is, how does Superman think of himself? The world calls him Superman and that's his life's mission, but since growing up on a farm is all he's ever known (in almost all versions of the story he's rocketed from Krypton as an infant, usually a newborn. In 1961's *Superman* #146, however, he looks to be about three and is already capable of constructing sentences.[14] In such a case the impressions of his formative years would manifest in his adult personality on Earth), it stands to reason that to him and his loved ones he's just Clark.

He's experienced several identity crises over the years as creators sought to explore the issue, the first significant one being "The Double-or-Nothing Life of Superman!" storyline in 1976's *Superman* #296–299. When he finds that he loses his powers when dressed as Kent but regains them once in Superman garb (part of an alien conspiracy to control him) he decides to temporarily hang his cape, hoping to "learn what the real *Clark Kent* is like in the process." It implies something of a dissociative state, evinced by his uncharacteristic behavior following. As Kent he manifests not only Superman's confidence but a newfound aggression. He talks back to his overbearing boss Morgan Edge, punches office bully Steve Lombard and even, it's heavily implied, finally sleeps with Lois—twice.[15] It suggests just how much he holds back both as Superman and as Clark Kent, and that perhaps neither is fully his true self.

He then tries it the other way, retiring Clark and becoming Superman full-time, but soon realizes that, just as he can't abandon his responsibilities as Superman, he can't stop being Clark Kent because it's the only way for him to interact freely with his friends. The story ends with him recognizing, "I tried to decide whether *Clark* or *Superman* is more important ... and realized that to do away with *one* would be to *kill* half of myself—*whoever* I really am!"[16]

Superman's struggle for self-definition and place in the world is something everyone faces, but this is a man whose abilities are unparalleled and so his role, his responsibility, is the most complicated. His actions and inactions require constant reflection and choice. He champions great, abstract ideals that turn his every utterance into gospel. He's regularly called upon to save the lives of everyone in the world, entrusted with the fate of humanity entire. But his powers are only physical. His cognition is the same as a human's, making his burden impossibly daunting, and he's had to shoulder it, for the most part, alone, without a partner, lover or family. He's a hero tested in every conceivable way, and Clark Kent is his only respite. An act or not, he can only connect to other people when he's Clark, and it's only as Clark that he can feel like one of them. Perhaps he also humbles himself daily as a timid stumblebum to atone, in a way, for being a Superman among men.

Alvin Schwartz, who wrote him for a decade, holds another view on his dualism. "These rationalizations for maintaining a secret identity had little to do with the real reasons, which lay in the nature of the character himself—his capacity for asserting his autonomy."[17] Psychoanalyzing Superman is futile, as he sees it, because he himself is a psychoanalysis of humanity. When he transforms he becomes at whim undefeatable, undeniable, insuppressible. The fantasy is universal; to have a secret Super-me. To be impervious to any harm, stronger than any challenge. Always confident, noble, regal, virile. To be able to soar above the petty woes of everyday life. Superman is the opposite of the Jungian Shadow; a hidden nature that's bright, a proclamation of power. He's neurotic catharsis in a cape.

This theme of transformation and transcendence is the through-line of Chabon's *Kavalier & Clay* and the reason he named its superhero character the Escapist, the understanding that the greatest form of escape is not just from surroundings but from self. At the same time, the fantasy Superman embodies isn't to become someone else entirely but rather a supreme version of the familiar self. Fingeroth phrases it as the common desire to "simultaneously be superior *and* common,"[18] to stand above but not apart, to be special without being different. To be Superman *and* Clark Kent.

It's a fantasy particularly resonant with Jews, for whom success has often meant being noticed and resented. It also touches upon the Jewish superiority-inferiority complex—found in many persecuted people, though possibly none more so than the Jews—by which "the chosen people," those favored by God above all others and the founders of arguably the most revolutionary social movement in human history, are also the most vilified, threatened and persecuted throughout their existence. It's a paradox that's at the heart of Jewish humor, from the Marx Brothers to Mel Brooks, famously combining incessant self-deprecation with incisive social satire. According to Maggin it's also part of the point of Superman, who's "virtually omnipotent and has *mishigass* anyway."[19]

In her bestselling book *The Tenth Circle*, a work suffused with comic book lore, Jodi Picoult writes that "Superheroes were born in the minds of people desperate to be rescued."[20] Of course, the perennially victimized would be the ones to dream of unstoppable saviors. But Picoult somewhat misses the point. Superheroes aren't a wish to be saved. Their Jewish creators didn't fantasize about helplessly depending on the mercy of others. They yearned to be mighty themselves, and for the world to see them for their true strength and love them for it. Yet to become something else also meant abandoning who they were, and so the secret identity was born. The ability to remain weak but at the same time strong, to stay themselves but also transform into super-selves, to only appear to need rescuing but secretly be the rescuers.

It also made literal what not only Jews but all immigrants and their children went through, split between worlds and identities. It's why "Clark cares about his secret identity a lot more than any other superhero," Maggin explains. As not a gifted superhuman but an alien being, "it makes him just a little more like the people he has to come in contact with."[21] Other secret identities were meant to conceal the person, while Superman, like Jews, used his to take part in society. And so the Hebraic-sounding Kal-El had his name and mannerisms Anglicized when he was raised by the Kents, Midwestern stock figures (largely still).

But despite his yokel upbringing, upon moving to Metropolis Clark was, along with his mild-mannered mien, clever and wry. He was a superhero with the looks and charm of a Hollywood star and an alter ego with the idiosyncrasies of a Hollywood accountant. "His fake identity was our real one," Feiffer declared. Specifically, he was Siegel and Shuster's alternate identity, meek and bespectacled and writerly. When, for his 45th Anniversary issue, Siegel called him "The Kid from Krypton who made it big," it was pretty clear it wasn't just Superman he was talking about.[22]

Clark Kent looked and behaved like his creators and he dressed like their fathers. He wore suits as exclusively as Superman wore his costume, even well past their vogue. Both Siegel and Shuster's fathers were men's tailors, and suits, both grew up learning, were what put food on the table and what poor immigrant Jews could wear to present a more respectable and gentile appearance. For Siegel they meant even more; he was the orphaned son of a suit salesman killed in a robbery, who then invented a crime fighter that hides his invulnerability under suits.

Their feelings of social inadequacy and fear and resentment of bullies, which manifested in Kent's air of unease and Superman's early zeal to teach predators a lesson, mirrored those of Jews within larger society. It made Superman more than an aspirational fantasy; he was a reaction formation to the nebbish Jew stereotype. In an era that increasingly revered vigor and ferocity as part of fascist ideology, gentleness and intellectualism were seen by many as weak and degenerate, a corruption of manly virtues. Jews, particularly by the Nazis, were labeled feeble and craven, a stereotype Clark Kent embodied. But Kent's intellect and determination were a powerful force for good, disarming the negative connotations of the stereotype, and his timidity belied the power and nobility of Superman, a reclamation of Jewish physicality.

What's more, the Antisemitic trope was a catch-22, portraying Jews as simultaneously infirm and all-controlling, inept and Machiavellian. Superman was the inverse, mighty and benevolent, using his great powers to help his fellow man. He was the *golus Yid*—the cowering, insecure exilic Jew—transfigured into an unstoppable champion of the oppressed, assuaging also the inherent Jewish ambivalence toward power.

All this leads to the central paradox of Superman's secret identity; not the realness of either of his personas, but their seeming inconsistency as Jewish allegory. If Kal-El from Krypton is a Jew from the shtetl and Clark Kent is his gentile pretense, why is Kent the one possessing characteristics associated with Jews? Shouldn't he be plainer, with a perfectly average job, posture and confidence, not a crusading journalist with the constitution of a mollusk? The answer is that both represent Jewish facets. Kent is the ambivalent assimilation while Kal-El is the proud ethnicity. One is Siegel and Shuster's self-image and a prevailing Jewish stereotype while the other is who they wished to be and be seen as. It's a mixed metaphor to be sure, but one with a simple premise at its core; it's not what you are that defines you, it's who you are—relevant today as it was then.

Famed deconstructionist Jacques Derrida stated that "every culture is haunted by its other," meaning that cultural and national identities form through juxtaposition to others, differentiating between those included and those excluded. Identifying "them" helps create "us." This "othering," combined with Jews' small numbers, is what Freud saw as being at the heart of Antisemitism.[23] Superman challenged the convention of other as enemy in popular fiction, by which adversaries were often outsiders, foreigners, invaders or aliens, all different from, incompatible with and hostile to dominant American culture. He turned Eurocentric America into the lesser developed civilization and the visiting stranger into a peaceful and munificent advanced man, one who not only strengthened but saved the group by entering it.

Yet despite his inherent superiority, he didn't want to be treated like a strange visitor. He wanted to be treated like, as he considered himself to be, a regular American, part of the normative "us." So he created a second identity, cast off what Lester Friedman calls "foreignisms" and adopted a whitewashed name that Chabon declares only a Jew would pick for himself. It's a name Siegel and Shuster took from Clark Gable and Kent Taylor and a deportment they took from themselves. According to Kaplan they also modeled Kent's mannerisms after Cary Grant's,[24] though Grant, as genial as he may have been, was a far cry from the bumbling Kent. He never stammered or knocked things over or cowered in a corner. He was no *schlemiel*—a klutz who breaks everything around him—nor a *schlimazel*—a hapless sort who can't catch a break—both of which Kent was. Kent was an exaggeration of his creators, and through them the Jewish cliché they fit.

What Superman also got from his creators and their assimilated brethren is the carefulness with which he interacts with the world as Clark Kent. He has to maintain a high level of self-awareness, be mindful of everything he says and does, lest he let slip and be exposed. It's a gingerliness familiar to immigrants living in foreign cultures. Even if not the dramatic fear of being discovered (though for Jews, even in the U.S., there was that, too) then of being seen as different, of saying something that isn't idiomatic or doing something that isn't normative and placing themselves apart. Being Superman, like any immigrant, means speaking in a second language and behaving in a second culture.

In the *Superman* movie, Jor-El tells his son, "Live as one of them, Kal-El.... But always hold in your heart the pride of your special heritage." It's the wish of every parent whose child is embedded in a new culture, to see them integrate and thrive but also preserve the identity and traditions of their legacy. Superman's success in doing so is the result of both the uniqueness and compatibility of his two cultures, much like the success Jews found in the U.S., as well as, like them, his ability to flit between identities. It makes him, as Feiffer calls him, "the ultimate assimilationist fantasy."[25]

At the same time, Superman is also a tragic figure. He's not just a refugee; he's the last of his kind, a minority of one. Kurt Busiek, who penned *Superman* and *Action Comics* between 2006 and 2011, sees his "sense of isolation, of loneliness, of being the only being like himself in the entire universe" as having "a grand and operatic power."[26] It's a survivor's solitude, of one who escaped the holocaust of his people, of postwar American Jews, both those who were stateside and those who came from Europe.

It's also the identity void of a living remnant. In 1933, approximately 9.5 million Jews lived in Europe, the majority of world Jewry.[27] By 1945, the extermination of six million of them—over 60 percent—meant that American Jews were the de facto Diaspora, and theirs became the universal image of Jews, the same image Clark Kent played into and also subverted. More importantly, they became the torchbearers of Judaism, tasked with keeping alive an endangered culture. Like them, the Last Son of Krypton is the sole custodian of an otherwise extinct society, shouldered with the dual responsibility of protecting his new world and preserving the memory of the old. He alone is left to define what a Kryptonian is, making his personal identity inexorably his cultural one.

Yet, Kal-El came to the U.S. as a baby. He grew up as an American boy. In his early comics he didn't even know he wasn't human, and in every version of his origin since 1978 he only learned it in his teens. Siegel wasn't an immigrant, his parents were, and Shuster came from Canada, hardly an exotic foreign culture, at the age of ten. They're both essentially homegrown Americans, which Superman, despite his exobiology, can also be regarded as. *Tablet* writer Rich Cohen describes first generation American Jews like them as having "the freedom to work and to pray but also to stop being Jews. Unlike Germany or England, there is no host population in America, no single race that can be threatened. America is a nation of nations, a nation of mutts."[28] They were the first Jews in millennia to define their own identity without outside restriction. To be able to live, dress, speak, worship, associate, marry and work as they wish, freedoms previously denied them in part or in full.

They were also a generation caught between two worlds, neither fresh-off-the-boat from the Old World nor established or respected in the new one. Many had one identity at home—Jewish, speaking Yiddish, wearing a *tzitzit* and yarmulke—and another at work or the outside world—American, speaking English, wearing a suit and fedora. It was the cost of the freedom to reinvent and assimilate. "Everyone has to figure out who they are as they grow up, but there's extra work for the children of immigrants, because we have at least two cultures to contend with," says Gene Luen Yang, the first graphic novelist to be named U.S. National Ambassador for Young People's Literature and writer of *Superman* Vol. 3 #41–50 and *New Super-Man* #1–24. "We have to figure out how these cultures speak to each other, where they contradict, and how they might fit together."[29] Superman contends with the same tug between identities, the ethnic Kryptonian and the assimilated Kent, not quite sure which is truer, when and where either is called for.

For American Jews, a dual identity could serve to either maintain a connection to Jewish tradition, renounce it, or slyly assert it without anyone being the wiser. Often it was two or all three of the above, mirroring the inherent ambivalence many felt about their heritage. The ability to decide at any given moment which identity will interact with the world is precisely what Superman does every time he changes from Clark Kent to Superman and back again, changing not just his behavior but effectively his race.

Though not incompatible, his two sets of values, Kryptonian and Earthly, have at times been at conflict, like in 1978's *Superman*. Krypton was remade from a utopian to a cold society, highly rational but emotionless, with architecture and technology based on ice crystals. Everything from machines to clothing is in stark black and white, awash in blinding fluorescence surrounded by pitch blackness. Smallville, by contrast, is elevated from small town America to nostalgic fantasy, a world inside a Rockwell painting full of warm emotions and colors. This esthetic polarity reflects Superman's internal conflict, his place and purpose in a world he wasn't born into.

On his voyage to Earth, Jor-El's recording cautions him, "it is forbidden for you to interfere with human history." But, as he grows up, Jonathan Kent tells him, "you are here for a reason." His biological father wishes him to remain hidden and uninvolved while his adoptive father urges him to harness his unique abilities in service of the society that took him in. At the film's climax, as both men's words echo around him, he's forced to choose between old and new, insulation and integration, to save Lois's life. He chooses the latter, interfering with history in the most literal sense by reversing the flow of time. But while he ultimately embraces the ideals of Earth as personified by Pa Kent, he doesn't reject his Kryptonian heritage. As the source of his powers it's the very value he brings to his new home, and it's Jor-El's hologram that teaches him how to use them.

Cold, deadly Krypton and idyllic, sheltering Smallville are apt stand-ins for Europe and the U.S. at the time of Superman's creation, and his dilemma is that of Jewish identity formation as a choice between assimilation and tribal loyalty, Americanism and Jewishness. Friedman writes

> These immigrants … quickly discovered that any commitment to the tenets and traditions of Judaism received its stiffest challenge not from brutal pogroms or cruel inquisitions, but from the seductive and intoxicating receptiveness of America. Since America offered new beginnings for everyone and presented only limited social and economic obstacles, the Jew's potential field of success was no longer confined to a small community of brethren or measured by his mastery of Talmudic law…. Thus the increasingly strong dichotomy between America as a place of economic salvation and one of spiritual peril.[30]

The clash of tradition and modernism was characteristic of the period as a whole, but it was more acute for Jews, members of the most ancient religion in the world (save perhaps Hinduism, counting the Vedic period). Four thousand years of cultural momentum collided with modern American culture, schismatizing Jewish identity. First-generation Jewish-Americans especially were torn between being the last of one tradition and the first of another. Whenever Clark stepped out on Lois with a flimsy excuse because his duty as Superman called it was the Jew turning down a Friday night date with the girl he liked because it was Shabbat. It was Sandy Koufax, star pitcher of the Los Angeles Dodgers, refusing to pitch at Game 1 of the 1965 World Series because it fell on Yom Kippur. Superman's secret identity was identity politics as high drama.

His desire to blend in and live as Clark Kent can also be seen as his creators' favor of acculturation and criticism of unassimilated Jews. Norms were different then, and the ideal to strive for, at least in the public sphere, was homogeneous. Immigrants often felt conflicting shame and pride in their heritage, and more conservative Jews were often seen by their more conformed, better-integrated tribesmen as clannish "domestic foreigners" rather than true citizens (to an extent, also an internalization of the racist trope). Siegel's mother Sarah came from Lithuania but considered herself, as Tye reports, "a proud American Jew … the kind who learned the language and how to get by … and she couldn't abode people … who hadn't adjusted."[31] Siegel came from a household that didn't deny its Jewishness but was assimilationist and Americanized, and took umbrage with Old World Jews who held on to the old ways.

The old ways were what made a culture of otherwise cerebral people refuse to acknowledge their impending doom, on Krypton and in Europe. Adapting to the new reality in America was necessary if Jews were to escape their confines, the specter of their history and perhaps chocking parochialism. If the diffident Kent was the old Diaspora Jew then Superman was the New Jew, a Super-Jew, enabled by the American way of life.

In 1959, six years before his book, Feiffer deconstructed the Man of Steel in a single-page, nine-panel cartoon in the *Village Voice*. Alone against a blank background, Superman describes how "this chick" he saved psychoanalyzed him, causing him to reconsider his life, give up superheroics, get an office job and settle down with her in the suburbs.[32] With true *sprezzatura*, Feiffer managed to encapsulate the driving neuroses of the character. He's a fantasy of manhood, an expression of male libido, and the cartoon evokes the corresponding fear of emasculation by a strong woman and the bondage of commitment. It's also a metaphor for the adventuring of youth giving way to the mundane responsibilities of adulthood and the inevitability of bourgeois living. More subtly, it's a hook-nosed Superman's conflict between his desire to be normal and what is perhaps less a moral imperative than a compulsive need to prove himself, exhibitionistically. He's the Jew who longs to abdicate the responsibility of his birthright and finally become, for better or worse, a regular American.

That, eighty years going, his identity is still subject to debate is testament to his appeal. Comics creators and fans alike, in interviews, online forums, comic book conventions and shops continue to argue who is the real person, Superman or Clark.

Feiffer and Tarantino are right that he's a stranger among us and that, unlike Batman or Spider-Man, he didn't become Superman, he was born Superman. It's "disguised as Clark Kent," after all, not "disguised as Superman." But that distinction gradually blurred throughout the 1970s in stories like "The Double-or-Nothing Life of Superman!" and eventually everted in his 1986 relaunch. The prevailing wisdom since has been, as one memorable exchange from the *Lois & Clark* TV show put it, "Superman is what I can do. Clark is who I am."[33] It's a pithy line, and it does make sense. Clark is the only identity he's known for most of his life. He's the earnest, virtuous, hardworking farm boy with small-town values (but not insularity). Superman is the role he took on by virtue of these qualities, as Earth's defender and a living billboard for truth and justice. That he carries himself differently as Superman isn't incongruous. Police officers and doctors assume a different demeanor when in uniform. It's a humanizing, relatable approach to the character. It's also wrong. Biology precedes psychology: he can think of himself any which way he wants, his DNA is Kryptonian. His superpowers are endogenous. Clark may be who he is, but Superman is what he is.

This dynamic wasn't clearly defined early on, but was entrenched with the introduction of Superboy in 1945, his retconned (retroactive continuity) costumed persona as a child and then teen, who remained canonical for forty years. Though there wasn't much distinction between Superboy and Clark (he didn't even bother wearing glasses for the first year[34]), he led a double life from around the age of ten, meaning that Clark Kent was almost always a guise while Superboy grew into Superman. It's arguably a semantic difference, but in this version of the character Superman is the clear true identity.

That said, it's a false binary. Superman doesn't have two personas, he has three. First there's Kal-El, scion of the House of El of Krypton. He wears a costume modeled after traditional Kryptonian garb, spends his time at the Fortress of Solitude, a monument to Krypton, and beginning in the 1950s, has an entire Kryptonian social circle, including cousin Supergirl (Kara Zor-El), old pet Krypto and the survivors' colony of Kandor. It's the cultural heritage aspect of his identity and the set of responsibilities that go along with it, of remembrance, tribute and conservation.

Second is Clark, the son of Jonathan and Martha Kent of Smallville. He's just a kid from Kansas who can do things others can't. It's his truest personality, which he retains when he becomes Superman. He changes his name and clothing, but Superman is simply a continuation of who he's always been. Yet, he's only Superman when there's a job to do.

Third is the Clark Kent of Metropolis, the pusillanimous, nearsighted *yutz* in boxy suits. He's an artificial construct meant to hide his true identity, but at the same time he's also a bright investigative journalist with a snappy, punchy prose style, and who he spends his daily life as and how he interacts with regular people, from friend Jimmy to love interest Lois.

Varying creative teams have approached this psychodrama differently throughout Superman's history, but for the most part have portrayed his secret identity as something that isn't so clear-cut. Each of its three aspects is true to a degree, and each reflects and informs who he is.

This consubstantiality makes him a richer, more layered, more realistic character than simply a hero in a mask. He's an individual struggling to reconcile the different sides of himself and to find balance between personal and social actualization.

It's the same strive for equilibrium that Jewish immigrants experienced, a constant tug-and-pull between their cultural heritage, individuality, and society at large. Young Jews, whether immigrants or children of, had to balance the old culture—social insulation, religious orthodoxy, and different language—with the challenges of the new—prejudice, harsh poverty, and a dynamic, pluralistic, secular urbanity—as well as their own private aspirations. They were people of two worlds, the home and the outside, often at odds with each other, trying to appease both. Superman's triple identity was their own—who they were, who they were expected to be, and who they wished to be.

Jewish identity, like all identities, is pliable, and the freedom in America to reinvent and self-define created uncertainty along with opportunity. Jews' unique heritage as religion, ethnicity and peoplehood was reexamined, for the first time in millennia in a substantial way, giving rise to new denominations of Judaism, like reform, conservative and modern orthodox, still predominant to the U.S. A Jew could be devout (*frum*), casually observant (*frei*), lapsed (*apikoros*), convert to gentilism (*mumar. Gevalt!*) or just pretend to be a gentile in public. Superman faced the same conflicts—Krypton and Earth, Smallville and Metropolis, legacy and autonomy, responsibility and fulfillment. He was a vehicle of self-expression for Siegel and Shuster to define, if not who they were, then who they wanted to be. His great promise was that Kal-El and Clark Kent reach homeostasis, and find success, in Superman. (In their original oeuvre, Krypton's only role was as the source of Superman's powers. His heritage was glaringly something he knew or cared little about. Its significance was developed in the postwar era, including by Siegel.)

That balance is delicate, threatened by two opposite but equally disruptive forces: rejection and acceptance. The former is symbolized by Kryptonite, Superman's famous Achilles' heel. It's radioactive debris of his exploded home planet that made their way to Earth as meteorites, and they're extremely harmful to his physiology. Even short exposure to a small fragment weakens him considerably, and prolonged contact would be lethal.

An incipient version appears in "The Reign of the Superman," but with reverse effect: Vagabond Bill Dunn is transformed into a Superman after ingesting a serum distilled from a meteorite. The familiar form first appeared in 1943 in the radio show,[35] but it didn't make its comic book debut until 1949's *Superman* #61 (where it's shiny red. It started glowing green in 1951's *Action Comics* #161).

It was conceived, however, in 1940, in an unpublished Siegel and Shuster story later titled "The K-Metal from Krypton." The official reason for its cancelation remains unknown, but it's likely due to the change it made to the status quo—aside from introducing "K-Metal," Superman discovers his alien origins for the first time and Lois discovers he's Clark Kent.[36] This version of Kryptonite bestowed superpowers on humans as it robbed Superman of his, a concept reintroduced by Siegel twenty years later in 1960's *Action Comics* #261 as X-Kryptonite, which empowers Earthly lifeforms (creating Streaky the Supercat), and in 1962's *Adventure Comics* #299 as Gold Kryptonite, a variant that removes Kryptonians' powers. Green Kryptonite was again given this ability in the *Smallville* TV series ('01–'11), used *ad nauseam* to empower each episode's villain.

Kryptonite is a baffling choice from a dramatic standpoint. The greatest threat to the world's mightiest hero—a man who can stop a speeding train and fly faster than a jet—isn't a similarly-powered villain or a giant monster or some doomsday machine. It's a rock. And yet it's proven popular with readers, who continue to follow a comic titled "Action" featuring a man fighting a mineral. It's a testament to the concept's resonance, a symbol fitting Superman's metaphorical framework.

It's no coincidence that Kryptonite first appeared as Superman learned of his origins, both in Siegel and Shuster's original concept and in *Superman* #61. It's literally a piece of his homeland, a deadly reminder of his true nature. Whether or not he feels himself human, Kryptonite is always there to remind him otherwise. If Superman represents wish fulfillment then Kryptonite is the harsh dose of reality.

Siegel pulled the name Krypton from the periodic table,[37] and while he likely picked it because it sounded exotic and was relatively obscure, it's derived from the Greek *kryptos*, meaning "hidden," the same derivation as Crypto-Jews, who, like Clark Kent, maintained their ancestral tradition in private while publicly pretending to follow another (Jews throughout history were coerced into following other religions, beginning with Hellenization, and many continued practicing their faith furtively. "Crypto-Jews" usually refers to either *Anusim*, late 11th-century German Jews, or *Marranos*, late 15th-century Iberian Jews, who as forced converts are also known as *Conversos*). Kryptonite is dangerous to Superman not just because it's lethal but because exposure means being exposed; it's a weakness all his own, one which singles him out. Brief contact is safe for humans but it pains him instantly and overwhelmingly, leading to numerous instances of Clark Kent almost being found out in its presence. It's the fear of failed assimilation, of rejection and alienation, given form. Kryptonite is weaponized Jewish anxiety.

The metaphor isn't limited to the fear of being ousted as Jews. Almost all youth, particularly transplants, most particularly children of immigrants, feel embarrassed by their parents. The social identity they assume among their peers is enfeebled, like Kent around Kryptonite, by a parent's accent or clothing. It can also be seen as the toxicity of bounden heritage to individuality, tradition as a cause of otherness. Ultimately, though, Kryptonite originates in the same place as Superman's powers. His heritage is simultaneously the source of his strength and of his weakness. It bespeaks to the ambivalence of American Jews who left the old world and ways behind only to find that they had followed them over. Their ethnicity and culture were a source of pride and strength, but also an impediment to acceptance and success.

The acceptance they sought also threatened to subsume their unique identity as Jews. Upholding their Judaism meant being marginalized, considered less American. Fully acculturating meant relinquishing their Jewishness. If Kryptonite exposed Clark Kent as Superman it would rob him of his human persona, leaving only the Kryptonian, but it's Kal-El that he would lose if he surrendered to the siren call of the *shiksa*, the gentile woman—Lois.

Superman and Lois Lane are the First Couple of comics, and together with Clark Kent, the first love triangle. If the Man of Steel is Jewish and the ace reporter is Catholic, as Maggin suggests (though her complete lack of religious expression in the comics implies she's lapsed and her skeptical, cynical nature make her a good candidate for atheist),[38] then their interstellar, interspecies romance is also one of interfaith.

Because Judaism is matrilineal, the religious and cultural pressure on men to marry within the faith is greater than on women, to ensure their children are Jewish. Intermarriage is seen by many as a rejection of Jewish lineage and practice and the biggest existential threat facing the Jewish people today. (It is, in truth, the leading cause of negative population growth among western Jews, approaching 50 percent of all Jewish marriages in the U.S. Of those, only a third raise their children Jewish. Some go so far as calling it "The Silent Holocaust."[39]) The assimilation wishes of yesteryear have become a fear of dissipation, but for Jewish-Americans, who like all people of hyphenated identities seek to fulfill both, the *shiksa* (or *shegetz* if male) holds "shiksappeal"; the allure of the new, the forbidden, the outsider to their community, and in a more discriminatory time a social mobility status symbol. Superman could find a more fitting match in any number of superheroines and aliens like himself (even Kryptonian, in more than one storyline), but Lois's difference from him, her humanity, is part of what draws him to her, and perhaps what he hopes to achieve through her.

The cost of their love was explored in 1980's *Superman II*, which saw the hero give up his powers so he could be with her. After Lois discovers his secret identity (ostensibly because he unconsciously let her) they fly to the Fortress, where the hologram of Lara, not Jor-El, awaits: he finally brought his girlfriend home to meet his mother. But Lois is a human, and he cannot be with her while still remaining Superman. He must choose. "You will become an ordinary man. You will feel like an ordinary man. You can be hurt like an ordinary man. Oh, my son, are you sure?" Lara implores him. "Mother," he answers defiantly, "I love her."[40]

In the director's cut of the film, featuring the original footage of Marlon Brando as Jor-El instead of Susannah York as Lara, a more deliberative exchange takes place. "Is this how you repay their gratitude, by abandoning the weak, the defenseless, the needful, for the sake of your selfish pursuits?" a disappointed Jor-El asks. His son replies, "Will there ever come a time when I've served enough? At least I get a chance for happiness." But Jor-El is unswayed. "Yours is a higher happiness, the fulfillment of your mission," he answers. "If you will not be Kal-El, if you will live as one of them, love their kind as one of them … you must become one of them."[41]

To be with a woman not of his people is to abandon his duty, the mission with which he's entrusted by virtue of being Krypton's last son. He would fully become Clark Kent, the assimilated costume, renouncing his true ethnic identity as Kal-El. Though he feels he's entitled to follow his heart, his parents, the older generation, see it as selfish waywardness. He's a chosen people of one, entrusted with a grave responsibility, and to shirk it is to betray his lineage. His dilemma is the quintessential Jewish guilt trip.

But he's in love, and faced with the choice between being Superman and being with Lois, he chooses the latter. It's the wrong choice, the story tells us, and he almost immediately regrets it. As the ordinary Clark he's powerless to stop Zod, Ursa and Non, the three Kryptonian criminals who escaped the Phantom Zone, from taking over the world. He comes to realize that there's not much to him without Superman, that his powers, his heritage, are part of what defines him (it helps that Lois falls out of love with him practically as soon as he stops being super).

He treks, like an atoning pilgrim, back to the Fortress, where in the theatrical cut of the film he regains his powers off-screen and without explanation just in time to defeat the villains, making it a rather confusing ending. The Donner cut, however, is much more satisfying, both in story and theme. "I've failed. I've failed you, I've failed myself, and all humanity. I've traded my birthright," he calls to his father for forgiveness. Jor-El of course does forgive him, as parents do, and restores his powers, and with them his legacy. He reaches out to reenergize his prodigal son like God in Michelangelo's *Creation of Adam*, likening Superman's transgression to Adam's original sin (while some Talmudic sages believe that Adam's temptation was punished in the form of mankind's mortality [Shabbat 55b], inherited original sin isn't part of Jewish doctrine, which holds instead that man is born pure and corrupted by his choices in life[42]) and the sacred duty he's entrusted with to the Jewish covenant with God.

Though Superman is able to restore his powers and reassume his duty, it's at the cost of his relationship with Lois. (He makes her forget about the whole thing with a "super kiss," a solution silly and disturbing in equal measure.) It's a poignant sacrifice for the greater good, and the moral of the tale; love cannot last if one must give up who they are for it. For Superman to relinquish his heritage is to no longer be Superman. For many Jews, the same holds for the abandonment of the responsibility concomitant with being Jewish, to ensure the survival of the people and culture, and a cautioning that to renounce it is to lose the spiritual and intellectual power it bestows.

Since the earliest days of Jewish immigration to the U.S. Jews wanted to fit in, to be Americans, for the first time in a hundred generations not be thought of first, and usually only, as Jews. The cultural fantasy, the image of success they aspired to, became the Jew who could pass for gentile, who partook in the Christian-dominated society unhindered, but who also stayed Jewish, honoring his tradition and practicing his faith.

In 1908, author and playwright Israel Zangwill's play about Jewish assimilation, *The Melting Pot*—which coined the phrase—described America as "God's Crucible, the great Melting-Pot where all races of Europe are melting and reforming.... God is making the American.... The real American has not arrived ... he will be the fusion of all races, perhaps the coming of superman."[43]

> *No man, for any considerable period, can wear one face to himself and another to the multitude, without finally getting bewildered as to which may be the true.*
>
>   —Nathaniel Hawthorne

The Galactic Golem

Adam, father of mankind in the Abrahamic religions, was a golem. The Hebrew word *golem* (גּוֹלֶם) originates in Psalms 139:16 as the adjective "galmi" (גָּלְמִי), meaning a formless, imperfect substance. It's likely a reference to Genesis 2:7, where "God formed man of dust from the ground, and breathed into his nostrils the breath of life; and man became a living being." The Talmudic exegesis of the passage describes Adam as a golem, whose gathered dust was "kneaded into a formless mass ... and his limbs were shaped" before he was brought to life (Sanhedrin 38b:4–5).

There are many tales in Jewish folklore of golems created by men, usually real historical figures, the first being 3rd-century Babylonian Rabbi Abba ben Joseph bar Ḥama (aka Rava), who formed a mute man from dust (Sanhedrin 65b:23–4). Then there are Rabbi Hanina and Rabbi Oshaia, who, curiously, created together a third-grown calf and ate it (Sanhedrin 65b:24–25). Other miracle-working rabbis and sages are said to have fashioned golems, but by far the most famous narrative is that of the Golem of Prague, created by the 16th-century Rabbi Judah Loew ben Bezalel (aka the Maharal). Like all folktales, there are several versions to the story of the golem created to defend the Jews of the Prague ghetto from pogroms, and in almost all, like in *Frankenstein*, the Promethean hubris of its creator proves deadly when his creation turns on him.[1]

(While the two tales share the central theme of creation rising upon its creator, the context is diametrically opposite; one is born of altruism, the other of egotism. *Frankenstein* relates to Superman in that, in the novel, the monster is anything but the mindless brute of film lore. Superhumanly intelligent and strong, he's a super-man himself. But while his life begins in a lab by his scientist "father" just as Kal-El is saved in a lab by his scientist father, he isn't sent away to safety but spurned by a fearful and selfish parent. He then isn't raised by loving strangers, he's shunned and persecuted by humans. And his appearance instills fear, not hope. His experiences lead him to become antisocial, a monster, rather than a hero. Thus, Superman is a reverse-Frankenstein's Monster. [Though Siegel and Shuster's first superman, Bill Dunn, a social victim experimented upon by an unscrupulous scientist, is analogues.])

As the tale goes, the Jews of Prague, already confined to the ghetto, were to be expelled or killed by order of Roman Emperor Rudolf II. Rabbi Loew fashioned the golem out of clay obtained from the banks of the Vltava River and vivified it using mystical incantations. The golem then became the protector of the Jews, fighting or frightening off marauders with his inhuman strength and invulnerability. When things go astray is where the story varies. In one version the golem is destroyed before he desecrates the Sabbath. In another he goes on a destructive rampage. In another he continues to grow uncontrollably. In at least one account the rabbi stops him at the cost of his own life. All of them end with the golem's body, either whole, as debris or as dust, stored in the attic of Prague's *Altneuschul* synagogue, where it lays waiting until he's needed again.

The golem bears several similarities to Superman, the obvious being his strength and invulnerability and his role as defender of the innocent. More subtle and more interesting is the source of his power. To animate the inert clay an invocation is used, either written on a scroll placed in his mouth, inscribed in an amulet hung around his neck, or etched into his forehead. The inscription is either a *shem*, an ineffable name of God (literally "name" in Hebrew) or, more commonly, *emet*, meaning "truth." (In the former, the golem is neutralized by removing the name. In the latter, the first letter of *emet* [אֱמֶת], *aleph* [א], is erased, creating the word *met* [מֵת], meaning dead. *Aleph* is the first letter of the Hebrew alphabet and itself a *shem* in Talmudic and Kabbalistic traditions, representing the oneness of God and God as the source and beginning of creation.[2]) Both fit the Superman mythos. His birth name "El" meaning god also makes it a *shem* and likewise denotes the celestial origin of his powers, and "truth," together with justice and the American way, is what inspires him to action.

The same rise in global Antisemitism in the early 20th century that led to the creation of Superman also inspired, or at least coincided with, a resurgence of the Golem figure in European culture. In 1915, German writer-director team Paul Wegener and the Jewish Henrik Galeen released the silent horror film *The Golem* (*The Monster of Fate* in the U.S.), followed in 1917 by *The Golem and the Dancing Girl* and in 1920 by the immensely successful *The Golem: How He Came into the World* (aka *The Golem*. The trilogy heavily inspired Universal Studios' 1931 *Frankenstein*, thematically and esthetically, to the point that the latter can be argued to be a blend of the golem legend and Shelley's novel). The same year, more than three centuries after Rabbi Loew, fellow Praguer Karel Čapek adapted the golem legend into his pioneering science fiction play, *R.U.R.* (*Rossum's Universal Robots*), coining the word "robot"[3] and introducing themes that have inspired countless narratives, like *I, Robot*, *Blade Runner*, *The Terminator* and *The Matrix*.

Building on the golem's popularity in the era and his relation to superheroes in particular, Chabon, among the first to make the connection, used him as a running thread in *Kavalier & Clay*. Josef Kavalier is a Prague Jew who manages to escape the Nazi-besieged city by hiding in the golem's coffin. He eventually arrives in New York, and together with his American cousin Sam Klayman (Clay), seeks work in what a classically trained Jewish artist could back then; comics. When a publisher asks them to create a new Superman, Joe first draws a strongman made of stone with four Hebrew letters etched into his forehead, explaining that he drew "the first thing I could think of that resembled…. To me, this Superman is … maybe … only an American Golem." To Joe it seems obvious that Superman, an indestructible, indefatigable defender of the oppressed is a golem, a "gesture of hope, offered against hope, in a time of desperation … one poor, dumb, powerful thing … exempt from the crushing

Superman: Man of Steel #82, August 1998. Written by Louise Simonson and illustrated by Jon Bogdanove. DC Comics.

strictures, from the ills, cruelties, and inevitable failures of the greater Creation."[4] They eventually invent a superhero named the Escapist, whose great success while being a publisher-owned property leads to years of frustration and heartache for them, making him a golem too—an artistic creation becoming independent of and eventually overpowering its creators, much like Superman did to Siegel and Shuster.

Superman has been compared to a golem within his own comics as well. In 1998's *Superman: Man of Steel* #82 he's time-tossed to World War II, where he defends the Warsaw Ghetto. Throughout, both Jews and Nazis recognize him as a golem, particularly two youths he rescues from a train headed to the death camps. "Thank you, Golem, for ***saving*** us!" the boys—odes to Siegel and Shuster—exclaim. "***We're*** the ones who ***invented*** you!"[5]

He's also fought several golems in his career, notably the Galactic Golem, a creature whose origin was borrowed wholesale from the folktale by Jewish writer Len Wein. First appearing in 1972's *Superman* #248, the Golem is assembled from "particles and pieces of galactic matter" from "the very birthplace of the universe" and brought to life by Lex Luthor using "galactic energy."[6] Like its namesake it eventually turns on its creator, and is similarly destroyed when the galaxy shape in its forehead is hit. It returned to plague Superman several more times, the latest being 2008's *Superman* #675.

Superman fought another golem, this one made of snow, in *DC Universe Holiday Special '09* #1, a short story anthology. In "Man of Snow," written by Arie Kaplan, the golem is unwittingly created by a superpowered Jewish boy on Chanukah.[7]

A clay golem with human appearance (which is how golems are described in the Talmud) also appears in the *Superboy* TV series, in the 1991 episode "The Golem."[8] When his neighborhood is plagued by a neo–Nazi gang, an elderly Jewish man uses his academic expertise in medieval mysticism to create a golem, vivified by the Hebrew word *chai* ("life" or "alive") carved into his chest. Immensely strong, bulletproof and mute but otherwise lifelike (especially when clothed in pleated chinos and a nice sweatshirt), the golem, like the original, gets out of hand, attacking the police and eventually his creator. A mysterious man bearing the same *chai* carving—presumably the storied golem, now human—tries to becalm him, but he ultimately chooses to destroy himself, parting with "shalom"; Hebrew for hello, goodbye, and peace.

Most noteworthy of these golems is Bizarro, one of Superman's most famous and enduring adversaries, who's a golem by any other name. In 1958's *Superboy* #68 a duplicator ray creates a simpleminded double of Superboy made of "non-living matter," with orthogonal, claylike features and chalk-white skin. Despite good intentions he's unruly and destructive, pacified only by a little blind girl who's unafraid of him—an idea taken from *The Golem* ('20) and later used in *Frankenstein*. Bizarro was reimagined in Superman's 1986 reboot as a flawed genetic clone created by Luthor, a gradually crumbling mute creature of instinct.[9]

Superman's parallel to the golem has been commented on in several books and articles. Fingeroth and Tye both briefly mention the golem. Andrae & Gordon discuss him at length, including as a precursor to Superman. Weinstein draws a similar parallel, as well as to other superheroes like the Hulk (convincingly) and Captain America (unconvincingly). Kaplan, who introduced a golem of his own to Superman's mythology, likewise points to shared themes, also noting them in other superheroes like the Hulk and Ragman. Curiously, none mention Wonder Woman, who, until her revised origin in 2011, was an actual golem, formed of clay and brought to life by the Greek gods, then sent on behalf of her people the Amazons to fight for peace and justice.[10]

According to Eisner, the golem legend underlies the superhero concept. "The Golem was very much the precursor of the super-hero in that in every society there's a need for mythological characters, wish fulfillment. And the wish fulfillment in the Jewish case of the hero would be someone who could protect us. This kind of storytelling seems to dominate in Jewish culture," he noted.[11]

Still, the wish for a mighty protector isn't unique to Jewish culture, even if perhaps it is more prevalent, and beyond Bizarro and the occasional golem foe, a direct influence on the creation of Superman would seem tenuous—except that Siegel did acknowledge the golem as an inspiration. He recalls in his memoir how, increasingly frustrated with rising Antisemitism, he was "very favorably impressed by a movie called the 'The Golem,' about an avenging being who used his awesome strength to crush a tyrant and save those who were being oppressed."[12]

Though Superman was influenced by the golem, the stronger parallel is to his role as a golem himself. Not textually but functionally, as a popular character. Like the story of the Golem of Prague, his story was created by his people at a time of great duress, shared far and wide with the larger world. He provided solace and raised awareness and empathy, an imaginary bodyguard sent to defend Jews from their assailants. And he, too, was fashioned into existence and given spirit through language and art, through writing and drawing instead of incanting and sculpting. Rather than a man of clay, he was a Man of Steel.

Siegel has described how Superman was his way of fighting the Nazis and helping his fellow Jews being persecuted, by giving the world a crusader of justice to inspire it. His Superman was a rallying cry, an anti-mimetic effort to influence public perception and policy. And it worked. Superman became, as editor Mort Weisinger called him, a Pied Piper. When he spoke, his readers, young and old, listened, and when he took action, they followed. He was a "war-time public relations expert," prompting scrap metal and wastepaper drives, war bonds sales and enlistment. As Tye writes, "He helped give America the backbone to wage war against the Nazis."[13]

All myths are reflective of their time and place, but Superman's was also performative, promoting the acceptance of immigrants and the imperative to oppose tyrants. He was a powerful symbol that effected real change, an edifying figure that, in whatever measure, truly bettered the world. (It can be similarly argued that he's since inspired generations of readers and viewers to be upright and selfless.) Superman wasn't just a fantasy, a wish. He was an incantation, a mythical creature created to save the Jewish people from annihilation, whose enemies were isolationism, nativism and Antisemitism.

This calling, never explicit, was eventually brought to the foreground in 1984's *Action Comics* #554, a tribute issue by Jewish industry veterans Marvin "Marv" Wolfman and Gil Kane. In an altered reality, human society is "devoid of resistance, the capability of violence, and the heroic concept," making it easy prey for alien conquerors. But two young, impractical dreamers from Cleveland, Jerry and Joey, imagine a hero with great strength and the power of flight to defend them. "Believe in **him!** He's our **only** hope!" They cry out to their fellow Earthmen. "We **need** someone like **Super Man!** He **must** exist!"[14] It's the boys' revival of mythic belief that eventually saves the world, creating a symbol that galvanizes people to unite and fight the invaders. In the hyperbolic, metaphoric world of comics, Jerry Siegel and Joey Shuster imagine their salvation into being. And from the perspective of Jews during World War II, the story is also a rebuke of pacifism and an argument for the need to sometimes use force.

Chabon's protagonists aren't based exclusively on Siegel and Shuster, but his choice to name one Clay in a novel heavily involving the golem denotes the creator as golem himself, molded by historical forces and animated by wishes, conscious and unconsciousness, in reaction to them. It also implies the role of the creator in effecting change through the creation: for what is a golem if not the power of art, manifest? The protection Superman awarded Jews by promoting social and political agendas urgently necessary for their survival at a time of grave danger is, ultimately, an act of heroism by his creators.

During the 1920s and 1930s, concurrent to the golem's resurgence in the zeitgeist, the preponderance of the American public and congress opposed involvement in Europe's conflicts. Isolationist pressure groups held great sway, particularly with German, Italian and Irish Americans, chief among them being the America First Committee. After famously spending his 1940 campaign promising that American boys would not be sent to foreign wars, Roosevelt also encountered fierce resistance in congress against selling arms to Britain, even as late as March 1941, when it was nearly bankrupt and the Axis forces had conquered much of Europe.[15] It did not at all seem likely that the U.S. would join the fight against Hitler, who was poised for victory.

Roosevelt, the man Jews had almost unanimously supported, proved apathetic to their plight. He refused to condemn Nazism when Hitler came to power, and later continually rebuffed pleadings from the Jewish Agency (led by David Ben-Gurion, future first prime minister of Israel) as well as his own War Refugee Board to bombard the railways leading to Auschwitz, despite knowing what transpired there through intelligence reports, choosing to stay silent on the matter. Reasons cited were that resources could not be spared from the war effort; that bombing the tracks or the death camp might prove ineffective; that any action to save Jews would validate the Nazi propaganda that it was a "Jewish war." Ultimately, the answer given was, "it would not warrant the use of our resources."[16]

While Jews were being relocated, incarcerated, starved, shot, gassed, experimented on, buried in mass graves and burned in ovens, the U.S. continued its strict immigration policy of the Johnson-Reed Act. Jewish refugee quotas were minimal, and even of that only a pittance got through thanks to the machinations of Breckinridge Long and his mandarins. Of the few visas granted, some entailed a waiting list of several years, rendering them death warrants. Ostensibly, it was out of fear of antagonizing Germany as well as jobless Americans still on the tail end of the Depression. Ultimately, though, the general public simply didn't want them in. A 1938 poll found that 86 percent of Americans opposed raising immigration quotas, while 67 percent wanted them reduced as much as possible. American Jews were noted as the exception, with 82 percent supporting raising quotas and actively encouraging refugees to come. Even a bill that would have admitted children above the regular quotas, introduced in Congress in the summer of 1939, after *Kristallnacht*, received no support from Roosevelt and failed to pass in committee. A Gallup poll at the time showed that 66 percent of Americans opposed taking in as few as 10,000 Jewish children.[17]

The public's antipathy toward Jews was bolstered on one end by the rise of Antisemitic organizations like the KKK, Bund and America First, personages like Father Coughlin, Charles Lindbergh and Henry Ford and publications like *Social Justice*, *Dearborn Independent* and *Mein Kampf*, and on the other end by the press, which by and large toned down or altogether ignored the ongoing Holocaust.[18] Infuriated and panicked, the Jewish community was desperate to reach their fellow Americans, to awaken them to the danger Hitler posed and the need to stop him. They needed an ambassador, a golem to defend their interests. Superman would be that vanguard, with the rest of the superheroes at his flank.

Longtime *New Yorker* film critic Richard Brody observes that "superhero and comic-book movies are so often fascinatingly and intricately political … it's worth paying attention to them and taking them seriously." (For example, 2014's *Captain America: The Winter Soldier* revolves around a clandestine mass surveillance and preemptive interception program by covert intelligence agency S.H.I.E.L.D., released a year after but written two years before Edward Snowden's exposure of the NSA's PRISM global surveillance program.) This holds even truer to the comics they're based on, a medium that more directly and unencumbered reflects the creators' philosophies. The vehemence of Golden Age Superheroes to take on the Swastika paralleled that one of group, American Jews. Superman kicked Nazi butt because Siegel and Shuster wanted to but couldn't. "Using comic book heroes for propaganda [i]s an honorable tradition," Frank Miller, one of comics' most celebrated creators (*The Dark Knight Returns, Sin City, 300*), told the *BBC*. "That's one of the things they're there for."[19] Beginning with Superman, they were conceived as a response to National Socialism's collectivism and hatemongering—empowered individuals caring for the innocent.

With the slew of anti–Nazi films by their cohorts in Hollywood putting wind at their backs, Jewish creators unleashed their superheroes on the Nazis, soundly defeating and humiliating the vaunted master race. The enemy combatants Superman faced progressively looked more like Nazis, until they were Nazis. And while most movie serials and animation films, many commissioned by the U.S. military, focused on the Pacific theater and the Japanese enemy, comics, despite their popularity, were mostly left to their own devices, thus free to focus on the European front and the German threat.

Like their landsmen out west, Jews making comics were *schlockmeisters*, purveyors of frivolity. But, while 60 percent of Americans disliked Jews almost 50 percent read their comics, and so instead of wringing their hands they typed and drew, using their platform to promote their cause. In his forward to Fingeroth's *Disguised as Clark Kent*, Stan Lee reflects that "Nothing could have been more natural than for our own Captain America to try to rally the nation against the Nazis, the worst enemies that the Jewish people ... ever had." Kirby, who already had experience lampooning Hitler in political cartoons, co-created the greatest Nazi-smasher of them all as "a way to help the war effort.... I was saying what was on my mind." While the press was downplaying Jewish suffering, the cover of *Captain America Comics* #46 (April '45) showed tagged inmates marched at gunpoint to giant ovens, human bones sticking out the ashes.[20]

Superhero comics were their four-color manifestos, agitprop for internationalism, rearmament, intervention and the New Deal. But they also knew they'd be more effective if they weren't seen as promoting narrow Jewish interests. As author and distinguished professor of English at the University of Houston David Mikics explains, "America's war effort depended on Americans not thinking that they were fighting, even in part, on behalf of European Jews. Indeed, in 1943 a substantial number of Americans still blamed the Jews for the war, just as Hitler did."[21]

Jews were portrayed as warmongers pushing the U.S. into a conflict not its own, and creators wishing to use their characters to convince the public otherwise had to be careful. They didn't collude to promote a secret agenda and manipulate public opinion. These were teens and men in their twenties, with a readership of mostly teens and children. It was a natural, grassroots reaction to the world, stories that, even when simply setting out to be fun, echoed their thoughts and emotions.

Still, their comics weren't anodyne. They pilloried Hitler and his followers relentlessly, and it didn't go unnoticed. In May 1940, Sterling North, literary editor of the *Chicago Daily News* (and later author of *Rascal*) called comics' support for interventionism and the New Deal "cheap political propaganda ... to be found on almost every page."[22] While the SS fumed against Superman in *Das Schwarze Korps*,

Mussolini barred outright all foreign comic strips and magazines from Italy, with the exception of Mickey Mouse, whom his children loved and so was allowed to remain, renamed *Topo Lino*, until he too was eventually banned in 1942 (Mussolini even barred the use of word balloons in Italian comics, considering them too modern and Anglo-Saxon, allowing only captions).[23] The Bund also took them seriously enough to send their creators and publishers death threats. But nevertheless, they persisted.

The *vox populi* wouldn't change until Pearl Harbor, but by then they had the pulpits they needed to rally support for their cause. Their efforts at propagandizing proved so successful that their comics coined popular epithets like "ratzi" and "Japanazi."[24] And beyond inspiring readers of age to enlist with gusto, their superheroes were good U.S. bonds salesmen, both through ads in the comics and the stories themselves, helping finance the war effort and thereby making an actual difference in the fight.

Superman bashed Bavarians and kiboshed Krauts with a mix of solemn consecration, righteous anger and cathartic glee. It was politicking through punching, a perfect reduction of the argument over entering the war to simplistic, binary—though by no means false—choices: to oppose the great evil, or to not. Siegel and Shuster, like most American Jews, understood what noninterventionists failed or refused to; that some things simply cannot be resolved through diplomacy. Sometimes the use of force is necessary and right.

But Superman used force to protect the weak, not oppress them. He was the counterargument to the Nazi ideology of natural struggle and dominance through strength. He was a hero with big muscles and an even bigger heart, just like America. He epitomized American largesse, as much part of the American ethos as fair play and upward mobility, repeatedly contextualized in his comics as British rearmament, New Deal welfare and refugee asylum. And when America finally followed him into battle, Superman changed from rabble-rouser to role model, from fighting the deficiencies of the American way to fighting fascism in its name. He became, and has stayed, the national hero, a symbol of American might and virtue. As propaganda goes, Little Boy and Fat Man were no match for Superman.

Siegel and Shuster created Superman in their image. He represented them in fiction, to enact what they couldn't, to fight bullies small and large. When hundreds of American jeeps, trucks, tanks, landing craft and planes bore his likeness or insignia and soldiers brought his comics with them on D-Day,[25] Siegel and Shuster got their wish. Their golem was right there on the frontlines, fighting Nazis.

But convincing Americans to fight was only half the equation. The other was immigration reform. The goal of American Antisemites was twofold: to keep the U.S. out of the war in Europe and to keep the Jews of Europe out of the U.S. Superman stood for exactly the opposite. "Given the nature of the U.S., it was only natural in the 1930s for our new hero to be the ultimate immigrant," Brian Singer, Jewish director of *Superman Returns*, said in an interview.[26] But the U.S. was failing to live up to its promise, at least for Jews. Americans needed reminding that America is a nation of immigrants, ultimately strengthened by taking in the weak. Superman's sensational abilities come from his alien heritage, serving as a constant reminder of the value of pluralism, and his origin story, a refugee from doomed Krypton taken in by the Kents as their own and instilled with the values and purpose of a hero, is a perfect allegory for the needy foreigner turning into the generous American. Superman is a promise to the American people that their hospitality will pay off with dividends.

His secret identity is an extension of the metaphor. Kal-El, the heritage of the immigrant, and Clark Kent, the mores of his adoptive culture, combine to create Superman, the most powerful being. And one who means well, even when he disguises himself as a "normal" American. It makes him equally a promise to immigrants: that coming to America is safe, that they will be taken in and taken care of, that they will be empowered, that they will make a difference.

Action Comics #40 and *Superman* #12, both published in September 1941, mark the beginning of Superman's covers serving openly as war propaganda, continuing until *Action Comics* #86 and *More Fun Comics* #104, both July 1945 (notably, two months after Germany's defeat but still two months away from Japan's surrender and the official end of the war). In those four years the Man of Tomorrow battled, terrified and mocked all manner of Nazi forces and called on Americans to take action and support the war effort.

When Superman rode an aerial torpedo toward its target on the cover of *Superman* #18 (September '42), it was not just an act of solidarity with America's forces but also a Freudian expression of masculine aggression and of naughty children waving their *schmeckles* in derision.

World's Finest Comics, a series Superman shared with Batman and Robin, depicts the trio similarly striding the canon barrels of a U.S. destroyer in issue #7 (September '42). On the cover of #8 they sell war bonds and stamps to kids, to "sink the Japanazis." They sell them again in #9 and in #11 they plant a victory garden. In #13 they call to fight paper waste to help the shortage, somewhat ironic considering the medium.

In the metatextual cover of *Action Comics* #58 (March '43) Superman prints propaganda posters of himself, in which he declares that "You can slap a Jap with war bonds and stamps!" He sells 7th War Loan bonds as Superboy in *More Fun Comics* #104, and in *Action Comics* #86 he buries Hirohito under a massive mound of the same bonds, announcing that "it isn't **Superman** who's doing this—it's the American people!"

So effective was he in soliciting bonds and stamps that the U.S. government recruited him to sell them in newspapers. His wide appeal allowed it to reach strategic demographics in publications like the *Los Angeles Japanese Daily News* (aka *Rafu Shimpo*).[27]

Superman was an emissary of his creators, a golem for their cause, a reimagined Moses exhorting Americans to save the Israelites from the pharaoh of the east, to let his people come. How successful he was, how much of a difference he ultimately made, is impossible to say. But to whatever extent that he did, it was a true job for Superman.

> *If I am not for myself, then who will be for me? And if I am only for myself, what am I? And if not now, when?*
>
> —Hillel the Elder

The Brave and the Bold

Superman vs. Übermensch

Superman has been compared to the Übermensch virtually from the start, at least as early as 1941, when the *New Republic* and *Saturday Evening Post* both discussed the connection. (Even though the demeaning *Post* article claimed that Nietzschean philosophy was "a concept neither Siegel nor Shuster could ever understand.")[1]

Catholic World published in 1943 a scathing critique of Superman, accusing him of being the Nazi Übermensch as well as a pagan false god. In 1954, then-famous child psychiatrist Fredric Wertham attributed Superman's origins to the Nazi ideal in his book *Seduction of the Innocent*, a notorious calumniation of comic books, asking, "How did Nietzsche get into the nursery?"[2]

While the attitude toward Superman's connection to the Übermensch has softened with time, it continues to be commented on in books and articles. In *The Comic Book History of Comics*, Van Lente and Dunlavey theorize that the original Bill Dunn Superman was heavily influenced by the Übermensch, while in *From Krakow to Krypton* Kaplan states it as fact, at least insomuch as the name.[3]

Saturday Night Live lampooned the parallel in a skit shortly after the release of *Superman*, "What If Superman grew up in Germany instead of America?" starring Dan Aykroyd as Überman, who, disguised as Klaus Kent, mild-mannered clerk for the Nazi ministry of propaganda, fights for "untruth, injustice, and the Nazi way."[4]

Though there's no evidence to support it—Siegel never mentions Nietzsche in any interview or in his memoir—the influence is more than likely, since the name would have inescapably carried the connotation then. Whether Siegel co-opted the idea or just the name, whether sincerely or ironically, the Man of Tomorrow is connected to the superior man of the future.

The name "Superman" first appeared in 1903, thirty years before "Reign of the Superman," in George Bernard Shaw's play *Man and Superman*, his translation of "Übermensch," more literally meaning over-man, a term popularized (but not coined) by German philosopher Friedrich Wilhelm Nietzsche (1844–1900) in his book *Thus Spoke Zarathustra: A Book for All and None*. It refers to the transcendent man, one who's surpassed humanity by rejecting the illusory morality dictated by a fictional God (famously, "God is dead") and thus free and empowered to create his own values, limited only by his will.

Superman certainly symbolizes power and superiority (or superiority through power), corresponding to the Nietzschean ideal. It's particularly evident in his early days, when he'd take the law into his own hands, dispensing his own brand of justice under no authority other than his unchallenged might. With indestructible machismo, he did what needed to be done without hesitation. (This in part is the secret to his success; he's super self-confident. A man who not only has the might to do the right thing but is assured about what the right thing is. Over the years writers, artists and actors have struggled to balance the portrayal of someone so alluringly comfortable in his own skin and so clear of purpose with his more humanizing, relatable dimensions as a man perpetually grappling with his identity and place in the world. He's at his best when he manages to strike both chords, which is partly why he's such a challenging character.) He was a fighting reformist who took on social and political orders both domestic and foreign, embodying an effort to transcend the limitations of old to something new and better. In this sense he was a true embodiment of Nietzsche's concept.

Superman was a man-god in place of the dead God, the epic hero reinvented bigger, stronger, faster—the American way. It's easy to see him as a fascist; by definition Superman is above man, and possessing "powers and abilities far beyond those of mortal men" is a central conceit of the fascist. That he enforces his will through superior might and violence, however well-intentioned, and even with the majority approving, is still the very essence of fascism. But to truly examine the claim that Superman is Nietzsche's Übermensch in tights, the original concept must be properly understood.

A pioneer of existentialism and postmodernism, Nietzsche's revolutionary and controversial ideas have arguably had a greater influence on 20th-century thought than any other thinker save Einstein. In several of his works (*Beyond Good and Evil, On the Genealogy of Morality*) he introduced the concept of *ressentiment*, the weak's resentment of the powerful. Those who are powerless and disenfranchised—whether by circumstances of birth or want of character—are subjugated and exploited by the powerful—those whose nature or will are superior—whom they inevitably resent. And so the oppressed have created "slave morality," a perversion of natural law; what in nature is good for the animal is a social evil and what is bad, good. Strength, triumph and dominance are portrayed as sinfulness, cruelty and oppression, while weakness is seen as a virtue, recast as humility and peacefulness. The superior beast of prey is thus subdued by the inferior lambs, convinced that its innate power is evil and deceived into relinquishing it.

These "moral prejudices" that have corrupted humanity were first introduced by Judaism. Nietzsche writes, "The Jews brought about that miracle of a reversal of values, thanks to which life on earth received a new and dangerous attraction ... with them begins the *slaves' revolt in morality*." It was Judaism that introduced to the world a single masterful God, the Ten Commandments and the Bible, and in them the false sanctity of life, freedom and justice, and a delusional dedication to the spiritual over the material. It begat a social revolution that has universalized the lowliness of the slaves and enslaved the masters. Its humanism—fairness, compassion and worst of all, selflessness—is a perversion of nature, as is the modern democracy that it spawned. Its promise of liberty and equality is a lie, a triumph of the *ressentiment* of the rabble and a "voluntary degeneration and stunting of mankind."[5]

It's important to note that Nietzsche meant this as an observation of origination, not an Antisemitic polemic, almost equally disavowing the Christian morality that followed. He held Judaism in contempt but not Jews, in fact speaking out openly against Antisemitism.[6]

His statement that "God is dead," a rebuff of religion and its moral dogmas, means that man no longer needs to depend on a value system dictated by others, whatever authority they claim to have or speak in the name of. The "Will to Power" is man's ascension to entirely subjective morality, dictated only by his own ambition and potency.[7] The embodiment of this idea is the Übermensch, whose superior will unshackles him from the false virtues of restraint and compassion to pursue his desires and fulfill his true potential for greatness. With God dead, man can and should take his place.

Nietzsche's views are doubtlessly harsh, but his nihilism is philosophical, not political. The Übermensch is superior and ruthless but not a fascist, since the self is the only purpose. Any authoritarianism, whether nationalist, racist or religious, subsumes individual will. Ideologies are cowardly escapes from the austerity of truth, degenerate preoccupations that distract from the real necessities of the world.

And yet, the concept of the Übermensch was one of the central tenets of Nazi doctrine, usurped and perverted in an intellectually spurious but politically successful enterprise to the extent that to this day the two are synonymous in the public's mind. The superman was espoused by Hitler to great propagandistic effect, equating him with the Aryan "master race." Nietzsche's morally transcendent being was reduced to a specimen of eugenics, his nihilistic philosophy replaced with National Socialism, and the call to leave humanity behind turned into the pretext to subjugate it.

Hitler also appropriated Nietzsche's views on the corrupting morals of Judaism, with two fundamental differences: he attributed them to race, not belief system, thus creating the *untermenschen*—under-men—for the Nazi Übermenschen to destroy as an imperative and, paradoxically, qualified Judaism's depravity as a calculated plot against mankind. He saw himself as the heroic savior of the world, or rather the superior races of the world, from the cancerous effect of Judeo-Christian morality (though he was careful not to challenge the church too overtly). "Conscience is a Jewish invention," he stated. "It is a blemish." To him, "The struggle for world domination is between me and the Jews."[8]

And so, to compare Superman and the Übermensch both the Nietzschean and the Nazi should be considered. To Nietzsche, the Man of Steel would have been heretical to the very idea of the Übermensch. They're philosophical opposites, the Übermensch being the ultimate individualist while Superman seeks nothing more than to be a public servant. The Overman is Freudian id made king while Superman is super-ego, dedicated not only to upholding but to enforcing existing morals and laws. He's the mightiest predator indoctrinated into servitude by the lesser masses. His nobility is really degeneracy, craven rather than heroic, a misguided devotion to the stunted ambitions of the "last men," who seek only the false happiness of peace, security and comfort.[9]

Nowhere is Superman more an antithesis to the Übermensch than in the seminal

1986 miniseries *The Dark Knight Returns*, where he's sent to stop an insurgent Batman by a corrupt president, feeling it's his duty to obey. Ironically, it's Batman who embodies Nietzsche's ideal in the story: a self-made hero who's risen to the level of superpowered demigods by sheer force of will, unstoppably determined, unencumbered by prevailing laws and norms and self-appointed arbiter of justice.

Lex Luthor is also something of an Übermensch. His origin has fluctuated between impoverished, middle-classed and wealthy, depending on the version of the character, but in all he's achieved power and influence through immense intellect and ruthless cunning, and he eschews the laws of man to suit his needs, whether openly or in secret. What prevents him from truly personifying the ideal is his obsessive hatred of Superman, born of jealousy of his unearned power and public adulation, what he himself aspires to but could never achieve to the same degree.[10] Ultimately, he's motivated by *ressentiment*.

Superman has been reimagined as a despot in countless alternate-reality stories, several based on or referencing the Übermensch (distinction between the two versions of the concept is rarely made). In the latest, 2015's *The Multiversity: Mastermen* #1, Kal-L lands in the Sudetenland in 1939, is raised by Hitler to become the Overman and leads the Nazis to world conquest.[11] But these counterfactuals only serve to demonstrate just how far removed the character is from Nietzsche's model.

As for the Nazi Übermensch, he is exactly what Superman was created to oppose. Siegel and Shuster, two unassuming Jewish teenagers, managed to subvert the idea of "superman" so successfully that, once universally associated with Nazism, it's come to almost exclusively evoke their hero, depriving Hitler of his ideological figurehead. From a German symbol of self-serving, atheist ideals, the superman became an American icon of altruistic, Judeo-Christian values, a rejection of the fascist call to rule over the weak in favor of the democratic belief in the innate value of human beings. Even the first version in "The Reign of the Superman" is a rebuke of the Übermensch; his power is ephemeral, his concerns petty, his character weak. All too late, he realizes that he isn't heroic, he's pitiful.

Seeing Superman as a fascist is a superficial reading. He's a dominant power, but the will he enforces isn't his own. It's the will of the people, as expressed through laws and norms. While he started off as a lawbreaker and a partisan activist, the fantasy he enacted wasn't fascistic. He showed restraint and compassion, strong-arming true abusers of power in defense of those they preyed upon. When in the real world democracy was failing to oppose fascism, in fiction Superman was strong enough to do so in its name.

His use of violence is a venial sin, considering it's always restrained—he never kills, maims or employs it beyond what is necessary to stop an aggressor—and it's always in service of protecting life, freedom and property. In this regard, he's no more a fascist than any agent of law enforcement. (Granted, he's self-appointed and acts extrajudicially, but he operates with the knowledge and blessing of the institutions of law and government, even being deputized by the mayor of Metropolis.[12])

He's an egalitarian hero, whereas the Übermensch is a social Darwinist. For the Übermensch there is no higher law than his own, no higher authority than himself. Superman is an abdication of self, a life spent in service of a higher ideal, like a biblical herald. He holds himself accountable to the same laws that govern every-one and to a deontological, objective morality that applies equally to all. "There was a right and a wrong in the Universe and that distinction was not very difficult to make," he muses in Maggin's novel, *Miracle Monday*, meaning not that the distinc-tion is always clear but that the choice is.[13] "Truth, Justice and the American Way" are values he represents that are external to himself, a contradiction to the Übermensch's egocentrism.

Superman seeks to also serve as an indirect force for good, by inspiring others to follow the same ideals. His morality isn't a mark of exceptionalism; it's a call to unity. "They can be a great people, Kal-El. They wish to be. They only lack the light to show the way," Jor-El tells him in *Superman*, then again in *Man of Steel*: "You will give the people an ideal to strive towards. They will race behind you, they will stumble, they will fall. But in time, they will join you in the sun. In time, you will help them accom-plish wonders."[14] As a rescuer and protector, Superman defends the status quo. As a beacon, he improves it. Nietzsche meant his Übermensch to be an aspirational figure as well—a continuous process of overcoming and becoming rather than a finite state of being—but he isn't a call to all like Superman is. He appeals only to the few with a will strong enough to transcend the rest.

The Übermensch is man aspiring to godhood; Superman is a god aspiring to humanity. Nietzsche would have held Clark Kent in the greatest contempt. His super-humanism, his unwavering faith in humanity, is perhaps an opposite response to the same dehumanizing, abstracting forces of the era that gave birth to the Übermensch. While Nietzsche saw his philosophy as a new form of enlightenment, Superman was a reaffirmation of foundational values and man's place in the world. The Übermensch is Gilgamesh, a man greater than man on a quest of personal glory and supremacy. Superman is Moses, or any biblical champion for that matter, whose heroism is mea-sured by goodwill, by his humble dedication and sacrifice for his community. It's a concept of valor and nobility rooted in a view of humanity as a collective, and theo-logically as part of a grand cosmology, mutually exclusive from Nietzsche's solipsis-tic nihilism.

The Nazi version is especially a man of brutal competition and complete lack of compunction, limited solely by the extent of his might. Superman, more powerful than the *Herrenvolk*—"master race"—could ever be, is a man of brotherly love, whose power only manifested thanks to the compassion of the strangers who found him. He's Siegel and Shuster's rebuttal to Hitler. The Übermensch is might makes right, Superman is right makes might.

Superman understands full well, from his own catastrophic experience, the value of collectivism. That Jor-El was a superior man, the only scientist on Krypton willing to challenge dogma and recognize the truth of their impending doom, was enough only to save his son, but not his race, loved ones or himself (though Nietzsche might argue that it was the democratic science council that doomed them, a view shared by the failed coupist General Zod). True power, Superman knows, lies not in the hands of the part but the whole, which is why he doesn't assume a more proactive position of leadership on Earth.

Superhero comics are inherently philosophical fiction, and Superman, as the first and most powerful, constantly wrestles with ethical dilemmas, first and foremost of power and responsibility. Not simply of using his power for the greater good and the price that incurs, but the conflict between his moral obligation to help others and his right to enforce justice. The same dilemma the U.S. faces as the world's greatest superpower.

Despite repeated temptation, Superman virtually never overreaches. He acts within the scope of the socially acceptable, limiting himself almost exclusively to emergency work. He saves bridges from collapsing but he doesn't help build them. He rescues innocents from disasters but he doesn't intervene in wars (since World War II). It's a measure of relativism that conflicts with his seemingly absolutist morality, one which Nietzsche would likely have argued is corrupt. Avoiding actions with far-reaching geopolitical consequences like toppling oppressive regimes or feeding the world's poor while apprehending bank robbers and saving cats from trees is an evasion of his true responsibility and a stance of moral cowardice.

As a fictional character, Superman can't be made to face the complex issues of the real world without the fantasy falling apart. Realism is his true Kryptonite. He would simply become entangled in too many consequences, from financial markets to governments to religious institutions. Siegel and Shuster realized this from the start, pitting him in 1940 against Hitler and Stalin in a safely isolated "imaginary" story in *Look* magazine.

Within the comics, the slippery slope to fascism is the theodicy usually used to explain why he doesn't operate on a larger scale. In 1997's *JLA* (Justice League of America) #4, for example, he fights Protex, the leader of an alien race invading Earth, white Martians who, seeing themselves superior to green Martians, had enslaved and exterminated them. Protex asks him, "How **stupid** are you? You let those human sheep do what they want when **you** could rule the world! Stunted slaves! They look at **you** and see what they **could** have become.... You know in your heart they're inferior!" To which Superman's answer is simple. "They **believe** in me. And in my heart I believe in them." After he and his fellow superheroes had won the day, they stop to reflect on their role as world saviors. Wonder Woman asks, "Are we doing too much or too little? When does **intervention** become **domination?**" "Humankind has to be allowed to climb to its **own** destiny," Superman replies, resolutely. "We can't **carry** them there." Flash then asks, "Why should they need **us** at all?" Superman's answer, again, is simple. "To catch them if they **fall**."[15]

Underlying any story is the question of who should wield power.—Arthur Miller

Phone Booth, Voting Booth, Confession Booth

Superman's Religion and Politics

In the beginning, Superman was a political figure. He was a progressive liberal, a New Dealer, reformist, interventionist, pro-labor and pro-immigration. A propaganda golem. But this was a short period in his lifespan. He quickly became an icon and a paradigm, understood to represent the ideal man and the perfect American, and both liberals and conservatives have been staking a claim to him since.[1]

An expression of his creators' psyche and culture, he inevitably also reflected their politics. These are intertwined in America: Jewish-Americans form the most politically-aligned demographic in the U.S. While the core of American conservatism is closely associated with Bible Belt Protestantism, American Jews are overwhelmingly liberal, averaging over 70 percent Democrat voters in the past 26 elections, markedly more than any other demographic except black Americans and with the highest voter turnout of any ethnic group.[2] In examining Superman and the superhero concept as a Jewish creation, this decided partisan affiliation becomes relevant. Is the Man of Steel inherently political, and if so, what are his politics?

Broadly, modern American political philosophy extends between two polarities: liberalism, a collectivistic approach viewing universalized rights and government involvement as most conducive to the common good, and conservativism, an individualistic viewpoint of personal rights and autonomy free of government infringement as the greater good. Superheroes, who volunteer their time and abilities for their community without official sanction, arguably personify both. It's a seeming contradiction, equally Karl Marx—"From each according to his ability, to each according to his need"—and Ayn Rand—"The question isn't who is going to let me; it's who is going to stop me"—Great Man in the service of Great Society.[3]

On one hand, super-heroism is an inherently liberal act. Dedicating and risking one's life to help others, on an ongoing basis, and for no reward other than the belief that, as Spider-Man's motto perfectly sums up, "with great power comes great responsibility," is a concept of social obligation at the expense of the self. The genre is inherently egalitarian, as the exceptional abilities superheroes possess are almost always a result of blind fate, usually a mishap involving a radioactive something or other. Their strength of character is often the x-factor that wins the day, but it's only because they were given the opportunity to bring it to bear that it does. Essentially, the premise is that, given the chance, we can all achieve greatness.

On the other hand, superheroes are conservative in nature. They exemplify rugged individualism, the personal responsibility to act wisely and morally, and are almost always more powerful and effective than external authority in the form of law enforcement. They're clear advocates of the right to bear arms, be it guns, Batarangs or power rings, as well as the right to privacy and anonymity behind a secret identity. And considering they spend most of their time and effort beating supervillains into submission and jailing them, it stands to reason they believe in a tough approach to crime.

The very idea of vigilantism suggests state or police ineptitude, whether by lack of resources, corruption or simply the inability to act decisively and with timeliness, necessitating the individual to wrest the law into their own hands in order to defend themselves or others. The superhero brand of vigilantism involves doing so regularly and systemically, indicating a fundamental mistrust of legislative, judicial and executive capacity. This worldview of government that, whether by motive or means, cannot be entrusted with the best interest of the citizenry is essentially libertarian, giving primacy to individual judgment. Ultimately, the question of whether superheroes represent more social cohesion or personal agency depends largely on whether their actions are considered to be within their rights or their moral duty.

Superman is, of course, nonpartisan. Saving people, averting disaster and upholding the law are no more party-specific than an EMT or police officer doing their job. His background is open to interpretation, a man raised by churchgoing folk on a small farm in the Midwest who's a crusading journalist for a large metropolitan newspaper in the Northeast. There are, however, elements to his character that can be interpreted as liberal. He gives almost all his time and effort to others, he clearly believes in intervening on behalf of others' wellbeing, and he knows firsthand that man isn't God's sole creation in the universe, nor the only one created in his image.

His greatest enemies are Luthor, an industrialist tycoon, and Zod, an army general. Luthor's modern version in particular is a corporate plutocrat with military contracts and government clout who uses his power to further his own ends on the back of others—an archetype traditionally vilified by the left, making Superman by contrast a liberal. The Big Blue Boy Scout also won't kill under any circumstances, making it safe to assume he's opposed to capital punishment (with one very notable exception in canon: in 1988's *Superman* Vol. 2 #22 he faces alternate versions of Kryptonian criminals Zod, Quex-Ul and Zaora from a "pocket dimension," where they've annihilated all life on Earth. He ultimately makes the decision to execute them using their version of Kryptonite, harmless to him, a decision that haunts him for years to follow[4]), and it's hard to imagine him taking a conservative stance on immigration considering he's an illegal alien himself.

The press pegged him as a leftist early on, even past his Roosevelt years. "Superman is a Liberal," the *New Republic* declared in the title of a 1947 article. His radio show tackled a host of social issues, they reported, primarily interracial tolerance, earning praises from the National Conference of Christians and Jews and the Calvin

Newspaper Service, a black newspaper chain, and denunciations from the KKK and the America First Party (an unaffiliated successor to the Committee).[5]

But he can just as easily be seen as a conservative. He's the ultimate defender of the status quo, more traditionalist than reformist. He seeks to preserve social order, avoiding actions that would upset the balance of things like pressing coal into diamonds for the poor, flying crates of food to the starving, building houses for the homeless or carving riverbeds into arid regions. Nor does he proactively seek to alleviate social ills and human rights violations, leaving them to the responsibility of mankind. While unmistakably a progressive liberal in his early years, over time, particularly during the 1950s and 1960s, he became a symbol of conformity and authority, making him perhaps a neocon.

He's also changed his stance on interventionism since World War II. Once a fervent supporter, he now refrains from interceding in global politics. It's the rare story that pits him against a foreign government, toppling a dictator or destroying a terrorist organization (and those instances usually involve fictional countries like Qurac or Bialya). But seeing as U.S. foreign policy has historically been more a matter of administration than party line, it could place him on either side of the aisle.

His credo, "Truth, Justice and the American way," is likewise multivalent. Truth and justice are universal values, and all political philosophies, including totalitarian ones, lay claim to them. "The American way" is a little less broadly interpretable. A nationalistic ethos, it's something of an anachronism, for better or worse, and to many uncomfortably ethnocentric, which is why it's largely been omitted in recent years. (In *Superman Returns* it's "Truth, Justice ... all that stuff."[6]) From this perspective, Superman can be viewed as a champion of American exceptionalism, a belief typically associated with the conservative right. Still, "the American way" presumably refers to the inalienable rights of life, liberty and the pursuit of happiness, freedoms equally espoused by the liberal left.

Like the country he represents, Superman is a combination, sometimes a contradiction, of attitudes and actions. After all, if he stands for the red, white and blue, then he stands for both the red and the blue.

Textually, the evidence is clear until the Eisenhower era. Early Superman stories have a clear bent, beginning with Bill Dunn, a commoner taken advantage of by the rich Smalley. Smalley believes the misfortune of the poor is deserved, that "if they had the slightest ambition at all they could easily lift themselves from their terrible rut."[7] It's a view of personal accountability as the determiner of success, traditionally a conservative attitude, in contrast with the liberal belief that it mainly owes to socioeconomic circumstances, and in the context of the story, the perspective of a villain.

The Man of Tomorrow, in addition to being an unequivocal New Dealer, was also not a proponent of the Second Amendment. In 1940's *Superman* #6—when gun control was becoming a hot-button issue following FDR's Federal Firearms Act of 1938—he crumples a gangster's Tommy Gun, announcing that he'd like "to do this to every weapon in the world!" What he did support was welfare programs, including government housing in 1939's *Action Comics* #8 and, thirteen years later in issue #187, healthcare, in a one-page PSA calling on people to "hop on the welfare wagon."[8]

He eventually stopped supporting specific policies, though politics have remained present. He's answered the call of almost all American presidents during his time—including Roosevelt, Truman, Kennedy, Johnson, Nixon, Carter, Reagan, Clinton, Bush, Obama and even Washington and Lincoln, through time travel—and in a 1991 story taking place in a possible near future even becomes president himself, though his party affiliation is never revealed and his campaign rhetoric is carefully nonspecific. Perhaps a clue can be gleaned from a parallel dimension version of him from Earth-23, introduced in 2009, who's a black U.S. president modeled after Barack Obama.[9]

In 2011's *Action Comics* #900 Superman renounced his U.S. citizenship. Feeling it necessary to disassociate himself from American policy so that he could better serve the world, he tells a stunned U.S. national security advisor, "'Truth, justice and the **American** way'—it's not **enough** anymore." Unsurprisingly, the move sparked controversy, receiving national media attention, including a diatribe in the *Wall Street Journal* titled "How Liberalism Became Kryptonite for Superman." Written by conservative industry veterans Chuck Dixon and Paul Rivoche, it called the story "the most dramatic example of modern comics' descent into political correctness, moral ambiguity and leftist ideology" and accused the industry of being overwhelmingly liberal and discriminatory against conservative professionals.[10]

While the accusations of biased hiring practices and lopsided storytelling merit serious attention, which they don't seem to have received, the arguments made in the op-ed only serve to undermine its premise. Dixon and Rivoche extol the Comics Code Authority, a defunct regulatory organization created in the 1950s, as a protective entity, when in fact it was a Big Brother censorial body that infantilized comics for decades. They also falsely equate "classic" Superman's moral clarity with conservative values, conveniently ignoring his origins as a New Dealer. The point, however, was rendered moot seven months later when Superman was rebooted as part of DC's "New 52" line-wide relaunch, making the story uncanonical and quickly forgotten.

The question of whether Clark Kent votes Democrat, Republican or something else remains unanswerable, and for obvious reasons will likely remain so. Even Lois doesn't know. In the 2008 miniseries *DC Universe: Decisions*, Lois, at that point already his wife and confidant, states that she's "proudly for a strong military, small government, low taxes and maximum individual freedom," pegging her as a conservative, but Clark squarely refuses to disclose his vote, believing in "the time-honored tradition of the secret ballot."[11]

In contrast to Superman's political leanings, which started out fairly explicit and have attenuated over time, expressions of religiosity have increased over the years. He was raised in Kansas, part of the American Bible Belt by most definitions, where religion is part and parcel of small-town life. Demographically, he's likely to be a Protestant or Methodist, perhaps a nondenominational evangelical, but, with a population of about 0.6 percent of the state, all but certain not Jewish.[12]

Elliot Maggin and Mark Millar both agree that Clark was raised Methodist, though Maggin makes a distinction to Superman, who he believes "adheres to a kind of interplanetary-oriented Kryptonian-based belief system centered on monotheistic philosophy.... I think he prays by rote, and constantly, the way some of us talk to ourselves in the shower." It's a somewhat opaque description of the hero's belief system (and a contrast to Maggin's later claim that Superman's Jewishness is "so self-evident that it may as well be canon"),[13] and it's unclear if an extraterrestrial could even be considered a member of the Christian or Jewish faiths.

Themes and signifiers aside, there's of course no evidence in any of the comics, novels, films, TV or radio series to support the notion that Superman is Jewish. On the contrary. During the 1970s, known as the Bronze Age of comics, Krypton was made into a heliolatrous society. They worshipped a pantheon of gods lorded over by the sun god Rao, the personification of Krypton's red giant sun (or red dwarf in some accounts) of the same name. There's nothing to suggest that Superman practiced his ancestral religion, though he did exclaim "Great Rao!" with frequency in those days, and in 1978's *Action Comics* #484, a 40th anniversary issue, the Golden Age Superman—now considered a separate character in the parallel dimension of Earth-Two—marries Lois Lane, first as Clark Kent in a church ceremony and then as Superman in a Raoist service.[14] The 1986 reboot returned Krypton to the science-based culture it began as, relegating Raosim to its distant past. (Though the 2018 *Krypton* TV show made it a theocracy.)

The *Superman* film, striving for naturalism, incorporated more of the Kents' religious life. They're clearly wearing their Sunday best, en route to or from church, when they discover baby Kal-El's ship, and Martha is quick to make the connection. "All these years," she says to Jonathan, "how I've prayed and prayed the good Lord to see fit to give us a child." Later, when Jonathan dies, they bury him in their churchyard. In fact, Puzo's script describes them as "Christian folk whose morals are as basic as the soil they till," along with an unused explanation that Clark was named after Martha's uncle, a church sexton.[15]

In Maggin's 1978 novel *Superman: Last Son of Krypton* (a promotional tie-in to the movie but set apart) it's revealed that Jor-El had actually sent a probe to Earth ahead of his son, to find the world's most developed mind, choosing none other than Albert Einstein. Evocative of the Annunciation, Einstein is recruited by the voice of Jor-El to watch over his son, but he humbly declines. Calculating that the rocket ship will land in Smallville, he helps make sure the Kryptonian baby is given a good home by orchestrating for the Kents to find him.[16] It's an interesting twist to the story, mostly for the alternative it imagines; Superman might have grown up in a Jewish home in Princeton, New Jersey.

The 1988 miniseries *World of Smallville* provides further insight into the role of religion in Clark Kent's upbringing. Its title logo is Smallville's skyline, a steepled church prominently at the heart of town. The first issue's opening image is of Superman soaring above it. The series also reveals that Pa Kent comes from a Puritan heritage. There is, interestingly, one Jewish character in Smallville, the general store owner, Mr. Schwartz.[17]

In the few instances Superman's religion has been explicitly shown or discussed, all in more recent years, he's been portrayed, unsurprisingly, as a Christian. In 1996's *Superman: The Wedding Album*, a standalone issue in which Lois and Clark marry, the wedding is held at the nondenominational Metropolis Chapel of United Faiths (with Jerry Siegel officiating as "Chaplain Herbert"). And when Clark Kent is mistaken for dead in the *Superman: The Animated Series* episode "The Late. Mr. Kent," his funeral service is held by a nondescript priest.[18]

He's sought counsel from clergy as both Clark and Superman, first in *Superman for All Seasons* #1, where he pays a visit to Pastor Lindquist, a Protestant minister, at his family church. In the "For Tomorrow" storyline in *Superman* Vol. 2 #204–15 he visits a Catholic priest named Father Daniel Leone several times, including for a confessional, which indicates either Catholic faith, an ecumenical approach to his Christianity or a general regard for religious authority figures. Father Leone also appears in *Man of Steel*, this time as a Smallville priest Clark consults about revealing himself to the world, and again in *Batman v Superman*, leading Clark's funeral service.[19]

The question of Superman's denomination was resolved canonically in *Action Comics* #848–850. He was raised Methodist, attending church regularly in his childhood with his mother, while his father, not much of a churchgoer, raised him on Protestant values. He eventually eschewed organized religion in favor of putting his faith in "the best that humanity has to offer."[20]

In *Superman* Vol. 4 #41, an unsubtle allegory about religious dogma, Superman is innocuously agnostic. When asked if he believes in God, he answers, "I've seen too much not to believe in '**something.**' But this is the **important** part … 'something' **isn't** everything." (The point also being, presumably, that man is judged by his actions, not beliefs.)[21]

He still, of course, celebrates Christmas. In 1946's *Action Comics* #93 he helps a group of war-traumatized Russian children get in the holiday spirit by decorating a large Christmas tree with radium to make it glow in the dark (likely giving them all cancer). In *Superman* Vol. 2 #165, a Christmas issue, he delivers gifts to his Justice League colleagues and takes Lois on holiday to the bottle city of Kandor. And, in the *Justice League* cartoon series episode "Comfort and Joy," he invites the Martian Manhunter to celebrate Christmas with his family in Smallville.[22]

Superman has even met Saint Nicholas himself on several occasions, a tradition of particularly whimsical escapades. In 1940's *Superman's Christmas Adventure* Santa Claus isn't just real, but the one responsible for manufacturing all Superman merchandise, which the Man of Steel helps deliver. In 1947's *Action Comics* #105 Superman helps Santa again, this time by putting him through a rigorous exercise routine to shed all the weight he'd gained overindulging on candy so he can fit back down chimneys. They meet again in 1984's *DC Comics Presents* #67, where Saint Nick finally returns the favor by helping Superman defeat, appropriately enough, the Toyman.[23]

The world Superman inhabits even has evidence for the existence of Jesus. The Spear of Destiny, the lance that pierced the side of Christ, is an artifact of great mystical power that fell into the hands of Hitler during World War II, allowing him to ward off any superheroes from Fortress Europe. First appearing in 1977's *Weird War Tales* #50, it was used to explain retroactively why the Golden Age Superman never defeated the Nazis. Superman later used the Spear to confront the Spectre, the embodiment of God's wrath, in 1994's *Spectre* Vol. 3 #22.[24] The existence of the Spear and its power indicates the existence of Jesus, though it remains unclear whether he's meant to be *the* divine son. In a world filled with men and women who fly, travel between dimensions and manipulate matter with their mind, the divinity of angels

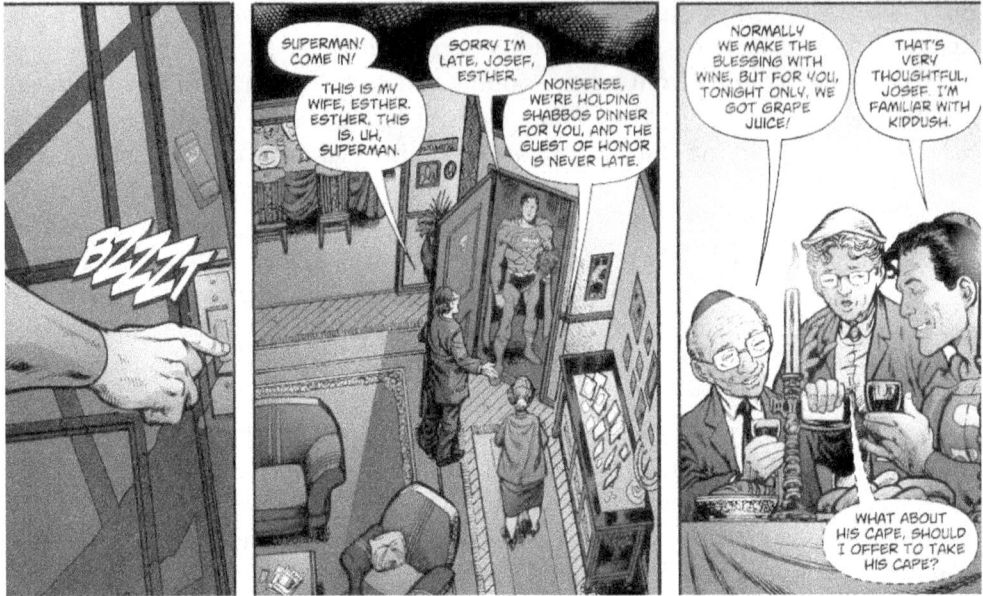

Action Comics #835, March 2006. Written by Gail Simone and illustrated by John Byrne. DC Comics.

and demons and figures like Jesus or even God himself could be questioned, perhaps no more than an ancient understanding of superhumans. Superman himself has been mistaken for a deity and worshipped in several instances.

Whatever else, 2006's *Action Comics* #835 makes clear that Superman isn't Jewish. When he's invited to Shabbat dinner by *Daily Planet* staffer Josef Schuman, an observant Jew (and perhaps a nod to Joseph Shuster), he attends wearing a yarmulke, also noting, "I'm familiar with Kiddush" (blessing over wine). But it's a duck out of water scenario; it's inherently comical to see the world's mightiest superhero sit down to eat kugels, especially with a stereotypical *yiddishe mama* shoveling more onto his plate. The scene is even more amusing because he makes quite a few gaffes in the span of two pages, entirely unintentional on the part of the writer, it seems, and unnoticed by anyone on the editorial team. To start, he rings the Schumans' doorbell, an electric device, on the Sabbath. Adding insult to injury, he brings them a bouquet of flowers, which are prohibited for religious Jews because of the labor involved in moving and putting them in water. And after dinner he kisses Josef's wife Esther goodbye on the cheek, which, depending on their level of orthodoxy, might be seen as inappropriate, though she doesn't seem to mind.[25] With such blatant lack of familiarity with Jewish religious customs, it's safe to say that Superman doesn't come from a kosher household.

I don't intend to show anything. I have no intentions.—Jorge Luis Borges

PART IV

Postwar to Postmodern
Redefining Superman, Comics and Judaism

Superman vs. the Mad Scientist

The Postwar Era

While by no means a consensus, comic book scholars generally divide comic book history into five epochs. The first, and largely overlooked as merely a prelude, is the Platinum Age, 1897–1938, beginning with *The Yellow Kid in McFadden's Flats*, a reprint of the famous strip in book format, and ending with *Comics on Parade #1*, an anthology featuring Tarzan, Li'l Abner and others. Following is the Golden Age, launching with Superman's rocket ship in 1938's *Action Comics* #1 and brought to an end by the censorious Comics Code Authority in 1954. The Silver Age began in 1956, when DC's *Showcase* #4 introduced the new Flash and revitalized the superhero genre, and ended in 1970 with *Green Lantern/Green Arrow* #76, which instigated a trend of socially conscious realism in superhero comics and begat the Bronze Age. It lasted until *Crisis on Infinite Earths*, a 12-issue series published in 1985–'86 that expunged and restarted DC's canonicity. Eschewing metallurgical hierarchy, the next era is known as the Modern Age, extending from 1986 to date, beginning with the brooding, deconstructionist sagas *Watchmen* and *The Dark Knight Returns*.

Though considered part of the Golden Age, and at the onset commercially thriving, the postwar era of 1945 to 1956 is more of an interregnum, sometimes called the Atomic Age but better described as the Witch Hunts Age or, as author and Columbia University Graduate School of Journalism professor David Hajdu suggests, the Comic Book Scare, paralleling the anticommunist Red Scare of the period.[1] The era saw further evolution of the medium, introducing new genres and seminal writers, artists, stories, characters and themes, but its later years are hallmarked by ostracism and persecution, all too familiar to the Jews that still populated it in the main.

After the war superheroes fizzled. With the Axis vanquished they lacked purpose, champions without a cause. The popularity they enjoyed fighting for Uncle Sam became awkward jingoism, first in the peacetime nation-building, then in the 1950–1953 Korean War. Americans were dying in droves again, but with a far less clear moral and national imperative. And there was the looming possibility of nuclear warfare with the Soviets.

"Mass popular interest dwindled sharply after 1945, and superhero titles disappeared to be replaced by genre books that tripled the overall sales of the comics business between 1945 and 1954," Grant Morrison writes in *Supergods*.[2] The superhero genre may have been moribund but the medium flourished in the postwar prosperity, expanding into new or newly popular territory like horror, comedy, science fiction, crime noir, jungle adventure, war stories, funny animals, Westerns and similarly non-spandexed genres.

Most successful by a margin was teen romance, a genre introduced to comics by Simon and Kirby in 1947's *Young Romance*, a runaway hit selling over one million copies. It quickly grew to 99 different series,[3] whose soap opera melodrama captivated adolescent readers in a way superheroes couldn't hope to.

America loved comics more than ever before. Writing for *Scientific American* in 1944, Dr. William Moulton Marston—former chairman of the psychology department at American University, professor at Columbia and Tufts, co-inventor of the early polygraph and, most importantly, co-creator of Wonder Woman—estimated that 18 million comics sold on newsstands every month, each read by four or five people, reaching a total of 70 to 90 million readers, about half of which were adults. These were just the magazines: Out of 2,300 daily newspapers in the U.S. only two didn't publish comic strips, the *New York Times* and the *Christian Science Monitor*. The Sunday newspapers collectively published a staggering 2.5 billion copies of strips.[4]

By 1947, one in three periodicals sold in the U.S. was a comic book. By 1949, monthly sales ballooned from 18 to 60 million. In his book *The Ten-Cent Plague: The Great Comic Book Scare and How It Changed America*, Hajdu writes that "the comic book was the most popular form of entertainment in America … reaching more people than movies, television, radio, or magazines for adults. By 1952, more than twenty publishers were producing nearly 650 comics titles per month, employing well over a thousand artists, writers, editors, letterers, and others."[5] These were the halcyon days, and while they were a twilight for superheroes, they also mark a maturation of the medium, which can and should tell different types of stories for different audiences, and serve as testament to its wide appeal.

As for the superhero genre, it was kept alive almost exclusively by Superman, Superboy, Batman and Robin, and to a lesser extent Wonder Woman. Out of the hundreds if not thousands of characters created in the 1930s and 1940s, these are the only ones to appear continuously to this day. Living up to his moniker, the Man of Tomorrow in particular did well. If in 1942 his series sold over 1.5 million copies, in 1946 he sold 3 million and was still syndicated in newspapers. The Supermen of America Club, which had a membership of 250,000 in 1941, reached 1.3 million in 1946.[6] 1949's spinoff, *Superboy*, was the first new superhero comic to succeed postwar. Superman's popularity was largely the result of his expansion into other media. His radio show continued until 1951 and the George Reeves television show, running from 1952 to 1958, elevated the character from a household name to an American icon.

At the same time, his comics seemed to have run out of stories to tell. On the cover of *Superman* #41 (July '46) the Action Ace can be found sitting, frustrated, in front of an empty art board of his own comic. With no more Nazis to fight he was left with somewhat lesser challenges, like the one announced on the cover of issue #61: "*Does Superman prefer Lois Lane as a blonde, brunette or red-head? See inside!*"[7] Having spent the war years swatting bombers and tearing battleships asunder, between 1946 and 1950 he turned his attention, together with Batman and Robin in *World's Finest Comics*, to sports. The covers feature them playing baseball (#15), rock climbing (#16), rickshaw racing (#17), doing a tightrope walk (#18), tug-o'-war (#19), basketball (#21), grip strength test (#23), speedbag boxing (#24), tennis (#25), unicycling (#26), powerlifting (#27), boxing (#28), racing (#29), juggling (#33), boxcar racing (#34), surfing (#36), logrolling (#38), fishing (#43) and roller-skating (#47), as well as other recreational activities like collecting autographs (of each other, #22) and making fun of Robin's weight (#20).

What eventually helped restore his cultural relevancy and keep Super-mania going was the purported arrival of real aliens on Earth. 1947's famous UFO crash-landing in Roswell, New Mexico, ignited the collective imagination, reaching a fever pitch in the 1950s with films like *The Day the Earth Stood Still* ('51), *The War of the Worlds* ('56), *Invasion of the Body Snatchers* ('56) and dozens of others. It provided Superman with exciting story fodder to compete with the new fads and adversaries worthy of his abilities. Even gritty, urban vigilante Batman started chasing around little green men.

Who was seen as irrelevant were Siegel and Shuster, at least in the eyes of Don-enfeld and Liebowitz. Their relationship had been contentious almost from the start, particularly between Siegel and Liebowitz. In December 1938, five months after *Action Comics* #1 debuted and when DC's owners realized they had a hit on their hands, Liebowitz wrote to Siegel to remind him "that we own the feature 'Superman' and that we can at any time replace you."[8]

Siegel and Shuster's ten-year contract guaranteed, in exchange for exclusivity, $500 for each thirteen-page story in the comics (adj. $8700), 50 percent of the net profits from the strip and 5 percent from movies, toys and other merchandise. As a work-for-hire agreement it was generous, magnanimous even, but as the share of the property's creators it was pittance. According to Siegel, in June 1941 Liebowitz informed them that DC had actually been losing money in overhead, and therefore they weren't entitled to any royalties. This is where unfairness turned into fraudulence. DC earned $1.5 million ($25.5 million) that year, as reported in the *Saturday Evening Post* (the same also indicates the duo were in fact being paid royalties, to whatever extent).[9]

The relationship curdled as Superman's success grew. Siegel's plots and Shuster's art were increasingly scrutinized, they were forbidden to give any interviews relating to Superman (ostensibly because the disgruntled Siegel was badmouthing DC to the press) and they were reminded of their expendability. When Siegel was drafted in July 1943, DC wrested production of the Superman strip from his and Shuster's studio in Cleveland to their in-house staff, refusing to return it upon his discharge.[10]

The *casus belli*, however, was Superboy. The first pitch for the character—an expansion of the brand with a younger, more lighthearted version targeted at younger readers—was originally made by Siegel in November 1938. DC turned it down, as well as a second pitch two years later. The 1942 *Post* article mentions that Siegel and Shuster were in the throes of developing a new *Superboy* strip together, but this too was rejected.[11] It wasn't until the appeal of kid superheroes had been demonstrated by the success of Robin, the Boy Wonder ('40), Captain America's sidekick Bucky ('41) and the Boy Commandos ('42) that DC reversed course, and in January 1945 debuted a Superboy feature in *More Fun Comics* #101. The problem was that they did so without Siegel's knowledge or consent.

Though he received writing credit, Siegel was livid. Making things worse, Shuster had supplied the art, negotiating a raise for himself in the process, and didn't tell Siegel either. Despite having collaborated with other artists to create new characters (Spectre with Bernard Baily in 1940, Star-Spangled Kid with Hal Sherman in 1941 and Robotman with Leo Nowak in 1942), Siegel saw it as a betrayal, conditioning their continued partnership on a formal written contract when he returned from service.[12]

Both regretted signing away their brainchild, one of the most popular, and lucrative, properties in American entertainment. As they saw it—especially Siegel, always the more committed of the two—Superboy was a separate character, and DC had stolen it from them outright. In April 1947 they sued, seeking $5 million in arrears and the ownership rights. The claim was that, since they'd developed Superman on their own, it didn't fall under their work-for-hire agreement, and what DC had bought for $130 back in 1938 were the rights to the first story but not the intellectual property. The lawsuit also accused the rest of company's superheroes of being plagiaries.[13]

Donenfeld and Liebowitz counterclaimed that the duo signed the original contract fully aware of the implications (which the *Post* interview seems to confirm); that the contract language was straightforward ("I hereby sell and transfer such work and strip, all good will attached thereto and exclusive right to the use of the characters and story, continuity and title of strip contained therein, to you and your assigns to have and hold forever and to be your exclusive property … to give you exclusive right to use and acknowledge that you own said characters or story and the use thereof, exclusively"); that they had been churlish ingrates, particularly Siegel, when their rate was 40 percent higher than anyone else DC employed and they'd been paid to date over $400,000 ($6 million); and that Superman's success owed more to his owners' business acumen than his creators' talent.[14]

After a year of litigation the court granted Siegel and Shuster ownership of Superboy, but not Superman. With little recourse, they accepted DC's offer of $94,000 ($1 million) for the character, which also included the surrender of any claim to either character in perpetuity. Like all ugly divorces most of the money was spent on lawyer fees, leaving them with about $29,000 to split between them.[15] After the dust had settled, they'd lost their creation, their byline as the creators, and their job. They would no longer have anything to do with Superman.

Afterward, science fiction editor and literary agent Mort Weisinger became the guiding force behind Superman. Siegel had been the one to recommend him to editorial director Whitney Ellsworth in 1941, having known him both from his days as a subscriber to Weisinger's *The Time Traveler*, the first nationally distributed fanzine, and as a contributor of fan fiction to his own *Science Fiction*. This didn't prevent Weisinger, by most accounts a bumptious character, from habitually talking down to Siegel and Shuster.[16]

Siegel's duties were handed to writers like *Superman* strip veteran Alvin Schwartz and Don Cameron, who'd ghosted for Siegel during the war and was the one who wrote Superboy's first appearance. Shuster was replaced principally with Wayne Boring, a longtime artist from his workshop, along with Al Plastino and Curt

Swan. Boring redefined the Man of Steel's look for the 1950s, giving him a thick-set, barrel-chested body and an oblong face with a high hairline and pronounced eyebrows. His storytelling was cleaner and more skilled than Shuster's, but not as energetic.

Siegel and Shuster were despondent. Siegel reportedly sent letters to DC's competitors announcing he'd commit suicide by leaping off the Grand Central Palace Building dressed like Superman. It drew a small crowd to the time and place he named, but he never showed.[17]

Siegel went on to serve as art director for Ziff-Davis's Approved Comics, a small line of books like *Cinderella Love*, *Kid Cowboy*, *Wild Boy of the Congo* and, most famous, *G.I. Joe*, though it didn't last long. He then wrote for publishers like Charlton Comics in the mid–1950s, where he co-created duds like Nature Boy and Mr. Muscles. He also wrote newspaper strips, co-creating *Ken Winston* for General Features and writing *Tallulah* and *Buck Rogers* for the John F. Dille Company. It was all freelance, part-time, short-run work. By 1959 he was facing eviction from his one-bedroom apartment in Long Island and couldn't afford milk or diapers for his baby daughter Laura. He found himself pleading to DC for work, which he got, writing Superman as a freelancer, at 20 percent his previous pay, uncredited.[18]

Shuster fared worse. Secretly, he took on a job providing erotic fetish art for an under-the-counter S&M magazine titled *Nights of Horror*, mostly drawing scenes of flagellation featuring lookalikes of Superman, Lois Lane, Lex Luthor and Jimmy Olsen. When he was no longer able to draw due to his advancing blindness, he became a janitor. He had given form to mankind's greatest aspirations and was now reduced to its squalor. He moved in with his invalid mother in Queens, later sharing a ramshackle apartment with his brother. When janitorial work became too arduous for the middle-aged man he became a delivery boy, delivering messages to, among other places, DC's office building.[19]

There's relatively little Jewish signification to Siegel or Shuster's postwar work, or to Superman at that time (despite still having two Jewish handlers, Weisinger and Schwartz). A big exception to this, however, was their next joint creation, Funnyman.

, They were still known as the creators of the world's most popular superhero, which allowed them to sell Magazine Enterprises on their new surefire hit. *Funnyman* #1 debuted in January 1948, a screwball comedy in the tradition of the Three Stooges and the Marx Brothers and a deconstructionist character only ten years into the construction of the genre, and years ahead of similar efforts.

A crime-fighting clown, Funnyman's alter ego was Larry Davis, a skinny red-headed comedian clearly based on Jewish comedian Danny Kaye. Eschewing the subtle metaphor of Superman, Funnyman was all but explicitly Jewish, using Yiddishkeit humor and shticks straight out of the Borscht Belt and speaking with an immigrant, urban inflection, like "Looky wot I got fer ya! Free fer nuttin'!" In issue #4, the time-traveling hero incurs the wrath of the wizard Schmerlin—"sch" being a Yiddish prefix of derision now in common American usage—who tricks King Artery by seemingly turning water into blood, the same as Pharaoh's false magicians in Exodus 7:22. Issue #5 introduces the villain Noodnik Nogoodnik, Yiddish-English for "pestering malcontent." The series ended with issue #6.[20]

Despite Shuster's art having evolved considerably and Siegel's vigorous pacing and dialogue, *Funnyman* didn't strike a chord with audiences. Perhaps its ethnic flavor was too strong, but more likely because it simply wasn't that funny. It was Siegel and Shuster's last collaboration, though according to Tye also their most joyous.[21]

Horror comics had been around almost as long as superheroes, but the early 1950s, with their postwar cynicism and rock & roll revolutionism, brought with them a cultural obsession with prurience. Even books like *1984* and *The Catcher in the Rye* were reissued as pulp paperbacks with salacious covers. *Catcher*'s read, "This unusual book may shock you," showing Holden Caulfield walking past a row of strip clubs and a man soliciting a prostitute. It sold 1.25 million copies in 1953 alone.[22]

EC Comics, founded as Educational Comics in 1944 by Max Gaines as a publisher of series like *Picture Stories from the Bible* marketed at schools and churches, became Entertaining Comics in 1950 when his son Bill inherited it, and began publishing series like *The Haunt of Fear, The Vault of Horror, The Crypt of Terror* (later renamed *Tales from the Crypt*), *Crime SuspenStories* and *Weird Science.*

Other publishers put out titles like *Horror from the Tomb, Tomb of Terror, Witchcraft, Adventures into Terror, This Magazine Is Haunted, Journey into Mystery* (which years later would introduce and be retitled *Thor*), *Weird Fantasy, Weird Adventures, Weird Horrors, Weird Chills, Weird Mysteries, Weird Terror, Ghostly Weird Stories* and quite a few other *Weird*s. Even *Captain America* became *Captain America's Weird Tales.*

By the end of 1952 nearly one in three comics were horror/macabre, making for about 200 monthly titles on newsstands. Though often cautionary tales, most stories were grisly, featuring vicious versions of the usual gunsels along with homicidal housewives, serial killers, witches, werewolves, vampires, ghosts and other malefic monstrosities. Many were also saturated with salaciousness to a degree that, for a predominantly children and teens' medium in the 1950s, bordered on pornography. It was *Grand Guignol*, shock schlock, epitomized by the jolting cover of *Crime Suspen-Stories* #22; a man with a bloody axe holding his wife's severed head by the hair, her body splayed on the floor, her eyes rolled back and blood dripping out her mouth.[23] Ironically, horror comics, particularly EC's, also contained the best art and storytelling of the period.

The thriving of the horror genre was perhaps a response to a post–world war, post-genocide world. Americans had woken up to an uglier, meaner, scarier world. The television industry dealt with it through its famously saccharine period, with shows like *Leave It to Beaver, Father Knows Best* and *The Donna Reed Show*, rejecting reality in favor of idealized, sterile depictions. But in film America explored its fears in a deluge of horror pictures, from Hitchcock's psychological thrillers to the more grotesque "creature features" like *The Thing from Another World* ('51), *Creature from the Black Lagoon* ('54) and the perfectly-titled *Them!* ('54).

It's this latter subgenre that comics took to, then took to its extreme. Though still more popular than film, they were perceived as trivial enough to operate under the cultural radar. They displayed man's inhumanity to man in a bacchanalia of torture and murder that included human experimentation, decapitations, dismemberments, live burnings and anything else the writers' perverse imaginations could conjure, none of it equaling the actual atrocities of the Nazis.

The horrors of the camps shocked international opinion when they were uncovered to their full extent after the war. Jews were horrorstruck to learn that six million of their brethren had been murdered, and by the images of piles of corpses in mass graves and the emaciated, lice-ridden survivors. Their shock and outrage fueled their work and worldview; Freud theorized the death drive (Thanatos); Elie Wiesel wrote the *Night, Dawn*, and *Day* trilogy; Theodor Adorno famously disavowed all poetry after Auschwitz as barbaric; and the Jews of the comic book industry spoke the unspeakable, as loudly and angrily as they could.

DC, cautious about its more public image from early on, published relatively innocuous titles like *House of Mystery*, macabre moralistic tales without the gruesomeness. With Superman, whatever PTSD his writers wished to work out would manifest as metaphor and euphemism. There could be no murder and mayhem in the comics of the world's favorite hero. Instead, he increasingly faced adversaries like Bizarro, a havoc-wreaking clone, Braniac, an alien who shrinks and bottles entire cities, and Mr. Mxyzptlk, a fifth-dimensional imp who warps reality—menaces not just to his physical wellbeing but to the safety and stability of everyday life, of society, community, family and personal identity.

There was one enemy, however, who would prove to be more dangerous, the first to ever defeat the Man of Steel. He was a mad scientist, but what made him different from the scores that came before was that he was real.

Dr. Fredric Wertham (Friedrich Ignatz Wertheimer) was a German Jew who immigrated to the U.S. following World War I. A distinguished psychiatrist specializing in forensic psychiatry, he served as the Chief Resident Psychiatrist at Johns Hopkins University's Phipps Clinic in Baltimore from 1922 to 1934, then as the senior psychiatrist for the New York Department of hospitals. He was a professor of clinical psychiatry at NYU, the director of Bellevue's Mental Hygiene Clinic and the head of the new psychiatric clinic of the Court of General Sessions (later renamed the State Supreme Court), responsible for the evaluation of every convicted felon in New York. He was a prolific author of textbooks and articles in peer-reviewed journals, a recipient of prestigious fellowships and an expert witness in high-profile trials.[24]

He was also a social crusader of true conviction. In Baltimore he treated black patients when no other psychiatrist would and testified on their behalf in court, which only few of his colleagues did. In 1946, instead of opening a lucrative private practice, he founded the Lafargue Clinic in Harlem, the first to provide low-cost mental health care mostly to people of color. Much of his practice was devoted to diagnosing and treating children considered juvenile delinquents. A champion of desegregation, his testimony was important, perhaps instrumental, in the 1954 Supreme Court case *Brown v. Board of Education*.[25]

What would make him the bane of the comic book industry was that, though a progressive, Wertham was also a priggish, starched personality, who fancied himself a cultural critic as well as moral authority and used his expertise to lend credence to his personal opinions. He disliked anything born of mass culture, including film and television, but his strongest disdain was reserved for comic books.

He wasn't the first critic of comics by any means. As early as 1908, librarians warned against the strips' "poor drawings, worse colors and bad morals." Even further back, in 1846 famed British poet William Wordsworth wrote a poem lamenting the advent of illustrated texts. Various accusations against comic books popped up in education journals, homemaking magazines and church sermons since before Superman debuted. But these were largely ignored, the usual clucking of tongues at anything new. The first notable detractor was Sterling North, Literary Editor of the *Chicago Daily News*. In a May 1940 op-ed titled "A National Disgrace" (later reprinted in *Childhood Education*) he dubbed all comics "a poisonous mushroom growth" and "graphic insanity," the bulk of which "depend for their appeal upon mayhem, murder, torture and abduction." They were "a strain on young eyes and young nervous systems—the effect of these pulp-paper nightmares is that of a violent stimulant.... Unless we want a coming generation even more ferocious than the present one, parents and teachers throughout America must band together to break the 'comic' magazine." Not mincing words, he found comic book publishers "guilty of a cultural slaughter of the innocent."[26]

Even William Moulton Marston, a Harvard-educated psychiatrist who loved comics and would soon work in them, conceded in an October 1940 interview for *Family Circle* that he believed they impaired the ability of children as well as adults to differentiate fantasy from reality.[27]

It didn't help that there were several cases of enthusiastic young Superman fans who'd jumped off the roof of their house. The first case was reported in *Time* on September 11, 1939, just a year after his debut. The child survived, but other children, reportedly reenacting scenes from other comics, weren't as fortunate.[28]

In March 1948 Wertham began his public crusade against comics with an interview in *Collier's* titled "Horror in the Nursery," where he first propounded his thesis; since almost all his young patients read them, it was clear that "comic books are an important factor in juvenile crime." By May he'd presented at a symposium about "The Psychopathy of Comic Books" and published articles in the *American Journal of Psychotherapy* and the *Saturday Review of Literature* (later reprinted in part in *Reader's Digest*).[29]

Wertham was the right man at the right time. With impeccable credentials, he rode the wave of American postwar paranoia about youth culture and juvenile delinquency. Things reached critical mass in April 1954 with the publication of his book, which would become the work he'd be most famous, and infamous, for; *Seduction of the Innocent: The Influence of Comic Books on Today's Youth.*

Seduction declares itself the result of seven years of scientific study,[30] though it's more of a personal screed, an expression of Wertham's monomaniacal fixation on comics as not just a catalyst but a root cause of delinquency, a brainwashing of otherwise well-adjusted or mildly susceptible youths into lecherous, murderous hooligans.

The book opens with the urgent warning that "comic books are an invitation to illiteracy, create an atmosphere of cruelty and deceit, stimulate unwholesome fantasies [and] suggest criminal or sexually abnormal ideas." Their effect on children is "a blunting of ... conscience, of mercy, of sympathy ... [and of the] taste for the finer influences of education, for art, for literature, and for the decent and constructive

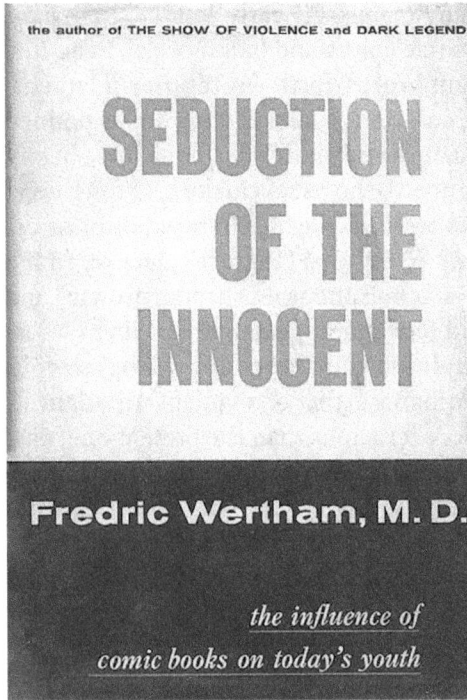

Left: *Seduction of the Innocent*, by Fredric Wertham. Rinehart & Company, 1954. *Right:* Fredric Wertham. Library of Congress, Rare Book & Special Collections Divisions.

relationship between human beings."[31] To an aesthete like Wertham comics were a cacophony of tastelessness, and many of his gripes are about their garishness, emphasizing that they elicit, in addition to psychotic tendencies, bad taste.

Curiously, he makes a point to distinguish between the lurid magazines and the upstanding newspaper strips, ignoring the roughhewn art and humor of popular strips like *The Katzenjammer Kids* or violence of *Dick Tracy*. Similarly, he considers funny animal comics harmless, while series like *Looney Tunes* and *Tom and Jerry* often contained slapstick violence like pianos and anvils dropped on heads.[32]

He makes numerous incendiary claims throughout, not the least of which is that reading comic books may lead to heroin addiction and trafficking. The proof? All the delinquents he interviewed who used or dealt drugs also read comics.[33]

At particular fault are the "crime comic books," which he classifies as anything depicting a crime being committed, from Westerns to supernatural tales. He even includes the comic book adaptation of *Macbeth*. But he takes particular umbrage with superheroes, especially the big three: Superman, Batman and Wonder Woman, which he considers "a special form of crime comics."[34]

Wonder Woman tortures men as a "cruel, 'phallic' woman. While she is a frightening figure for boys, she is an undesirable ideal for girls, being the exact opposite of what girls are supposed to want to be."[35] Meaning, ostensibly, demure.

When the comics didn't provide enough to work with, his criticism focuses on subtext, inferring that "Batman stories are psychologically homosexual. Our researches [*sic*] confirm this entirely." To support the claim, he declares that "Only someone ignorant of the fundamentals of psychiatry and of the psychopathology of sex can fail to realize a subtle atmosphere of homoerotism which pervades [them]."

Conflating homosexuality with pedophilia (common then), he diagnoses that they "fixate homoerotic tendencies by suggesting the form of an adolescent-with-adult ... type of love-relationship." His evidence is that Bruce Wayne's ward is named "Dick," whom he shares "an idyllic life" with in "sumptuous quarters, with beautiful flowers in large vases."[36]

But it was Superman who elicited Wertham's ire the most. He "undermines the authority and the dignity of the ordinary man and woman in the minds of children" because parents and teachers can't possibly compete with an invulnerable flying man. He promotes fascism and racism because, by opposing a variety of bigoted and repressive enemies, he's in fact providing their ideologies with a platform. His heroism "engenders in children either one or the other of two attitudes: either they fantasy themselves as supermen, with the attendant prejudices against the submen, or it makes them submissive and receptive to the blandishments of strong men who will solve all their social problems for them—by force."[37]

In short, Superman is a super-fascist, whose very "conceit gives boys and girls the feeling that ruthless go-getting based on physical strength ... is the desirable way to behave." Even his costume conveys this. It's a "fancy raiment that is a mixture of the costumes of S.S. men, diver and robots," prominently displaying (in addition to robot couture) "the big S ... we should, I suppose, be thankful that it is not an S.S."[38] Siegel and Shuster's champion of the oppressed, according to Wertham, was a Nazi.

Seduction of the Innocent was the *Reefer Madness* of its day, a work of panicked propaganda that seems farcical today, expect that it found a credulous audience, leading to nationwide public invective. It was an instant bestseller and a Book of the Month Club selection, as well as Book of the Year by the National Education Association. Wertham was invited to speak in influential forums like the Women's National Book Association, Columbia University's Teachers College and the American Prison Association.[39] Eventually, it played a pivotal role in the hearings before the Subcommittee to Investigate Juvenile Delinquency of the Committee on the Judiciary.

What truly catapulted the issue to the forefront of national attention was the case of the "Brooklyn Thrill-Kill Gang," surprisingly overlooked in most discussions of the anti-comics hysteria of the 1950s. In August 1954, four middle class Jewish teenagers from Brooklyn—Jack Koslow, Melvin Mittman, Jerome Lieberman and Robert Trachtenberg, ranging fifteen to eighteen—were arrested for a string of harrowing crimes that included beating two homeless men to death, setting a third on fire, assaulting two women in a park at night and a litany of other violent offenses.[40] The case made front page headlines nationwide and the four became the public face of juvenile delinquency.

As recounted in Mariah Adin's *The Brooklyn Thrill-Kill Gang and the Great Comic Book Scare of the 1950s*, the teens were said to have been influenced by violent comic book heroes and horror comics, particularly *Nights of Horror*. Not actually a comic, it was an underground black and white illustrated magazine depicting women in lingerie and fetish gear engaged in sexual acts, bondage, and torture. It featured spanking, whipping, pot smoking, and interracial and lesbian couplings, though ultimately little actual nudity or explicit intercourse. It was the magazine Joe Shuster secretly drew, the characters resembling his Superman cast. Sadly, it's his last known work.[41]

Wertham was the court-appointed expert, blaming comics as a direct cause of the four youths' heinous acts. It brought the anti-comic book frenzy to a crescendo. Civic officials rushed to denounce them as "obscene, lewd, lascivious, filthy, indecent and disgusting literature accessible to the youth," vowing to eliminate them. It also didn't take long for the Antisemitic undercurrent to manifest. Among the various explanations given for the youngsters' sociopathic rampage was their "limited, soul-less Jewish education."[42] Little did Wertham realize that the co-creator of Superman had also provided the lurid art for *Nights*. One can only imagine how Shuster felt learning about the matter. There's no record of him ever mentioning it. (Evidence unearthed in a 2005 journalistic investigation casts doubt on the four's culpability, indicating they may have simply been hooligans who'd been coerced by an overzealous police and DA's office into false confessions.)

Historians vary in their treatment of Wertham. In *Fredric Wertham and the Critique of Mass Culture*, Bart Beaty, author and head of the English Department at the University of Calgary, is largely forgiving, pointing out the complexity of his opinions and his supposed change of heart about comics in the 1970s. He laments that, as a result of both resentment against Wertham and his questionable methodology, he isn't mentioned in many of the texts dealing with the history of pop culture, comic books, mass effects of media and delinquency.[43]

Fingeroth's view is more impartial, particularly for a comic book writer and editor. He portrays Wertham as quixotic if overzealous, motivated by sincere concern for the welfare of children. He also notes Wertham's later book, 1973's *The World of Fanzines: A Special Form of Communication*, which looked positively upon the self-published magazines, including those dedicated to science fiction and superheroes.[44]

Though less so, Kaplan and Van Lente are also fairly sympathetic toward the man and his motivation, if not his means. Hajdu, in contrast, depicts him as a publicity hound, sometimes at the risk of his own patients' case in court, and a scientist who knowingly mispresented his polemic as scholarly work. As far as Stan Lee was concerned, "He was a good huckster, got a lot of publicity, and it almost destroyed the comic book business."[45]

Not all of Wertham's claims are spurious. The content of comics, even superhero comics—perhaps especially—isn't above scrutiny. The strong association between exposure to violence in the media and the perpetration of violence, particularly among children, has been firmly established,[46] though still largely ignored, and Wertham wasn't wrong or alone in pointing to this.

Like the pulps that birthed them, comics were often lowbrow, raunchy and pandering to sexual and racial stereotypes. As an art form they were almost equally transgressive. Though they were often dynamic and engaging, their creators were commonly untrained and the results were fittingly unstructured and unrefined. By the 1950s they'd become the unloved bastard grown into an incorrigible wild child, which was precisely their appeal. But many were inappropriate for young readers, and without a rating system like today's MPAA in film (G to NC-17) they were accessible to anyone on a newsstand or spin rack regardless of their intended audience, which was often teens and older.

Even Superman, in his earliest days (though long past by Wertham's time), was a violent vigilante whose flagrant disregard for the law can be seen in stories like *Action Comics* #12, where he wages a crusade against reckless drivers that includes wanton destruction of private property and assault, including against police and the mayor, making him the most wanted man in Metropolis. He routinely threatened crooks that he'd kill them, and though it was meant to be an obvious bluff to the reader, he sometimes actually did, even if it wasn't explicitly shown; in *Action Comics* #2 he throws a man over a likely fatal distance and he frequently knocked aircraft out of the sky.[47]

That said, when Wertham's research archives for *Seduction* were made public in 2010 and Carol Tilley, professor of library and information science at the University of Illinois, reviewed them, she encountered "numerous falsifications and distortions," through which Wertham systematically "manipulated, overstated, compromised, and fabricated evidence." He "edited and altered children's statements and clinical presentations," ignoring altogether that many were poor and uneducated, and in some cases it seems even created evidence out of whole cloth. Ironic, considering he claimed to have found "an appalling lack of scientific method on the part of professionals who have for years paid no attention to comic books."[48]

Seduction is rife with facile arguments, first among them being that, since almost all the youth Wertham treated read comic books, they must be to blame for juvenile delinquency. He could have equally blamed air. And by the standard he established for the corrupting "crime comics"—any depiction of crime or violence of any kind—the Bible, Homer, Shakespeare or Twain wouldn't have passed muster.

His psychosexual fixation with superheroes is similarly misguided. "Dr. Frederic Wertham was an idiot," Chabon writes in *Kavalier & Clay*. "It was obvious that Batman was not intended, consciously or unconsciously, to play Robin's corrupter: he was meant to stand in for his *father*, and by extension for the absent, indifferent, vanishing fathers of the comic-book-reading boys of America." Superman's authority likewise wasn't homoerotic or fascistic. It was patriarchal, that of a reassuring father to millions of American children who missed or lost theirs. Despite conjuring Freud twelve times in *Seduction*, Wertham failed to realize, or chose to ignore, Freud's belief that humanized gods—like superheroes—are all father figures, totemic stand-ins for a child's veneration of the omnipotent father.[49] (Following that thought, supervillains can be seen as Oedipal threats, the fear of the father's power and disruptive capacity on a child's autonomy.)

It also didn't occur to Wertham to correlate the supposed rise in juvenile crime with the absence and death of fathers sent off to wars, the militarization of culture during wartime, secularization, the baby boom growth in youth population, urban crowding or simply the increased interest and reporting capacity of the media.

It didn't matter that the *Adventures of Superman* radio show was recognized by many of his peers, as well as several education professionals and parent organizations, for promoting tolerance and acceptance, or that Superman comics were being successfully used by savvy teachers to teach grammar, civics, geography and other subjects to otherwise disinterested students.[50] To Wertham, Superman was a fascist because the very concept of superpowers was inherently fascistic. The superhero was a man of action over intellect, force over reason, the hallmark of fascist and Nazi ideology.

He missed the point entirely. Superheroes carried a message not of power over others but of personal empowerment. Superman used his abilities not to expand his own hegemony and *Lebensraum* but to protect the freedom and security of others. What he did was no different than what millions of American GIs did. What's more, he was far from a brainless brute. He spent most of his time as Clark Kent, a cerebral and conscientious journalist, and while he easily overcame pedestrian thugs and crooks, his supervillains—Ultra-Humanite, Luthor, Prankster, Toyman, Mr. Mxyzptlk—were almost always defeated in battles of wits, demonstrating the superiority of logic and virtue, not force. In short, Wertham failed to grasp what every child knew. Superman is a good guy.

Some give Wertham the benefit of the doubt of noble intentions, pointing to his impressive record—a doctor dedicated to treating poor children and to promoting racial equality is hard to vilify—and to *The World of Fanzines* as something of a retraction and apology. But whatever contrition Wertham expressed in later years was halfhearted at best, a revisionist claim that he was never an advocate of censorship or had anything against comic books per se. Not only did he never recant his claims or express regret over their consequences, he continued to stand by them. Shortly before his death, in the 1981 BBC documentary *Superman: The Comic Strip Hero*, he took the opportunity to lambast Superman one last time, calling him "a symbol of force, power and violence. That is what he represents. And that has had an enormous influence, which one cannot possibly exaggerate, on the youth, not only of this country but … of many other countries."[51]

It may not have been an insidious plot, but Wertham's crusade against comics was sanctimonious and willfully misguided. As a man of science, versed in methodical examination and critical analysis, he should have known better. His methodology wasn't just sloppy—his consistent use of omissions, distortions, misattributions, paralogisms and fabrications could only have been deliberate. It was sophistry and demagoguery in service of an agenda, for which he'll remain forever maligned as the puritanical zealot who crippled and nearly killed the comic book industry.

Wertham succeeded in sparking mass hysteria and stigmatizing comics to a degree that still lingers today. Worse, he was a Jew fomenting animosity toward a Jewish industry, which he undoubtedly knew it was. Morality trumps tribalism, but Wertham didn't just take a stand. He fervently crusaded against comics, accusing fellow Jews of fascism and Nazism not a decade after the Holocaust. *Seduction of the Innocent* was the new *Protocols of the Elders of Zion*, a blood libel.

Whatever personal drives motivated him, Fingeroth suggests that his specific Jewish ethnicity played a part. "Consciously or not," he writes, "Wertham's attacks on comics (and Hollywood, as well) took on aspects of the rivalry between Our Crowd and the Eastern European immigrants and their decendents."[52]

The term "Our Crowd" is borrowed from Stephen Birmingham's 1967 book, *Our Crowd: The Great Jewish Families of New York*, which examines the lives of prominent 19th-century New York Jews like Loeb, Goldman-Sachs, Straus, Seligman, Lehman,

Guggenheim and others, almost all of German origins. It has since come to refer to other socioeconomically exalted German Jews, including in the 20th century, an example being *New York Times* owners, the Ochs-Sulzberger family.

Most German Jews immigrated to the U.S. in the 1840s, decades before their Eastern European cousins. They were cultured bourgeoisie who, though fleeing persecution, often arrived with their finances largely intact. The shtetl *Ostjuden*—East Jews—were the poor country mouse to their city mouse, "an embarrassment, to be helped only at arm's length through charitable institutions."[53]

It was the great schism of Jewish-American society; rich and poor, educated and unschooled, urban and rural, secular or reform and orthodox, assimilated and segregated. The 2008–2009 exhibit *East European Jews in the German-Jewish Imagination* at the University of Chicago Library explained

> The long and difficult path toward emancipation during the nineteenth century led German Jews to reject traditional notions of Jewish nationhood and to refashion themselves as "German citizens of the Mosaic faith." In their efforts to assimilate, they deliberately adopted German middle-class gentility, politeness, and aesthetic refinement, and contrasted these traits with a crude stereotype of East European Jewish life.[54]

Yiddish was largely scorned as a vulgar bastardization of German. Moses Mendelssohn, the foremost proponent of the 18th to 19th-century Jewish Enlightenment (*Haskalah*), called it "a language of stammers, corrupt and deformed, repulsive to those who are able to speak in a correct and elegant manner." These attitudes remained well into the following century. Novelist Jakob Wasserman wrote in 1922, "If I spoke with a Polish or Galician Jew and tried to understand his way of life and thinking, I could stir myself to feel compassion or sadness, but never a sense of brotherhood. He was entirely strange and, when individual human sympathy was lacking, even repulsive."[55]

The cultural gap was so large that some German Jews even held Antisemitic views of their Eastern cousins. Writing for the *Atlantic* in 1908, Edwin J. Kuh called them "the undesirable members of their race," belittling their suffering and calling on Americans to bar them from respectable institutions.[56]

This rift can be traced back to the westward migration of Jewish refugees fleeing pogroms, making them a visible presence in Germany,[57] much to the chagrin of the genteel Jews who'd assimilated and prospered there with little fanfare. It carried over from the Old World to the new like a disease in the belly of a ship, reemerging with the growing presence of Eastern European Jews in New York. They, on their part, saw German Jews as Hellenized apostates, intermarriers and self-haters, and themselves as noble torchbearers of Jewish tradition and spirituality. (A similar culture clash took place in newly-established Israel between Ashkenazi Jews—the Western and Eastern groups of which were far less divided—and Sephardic [Mediterranean and Balkan] and Mizrahi [Middle Eastern and African] Jews. A sad testimony to mankind's infinite capacity, even among its smallest, most persecuted groups, to find ways to distinguish and discriminate.)

With the postwar rise in prosperity, as well as tolerance toward them, Jews were able to leave the Lower East Side's rookeries and better-off South Bronx for comfortable suburban living and move their businesses from the winding old streets of downtown to the sprawling neoclassical avenues of midtown. They largely weren't welcome by the established German Jews, who didn't care to share space with the uncouth arrivistes. Comics in particular were a sore, with at least fourteen publishers and studio shops ("packagers") in the area.[58] DC's offices, a multimillion-dollar corporation owned by two Jews from the tenements, were at 480 Lexington Avenue at 46th Street, a block away from the Yale Club.

Siegel and Shuster, Simon and Kirby, Kane and Finger, Eisner and (studio partner) Jerry Iger, Goodman, Lee and most others in comics were first generation Americans to Eastern European parents. The comics they produced—unassuming, of limited literacy, frequently crass and often insurrectionary—were everything they were said to be, and an affront to a culturati like Wertham.

Fingeroth ultimately rejects the Our Crowd vs. Ostjuden argument on the grounds that Wertham doesn't fit the right immigration wave and social circles. He offers instead that it was more a class clash, which Kaplan similarly argues, whereas Van Lente and Dunlavey see it more as political, the socialistic doctor taking on exploitive big business.[59] All are viable, but Wertham, despite having immigrated to the States almost eighty years after the main influx of German Jews and not quite so upper class, was still a learned, eminent, Western European Jew, who echoed in his condemnation of comics the same prejudices against Galician Jews. He was a *yekke*; Yiddish for "jacket," referring to pompous, persnickety and overly formal German Jews who fancied themselves refined Westerners (*yekke* has since come to refer to Jews of German descent in general, carrying a light connotation of fastidiousness), and the hostility he expressed toward the Jews in comics carried undertones of casteism. Of course, Antisemites cared little to distinguish between Eastern and Western Jews, and Wertham's rhetoric helped inflame their hate.

While the era's backlash against comics hasn't typically been associated with Antisemitism, its presence, implicit and explicit, is impossible to ignore. The rhetoric was thinly veiled, as it always is, with WASP publications like the *Hartford Courant* calling comics "the filthy stream that flows from the gold-plated sewers of New York." Bishop John F. Noll, founder of the pressure group the National Organization for Decent Literature and at best a casual Antisemite, led Catholic organizations in a campaign against comics that referred to their publishers as "parasites," an Antisemitic cliché. Comic books were "Northeastern, urban, and vaguely ethnic, if not overtly Jewish," Hajdu writes,[60] a flavor not always appreciated by Christian heartland folk and cultural tastemakers.

Wertham's histrionics appealed to retrogrades, predisposed to suspect anything printed that isn't scripture, particularly if originating in modern-day Sodom and produced by Jews. They equally appealed to McCarthyists, who revived the prewar association of Jews with communism, notoriously persecuting mostly Jewish Hollywood moviemakers.[61] (Ironic, considering Wertham's own work carried echoes of the Frankfurt School's critique of mass media and culture as products of capitalist consumerism.)

Jews again found themselves depicted as subversives, corrupters, and disloyalists, this time by the American government in the form of Senator Joseph McCarthy

(R–WI) and the House Un-American Activities Committee. It didn't help that the Superman radio show worked with the Jewish NGO the Anti-Defamation League (ADL) to incorporate democratic and anti-racist themes in its storylines. State Senator Jack Tenney (R–CA), chairman of the California Un-American Activities Committee, was an outspoken Antisemite (as well as segregationist and interment supporter) who was convinced the ADL was a nefarious façade and their tolerance campaigns were Zionist communist propaganda.[62] (As a European-style social democracy, replete with *Kibutzim* [agrarian collectives], Israel was suspect by some in American government as having split loyalties. That its neighboring enemies were all backed and armed by the USSR didn't seem to matter. Divided loyalties and factionalism are longstanding Antisemitic canards.)

Of course, like in Hollywood, publishing and academia, socialism was the bon ton of many liberal and artistic people at the time, the comic book field included. In Superman's case, Alvin Schwartz was a declared Trotskyite, while his editor Jack Schiff was a Stalinist. Some of that worldview did trickle into the comics, though not in the seditious way McCarthy or Tenney imagined. "I tried to change Superman from being a meathead who simply had a harder punch," Schwartz told Tye, "into something more human and philosophical."[63]

The national panic over comics led to the creation of the Senate Subcommittee to Investigate Juvenile Delinquency of the Committee on the Judiciary, focusing specifically on the effects of mass media and particularly comic books on youths' mental wellbeing and criminality. Hearings opened in Manhattan federal court on April 21, 1954, led by the overzealous Senator Estes Kefauver (D–TN). They were front page news, televised and broadcast on the radio around the country.[64]

Kefauver was by no means Antisemitic, and in fact an ardent supporter of nascent Israel. His fervor may have been more personal; three years prior he chaired the Special Committee on Organized Crime in Interstate Commerce. Known as The Kefauver Committee, it was much-publicized, though its legislative achievements were modest, at best, resulting in an exhausted Kefauver stepping down. Perhaps he needed the bully pulpit as he was gearing up for his 1955 vice-presidential run with Adlai Stevenson.[65]

Wertham understood these were show trials, and he made sure to play his part. On the very first day of the hearings, full of froth and fury, he announced that "Hitler was a beginner compared to the comic book industry. They get the children much younger."[66] Here was a Jew, testifying against other Jews in the wider context of McCarthyism which predominantly targeted Jews, accusing them of being worse than Hitler himself on the heels of the Holocaust.

Testifying under oath, he reiterated his claims from *Seduction*, despite many of them being misleading or false. Perfectly healthy, normal children with a good home life may be seduced into criminality by reading comics, he claimed, and so comics should be treated like infectious diseases, as a public health problem, and their sale to persons under fifteen illegalized.[67]

Despite all the gory and lascivious comics exhibited as evidence he chose to single out Superman—the most famous character—first implying that women were being raped in his comics and then stating that they were "particularly injurious to the ethical development of children.... They arose in children phantasies [*sic*] of sadistic joy in seeing other people punished over and over again while you yourself remain immune. We have called it the Superman complex."[68]

Other pundits and claimants were invited to testify or write op-eds for the papers, most railing against comics and their creators. They were portrayed as a cabal of degenerates, opportunistic Fagins peddling lurid smut to impressionable children. There were voices of reason, however. A colleague of Wertham's from Bellevue, Lauretta Bender, a noted child neuropsychiatrist and an expert on child schizophrenia, suicide and violence, who was the head of the children's psychiatric service at the hospital until 1955, actually extoled the virtues of Superman as an inexpensive form of therapy, noting that he offers "the same type of mental catharsis that Aristotle claimed was an attribute of the drama."[69]

Marston called them a "mental vitamin," explaining that "the wish to be super-strong is a healthy wish.... The more the *Superman–Wonder Woman* picture stories build up this inner compulsion ... to battle and overcome obstacles, particularly evil ones, the better chance your child has for self-advancement in the world." He himself was a consulting psychologist on DC's advisory board, along with various distinguished academics.[70]

As Superman, George Reeves was the national chairman of City of Hope, helping raise money for children's cancer research and treatment through fundraising campaigns, including appearances in costume in parades around the nation. While Wertham was accusing Superman of corrupting children the real one was saving their lives. Reeves, along with the showrunners, was conscientious about the role: "In *Superman*, we're all concerned with giving kids the right kind of show. We don't go too much for violence.... We even try in our scripts, to give a gentle message of tolerance and stress that a man's color and race and religious beliefs should be respected." A laden message, considering the Jewish origins of the comic and the show. But Wertham saw it differently, writing that "The comic-book Superman has long been recognized as a symbol of violent race superiority. The television Superman ... does not only have 'superhuman powers,' but explicitly belongs to a 'super-race.'"[71]

Just as Wertham fabricated facts, he ignored others. From 1949 to the mid–1960s, DC collaborated with various welfare organizations and agencies to create public service ads that ran through their various titles, several starring Superman, under the guidance of Jewish Superman editor Jack Schiff.[72]

In one such ad, Superman lectures a group of teens on the values of tolerance. "And remember, boys and girls, your school—like our country—is made up of Americans of <u>many</u> different races, religions and national origins," he says with a wag of his finger. "So.... If YOU hear anybody talk against a schoolmate or anyone else because of his religion, race or national origin—don't wait: tell him THAT KIND OF TALK IS <u>UN-AMERICAN</u>." In another ad, a boy named Sam Levy is excluded from a kids' clubhouse for being Jewish until Superman arrives to lecture them, looking straight at the reader: "It never should matter what a person is—Protestant, Jew or Catholic. Nor should it matter what the color of a person's skin is, or where his parents were born." At least one ad was made into book covers and posters for schools.[73]

What's more, while the U.S. government was attacking comics creators it continued hiring them to produce comics for its own needs, including propaganda pamphlets, army manuals, recruitment posters and ads, and guides for various departments, from Treasury to Health.[74]

None of it mattered. It also didn't matter that the legal counsel for the subcommittee questioned Wertham's methods, noting that he represented the extreme position among psychiatrists and that in fact most of his colleagues saw no meaningful correlation between comics and delinquency.[75] Like all McCarthy-era hearings it was less of an inquiry and more of an inquisition, with Kefauver in the role of Torquemada. And soon enough came the Auto-da-fé.

Superman "Help Keep Your School *All American!*" ad, 1949. Written by Jack Schiff and illustrated by Wayne Boring. DC Comics.

Public outcry reached a piercing falsetto when comic books were being burned across the U.S. Schools, churches, scout troops and other civic groups, along with parents, collected or confiscated kids' comics, then burned them in public bonfires, some consuming thousands of comics and reaching 25 feet[76] (which is partly why Golden Age issues are so rare and valuable).

The same Americans who'd just now laid their lives on the line and lost loved ones in the fight against the book burners of Berlin were doing the same thing in their own back yards. For Jews, whose books had been burned shortly before they were, the sight was frightening.

Flames were fanned by the press, as always, with stories of kids tying towels around their necks and jumping off rooftops and out windows, despite very few such recorded incidents. The *New Yorker* wrote that "Superman and his pals are ... perverse, fantastic, and foolish." *Catholic World* described him as "very much in the style of a Nazi pamphleteer." The odium wasn't limited to American conservatism. French

"Superman's Code for Buddies" ad, 1950. Written by Jack Schiff and illustrated by Al Plastino. DC Comics.

Communist paper *L'Humanité* saw him as a symbol of "the overweening vanity of atomic capitalism" and called for "a law for the material and moral protection of our child's press"—the same goal the "capitalist imperialist gangsters" in America were after.[77] Superman had become, like the Jewish community he came from, the Other.

Groups like the National PTA called for a housecleaning of comic books, while public figures rushed to pillory their creators. Ever the moral paragon, FBI Director J. Edgar Hoover called them "unquestionably base individuals who spread obscene literature across our land" and thus "threaten the morality of our Nation and its richest treasure—our young people."[78]

Wertham agreed. He felt the committee didn't do its job, so he took his case once again to the court of public opinion. Titling his *Saturday Review* article "It's Still Murder: What Parents Don't Know about Comic Books," he claimed, among many other things, that "the connection between crime comic books and the more violent forms of juvenile delinquency is now well established." It was quite the opposite, which he knew, but he still declared that "never before in the history of civilized countries have adults been more deficient in their duty to the young." Not only were comics the single greatest threat to children, they were now the greatest evil perpetuated upon them in human history. "Mammon is at the root of all this." He stated, using, perhaps not coincidently, a Hebraic word. "The comic-book publishers, racketeers of the spirit, have corrupted children in the past, they are corrupting them right now, and they will continue to corrupt them unless we legally prevent it."[79]

More than a hundred acts of legislation were introduced across the U.S. to restrict or outlaw the sale of comics. In Canada, the 1949 Fulton Bill outlawed the production and sale of all crime comics (i.e., depicting crime), not officially repealed until 2017.[80]

For authorities and authority figures alike, the growing youth culture revolution—with a new breed of movie stars like Marlon Brando, James Dean and Natalie Wood and Beat Generation figures like William S. Burroughs, Allen Ginsberg and Jack Kerouac—threatened the existing order, but was harder to take on. The comic book industry, particularly with its implied Jewishness, was an easy target.

Van Lente and Dunlavey speculate that violence as a whole fell into disfavor after the war, but the proliferation of Westerns and noir in film, television and radio, as well as horror and action-heavy sci-fi movies, indicate otherwise. It didn't help, though, that Bob Wood, co-editor of *Crime Does Not Pay*, the first and most successful of the (actual) crime comics, beat his lover to death with an iron in a hotel room in August 1958.[81]

In the blink of an eye, America's favorite pastime became abhorrent. Working in comics became ignominious. "Comics were a dirty word.... If you said you drew comic books, it was like saying you were a child molester," Silver Age icon Carmine Infantino (among many accomplishments, co-creator of the second Flash, Editorial Director of DC 1967–1971 and Publisher 1971–1976) told Hajdu.[82] The superhero genre had already been in decline over the past decade, but being lumped in with the gruesome and prurient comics tolled its knell. Siegel and Shuster, who were already dispossessed of their creation and income, were also forced to watch as it was being dragged through the mud.

The spring of 1955 saw the release of the committee's interim report. While it did find that comic books had "questionable aspects" and noted that emotionally disturbed children may show excessive interest in crime and horror comics, it concluded: "Surveying the work that has been done on the subject, it appears to be the consensus of the experts that comic-book reading is not the cause of emotional maladjustment on children." Furthermore, the report echoed William Marston's opinion, remarking that "the child with difficulties may find in comic books representations of the kinds of problems with which he is dealing, and that comic books will, therefore, have a value for him which they do not have for a child who is relatively free of these troubles."[83]

It received little media attention, but regardless, it was already too late. Wertham and Kefauver's public crusades decimated the industry. There were other factors involved: The century-old American News Corporation, distributor of nearly half of all comics in the U.S., shuttered in 1957. Van Lente and Dunlavey also point to postwar suburbanization, which cut off easy access to points of sale like newsstands and drugstores, and to the shift from public transportation to cars, which further reduced opportunities for reading.[84] And there was also television. But the industry didn't decline, it was purged.

After tripling in the decade prior, sales plummeted from about a billion issues a year to about 180 million—a 72 percent drop. When Eisenhower took office in 1953 there were some fifty comic book publishers. By the time he left in 1961 there were fifteen. Thousands of characters, superhero and otherwise, disappeared, most never to return. The first comic book series, *Famous Funnies*, which had launched in July 1934, came to an unceremonious end in July 1955. Horror publisher EC Comics folded the same year. In 1957 Marvel fired its entire staff save one, Stan Lee, who remained as editor in chief as well as the only writer, hiring freelance artists to produce mostly Godzilla-style monster comics.[85]

Many, who could no longer support themselves and their families through the rapidly dwindling industry, left for fields like advertising, which were now open to Jews—the same ones whose segregation sent them into comics in the first place. The upward mobility of Jews in the 1950s also played a part, creating better opportunities for employment. Some never looked back.

By the time the dust had settled, more than eight hundred people lost their livelihood. Some became homeless.[86] *The Ten-Cent Plague* ends with a haunting fifteen-page long "black list" of publishers, editors, writers, artists and others whose careers were destroyed, a poignant lesson in the danger of righteousness.

To save itself, the beleaguered industry formed the Comics Magazine Association of America (CMAA), which, on October 26, 1954, created the Comics Code Authority (CCA), an independent, self-censoring body that imposed the strictest regulations of any mass media. Obsequiously, it promised "sound, wholesome entertainment," with diktats like banning the words "horror" or "terror" in titles; prohibiting any depiction of zombies, vampires, ghouls or werewolves; dressing all characters "appropriately"; emphasizing the sanctity of marriage; and fostering respect for authority like parents and the government.[87]

Every issue had to pass a review prior to publication to carry the CCA seal of approval, a postage stamp–shaped imprimatur in the upper right corner of the cover, if publishers wished to appease distributers, advertisers, parents, clergymen and politicians. The only publishers that could afford to refuse were Elliot, who published the literary adaptations series *Classics Illustrated*, and Dell, who published Disney's brand-safe comics. The seal remained in place for 57 years, before quietly disappearing in 2011 (in 1971 the code was revised to allow, under certain provisos, depictions of crime, sexuality, drug abuse and the supernatural. Thirty years later Marvel was the first to defect, adopting an in-house rating system, followed by DC in 2011[88]).

"To survive, the superheroes surrendered their dignity," Morrison laments. The CCA made comics, superhero and otherwise, inoffensive to the point of insipid, infantilizing them and rendering them unappealing to teens and adults. "It instilled that belief in the American public that comics are strictly a kid's medium," Marvel chief creative officer and former editor in chief Joe Quesada said. "We're still fighting against that stigma today."[89]

Unsurprisingly, the draconian code wasn't enough for Wertham. He wrote, "The problem is really simple. You either close down a house of prostitution or you leave it open."[90]

Acutely aware of the visibility that came with Superman, DC had been careful from early on. In 1940, long before Wertham, Whitney Ellsworth instituted an editorial policy for Superman's comics, not always to Siegel's liking. It included strictures like "the inclusion of females in stories is specifically discouraged. Women, when used in plot structure, should be secondary in importance"; "Expressions having reference to the Deity are forbidden"; "Characters—even villains—should never be shown bleeding"; and "Good people should be good, and bad people bad, without middle ground shading."[91]

The house that Superman built weathered the storm partly because his comics, despite it all, were seen as safe by many parents. But his Golden Age was over. If his three series (*Action Comics, Superman, World's Finest*) sold 3 million monthly copies in 1946, by 1960 the same titles sold under 1.8 million—a 40 percent drop—although total sales grew to about 3.7 million with the addition of spinoff titles *Superboy, Adventure Comics, Superman's Pal, Jimmy Olsen* and *Superman's Girl Friend, Lois Lane*.[92]

What also prevented him from becoming a pariah like most other superheroes was the immense popularity of the *Adventures of Superman* television show. Launching in 1952, a year after the radio show had ended, it was broadcast around the world, spreading the superhero's fame far and wide, with 35 million viewers in the U.S. alone.[93] And while the first season had noir overtones, the following five seasons were sunny and sanguine, safe for young children. It was star George Reeves, however, who truly made the show a success. With his square jaw, cleft chin and commanding presence—and despite his foam-padded shoulders, flesh-padded midsection and age of 44 showing in the last season—he imbued Superman with Hollywood charm and bravura.

In the comics, the CCA brought about Superman's third metamorphosis (debuting on his March 1955 covers, *Action Comics* #202 and *Superman* #96), from a Depression-era taciturn, two-fisted reformist to a wartime jingoist to an agent of law and order. Like the other great illustrated American icon, Mickey Mouse, who started out impish but in short order became domesticated, Superman was now a symbol of orthodoxy, a sermonizing father figure in the vein of Ward Cleaver.

The threats he faced were similarly blunted. Whereas his early adversaries were predatory officials, ruthless criminals and Nazis, his 1950s comics took their cues from the TV show, pitting him against parochial, often slapstick mobsters, tricksters, demented scientists and, with increasing regularity, Lex Luthor.

While the Beats were experimenting with narrative form, Eastern philosophies, existentialism and the blending of the romantic and surreal, Superman's writers, abiding by the Code, produced stories that, for all their charm, inventiveness and occasional poignancy, were also safely conservative and formulaic. They were homogenized and pasteurized for 1950s America. Fun, cheerful, inane and desultory.

In this era of sanitized asexuality, where even real-life married couple Ricky and Lucy Ricardo slept in separate twin beds on *I Love Lucy*, Superman went from flirtatious to celibate. His brimming libidinous masculinity—a large part of his wishful appeal to pubescent and older readers—turned into a disinterest in women. Romantic interest was still present, with Lois as well the occasional "safe" character like mermaid (and therefore agynary) Lori Lemaris (*Superman* #129), but it was platonic and innocent, a summer camp crush. He was still super, but less man than ever before.

The CCA effectively lobotomized Superman, at least for a short while. Until editor Mort Weisinger was given the reins in 1958, beginning with *Action Comics* #241 and *Superman* #122,[94] helping introduce many new concepts to the mythology, several with Jewish meaning.

Clark Kent was mostly sidelined, a bookend to Superman's adventures, and he, too, was denatured. As Superman became magisterial Kent also gained confidence, going from a mild-mannered reporter to "the Daily Planet's ace newsman."[95] Gone was the hapless, timorous neurotic. That Jewish cliché wouldn't resurface in comics until Peter Parker became Spider-Man in 1962. Inspired by Reeves' performance, Kent and Superman became indistinguishable, hopping in and out of frame with the same reassurance and fourth wall-breaking wink. Ostensibly, a leading man on TV simply couldn't be that anemic, even if by pretense. Kent wasn't charismatic, wasn't WASPy enough (it would be nearly a decade before the U.S. had its first Catholic president in JFK), wasn't a wholesome role model. Which, of course, was the point.

It was in this era that Superman's deification began. A steadfastly chaste, always on the job Puritan and a man of wisdom and composure (not always, but certainly compared to his earlier hotheadedness), he achieved a level of saintly perfection that, while making him almost antiseptic, also helped him attain venerability in the larger Christian culture. The antiauthoritarian had become the ultimate authority figure. The ethnic refugee had not only assimilated, but came to embody the American mainstream.

He also gained a new archenemy; Rosie the Riveter, scheming to emasculate him at every turn. As able-bodied men were deployed overseas during the war, women took their place in factories and offices, gaining newfound power and independence many were reluctant to surrender once the men returned. They, in turn, largely didn't like returning as conquering heroes to filled positions and empty households. Lois, a self-determined, confident, opinionated career woman was now a shrew in need of taming, and super-manly-man would have to show her what's what. (Lois wasn't alone in dealing with the sexist regression of the period. Wonder Woman, having fought the Axis, was pitted against new nemesis Egg Fu—a giant sentient mustached Chinese egg—ticking the checkboxes for frivolousness, Yellow Peril stereotype and metaphor for women's cookery duties.[96])

Lois was popular enough to not only receive her own series, *Superman's Girl Friend, Lois Lane*, but for its sales to match *Action Comics*.[97] In it, she spent virtually all her time trying to either uncover Superman's secret identity, convince or trick him to marry her, or both. When at its best, it featured *His Girl Friday*–style hijinks. At its worst, it was chauvinistic and paternalistic, constantly putting Lois in her place. Tellingly, the cover story of the first issue saw her transformed into a broomstick-riding witch.

In one memorable instance, Superman has one of his doppelgänger robots (a recurring trope of the era) put her over its knee and spank her, to teach her a lesson for being so snoopy. She occasionally gained superpowers of her own, either in "imaginary tales" or some other artifice, but was less concerned with saving lives and fighting crime than whipping up a literal ton of flapjacks and catfighting with a similarly-powered Lana Lang for Superman's hand in marriage. A Super-Lois was inherently "a super-headache."[98]

The through-line of the series, however, was Lois's obsession with revealing Superman's secret identity—an assimilationist Jew's worst nightmare, particularly in light of the role seeking out and exposing Jews played in the Holocaust, as well as its recent echoes in McCarthyism.

Despite the CCA's bowdlerizing, mature subject matter and themes did find their way into comics, particularly Superman's. "These stories were all about emotion," writes Morrison. "Superman plunged into great surging tides of feelings so big and unashamed that they could break a young heart ... cataclysmic tales of love and loss, guilt, grief, friendship, judgement, terror, and redemption."[99] They were adventure stories full of passion and pathos, a curious amalgam of sullen and silly. Even when he was depicted as virtually omnipotent Superman was never insouciant. The Last Son of Krypton was a haunted man, burdened by the weight of two worlds, the one he'd lost and the one he was desperately trying to save. The Holocaust had made his drive and fears real, adding an unprecedented level of gravitas to superhero comics and giving his saga the heft of a Shakespearean tragedy.

Fingeroth, the only author to discuss the development of Krypton's destruction as a Holocaust metaphor in the postwar era, writes that Weisinger, a hands-on "auteur editor," encouraged his writers and artists to explore "the dramatic potential inherent, in a post–Holocaust world, of Superman as the 'sole survivor' of the planet Krypton."[100]

While Batman's origin became a thing to only ever allude to, never show, Superman's comics repeatedly featured scenes of his planet's destruction, with entire storylines devoted to its meaning and consequences. It came to symbolize humanity's great sin, its vanity and obtuseness, equally reflecting Cold War anxieties about atomic warfare.

Freud saw as an essential condition to the creation of myths and epics a vibrant culture that comes to a catastrophic end.[101] In Superman's case, the death of Krypton provided motivation and melodrama, while the death of European Jewry provided inspiration for Krypton. The idea predated the war and was little more than a footnote until after it, but the *Shoa*—Holocaust—is a singular event in Jewish history only in scope. Its timeline is a bloody thread of persecution, expulsion and near-genocide spanning the world and the ages, a cyclical trauma of a civilization built and destroyed that, for better or worse, is an integral part of Jewish identity and culture, found in its stories, songs, prayers and holidays, from Passover to Yom Kippur. It's this collective memory that Siegel and Shuster drew from when conceiving Krypton, made all the more poignant by the timing.

Chabon also draws a parallel between Krypton and the Holocaust. In the 2003 History Channel documentary *Comic Book Superheroes Unmasked*, he comments, "Superman comes from this other place to America. He can never go back there, it's been destroyed, very much as the Europe…. Jews left behind was eventually destroyed."[102] He's an orphan who's lost his family, his home and his entire race, the last vestige of an extinct civilization, and that knowledge is inescapably present in everything he does. Jews, particularly Ashkenazi, all saw themselves as survivors. Either they themselves endured the Holocaust, or they lost family members, or they were simply next in line had Hitler had his way. The trauma was so pervasive, so strong, that it arguably became the defining characteristic of modern Jewish culture. Whatever they did, whatever they accomplished, was in spite of, in defiance of and because of their attempted murder.

Jews who, like Kal-El, escaped in infancy also inherited this PTSD. Even the baby boomers born after the war came to be known as "second-generation Holocaust survivors." It was upon their shoulders that the responsibility of continuation, restoration and remembrance was placed, a calling and a burden the likes of Herman Wouk, Philip Roth, Paul Auster and Art Spiegelman would wrestle with in their works. Superman, like his writers, *for* his writers, was working out his survivor's guilt.

Superman didn't get a full-length origin story until 1948, a decade after his debut, and when he finally did it wasn't by either of his creators. Batman and Green Lantern co-creator Bill Finger and artist Wayne Boring were tasked with fleshing it out, harvesting what Siegel and Shuster had sown. The cover of *Superman* #53 proudly touts the 10th anniversary of "the world's greatest adventure character," but the opening image inside, instead of exciting or celebratory, is a close-up of a morose Superman clutching his head. The story follows Jor-El as he beseeches the Council of Five—a governing rabbinical council still a fresh memory from shtetl religious life—to mobilize a mass evacuation of Krypton using colossal rocket ships. His prophesy is greeted with laughter, condemning the entire race to extinction save for his son, whom he manages to send away.[103]

The story resembles the flood narrative of Genesis 6–9, in which Noah is the only man to recognize the coming end of the world and builds a large craft to save himself and his family. It particularly corresponds to the Midrash account depicting Noah's futile attempts to warn his fellow men, who ridicule him in return (Gen. Rabbah 30:6–9). It's also suggestive of leaders of some ghetto and shtetl communities, as well as world leaders, who dismissed the approaching tidal wave of Nazism.

Superman himself only learned of his heritage the following year, in *Superman* #61. "Superman's Return to Krypton" was also written by Finger, who dusted off Siegel's unused concepts from his 1940 unpublished "The K-Metal from Krypton" story, reintroducing them at a time where they resonated the most. Again the story opens with Superman clutching his head, this time in horror. Travelling through time, he returns to Krypton right before its destruction, but for all his powers is powerless to stop it. As a time-traveler he's invisible and inaudible to them, but, the story being told from his perspective, it is they who are the walking ghosts of the past. It's a melancholic, unsettling science fiction fantasy,

Superman #53, August 1948. Written by Bill Finger and illustrated by Wayne Boring. DC Comics.

ending with a strongly evocative message for Jews as Jor-El entreats his departing son, "You will be the last survivor of our great civilization! Be worthy of it!"[104]

Under Weisinger's aegis, Superman's writers showed almost a compulsion to revisit his homeland, reconnect him with his lost family, give him a sense of closure as well as of purpose. "The Return of Planet Krypton!" (1953) in *Action Comics* #182 brought the mountain to Muhammad when Krypton suddenly appears in Earth's solar system, only to be revealed as a replica.[105]

In a second story titled "Superman's Return to Krypton," in 1958's *Superman* #123, Jimmy Olsen comes into possession of a mystical Native American totem, using it to grant Superman's fondest wish and send him back in time to Krypton to meet his parents. And in 1959's *Superman* #132, "Superman's Other Life," he watches a morbid computer simulation of his life on Krypton had it not exploded.[106]

The apotheosis of postwar pathos, however, was in 1960's *Superman* #141. In yet

another story titled "Superman's Return to Krypton," the Man of Steel accidently goes back in time again and returns to his home world, where he falls in love with actress Lyla Lerrol—unlike Lois, one of his own—and befriends his parents as an adult, even attending their wedding. Ultimately, though, he's powerless to change history, and is forced to witness his planet's detsruction.[107] Written by Siegel—whom Weisinger allowed to return as an uncredited freelancer—it's the best of these stories, including the many that followed. It plays out the wistful fantasy of every survivor, and ends with the same heartbreaking, undeniable reality, filled with guilt and sorrow.

Although Superman was created by tragedy and is driven by it, what truly defines him is the love and acceptance he found in America. Like Jewish survivors, it's where he found hopefulness and, like them, it's where years later he discovered others of his family and community who'd survived, including his cousin Supergirl (*Action Comics* #252, May '59) and even his childhood pet Krypto (*Adventure Comics* #210, March '55).

Comic books weren't the only medium in which Superman displayed, alongside daring-dos, emotional gravity and social conscience. His radio show, reaching millions of listeners, spent a great deal of time preaching tolerance and acceptance. Its original opening sequence ('40–'41) declared him a "champion of equal rights, valiant, courageous fighter against the forces of hate and prejudice."

This wasn't unintentional. Jewish showrunner Bob Maxwell enlisted Jewish *New York Times* journalist Ben Peter Freeman to help write the show, with feedback from education consultants, organizations like Big Brothers of America and the National Conference of Christians and Jews, and even famed cultural anthropologist Margaret Mead. It was goodwill propaganda, even given a codename: "Operation Intolerance."[108]

In an epic 38-episode story airing October 11–December 03, 1945, Superman squares off against Atom Man, imbued with the radioactive power of Kryptonite by his father, an escaped Nazi, and mad Nazi scientist Der Teufel (The Devil). He's Superman's counterfoil, with a funhouse mirror origin and even an undercover job at the *Daily Planet*, but he is driven by hate and power-lust, a reminder of their danger not two months after the war ended. He's also Superman's first supervillain proper, with powers, moniker and a costume, consisting of meshed metal gloves and a control box on his throat.[109]

Five months later Superman fought "the Guardians of America," a white supremacist organization whose leaders lure poor and troubled youth into their ranks. Seeking to prevent the building of an interfaith, interracial "Unity House" for children, they engage in vandalism, battery and attempted murder before Superman exposes their leader as a wartime Nazi spy, making clear the connection between American racial intolerance and Nazi evil.[110]

The following month aired the most famous storyline of the radio show, "The Clan of the Fiery Cross." An obvious reference to the Ku Klux Klan, it took on the organization at a time when segregation, quotas and other forms of institutional racism were still the norm. Instead of the romantic aura of a secret cabal that often accompanied the KKK's portrayal, the Clansmen are shown to be ruthless thugs, jealous of the accomplishments of those they deem not "true Americans." Hiding under

George Reeves as Superman in *Superman and the Mole Men*, 1951. Lippert Pictures.

white robes, they seek to intimidate an Asian family by spreading libels and burning a cross on their lawn, eventually attempting to murder them. They even resort to placing a bomb under the child's bike. In the end, Superman puts a stop to their plans while Clark Kent exposes them in the *Planet*.[111]

The story was meant to demystify and trivialize the real Klan, using to this end actual secret code words and rituals supplied by folklorist and author Stetson Kennedy, who infiltrated the organization to provide information to law enforcement agencies, civil rights organizations, and Superman.[112]

The 1948, 15-part Columbia movie serial *Superman*, produced by Sam Katzman and starring Kirk Alyn as the first live-action Man of Steel, also saw the hero using his powers "in the interest of truth, tolerance, and justice."[113]

Tolerance was also the theme of 1951's *Superman and the Mole Men*, the first Superman motion picture (which also doubled as the launchpad for the TV series). Starring a young, lithe George Reeves, it was produced by Barney Sarecky, directed by Lee Sholem and written by "Richard Fielding," alias for the team of Bob Maxwell and Whitney Ellsworth, the token gentile of the group. The plot has Superman stop a town mob from lynching a group of short, hairy mole men (Jews?) who emerged from their subterranean realm because oil drilling had invaded their sanctum. He recognizes that fear of the unfamiliar is the cause of prejudice, reminding audiences that he, too, is a strange visitor from elsewhere and that evil can be perpetrated by good people swept up in a tide of anger and hate.[114]

It's a timeless lesson, but never more timely than soon after the Holocaust and in the midst of McCarthyism. By championing peaceful coexistence—in comics, radio, cinema, PSAs and elsewhere—Superman was a Jewish golem who defended and advocated for all oppressed minorities. In good times and in bad, glum or gleeful, he is a hero forever defined by the circumstances of his birth, in his world and ours.

Your destroyers and those who lay you waste shall come from within you.—Isaiah 49:17

If I Were a Superman

The Silver Age

If the Golden Age of comics began with a big bang, the Silver Age started with lightning strike. Julius "Julie" Schwartz had been a close friend of Weisinger's from the Bronx since they were sixteen. Part of the early clique of sci-fi fans, they'd cofounded the fanzine *The Time Traveler* and both had contributed fan fiction to Siegel's *Science Fiction*. At nineteen, Schwartz became a literary agent specializing in science fiction and fantasy, a niche at the time, representing the likes of H.P. Lovecraft and Ray Bradbury.[1] In 1944 he joined DC as an editor, the affable counterpart to the surly Weisinger.

Schwartz was there for comics' heyday, and he was there for their vicissitude. Trying to keep DC afloat, in 1956 he launched a new series, *Showcase*, a testing ground for new concepts in standalone stories. The first few issues featured stock adventure characters like firemen and frogmen, but in October's issue #4 he introduced, together with Jewish writer Robert Kanigher and artist Carmine Infantino, a reconceptualized version of the Flash. Keeping only the name and power of the 1940 superhero, the new Flash was Barry Allen, a police scientist who was struck by lightning and flung through a cabinet of chemicals, endowing him with super-speed. Decades ahead of shows like *CSI*, he used his scientific prowess as much as his super-powers to solve crimes and apprehend criminals.

The electric shock that gave the Flash his powers also defibrillated the super-hero genre back to life, revitalizing the comic book industry and kicking off the Silver Age. Applying his science fiction background to other stale characters, Schwartz helped revamp Green Lantern, Hawkman, the Atom and others, giving each a modern twist. Green Lantern's power ring, for example, was now the product of advanced alien technology rather than magic.

A cavalcade of new and reimagined characters followed, a superhero renaissance that Fingeroth compares to the Second Temple period.[2] But, while the industry experienced a revival, it wasn't yet a revolution. For that, something marvelous had to happen.

Inspired by DC's success, Marvel editor in chief Stan Lee decided to try his hand again at superheroes, this time inventing his own instead of writing others.[3] Together with Jack Kirby he co-created the Fantastic Four, debuting in November 1961, sparking a manic period of brilliant creativity in which they created together an entire pantheon, including the Hulk ('62), Thor ('62), Iron Man ('63), Avengers ('63), X-Men

('63), Silver Surfer ('66), Black Panther ('66) and countless others, while Lee also co-created Spider-Man ('62) and Doctor Strange ('63) with Steve Ditko and Daredevil ('64) with Bill Everett.

More than just new characters, they created a new approach to the genre, introducing greater realism and deeper characterization. They also infused it with the melodrama of teen romance comics and recast monsters as outcast heroes, which appealed to teenage readers in particular. Marvel became, and stayed, the industry innovator, coming to be known as "the House of Ideas," while Lee and Kirby earned the monikers "Stan the Man" and "King of Comics." They may not be widely thought of as such, but their output and its impact on modern culture makes Lee one of the most influential writers of the 20th century and Kirby one of its most influential artists.

Just as comics were invented by young Jewish novices in the 1930s, they were reinvented by middle-aged, seasoned warhorses like Schwartz, Lee and Kirby in the late 1950s and early 1960s. A new crop of young Jewish creators would soon join, while Jewish youths also helped establish comics as a viable, if still stigmatized, industry: In July 1964, five teens—Bernie Bubnis, Ethan Roberts, Ron Fradkin, Art Tripp and Leonard "Len" Wein (who'd go on to write Superman, among other characters, and co-create new ones like Swamp Thing and Wolverine)—organized the first comic book convention, held in New York's East Village neighborhood, in a small hall on the second floor of a Jewish fraternal organization. It was a modest gathering of 43 attendees, which would grow to become today the pop culture Mecca that is San Diego Comic-Con (aka Comic-Con International: San Diego), with 130,000 attendees, and its East Coast counterpart, New York Comic Con, with 250,000. The very first ticket was bought by a sixteen year old named George R.R. Martin, future author of *Game of Thrones*.[3]

In many ways the Silver Age was Superman's true golden age, a period of grandeur and fertile invention that shaped much of who he is today. Many of his Jewish themes were also expanded upon, though this has been all but ignored by scholars. With the exception of Fingeroth, what literature exists on the subject of his Jewish signification limits its attention to his formative years, from 1938 to 1954.

Much of Superman's enrichment during this era, Jewish and otherwise, owes to the indelible influence of Mort Weisinger. Weisinger had been a Superman editor since before the war, working during the 1950s under editorial director Whitney Ellsworth. When the *Adventures of Superman* show was cancelled in 1958 and Ellsworth, who served as its producer, editor and writer, opted to stay in Hollywood, Weisinger became the demiurge of Superman's world (beginning with *Action Comics* #241 and *Superman* #122).

Even under the Sauron eye of the CCA, comics were still largely targeted at adolescents and young adults. Weisinger decided to aim his at children, a large and quickly growing market following the baby boom. (He even hired them, assigning thirteen-year-old prodigy Jim Shooter, a future industry luminary, to write an immensely successful Superman spin-off, *The Legion of Super-Heroes*.[4])

The kid-friendly nature of Superman's adventures became the hallmark of his Silver Age tenure; colorful, whimsical and outlandish. They were frequently "imaginary stories" in which Krypton is never destroyed, or he's never found by the Kents, or Lois exposes his true identity or tricks him into marrying her (or marries Luthor, or Luthor marries Martha Kent), or his powers temporarily change or disappear. The latter also frequently occurred in his "real" stories, forcing him to rely on his wits, which Weisinger believed made him more likeable.[5]

Weisinger co-created or helped introduce a great many new elements to the mythology, notably Superman's powers resulting from exposure to Earth's yellow sun, the Fortress of Solitude, the Phantom Zone, the bottle city of Kandor, the various color types of Kryptonite, and new characters like Supergirl, Krypto the Super Dog, Bizarro and the Legion of Super-Heroes.[6]

His greatest contribution, however, in his own opinion, was to give Superman "a 'mythology' which covered all bases."[7] The norm in pulps and comics until then was a central idea—a hero and his mission—without much character development or storyline progression. But Superman, Weisinger understood, was more than just popular. He meant something. He also understood that without continuity, without the stakes meaning something and things having repercussions, readers, even young ones, wouldn't be that invested. And so, with the diligence of a Midrashic sage attempting to answer questions and inconsistencies in the Bible, he established canonicity in Superman's lore, the first in a comic book property and one more vast and detailed than arguably any other character's in popular fiction.

It was made possible by the complete control he was given over the character, the aid of his assistant editor, E. Nelson Bridwell, who had "an encyclopedic memory for everything comics … and the bible,"[8] and, instrumentally, his choice to rehire Jerry Siegel in 1959 to continue charting the course for his creation. Siegel was 45 now, and he brought a new level of depth and maturity to his writing.

"Jerry, whom I consider the most competent of all the Superman writers, established the foundation for the series," Weisinger said. "What his successors did was just embroidery, including my own contributions. Siegel was the best emotional writer of them all." Schwartz likewise considered Siegel "a genius." The feeling wasn't mutual. Siegel detested Weisinger's constant rejections and revisions of his writing on his own character, which dated back to his time working under him in the 1940s. But he was destitute, had a baby to feed and it was a chance to be reunited with his brainchild. After eleven years of estrangement he was back at DC, quietly writing his Superman again, now as a freelancer, without a byline and at a fraction of his former pay (beginning presumably with *Action Comics* #259 [December '59] and *Superman* #135 [February '60] and lasting until *Action Comics* #326 [July '65] and *Superman* #202 [December '67], though his assignments were irregular and his stories from that time were uncredited).[9] Still, it was a prolific period. He wrote issues of *Action Comics*; *Superman*; *Superboy*; *Supergirl*; *Superman's Girl Friend, Lois Lane*; *Superman's Pal, Jimmy Olsen*; *Legion of Super-Heroes* and others, creating many new characters and concepts that are still in use today.

The years since he last worked for DC had been difficult. He found himself itinerant between short-lived jobs for different publishers, hiding behind pen names like "Joe Carter" and "Jerry Ess." He even did work for Marvel while already back at DC, writing the Human Torch lead feature in *Strange Tales*, but after only two issues

(#112–113, September–October '63) he was deemed "too campy" and let go. Lee, who'd known him for years, gave him some work as a proofreader. "Everybody liked him," Lee remembered. "He was a hard worker."[10]

His low pay and lack of benefits or job security at DC, coupled with his lowly status and Weisinger's overbearingness, brought his resentment to a boil. In 1966 DC's copyright registration of Superman was about to expire (the law then limiting ownership to 28 years), and he and Shuster planned to sue for ownership again. Again DC caught wind, and again he was fired. The lawsuit was eventually filed in 1969, arguing that, since they'd created Superman before selling him to DC, the intellectual property was not a "work for hire" and wasn't DC's to renew ownership over. Accounts of the events vary; Tye writes that the case was ruled in favor of the defendants in 1973, while Van Lente writes that they dropped the suit in exchange for a promise of a generous stipend that was never delivered upon.[11] Either way, they never worked on Superman again.

Like in the Golden Age, Silver Age superhero comics reflected the preoccupations of the time. Most new characters owed their origins to atomic power or radiation, usually by accident, from DC's Captain Atom to Gold Key's Doctor Solar to virtually all the Marvel heroes. With the launch of *Sputnik* on October 4, 1957, the space age began, and with it science fiction, which was already popular, became all the rage. The good guys and bad guys took their fight from city streets and battlefields to outer space, which also proved a new canvass for literary exploration in the hands of "serious" authors like Isaac Asimov and Ray Bradbury.

Then in 1965 came *Star Trek*, merging action and philosophy in what was the most progressive show on television for years to come. A pioneer of earnest utopian science fiction (as opposed to Thomas More's sarcastic *Utopia*, George Orwell's dystopian *1984* or the phobic films of the 1950s), in the midst of the Cold War it portrayed a peaceful future based in large part on socialistic ideals (no capitalism, collective mission, full equality, world government) featuring multinational, multi-ethnic characters.

For the first time in human history the stars themselves, the stuff of dreams and legends, were within reach. It was only natural that Superman would epitomize it. While his powers and origin unmistakably count as science fiction, the genre he debuted in was socially-minded crime noir, quickly adding elements of movie serial grand adventure, then war stories. There were ray guns and experimental gasses and the occasional rocket ship or giant robot, but these were props. His stories were earthbound, dealing with crime, corruption and war, and his enemies mostly wore suits or military uniforms. But by the late 1950s he was regularly visiting distant planets, encountering other beings and traveling through time. It was then that his core genre became science fiction, which it remains today.

It was this space opera and superpowered spectacle that also gave rise to the majority of Superman's rogues' gallery. Curiously, though the concept of supervillains already existed (the first costumed villain with supernatural abilities was likely Fawcett Comics' Captain Nazi, first appearing in December 1941's *Master Comics* #21 as an adversary of Captain Marvel and Bulletman), the idea of providing the world's mightiest hero with formidable antagonists hadn't occurred to his handlers. He spent most of his time fighting gangsters and renegade scientists, often in overwrought plots that provided the needed tension (partly no doubt to match the TV series, the scope of which was limited by budget). Finally, he was pitted against genuine threats like Brainiac, Bizarro, Metallo, General Zod and the Parasite.

In truth, the Silver Age consists of two periods for Superman, the latter being one of steady decline. All the innovation—the supervillains, Fortress of Solitude, Kandor, Supergirl, sun-based powers, Phantom Zone—took place before 1965, with the Parasite being the outlier in 1966. His stories in the latter part of the Silver Age, while maintaining the same overall tone, largely recycled the same concepts, wearing them thin. Partly, it could be because Weisinger's intense workload and pressure, coupled with his nerves and an overuse of prescription drugs, led to an ulcer, hypertension, insomnia and eventually a nervous breakdown,[12] leaving the ship without its captain.

More likely, the culprit was the space race. Space was the new frontier, the new Manifest Destiny. It was science fiction made fact, instilled with the moral imperative of the Cold War. Astronauts wore iconic uniforms and risked their lives in the name of high ideals and patriotism and flew around in rocket ships and had adventures in outer space. They were real-life superheroes, and the make-believe ones just couldn't compete. Leaping tall buildings in a single bound was mundane compared to Neil Armstrong's one giant leap. Superman was the past. John Glenn was the shiny chromed future.

While *Superman* was the top comic from 1962 to 1965 (not to mention his comics being translated into different languages in 42 countries), between 1965 and 1969 monthly sales dropped by 38 percent, roughly from 824,000 to 512,000, and would continue to decline throughout the following Bronze Age.[13] Superman's legend would only grow, but his comics would never be best-sellers again for any sustained period of time.

The 1960s didn't just change Superman. They were, as *Life* magazine dubbed them, "The Decade When Everything Changed."[14] Everything was in ferment—politics, war, gender relations, race relations, esthetics and entertainment. Americans faced frightening new realities like nuclear Armageddon, the Berlin Wall and the interminable Vietnam War; social change movements like the Sexual Revolution, Women's Liberation, Civil Rights, Antiwar and Flower Children; and watershed moments like the Cuban Missile Crisis, George Wallace's "Stand in the Schoolhouse Door," Kennedy's "Camelot" presidency and assassination, Washington and Selma marches, the Voting Rights Act of 1965, Martin Luther King's assassination, Robert Kennedy's assassination, the Manson Family Murders, Stonewall riots, Summer of Love, Woodstock and the moon landing. It was an age of anomie and aspiration, turmoil and transformation.

It was also when emergent mass media and youth culture birthed pop culture, in turn giving rise to the pop art movement. Challenging dogmas of high and low art, it incorporated elements from film, music, politics, industry, advertising and comics. In fact, comic book art is at the origin of pop art; Richard Hamilton's 1956 collage, *Just what is it that makes today's homes so different, so appealing?*, considered the first significant pop art, includes at its center Jack Kirby's cover of *Young Romance*

#26. Out of the five pop paintings Andy Warhol first exhibited in 1961, one was *Superman*, based on Kurt Schaffenberger's art from *Superman's Girlfriend, Lois Lane #24*.[15] (He'd make another in 1981, using Curt Swan art.) Roy Lichtenstein used comic books as source material in many of his works, copying panels and images from romance, war and superhero comics, then simplifying the art to highlight its commercialism. Whether or not in doing so he made real art out of comics or simply plagiarized them is subject to debate, though several of his pieces show little actual change from the originals.

It's ironic that pop art, championing the artistic merit of the common and the commercial, patronized comics as something to critique rather than recognizing their value, particularly as an original art form in itself. Still, the rise of pop art gave comics the boost they needed to reach the mainstream. America fell in love with camp, with psychedelia, with over-the-top everything, the louder and more colorful the better, and superheroes found themselves celebrated again, if in a new way.

The short-lived but immensely popular *Batman* TV series starring Adam West ('66–'68), while further stigmatizing comics as kitsch, also brought into wide culture the iconography of comics, a world of symbols in action, as well as the famous, or infamous, *Pow! Zap! Wham! Kapow!*

Comics, particularly Superman's, also pervaded the English language. "Brainiac" formally entered the Oxford Dictionary, becoming a common term for someone who's highly intelligent or a know-it-all, along with "Bizarro" for someone who's strange or does things in an opposite manner than expected and "Kryptonite" as a synonym for Achilles' heel.[16]

Artistically, no single comic book artist has had the influence "King" Kirby had, particularly his 1960s–1970s oeuvre. Fusing a mishmash of influences—midcentury commercial, European avant-garde, surrealism, expressionism, cubism, op art, Piranesi—into a visual language all his own, his innovation in composition, dynamism and design can be found today in almost all forms of visual communication.

Superman reflected very little of all this. Artistically, his comics were solid but conservative. Curt Swan, arguably the definitive Superman artist, drew his Man of Steel to look younger, pushing thirty instead of forty, more muscular than stocky and with softer features that made him more handsome. His storytelling was more naturalistic and nuanced, which grounded Superman in the real world and, in doing so, emphasized his incredible powers and exploits, but it also made things appear stiff and static sometimes.

Narratively, Superman disengaged from the real world. If his Golden Age comics were dark but exuberant, and his postwar era listless, his Silver Age escapades were largely bright, boisterous and vapid. Following his social and political activism in the preceding decades, found in all his media manifestations, his concerns in the 1960s became as fictional as he is. The Red Menace was conspicuously absent from his comics. There were no Soviet nukes to stop, no spies or saboteurs to apprehend. He remained safely homebound in Metropolis, focusing his attention on the parochial—the endless parade of criminals who thought it was a good idea to rob a bank in Superman's town—and the celestial—invading aliens, usually in armadas of one or two small ships.

Metropolis felt like no place in particular, clean, orderly, sunny, a Stepford city, with no signs of socioeconomic disparity or racial diversity. So did Smallville, caught in nostalgic yesteryear like a fly in ember. The Man of Tomorrow fell behind the times. His first regular black cast member, *Daily Planet* colleague Ron Troupe, wouldn't appear until 1991.[17]

There were also no wars to fight after World War II. Having battled the Nazis with fervor, he ignored the Korean War and involved himself with the Vietnam War, an intractable twenty-year campaign, only once, in May 1969's *Superman* #216. Even then, he intervened briefly to stop a superpowered enemy and returned home, in a story that's neither jingoistic nor critical.[18]

Weisinger deliberately kept Superman out of the social upheaval of the era and, presumably, any contentious subject matter. He was after all a corporate property now. Tye also suggests that, as a right-wing man in a largely left-wing industry, Weisinger opted to avoid any potential conflicts. But it also had to do with his own predilections. "Dreaming up socially conscious plots on the kid level really turns me off," he admitted shortly before retiring.[19]

Instead, Superman went cosmic. He was still a hopeless square, but his comics went from charmingly silly romps to unbridled absurdism, hallucinogenic miasmas that appealed to the very young or the very high. Jimmy Olsen routinely switched brains with gorillas (*Superman's Pal, Jimmy Olsen* #24, #49, #86, #116) and nearly married one (#98). Superboy and the Legion of Super-Heroes stopped a colossal space amoeba from eating the sun in *Adventure Comics* #352. In *Superman's Girl Friend, Lois Lane* #30, one of Superman's doppelgänger robots built a robot-mermaid wife and son on the distant planet Yorrp, breaking a confused Lois's heart. (The Superman-Clark-Lois love triangle also morphed from a dramatic element to more of a *commedia dell'arte*.)

There was Superbaby, a recurring backup feature about the mischiefs of an infant Superman, wearing a barelegged onesie version of his costume. There was also a Super-retinue that included his teenage cousin Supergirl and the Legion of Super-Pets, a menagerie of animals with superpowers and capes that included Krypto the Super Dog, Streaky the Supercat, Beppo the Super-Monkey, Comet the Super Horse, and Proty II, a cute protoplasmic alien blob (the first Proty, alas, had died). Superman was no longer the sole survivor of his planet and no longer alone, though he may have wished he was.

It was also when his powers grew to be virtually limitless, in both might and variety, elevating him from a super-man to a god and making him his own *deus ex machina*. His super-speed increased to the point that he could travel through time at whim; he gained the powers of super-hypnosis; super-ventriloquism; super-weaving; super-memory; super-mathematics (which he gets wrong); even super-kissing. He accidently destroys a barren solar system with a super-sneeze, and in a particularly memorable story temporarily gains the ability to produce a homunculus replica of himself out of the palm of his hand, fully costumed and imbued with all his powers.[20]

Other DC characters had similarly outlandish stories, notably Batman, but Superman's trippy exploits came to symbolize the frivolity of the Silver Age. His power increase and gimmicked plots were doubtlessly in part a response to growing competition from Marvel and other DC superheroes, a challenge faced by every original idea. But it was perhaps also a response to the changing perspective of American Jews, a reckoning with their past inadequacy, their changing place in American society and their future identity.

The theme of the sixties was reinvention. Of self, personal and group relationships, cultural structures and mores and, for Jews, their Judaism and Jewishness. The reality of the Holocaust was sinking in, with books like Elie Wiesel's *Night* ('60), *Dawn* ('61) and *Day* ('62), *The Diary of Anne Frank*, which early in the decade became part of the national school curriculum,[21] and films like *Judgment at Nuremberg* ('61) and *The Pawnbroker* ('64). The trial of Adolf Eichmann was a true "trial of the century," dominating world headlines for two years and leading to Hannah Arendt's landmark *Eichmann in Jerusalem: A Report on the Banality of Evil* ('63).

There was an understanding, for the first time, that the stereotypes, stigmas and intolerances toward Jews have a direct causal relation to the violence against them. With that, Jews were freer to shape their own social image and their own path in society. Their contributions to the culture had been significant throughout the first half of the 20th century, but they were also largely veiled to both appeal to and avoid the scorn of the general public. The counterculture revolution, however, replaced conformity as a value with the challenge of authority, and American tastes changed to prefer caustic, irreverent entertainment that "stuck it to the man." Jews, with centuries of experience in exactly that, finally brought out their Jewishness from behind the curtain.

When in September 1964 *Fiddler on the Roof* premiered on Broadway, named after a Marc Chagall motif and starring Zero Mostel, it was their collective "coming out." They could finally breathe a sigh of relief and have a good laugh at past hardship. They turned the longstanding suffering of the shtetls and the brutal violence of the pogroms into whimsical song and dance. The critical acclaim and massive popularity of the musical, followed by a successful film adaptation in 1971 starring Israeli actor Chaim Topol, only added to the sense that, finally, the storm had passed.

It was also safe now for Jews to poke fun at their great champion. *Fiddler*'s producer Harold Prince also produced and directed a short-lived, though not badly received, whimsical musical in 1966 titled *It's a Bird…. It's a Plane…. It's Superman,* written by duo Robert Benton and David Newman, the latter Jewish, who'd go on to write the second treatment of the Superman movie script. Shuster would go down to Broadway to see the celebrities attending, like Frank Sinatra and President Lyndon Johnson, but he was never able to watch the show himself. He couldn't afford the ticket.[22] It's unclear if Siegel ever bothered.

For decades, almost everything in film and television was produced, written and directed by Jews and almost nothing starred or discussed them. All of a sudden, on camera, radio and stage, in literature and politics, Jews were everywhere. It was as if, like the cartoon Road Runner, they had been gathering momentum in place, just waiting for the opportunity to zoom ahead.

The American cultural landscape became filled with figures like Eddie Cantor (Edward Israel Itzkowitz), Sid Caesar (Isaac Ziser), Milton Berle (Mendel Berlinger), Lenny Bruce (Schneider), Mel Brooks (Melvin Kaminsky), Rob Reiner, Bob Dylan

(Zimmerman), Paul Simon, Art Garfunkel, Primo Levi, Saul Bellow, Philip Roth, Bernard Malamud, Joseph Heller, J.D. Salinger, Arthur Miller, Norman Mailer, Neil Simon, Stephen Sondheim, Bette Midler, William Shatner, Leonard Nimoy, Stanley Kubrick, Peter Sellers, Kirk Douglas (Issur Danielovitch), Paul Newman, Elliott Gould (Goldstein), George Segal, Barbara Walters, Mike Wallace (Wallik), Billy (Samuel) Wilder, Tony Curtis (Bernard Schwartz), Walter Matthau, George Burns (Nathan Birnbaum), Henry (Heinz) Kissinger and American-Israeli Golda Meir (Meyerson).

For many, it was time to transform their parents' surreptitiousness into a new brand of Jewishness, ethnically loud and proud. And America embraced them. When baseball legend Sandy Koufax (Sanford Braun) refused to pitch at the 1965 World Series because it fell on Yom Kippur, it garnered national attention. Barbara Streisand became a sex symbol not despite but because of her *schnoz*. And Dustin Hoffman and Woody Allen (Allan Konigsberg) overturned conceptions of manliness, from broad-shouldered, assertive macho to intelligent, sensitive and funny.

As Rich Cohen writes, "For perhaps the only time in history, you might actually want to be a Jew." And some of America's biggest celebrities did. In 1956, the ultimate blond bombshell, Marilyn Monroe, converted to Judaism when she married celebrated playwright Arthur Miller, an improbable match that enraptured the country and helped bring Jewish life, particularly intellectualism, into the mainstream. She remained Jewish even after their divorce in 1961, until her untimely death a year later. Elizabeth Taylor, arguably the biggest movie star in the world at the time, converted in 1959, becoming a passionate supporter of Israel through charity work and visiting the nascent state several times. Sammy Davis, Jr., likewise converted in 1961.[23]

Jewish staples like bagels and cream cheese, corned beef on rye, dill pickles and chicken soup became not only part of the New York diet but spread to heretofore bastions of burgers and BBQ. "Schmuck" became American vernacular, along with other Yiddishisms-turned-New Yorkisms-turned-Americanisms like glitch, klutz, putz, nebbish, oy, shtick, spiel and spritz.

Rachel Shukert, author, journalist and staff writer on the *Supergirl* TV series, wrote in *Tablet*, "That's irony for you. For all the hand-wringing about assimilation, we didn't turn into them. We turned them into us."[24]

It was also the golden age of Jewish-American writing, perhaps not coincidently of American literature in general. In particular, Jewish writers, some of which appeared on the scene the decade prior, dealt with Jewish themes with increasing explicitness, often through semi or fully autobiographical works, including Levi, Heller, Salinger, Bellow, Malamud, Miller, Roth, Mailer, Ginsberg and, of course, Siegel, Finger, Weisinger, Schwartz, Lee and Kirby. Many of these themes—Antisemitism, the Holocaust, survivor's guilt, assimilation, conflict of identity, interfaith relationships—had been reflected in Superman's texts for years, now explored freely and more deeply in literary prose.

Mordant, anarchic Jewish humor transformed American satire from cuddling to biting, pioneered by stand-up and sketch comics like George Burns (Nathan Birnbaum), Lenny Bruce, Don Rickles, Woody Allen and Joan Rivers (Molinsky), who threw darts at political, religious, racial, sexual and social norms, usually vulgarly, merging the Talmudic tradition of observation and endless reflection with the role of the court jester. So did Carl Reiner and Mel Brooks in their "2000 year old Man" series of TV skits and hit comedy albums. Brooks, on his part, went on in 1968 to create *The Producers*, with its play within a play, *Springtime for Hitler: A Gay Romp with Adolf and Eva at Berchtesgaden*, the supreme cathartic act of Jewish-American comedy.

Jerry Lewis (Levitch), the living embodiment of Borscht Belt humor, with his frenzied neurosis and fitful Yiddish exclamations like *froinlaven!* (loosely, "nice lady"), even met Superman in his own DC series, *The Adventures of Jerry Lewis* #105, where he tries on the costume and—what else—is mistaken for a masked Man of Steel by Lex Luthor, hijinks ensuing.[25] Juxtaposed, the mild-mannered, bumbling Clark Kent isn't nearly as slapstick as Lewis, but the two do share a restrained timidity that promises to explode into hyperkinetic action at a moment's notice.

And then there was *Mad*. Born in 1952 as a comic book by industry black sheep EC Comics and switching to magazine format in 1955 (among other reasons to avoid the CCA), by 1973 it reached a circulation of 2.8 million, more than most newspapers. Edited and at first entirely written by Harvey Kurtzman, it featured what Fingeroth accurately describes as a "very New York Yiddish sense of humor and irony,"[26] a mix of trenchant satire, gallows humor and a strong liberal bent, which have since become the norm in American comedy, from *Saturday Night Live* to *Seinfeld* to *The Simpsons*. It also regularly incorporated Yiddish, like *furshlugginer*, *schmaltz*, *oy*, *feh*, *ganefs* and *kaputnik*. Even the catchphrase of *Mad's* famed mascot, Alfred E. Newman—"What, me worry?"—is a translation of the Yiddish idiom *isch ga bibble*.

Of particular note, issue #4 introduced what would become a recurring spoof, "Superduperman." Just as hapless in costume as when disguised as lowly Clark Bent, the befuddled hero asks, "Shazoom? Vas ist das Shazoom?" A random use of Yiddish that hints at the all-American hero's hidden ethnicity. (Although to be fair, he also exclaims "*pastafazoola!*")[27]

Jewish culture also manifested in science fiction. Unprecedented, both of *Star Trek's* lead actors were openly Jewish. William Shatner and Leonard Nimoy both came from Orthodox Jewish families that fled the pogroms and both spoke Yiddish as their first language. "Everything I do is informed by my Judaism," Nimoy said in an interview. "A lot of what I've put into Spock came to me through my Jewish orientation." A half-human, half-alien from an advanced race dedicated to logical thinking and scientific pursuit, Mr. Spock is essentially a Jewish stereotype in sci-fi clothing. More specifically, Spock's famous Vulcan Salute was created by Nimoy based on *Birchat HaKohanim*—the ancient blessing performed by the Jewish high priests, using the hand to form the Hebrew letter Shin (שׁ), standing for Shaddai (שַׁדַּי), one of the biblical names of God.[28] The accompanying greeting, "live long and prosper," is from Deuteronomy 5:33, where Moses, after forty years of wandering through the desert, finally delivers the Hebrews to the Promised Land, which he cannot enter, wishing them, "live and prosper and prolong your days."

The biggest change in Jewish representation was on the big screen. Film critic J. Hoberman identifies Mike Nicholas' (Peschkowsky) 1967 hit *The Graduate* as the first in what he calls "the Jewish new wave," lasting until 1972, featuring Jewish actors,

Jewish protagonists, a Jewish sensibility and often Jewish subject matter. While as a trend this may true, the real game changer was 1960's *Exodus*. Based on Leon Uris's 1958 novel of the same name—the biggest bestseller in the U.S. since 1936's *Gone with the Wind*—it starred Paul Newman and Eva Marie Saint (who'd go on to play Martha Kent in *Superman Returns*). The film portrayed Israel's creation and fight for survival through the story of Ari Ben-Canaan (based on real-life Yossi Harel), a Holocaust- and battle-hardened commander of the Haganah militia.[29]

In *The Jewish Image in American Film*, Lester Friedman describes, "American audiences met a character far different from Hollywood's earlier portraits of weak, ineffectual, and passive Jews that had dominated America's screens since the silent days." Both Newman and his character were handsome, confident, secular Jews, the difference being Ben-Canaan's anti-assimilationism and mistrust of gentiles.[30] A Jew finally got to be the hero, inspiring a small wave of similar action-dramas, notably 1966's *Cast a Giant Shadow*, a star-studded production starring Kirk Douglas as the real-life Colonel David "Mickey" Marcus, a Jewish-American World War II hero who left to become the first Israeli general, and so the first commander of a Jewish army since Simon Bar-Kokhba. It also starred John Wayne, Frank Sinatra, Yul Brynner and Angie Dickinson.

Philip Roth would later write, "I find that I am suddenly living in a country in which the Jew has come to be—or is allowed for now to think he is—a cultural hero … the image of the Jew as patriot, warrior, and battle-scarred belligerent is rather satisfying to a large segment of the American public…. It fills any number of Jewish readers with pride … and gentile readers … with relief."[31]

What ultimately transformed the Jewish image, however, was Israel. With Jewish irredentism reshaping millennia-old barren desert into a vibrant, modern country, Diasporic Jews looked to their ancestral homeland as the state of the future. It was a place of modern miracles and of divine providence to some, surviving and thriving despite inhospitable terrain, increasingly hostile British rule and the 1948 War of Independence: The newly-formed Israel Defense Forces, vastly outnumbered and without a single cannon or tank, won against the combined might of five invading Arab armies promising "a war of annihilation … a momentous massacre in history." It was the victory of David over Goliath, though a costly one. Nearly 1 percent of the entire Jewish population were killed.[32]

It was also the crucible in which the New Jew was born. Israel's founding father and first prime minister, David Ben-Gurion ('48–'53), declared, "Israel has created a new image of the Jew in the world—the image of a working and an intellectual people, of a people that can fight with heroism."[33] No longer seen as merely timid and cerebral, Jews were now rugged pioneers, a new mythological creature that was farmer, warrior, builder and scientist, muscular and erudite, olive-skinned and blue-eyed. They were Captain America, meek denizens of ghettos transformed into super-soldiers, Clark Kents turned into Supermen through field labor and military service.

The 1967 Six-Day War in particular changed attitudes toward Israel, as well as toward, and by, American Jews. Brandeis University professor of American Jewish History, Jonathan D. Sarna, and Jonathan Golden, write; "The paralyzing fear of a 'second Holocaust' followed by tiny Israel's seemingly miraculous victory over the combined Arab armies arrayed to destroy it struck deep emotional chords among American Jews." In yet another victory against overwhelming odds, this time swift and decisive, the Jewish state's future was no longer tenuous. For Jews, it was the first true sign of optimism in a century of horrors. America was also no longer the center of world Jewry, and Israel offered a new version of Jewish practice, culture and self-definition, inspiring "something of a spiritual revival ... [in] the American Jewish community ... many turned religiously inward, some were 'born again' into Orthodoxy, and every movement in American Judaism witnessed new interest in traditional religious practices, heightened appreciation for mystical and spiritual sources, and an enhanced desire for Jewish learning."[34]

Israel's triumphs also inspired a willingness to fight social wrongs. It's no coincidence that the Civil Rights Movement came on the heels of the Holocaust; for many Americans it brought about a sobering realization about the nature of bigotry, and for Jews it created a moral imperative. Having survived genocide, and as nonwhites who could pass for whites and, for the first time, were accepted, at least provisionally, as whites, American Jews were in a position to understand and to help. Most were "truth to power" progressives, and the fighting spirit they saw in their Middle Eastern brethren emboldened them.

Jews comprised over 30 percent of white Freedom Riders, the activists who rode buses to the South to picket segregated establishments and register blacks to vote—more than ten times their share of the population. President of the American Jewish Congress, Rabbi Joachim Prinz, spoke at the March on Washington about Jewish solidarity with the black cause, born of a shared painful history of slavery, segregation and ghettoization. When Martin Luther King gave his historic "I Have a Dream" speech, it was one he'd co-written with his close friend and advisor, Stanley Levison.[35]

The transformation of Jewish identity, image and place in American culture was reflected primarily in Marvel Comics' new wave of superheroes, which brought the themes that had been part of the genre since its inception close to the surface. While DC offered byzantine plots and safe escapism, Marvel brought a more familiar scale to even their most far-fetched adventures through the use of deeply flawed, identifiable characters, making them humans with superpowers rather than superhumans. And they told their stories with the flavor of Yiddish theater plays, effusive melodramas spiced with cynical humor. As discussed by Weinstein and Kaplan and in greater detail by Fingeroth, their comics were brimming with Jewish signification.

While Marvel supplanted DC as Jewish metaphor-maker, DC was still firmly the industry leader,[36] and Superman's Jewish themes continued to express themselves, if in new ways (and despite Weisinger's distaste, subtly commented on contemporary issues, especially under Siegel's hand). As absurd and jocular as his comics of the era may have been, they were also full of poignancy, exploring much more readily his status as an orphaned refugee and lonely alien.

Superman spent the sixties in mourning, a tortured soul traumatized by the tragedy of his past and wistful for his lost parents and people. The threats he faced grew direr, often with the fate of the entire world hanging in the balance. Nuclear proliferation and the popularity of space invader films raised the stakes, but his sense of burden and urgency evoked a deeper, more visceral understanding of annihilation.

The evil of his new breed of villains was also more personal. Each of the Phantom Zone criminals could potentially overcome him, and their worst, Zod, carried over his blood feud with his father. Brainiac had been an enemy of Krypton, a powerful spacefaring alien who, several years before the planet was destroyed, miniaturized and abducted its entire capital city Kandor, keeping it in a bottle with all its inhabitants. When Superman stopped him from doing the same to Metropolis, he found it aboard his ship, bringing it to his Fortress until he could restore it to size.[37]

The idea of an entire community—and by virtue of being the last of its kind, an entire race—forcibly displaced and deprived of freedom, and that its people were later counted to number six million,[38] inescapably evokes the Jewish plight as uprooted refugees and of the Holocaust. At the same time, it's the fantasy of a community preserved, a remnant of the Old World and the old way of life. That it remains in a bottle means that the past is both within reach and safely separate from the new life. (Why they choose to remain bottled simply because of their size, or why Superman and Supergirl are able to shrink themselves to visit the city and then enlarge themselves back but not the others, is never explained.)

A rich metaphor, it could equally stand for Israel, a tiny bastion of a remaining people, preserving a culture nearly lost and continuing its ancient splendor. Kandorians are the *sh'erit ha-pletah*—the escaped remnant—of their people, a biblical term (Ezra 9:14, I Chron. 4:43) used to refer to the Holocaust survivors who helped form the Jewish state.

Superman, meanwhile, was made an honorary citizen of every nation in the UN in *Superman* #146 (July '61)—talk about Jewish wish fulfillment. But his proudest moment was also his saddest; the same issue made a small but pivotal change to his origin, portraying him jettisoned from Krypton not as a newborn but as a three year old, giving him memories of his family, culture and language (Kryptonese, later called Kryptonian).[39] He was no longer an immigrant who'd only ever known his new home. He was now a man whose childhood was taken from him, who witnessed his family wiped out. It deepened his pain and gave his ethos a greater dimension of tragedy.

The peak of Superman's Silver Age gravitas—and Jewish signification—is "The Death of Superman" in *Superman* #149 (November '61), written by Siegel. Several influential Superman handlers cite it as their favorite Silver Age comic, including Marv Wolfman, Roger Stern, Jerry Ordway, Kurt Busiek and John Byrne, as well as Jerry Siegel himself. In his unpublished memoir, he takes particular pride in two uncredited stories: "Superman's Return to Krypton" in *Superman* #141 and *Superman* #149.[40] Both are exceptional stories, captivating and emotional, but seemingly there's nothing thematic connecting the Last Son of Krypton visiting his home world and an "imaginary" tale in which Luthor murders him.

In the latter, Luthor finally manages to outwit his sworn enemy and kill him. He goes into hiding, believing he got away with it, until he's nabbed by Supergirl, whose existence then was still a secret, working as Superman's covert operative. She brings Luthor to trial not in Metropolis or the World Court but in Kandor, where he's told "you killed a Kryptonian, and so you will be tried **by** Kryptonians!" Televisions around the world show him gloating behind an enclosed glass stand, until he's eventually sentenced to death.

The story was published during the height of the Eichmann trial and is clearly based on it. The worst Nazi criminal to ever be caught, Eichmann was the chief architect of Jews' deportation to the extermination camps. He'd fled to Argentina, a non-extradition country, where in May 1960 he was captured by the Mossad, Israel's clandestine intelligence agency. He was brought to stand trial in Jerusalem, by the people of his victims in their own sovereign state, where the remorseless Eichmann stood behind bulletproof glass, receiving front-page and primetime coverage worldwide, until in December 1961 he was convicted and sentenced to death.

Siegel wasn't being subtle. Luthor is even called "the greatest villain since Adolf Eichmann!" But the explicit comparison between Superman's worst enemy and the Jews' worst living enemy, and of the Jewish and Kryptonian people's right to self-determination as the judges of their persecutors, wasn't enough. Luthor smugly believes he'll avoid paying for his crimes by offering his scientific brilliance to provide Kandor with their greatest desire. "Punishing me won't bring **Superman** back!" he tells the court. "Let's compromise! Let me go, and I'll build a ray that'll enlarge Kandor." To his utter surprise he's rebuffed, informed that "We Kandorians don't make deals with murderers!"[41]

Luthor here stands for the 1,500 Nazi scientists who, despite being war criminals, were moved to the U.S. as part of Operation Paperclip, the most noted and notorious of which being Wernher von Braun, inventor of the V-series rockets that blitzed London, killing 30,000 and injuring 50,000. A colonel in the SS, von Braun also oversaw the slave labor of camp prisoners and resultant death of thousands, mostly Jews, but after the war was provided full amnesty and citizenship by the U.S. in exchange for helping it win the arms and space races. He developed the rockets for America's first space satellite and first series of moon missions, making him a celebrated hero. The Smithsonian annual lecture, National Space Society award and American Astronautical Society symposium are named after him to this day.[42] The pardoning and then veneration of Nazis enraged Jews around the world, who felt that justice for their families had been denied in the name of American interests. As far as they and Kryptonians were concerned, no deals should be made with devils.

Kaplan also points out another story of Siegel's, "The One Minute of Doom!" in *Superman* #150, as Jewish allegory. In it, the surviving Kryptonians hold a moment of silence on Krypton Memorial Day, remembering the countless lost, as is customary in Israel on Holocaust Memorial Day.[43]

In *Superman* #190 (October '66) the Man of Steel faces off against Amalak the space pirate, a recurring villain until the 1980s, who harbors deep hatred of all Kryptonians because one had destroyed his world (later revealed to be Zod).[44] Amalak's name is just a slight variation of the biblical Amalek, nomadic marauders descendant from Esau and mortal enemies of his brother Jacob's descendants, the Israelites (Gen. 36:12, 1 Chron. 1:36).

Superman was also no longer the last of his kind. There was his cousin Supergirl, her parents, meaning his uncle, various criminals who survived in the Phantom

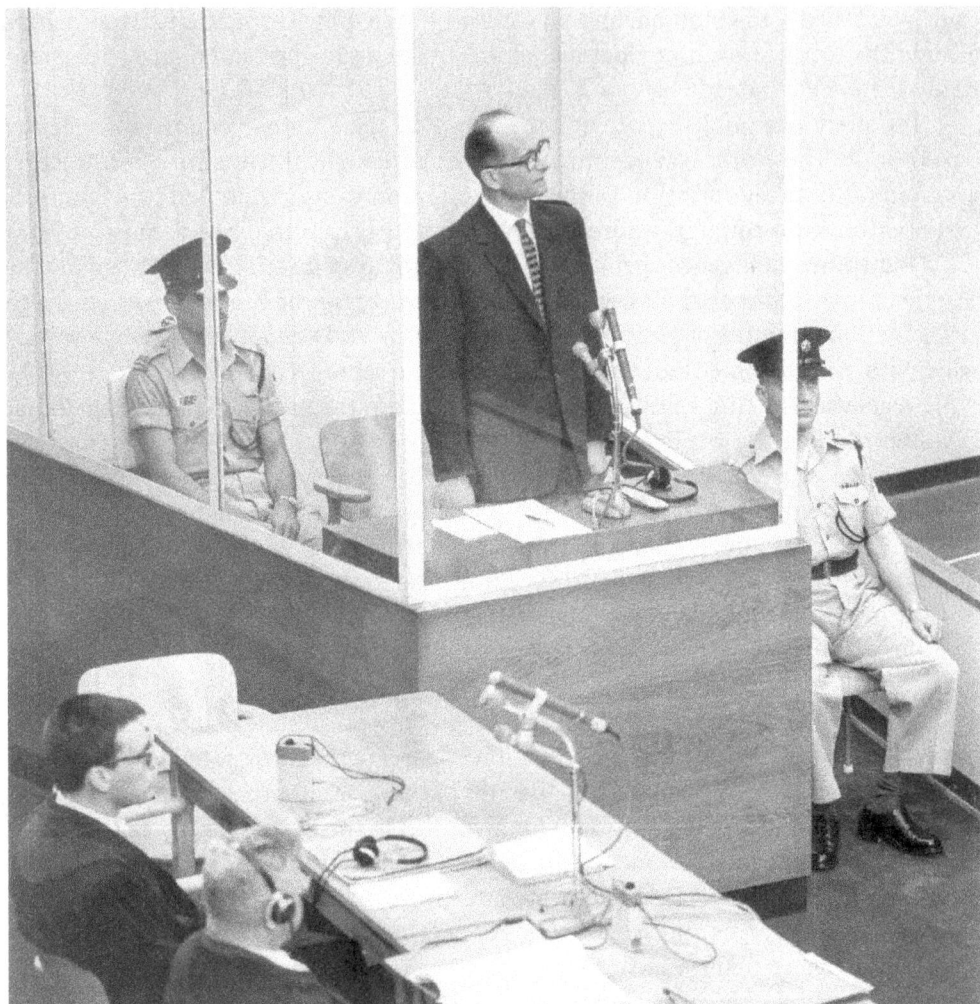

Eichmann in court. Jerusalem, Israel, 1961. Yad Vashem, item ID 65275.

Zone, his childhood pets Krypto and Beppo (Streaky and Comet were Earthlings), and an entire city from Krypton. In one story even his parents turned up alive, in continuity, although they had to return to hibernation.[45]

This "Superman family," as they came to be known, diluted Superman's uniqueness and detracted from his pathos, though they enriched his mythology in other ways. They were, as Superman writer Karl Kesel notes, "a displaced community of refugees (touching on that immigrant theme again)."[46] The family, friends and neighbors who'd survived, unbeknownst, only to meet years later, like so many Jews after the war.

Even Zod and the other Zone inmates can be seen as representing the frustratingly, heartbreakingly unfair survivors of the Holocaust. Not everyone who made it was a saint, and sometimes it was the worst qualities that allowed people to survive. That there were bad Jews who lived on to do bad things while so many good ones perished only added to the tragedy.

Above and right: *Superman* #149, November 1961. Written by Jerry Siegel and illustrated by Curt Swan. DC Comics.

While Superman's sense of loss and grief grew, along with his connection to his culture and people, so did his insecurity. He spent numerous stories carrying out elaborate and sometimes cruel hoaxes involving Lois, Jimmy and Supergirl, testing their love and loyalty. He was the outsider making sure his acceptance was not conditional.

He spent even more time avoiding the bonds of matrimony with Lois. Lois fantasized about domesticating the gallivanting hero, which simply wouldn't do for a man of his responsibilities and coolness, but like much else of his Silver Age behavior it was rooted in more serious anxiety. It was the post–Holocaust conflict of Jews who had resettled in freer societies, leading to the opportunity, and peril, of intermarriage. On one hand, what better revenge against Hitler than to settle down, claim a place within society rather than at its periphery, and propagate the Jewish race? On the other hand, how could Jews settle into comfortable family life after the horror that'd just swept through them? There was too much to do, to rebuild, to remember. They were an endangered species now, and to marry a gentile, to raise non–Jewish children, was to spit on the graves of the dead.

By and large, the dominant theme of Superman's 1960s adventures was change. In the Kennedy era of clean-cut cosmopolitanism he constantly transformed into monsters or gained abilities he couldn't control, grotesqueries that were alien in a way he'd never been. He was quite literally the hero with a thousand faces. By no means an exhaustive list, Superman became: a cat; a baby, six times; old; a tree-man; a devil; fat, four times; minuscule, three times; a giant, five times; a mind-reader; split in two, five times; a parade balloon; a sphinx; magnetic; a double of Jesse James; a Kryptonian monster; a caveman; a monkey; a giant gorilla; a leper; his shape warped; he glowed like a rainbow; gained a Midas touch; a lion's head; an ant's head; a third eye in the back of his head; fire breath, twice; diamond-vision; long hair and fingernails; an extra finger on each hand; and his face changed colors with his emotions. His supporting cast wasn't spared these metamorphoses either, from acquiring various superpowers to turning into hideous human insects.[47]

They also extended to his new villains, warped mirror images like Metallo, a cyborg who's not only his spitting image but joins the *Planet* as an unscrupulous reporter, successfully woos Lois, uses his super-strength to commit crimes and is powered by a heart of Kryptonite.[48]

Superman became an avatar of identity fluidity, embodying the sixties' search for, struggle with and redefinition of self and society. With psychoanalysis at the peak of its popularity and the concepts of unconsciousness and neurosis becoming part of the cultural lexicon, Superman, the ideal man, was used to explore the desires, anxieties and projections of his writers. He was existential angst manifest: If Kafka took humanity away from man by turning him into a bug and Siegel and Shuster enhanced it with the proportionate strength and leaping ability of one, man was now both less and more, dehumanized but super.

It was a potent metaphor for American culture. The U.S. had cemented itself as the World's greatest superpower, but it was also in flux and doubt. Americans found themselves in a house of mirrors, faced with warping, unrecognizable reflections. Superman's increase in power to near-omnipotence paralleled that of the U.S., and Weisinger's favorite shtick of taking his powers away served to reexamine their nature and the personal ethos that drives him, much the same as America was doing.

But Superman's constantly mutating physiology also marked him as something other than human, particularly when some form of Kryptonite was involved (which was often). In reflecting his handlers' American neurosis he also inexorably reflected their Jewish-American preoccupations. Jews were free to define their identity after it had been defined for them by murderous Europeans, but with intermingling, intermarriage and a growing spectrum of denominations, the question was harder to answer than ever before.

A generation after the war they were mostly native, not immigrant, and enjoyed a level of security, comfort and status unparalleled in their history. But the Holocaust was still an ember, and there was the underlying fear that the rug would be pulled from under them. That they would be rejected, ostracized again, return to being the Other so ingrained in their historical memory.

Many also felt conflicted about the freedom and power that secularism and integration brought. It was the same ambivalence embodied in the Clark Kent/Superman dynamic, except now Superman himself was in question, unidentifiable at times, capable of accomplishing anything one moment and forced to prove he can survive without his powers the next, just like they were.

> *Change is the law of life. And those who look only to the past or the present are certain to miss the future.*
> —John F. Kennedy

Nazis in Space and Superman on Screen

The Bronze Age

Stretching from 1970 to 1986, the Bronze Age can perhaps be defined as the era of social consciousness. It continued much of the Silver Age's grandiosity and out-landishness, while re-introducing the Golden Age's darker realism. The Comics Code's amendment in 1971 allowed for more mature storytelling, enabling creators to explore, among other things, themes of culture and ethnicity, increasingly more explicitly. Comics were now also targeted at more specific demographics through the emergent direct market, consisting of about 30 comics specialty shops in 1972 and about 3000 a decade later.[1] It created a more stable market and organized fandom, allowing mainstream superhero stories to be told in greater breadth and depth as well as providing a venue for experimental ventures and underground comix.

World-saving heroes began paying attention to real-world issues, engaging with questions of sexuality, substance abuse, urban decay, racial and economic inequal-ity, systematic injustice, environmentalism, and political and economic corruption. Jewish creators, particularly outside "big two" DC and Marvel, increasingly brought their background to the foreground, producing loosely or fully autobiographi-cal works like Art Spiegelman's 1972 short stories "Maus" and "Prisoner on the Hell Planet" (which would eventually become his 1992 Pulitzer winner *Maus*), Trina Rob-bins' 1972 *Wimmen's Comix* series, Harvey Pekar's 1976 *American Splendor* series and Will Eisner's 1978 *A Contract with God and Other Tenement Stories*, considered the first graphic novel. Mainstream creators also started telling more personal stories, like Howard Chaykin's 1983 *American Flagg!*—a prescient futuristic series starring Reuben Flagg, the first openly Jewish action hero. "I'm no longer afraid, ashamed, or uninterested enough in my personal background to keep it out of the work," Chaykin said. "I'm no longer a Jew masquerading as a gentile through comics."[2]

Though perhaps no longer the supermajority, Jews were still the dominant pres-ence in comics, and an influx of new Jewish professionals, mostly young, middle class and college educated, brought new perspectives to stories.

In 1967, Jack Liebowitz sold DC to conglomerate Kinney National Ser-vices, which in 1969 acquired Warner Bros. and in 1972 reorganized into War-ner Communications (becoming Time-Warner in 1990). Like Warner, Kinney was a Jewish-owned and run businesses, which is why, at least in part, Liebowitz was willing to sell his company to them. He later wrote, "I liked the people.... Jewish, Jewish oriented."[3] They were fellow tribesmen and spoke his language, figuratively and literally. They were *mishpucha*, and he could trust that they'd provide a good home for his Superman.

In 1976, at only 28 years old, Jenette Kahn, the daughter of a conservative rabbi, became the new publisher. The youngest executive in the Warner corporation, by 1981 she became president of DC, also assuming the title of editor in chief in 1989. She was of a different generation of American Jews, not the Depression-era incult immigrants and their sons but a baby boomer and a Harvard-educated woman.[4] Her first order of business was to officially change the company's name from National Periodical Publications to DC Comics, as it was already known by fans. Making comics was something to be proud of, not hide.

When Weisinger, who'd charted Superman's course longer than anyone before or since, retired in 1970, Julie Schwartz took his place, bringing a new, more sober tone, closer to Siegel and Shuster's original vision. He also brought on a team of Jewish *wunderkinds* to revitalize the Man of Tomorrow. Paul Levitz, whose grandmother came from the same Russian shtetl as Siegel's father, became the editor of *Adventure Comics* and the writer of *The Legion of Super-Heroes* in 1971, at only 20. Len Wein, who at 16 had organized the first comic-con (and ostensibly coined the term), was now a stately 23, taking over writing *Superman*—"the granddaddy of the whole megillah," as he called him[5]—the same year. He shared duties with writing duo Elliot Maggin, 21, and Cary Bates, not Jewish, 23.

A 26-year-old Marv Wolfman was assigned to write *Adventure Comics*, *Superman* and *Supergirl* in 1972, later also *Action Comics* and *The Superman Family*. Chaykin was 29 when he drew the *World of Krypton* in 1979, the first comic book miniseries and a trove of Jewish signification. It was written by Paul Kupperberg, 24, who, beginning in 1982, became the prolific writer of *Action Comics*, *Superman*, *Superboy* and *Supergirl* (and later the author of literary treasure *Jew-Jitsu: Hebrew Hands of Fury*). Alongside Maggin, his was the most distinctly Jewish voice in Superman's Bronze Age oeuvre. "When these characters were first created, anti–Semitism was so prevalent, even in an industry run by Jews," he later said. "We finally reached a time when you stopped hiding being a Jew." At 55, Robert Kanigher was the elder of the group, a Golden and Silver Age veteran who'd helped Schwartz relaunch the Flash, known for the social consciousness and "fatalistic, moralistic Jewish attitude" of his stories.[6] He was assigned to write *Justice League of America* as well as *Lois Lane*, which he seems to have approached with mixed feelings.

The public mood at the time was jaundiced. It was the decade of the Vietnam War morass, the government-indicting Pentagon Papers, the Watergate scandal and the disgraced downfall of Richard Nixon. There was stagflation, dramatic decline in manufacturing jobs, inner city ghettoization, rampant urban crime and the beginning of the drug epidemic. It was a time marked by disillusionment and cynicism, more toxic to Superman than Kryptonite.

The Bronze Age has an overall bitter flavor to its comics, and despite some outstanding works, was a creative and commercial nadir. Superman in particular struggled. It was difficult for young writers and artists to see America as the land of opportunity and embrace a character so earnest about its promise.

Schwartz excised some of the Silver Age *mishigas* like the Legion of Super-Pets and the multicolored, identity-warping Kryptonite, favoring a more grounded approach. With Maggin and Bates in particular, he fleshed out Superman's mythology, adding detail and interconnectivity with other DC characters. Superman became the hero of heroes, their leader, casting him even further in a messianic role. Lois was back to form as a strong, intelligent woman, though she often came across as disgruntled, missing her sly sense of humor, and protested a bit too much about not needing Superman.

Still, despite the changes, things felt stodgy. Even the better stories of the period were part of a stultified routine, lacking passion or purpose. That the 1978 album-sized *Superman vs. Muhammad Ali* is perhaps his best and most exciting comic of the decade speaks volumes. The Man of Tomorrow had become the man of yesterday, drifting into irrelevance as a nostalgic period piece.

While Wonder Woman appeared on the July 1972 inaugural cover of Gloria Steinem's *Ms.* magazine, the first national feminist publication, Superman appeared in old TV reruns. Stephen Schwartz's 1971 musical *Godspell*, as well as its 1973 film adaptation, featured Jesus wearing a Superman T-shirt. Barbra Streisand also wore one, sexily, on the cover of her 1977 album, *Superman*, also its title song. Henry Kissinger was illustrated in full costume, with a "K" replacing the "S," on the June 10, 1974, cover of *Newsweek*. These weren't reverential; he had become an ironic meme.

Siegel himself offered in 1979, "I think Superman's greatest challenge is that he has been published for forty years … his super-deeds are now known to millions everywhere and do not elicit the same utter amazement." He was also no longer unique. "Many competing super-heroes have … inundated the public with a veritable avalanche of super-deeds." Sales reflected the public's disinterest. If in the Golden Age *Superman* sold 1.3 million monthly copies, and the Silver Age saw a gradual decline to about 512,000, the Bronze Age saw an even steeper drop, from 447,000 in 1970 to 297,000 in 1975, to 179,000 in 1980, to under 99,000 by 1985.[7]

"The folks making decisions about Superman actually seemed seriously desperate as to where to turn in those days," Maggin remembers. One solution was to tap into the popular trend of sociopolitical themes. Even though he was the original socially conscious crusader, the witch hunts and Weisinger's aversion to social realism had left Superman behind the times. His political evolution since the war was marked mostly by longer sideburns. "Boundaries were being pushed elsewhere, but with Superman, such a high-profile vehicle, they waited until pretty much the rest of comicdom shamed them into change," artist Alex Ross explains.[8]

While Iron Man dealt with alcoholism (*Invincible Iron Man* #120–128), Spider-Man with the murder of his longtime girlfriend (*Amazing Spider-Man* #121), Green Arrow with his teen sidekick's heroin addiction (*Green Lantern/Green Arrow* #85–86) and Aquaman with the kidnap and murder of his toddler son (*Adventure Comics* #451–452), Superman continued to battle sundry doppelgängers, like a parasite from another dimension that assumed his shape (*Superman* #233–242) or a man named Rufus who stole his powers and dressed like Caesar (*Action Comics* #404).

New villains created were equally uninspired. Terra-Man, first appearing in March 1972's *Superman* #249, was a blatant takeoff of Clint Eastwood's Man with No Name, a cowboy from space striding a flying Pegasus. Even worse was the Supermobile, introduced in March 1978's *Action Comics* #481, a vehicle made of indestructible "Supermanium" that allowed a depowered Superman to not only fly but punch bad guys with its extendable mechanical fists. (That it coincided with the sale of Corgi Toys die-casts might explain its existence.)

The first attempt to invigorate things was giving Clark Kent a new, modern job. Beginning in *Superman* #233 (January '71), he left the *Planet* to become a TV news correspondent and then anchorman at Galaxy Communications' WGBS-TV. It added drama by placing him in different predicaments, but it was also incompatible with his need for obscurity and mousy pretense and quickly became tedious.

A welcome addition to the cast was Dave Stevens, the first black journalist at the *Daily Planet*, first appearing in *Superman's Girl Friend, Lois Lane* #106 (November '70). But Stevens appeared six times in all before disappearing in 1979, and was the only recurring black character in Superman's comics until 1991's Ron Troupe.

Other attempts, while noble in intention, were misguided, even cringeworthy by today's standards. *Superman* #239 (July '71) introduced Vathlo Island on Krypton, a racial separatist utopia. The idea being, since slavery never existed on enlightened Krypton, black Kryptonians—never before seen or mentioned—had never left their indigenous land, conveniently an island. The concept was repurposed in *Superboy* #216 (April '76) for Marzal Island, this one on 30th-century Earth, where Superboy and the Legion of Super-Heroes meet Tyroc, an angry black man dressed like a disco space pimp.

Most dumbfounding, however, was Lois in blackface. In a story titled "I Am Curious (Black)!" in *Superman's Girl Friend, Lois Lane* #106 (November '70)—an odd reference to a 1967 R-rated, nudity-filled Swedish film named *I Am Curious (Yellow)*—the intrepid reporter is given an assignment to write about Metropolis's slum, Little Africa. The residents refuse to speak to her because "whitey" is the enemy, so Superman helps out by letting her use an alien transformation chamber to become black for a day. Undercover, Lois finds that they are the nicest people possible, and once she has gained their trust they accept her hand in friendship even after she reveals herself.

It's hard to gauge how seriously writer Robert Kanigher took the story. It's fairly silly, not the least of which is the "plastimold" operated by a "Transformoflux pack" that turns her black. But it's also bold for a Superman comic at the time, and there's a clear didacticism to it. It's the first overt recognition of poverty, inequality or racism in Superman's comics since the Golden Age, as well as the first discussion of his racial status. When Lois confronts him about the reality of being a black outsider in America, he exclaims, "You ask that of *me.... Superman?* An alien from *Krypton ...* another planet? A *universal outsider?*" But she now understands the difference, replying, "your skin is the *right color!*"[9]

Superman is biologically, and to an extent culturally, an alien, a strange visitor, but he looks white, which allows him to be accepted into mainstream society, both as Clark and as Superman. As a Jewish metaphor, another layer is added in the context of the times. Like Jews, he can choose to hide his ethnicity, but also to reveal it and still have relatively little fear of rejection, because he looks like the dominant population. Even as unwashed immigrants, for all the bigotry and impediments Jews faced in America, they were still treated better than minorities of color, particularly blacks. Now, in the 1970s, these "universal outsiders" were finally welcome, and their preoccupations in fiction began reflecting, along with their own changed status, the plight of those still left outside.

January 1971's *Superman* #233 marks the end of the Silver Age for Superman (and perhaps the beginning of the Bronze Age in general). It was Schwartz's first issue on the title, and he immediately set about reinvigorating the character. Not quite a reimagining like with DC's other characters, he instead launched a storyline that promised "a return to greatness!"[10] To this end he enlisted the superstar team of writer Dennis O'Neil and artist Neal Adams, who'd helped him do the same for Batman the year prior in *Detective Comics* #395 (January '70), rescuing the Dark Knight from his 1960s campiness and restoring him to his noir, gothic roots.

O'Neil's hardboiled realism worked well with Curt Swan's style, at the top of his game here (especially when paired with inker Murphy Anderson to form "Swanderson"), and with Adams' photorealistic, kinetically-charged covers. In a nonconsecutive eight-part epic (*Superman* #233–235, 237–238, 240–242) titled "Kryptonite Nevermore" (aka "The Sandman Saga") Clark Kent becomes an anchorman, all Kryptonite on Earth is rendered inert, and Superman's power is reduced by a third. His Silver Age continuity still stood, but decreasing his powers and removing Kryptonite as an overused plot device was meant to give him sorely-needed conflict to work with.

Superman had gotten too powerful to be interesting, too godlike, too abstract, and resultantly unheroic; there was rarely any real risk or sacrifice. But, while a valiant effort, the Man of Might was left too mighty still. Reducing by a third the power of someone who can push planets out of orbit doesn't have much of a dramatic effect. It proved to be a scattershot attempt, ignored as soon as O'Neil and Adams left, with #243 (Adams continued to provide occasional covers).

The duo moved on to collaborate on a highly-acclaimed, socially-relevant run on *Green Lantern/Green Arrow*, successfully transforming Green Arrow, a second-rate Batman knockoff (with Arrowcar and Arrowcave), into DC's new champion of the oppressed.

Superman may have been languishing creatively, but the era produced some of the most important stories to his mythology, including significantly more overt Jewish themes and allusions. The Galactic Golem, adapted from Jewish legend, was introduced in *Superman* #248 (February '72). Issue #264 (June '73) retooled Exodus as the tale of ancient Kryptonians overthrowing the evil pharaoh Taka-Ne with a plague. The *World of Krypton* miniseries (July–September '79) depicted a culture devoted to education and knowledge, with a displaced community thought dead numbering six million. "The Double-or-Nothing Life of Superman!" storyline in *Superman* #296–299 (February–May '76) was a milestone in Clark Kent's gradual journey to become a more real aspect of his personality, paralleling the fading existential dread and social unease among young Jews and their own questions of place and identity.

When the very genesis of Krypton was explored in *Superman* #238 (June '71), it was the story of stranded astronauts Kryp and Tonn, an Adam and Eve who were cast from elsewhere to cultivate and populate the planet. The *Krypton Chronicles* miniseries (September–November '81) told of their progeny, the El lineage—consisting of lawgivers, kings, priests, prophets, novelists, entertainers, and various types of scientists and inventors—who guided the development of their civilization since its earliest days.[11] While it weakened the concept of Superman as a refugee saved by chance (and added a troubling dimension of eugenics), it cast the El family—the "god" family—as a chosen people, a few who inspired the many and revolutionized their world through spirituality and reason.

Particularly familiar of these is the story of ancient prophet Jaf-El, who futilely sought to warn his fellow Kryptonians against their evil ways and worship of false idols in the face of an impending flood sent by the sun god Rao. Mirroring the story of Noah and foreshadowing Jor-El's, it ends with a twist; the righteous are saved by the animals rather than the other way around, carried to high ground by winged creatures, inheriting a cleansed world once the waters recede.[12]

More than any other writer since Siegel, Maggin was informed by his Jewish background, freely borrowing from religion and folklore. Of particular note is his multipart "Miracle Monday" opus, beginning in *Superman* #293 (November '75). It features a historian from the 35th century who time-travels to witness the Man of Steel perform a famous miracle, a plot reused six years later in *Superman: Miracle Monday*, the second of Maggin's bestselling prose novels. The name of a holiday celebrated thousands of years in the future on the third Monday of every May, it commemorates Superman defeating Samael, the ruler of hell, and saving humanity.

A prominent figure in Talmudic mysticism, expounded upon in later writings, particularly medieval Kabbalism, Samael (סַמָאֵל) isn't the Christian devil he's amalgamated with in the novel. Associated with the angel of death, his name translates as "venom of God" (סם-אל), understood as "God's blinder," one who blinds, or obfuscates, for God (with no devil, supernatural evil is attributed in Jewish tradition directly to God, carried out in the name of a greater good). He's the incarnation of the evil urge, the *yetzer hara*, which clouds, like a poison, the good inclination, *yetzer hatov*, not unlike the role of the devil as corruptor.[13] And like the devil of the gospels, that of the novel is outwitted by Superman, who wins the day through his unwavering virtue.

DC Comics Presents Annual #2 (July '83) continues the saga, in which the time-traveler (renamed Kristin Wells in the book and made a history professor here) uses future technology to become Superwoman and aid Superman against King Kosmos, a conquering warlord from a possible future. An otherwise generic villain, he's a "***despot*** who enslaved a ***nation*** on his native world,"[14] specifically not a world-ruling tyrant but an oppressor of a single nation of people, evoking the pharaoh of Exodus, even wearing a pharaonic-looking crown.

It casts Superman yet again in the role of Moses, and just as the story of Exodus and the Hebrews' deliverance is celebrated in the Jewish holiday of Passover, held "in the month of the spring" (Ex. 23:15), so does Miracle Monday, which the novel notes "came in the spring."[15]

The equivalence is made obvious in *Superman* #400 (October '84), nearly a decade after the epic began, in the tale of a family celebrating Miracle Monday in the year 5902. The festive dinner is modeled after the Passover Seder; it's referred to as "a night of the year that is different from all other nights," the opening phrase of each of The Four Questions of the Haggadah—"Why is this night different from all other nights?" ("*ma nishtanah*"). The father toasts, "Across the galaxy tonight ... families gather ... for the **Miracle Monday** dinner—a celebration of our **freedom!**" describing the Seder exactly—a family dinner celebrating freedom from bondage, its blessings held over wine. His son recites, "We celebrate today because thousands of years ago—Superman ... taught us to live as a free people!" similar to the Haggadah's decree that the story of Moses be told and retold by each generation as if anew. "Let all who are hungry come and eat!" the father says, quoting verbatim from the Haggadah ("*kol dichfin*"). Each member of the family then symbolically puts a portion of their food onto an empty plate reserved for Superman upon his return, like the Seder custom of setting aside a glass of wine for the return of the prophet Elijah. Lastly, the father's name is Herzog, the same as Chaim Herzog, the President of Israel at the time the story was published, to whom he also bears a strong resemblance.[16]

Shortly thereafter, in *Superman Annual* #10 (November '84), Maggin traces Superman's origin—and signification—to biblical creation itself. "Once there was the

Superman #400, October 1984. Written by Elliot S. Maggin and illustrated by Klaus Janson. DC Comics.

void ... when *chaos* held sway—until there were spoken the magic words! *Let there be light!* Some called this event *Genesis*," the story opens. It tells of a sword-shaped object formed from the primordial matter of the universe and imbued with the power of its creation. Intangible, it follows baby Kal-El on his voyage from Krypton to Earth, the "S" shape at its pommel unbeknownst inspiring his insignia as Superman. When eventually it does manifest physically, like a cosmic Excalibur, he rejects its great and terrible power. "*You have done well, my son,*" a disembodied voice tells him, presumably that of God himself. "*You have earned your name, your future is yours to make. Your greatness among living things is assured. So shall it ever be.*"[17]

Maggin brought a more philosophical bent to his work, using Superman like a Midrashic parable to question beliefs and convictions. "He has to think and he has to make the readers think," he said, "and that's what separates Superman from everything else."[18]

Most memorable is his groundbreaking "Must There Be a Superman?" in *Superman* #247 (January '72), which examined, for the first time, Superman's role and effect on human civilization. Several months before Umberto Eco did the same on a wider canvas in his essay "The Myth of Superman," the story saw Earth's mightiest hero accused of interfering with humanity's natural progress by making it over-reliant on him. It questions not the responsibility that comes with power, the central tenet of superheroics, but rather the responsibility to limit its use—timely in the midst of Vietnam and just before Watergate, and always carrying an added layer of meaning when asked by a Jew. It stops short of delving into the inevitable impact Superman would have on the world by his mere presence, regardless of any specific action he takes or avoids, but it nonetheless marks the first serious handling of these issues, years ahead of deconstructionist works like *Watchmen*. The story also manages, in its mere seventeen pages, to remind readers that Superman is an immigrant, paralleling his origin with that of an undocumented boy from Mexico sent by his dying father in hopes of a better life.[19]

The theme of Superman as an immigrant continued developing throughout the Bronze Age. In *Superman* #354–355 (December '80–January '81), an eerily prescient tale set in 2020, his grandson, Kalel Kent, is attacked by American race supremacists calling themselves "the Purists." Wearing a variation of the Swastika and saluting *sieg heil*–style, they see Superman as a polluter of Earth culture who spreads Kryptonian customs and interbreeds with humans to "destroy the genetic *purity* of our glorious *race!*" To them, even the second-generation earthborn, quarter-Kryptonian Kalel is an alien "*mongrel.*" Like his grandfather, Superman III smashes the Nazi gang. Also noteworthy is his plan to be "a super-hero with *multiple identities,*" a freedom of self-definition that wasn't afforded to his father and grandfather.[20]

Not just themes and signifiers, the era also saw the introduction of explicitly Jewish characters to Superman's comics. The first was Morgan Edge, created by Jack Kirby in *Superman's Pal, Jimmy Olsen* #133 (October '70). The president of Galaxy Communications, owners of WGBS and the *Daily Planet*, Edge was Clark Kent's boss, a complicated personality who was a ruthless capitalist but also an honest and friendly man, which turned him into a conflicting metaphor when he was revealed to be Jewish, born Morris Edelstein, in *Action Comics* #468 (February '77). Whether

Kirby intended him to be Jewish is unclear, but the character was revamped in 2011 as black, with no indication thus far of being Jewish.[21]

Supergirl foe Blackstarr, created by Kupperberg and Carmine Infantino, was the first, and to date last, openly Jewish villain in the super family's opus, appearing in *Supergirl* Vol. 2 #13 (November '83). A fascinating character, she's the leader of a violent neo–Nazi organization who is actually Rachel Berkowitz, a camp survivor whose trauma led her to embrace Nazi ideology.[22] She made only one more, forgettable appearance in *DC Comics Presents* #86 (October '85), where she fought Supergirl and Superman.

Superman even made a visit to the Holy Land, in the uncanonical *Super Friends* #7 (October '77). In a laughably archaic Israel, showing mostly ultra-orthodox Jews and wooden pushcarts, he meets Chaim Lavon, a schoolteacher who's secretly Seraph, a yarmulke-wearing superhero who derives his powers from the cloak of Elijah, the ring of Solomon, the staff of Moses and long hair like that of Samson's.[23] Seraph entered the canon in *DC Comics Presents* #46 (June '82), also a Superman story, appearing sporadically until the mid–1990s. He holds the distinction of being the first explicitly Jewish superhero.

In their most momentous initiative to fight off the doldrums, DC hired Jack Kirby away from Marvel. For a founding father of Marvel to defect to the Distinguished Competition was seismic, as if John Lennon had left the Beatles for the Rolling Stones. In an era when creators rarely received cover credits, DC proudly announced "***Kirby is HERE!***" above the title of his first issue.

Kirby chose to take on, of all things, the ancillary series *Superman's Pal, Jimmy Olsen*. It served as the launch pad for what would come to be considered his magnum opus, the "Fourth World" saga—a metanarrative told throughout various series between 1970 and 1973, all written, drawn and some edited by him, primarily in three new, interrelating titles: *New Gods, Forever People* and *Mister Miracle*. Until then, Marvel had a rich, quickly expanding cosmology while DC had virtually none outside the pages of *Green Lantern*. Kirby crafted a grand space opera, years before *Star Wars*, filled with high-minded concepts and dozens of new characters which have since become cornerstones of DC's shared universe.

Super Friends #7, October 1977. Written by E. Nelson Bridwell and illustrated by Ramona Fradon. DC Comics.

He came out swinging,

each issue bursting with original ideas and raging with artistic vitality. His Superman was "the most dynamic and heroic super-hero to cross a page of DC art since the 1940s," according to longtime Superman writer-artist Jon Bogdanove. "His stories were so fast-paced, majestic, more mythic than anything DC had ever done."[24]

Kirby had always worn his Jewishness on his sleeve, and for DC's flagship character he "took his youthful fights in the slums of NY, his battles with Nazi armies and forged them into a visual vocabulary," Levitz writes. His first issue, *Jimmy Olsen* #133 (October '70), added to Metropolis the neighborhood of Southside, nicknamed Suicide Slum, which he'd originally created as New York tenements in April 1942's *Star Spangled Comics* #7 and now used to bring to Superman's city a "texture and flavor informed by his Lower East Side childhood."[25]

In issue #134 he introduced Darkseid. Kirby's villains tended to be fascists rather than criminals or lunatics, like the Nazi Red Skull and European monarch Dr. Doom, but with Darkseid he took the concept to its conclusion; a tyrant god who subjugated his world, enslaving or exterminating those he deemed inferior, perpetually striving for greater conquest. He was more than just a genuine threat to Superman and the Justice League. If Superman embodies the American dream then Darkseid is the nightmare, particularly in the Jewish perspective. He's essentially space Hitler.

Bogdanove, who's Jewish, notes the parallels:

> You have a *"fuhrer"* character, whose name is Darkseid [pronounced Darkside], but the "seid" is spelled like a German word. And then there's the image of sooty Apokolips, with its open fire pits, which is evocative of the industrialized war machine of Nazi Germany. Armagetto (the slums of Apokolips whose wretchedly impoverished denizens were known as "Hunger Dogs") was really about the ghettos in Poland and elsewhere. All these people who slave and die for Darkseid are subjected to dispiriting slogans, like "Work Is Life, Death Is Freedom," a clear allusion to the Nazis' "Work Will Make You Free."[26]

Darkseid is exactly that—the dark side of humanity, and the peculiar spelling of his name can be read either as Germanic (though "side" is actually "seite") or referring to the Germans, "seid" meaning "are," as in "we are dark." Darkseid himself is a jackbooted dictator and warlord, often found on his balcony overlooking or speechifying at his Parademons—masses of hive-minded airborne soldiers. His planet, Apokolips—the "k" taken from the German spelling—is a militant society dedicated to ceaseless universal war, while those deemed inferior are enslaved in the Armagetto fire pits, work camps built around perpetual furnaces that inexorably call to mind the crematoriums of the Holocaust.

Subtlety wasn't Kirby's strong suit, nor interest. Apokolips is "an armed camp" with uniformed guards and gaunt slave laborers wearing striped headwear. Its ruler, in his first full appearance, is addressed, "Hail **Darkseid ...** wielder of holocaust!"[27] He's the platonic ideal of totalitarianism, seeking not banal territorial conquest but the Anti-Life Equation, mathematical proof of the futility of living, giving, in turn, total control over the minds of sentient beings. He's a warning, that if the right formula—the right conditions, right demagoguery—is in the wrong hands, we might find ourselves swept up mindlessly in a madman's quest for power.

The villain of the 2017 *Justice League* movie, Steppenwolf is another of the New Gods, uncle to Darkseid and general of his armies, introduced in *New Gods* #7

New Gods #1, March 1971. Written & illustrated by Jack Kirby. DC Comics.

(February '72). His name is German for the steppe wolf, or grasslands wolf, a likely wordplay on General Rommel, the Desert Fox.

Other members of Darkseid's Elite have Germanic names, including Brola and Virman Vundabar. The latter, first appearing in *Mister Miracle* #5 (December '71), also looks the part: though in *Tales to Astonish: Jack Kirby, Stan Lee, and the American*

Comic Book Revolution author Ronin Ro attributes his design more to Mussolini,[28] and Vundabar does wear a sash, his dress is otherwise a hybrid of Prussian and Nazi uniforms, including a tunic, shiny black knee-boots, armband and monocle. His mannerisms are equally satirical, including fastidiousness and heel-clicking, as is his name, "Virman" combining "vermin" and "man" and "Vundabar" being a phonetic spelling of *wunderbar*, German for "wonderful."

In contrast, the gods of New Genesis—enemies of Apokolips and alleys to Superman—are brimming with Jewish signification. Mister Miracle, aka Scott Free, debuted in his own title in April 1971 as a Houdini-inspired hero long before *Kavalier & Clay*'s the Escapist. His wife Big Barda was based physically on Jewish singer-actress Lainie Kazan and the disposition of Kirby's wife, Rose.[29]

The knowledge-seeking Metron (*New Gods* #1, March '71) was given Leonard Nimoy's likeness and mannerism,[30] while his name and role are patently derived from the angel Metatron, described in the Talmud and Kabbalah as a celestial scribe and guardian of secrets. Metatron (alt. Mitatron or Mattatron) is noted to be sitting when performing his heavenly duties, the only being allowed to do so before God (Chagigah 15a), much the same as Metron perennially sits on the spacefaring Mobius Chair, which allows him to travel through space and time to observe and record the universe. His outfit is a pattern of interconnected spheres and lines—one of Kirby's hallmark motifs, used in numerous designs—resembling Kabbalah's Tree of Life cosmological diagram.

Himon, a homophone of the Yiddish name Hyman, whose daughter is named Bekka, was based on the Jewish Sheldon "Shel" Dorf, architect of the first San Diego Comic-Con in 1970. (A longtime Super-fan, Dorf sent Schwartz a letter in 1981 speculating about Superman's Jewish heritage, including an illustration of the Man of Steel wearing a yarmulke and a tallit for a cape.) A scientist and mystic, Himon is the inventor of the Mother Boxes; small, rectangular super-computers carried in armbands that connect to the all-knowing "Source." Not just a precursor to smartphones, they also, as pointed out by *Tablet*'s Gabriela Geselowitz, recall the Tefillin, the Jewish prayer phylacteries. In their first appearance in particular (*Mister Miracle* #9, August '72) they're depicted as black cubes worn with straps wrapping down the arm, making it hard to argue.[31]

The most hermeneutically rich character, however, is Highfather (originally High-Father), prophet-leader of the evocative "New Genesis," first appearing in *New Gods* #1 (March '71). A white-bearded, robed sage, he carries the "wonder staff," shaped like a shepherd's crook, a conduit for the Source—a higher power that speaks to him in flame, bestowing "the written word." The Source is described, "It is ***eternal!***" and "beyond all the knowledge and sweeping concept at our command ... serene—omnipotent—all-wise!"[32] making it, clearly, God. It communicates with Highfather through "the Wall," the last remnant of the old gods, suggestive of the Western Wall in Jerusalem, Judaism's holiest site and the last remnant of the ancient Temple, where priests communed with God.

Before becoming Highfather, he was Izaya the Inheritor, a homophone of the biblical prophet Isiah (Yeshayahu), whose name means "God is salvation." He sojourns into the desert wasteland of New Genesis in search of enlightenment,

Left: Mister Miracle #9, August 1972. Written & illustrated by Jack Kirby. DC Comics. *Right:* Jewish boy wearing a yarmulke and a prayer mantle prepares to put on the belts (tefellin). Israel, January 1963. Van de Poll collection, National Archives of the Netherlands. Cat. 2.24.14.02.

where he first encounters the Source, which confers upon him his destiny and grave responsibility.[33]

Highfather is clearly Moses. This isn't subtext but text—a deliberate evocation of the narratives and themes of the Bible. Kirby also told his stories with biblical resonance, grandiose and stentorious tales of awe-inspiring things, full of pseudo or outright biblical language, from the very overture to his epic "An ancient era was *passing in fiery* holocaust! … **Then—there was new light!**"[34]

Kirby essentially based his good gods on famous and familiar Jews and the evil gods on Nazis, and in doing so cast the celestial struggle of the Fourth World in terms of Judaism vs. totalitarianism.

Back on Earth, Kirby introduced to Superman's world two more characters based on Jews: Stan Lee and himself. Detective Dan "Terrible" Turpin, a member of Metropolis PD's Special Crimes Unit, appeared in *New Gods* #5 (November '71). A squat, crusty, bushy-eyebrowed cop from Suicide Slum, he was a manifestation of Kirby in fiction, like Captain America and the Thing and other Kirby creations. The other was conman Funky Flashman, appearing in *Mister Miracle* #6 (February '72), an unflattering satire of Lee, whom he parted ways with on unamicable terms.[35]

Ultimately, although he immensely enriched Superman's mythology and injected it with much-needed fervor, sales continued to slump. His offshoot series were soon cancelled, and his contributions weren't fully appreciated until years later. Even the great mythopoet "King" Kirby couldn't save Superman.

Like their creation, Siegel and Shuster were also in dire need of rescuing, and for all three salvation would come with *Superman: The Movie*. Siegel was still writing comics occasionally, notably Walt Disney properties for licensee Gold Key Comics (*Donald Duck* #146 [November '72] and *Huey, Dewey and Louie Junior Woodchucks*

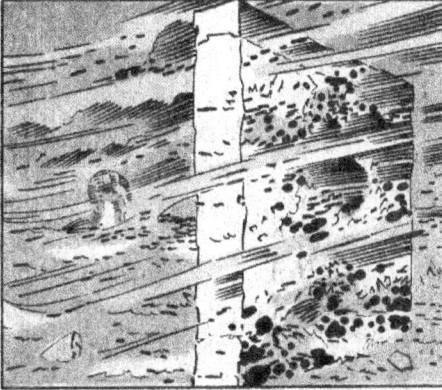

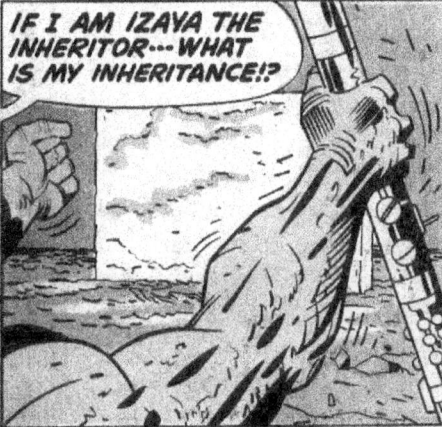

New Gods #7, March 1972. Written & illustrated by Jack Kirby. DC Comics.

#16–17 [September–November '72], as well as several issues of *Topolino* [Mickey Mouse] for Italian licensee Arnoldo Mondadori Editore, under the penname "soggettista e sceneggiatore" [both words meaning "scriptwriter"]). By 1975, however, he moved out west and was working at the California Public Utilities Corporation as a mail clerk for around $7,500 a year ($36,000 adj.). He also suffered from a heart condition, and his wife Joanne took up a job as a car saleswoman. He became a recluse, shunning friends and colleagues, reportedly every so often contemplating suicide.[36]

Shuster, unmarried and now legally blind, didn't have an income. He was living under his brother's care in his threadbare apartment in Queens, sleeping on a cot next to a broken window. At one point, a patrolman found him sleeping on a park bench and bought him a hot meal.[37]

Both men were in their sixties now, poorer than they'd been as youths during the Depression. Adding to their indignity, their names had been erased from the Superman legend. (Even today, while everyone knows Superman, relatively few have heard of them.)

At the same time, Mario Puzo, fresh off his second Oscar win for *Godfather II*, was reportedly being paid an unheard-of $3 million for writing the script for a new Superman movie. (Fourteen million dollars adjusted, making it the most expensive screenplay in history by a margin.) When Siegel read this, he became apoplectic. "Jerry was very bitter," Neal Adams remembers. "Joe didn't seem to have anything to say. He was the super-nice-guy partner." Shuster had also felt slighted by DC and fought them alongside Siegel, but he wasn't as acrimonious or as aggressive. His was a different personality, in ways more like the mild-mannered Clark Kent than Siegel was. In one interview, he said that it was hard to feel bad about his lot in life when millions of children were reading comic books with his character.[38]

Siegel decided to change tactics. What they failed to do in the court of law they'd do in the court of public opinion. The dramatist that he was, he knew it would make for a great human interest story, and in October 1975 he self-issued a ten-page, single-spaced press release to a thousand news outlets across the nation. It read:

> I, Jerry Siegel, the co-originator of Superman, put a curse on the Superman movie! I hope it super-bombs. I hope loyal Superman fans stay away from it in droves…. Joe Shuster and I … got nothing from our creation, and through many of those years we have known want, while Superman's publishers became multimillionaires…. National Periodical Publications, Inc., killed my days, murdered my nights, choked my happiness, strangled my career. I consider National's executives economic murderers, money-mad monsters. If they, and the executives of Warner Communications which owns National, had consciences, they would right the wrongs they inflicted on Joe Shuster and me.[39]

He also sent his diatribe to the Academy of Comic Book Arts, which Adams was president of at the time. Adams was shocked to learn of their misfortune, and took up their cause. He reached out to the National Cartoonist Society, of which Jerry Robinson was the president, and together they helped arrange newspaper and TV coverage, including in the *New York Times*, *Washington Star*, *Today* and *Tomorrow*.[40]

With Hollywood star looks, gumption and a developed sense of justice, Adams was a real-life superhero. He was also one DC's top talents, and he put his career on the line to help Siegel and Shuster fight the good fight against his own employer.

(Adams would continue crusading for various causes, from convincing DC and Marvel to return pages of original artwork to their artists to more recently leading the effort to pressure Poland's Auschwitz State Museum to return portraits painted by a survivor of the camp.[41])

As with any faceless corporation, it's hard to say where human decency and PR interest each begins and ends, but Warner Bros. eventually agreed to pay. According to longtime Superman inker Murphy Anderson, Liebowitz's nephew, Jay Emmett, then a senior executive at Warner, had campaigned on the duo's behalf,[42] perhaps to atone for his uncle's sins.

Following 27 years of failed litigation, an agreement was reached after two months of public campaigning. They each received a $20,000 annual stipend ($96,000 adj.) plus medical benefits. All things considered a paltry sum, but a big help nonetheless. Just as important for the prideful creators, their byline was restored—"Superman created by Jerry Siegel and Joe Shuster"—to all appearances of the character in comics, movies and elsewhere, excluding merchandise. In return they agreed to relinquish any further claims of ownership. Fearful of jeopardizing their hard-won compensation, they shunned publicity for the remainder of their days, giving only the rare interview.[43]

Joe Shuster (L) and Jerry Siegel (R). Publicity photograph for campaign against DC Comics, 1976 (Hake's Auctions).

There were two seminal events in Superman's life in the 1970s. The first was Jack Kirby, the industry's biggest artist, taking on its biggest icon. The second didn't take place in the comics. It was *Superman: The Movie*.

Opening on December 15, 1978, *Superman* changed everything. It was so pitch-perfect, capturing the character's magic and grandeur, that it redefined him forevermore. His first movie (serials notwithstanding) was the same as his first comic; pure wonder, and though its effect wasn't as immediate, it would launch the superhero genre in cinema as it did in comics.

The idea of a big-budget, wide-audience movie based on a comic book, let alone a forty-year-old one, was revolutionary. It called for the vision and *chutzpah* of independent producers Alexander Salkind, a Russian-German Jewish Holocaust survivor, and his son Ilya, who bought the rights from a disinterested Warner Bros.

They hired Richard "Dick" Donner, who'd made 1976's hit *The Omen*, to direct, the first comic book fan to make a comic book film. He even looked like a shorter, longer-haired Clark Kent.

Puzo was chosen for his heft and prestige, though he was no stranger to pulp fiction, having worked on Marvel publisher Martin Goodman's *True Action* magazine during the 1950s and 1960s.[44] But his script, despite costing a king's ransom and becoming a venerated part of the movie's success, and even with doctoring by David and Leslie Newman and Robert Benton, was deemed too puerile by Donner, who favored verisimilitude.

The shooting script, written by Donner's close friend Tom Mankiewicz, followed the same outline and included several of the same scenes and dialogue, but it was less farcical and, paradoxically, less violent and cynical. (Puzo's Metropolis was grimier and closer to the real New York of the seventies. His script included a greater death toll of policemen, featured an escaped Nazi as Luthor's henchman and had Superman dispense with Luthor by throwing him into an alligator tank.) The end result was a screenplay that Brando called "a bleepin' valentine,"[45] winning the 1979 Hugo Award.

The real challenge, however, and the keystone of the film, was casting Superman. Among the actors considered was Charlton Heston, which would have made for an interesting Moses connection, and among those offered the role were Paul Newman and Dustin Hoffman,[46] two Jewish, but very different, choices. Eventually, Donner decided to cast an unknown in the lead, another radical concept for the time, choosing 26-year-old Julliard graduate Christopher Reeve.

Superman cost $55 million to make, more than any film before it (co-producer Pierre Spengler later claimed it was actually closer to $75 million), causing the Salkinds and Warner Bros. to fear it would prove unprofitable. But the public's excitement was palpable. Leading up to its release, *Superman* is said to have appeared on more national magazine covers than any film in history. It opened to rave reviews and sold-out theaters. A hundred and twenty million people watched the movie, which grossed over $300 million worldwide. (A Hollywood blockbuster today, costing roughly $250 million to produce, would have to earn over $1.4 billion, a feat that to date only eleven movies have accomplished.)[47]

It lived up to its tagline—"you'll believe a man can fly"—winning the 1979 Special Achievement Academy Award for Visual Effects and three other nods (Best Film

Editing; Best Music, Original Score; Best Sound). It was the first superhero block-buster, and together with the previous year's *Star Wars* and *Close Encounters of the Third Kind*, changed cinema forever. It also made Superman more iconic than ever before.

Superman was a rousing display of unbridled optimism, shining brightly at a time of national anxiety and cynicism. It was thrilling and uplifting, everything Superman should be. "People were looking for some kind of fantasy," Ilya Salkind remembers. "They were depressed and bored, had problems. They were looking for Superman—something special, something good, something powerful."[48]

The first, and for a long time last, comic book-based movie to approach the source material earnestly rather than sarcastically or apologetically, it cast serious, famed actors around an unknown who was so perfectly cast it was as if Donner had reached into the comic and plucked Superman out. His inspired directing, with a script crackling with energy and emotion, cutting-edge effects, and composer John Williams' triumphant score—a frisson of horns and strings that perfectly captured the essence of Superman—made *Superman* lightning in a bottle. More importantly, and the reason it remains arguably the best superhero movie of all time, is that the spectacle is in service of something greater. More than just entertaining, it's inspiring, a stirring call to become better. And that's what separates, or at least should, superheroes from other action heroes.

"If Richard Donner hadn't done that movie, there wouldn't be superhero movies," *X-Men* and *Superman Returns* director Brian Singer said.[49] It not only proved the appeal and value of the genre, it managed to surpass the comics it was based on, a rarity for an adaptation of any kind. It isn't a perfect movie, for all its merits. It suffers from somewhat erratic pacing, as well as shifts in tone between Reeve's sincere performance and Gene Hackman and Ned Beatty's Lex Luthor and Otis the henchman, played more for camp. Luthor's plot—buying worthless desert east of California and sending a nuclear missile into the San Andreas Fault to plunge it into the ocean, thus becoming the owner of the new West Coast—is both preposterous and pedestrian, a glorified real estate scheme. And it doesn't help that Superman thwarts it by confusingly reversing time.

But what's really at the heart of the film is Superman's *bildungsroman*—the young hero's journey of self-discovery—and his romance with Lois, the most famous love affair in literature after Romeo and Juliet. It features a Clark Kent properly restored to his schlemiel-schlimazel ways, and with it what was there at the beginning but had been lost over time; humor, particularly in the delightful banter that had characterized Siegel's dialogues.

Brando brought Jor-El to life with Shakespearean gravitas, if also stiffness, and Margot Kidder's neurotic livewire Lois, based on Jewish feminist icon Gloria Steinem,[50] played perfectly against Reeve's poise. It was Reeve, however, who was the film's breakout star. Looking like the Neal Adams or José Luis García-López depiction of the character—tall, mesomorphic, with sharply-defined features and thick, wavy hair—he not only looked the part, but proved to be a genuinely gifted actor.

Reeve understood that Clark Kent isn't just Superman in thick glasses. He modeled him after Cary Grant,[51] but he portrays him the way Siegel and Shuster did, an intricate charade which the audience is in on. He hides his 6'4" frame as a lumbering, chronically slouched man, oversized for the world around him, always occupying spaces awkwardly and knocking things over. He avoids eye contact, tucks his cleft chin in and speaks through his nose, stammering and hesitant, with over-animated expressions and puppy-wide eyes. He's naïve to the point of clueless, lost without even knowing it, hopelessly dependent on Lois to watch out for him. He's like a mix between a yokel and a yeshiva student, a farmer's son in the big city but with the cerebral, impractical attitude of someone who's studied the world, not experienced it. And yet, Reeve manages to convey, he loves being Clark. It's at once an act and his truest self. It's through Clark that he can communicate with people as an equal, to form relationships, without their awe of the superhero standing between them.

And when Reeve becomes Superman, he transforms. He carries himself with perfect posture, upright and square-shouldered but completely relaxed, even taller now but perfectly proportioned. His voice turns deeper, slower, steady. His demeanor is masculine but graceful, regal but unassuming, and he looks people in the eye with a stare that's reassuring and captivating. He exudes self-confidence, not only from being physically invulnerable but also emotionally secure, with a clarity of place and purpose that can only exist in fiction. What Reeve expresses, in a way that none have before or since, is the fantasy at the core of the character—that all our failings are separate from who we are, that how others see us is a deceptive echo of our true power, that the circumstances of our life are subject to our will, that underneath it all we are assured, capable and good. That in all of us there hides a Superman.

The movie made audiences believe a man can fly, but Reeve made them believe *in* the man, and that he can hide in plain sight behind a pair of glasses. It's why he remains the definitive Superman.

Ultimately, it's a movie worthy of its hero, and of its highest praise. At the end of the premiere Siegel and Shuster approached Donner with teary eyes, thanking him for bringing their creation to life just as they'd imagined it.[52]

It's also a movie suffused with Christian themes. A godlike Jor-El sends his son to Earth in a Star of Bethlehem/Christmas tree topper-looking ship, where he grows to save mankind from its own sin in the form of Lex Luthor's greed (though with a twist; he does so in an act of apostasy, by disobeying his heavenly father—literally, as his memory materializes in the clouds—choosing to interfere in human history). It's here that the Superman as Christ allegory began, fittingly embodied by an actor named Christopher. It may have always been present to some extent, but the movie fleshed it out, to the degree that Donner received death threats over the sacrilege.[53]

The movie isn't without Jewish signification, however. Kal-El is still a child refugee, and central to his character arc are his racial identity, cultural heritage and incumbent responsibility. These contending religio-cultural undertones didn't escape notice. Pete Hamill of the *Daily News* (which played the *Daily Planet* in the film) wrote in 1977: "Metropolis was … invented by Jerry Siegel and Joe Shuster almost 40 years ago, but it was Protestant. And Superman/Clark Kent was a terminal Protestant.… They had a hero who said 'swell.' In short, they had to write about a goy."[54]

More interesting in this respect is the context of the movie's creation. Superman's success as a comic book character was the result of a Jewish quartet: two who dreamt

Top and above: Christopher Reeve as Clark Kent and Superman. *Superman*, 1978. Warner Bros.

him up, Siegel and Shuster, and two who made that dream a reality, Donenfeld and Liebowitz. Superman's cinematic triumph was the result of a similar dynamic, this time the visionary duo being Donner and Mankiewicz and the practical pair being the Salkinds.

The Salkinds were *machers*—shrewd, resourceful and aggressive salesmen—and they recognized Superman's value as a cinematic property when nobody else did. Donner was the perfect choice to direct. Born Richard Donald Schwartzberg in 1930 in the Bronx, he came from the same background of wisecracking, vivace-tempo New York Jews that birthed comics, a sensibility he successfully brought to the movie, particularly the Metropolis scenes, together with Mankiewicz.

Just as Superman had been born of a Jewish perspective he was reborn of one, and for the second time in his life two sets of caretakers, creative and entrepreneurial, were at odds. They clashed over budget, schedule and vision, until eventually Donner was fired halfway through *Superman II*, which was being filmed concurrently.[55]

This dualism of creativity and pragmatism, inspiration and implementation, the heavenly and the earthly, is a central tenet of Judaism, the first religion to posit an omnipotent, omnipresent, intangible god and at the same time stipulate a complicated set of laws as its practice, 613 immutable *mitzvahs* (meaning both commandments and acts of charity) in the Hebrew Bible and its accompanying oral traditions (Oral Torah) and countless hermeneutical applications, known collectively as *Halacha*, guiding everything from prayer to diet.

Idea and action being codependent yet conflicting is a notion deliberated on throughout the Talmud, exemplified in the relationship of Jacob and Esau, the original dreamer and doer. The sons of Isaac and Rebekah, they were at odds from the womb, where they "jostled each other" (Gen. 25:22). As identical twins, the Midrash tells, they were distinguishable only by their character, two sides of the same coin. Esau was a man of the field, a great hunter and fighter, while Jacob spent his time at home, engaged in study (Rashi Gen. Parashat Toldot 25:27–30). Esau was also materialistic and deceitful, forever remembered in infamy, while the spiritual and pious Jacob, renamed Israel (connoting empowerment by or a path to God) earned his place in posterity as the begetter of the Israelites (Gen. 32:28–32). By the same token, Donenfeld and Liebowitz and the Salkinds came to be maligned for their unscrupulous treatment of the creative talent while Siegel and Shuster and Donner and Mankiewicz have earned acclaim.

Though it did well, 1980's *Superman II* failed to replicate the success of the first. Donner was replaced with British director Richard Lester (Liebman) to finish the film, who eschewed Donner's "grandiose myth" in favor of "quirky ... slightly more unexpected silliness."[56] His approach to the material resulted in an uneven patchwork with Donner's earnestness, particularly the inexplicable addition of superpowers like invisibility, telekinesis and, most oddly, the ability to transform the "S" symbol into a giant, cellophane-like offensive weapon.

The movie does, however, continue many of the themes established previously (though not nearly as satisfyingly as 2006's *Superman II: The Richard Donner Cut*), even deepening the scriptural allegory with the diabolical Zod, played swaggeringly by Terence Stamp. It also contains a discreet, metatextual joke; after Superman saves a boy who tumbles over the rails into Niagara Falls, an old lady exclaims, barely audible in the melee, "What a nice man! Of course he's Jewish!" Neither Puzo's nor Mankiewicz's script includes the line, most likely inserted impromptu by Lester during filming.[57]

Superman III followed in 1983, critically panned though modestly successful. Directed by Lester, it costars an out of place Richard Pryor, whose slapstick shenanigans grate loudly against Reeve's sincerity. Worse, as if to counterbalance, other elements are strangely morbid, including a schizophrenic Superman, under the influence of artificial Kryptonite, impliedly bedding a ditzy henchwoman, and a scene befitting a horror film of a woman swallowed up screaming by a super-computer and turned into a mechanical Frankenstein.

Though it remains derided by fans, the film does possess redeeming qualities. Reeve looks his best, having matured into the role and at his physical prime. His visit to Smallville and rekindling of romance with childhood crush Lana Lang, played by a charming Annette O'Toole, is poignant, and serves as a simplistic but effective theme of heartland wholesomeness vs. sterile industrialism. The latter is embodied by Robert Vaughn, convincingly offhanded as sociopathic financier Ross Webster.

Christopher Reeve transforming from Clark Kent to Superman. *Superman III*, **1983. Warner Bros.**

(Prefiguring, and likely influencing, Lex Luthor's reinvention as a corporate raider in the comics three years later.) The special effects, particularly flight, are possibly the best of the tetralogy, and the film contains some engaging action, chiefly an early sequence involving a chemical plant fire, on par with the first two films.

Unfortunately, 1987's *Superman IV: The Quest for Peace* possesses none of these strengths. The Salkinds sold the rights to Israeli cousins Menahem Golan and Yoram Globus, whose production company Cannon Group specialized in action B-movies starring the likes of Chuck Norris and Jean-Claude Van Damme, though they also produced comics-related schlock like *Masters of the Universe* ('87) and *Captain America* ('90). Superman was by far their highest cachet property.

Though ambitious in its approach—questioning Superman's self-imposed limitations on interfering with world order in light of nuclear proliferation—the film is dreadful. Cheap-looking and silly, even its co-screenwriter Mark Rosenthal admits it was "dumbed down." Both Reeve and Kidder look tired (and Reeve is noticeably less muscular), and so were moviegoers. The international box office didn't even make back the film's meager $17 million budget. The same year's *Police Academy 4: Citizens on Patrol* made almost double.[58]

There is also a *Supergirl* movie, produced by the Salkinds in 1984. Following the same formula of a newcomer in the lead surrounded by renowned actors—Peter O'Toole, Mia Farrow and a hammy Faye Dunaway as villainess Selena—the spinoff is more lyrical but also inane, ultimately proving forgettable. Reeve makes a cameo in the form of a dorm room poster and Mark McClure reprises his role as Jimmy Olsen (the first instance of a "shared cinematic universe"), supporting 21-year-old Helen Slater in the titular role—the first Jew to play a superhero and a well-cast *Maidel* of Steel.

Unfortunately, it would take years for the lessons of *Superman* to be learned, in both cinema and comics. Superman's comic books continued the course, and sales continued to decline. The rising cost of paper, printing

Helen Slater as Supergirl. Publicity photograph for *Supergirl*, 1984. Warner Bros.

and distribution, combined with irregular shipping, led DC to increase its prices, from 15¢ in 1970 to 50¢ in 1980 to 75¢ in 1984—500 percent, three times the rate of inflation—which resulted in further decline in sales. By some estimates, 60 percent to 80 percent of comics on newsstands were being returned unsold each month for a refund.[59]

Attempting to compensate, in 1978 DC aggressively over-expanded, adding 57 new titles in just three years. Met with little interest, the publisher was forced to cancel 31 of them in what came to be known as "the DC implosion." Compounding misfortune, that winter saw a series of blizzards that disrupted distribution as well as foot traffic, leading to sweeping cancellations and layoffs. "A lot of us were wondering if there would even be a DC a year from then," Kupperberg remembers.[60]

The success of *Superman*, plus an eventual pickup in sales, saved the company. But the real game changer came about the year before. July 1977's *Star Wars* comic, licensed by Marvel, singlehandedly saved the also-struggling publisher and with it likely the industry. It was the first series to sell over a million copies per issue since 1960, far outperforming market leaders like *Amazing Spider-Man* (282,000), *Superman* (235,000) and *Batman* (165,000).[61]

It also helped cement Marvel as market leader. By 1984 DC was a mere irritation, with an 18 percent market share compared to Marvel's 70 percent. Its flagship title, *Superman*, didn't even breach 100,000. Warner, at a loss of what to do with their hemorrhaging subsidiary, even planned to license the publishing rights to Marvel. Jim Shooter, who'd started under Weisinger on *The Legion of Super-Heroes* when just

thirteen, was now Marvel's editor in chief. He recalls how an excited John Byrne, the immensely popular cowriter-artist of *The Uncanny X-Men* and writer-artist of *Fantastic Four* and a huge Superman fan, even created, unsolicited, a plot synopsis and a fully rendered cover for the first Marvel issue of Superman.[62] However, legal complications ended up thwarting the deal, and probably for the best.

Another factor in DC's continuingly abysmal sales was its baroque canon, particularly Superman's. Stretching nearly half a century, it'd become overstuffed with elements that, even when brilliant in their own right, created a convoluted world for new and casual readers to follow, while longtime fans faced a welter of contradictory and outmoded stories (like a Superman who at first could only leap tall buildings in a single bound but flew around as Superboy).

Partly to solve this, DC had developed the "multiverse," an idea imported from science fiction (though popularized in comics) by Schwartz and Gardner Fox in *Flash* #123 (September '61), comprising an infinite number of parallel dimensions in which different stories took place. There was Earth-One, in which the current continuity was set, starting at the Silver Age. There was Earth-Two, counterintuitively home of the Golden Age versions of the characters (and so the rebellious Superman who fought Nazis was not the straight-laced Superman who fought aliens). On Earth-X the Axis won World War II and the remaining heroes became Partisans. There were many more, and whether they made things less or more confusing, DC's continuity had become too much of a Gordian knot.

Crisis on Infinite Earths, a 12-issue limited series stretching between April 1985 and March 1986, was the sword. Published at DC's 50th anniversary (dating to 1935's *New Fun: The Big Comic Magazine* #1), *Crisis* was, quite literally, its midlife crisis. A Superman story at its core, it was DC's first-ever company-wide crossover event, a requisite nowadays, featuring its entire pantheon past and present. Heroes from across the multiverse joined forces to stop a cosmic menace from destroying all of creation, an end of days brought about by the almighty of Superman's world; Marv Wolfman, Len Wein, Robert Greenberger and George Pérez. By the story's end, the multiverse had gradually constricted until all the different earths were folded into one, dubbed New Earth, in which various surviving elements were amalgamated.

The story strongly resembles the Kabbalistic concept of *shevirat ha-kelim*—"the shattering of the vessels"—derived from the Midrashic account of the building and destruction of the primordial worlds that preceded our own (Gen. Rabbah 3:7, 9:2). Weinstein is the only one to reference it, though he compares it to Krypton's destruction.[63] That parallel mostly works metatextually, seeing Krypton as prologue to Superman's narrative. The parallels to *Crisis* are more significant, particularly when comparing to the concept's metaphysical sense. Kabbalah, especially the writings of famed 16th-century mystic Rabbi Isaac ben Solomon Luria Ashkenazi (aka the Arizal) of Safed (in what was then Ottoman Syria and today Israel), posits a multiplicity in creation, similar to the multiverse and to modern quantum mechanics' many-worlds interpretation (different, though, in that it associates spiritual dimensions with physical ones). By this model, the whole of creation was infinite (*Ein-Sof*), which God then folded into a finite world in a series of contractions (*tzimtzumim*), resulting in our known world (Etz Chaim 1:2).

Inspired by Jewish ontology or not, *Crisis* marks a shift in Superman lore toward Christian iconography with the cover of issue #7 (October '85), in which he cradles the dead Supergirl in his arms like a Pietà, in place of the slain Jesus in Mary's, with the sun serving as a nimbus behind him.[64] It's one of the most famous and homaged comic book covers.

Crisis was also the bridge from the Bronze Age to the Modern Age, a rebirth of DC that gave readers the best of all possible worlds. Superman, who had ushered in the Golden Age, was allowed to say his goodbyes, which he did in the two-part story "Whatever Happened to the Man of Tomorrow?" in *Superman* #423 and *Action Comics* #583 (September '86).

Schwartz's first choice to write it was Jerry Siegel,[65] which would have made for a perfect bookend, but it didn't come to pass. Accounts differ on whether Siegel turned it down or legal complications prevented it, but Schwartz eventually went the opposite direction and hired British upstart Alan Moore, whose experience writing Superman was sparse but well-received, including the moving "For the Man Who Has Everything" in *Superman Annual* #11 (November '84) and a team-up with Swamp Thing in *DC Comics Presents* #85 (September '85). Swan, Superman's longest-running artist, was chosen to illustrate.

More a series of battles and tragic deaths than a story, the deft characterization of Superman and his supporting cast and the systematic breakdown of his tropes make for a powerful, brutal, melancholic tale. It's a worthy, if bittersweet, coda to the classic Superman.

The cover of *Action* #583 features Superman flying at the reader with his supporting cast waving goodbye, alongside Schwartz, Swan and Kahn. Swan, who thought that "comic books were only a passing fad and would never survive the '40s" when he started,[66] bid farewell to the character he defined for thirty years. It was also Schwartz's sendoff after sixteen years at the helm. Despite overseeing one of the weaker periods in Superman's history, Schwartz is remembered fondly for being the creative force behind the revitalization of the genre and for streamlining the Man of Steel.

"Whatever Happened" ends with Superman, having relinquished all his powers following his ultimate battle, living under a new secret identity, married to Lois with a son named Jonathan, leading a normal life. Or so it seems. Because baby Jonathan, despite his father's chestnut-dyed, now-graying hair, sports black locks and a familiar-looking spit curl. And on the very last page, right before the end, we catch him playfully pressing a piece of fireplace coal into a diamond.

It's a perfect ending for the Jewish metaphor that's at Superman's core. He can hide who he is, abdicate his special gifts and responsibility, fully assimilate into humanity, but in the end, he can't disavow his heritage, nor can his child. Judaism is different from other religions in that it's also a race, a peoplehood and a culture (and for nearly half a nationality). Jews may renounce their faith, but they cannot renounce their Judaism any more than the color of their skin. The same extends to the comic book industry. Though Jews continued to play a vital role, and were still represented in comparatively high numbers, from the mid–1980s onward comic book publishing was decreasingly a Jewish industry. Themes gradually became anecdotes until they all but disappeared, leaving only the metaphorical underpinning. But that's still there, and in Superman's case forever will be, a Jewish heritage that, even if disavowed, ignored or forgotten, is an inseparable part of who he is.

> *So many of our dreams at first seem impossible, then they seem improbable,*
> *and then, when we summon the will, they soon become inevitable.*
> —Christopher Reeve

Second Coming

The Dark Age

Though naming a comics era "the Dark Age" brings to mind medieval Europe, it was in fact a vibrant time of reinvention, revitalization and resurgence. It was also possibly the most eventful period in Superman's opus.

The different ages of comic book history are usually counted from watershed moments, like 1938's *Action Comics* #1 or 1956's *Showcase* #4. These are just demarcations, since like all epochs each is less a break from than an extension of the previous, its trends an effect to an earlier cause. The Dark Age, also called the Modern Age (and sometimes the Iron Age), isn't as well defined or agreed upon as previous eras. The issue is partly semantic; some regard the Dark Age as a shorter span within the Modern Age, like the Renaissance within the early modern period, some as a preceding era and others as synonymous. Either way, most seem to agree that it began in 1986, with *Watchmen* and *The Dark Knight Returns*, both DC works.

Heritage Auctions, owners of the *Overstreet Comic Book Price Guide,* define the Modern Age as beginning in 1980 and continuing to present. In contrast, *Life* magazine delineates the Dark Age between 1984 and 1989. Kaplan, curiously, defies consensus by disregarding them altogether, counting the Bronze Age from 1979 to today. But these goalposts are either too capacious or too confined, especially given the previous ages have all been around sixteen years long. Levitz offers a more useful periodization; the Dark Age began in 1984 and ended in 1996. The Modern Age is separate, beginning in 1998 and lasting until 2010, when the current Digital Age began.[1]

The 1980s was a decade of change. Counterculture hippies became yuppies, trading in their bellbottoms for briefcases in a jolted economy. Societal existentialism was replaced by an embrace of capitalism, consumerism and neoconservatism. The Reagan Revolution was a cultural analeptic, an exciting promise by a charismatic new leader to return to strength, pride and conviction. It was "Morning in America."

The Cold War was heating up quickly, with Americans determined to oppose the Evil Empire with jingoism not seen since World War II. The Middle East increasingly exported Islamist terrorism, targeting American barracks, embassies and planes. Domestically, growing inequality and the drug epidemic lead to an increase in urban crime, particularly gang violence. These threats, real and perceived, all contributed to a return to a good vs. evil narrative and provided superheroes with new faceless evildoers to battle.

Hollywood produced bombastic blockbusters starring blustering bodybuilders, while the soundtrack of the era was a mixtape of Michael Jackson and Van Halen, Madonna and Iron Maiden. Its esthetic was the provocateuring East Village art scene, with the likes of Keith Haring, Jean-Michel Basquiat, Barbara Kruger and a resurgent Warhol.

Comics were part of this American cultural explosion. Following the relatively torpid 1970s, the newfound enthusiasm, coupled with cynicism as its counteraction, gave superheroes "a new lease on life," as Morrison puts it, in "books that were philosophical, postmodern, and wildly ambitious."[2] It was a coming of age for comic books, with many longstanding characters being reinvented, including Superman.

Storytelling evolved to include greater thematic and psychological complexity and rounder characters, while artwork embraced new styles and visual language. Non-superhero genres enjoyed a revival, like horror, fantasy, crime noir, melodrama and vérité. The quietly amended 1989 Comics Code marked the end of most content restrictions,[3] allowing for greater creative freedom and more adult fare.

This brave new world attracted new frontiersmen, many from the British comics scene. Dubbed the "British Invasion," it included writers like Alan Moore, Neil Gaiman and Grant Morrison, who brought with them a romantic-gothic sensibility marked by heavy authorial presence, an emphasis on lyricism and theme over plot, and drollness.

They also brought to their work Jewish thought, though only Gaiman is Jewish. Gaiman routinely borrowed Midrash parables for his stories, including its storytelling style of blending surrealism and naturalism. Moore, who had ended the classic Superman's career in "Whatever Happened to the Man of Tomorrow?" (*Superman* #423 & *Action Comics* #583), is a mysticist who heavily incorporated Kabballah into his writing. Morrison has been the most impactful on the Man of Steel, authoring immensely popular runs like *JLA* ('97–'00), *All-Star Superman* ('06–'08) and *Action Comics* ('11–'13). He brought a psychedelic, New Wave and Punk Rock vibe to an industry largely still fixed in Folk and Funk, along with frequent Kabbalistic references and a "caustic … dark and skeptical Jewish surrealism" which he credits to the influence of Jewish comics writer Steve Gerber.[4] (Best known as co-creator of Howard the Duck, Gerber also brought this sensibility to his 1982 *Phantom Zone* miniseries with Gene Colan [Coen] and its conclusion in *DC Comics Presents* #97 [September '86], a parallel envoi to Moore's "Whatever Happened" depicting an outlandishly gruesome end to Superman's saga.)

Jewish presence in the industry continued to wane during this period, but ironically Jewish representation in the comics themselves increased to unprecedented— and for the first generation of comic book makers, undreamt of—degree. While Siegel and Shuster hinted that their hero was "strictly non–Aryan" and Simon and Kirby sent theirs from the Lower East Side to punch Hitler, in January 1980's *Uncanny X-Men* #129 Jewish writer Chris Claremont and cowriter-artist John Byrne introduced the aptly-named Kitty Pryde (Prydeman), aka Shadowcat, the granddaughter of Polish Holocaust survivors who wears a Star of David necklace in and out of costume.[5]

Also from the X-Men oeuvre, archvillain Magneto is the most prominent explicitly Jewish character in comics. He wasn't created as such, but over time his story has come to not only reflect but openly engage with questions of Jewish identity, people-hood, Antisemitism and the Holocaust. Born Max Eisenhardt, he was revealed in August 1981's *Uncanny X-Men* #150 to be a survivor of Auschwitz. Following the war he became a Simon Wiesenthal–like Nazi hunter, before moving to Israel, where he volunteered in a psychiatric hospital for Holocaust survivors. There, he befriended future X-Men founder Charles Xavier (Professor X), whose romance with Dachau survivor Gabrielle Haller produced a love child, David. Gabrielle would go on to become the Israeli ambassador to the UK while David became the super-powered Legion in March 1985's *New Mutants* #25.[6]

Throughout the 1980s, Marvel continued to Judaize characters like Iceman (yet another mutant) and produce new ones like Captain America's girlfriend Bernie Rosenthal and childhood best friend Arnie Roth. They also created an Israeli super-heroine, Sabra (Ruth Bat-Seraph), named after an indigenous prickly pear, an epi-thet for native-born Israelis for their purported tough, thorny exterior and soft, sweet interior.[7]

DC was less daring, settling for telltale surnames for less prominent characters. Firestorm is a hero created through the melding of two personas, high school football star Ronnie Raymond and Nobel laureate physicist Martin Stein. Raven of the Teen Titans is Rachel Roth. Nuklon (later Atom Smasher) is Albert Rothstein. In one story, the immortal Phantom Stranger was hinted to be none other than the fabled Wander-ing Jew, the man who mocked Jesus at the crucifixion.[8]

Noteworthy is Colossal Boy, a member of the 30th-century Legion of Super-Heroes. Originally created by Jerry Siegel and Jim Mooney in August 1960's *Action Comics* #267, he was later given the Hebraic name Gim Allon and in April 1980's *DC Special Series* #21 was identified as Jewish.[9] There's nothing to indicate Siegel meant for him to be Jewish, though for a character introduced only fifteen years after the Holocaust, he serves as a reassurance that Judaism will continue, and continue to be welcome, far into the future. Superman, meanwhile, gave no sign of embracing his heritage. On the contrary, he was about to shed many of its trappings.

The pinnacle of Jewish subject matter in comics was *Maus*. It's the memoir of writer-artist Art Spiegelman's relationship with his father, Vladek, and of his father's experiences in the Holocaust. Though nonfiction, it depicts Jews as mice (*Maus* is German for mouse), Nazis as cats, Americans as dogs, etc. Starting off as two vignettes in 1972 and expanded into a serial published in *Raw* magazine between 1980 and 1985, it eventually came out in collected form in 1986, with a second volume in 1991.[10]

It wasn't the first Jewish graphic novel—Will Eisner's 1978 *A Contract with God and Other Tenement Stories* is a semi-autobiography about Jewish immigrant life in the Bronx during the Depression—but *Maus* achieved unprecedented mainstream success. It's an artistic triumph, both in its novelty and its thoughtful communica-tion in ways proprietary to the medium, foremost the jarring disjunction between the horrific events and the anthropomorphized animals. It helped comics come into their own as an art form and storytelling medium and revolutionized the industry. Nonfiction, particularly biographical comics, remain one of its bestselling and most celebrated genres. *Maus* received the 1992 Pulitzer Prize, the only graphic novel to ever do so.[11]

The year of 1986 was pivotal for comics. It fundamentally changed the industry and the superhero genre, Superman included. So much so that popular news site CBR (Comic Book Resources) called it "comics' most important year, ever."[12] Along with *Maus*, two DC miniseries released that year became the defining works of the era: *Batman: The Dark Knight Returns* (June–December '86) and *Watchmen* (September '86–October '87). Other less extolled but likewise impactful milestones include the Superman miniseries *The Man of Steel* (October–December '86) and Marvel's "Born Again" storyline in *Daredevil* #227–#233 (February–August '86). It was also the year Dark Horse Comics was founded, the first successful independent publisher of mainstream comics (as opposed to head shop comix).

More landmarks followed in rapid succession, like "Batman: Year One" (*Batman* #404–407, February–May '87), new *Wonder Woman* (Vol. 2, February '87–February '92), *Batman: The Killing Joke* (May '88), *V for Vendetta* (September '88–May '89), *Arkham Asylum: A Serious House on Serious Earth* (October '89) and *Sandman* (Vol. 2. January '89–February '96).

What characterized these are greater emphasis on character, psychological realism, experimentation with form and new, palpable energy. Their themes, prefigured in the Bronze Age, favored terra firma over psychotropic space, including sociopolitical commentary. The dominant trend they ushered in, however, was of somber, hardboiled stories featuring brooding antiheroes and graphic violence and sexuality—hence "the Dark Age."

Also known as "grim & gritty," this flavor of comics was by no means the only popular one, but it did set the industry palate for years to come, with an aftertaste that still lingers. Readers responded well to the new breed of picaresque heroes who straddled, and sometimes crossed, the line. Superhero comics took on a subversive attitude, deconstructing every tried-and-true trope of the genre, often ending in disenchantment. If superheroes originally meant to embody the Judeo-Christian conception of godly benevolence they were now more like pagan deities, with the same failings as men, prone to pettiness, arrogance, lust, anger and vengefulness.

It was a double-edged sword. When these stories were good they were more mature and more intelligent, more satisfyingly challenging, and their realism helped anchor the fantasy and make it more immersive. Even when overwrought with philosophizing, it was usually at just the right level for teens and young adults. When they weren't good, however, they were more pretentious than ambitious, confusing depravity with gravity and psychobabble with insight. Their self-seriousness and relentless cynicism often crossed unintentionally into farce, and ironically stifled the exploration of identity, place and purpose that earlier, more playful comics allowed.

The darker themes and depictions of sex and violence rarely exceeded those of a PG-13 film, but they incurred the usual outcries, including from liberal publications like the *New York Times*, which called modern comics "vindictive" and "sadistic" and accused the industry of "playing with the same fire that nearly destroyed it in the early 1950's."[13]

Not unlike the American Jewish culture that birthed it, the comic book industry is ever self-deprecating and insecure. Partly in an anxious bid for recognition, it embraced postmodern hallmarks like skepticism, moral relativism, irony and self-reference. Rebellious by nature, comics also reacted, almost kneejerk, to Reagan's rah-rah America. They were more punk subculture, and they railed against neoconservatism and neo-puritanism, conspicuous consumption and corporate greed, AIDS hysteria and environmental complacency.

The same forces that'd shaped superheroes half a century earlier—poverty, crime, urban decay, class struggle, racial tensions, looming prospect of war—were now reshaping them, but more cynically and less hopefully. With the world perpetually under a Doomsday Clock nearing midnight, when the global superpowers seemed constantly on the verge of wiping humanity out, it was impossible not to recast men and women with superpowers in a skeptical light. If "with great power comes great responsibility," then too great a power is itself an irresponsibility.

The Dark Age also brought about a new world order, as the industry shifted its balance from newsstand to direct market sales. If previously comic books were found in street kiosks, supermarkets, toy stores and malt shops, they were now sold primarily through dedicated specialty stores. It was the most significant change to the business since it transitioned from promotional giveaways commissioned by retailers to newsstand and magazine rack sales in 1934.

Comics changed from impulse buys picked up by casual readers to planned purchases by habitual consumers, and comics stores became spaces of interaction that turned fans into a community, or "comicdom." It became a niche market, an ecosystem of enthusiasts that stabilized the industry but also warded off newcomers.

The direct market expanded rapidly. On the onset it had included around 30 shops in 1972, growing to 800 by 1979. By 1986 there were 4,000, and by 1993 about 10,000. The industry more than doubled in size during the 1980s, with DC and Marvel more than tripling their titles and raising their price by 250 percent—from 40¢ in 1980 to $1 in 1990—quadruple the national inflation rate.[14]

Comic books also weren't aimed at young children anymore, which they'd been since the fifties. Readership was mainly 13–29, and still almost entirely male (as was creatorship. The first female writer on a Superman comic wasn't until April 1985, when the Jewish Mindy Newell wrote a backup story in *Action Comics* #566).[15] Gen X teens were drawn to comics' new gloomy, grungy tone, which elicited in turn increasingly edgy works.

The cynical attitude toward superheroes inevitably targeted Superman, the prime thesis of caped wonders. The first work to offer a meaningful take from this angle was a Batman miniseries, *The Dark Knight Returns*, writer-illustrator Frank Miller's auteur opus.

As much political cartoon as comic book, it's an industry touchstone, an ambitious and accomplished deconstruction of Reaganism and of Batman's mythology, which author Stephen King calls "probably the finest piece of comic art ever to be published in a popular edition."[16] A bold and brutal noir story sketched in bristly lines and stark chiaroscuro, it's set outside continuity in a grimdark near-future where Gotham is entirely overrun by crime and corruption, Reagan remains the president, a callous and clownish authoritarian figure, and the specter of imminent nuclear war with the USSR looms. A grizzled Batman, looking like a human cinderblock, comes out of retirement to mete out hard justice, an apostate from noble law-enforcement to merciless vigilantism.

Relatively little has been said about Superman's role in the story, despite him being a key character and its influence on his future portrayals. The very first image—the iconic cover of issue #1, used for the collected edition and frequently homaged and parodied (an industry norm since the Dark Age)—is of a silhouetted Batman midair, right arm outstretched and left arm raised above his head. It's an inverse, nearly identical pose to the cover of 1939's *Superman* #1. Though possibly coincidental, the strong similarity and the uncommon pose suggest otherwise. Either way, the likeness seems to have gone unnoticed.

Future Superman is the only "legal" superhero left, at the cost of becoming Reagan's flunky and tool of government policy. He's sent after the rebellious Batman, leading to their first great and still most famous grudge match. Batman is a true Nietzschean Übermensch, a radical, uncompromising individualist determined to upset a dystopic status quo enabled by both well-meaning bleeding-hearts and opportunistic conservatives. Superman meanwhile is an agent of the establishment, at best a misguided idealist and at worst a damned-soul pragmatist.

For Miller, a baby boomer, Superman was a sellout, the opposite of the rabble-rousing reformist he started out as. Particularly in the context of Reagan-era neoconservatism, it can be read as a disgruntled, cautionary tale about how America was losing its way, how the Superman character had been handled, and how one reflected the other.

By the end, though, the Man of Steel is redeemed. He comes around to recognize the need to challenge and create change, and implicitly endorses Batman's anti-establishmentarianism. With a classic, reassuring wink, he lets the reader know that, despite his sanctification, he hasn't lost his humanistic *chutzpah*.[17]

Following the events of *Crisis on Infinite Earths*, and invigorated by the success of his films, DC set about revamping Superman. Several people pitched concepts, including Cary Bates, Frank Miller, Steve Gerber and Marv Wolfman,[18] but the task of reimagining comics' biggest hero was eventually given to comics' biggest superstar at the time, John Byrne.

Known for his property-reviving runs with Chris Claremont on *The Uncanny X-Men* and solo on *Fantastic Four* (*The Uncanny X-Men* #108–#143 [December '77–March '81], *Fantastic Four* #232–#295 [July '81–October '86]), the 36 year old was lured away from Marvel with the offer to both write and illustrate the new Superman, leading not just a tweak or retcon but a full reboot, a Superman 2.0—one of the biggest brand relaunches ever. Byrne was given a six-issue series, *The Man of Steel*, to retell the origin, between October and December of 1986, followed by a new *Superman* series beginning with issue #1 in January 1987.

The first volume of *Superman* was renamed *Adventures of Superman* with issue #424 the same month and entrusted to writer Marv Wolfman and co-plotter/illustrator Jerry Ordway. *Action Comics* was originally offered to Alan Moore, but the prolific Byrne ended up writing and illustrating it as well, beginning with issue #584

Left: Batman: The Dark Knight Returns #1, June 1986. Cover by Frank Miller. DC Comics. *Right: Superman* #1, June 1939. Cover by Joe Shuster. DC Comics.

(as well as occasionally writing or co-writing *Adventures*).[19] Andrew Helfer replaced Julius Schwarz as editor on all three titles, under the aegis of executive editor Dick Giordano. For the first time since his creation, Superman's handlers were mostly gentile.

Byrne felt it was as if he'd been "given the Bible, and told to jazz it up." His mandate, as he saw it, was "not so much a renovation, as much as a reaffirmation" of Siegel and Shuster's original version, to preserve and update the core elements for a modern audience. He incorporated elements from his 1984 pitch for the aborted Marvel issue of Superman as well as heavy influences from the *Superman* film, which he saw by his count 112 times.[20]

A creative powerhouse firing on all cylinders, Byrne's work was bursting with vitality. His style was clean and crisp, with layouts that favored wide and tall panels, giving him room to show off Superman's epic feats, and tight spacing, giving his stories the rapid pulse of a summer blockbuster. His Superman was majestic, exuberant and sexy, in a way he hadn't been for some time.

Here Superman didn't lead the trend but buck it, shining bright at an age hallmarked by darkness. He was earnest rather than cynical, reconstructed instead of deconstructed, not so much a rejoinder to *Dark Knight Returns* and *Watchmen* as much as an alternative reaction to the same cultural forces.

The reinvention of Superman was a cause célèbre on par with New Coke the year prior, earning national headlines. Other rebooted stalwarts like Batman and Wonder Woman didn't receive nearly as much attention, a testament to Superman's place in the culture as not just an American icon but an expression of American idealized self-image. Some considered the change sacrilegious, decrying his reduced powers (though in truth this simply made official what he'd undergone regularly throughout the Silver and Bronze Ages by way of various artifices) or that he'd been "Marvelized" (which he had, in that he now lived in a more recognizable world and was less saintly and more relatable, but both companies had really been cross-pollinating for years). Most readers, however, seemed to enjoy a Superman who enjoyed himself. Sales had slumped to 60,000 copies for *Superman* #413 and a woeful 29,000 for *Action Comics* #573 by November 1985, but *The Man of Steel* #1 sold over a million, the highest sales in forty years.[21]

DC's flagship character has been reinterpreted before and since, but it was Byrne's take that proved the most resonant and lasting. *The Man of Steel* was epochal, an extensive retelling of possibly the most famous origin story in fiction. It details Kal-El's journey to Earth, Clark Kent's life in Smallville, his decision to assume the mantle of Superman and his earliest adventures in Metropolis, told largely from his perspective.

It's a syncretic fusion of past lore and modern elements, apparent from the opening image of a redesigned Krypton. No longer the colorful Buck Rogers–style technosocial paradise it had largely remained since Wayne Boring designed it in 1948's *Superman* #53 (Shuster's was made of skyscrapers in *Action Comics* #1 and Bauhaus towers in the first newspaper strip), it now resembled the movie's Krypton, a harsh, antiseptic environment (though desert instead of glacial) in which physical contact was forbidden and, curiously, everyone shaved off their eyebrows. It was still a knowledge society, but "cold and heartless ... stripped of all human feeling, all human passion and *life*," one that, Byrne intended, "deserved to blow up."[22]

One small and largely unnoticed yet meaningful change to Superman's mythology is the circumstance of his birth. Rather than being born on Krypton and rocketed to Earth as an infant, he was artificially conceived in a "gestation matrix," which Jor-El then attached to a "hyper-light drive" and launched.[23] Consequently, when Kal-El hatched from the artificial womb he was actually born on Earth, in Kansas, changing him from an immigrant to a first-generation American. (The point has been generally ignored, with the exception of 1991's *Action Comics Annual* #3, an alternate future tale which used it to make him eligible to run for president.)

A more dramatic change to the lore, the Kents were now alive and well, whereas past accounts had them die during Clark's youth. Their continued presence in his life served as an anchor for his humanity and added the theme of family to his narrative. It counterbalanced, and to a large extent annulled, his social isolation and otherness. It also matured the fantasy, giving Superman an adult relationship with his parents, going against the superhero desideratum, which he himself established, of a completely autonomous hero.

His powers now didn't fully manifest until adulthood, allowing him to live a relatively normal life. He was never Superboy, and as Superman was far less powerful than before, though still far stronger than in his early days. For the first time he had an official age—28—and he was again the sole survivor of Krypton, with no diluting elements like escaped cousins, pets, criminals or bottled colonies. Kryptonite only came in a single chunk of verdant, and there was no Fortress of Solitude to safeguard it in. There was no need for solitude, for remembrance and preservation of a culture he knew almost nothing about. In contrast to most Dark Age superheroes he maintained an amicable relationship with authorities, even taking direct orders from President Reagan.[24] He may have been returned to roots, but the dissident reformist was gone for good.

Metropolis, meanwhile, became all but explicitly New York, and Lois finally got her groove back. Byrne based his take on Rosalind Russell's portrayal of reporter Hildy Johnson in 1940's *His Girl Friday* (apt, given that Johnson was influenced by Torchy Blane, the original inspiration for Lois),[25] as well as Margot Kidder's neurotic livewire. She was confident, driven and sharp in a way she hadn't consistently been since the Golden Age and befitting a post-second wave feminist. She was also hard-bitten and again had a distaste for Kent, though more because of professional rivalry than his spinelessness. Her flirtation with Superman, meanwhile, became more sexually charged.

Superman also had a different relationship with Batman, more an entente than a partnership, resulting from their changed, clashing personalities (which Byrne coordinated with Miller, who rebooted Batman in issues #404–407[26]). They were still the world's finest, but no longer super friends.

The most altered character was Lex Luthor. He was still a mad genius, but gone were the gray prison jumpsuit of the Silver Age and the silly green and purple tights with a Dracula collar and ankle jets of the Bronze Age, replaced by the 1980s guise of the devil; a dark Italian suit. He was now an industrialist and financier, Gordon Gekko with ten times the intellect and means and ego, no longer the most wanted criminal in the world but its most successful entrepreneur. He traded in his secret subterranean lairs for a penthouse office atop LexCorp Tower, modeled after the Citigroup Center skyscraper in Midtown Manhattan.[27]

Luthor's backstory also changed. Not one of Siegel's finest ideas, in April 1960's *Adventure Comics* #271 it was revealed that he had been Superboy's best friend in Smallville, but when Superboy accidently burned off his hair when saving his life, he swore eternal vengeance. His motivation was now more straightforward—envy. Marv Wolfman, who reinvented Luthor as a corrupt plutocrat, explains, "He hates him because he's no longer the best man in Metropolis. And in Luthor's mind, how can you conceive of being anything less than the best?"[28]

This new version of Superman's oldest foe successfully tapped into the strong public sentiment against corporate racketeers like Michael Milken and Jordan Belfort (who even had villainous monikers, the Junk Bond King and the Wolf of Wall Street), especially after the 1987 Black Monday market crash. Making him the potentate of Metropolis, with influence over its economy and politics, essentially gave him real-world superpowers and made him a more worthy adversary. He was a social predator, an embodiment of the oppressive establishment, in the tradition of

Superman's earliest enemies; the slumlord, the gangster, the corrupt politician, the lobbyist, the war profiteer. In particular, he was a recast of Professor Smalley, the sneering, exploitive elitist from Siegel and Shuster's 1933 "The Reign of the Super-man." With that, Superman became socially relevant again, an egalitarian crusader against injustice, a Champion of the Oppressed.

Interestingly, neither Wolfman nor Byrne point to Smalley as an inspiration. Rather, Luthor was largely based on Donald Trump, a real estate mogul both admired and reviled in New York circles, with added influences of Ted Turner, Howard Hughes, Thomas Edison and Satan. He lived in a glass tower, behaved ostentatiously, dated models and plastered his name in giant letters on every building and business he owned. The standalone comic *Lex Luthor: The Unauthorized Biography* (July '89) took it further, featuring a cover imitating Trump's *The Art of the Deal*, with a character even declaring that it "could do better than Trump's book."[29]

In a prescient, anti-mimetic twist, Luthor became president in 2001, winning on a platform of manufacturing growth, defiance of partisan interests, whitewashed impropriety and a strongman image. As president, he stoked xenophobia against "the alien," declaring him a wanted public enemy. He was ultimately exposed over illicit dealings with the despot Darkseid and enabling an attack against the world for political gain, bringing his presidency to an end.[30]

The biggest change, however, was to Superman himself. He got a makeover; Byrne gave him a physique every bodybuilder dreams of, with a slim waist, massively broad shoulders, arms the size of legs and legs the size of tree trunks. His features resembled Reeve's, with prominent cheekbones and a tapered nose, and his famous spit curl became a tousled forelock. This being the eighties, everything got bigger—muscles, hair, "S" symbol, cape—Superman looked like Reeve trained by Schwarzenegger and styled by Liberace.

More meaningful, he underwent an alter ego role reversal. After nearly fifty years of being a "strange visitor from another planet … disguised as Clark Kent" it was now Clark who was the true persona and Superman the disguise. "Superman isn't *real*. He's just a fancy pair of long johns that lets me operate in public without losing my private life," he states.[31] The reasoning was valid. Since in this version he only learned of his Kryptonian origins in adulthood, Clark Kent is all he'd ever known and who he grew up thinking of himself as. Superman and Clark were also no longer dissonant egos, just a change of mannerism between roles, like a doctor or police officer on the job.

Accordingly, Kent transformed from an anxious, bunglesome wimp into a genial but markedly more confident personality, only "a trifle *unsure* of himself,"[32] a shrewd newshawk who gave as good as he got in his rivalry with Lois, whom he still fancied but no longer pined for. He became a consummate yuppie, a set of silk suspenders away from an investment banker.

As Superman, meanwhile, he became "more aggressive … not so squeaky-clean … a little more like Dirty Harry," back to his no-nonsense crimebusting roots, if less rough-edged. He may have been created as a crusading New Dealer, and there was a new blue vs. white collar dynamic to his enmity with Luthor, but he was now, in

Byrne's words, a "Super Republican," embracing Reagan's flag-waving patriotism.[33] This Prouder, Stronger, Better Superman was well-adjusted, charming, uncynical and unafraid to plant tongue in cheek.

Byrne succeeded in making him less icon and more man, with greater depth and dramatic appeal. Thematically, however, he missed the point. The fantasy of Superman isn't merely the ability to pick up a car. It's the promise of great power, as well as great confidence and great popularity, hidden within, waiting to manifest at the right time. Of a secret truer, better self, realized.

From Siegel and Shuster onward, Superman writers and artists have been informed by their life experiences. Byrne was born in England, raised in Canada and immigrated to America, which he proposed gave him "a little cleaner view … what I'm bringing to Superman is the alien view."[34] As an immigrant he understood that the outsider's perspective and challenges of integration were part of what shaped Superman, but he was also white, Christian, from a Western country, didn't flee danger and grew up speaking English. To him, cultural differences were semantics.

The Man of Steel concludes with Superman learning of Krypton, then dismissing the knowledge of his ancestral home as "***curious mementoes*** of a life that ***might have been.***" Breaking with the past, he doesn't see himself as a refugee immigrant, burdened with survivor's guilt or the obligation of his birthright. Instead he declares, "It was ***Krypton*** that made me ***Superman …*** but it is the ***Earth*** that makes me ***human!!***" His bloodline is important only insofar as his powers, his ethnocultural heritage being "ultimately ***meaningless.***"[35] Even his outfit, traditionally Kryptonian garb or fabric, became a costume Ma Kent made for him.

In this sense he did harken back to his original Golden Age version. Krypton was just a pretext for his physiology, and though Clark Kent was a charade mostly played for laughs, Siegel saw Superman as "simply a human with powers ordinary humans do not possess." But it also abdicated much of the character's growth since, including that made by Siegel himself. It also wasn't quite the paradigm shift it was seen as and made out to be. Bates and Maggin had developed both personae as coessential, with the understanding that "this is a boy that was adopted at age one. He grew up here on earth; for all intents and purposes he's one of us," while also "the entire Superman idea is unique because he has been Superman since the day he was born, and he's been Clark, too."[36]

Byrne, though, favored a decisive binary, in which the farm boy was real and the spaceman a role. Kent was no longer an act of self-abnegation but of self-actualization, a homegrown American whose foreign ancestry was part of his genetic makeup but otherwise had no real bearing on his life.

Not everyone agreed. Smithsonian curator Carl Scheele, who directed the year-long exhibition "Superman: Many Lives, Many Worlds" in honor of his 50th anniversary, described him as "the essence of the great immigrant tradition." Writer Mark Waid, who readapted the origin story nearly twenty years later in 2003's *Superman: Birthright*, remarked that "one thing that struck me off-note with John Byrne's big revamp was the reversal of those roles, with Superman just another disguise. It struck

The Man of Steel #6, December 1986. Written & illustrated by John Byrne. DC Comics.

me as taking away one thing that made him unique and it gave short shrift to his alien heritage."[37]

It also forsook much of the character's Jewish heritage. If Superman was created as a reflection of Siegel and Shuster's self and culture, changing him also meant reshaping the metaphor. These changes mostly detached him from his Judaic underpinning, though they also created new, if unintended, parallels.

He was still technically from elsewhere but he was no longer the Other, the perpetual outsider struggling to assimilate and to define his identity. As Clark he had no need to pretend, to adapt unnatural affectations and appearance in order to fit in. He was now a late baby boomer/Gen Xer, and American Jews of his generation grew up in a more integrated society than their parents and grandparents. They weren't as relegated to distinct neighborhoods or social and professional circles, and for most English was the first or only language spoken at home. Who they were was no longer dictated by what they were. They were American, and other identifiers were unimportant or at most hyphenated, consigned to the role of backstory.

For many, like Superman, the Old World held no romantic appeal, nor did they have the complicated relationship with it that their immigrant parents did. It was a place connoting only desolation, a past best left in the past. Superman still embodied a Jewish fantasy of self-definition, but it was one of differentiation rather than assimilation, the empowerment of heritage without the encumbrance of its traditions. If in 1978's *Superman* Clark Kent avoids playing high school football in fear of abusing or revealing his powers, by 1986's *The Man of Steel* #1 he's Smallville High's star quarterback.[38]

In "The American Jewish Experience in the Twentieth Century," Jonathan Sarna and Jonathan Golden write that "History had proved that East European Jews would Americanize with a vengeance. The question now was whether, as Americans, they would still remain Jews." Jewish immigrants and their descendants had assimilated, Americanized and secularized, leaving behind many of the observances, traditions and mores of Judaism. Superman went even further, seeing his Kryptonian heritage, after decades of wistfulness, as "anathema."[39] Whether or not it made him more fully American, it reflects the cultural loss inherent in assimilation, the same ambivalence he'd embodied in the Golden Age as he transformed back and forth between Kent and Superman, the assimilated costume and the ethnic pride. For Jews, whose culture and community are uniquely deep-seated in their religion, it brought about a reckoning of identity.

The Jewish identification and erudition of some was nominal, especially compared to their parents', consisting of traditional foods, Yiddishisms and a liberal attitude. Others, meanwhile, explored their Judaism to broaden boundaries of worship and self-definition. By the end of the 1980s the Jewish reform movement rivaled in size the traditional conservative movement, and roughly half of American Jews were marrying gentile spouses. That Superman no longer had a Fortress of Solitude, a place to connect, learn and reflect on his heritage, was essentially him not attending shul anymore. (Adding insult to injury, when it was reintroduced in December 1989's *Adventures of Superman* #461, it was compared to a cathedral.)[40]

Jewish identity was also being redefined in Israel, not through assimilation but its opposite, reclamation. Jewish life was everyday life in a nation where even comic books were read in the language of the Ten Commandments. The first generation of Sabras, born and raised in the modern Jewish state, were still in their thirties, and they'd grown up not as outsiders, strangers in a strange land, but as natives of a secure and prosperous ancestral homeland. For American Jews, Clark Kent's newfound assuredness came not because Krypton didn't matter but because it had been reborn.

Superman's declaration, "It was **Krypton** that made me **Superman ...** but it is the **Earth** that makes me **human**," on the face of it, is a simple choice, to define himself by the new rather than the old, to be a Man of Tomorrow rather than yesterday. But it belies the inherent contradiction of his alter ego reversal. The hero is still Superman. His mission, his calling, is as Superman. It's his heritage that makes him special, that enables him to actualize the teachings of his upbringing. He is, first and foremost, whether he cares to admit it or not, a Kryptonian.

In this regard Superman is different from other heroes, and Judaism is different from other religions. All faiths are integral to the personal identity of their adherents, but Judaism is unique in that it inseparably comprises race, culture and faith distinct to a group of people. Religiosity isn't its defining standard. One doesn't need to believe in or practice any form of Judaism to be Jewish. It's acquired by either birthright or conversion and cannot be abjured: although a complex and historically controversial issue, most Jewish thought, including rabbinical institutions, considers apostate Jews as still Jews (Sanhedrin 44a).

"Superman suffers from a duality of interpretations that are inherently conflicting," Bogdanove admits. "Is Clark the man and Superman the job, or is Superman the alien the real person and Clark the disguise?"[41] The answer is really the question itself, and it's not the reader who's asking it, it's the character. It's his driving inner conflict, a search for identity equilibrium.

In a way, he stopped being Clark when he discovered he wasn't simply a gifted Midwesterner but an extraterrestrial. Like Moses, who grew up as Egyptian royalty but came to identify as an Israelite because of his birthright, Clark didn't so much assume the guise of Superman as much as realize he's always been Superman. It's why farm Clark and Superman are coterminous, essentially one and the same, while city Clark is a pretense. Even Byrne's yuppie Clark, for all the talk about him being the real persona, was still more mild-mannered than the hero, still hid his strength, still combed his hair back tightly and wore glasses he didn't need. His identity as Clark Kent may have preceded Superman, but afterward it was as Superman that he was his true, or at least truest, self.

And, try as he might, he's still super first and man second. Batman isn't half bat, his costumed identity is totemic, not biological. But Superman's identity, regardless of how he sees himself, is determined by his alien biology. He may be a Kansas farm boy at heart, but his heart isn't human.

What's more, the duality of interpretations Bogdanove talks about is really a false dilemma. Superman's personality is more complex, a trinity—Kal-El, Clark Kent, Superman—coexisting in cognitive dissonance. Testament to this are *The Man of Steel*'s three miniseries companions, *World of Krypton* Vol. 2 (December '87–March '88), *World of Smallville* (April–July '88) and *World of Metropolis* (August–November

'88), each dedicated to a formative setting in his life. Kal-El is his nature, Clark Kent his nurture, and Superman the fulfillment of both.

"I don't think even Siegel and Shuster realized what they were doing…. Superman's like Moses, cast away and brought to another land, or Christ." Wolfman, Byrne's collaborator, said in a 1986 interview.[42] Perhaps owing to his own Jewish background, he recognized the core allegory at play, which, for all the changes made post–*Crisis*, was still present in the Superman mythos.

A wimpy neurotic or not, Kent was still a bespectacled intellectual in a cerebral vocation, still in his creators' image and a Jewish stereotype. And Superman still fought for truth, justice and the American way, values that, in their Western understanding, derive much from Judeo-Christian tradition. The new Krypton was colder but more numinous, and the physical isolation of its giant city-citadels, separated by harsh climate, resembled more the scattered shtetls of Eastern Europe. Like the Jewish Diaspora, this state of affairs was brought about by a bygone war that dispersed the population across the planet (a civil war fought over the human rights of clones, ignited by a deranged mother who wed her son to her own clone because no woman was good enough for him, a Jewish cliché if there ever was one) and led, ultimately, to its destruction "in a terrible fiery holocaust."[43]

Being born from the gestation matrix in Smallville made Superman more of a Jesus figure, a savior sent from elsewhere but born, without carnal sin, among the people. At the same time, the holographic recording made by Jor-El (with Lara conspicuously absent), a carryover from the film, brought into canon the parallel to Moses's burning bush (and to the Kindertransport letters, disinterring the element from Siegel and Keaton's early version).

New additions included a Jewish mayor of Metropolis, Frank Berkowitz, who's the one to officially deputize Superman as an agent of the law, and Superman's "number one fan" from Metropolis's Suicide Slum, based originally on the Lower East Side, Bibbo Bibbowski, based on real-life Jewish friend of artist Jerry Ordway, Jo Jo Kaminski.[44]

Lex Luthor received a new backstory of an impoverished childhood in Suicide Slum, lending credence to Maggin's claim that he was Jewish.[45] (In this regard, his character arc reflects the upward mobility of American Jews from poor laborers and merchants to prosperous lawyers, doctors and bankers.) Conversely, his villainy was more in the Antisemitic vein than ever before. Beginning with Byrne and Wolfman's characterization and coming into sharper focus in following years—notably *Superman: The Animated Series* ('96–'00) and in comics the *Superman: Birthright* ('03) and *Lex Luthor: Man of Steel* ('05) miniseries—his grudge against Superman became rooted in bigotry and xenophobia. Referring to Superman as "the alien," he views him as an inherently corrupting presence that stymies and atrophies humanity. Intent on preserving his own power and hegemony and seeing himself as the true savior of mankind, Luthor is a Henry Ford figure, an Other-hater like countless supremacists and nationalists who've targeted Jews throughout history.

If the new Superman exemplified successful assimilation, his doppelgänger, the new Bizarro, was its nightmarish failure. Introduced in *The Man of Steel* #5 (December '86), he was now a malformed clone that believes he's Superman, even showing up at the *Planet* in a disheveled suit and glasses.[46] But his ghastly appearance, addled mind and muteness immediately cast him as a monster and he is feared and rejected by those around him. He's the "fresh off the boat" (or in this case bio-matrix) foreigner, instantly recognized as different, confused by behavioral norms and struggling to communicate through a language barrier.

The new Metallo likewise worked as a metaphor of dissimilation and rejection by the dominant group. Originally a funhouse mirror version of Superman, he was now a living weapon created by a mad scientist (naturally) who saw Superman as a parasitical invader coming to subvert and conquer from within.[47] His hostility became personal, rooted not in a criminal agenda but in racism, the same paranoid hate that has framed much of the violence against Jews, including the Holocaust, as an act of self-defense.

The biggest new Jewish element was Darkseid, who Byrne rightly felt would make "a perfect Superman villain."[48] Even though he was created in the Superman spinoff *Jimmy Olsen* in 1970, the Hitler-inspired evil god didn't clash with the Man of Steel until October 1980's *Justice League of America* #183. And it wasn't until *Legends*, DC's first post–*Crisis* crossover, and the tie-in issues *Action Comics* #586 and *Adventures of Superman* #426 (March '87), that the Lord of Apokolips truly became one of Superman's main adversaries and arguably the most powerful. It may have been fifty years later, but Superman was still doing what he was created to do—punch Nazis.

The year of 1987 also saw the publication of *Superman at Fifty: The Persistence of a Legend*, an essay collection that includes the first public deliberation on the character's Judeo-Christian undertones and his metaphor as a Jewish immigrant assimilating through a WASP disguise. It even humorously addresses the question of whether or not he's circumcised, concluding that he isn't because of his invulnerability as a baby.[49]

Despite 1987's calamitous *Superman IV* ending his cinematic career for a generation, the Man of Tomorrow was soaring his highest since the Golden Age. In addition to *Superman at Fifty*, *Time* dedicated their March 14, 1988, cover story to his golden jubilee. They also wondered about his Jewishness, but quickly dismissed it since "the man has all the ethnicity of Formica."[50]

The *Superman 50th Anniversary* TV special, a mockumentary produced by the *Saturday Night Live* crew and starring several of the cast, aired in June. In September, a Saturday morning cartoon featuring the new version of the character, simply titled *Superman*, aired on CBS. It lasted only thirteen episodes, but it marks the beginning of a more or less uninterrupted 23-year presence on the small screen. In October, a live-action *Superboy* show debuted in syndication (renamed *The Adventures of Superboy* in the third season), lasting until 1992. Produced by the Salkinds and taking its cues from the films (though set apart), it starred John Haymes Newton in the first season and Gerard Christopher following as college student Clark Kent, in Florida of all places. As a property, Superman's estimated value surpassed $1 billion ($2.2 billion adj.).[51]

October 1988 marks the end of Byrne's tenure. He'd originally declared his aim to complete a hundred-issue run, but *Superman* Vol. 2 #22 was to be his last (he'd already left *Action Comics* with May's #600). Claiming DC was constrictive and undermining, he ended up regretting his involvement, calling it "death by a thousand cuts."[52]

His last issue is notable in that it introduced possibly the most controversial change to the ethos. Superman violated his one immutable moral code, to never kill. In a "pocket dimension" in which the Phantom Zone criminals (in this case Zod, Quex-Ul and Zaora) wiped out the entire population of the Earth, as the only arbiter of justice, Superman executes them using their version of Kryptonite. It's not retributive, it's the only way to stop their imminent threat to his own world, making it understandable and even justified. But this was Superman. The Big Blue Boy Scout, the heroes' hero, known for saying "there's always a way."[53] It tarnished him, showing that even he was susceptible to the grim & gritty fad and the zero tolerance zeitgeist.

Figures for *Superman* Vol. 2, Byrne's home title, are unavailable, but sales of *Action Comics* tripled during his time (though still a modest seller in the market, especially compared to its heyday).[54] Byrne's indelible mark, though, is in redefining the character and his mythology. Many of the elements he introduced have since been changed, but his remains the most influential and lasting of Superman's many revisions and tweaks, and one of the best arcs in his storied eighty-year career.

After Byrne Superman's comics trundled along, but did well enough to merit a fourth series, *Superman: The Man of Steel*, launched in July 1991, allowing DC to offer a new Superman comic each week. It was helmed by Louise Simonson, the first woman to regularly write the character, and Jon Bogdanove, the most stylized of Superman's core artists and a new Jewish addition, along with writer Roger Stern on *Superman*.

The Man of Steel, meanwhile, continued to undergo changes. Some overturned Byrne's, like familiarizing him with Krypton and making it an integral part of his identity again. In February 1991's *Action Comics* #662, five years into his relaunch and 53 into his courtship of Lois, he revealed his secret identity to her and proposed. After half a century of dramatic tension the big moment felt underwhelming and unromantic, given less than six pages over two issues and ending in a muted response from Lois.[55] But she eventually accepted, and the two are still married.

Jewish themes and preoccupations could still be found, though with decreasing frequency. One noteworthy instance is when the Joker almost blew up Tel Aviv. In the landmark Batman story "A Death in the Family" (*Batman* #426–429, December '88–January '89), the Joker steals a nuclear cruise missile and attempts to sell it to Lebanese terrorists, unnamed but clearly Hezbollah, who aim to launch it at Tel Aviv. Batman foils the plan, but Iran's Supreme Leader, Ayatollah Khomeini himself, rewards the Joker by appointing him as the Iranian ambassador to the UN, under full diplomatic immunity (a twist that, given the regime, only slightly strains credulity). The Clown Prince of Crime gives a rambling speech at the General Assembly in which he compares the Islamic Republic's zealously to his own insanity, then predictably tries to kill everyone with his laughing gas. Superman, attending undercover, saves the day.[56]

In "The Warsaw Ghetto," *Superman* Vol. 2 #54 (April '91), a time-tossed Champion of the Oppressed finally got his chance to save Jews from Nazis. First he does what the U.S. government had refused to and stops a cattle car full of Jews from reaching its destination (giving a whole new meaning to "more powerful than a loco-motive"). He then stops a Nazi atomic bomb from detonating and is taken for an angel. It marks the first time the extermination of Jews is explicitly mentioned in a Superman comic.[57]

The 1990s were an era of extremes. The Soviet Union's collapse in 1991 led to the creation of more than a dozen democracies (and freeing 1.6 million Jews, about 12.5 percent of world Jewry, to emigrate, mostly to Israel[58]), as well as to several coups and wars in former Eastern Bloc states. Israel and the PLO signed the Oslo Accords ('93–'95) and England and Northern Ireland the Good Friday Agreement ('98) while genocide took place in Bosnia ('92–'95) and Rwanda ('94). The Berlin Wall fell and the European Union was formed ('91–'93) while multinational war was waged in the Persian Gulf ('90–'91). The World Wide Web revolutionized human communication and the dotcom bubble crashed global stock markets ('00–'02).

Cultural tastes changed, and superheroes changed with them. The rock & roll sixties that gave birth to Spider-Man and the X-Men were now grunge and thrash, breeding the likes of Justice League spinoff *Extreme Justice*, *X-Treme X-Men* and *Adam X the X-Treme*, a soul-patched superhero with the power to set a person's blood on fire.

The Dark Age, which started out as "grim & gritty," became "extreme," character-ized by ultraviolent gun-toting antiheroes with perpetually gnashed teeth who reg-ularly maimed and killed their enemies. Names of villains and heroes alike evoked death and violence, like Carnage and Ripclaw. There were even two different ones named Holocaust. The most common theme, though, was blood: there was Bloodaxe, Bloodbath, Bloodbow, Blood Claw, Bloodhawk, Bloodklott, Bloodlust, Bloodpool, Bloodscream, Bloodshed, Blood Spider, Bloodsport, Bloodshot, Bloodstorm, Blood-strike, Bloodthirst, Blood Syndicate, Bloodwraith, Bloodwulf, Bloodwynd, Bloody Mary, Youngblood and other such sanguinary sobriquets, all created during the decade.

Everything was in excess. Anatomy ran amok with impressionistic bulges that swelled, stretched and striated like Silly Putty. The streamlined tights and cape look that Superman pioneered was abandoned in favor of rococo suits of armor (or in Thor's case, a crop top), chromed bionic prosthetics and giant shoulder pads. Char-acters were armed to the teeth, with guns the size of cannons and a glut of ammo pouches on belts, thigh straps and bandoliers, looking like battleships on legs.

The 1980s trend of overserious but transgressive superheroes became caricatur-ized, a claim to radicalness that was ultimately banal. Superheroes behaved like petu-lant teenagers in comics that favored style over substance, featuring vacuous themes, fatuous dialogue and gratuitous violence. Still, even the less accomplished works were exuberant, exploding with high-octane action and new concepts that reinvigo-rated and grew the industry. The quality of art, as well as of paper and print, leapt for-ward, and the launch of DC's adult content imprint Vertigo in 1993 (headed by Jewish editor Karen Berger) brought avant-garde, high-minded, non-superhero fare to the forefront, like *Sandman*, *Hellblazer*, *Preacher*, and *Y: The Last Man*.

While the era is marked by a general focus on art over story and the formation of new publishers like Image Comics that allowed creators to own the rights to their work, it ironically also produced countless derivative characters, often barely redesigned plagiarisms. Superman fared better than most, with analogues clearly done in homage, parody or commentary. There were many, including Supreme, Samaritan, Apollo, Caped Wonder, Captain Power, The High, Legacy, Mighty Man, Mister Majestic, Icon and Prime. None picked up on any of his Jewish themes.

The real deal of steel, meanwhile, meandered. Despite the addition of vivid writer-artist Dan Jurgens to the roster, who'd eventually succeed Byrne as the main creative force on the character, and memorable storylines like "Panic in the Sky," sales continued to falter. *Superman: The Man of Steel* #1 was the only issue of his to crack the top 100 list in 1991, placing at 83.[59]

In the era of "extreme," Superman remained reasoned and compassionate, optimistic and unarmed—"a world-class bore," the *Times* called him.[60] For teenagers, an action hero who was also a responsible adult was unexciting, a stuffy cornball.

There was also the question of what, exactly, was "a job for Superman." Now that America was the only superpower left, what need was there for its superpowered champion? The Cold War was over and Western liberal democracy seemingly won out over communism, fascism and militant nationalism (what political scientist Francis Fukuyama myopically called the "End of History"). The American Way prevailed, the never-ending battle ended. Superman was left with no grand cause, no urgent threat, no tangible adversary. And there were only so many costumed criminals and invading aliens he could fight and stay relevant.

Joe Shuster died on July 30, 1992, at the age of 78. Like in their childhood, he and Siegel lived only three blocks from each other, in West LA. He died alone, unmarried and childless, leaving behind no insurance policy or will. His one-bedroom apartment was found cluttered with a lifetime of Superman memorabilia, most of which he likely had to buy with his own money.[61]

DC ran a full-page commemoration in all issues cover-dated November 1992. They also paid his estate a douceur of $600,000 and other benefits, including a modest annual pension for his siblings, in exchange for relinquishing all claims to the property. Shuster's last words on record, less than three months before his passing, were "[t]here aren't many people who can honestly say they'll be leaving behind something as important as Superman. But Jerry and I can, and that's a good feeling."[62]

Superman died shortly after his creator. It had only been six years since his rebirth, but it seemed that whatever alchemy Byrne used to rejuvenate him had worn off, and he was back to languishing in the doldrums. So DC decided to kill him. It was perhaps inevitable that the Dark Age would extinguish, if only for a time, comics' lodestar.

The timing proved propitious. The issue of his death, *Superman* Vol. 2 #75, was released on November 18, 1992 (cover dated January 1993), an exceptionally slow news day (the *Times* headline read, "Young Believe Malcolm X Is Still Speaking to Them"[63]). It grabbed media attention worldwide, resulting in a frenzy by longtime fans, curious newcomers, nostalgics and collectible investors, lining up around the block to comic book stores by opening time.

It sold three million copies overnight, the highest single-day sales of a comic book, earning $30 million ($54 million adjusted). Including various cover iterations and reprints it ultimately sold more than six million copies, the second highest figure of any American comic book (after October 1991's *X-Men* Vol. 2 #1, which sold nearly 8.2 million).[64]

Sales remained strong throughout the storyline. April 1993's *Action Comics* #687 topped a million copies while June's *Adventures of Superman* #500 likely surpassed two million. Superman titles dominated sales with the top five spots in 1993, which Jenette Kahn called "the most successful year in the history of DC, and probably in the history of comics." The *Death of Superman* collected paperback became the best-selling American graphic novel of the 20th century.[65] In death Superman became more popular than he ever was in life.

The narrative, a triptych—the "Death of Superman," "Funeral for a Friend" (renamed in paperback "World Without a Superman") and "Reign of the Super-men," often referred to collectively as "The Death and Return of Superman"—was a multi-series opus stretching from November 1992's *Superman: The Man of Steel* #17 to October 1993's *Adventures of Superman* #505. It features a new enemy called Dooms-day, a spiked gray hulk created as a mindless bioweapon in Krypton's ancient past who eventually finds his way to Earth. More force of nature than character, he's a symbolically "extreme" and, at the time, forgettable ad hoc villain.

The plot is likewise utilitarian, a trail of mayhem and destruction ultimately stopped by Superman at the cost of his own life. *Superman* Vol. 2 #75 is a 26-page-long slugfest drawn entirely in stentorious full-page panels ("splash pages").

"Funeral for a Friend" is an affecting second act, showing the world's reaction to the loss of its greatest hero and examining the impact he's had, as both Clark and Superman, on loved ones, colleagues, adversaries and everyday people.

In "Reign of the Supermen," a nod to Siegel and Shuster's 1933 story, four Super-men appear, two claiming to be the original. Each is meant to represent an aspect of the character: Steel, a high-tech engineer inspired by Superman to don an Iron Man–like suit of armor, who shares the same rectitude but lacks the power; Super-boy, a clone teen of steel, who possesses similar powers and goodness but is a reckless hothead; the Eradicator, a Kryptonian artificial intelligence with Superman's appear-ance and abilities but none of his compassion; and Cyborg Superman, a villainous pretender who proves just how terrifying Superman's power in the wrong hands can be.

The true blue eventually does return, of course, having been resuscitated with convenient Kryptonian technology, to save the world in the nick of time. (Sporting, and keeping for over three years, long hair, unfortunately drawn by some to look like a mullet and to this day remembered as such. As Clark he had an equally unfortunate ponytail.)

The *Times* wasn't impressed. "Superman was a goner long before Doomsday arrived," it ridiculed,[66] a relic of a bygone era of Cold War and warm apple pie. But that was precisely the point. Superman had become superannuated, or so the think-ing went. His death was meant to remind people how special he was and to restore his relevance. His four epigones epitomized trends of the Dark Age—armored, leather-clad, bionic, body-horrific, irresponsible, snarky, ruthless, murderous—shown to be corruptions of the heroic ideal. It was a call for the wayward flock, seduced by postmodern, heterodox antiheroes, to return to the fold, to re-embrace the prelapsarian icon, the superhero who started it all.

Superman was by no means the first comic book character to die and come back, nor did any fan truly believe DC had killed him off for good. But the response of shock, outrage and mourning was unlike anything seen before or since. (His death actually started a trend; Mr. Fantastic, Green Lantern, Green Arrow, Wonder Woman, Captain America, Spider-Man, Starman and Iron Man all died and were resurrected, though none elicited reactions remotely as strong.) His death was understood to mean something. It was, as the *Washington Post* wrote, the passing of a "mythic American icon."[67]

This is also when the reframing of Superman as a Jesus figure carried over from the Christopher Reeve films into the comics.

Doomsday is named in direct reference to the end of days,[68] and Superman endures a Passion to stop him—he's stigmatically beaten and cut to death, Doomsday's bone spikes in place of thorns, nails and spears—ultimately sacrificing himself for mankind's salvation. The closing images of *Superman* Vol. 2 #75 are of Lois cradling his body, Pietà-style.

The funeral procession and service are nonspecific, but the Christ allegory becomes unmistakable when his body mysteriously vanishes from its sepulcher, followed by his revenant return to save humanity yet again. When he appears it's essentially via birth, flushed out in liquid from between the legs of a giant Kryptonian war suit,[69] a savior manifest corporeally from both the other world and another world.

Prior to his second coming, Metropolitans holding vigil at his monument carry signs reading "Savior" and "**He** died for you."[70] Then four false messiahs capable of performing great signs and miracles appear, claiming to either be him or assume his mantle, just as Jesus warns in Matt. 24:5–26 & Mark 13:6–22: "For many shall come in my name, saying, I am Christ; and shall deceive many." Essentially, Superman died a Jew and was reborn a Christian.

The massive success of the "Death and Return" saga helped create an industry boom. Nearly sixty years after their inception, comic books reached their apogee in April 1993, which saw 48 million books sold to the Direct Market alone, making an estimated $850 million.[71]

Fueled by demand, publishers offered more titles and at higher cover prices (from $1 in 1992 to $1.95 in 1996) while the cost of back issues skyrocketed. *Action Comics* #1, the Holy Grail of collectors, cost around $400 in 1974. By 1984 it fetched about $5,000. By 1988 it jumped to $35,000. By 1991 it was $82,500. A near-mint copy would ultimately sell for $3.2 million in 2014.[72] Comics, once considered disposable items (at least by parents), were now prized collectibles, seen as nest eggs, creating a speculator market.

But after the rise comes the fall, and inevitably the bubble burst. The market was flooded with comics that were uninspired and rushed, marked-up "special editions" with gimmicks like holofoil covers, and contrived "events" that took place across multiple series, strong-arming readers to buy them all. The growth of videogames and cable television didn't help; neither did financial brinkmanship by publishers and retailers and warring between distributors. Two days after Christmas of

Superman Vol. 2 #75. Written by Dan Jurgens and illustrated by Dan Jurgens and Brett Breeding. DC Comics.

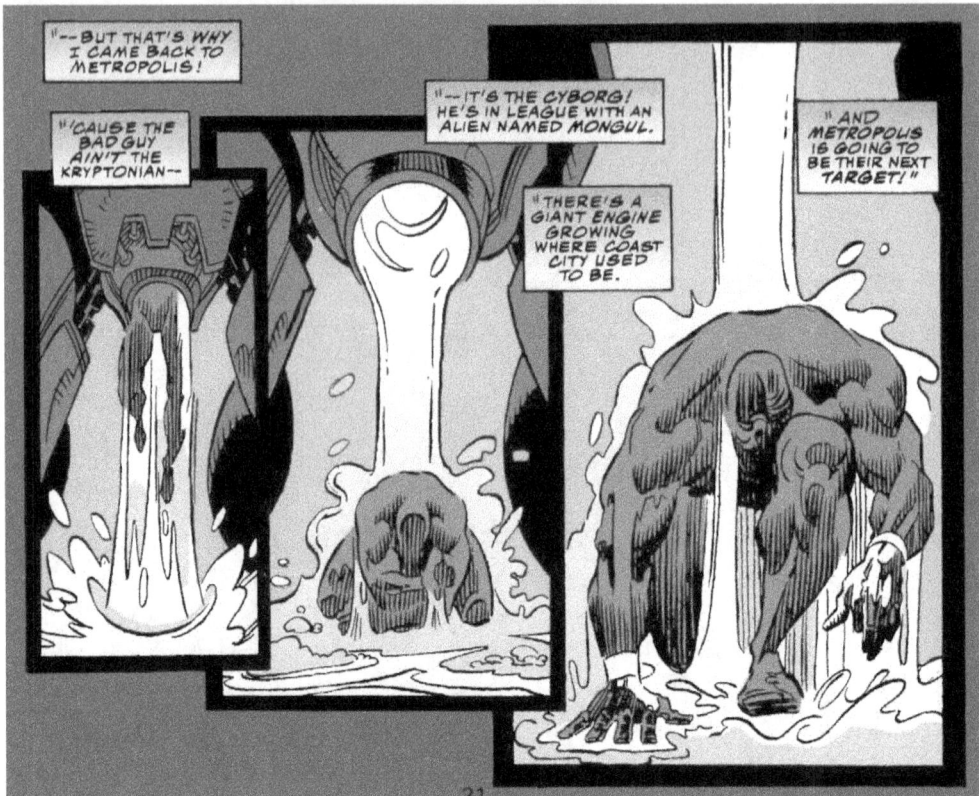

Superman: The Man of Steel #25, September 1993. Written by Louise Simonson and illustrated by Jon Bogdanove. DC Comics.

1996, an overleveraged Marvel declared Chapter 11 bankruptcy. (A drama whose dramatis personae are Jewish, including owner tycoon Ron Perelman, corporate raider Carl Icahn, and Israeli-American savior stakeholders Ike Perlmutter and Avi Arad, as recounted in Dan Raviv's 2002 *Comic Wars: Marvel's Battle for Survival*.) Its weight dragged the industry down with it. Monthly sales nosedived by 85 percent and as many as 90 percent of comic book stores closed their doors. From about 10,000 shops in 1993, there are about 2,000 in the U.S. today.[73]

From his historic high in 1992 and the top five spots in 1993, Superman comics dropped by 1994 to spots 33, 44, 48 and 69. By 1996 only one breached the top 100, placing at 82. And by 1998 none did.[74] (A fifth title, *Superman: The Man of Tomorrow*, debuted in June 1995, lasting sixteen issues.)

Although the conditions that led to the market crash can be traced back to the late 1980s, the success of the "Death of Superman" and the tsunami that followed have marked it as the flashpoint. It remains hotly debated whether it was ultimately a harmful publicity stunt, a pyrrhic victory or a legitimate, accomplished story. Whichever the case, its enduring legacy is undeniable, on the industry, on Superman's canon and on his symbolism.

While Superman resumed his never-ending battle for relevance in comics, he enjoyed a resurgence on television. Improbably, he became a recurring motif and de facto cast member on "the greatest sitcom of all time," *Seinfeld*. In virtually every one of the show's 180 episodes between 1989 and 1998 he appears as a statue on a shelf, fridge magnet or other piece of memorabilia in Jerry's apartment. He's referenced countless times in dialogue and features prominently into several episodes' themes and plots (in one, Jerry goes by the alias "Kal." In another he contends for his friend Elaine's affections against "Bizarro Jerry," an eerie opposite of himself. In another, he dates a woman named Lois and runs a race to impress her to the *Superman* score[75]). *Seinfeld*'s cultural impact was immense. It changed the sitcom formula from preposterous scenarios to the preposterousness of everyday life, bringing New York Jewish culture, neurosis and existentialist, fatalistic humor to mainstream America and the world, helping make them postmodern hallmarks.

The connection to Superman wasn't happenstance. Part of Seinfeld's preoccupation with the character came from recognizing him as a "Jewish brother-in-arms." Conversely, Seinfeld credits his own influence on the superhero genre: "There's a certain tone, a certain *chutzpah*, that we had, [that I see today] in comic book movies. Superheroes speak like we spoke. Very sarcastic, very witty, very matter-of-fact, while the world is being destroyed ... they're trying to do me as Thor!"[76]

Superman also starred in two shows of his own. From 1993 to 1997, *Lois and Clark: The New Adventures of Superman* aired on ABC, not a Saturday morning cartoon but a primetime drama focusing on the titular characters' relationship—and giving Lois top billing. Starring Dean Cain and *Seinfeld* alumnus Teri Hatcher, the soap opera/rom-com hybrid showed that the romantic triangle alone was a rich enough vein of the mythology. It was lighthearted and spirited, mostly thanks to the chemistry between its leads, who largely followed Byrne's characterization but brought their own charm to the roles.

Cain was an endearing everyman Superman, and to date the only actor to play him who wasn't fully Caucasian. Born Dean Tanaka,[77] his Anglo-Japanese heritage was gently evident in his features and coloring, proving that, as an American icon, the Man of Steel could represent a more diverse modern America. Interestingly, this change doesn't seem to have been noted in the press.

Despite strong first two seasons the series gradually derailed into camp and *schmaltz* and was cancelled after the fourth. Showrunner Deborah Joy LeVine is Jewish, but otherwise representation is limited to two presumably Jewish characters, recurring scientist Dr. Bernard Klein and Superman's talent agent Murray Brown. The only notable instance of Jewish themes is in the episode "Just Say Noah," in which Lois's neighbors the Sitkowitzes are addressed by a disembodied voice emanating from a burning bush—a rigged flowerpot in the entrance to their building—telling them not to fear and that they've been chosen. A madman who believes God is talking to him plans to bring them, along with other couples, onto his giant wooden ark and flood the earth. His inspiration are the apocalyptic Dead Sea Scrolls, for which the show uses a copy of *Shulchan Aruch*, a comically mismatched text of technical rulings and practices.[78]

In September 1996, while *Lois and Clark* was in its third season, *Superman: The Animated Series* debuted on the WB Network, starring Tim Daly. A sequel to the highly stylized, multiple Emmy Award–winning *Batman: The Animated Series*

Dean Cain and Teri Hatcher as Superman and Lois. Publicity photograph for *Lois and Clark: The New Adventures of Superman*, 1993. ABC.

Lois and Clark: The New Adventures of Superman, season 3 episode 5, "Just Say Noah," 1995. ABC.

('92–'95), the show was a mix of science fiction, noir and social drama, featuring a relatable, less powerful and more headstrong hero. Clark Kent was likewise less mild, in line with the now decade-old depiction of him being the true persona. Of note, Lex Luthor was loosely based on Greek-American actor Telly Savalas (*Kojak*),[79] but given a darker complexion and thick lips, seeming to imply, though never discussed, that he was at least partially black.

Another noteworthy change was to detective Dan Turpin, drawn to look like creator Jack Kirby. Despite uttering Yiddishisms like "oy" he wasn't made explicitly Jewish until his death in the show's second season, in an episode dedicated to Kirby, where a rabbi reads the *Kaddish* prayer at his funeral. (Though the rabbi is voiced by a real cantor, he's drawn with a tallit, which isn't worn in funerals, and he wears it wrong, like a scarf.)[80]

On the big screen, meanwhile, the Metropolis Marvel's fortune wasn't as favorable. Despite Warner Bros.' hope to jumpstart the franchise, successive productions kept floundering in development hell for nearly twenty years.

On January 28, 1996, at the age of 82, Jerry Siegel passed away. DC published a full-page tribute in their April and May issues. It was more elaborate and heartfelt than Shuster's.

His obituaries and the thought pieces that followed mark the beginning of the discussion about Superman's Jewish signification in the public sphere. Gary Engle

Superman The Animated Series, season 2 episode 26, "Apokolips…. Now! Part II," 1998. The WB/Warner Bros.

had been the first to write about it in his 1987 essay, "What Makes Superman So Darned American?" in *Superman at Fifty*. He was ideally suited for it as a professor of literature, writing and popular culture at Cleveland State University and an ordained minister. The same book also contains the short satirical essay "Is Superman Jewish?" by author and journalist Scott Raab.[81] Their insights, however, failed to reach critical mass. It wasn't until Siegel's death that the press, and subsequent books, started examining the character, as well as other superheroes, in a Jewish light.

Journalist and interfaith leader Eric J. Greenberg wrote an article titled "Did Superman Have Biblical Roots?" in the *New York Jewish Week* in February 1996. He followed up in May with a *Jerusalem Post* piece, "Superman: A Jewish Hero." In November, Jules Feiffer spoke about it at the Library of Congress, then in December wrote an op-ed for the *New York Times Magazine*, "The Minsk Theory of Krypton." In 2000 Michael Chabon published *Kavalier & Clay*, exploring the subject in fiction and in depth, followed in 2003 by Arie Kaplan's "Kings of Comics" three-part series in *Reform Judaism*. In 2008 Kaplan turned it into a book, *From Krakow to Krypton*, by which point Simcha Weinstein's 2006 *Up, Up, and Oy Vey!* and Danny Fingeroth's 2007 *Disguised as Clark Kent* had also come out.[82]

Back in the comics, while his ongoing series struggled, the four-issue superhero opera *Kingdom Come* (May–August '96) would prove epochal for Superman and, as often follows, DC and the industry. Written by Mark Waid and Alex Ross and fully painted by Ross, it's an uncanonical "Elseworlds" story set about fifteen years in the future.

Superhumans have proliferated, but the younger generation has sloughed off the hero's code of honorable conduct and minimal, nonlethal force. They revel in blithely violent squabbling, unconcerned with bystanders, until disaster inevitably strikes. A graying, thickset Superman returns from self-imposed exile, along with other old guard heroes, to restore order and people's trust. The superhumans, young and old, divide into factions and square off, with the fate of the world, as always, in the balance.[83]

It's a cautionary tale, and a metatextual rebuke of the Dark Age. It passes judgment on postmodern, "deconstructed" superheroes and finds them wanting, showing them to be little more than adolescent, morally vacant narcissists. It's a dark but not cynical story, a convincing reconstructionist argument that superheroes are at their best as bright inspirational figures. Together with Grant Morrison's *JLA* run and Marvel's "Heroes Return" relaunches in 1997, *Kingdom Come* is the closing chapter of the Dark Age. Grim & gritty would forever remain part of superhero comics, but it no longer eclipsed their innate hopefulness.

Kingdom Come is also likely the most blatantly Christian work in mainstream comics. What "The Death and Return of Superman" did thematically it did with intended explicitness, casting Superman firmly in the role of Jesus. It's not an evangelizing text, it borrows from Christian dogma as a cultural blueprint, but even its name is taken from the Lord's Prayer (Matt. 6:10, Luke 11:3). It's rife throughout with quotes and omens from the Book of Revelation (8:5, 11:19, 16:18, etc.) and other religious and Christly imagery. And it's narrated by a preacher, Norman McCay, modeled and named after Protestant minister Clark Norman Ross, Alex Ross's father.[84]

Plagued by prophetic, increasingly apocalyptic visions, McCay is visited by the Spectre, God's spirit of vengeance, and the two bear witness to events unfolding until McCay intervenes at a crucial moment to stay Superman's hand, saving the world. He serves in the role of John, visited by an angel of the Lord (Rev. 1:1), and together they are the Two Witnesses (11:1–14). His intervention is the unexpected departure from Revelation, though he's a man of faith who restores Superman's—the returning messiah—faith in mankind, thus saving it, just as faith promises to be mankind's salvation in the end days (3:20 et seq.).

Superman's Christianization was complete. The Jewish elements would remain an inseparable part of his core mythology, but his standing as a Christ figure was cemented hereafter.

Meanwhile, Jewish subject matter was front and center in *Supergirl*. Written by Peter David and drawn by Gary Frank, the new series launched a month after *Kingdom Come*.

David, best known for his eleven-year run on *The Incredible Hulk* (where he made supporting character Doc Samson a former yeshiva student), is the son of an Israeli mother and grandson of Holocaust survivors. He understood Superman was created as a Jewish reaction formation, writing that "few times in the history of mankind were Jews, as a race, disenfranchised as they were by Nazi Germany—deprived of property, family, livelihood, human dignity and, finally, human life. It was from this period of ultimate insult to the Jewish race that Superman was born."[85] Whether this affected his approach to *Supergirl* or not, his eighty-issue run (September '96–May '03) is suffused with religious themes, Jewish and otherwise, to a degree unprecedented and unsurpassed in the Superman mythos.

It makes sense for Supergirl to be more Jewish on the metaphor spectrum than Superman. If Krypton is a stand-in for Jewish heritage, then for Kal-El it's the legacy of his bloodline whereas for Kara Zor-El, who was sent to Earth as a teenager, it's the home and culture she knew and grew up in and lost. A postwar creation, she's the child Holocaust survivor making her way in a new, foreign land.

But David's Girl of Steel isn't Kara. She's Matrix, an extradimensional protoplasmic shapeshifting telekinetic artificial lifeform, who merges with Linda Danvers, a young Virginian from a devout Methodist family who is secretly a Satanist dating a fly-demon. Their combined being forms, of all things, an angel, endowed by God with wings and powers of fire.[86]

This was knowing absurdity told with a straight face, further enhanced by the simple-line art and bright colors. *Supergirl* was a paranormal teen drama prefiguring the trend of *Buffy the Vampire Slayer* and *Twilight* and a tour de force of theological themes worthy of its own treatise. These borrowed from Hebrew scripture, rabbinism, mysticism and folklore, as well as the Christian tradition's more fertile representation, angelology and demonology.

The series opens with a prayer to God,[87] and he's mentioned, discussed or invoked in virtually every issue of its seven-year span. The Bible is frequently referenced and quoted, along with matters of divine purpose, providence, worthiness of and fall from grace, creationism, sin, damnation, redemption, souls, heaven, hell, Jesus, the devil, angels, demons, commandments and prohibitions, free will vs.

determinism, epiphanies, prophecies, miracles, theodicy, and the parallel of hopefulness—Superman's raison d'être—and spiritual faith.

Supergirl also features an explicitly Jewish regular supporting character, reporter
Wendell "Cutter" Sharpe. Even more of a rarity, he has a darker complexion, implying Sephardic or Mizrahi ethnicity, showcasing Jewish diversity. He even remarks on
most American Jews' ability to pass for white. Other secular Jewish elements include
criticism of the Nation of Islam's inveterate Antisemitism and the general public's
willingness to overlook it and the return of holy relics to Israel,[88] but it's Jewish spirituality that provides the series' core themes.

Supergirl is an earthborn angel, a classification invented by David. They are
manifestations of the Shechina, the figurative female aspect of the Divine Presence,
interpreted by David as the loving side of God that keeps his Old Testament wrath-
fulness at bay. Supergirl even saves the Shechina, effectively saving God and all of
creation.[89]

Commonly spelled *Shekinah* (שְׁכִינָה), the polysemic word means "dwelling,"
denoting God's immanence in the material world (the Tabernacle, *Mishkan*, shares
the same root). In Talmudic and later Kabbalistic writings it's described as a holy,
cleansing fire and associated with the Sabbath, light, love, faithfulness and marriage (Avot 3:2, 3:6; Berachot 6a; Shabbat 12b, 30b; Megillah 29a; Sotah 17a, Sanhedrin 39a, 58a) and in prayer allegorically as a winged being carrying souls into and
out of the world, a Valkyrie-like link between the divine and the earthly (*El Maleh
Rachamim*). David literalized these elements, making Supergirl a fiery agent of
God.

As an angel, Supergirl saves the Garden of Eden (where the Tree of Knowledge
is depicted as an apple tree, a decidedly Christian rendition) as well as Heaven. She
encounters various scriptural and apocryphal characters, including Baalzebub, the
angel of the Ten Plagues, and the recording angel Metatron, portrayed here in the
Renaissance tradition as winged, fair-skinned and flaxen.[90]

A main adversary is Lilith,[91] the most famous demon of Jewish mythology and
the source of the succubus legend. Her name meaning "of the night" in Hebrew,
she's Adam's first wife and postlapsarian lover (Eruvin 18b, Zohar 1:34b, 1:54b, 3:19,
Yalqut Reubeni B'reshit 34b), mothering spirits and winged demons with him and
with their son Cain (Zohar 1:19b, 3:76b–77a). She roams the Earth seducing men to
bear demons (Shabbat 151b, Zohar 1:19b, 1:54b–55a), causes the birth of deformed,
winged babies (Niddah 24b), steals them (Zohar 3:76b–77a) or kills them (Zohar
1:19b, Alphabet of Ben Sira 23a–b). She's also considered Samael's feminine aspect
and consort, a fiery, chaotic counterpart to the Shekinah, and in this capacity associated with the Serpent of Eden (Zohar 23b, 55a, Zohar Sitrei Torah 1:147b–148:b).
A missed opportunity, the comic doesn't position her as Supergirl's counter-
force.

The Maid of Steel possibly even befriends God himself. Wally Johnson, a seemingly omniscient and omnipotent boy who appears sporadically to offer guidance or
intervention, may or may not be a living embodiment of the Almighty. Though he
calls himself "the God-Boy," the question is playfully left unanswered.[92]

David managed to make Supergirl a legitimate character in her own right rather than a Superman derivative, but in doing so strayed her too far afield. His offbeat experiment lasted a respectable eighty issues before getting cancelled, and he continued to explore themes of spirituality in other work, like *Fallen Angel* ('03–'11).

The Man of Steel, meanwhile, also evolved. Though originally planned for June 1993's *Adventures of Superman* #500,[93] in December 1996's *Superman: The Wedding Album* special he and Lois finally tied the knot. The story sidestepped any themes of interspecific, interracial or intercultural marriage and the questions of assimilation and family that come with it, but it nonetheless marks a rare progression in super-hero comics.

Lois and Clark were married in a traditional Christian ceremony held in an unnamed, nondenominational church (identified elsewhere as the Metropolis Chapel of United Faiths). In attendance were their close friends and family together with Superman creators past and present, from Joe Shuster to Jenette Kahn. Presiding was Chaplain Herbert Fine, who'd also administered Lois's christening, bearing Jerry Siegel's likeness and penname from "The Reign of the Superman."[94]

The issue was published in October, coinciding with the couple's nuptials in *Lois & Clark*. There, it was presided over by the affable and enigmatic "Mike," heavily implied to be none other than the archangel Michael.[95] Though not meant to be taken too seriously, it nonetheless established Superman as a subject of divine interest, if not providence.

In the span of a decade, Superman was reborn, reconceptualized, killed, resurrected, Christianized and, after 58 years, married to his lifelong love. It was fitting that, as a new

Supergirl Vol. 4 #17, January 1998. Written by Peter David and illustrated by Leonard Kirk. DC Comics.

Supergirl Vol. 4 #38, November 1999. Written by Peter David and illustrated by Leonard Kirk. DC Comics.

Supergirl Vol. 4 #19, March 1998. Written by Peter David and illustrated by Leonard Kirk. DC Comics.

millennium dawned, the character who embodied both Jewish culture and the spirit of 20th-century America redefined himself, as well as his past and future.

> *It was the best of times, it was the worst of times, it was the age of wisdom, it was the age of foolishness, it was the epoch of belief, it was the epoch of incredulity, it was the season of Light, it was the season of Darkness.*
> —Charles Dickens

Superman Supernal

The Modern Age

On September 11, 2001, the world changed forever. A madman straight out of a comic book, driven by a fevered ideology of world domination, attacked the U.S., murdering nearly three thousand people.

The Modern Age of comics had by most accounts begun a few years prior—definition varies widely, from 1980 according to Heritage Auctions to 1998 according to Levitz[1]—but 9/11 was the opening shot of the 21st century, and like with much else, marks a decisive turning point in comic book history. It's likely that when the Modern Age is looked back upon it will also mark its beginning.

The prevailing trend of the era is renaissance (apt, given that it follows the Dark Age), a creative and economic resurgence that saw a raised bar of writing and art and an influx of new talent from across the literary and entertainment landscape, new readers and renewed attention from culture at large.

There aren't any specific comics credited with kicking off the Modern Age (and DC for the first time wasn't the kicker), but noted works include the Ultimate Marvel imprint, particularly *Ultimate Spider-Man* (October '00–July '18) and *The Ultimates* (March '02–May '07); the ascendance of Marvel's *Avengers*, beginning with issue #500 (September '04) and culminating in the gargantuan movie franchise; the *Superman: Red Son* and *DC: The New Frontier* miniseries (June–August '03 and March–November '04, respectively); and Vertigo's provocative *Preacher* (April '95–October '00) and *Y: The Last Man* (September '02–March '08).

Other watersheds include auteur autobiographies like Marjane Satrapi's *Persepolis* ('00) and Alison Bechdel's *Fun Home: A Family Tragicomic* ('06), middle grade graphic novel series like Dav Pilkey's humorous *Captain Underpants* ('97–) and spinoff *Dog Man* ('16–), which have sold collectively 93 million copies worldwide,[2] and Japanese manga, which had gained success in the American market in the nineties and became a significant industry vertical, like *Shōnen Jump* (January '03–December '18) and *Naruto* (January '03–).

Together, these new genres and formats expanded readership to include more young females and people of color, gradually changing a landscape that's still predominantly white males in their teens and twenties. Comic book shops, though still the industry backbone, have gradually become outmoded, indicated by a clientele that's in the main 30–50-year-old men, while trade paperbacks (collected editions of previously published comics) and graphic novels have become bookstore and library staples.[3]

Digital comics, or webcomics, have particularly transformed the way comics are produced, sold and read, providing a wide variety of content that's affordable and accessible, a platform for unconventional material that might otherwise not see print and new visual tools. Levitz accordingly dubs the present period, counting from 2010, as the Digital Age.[4]

Superheroes and other comics-based material have proliferated in video games, television and especially movies, attaining mainstream popularity at a level rivaling that of the Golden Age.

In large part, this is a result of 9/11 and the subsequent zeitgeist, conditions that remarkably echo those of the 1940s. A surprise attack using suicide planes, an ensuing multi-front war, a Great Recession, a global refugee crisis, the welling of nationalism, tribalism and xenophobia and a fear of overpowering technology have given rise to the cultural dominance of superheroes.

The new millennium brought new anxieties and with them a new need for escapism and for reflection—both in the sense of introspection and of idealized self-image—a utopian counter-narrative to the pessimistic, cynical, solipsistic cultural climate. It's this desire for hopefulness, for the promise of a better tomorrow, that Superman so perfectly embodies. Which begs the question; in this current age of superhero dominance, why is he lagging behind?

Superman's death and return in 1993 was followed by a stroboscopic succession of "event" storylines, each promising a greater threat and greater change to the status quo. Metropolis was destroyed; his origin was altered by a time-traveling villain; he faked his death as Clark Kent; lost his powers; married Lois; gained new electric powers, new suit and blue skin; split into two entities, one red and one blue; met his descendent from the 853rd century; Metropolis was transformed into a futuristic city; Earth was embroiled in interplanetary war; Krypton's true nature was revealed; Joker gained godlike powers and altered reality; Luthor was elected president and declared him an outlaw.[5]

Upheaval became routine, and plain, self-contained stories harder to find. The Man of Steel seemed to have lost his way. (The trailer for the 2007 *Superman: Doomsday* home video animated film absurdly promised a Superman who's "darker, more dangerous than ever before.") Some of these stories were good, but event fatigue set in and they were met with declining sales. By 2000—the nadir of the industry as a whole, with direct market sales as low as $255 million—Superman titles were selling around 40,000 copies.[6]

Through it all, Jewish themes continued to manifest, including overtly. To commemorate his 60th anniversary, in *Superman: The Man of Steel* #80–82 (June–August '98) DC sent him traveling back in time to Nazi-occupied Poland, where he experiences firsthand the atrocities of the Holocaust. Except that nowhere in the three issues are Jews ever mentioned. Jon Bogdanove, who cowrote and drew the story, did identify the Nazis' victims as Jews in his script, but, despite his objections, then-series editor Joey Cavalieri excised any explicit reference (including to Catholics, Germans and the Holocaust) in fear that they might stir controversy and "be used derisively by young readers."[7]

It's hard to imagine who would have taken offense at the factual depiction of

Jews' persecution, but the result is a story full of characters with Hebraic names, some wearing yarmulkes, speaking in Yiddish, who are referred to only in euphemisms. When Superman enters the Warsaw Ghetto in disguise (where he joins the real-life leader of the Warsaw Ghetto Uprising, Mordechai Anielewicz) and helps dig a mass grave for the decomposing bodies, Jews are referred to as its "murdered residents," the "target population of the Nazis' hate." Even the Final Solution is attributed only to "ridding the world of peoples they hate." Issue #82 goes as far as reproducing the infamous "Warsaw Ghetto Boy" photo of the little boy in a cap raising his hands at SS gunpoint without identifying him as Jewish.[8]

The choice to censor any mention of Jews is doubly confounding considering that, only seven years prior, a similar story involving time travel to World War II—"The Warsaw Ghetto!" in *Superman* Vol. 2 #54 (April '91)—explicitly refers to Jews and the death camps.

Superman: The Man of Steel #82. Written by Louise Simonson and illustrated by Jon Bogdanove. DC Comics.

***Warsaw Ghetto Boy*, photographer unknown. Poland, c. April–May 1943.**

The story, and reactions, made the news. The Anti-Defamation League found it "extremely offensive," remarking, "in what was to have been a positive teaching lesson, Jews were not mentioned.... You can't be general when you talk about victims of the Holocaust. To rob the victims of their identity—when they became victims solely because of their identity, the fact that they were Jews—is just misguided." They added that, while they understood DC had good intentions, "one can get so locked in trying not to offend, you offend."[9]

DC issued a public apology, calling the omission "a lapse." Some Jewish groups, like the Simon Wiesenthal Center, called on them to include the apology, along with educative material, in the series' letter column and on the company website, but DC never did.[10]

In 2004, Jewish *Superman* writer Steven T. Seagle (*Superman* Vol. 2 #190–200 [April '03–February '04] and sundry issues), with artist Teddy Kristiansen, released the graphic novel memoir *It's a Bird* … through Vertigo. Using Superman as a vehicle for self-exploration, Seagle finds common ground in his sense of alienation as a social outsider. He also sees Superman as a Jewish metaphor, for the constant pull, and choice, between heritage and self-constructed identity and for sidestepping stereotypes and Antisemitism to find acceptance. He likewise notes the Hebrew connotation of "El" and Superman's Judeo-Christian iconography, though he doesn't explore them.[11]

In canon, meanwhile, Superman continued to Christianize. He was now officially 33, same as Jesus at the time of his struggle and sacrifice, and was assigned an explicit religious and denominational affiliation for the first time. He was raised

Protestant in September 1998's *Superman for All Seasons* #1, then a churchgoing Methodist with a lapsed Protestant father in July 2007's *Action Comics* #849.[12]

The "For Tomorrow" storyline in *Superman* Vol. 2 #204–#215 (June '04–May '05) glaringly omits any discussion of his religious belief, but otherwise entirely centers on his Christology. When he fails to save a multitude of people he falls from grace, losing the faith of humanity and his faith in himself. It makes the point that his comparison to Jesus or God is both unavoidable and impossible, since he's an all-powerful savior with ordinary human failings.

The story begins with the Man of Steel making a confession to Father Leone, a young Catholic priest experiencing a crisis of faith of his own, telling him, "My **sin?** Was to **save** the **world.**" It's the sin of hubris, of a savior complex, of both the hero and the character. The scene, and others following, is heavy with Christian iconography, like sunshine behind his head and crucifixes, crosses and angel statues around him. When the priest first sees him, he begins to utter "Oh my…" as he kneels down, presumably in shock but clearly allusive. Later, when Superman tells Leone, "that's a **play** on your beliefs I'd **never** do to you," the priest replies, "because you **can?**"

Scriptural intimations, particularly to Christ, are found throughout the narrative. Flash tells him, "the media are **crucifying** you." Two issues later, the cover is a play on a Pietà. The biblical Delilah even makes an appearance, stating that she'd once felled "another **like** him." (It's unclear if this was intended, but her inclusion draws parallels between Samson and Jesus, both men of God-given power who were betrayed by a confidant, tortured and mocked by heathens, and ultimately sacrificed themselves out of love for their people. Even their iconic outstretched poses are similar.) Another character is called Pilate, a living weapon programmed for a covert strike on Tel Aviv.

The adversary of the story is Zod, wearing here armor with giant red horns coming out his forehead. When Superman defeats him but then reaches out to save him, it's in the form of Michelangelo's *Creation of Adam*, with Superman in place of God and a fisted Zod as a defiant Adam. Like much else in the story it makes for a mixed metaphor, but its theme is nonetheless the nature of salvation, love being its acceptance and hate its rejection.

Over the course of the story Superman gradually drifts away from humanity. When Batman calls him "Clark," he corrects him, "**Kal-El,**" and he speaks of mankind in the second person. But in the end, he puts his trust in Father Leone to save the day. It's an act of faith in man, and a validation of Jesus' faith in mankind's worthiness. Leone sacrifices himself, and it's equally interpretable as an affirmation of religious devotion or of man's control over his own destiny.[13]

The standalone *Superman* #659 deals even more directly with the character's religious signification (February '07. *Superman* Vol. 2 came to an end with issue #226 [April '06] and *Adventures of Superman* reverted back to *Superman* Vol. 1 with issue #650 [May '06]). The cover shows the titular titan from an inferior angle, arms outstretched, his head engulfed in sun halo and his cape replaced by outspread wings, as he descends onto a crowd reaching up to him. It's an obvious conjuring of pietistic art, and in case the point is missed the issue is also titled "Angel."[14]

Superman **Vol. 2 #215, May 2005. Written by Brian Azzarello and illustrated by Jim Lee. DC Comics.**

It features Barbara Johnson, a devout Christian from Metropolis's Suicide Slum. When Superman saves her from a speeding car after she manages to mutter a quick prayer, she becomes convinced that he's a heavenly angel. Emboldened by her seeming providence, she sets out to rid the neighborhood of crime by placing herself in its path and praying for him. Again and again, his super-hearing allows him to arrive in the nick time, which only strengthens her conviction. Even when she is inevitably shot, while she comes to recognize her folly, she remains steadfast in her faith.

The story explores how Superman lends himself to different interpretations and where he fits on the continuum between religion and secularism. It compares him to an angel in its broadest sense, but angels are a theological tenet, found in many traditions, and differing considerably between them. It's the Christian version—winged men, somatic messengers and soldiers of God and guardians of man—that has been popularized in the world's imagination through Western art and entertainment, and which Superman is likened to here. But it isn't necessarily the most fitting.

The word "angel" comes from the Greek *ángelos* (alt. *ággelos*), meaning "messenger" or "delegate," a Septuagint translation of the Hebrew *mal'ach* (מַלְאָךְ), which means "one who is sent," a performer of a task or deliverer of a message. And so an angel is a description of duty, not nature, ascribed in some cases to human agents (e.g., Gen. 32:3, Num. 20:14).

Angels are largely depicted in the Bible as envoys rather than guardians, and even then mostly as ad hoc appointees, not tutelaries of individuals, places or nations. It's not until Psalms 91:11 that a guardian angel is first appointed.

Many instances of angelic manifestation in the Bible are considered to be of God himself, particularly when referred to as "angel of the Lord" or "angel of God."[15] Most famous of these is the burning bush in Exodus 3:2–6: "There the angel of the Lord appeared to him in flames of fire from within a bush.… God called to him from within the bush.… I am the God of your father."

Where the Jewish conception of angels primarily differs from the Christian one is in their hierarchal relation to man in the theological order. Christianity tends to see them as superior, certainly in Catholicism (Catechism 330), while Judaic thought stresses that, despite their divine nature, they are inferior to man. They are not born in God's image (Tehillim 17:8a) and, because they lack free will or evil inclination (*yetzer hara*) to overcome, they cannot rise in their spirituality and servitude in the same manner (Shabbat 89a, Chullin 91b, Gen. Rabbah 48:11, 65:21, Midrash Ps. 103:13. Jewish faith therefore doesn't include the fallen angel tradition [at least in the same manner], a foundational tenet of Christianity.) Even in Heaven pious humans rank above angels and dwell closer to God (Sanhedrin 93a, Nedarim 32a, Gen. Rabbah. 21:1).

Accordingly, angels are not worshiped or honored in Judaism and shouldn't be prayed to (Shabbat 12b), unless as emissaries of prayers to God (*Machnisei Rachamim*). This divergence between the two religions may trace back to Psalms 8:4–5, which in the Vulgate, and following in most English versions, reads, "what is mankind…. You have made them a little lower than the angels," whereas the original Hebrew reads, "you have made him a little lower than God."

This poses an interesting question about Superman. He's a being of extraordinary power and equally remarkable virtue, the former owing to his celestial nature and the latter to his earthly nurture. Humans look up to him for protection and inspiration. But is he superior or inferior to man, whose struggles and risks are greater? When a firefighter saves someone from an inferno, is their heroism not greater? This has been discussed in several instances, including in "For Tomorrow," though never conclusively.

The Man of Steel, the inhuman guardian of humanity, isn't a perfect fit for either tradition. He can be seen as an angel in the Jewish sense, a hero tasked, knowingly or not, with a divine mission, and he shares his theophoric surname, El, with the angels of the Hebrew Bible. But he equally works as a Christian angel, a flying man of great virtue and physical beauty dedicated to mankind's protection and enlightenment. In either case, who's to say that angels can't be from another planet?

Three years into the new century and eighteen into the new Superman's tenure, DC pressed the refresh button again. *Kingdom Come*'s Mark Waid was chosen to helm the new origin, titled *Superman: Birthright*, paired with artist Leinil Francis Yu. They were given twelve issues, double the space Byrne had with *The Man of Steel*, stretching between September 2003 and September 2004, with the goal of reinventing Superman "from top to bottom to reflect today's world and today's sensibilities."[16]

Noting Elliot Maggin's work as an influence,[17] Waid's narrative is fresh, charged and accomplishedly grand, if at times overburdened; the strength of Superman's origin is in its fable-like simplicity. Yu, a gifted artist with a dark style, is miscast. Presumably chosen precisely because it's nontraditional for a Superman comic, which tend to be clean-lined and realistic, his art is too edgy for the character, lacking the warmth that best suits him (that Yu frequently draws him without pupils only distances him further).

Birthright is a complete reworking of the legend, altering, discarding and in a few instances restoring elements of the lore. Byrne's revived Kents were kept around and

Lex Luthor is still a tycoon, but he's again Clark's childhood friend and again a mad scientist, his fortune built on inventions and discoveries. A new, redundant addition, borrowed from Batman, has Clark roaming the globe on his journey to heroism.

More meaningful, *Birthright* reinstates Superman as the real persona and Clark Kent as the disguise, though they're portrayed more as different demeanors than a stark binary. Moreover, Clark Kent of Smallville is shown to be his authentic self whereas Clark Kent of Metropolis is a pretense, demonstrating that the character juggles three, not two, identities.

"Birthright" thusly can be read as a reclamation. Byrne's Superman shirked the yoke of legacy, uninterested in his cultural heritage. Waid and Yu's Superman seeks it out, seeing it as defining and empowering. In doing so, he also restored that aspect of his Jewish birthright.

This is reflected in his costume once again being made from the fabrics he was wrapped in when rocketed to Earth, though this time it's also modeled directly after Kryptonian garb. It gives the outfit greater meaning, culturally and personally, and makes it a vital part of his self-definition. Cleverly, it tethers him to his lineage even further when, inspired by the '78 movie, the "S" emblem is shown to be his family crest, and in turn revealed for the first time to be the Kryptonian pictograph for "hope," found on flags and uniforms.[18] In adopting it for his own, the "S" then signifies his self, his ancestry and his ethnicity. It adds a new dimension to one of the world's most recognizable symbols, and further turns his act of transformation from Clark Kent to Superman into an act of declaration, the same as wearing a cross or, since it's the symbol of a people, a Star of David.

Waid and Yu don't employ any particularly evocative Christian themes or imagery in *Birthright* (interesting, given *Kingdom Come*), but there are a couple of anecdotal Jewish motifs. Judaism ascribes sanctity to the letters of the Hebrew alphabet: throughout the Talmud and in other Kabbalistic texts, letters are assigned both symbolic and metaphysical meaning. God is even said to have created the world using letters (Berakhot 55a). Examples of this in practice are the letter *Shin* (ש) on mezuzahs or the word *chai* (חי) on charms and necklaces. Making the "S" stand for hope places it within the Jewish tradition, a letter of talismanic power, representing an abstract but powerful concept (and, given that it's the symbol of Superman, one of faith in deliverance).

Issue #1 is titled "In the Beginning," also captioned on the cover, the opening words of the Bible. It's especially befitting given the Midrashic explication of the wording; in the original Hebrew the opening word is *Bereshit* (בראשית), meaning "genesis," which begins with the letter *Bet* (ב), the second letter of the alphabet. This is explained as signifying that the world created, our world, is not in fact the first one formed. "A time-order existed before this," the tractate describes, "the Holy One … went on creating worlds and destroying them until He created this one and declared, 'This one pleases Me'" (Gen. Rabbah 3:7–8). It makes for an interesting equivalent to *Birthright*, not the first permutation of Superman's world.

That canon was short lived, however. Revisionist changes began appearing not two years later, introduced by writer Geoff Johns. (Johns wrote or cowrote, with interludes, *Superman* Vol. 2 #179–Vol. 1 #653 [April '02–August '06] and *Action Comics*

#837–873 [May '06–March '09]. He also served as President and Chief Creative Officer of DC Entertainment from 2016 to 2018.)

Infinite Crisis, a seven-issue sequel to *Crisis on Infinite Earths* (December '05–June '06), restored the DC multiverse, including elements from different versions of Superman's origin, like his teenage adventures with the Legion of Super-Heroes. Shortly following, the "Last Son" storyline in *Action Comics* (#844–846, #851, *Annual* #11, December '06–July '08)—co-written by Jones with former employer and mentor Richard Donner—made further changes to Krypton's depiction.[19] (A grand story that, at heart, like so many Superman stories, is about legacy and the choice between cultures and identities.)

More significant, in "Brainiac" (#866–870, August–December '08), Jones and artist Gary Frank made Clark Kent a nebbish pretense again and Superman his decidedly true self.[20] Heavily influenced by Donner's *Superman* in both tone and visuals, even modeling Superman after Reeve, it also restored much of Siegel and Shuster's whimsical approach to the character's double life, adding sorely-needed humor.

Jones and Frank followed their run with the miniseries *Superman: Secret Origin* (November '09–October '10), officially replacing *Birthright*. But unlike *Birthright* and *The Man of Steel*, which largely reconceived the mythology, *Secret Origin* is more a synthesis of the past, amalgamating elements from the Golden and particularly Silver Age with more recent ones. Superman's early costumed career as Superboy, for example, is restored to canon, although he operates unseen around Smallville, inspiring an urban legend of a "Super-Boy," while adventuring openly with the Legion of Super-Heroes during his jaunts to the 30th century. Movielike, heartfelt and too rushed in six issues, *Secret Origin*'s main alteration is in emphasizing his journey of adjustment through childhood over his continuous alienation as an adult, as well as the welcome addition of Lara to the holographic recording in his rocket ship.[21]

There's nothing notably Jewish or Christian in *Secret Origin* (notwithstanding Clark's December birthday), but there certainly is in the contemporaneous, uncanonical *All-Star Superman*. A twelve-issue series by Grant Morrison and Frank Quitely (January '06–October '08), it was a commercial success, reaching over double regular Superman sales, and a critical hit, winning three Eisner Awards and ranking third in *Time*'s Top 10 Graphic Novels of 2007 as well as CBR's Greatest Superman Stories of All-Time.[22] In 2011 it was adapted into an animated home video film.

All-Star Superman is a romantic ode to the Silver Age, successfully capturing its spirit of the bizarre and wondrous, like sun astronauts and impossibly heavy keys made from white dwarf stars. It's also a fairly blatant Jesus allegory. Its Superman is Christlike in moral perfection, wisdom and omnipotence, and its plot revolves around his preparation for a death he knows is coming as he performs miracles and ultimately sacrifices himself to save humanity.

During the series he creates a world and imbues it with human life; reaches out and heals the incurably sick; confirms there's a guiding intelligence to the universe, which he alone can sense; and his sacrificial death is followed by the promise of his eventual return.[23] The first issue special edition cover, reused in the trade paperback and later as the basis for a DC Collectibles statue, is of Superman descending from the heavens, bent elbows away from a crucifixion pose, bright sunbeams emanating from behind his head.

Also in 2006, *Superman Returns* was even more nostalgic, sentimental and evangelizing. It ended Superman's nineteen-year truancy from the silver screen with a grandiose production estimated at $260 million, the most expensive movie ever made at the time. It was to be the first in a new franchise, seeded with plot points for future installments, but middling reviews and a disappointing global box office of $391 million made it a one-off, flatlining the property for another seven years.[24]

Superman Returns is, more than anything else, a melodrama. It focuses on his relationships with loved ones and the world, but though it has heart—more so than later iterations—it lacks action, despite its budget and running time of nearly three hours, and much of it is underwhelming. It's further burdened by a weak plot, misguided characterization and an unresolved ending, but mostly by its reverence to the Donner films at the expense of its own identity. Yet it misses their charm and exhilaration, instead adopting an off-key melancholy tenor and a muted sepia palette.

Winsome lead Brandon Routh, like the film, is entertaining but unspectacular. A Reeve lookalike, he never fully inhabits the role as much as impersonates his predecessor, except that the Superman of *Returns* isn't confident, comfortable and colorful but lonely, gloomy and dull. The suit is a drab maroon and cold blue, with conspicuous shoulder padding and two-inch soles. The "S" is too small, hard to make out at a distance, as if being coy.

Superman here is no role model. He saves people, but otherwise he's self-absorbed, self-pitying, even self-indulgent. The movie can more or less be summed up as him cleaning up his own mess. Ironic, given that it's also cemented him as Christ figure.

Returning from a five-year excursion to the site of Krypton's destruction, he's a celestial benefactor returning to an apostate world that doesn't want his protection or edification. Even Lois (a miscast 22-year-old Kate Bosworth in a bad wig) rejects him, both romantically, by becoming engaged to another, and by renouncing her faith, writing the Pulitzer-winning article, "Why the World Doesn't Need Superman."

The movie is rife with intrusive Christology, like Superman hovering in the heavens listening for cries of help or held by his mother Pietà-style. The movie poster shows him suspended above the world, legs pressed and pointed and arms extended, halfway between a crucifixion and a reaching-out pose.

The peak of it is at the end, when the Man of Steel, enfeebled by Kryptonite, suffers a Passion as Luthor and his henchmen take turns punching, kicking and dragging him on the ground, eventually stabbing him in the waist and leaving him for dead. It's a wince-inducing scene of almost fetishistic glee, unfitting for Superman, conforming mainly to the Catholic and Orthodox focus on the suffering of Christ. Superman then finds just enough strength to save the day, before plummeting down to Earth in a crucifixion pose, firmly and with finality establishing him as Christ in a cape. (Though this is undermined by his lackluster resurrection; he lands with a muted thud, is rushed to a hospital, flatlines, then wakes up inexplicably and off-camera and flies away.)

Director Brian Singer credits his background as a Jew growing up in a Catholic neighborhood for his understanding of the character. He acknowledges Superman's Mosaic origin, but his take is firmly "a story about Christ—it's all about sacrifice: The world, I hear their cries. So what happens? He gets the knife in the side and later he falls to the earth in the shape of a crucifix. It was kind of nailing you on the head, but I enjoyed that."[25]

What's subtler, and profounder, is the immigrant metaphor of the film. When Lois asks him why he left to visit his destroyed home world, Superman answers, "I had to see for myself." On the face of it, it makes little sense, and that he abandoned his post as Earth's protector for years makes him selfish. But his desire is no different than that of immigrants and their descendants who embark on family tree tours overseas to learn more about their origins.

Particularly, since he visits the ruins of a dead world, it's comparable to Jewish immigrants and their children who visit the remains of their culture in Europe, the old shtetls and towns and camps where their people lived and were killed. The annual International March of the Living alone has drawn over 260,000 Jewish youths from around the world to Auschwitz-Birkenau,[26] driven by a need that's more visceral than rational, to see for themselves, to understand, to reconnect, to remember.

Another reflection of the immigrant experience is the theme of generational bond across the gulf of time, place and culture, of Jor-El and Kal-El, and Kal-El and his son. When Superman learns that Lois's child Jason is his, he repeats to him his own father's sendoff from *Superman*, "you will see my life through your eyes, as your life will be seen through mine … the son becomes the father, and the father becomes the son."[27] It's a tenuous parallel to a heavenly father's divine mission since Jesus had no son of his own to bequeath it to. Rather, it reflects a father's hopes for his child, to excel and to exceed, and in the case of immigrants, to carry on their heritage. Superman is no longer the Last Son of Krypton; he's the last father. Jason is equal parts alien and human, a native son of an immigrant, with the blood of a race from elsewhere but no direct connection to its people. It carries the poignancy of Jewish continuation, especially in the Diaspora and in a mixed family, the personal responsibility for the survival of the people and the culture.

In television, meanwhile, the teen drama *Smallville*, debuting on the WB in October 2001 and lasting ten seasons, took things a step further. Like much of post–9/11 culture it had a palpable tone of angst even during its lighter moments, and its treatment of religious themes was unsubtle. It drew clear and constant parallels between Superman and Jesus, to the point that it was effectively a Christ story disguised as a superhero one.

The Metropolis Marvel had a strong year in 2004. Dubbed "The Year of Superman" by DC, it featured both *Birthright* and the new creative team of popular writer Brian Azzarello and superstar artist Jim Lee on *Superman*. Issue #204, the first chapter of their "For Tomorrow" opus, was the year's bestselling comic, and Super-titles occupied six of the top ten spots. But it wasn't to last. By 2005, issue #215, the closing chapter, ranked at 52.[28]

Then came the Great Recession of 2007–2009. Although the industry wasn't immiserated like some others, sales flattened. By September 2010, periodical sales reached their lowest in a decade, since the bottom of the crash. (It's arguable whether

DC and Marvel raising most cover prices from $2.99 to $3.99 helped or hurt.) Superman sales were further hampered by uneven quality between his different titles and storylines that were regularly protracted and sonorous while often feeling glib. He hit his all-time low in April 2010's *Superman* #697, with direct market sales around 31,500—a far cry from the million-plus copies he sold in the 1950s.[29]

He seemed to have lost his élan. Just as the Depression and prewar era gave the world a hardboiled, scrappy Superman and World War II made him a bright Super-patriot, 9/11 and the interminable, internecine War on Terror redefined him for a new generation of readers. He became more pensive, anxious, hesitant, his assured deontology replaced by consequentialist dilemmas. As Byrne saw it, he'd become a "conflicted whiner."[30]

This loss of direction is exemplified in the landmark *Action Comics* #900 (June '11), which saw Superman planning to renounce his American citizenship because he felt misconstrued as an instrument of U.S. policy. It's unclear why he suddenly felt the need to distance himself from American political reality and its complexities. He hadn't been associated with it since the 1940s. He was never a purely domestic hero; his first foray abroad was in *Action Comics* #2, and since then he's been rescuing people and dispensing justice all over the world, crossing sovereign borders on a daily basis. He's an international persona grata, even made global citizen by the UN in July 1961's *Superman* #146.[31] His never-ending battle for "the American way" was never really perceived as promoting specific U.S. interests as much as values.

It's worth noting that Superman, not Clark Kent, is the one renouncing his citizenship, and the meaning of that distinction changes depending on which one is considered his true self. But the point is moot, since he never actually got around to it and the matter was ignored thereafter.

The story was written by the Jewish David Goyer, and it makes for an interesting contrast with how Siegel wrote the character, as a reflection of the generational change in Jewish-American identity. Siegel and Shuster's Superman was a fervent assimilationist and American patriot, even a jingoist. They were an immigrant and a child of immigrants, part of an ethnoreligious group that sought acceptance, socially and, desperately, politically, as refugees fleeing Europe. Their immigrant hero embodied a wish to belong, and they were immensely proud that he'd become an American symbol.

Goyer and artist Miguel Sepulveda's Superman not only disavows representing America but outright abdicates his nationality. It clearly isn't essential to his self-definition, nor does he seek his country's validation. It's the assuredness of a homegrown American, removed from the prejudice and oppression of old, in a place and time where Jews are largely seen as part of the dominant culture. When he declares that "the ***American*** way ... it's not ***enough*** anymore,"[32] it's not because he finds it wanting, but because he can afford to not be solely defined by it.

In hope of invigorating the character and attracting new readership, fan-favorite writer J. Michael Straczynski (creator of TV's *Babylon 5*) was handed the reins with *Superman* #701 (September '10). But instead he embraced Superman's ennui, sending him on a thirteen-issue walk across the U.S. to reconnect with everyday America. Unsurprisingly the direction didn't prove popular, and Straczynski left halfway through to concentrate on other projects.[33] October 2011's *Superman* #714 was the final issue of the series, after 72 years.

With sales continuously flagging, a beleaguered DC decided to repeat what worked in 1985, this time even more daringly. The five-issue miniseries *Flashpoint* (July–October '11) provided the cosmic reboot, involving time travel instead of parallel dimensions, followed by "The New 52" initiative; all series were cancelled, and in September 2011 (cover-dated October or November) 52 were relaunched with a new #1 and a complete blank slate. Preceding continuity was expunged and characters were reconceived, redesigned and made younger.

The goal with Superman was to reposition him as the company's flagship property. He was pared down to two titles, *Superman* Vol. 3 and *Action Comics* Vol. 2 (the first interruption of the series' numbering since 1938), with three added later, *Superman Unchained* (August '13), *Batman/Superman* (August '13) and *Superman/ Wonder Woman* (December '13). Grant Morrison was chosen to headline the overhaul, paired with artist Rags Morales on *Action Comics*. Industry luminary George Pérez followed their lead as writer-artist on *Superman*.

The Man of Steel got a second makeover and fourth new origin story in 25 years. He was a ruffle-haired Millennial in his early twenties, less powerful and unable yet to fly. Impoverished, his costume for a good while consisted of tattered jeans, worn combat boots and a rotation of red, white and blue T-shirts bearing his "S" emblem.

When he did get a Super-suit, it was the first substantial lasting change to his iconic look since Shuster's design. Jim Lee, now also Co-Publisher of DC, designed the new costume. Instead of tights it was Kryptonian armor, a

Justice League Vol. 2 #1, November 2011. Written by Geoff Johns and illustrated by Jim Lee. DC Comics.

form-fitting hard glossy shell with line patterns and red accents. It had a high collar, pointed sleeves, no red trunks, a triangular cape and a more angular "S." It was overwrought and unattractive, and encasing him in armor only detracted from the character.

The New 52 Superman was earnest but callow, scrappier, and decreasing his power increased the stakes. "There's a distance between this one and the guy we saw throughout the 2000s, who was a bit more riddled with self-doubt and confusion," Morrison explained. "This is a Superman who absolutely believes what he does is right."[34]

He displayed the same pluck as Clark, now closer in age to Jimmy than to Perry. Only a year in, he quit his job at the *Planet* over the compromised state of modern journalism to become an independent news blogger. But this rendition of Clark Kent was little more than a charade. When he appears to be killed, Superman replaces him with another secret identity with little compunction, feeling that he has "outlived him." When he eventually does revive him, it's not because he's an integral part of his psyche but because he's an effective tool of fighting for justice as a journalist.[35]

Other changes include making Krypton a utopian society again, if leisurely to the point of decadent, and finally giving Lara a role in building the rocket ship. The Kents were killed off, a pointlessly tragic death in a car accident on the night of Clark's senior prom.[36] Equally tragic, he and Lois were single again, not even courting. (Married Superman worked—the character lent itself surprisingly well to it—but it also made him a humdrum grownup.) There wasn't even the Superman-Lois-Clark love triangle. The recast simply didn't have chemistry. Whatever the original plan, he soon became involved with Wonder Woman, forming the ultimate power couple.

The most meaningful, and positive, change was returning Superman to his New Dealer roots. No longer an establishment hero, he was an undomesticated dissident, a vigilante crusader taking on inequality and social predators. With the New 52, DC aimed to make its heroes more rebellious, unpredictable, cooler, and Superman was the most unruly. For the first time since the early Golden Age he was intent on fighting social and political corruption even if it required defying authorities.

On the cover of *Action Comics* Vol. 2 #1 he's chased and shot at by the police, signaling the departure from norm. In the first scene he barges into the penthouse of a corrupt mogul and throws him off the roof, catching him in time to get a confession. He still faced supervillains, but now also issues of the day, like police brutality in issues #41–43 (August–October '15).[37]

Morrison and Morales's eighteen-issue run was propulsive, fresh and ambitious, though burdened by metatextuality, disjointedness and distracting inconsistencies with *Superman* and other New 52 series, to which it was confusingly set five years prior.

Pérez stepped down from *Superman* after only six issues, citing frustrations over lack of coordination with *Action Comics* and constant editorial meddling. "The industry has changed so much, and now it's corporate comics," he said. "It was a book being done by committee … and yet they couldn't make up their minds what they wanted from day to day…. I don't blame the people at DC for it—they're following the dictates of Warner that now has a much more hands-on policy."[38]

Morrison and Morales, meanwhile, also returned Superman to his Jewish roots. "The rocket is Moses' basket," Morrison writes in the afterword to issue #2 (December '11). "So I made it a little more basket-y," Morales adds.[39] Giving Superman something of a temper also made him more Moses-like, less the gentle Lamb of God of previous years.

Before finding Kal-El, the Kents, made Baptists here, are compared by their minister to the Hebrew patriarchs and matriarchs that had difficulty conceiving and eventually gave birth to miracle babies who grew up to be great prophets and saviors.[40]

When the Man of Steel first dons the Kryptonian armor in issue #8, it changes colors and patterns as it calibrates to its new wearer. Distinctly, this includes a Star of David emblazoned across his chest in place of the "S."[41] Given both Morrison and Morales's penchant for detail, it's unlikely unintentional.

In issues #10 he faces Nimrod the Hunter, named after the biblical king who was "a mighty hunter before the Lord" (Gen. 10:8–9). The name in Hebrew (נִמְרוֹד) stems from the root *mered* (מרד), meaning rebel or rebellion, understood as iconoclasm (Gen. Rabbah 38:13). An idolater and adversary of Abraham, the comic book counterpart similarly fancies himself Superman's better, only to be handed a humiliating defeat.[42]

After leaving the series, Morrison was tasked with mapping out the DC multiverse. Together with artist Rian Hughes, he partly modeled the cosmological structure after the Kabbalistic Tree of Life, even dividing the universes into spheres (*sefirot*) and including metaphysical domains like heaven and hell.[43]

Motifs like these ended with Morrison, though Jewish parallels could still be found, like *Action Comics* Vol. 2 #25 (January '14), where Superman expresses kinship with undocumented immigrants as he saves them from murderous white supremacists. In *Superman* Vol. 3 #32–38 (August '14–April '15) the villain is a blue-eyed blond from an extradimensional society self-dubbed "The Great World," which sustains its utopia by sacrificing six million people to its burning furnaces. Despite the obvious Holocaust allegory, this hasn't been noted in any discussion or review of the story.[44]

The new, younger, brasher Superman started off with vivacity and charm, if occasional gruffness, but in less capable hands gradually grew surlier and less likable. DC aimed for irrepressible spunk but overshot, and the result just wasn't Superman anymore.

Sales declined again. Overall, the New 52 invigorated sales for a brief period, but as the novelty wore off so did interest. DC made several attempts to course-correct. Superman got a new outfit, closer to his classic look, softer and less fussy, though it still featured an awkward high collar and knuckle-length sleeves. He also got a new superpower, the first since the Bronze Age, an explosive "solar flare" that temporarily left him powerless.[45]

His secret identity was exposed to the world by Lois to save him from blackmailing, in a story that could have explored the inherent journalistic dilemmas or the problem of a moral person who regularly lies to his friends, but instead just wrote the character into a corner. He changed his look once more, back to jeans and a T-shirt, this time with a buzz cut and the Fleischer cartoons' "S" with a black background. He left Metropolis and rode a motorcycle across the U.S., eventually joining an underground fight club of pagan deities.[46]

These changes were increasingly more ploys than plots, desperate, desultory and with diminishing returns. Meanwhile, DC quietly brought the "real" Superman back.

The eight-issue miniseries *Superman: Lois and Clark* (December '15–July '16) revealed that the pre–New 52 Man of Steel had survived the end of his universe, along with Lois and their newborn son Jon. They

Action Comics **Vol. 2 #8, June 2012. Written by Grant Morrison and illustrated by Rags Morales. DC Comics.**

were living in the new world under assumed names, and he'd been operating anonymously as a bearded, black-clad hero.

Though not framed as a tragedy, it's possibly the saddest of all Superman stories. He had utterly failed in his life's mission. His Earth, like Krypton, had been wiped out. Everyone he'd ever known and loved gone save for his immediate family, now stranded refugees. He was the last son of two worlds.

"This Earth is so different from our own," the story opens with Lois narrating. "Suspicious. Doubting. Edgy. Without **faith**."[47] DC's New 52 brand was a less optimistic, more hostile environment for their heroes to face, adding drama and reflecting the real world post–9/11. But what introducing the older Supermen to it only served to highlight was how much a hopeful, inspiring Superman was needed, and how far astray the new version had veered.

The New 52 Superman lasted, appropriately, 52 issues. In *Superman* Vol. 3 #52 (July '16) he was disposed of unceremoniously, killed by a combination of Kryptonite poisoning and unstable powers. His body simply crumbled to dust, like a golem that mimicked but never truly attained life. He was promptly replaced by his predecessor in *Superman* Vol. 4 #1 and the relaunched *Action Comics* Vol. 1 #957 (August '16), and soon after it was revealed that he was never more than an aspect of Superman split off by the reality-warping Mr. Mxyzptlk. The two versions remerged to form a singular timeline retroactively, effectively erasing from canon the preceding half decade.[48] The abrupt change elicited notably little fan outcry.

In the meantime, the Action Ace got a fresh start on screen with 2013's *Man of Steel*. Promoted by an aggressive marketing campaign that included more tie-in promotions than any film in history, it grossed nearly $670 million worldwide, almost double what *Superman Returns* made.[49] But it still fell short of Warner Bros.' expectations, and reviews were mixed. In many respects it's a better movie than *Returns*, certainly more thrilling, and it deftly balances all the tropes in reinventing the mythology. But it's also a dour, joyless affair, set in desaturated color to a domineering score and featuring a cold, anguished, "Batmanized" Superman.

Star Henry Cavill looks more like Shuster's Superman than anyone else who's worn the cape, beefy, with a wide jaw and a thick neck. There's a quiet intensity to him, but he doesn't convey the same sheltering warmth that Reeve did. The costume also got an update, a navy blue Nouveau-influenced sculpted suit covered entirely in chainmail texture with no red trunks. Like the movie, it looks good but too dark.

Rushing to catch up to the Marvel Cinematic Universe—a successful series of interconnected movies launched in 2008—*Man of Steel* is the opening salvo of the DC Extended Universe, entrusted to auteur director Zack Snyder.

Snyder (*300, Watchmen*) is a gifted visualist, with a distinct style and penchant for compositions that look like Renaissance tableaus, but he isn't a particularly capable storyteller. His plots are often incoherent and his characters tend to strut, posture and speechify rather than feel and interact. His work is also relentlessly cynical, making him the wrong choice for Superman.

Likewise mismatched is screenwriter David Goyer, who, despite his credentials (the *Blade* and *Dark Knight* trilogies), is also the comics writer who decided Superman shouldn't be an American anymore.

The result is a rather bleak film with questionable ethics. In one scene, Pa Kent (Kevin Costner), traditionally Clark's guide to folksy heartland morality, is upset with his young son for risking revealing himself by saving a school bus full of classmates. "What was I supposed to do, just let them die?" Clark asks. "Maybe..." his father muses.[50] It's a far cry from telling him "you are here for a reason" in *Superman*.

Jonathan isn't motivated here by a utilitarian dilemma but by fear of Clark being resented, rejected and persecuted. It's the fear of an America embroiled in unpopular wars for twelve years, weary of using its power and favoring nonintervention. Exactly what Superman was originally created to campaign against.

The film's villain is General Zod, presented as less of a devil and more of a Nazi. On Krypton, he attempts a putsch against the government to "sever the degenerative bloodlines that led us to this state." When he arrives on Earth, rather than integrate and cohabitate he intends to replace the inferior humans, and then only with those Kryptonian lineages he deems worthy of reviving (using the Codex, a genetic registry).

Zod is also a refugee, like Kal-El, a survivor of his people's destruction, and in this respect embodies the xenophobic stereotype of the "bad immigrant"; insular, irreconcilable, coming to subvert, transform and conquer. Superman is the "good immigrant," defining himself as a native first and wishing only to be accepted and to contribute.

Zod forces upon him a choice between Krypton and Earth, between his two cultures and identities. He chooses both. He doesn't reject Zod or the idea of rebirthing their race, just doing it at the expense of his adoptive home. What he rejects is the mutual exclusivity of tribalism. He fights on Earth's side, but he does so while embracing his heritage, wearing an ethnic costume bearing his family crest and following the guidance of Jor-El's hologram. Through him, Krypton doesn't threaten but saves Earth. His self-actualization is in combining the best of both worlds.

This conflict is subtext in *Superman*, where in the finale he makes a choice between his fathers' differing views, that it is forbidden for him to interfere in human history or that he is there for a reason. But *Man of Steel* is not a movie of nuance, and his options are expressed repeatedly and often in yelling, until they reach a crescendo in a forty-minute revelry of nonstop wholesale destruction.

The spurned Zod lays waste to much of Metropolis (played by Chicago), and their fight showcases Superman's incredible power in full CGI glory for the first time. It's a sanitized battle, assiduously detailing the mass destruction while avoiding any explicit gruesomeness, and it's clearly meant to evoke the familiar sights of 9/11. Perhaps intentionally, this equates Superman with America, from its own perspective; peaceful, protective, reconciliatory, reluctant to fight but resolute when forced to, while Zod is the implacable, bloodthirsty fundamentalist.

His hand unconvincingly forced, Superman ultimately kills Zod to stop him, and is immediately consumed by obligatory, absolving guilt. The film seems to argue that, post–9/11, the urgent end justifies the harsh means, even for Superman. ("He's gotta do what he's gotta do," Snyder said in an interview.[51]) But this misses the point of him. He doesn't need to reflect the American reality; he embodies its aspiration.

It also undercuts the unsubtle comparison to Christ throughout the film. Jesus didn't punch Satan through Jerusalem's walls or snap Pontius Pilate's neck. Superman is an action hero, not a martyr, which is the inherent problem in making him a Christ figure. But it's particularly problematic when he's not only willing to kill but, until the very end, makes no discernable effort to spare or save bystanders or expresses any alarm over the massive death toll.

At the same time, the film introduces new Moses parallels. Before he becomes Superman, he responds to three plights: he saves roughnecks on a burning oil rig, rescues his schoolmates from a sinking bus, and aids a harassed waitress. Moses, before becoming his people's hero, helps in three instances: he saves a laborer from a slave driver, stops a fight between fellow Israelites, and defends bullied women at a watering hole. Like Moses, Superman is reluctant to be exposed or assume his birthright mantle when Jor-El's apparition calls upon him to, eventually doing so because he is the only one who can save his people (though adoptive) from a tyrant.

The religious themes continue, if less bluntly, in *Man of Steel*'s 2016 sequel, *Batman v Superman: Dawn of Justice*. Also directed by Snyder and co-written by Goyer, the movie is as portentous as its title. It's almost farcically grim, excessively violent (an R-rated cut was released on DVD) and clearly favors the Dark Knight, even giving him top billing.

To its credit, it's filled with beautiful shots, ideas that seek to challenge and possibly the best fight choreography for Batman on film. But these are threaded on a rambling plot and obscured by the sludging pace and shoehorned cameos of Aquaman, Cyborg and Flash (the exception being Wonder Woman, equally gratuitous but enrapturing thanks to actress Gal Gadot).

Superman and Batman are implausibly bitter enemies, manipulated by Lex Luthor into a juvenile, testosterone-fueled grudge match. Superman intends to stop the vicious vigilante, who in this movie maims and kills criminals, while Batman means to slay the powerful alien because, "if we believe there's even a 1% chance that he is our enemy, we have to take it as an absolute certainty."[52] The reasoning is about as convincing as Batman ultimately winning the fight, as well as his abrupt change of heart when, about to deliver the killing blow, he learns that both their mothers are named Martha.

The movie's Christian overtones, culminating in Superman's self-sacrifice, lead directly into 2017's *Justice League*, where he returns from the dead to save the world. Pointedly, his resurrection involves a baptismal submersion in water while a bright light shines from above, a final battle for the fate of humanity under red skies and facing Steppenwolf, an ancient, otherworldly, horned adversary from a fiery domain with a legion of winged, fanged "Parademons" at his command.

In the relatively little screen time he's given in *Justice League*, Superman is startlingly different from *Man of Steel* and *Batman v Superman*, a response to criticism of their dark tone. "Superman was a beacon to the world," it's explained. "He didn't just save people, he made them see the best parts of themselves."[53] Several such references to light and hope are made, entirely inconsistent with the previous two films, and he returns with a newfound sense of humor, smiling, laughing and quipping. It's a welcome change, but it isn't enough to save the movie.

Snyder was replaced partway through by writer-director Joss Whedon (*Avengers*), whose lighter approach turned the film from somber to schizophrenic. It was a critical and box office flop, coming in at a net loss of up to $100 million and ending, as of this writing, Cavill's turn in the role.[54]

In February 2016, six weeks before *Batman v Superman*, Siegel and Shuster's never-ending battle finally came to an end.

In 1976, the newly enacted Copyright Act allowed for copyrights to revert back to creators or their family after 56 years.[55] Siegel and Shuster had just reached an agreement with DC a few months prior, following their public relations campaign, which meant they couldn't sue for ownership again. But their heirs could. And so, in

1997, after Siegel passed away, his widow Joanne and daughter Laura moved to recapture the rights to Superman.

Negotiations dragged, and in April 1999 the termination notice took effect. It was a pyrrhic victory. While the original concept and earliest material were produced independently and then sold to DC, later elements were developed under a work-for-hire contract, which the Copyright Act didn't protect. The result was a catch-22 headscratcher in which the Siegels owned half the character, including the original costume and power set of leaping tall buildings, deflecting bullets and outrunning trains, while DC owned the other half, including his ability to fly, X-ray vision, Kryptonite, the *Daily Planet* and most of his supporting cast and villains, from the Kents to Luthor.[56]

DC disputed the notice, and negotiations continued until an agreement in principle was eventually reached in October 2001. Siegel's heirs accepted DC's offer in a letter, granting all rights to Superman, Superboy and related properties (and the Spectre) in exchange for a $1 million signing bonus, $2 million advance, forgiveness of a previous $250,000 advance, an annual guarantee of $500,000 for ten years and various other royalties. Most importantly, they were to receive 6 percent of gross revenue, which in global licensing fees and merchandise sales are estimated at $277 million annually, potentially totaling $16.6 million.[57]

But the deal was never formally finalized and eventually fell through, for various contested reasons. The Siegels repudiated it, served another notice of termination in 2002 and sued in 2004. Years of rancorous litigation followed, with rulings in 2006, 2007, 2008 and 2009, increasingly in favor of the Siegels, until in 2012 a California federal court declared that the 2001 letter constituted a legally binding contract. The Siegel estate, at this point consisting only of Laura, appealed the decision to the Ninth Circuit Court, which upheld it on April 18, 2013—the 75th anniversary of Superman's first appearance in *Action Comics* #1.[58]

Starting the following month, all comic books and other media featuring Superman and related characters include the credits, "Superman created by Jerry Siegel and Joe Shuster. By special arrangement with the Jerry Siegel family." (Originally a 2001 proviso. Instated in *Action Comics* Vol. 2 #20, *Superman* Vol. 3 #19, *Superboy* Vol. 6 #20, *Supergirl* Vol. 6 #20 and *Justice League* Vol. 2 #19.)

In 2016, the Ninth Circuit refused a request to revive the suit, reaffirming that DC owned all rights to Superman.[59] Though the Siegel estate can still appeal to the U.S. Supreme Court they haven't done so, and the Court is unlikely to reverse the ruling.

Shuster's heirs tried to recapture their rights in a similar lawsuit, eventually appealing to the Supreme Court in 2014, but were denied on the grounds that their 1992 agreement with DC following his death effectively relinquished all claims to the property.[60]

The seventy-year inextricable series of lawsuits and countersuits, one of the longest IP litigations in history, was finally over. Whether they were compensated fairly or not, Siegel's family secured a multimillion dollar annual payout and, no less important, a measure of justice in his name.

Following the New 52, and with a higher cultural profile thanks to the Cavill films, DC rebooted Superman again in 2017.

It was risky. Since 1986, Superman had undergone several restarts, retcons and retellings—including *Zero Hour* ('94), *Birthright* ('03–'04), *Infinite Crisis* ('06), *Secret Origin* ('09–'10), *Flashpoint/New 52* ('11), *Convergence* ('15) and *Rebirth* ('16), notwithstanding in-story revisions like *Superman Secret Files & Origins 2004* and *Batman/Superman* #1 ('13), uncanonical versions like *Superman for All Seasons* ('98), *All-Star Superman* ('06–'08), *Earth One* ('10) and *American Alien* ('16) and subversive takes like *Red Son* ('03) and *Injustice: Gods Among Us* ('13–'16)—with diminishing returns of fan interest. But the existing Man of Steel was untenable; an extradimensional original of an ersatz dead Superman who was a stranger to his own supporting cast. DC needed a mulligan.

The two Supermen were amalgamated, along with their personal histories but without the rigmarole of resetting everything else, in the four-part "Superman: Reborn" (aka "Rebirth") in *Superman* Vol. 4 #18–19 and *Action Comics* #975–976 (all May '17). Issues #977–978 served as a clip show, revisiting and reaffirming older element of canon. The cover to #977 added the classic "S" to the title logo and featured a smiling Clark opening his shirt to reveal the erstwhile costume, against a collage background showing him marrying Lois and flying the American flag, signaling a return to the status quo ante.

Superman's canon now comprised elements from *The Man of Steel*, *Birthright*, *Secret Origin*, the New 52, storylines like the Death and Return and the *Lois and Clark* miniseries, and touches of the Silver Age and *Superman: The Movie*.[61] It was an esemplastic feat that, while somewhat vague and paradoxical, created a platonic ideal of the character, both familiar and multivalent.

"The Bible and the Talmud are in essence collections of stories, which we continue to tell over and over," Will Eisner told the *New York Jewish Week* when discussing Jewish themes in comics.[62] Superman's origin has been told, retold and retooled countless times, a repetitive cycle of myth-affirmation that's typically reserved for religious stories. Greek dramas or Shakespeare plays, considerably older than superhero stories, are recontextualized every so often, but not as persistently, and legends like Hercules and King Arthur sporadically reemerge in new versions, but they don't hold a consistent place in the public consciousness as do Moses and Jesus, whose story is retold, in different contexts, virtually every weekend.

The very concept of a reboot or retcon fits within the Jewish mitzvah of telling and retelling important stories, itself reiterated in the Hebrew Bible (Deut. 11:18–19, 31:12, 19, Josh. 1:8) and various rabbinical texts (Chagigah 9b, Sanhedrin 99a, Menachot 99b). The Mishnah (מִשְׁנָה), the foundational work of Jewish exegesis and religious law, means by name both repetition and memorization (שִׁינּוּן), connoting, and containing, simultaneous reaffirmation and reinterpretation. Particular emphasis is given to Judaism's origin story—deliverance out of bondage, of the Torah and to the Holy Land—including that of its greatest hero, Moses (Deut. 5:15, Ex. 13:3, 8–16, 22:21, *Shema*, Haggadah), which provided the framework for Superman's own continually retold origin.

The Man of Tomorrow felt like himself again. Writer Peter J. Tomasi and artist Patrick Gleason on *Superman* Vol. 4 and writer Dan Jurgens back on *Action Comics* with sundry artists (beginning with August 2016's #1 and #957, respectively) restored brightness and optimism to the character. Back also was the tried and true iconography, meant to make an impact; a splash page of him standing akimbo on the moon next to Apollo 11's American flag, the caption reading "Superman is here to stay!"; a cover of him hovering above the clouds, staring reassuringly into the distance as the sun rises behind him; a double-spread of him soaring joyful among birds over scenic farmland.[63]

The only holdover was the costume, which couldn't be decided on. When the pre–New 52 Superman resumed the role, it was changed back to tights but made to resemble the current films, a darker outfit with metallic blue cuffs, blue boots with red trims and red waistline detailing in lieu of trunks. Twenty issues later, following "Superman: Reborn," he returned to his classic suit, except for a red belt with a golden shield buckle and still no trunks. Those made their triumphant return a year later, completing the iconic look after a seven-year hiatus. The one alteration that remains is a subtle version of the cuffs.[64]

DC's gambit paid off. The new direction was well-received, and sales surpassed 100,000 copies. Even after tapering off they held the line at a respectable 60,000 range. Superman, it seems, can't sustain significant monthly sales over time, but he does hold a unique place in public consciousness. When *Action Comics* reached its milestone #1000 issue in June 2018, marking Superman's 80th anniversary, even with a cover price of $7.99 it sold over 500,000 copies, making it the year's bestseller. *Superman* remains the highest-selling series over its lifespan, with estimates reaching 600 million copies worldwide.[65]

In May 2018, all DC comic books featured a double-page house ad announcing "BENDIS IS COMING!" alongside a smiling Superman.

Brian Michael Bendis was Marvel's premier writer, synonymous with the company after eighteen years of helming and revitalizing high-profile titles like *Ultimate Spider-Man*, *Daredevil* and *Avengers* and co-creating enduring characters like Jessica Jones and the second Spider-Man (Miles Morales). He received executive producer credits on several television shows and was a core member of the Marvel Creative Committee, overseeing the company's ventures in film and other media. His decampment to DC was as seminal as Kirby's and Byrne's, making national news.[66]

DC handed him both *Action Comics* and *Superman*, beginning with #1000 and a new Vol. 5 #1, respectively, which he continues to write. It's been a good fit. His signature style of naturalistic fantasy, a blend of the mundane and the miraculous bordering magical realism, suits a mythology that's equal parts personal drama, philosophy and action-packed spectacle. On *Superman* in particular he's bolstered by Ivan Reis, whose realistic and dynamic art is effectual at expressions as much as at explosions. Their Superman is boldly earnest, deeply empathic, intelligent, deliberate, but also passionate and whimsically self-aware. It's a take that proves that, more so than many other superheroes, Superman is, when handled right, a fully realized character.

Bendis conveys a similarly nuanced view of his dual identity. Rather than a zero-sum game it's an act of equilibrium. As Clark he confesses that "living up to the ideal of *Superman* gets to be so overwhelming," while as Superman he explains that being Clark allows him to "*Be* with people. Learn. Adapt. Be part of the conversation."[67] Either one is a role, and either one is a genuine aspect of himself.

Recently, Superman revealed his secret identity to the world, in an effort to better live up to his own creed of truth. Calling a press conference, he announces, "I'm so proud of my heritage … both from Krypton and Earth … and when I show up as Superman, I want to show up representing both parts."[68] (Consequences remain to be seen as of this writing, though the big change is all but certain to be overturned eventually.) That he phrases the personal moment in cultural terms, reconciling not just both sides of his personality but of his heritage, is not undeliberate.

Growing up in Cleveland, Siegel and Shuster's hometown, Bendis was an orthodox yeshiva student who loved comics and "studied them like the Torah." He got his start doing caricatures at bar and bat mitzvahs, and when he broke into comics he brought his background with him. His Spider-Man in particular, which he wrote longer than anyone else, wisecracked like Seinfeld, peppered Yiddishisms like *oy*, *mishugas*, *fakakta* and *shmendrick* and referenced holidays like Shavuos. Although it was obvious he was Jewish it was never made explicit, and Bendis limited himself to confirming it in interviews.[69]

He's brought similar influences to Superman, with supporting characters like Metropolis PD Captain Maggie Sawyer complaining about a "pain in the tuchas" and Myand'r, king of the planet Tamaran and father of the Teen Titans' Starfire, mentioning his science advisor attending a cousin's bar mitzvah (connecting, in a happy coincidence, to Starfire mentioning she once visited a Lubavitch center on Tamaran in the comedic *Teen Titans Go!*). Perry White is possibly meant to be Jewish, telling his staff that "Lois Lane would have broken this story and we'd be home for Shabbat dinner!"[70]

Unlike Peter Parker, Clark Kent isn't Jewish, and Bendis doesn't imply otherwise, but he has expressed a kinship to Superman that's "very, very deep, genetically."[71] He recognizes the character's Jewish DNA, and he's threaded Jewish themes, new and old, throughout his run.

It's revealed that Krypton was destroyed as a result of orchestrated genocide, not natural cataclysm, at the hands of villain Rogol Zaar, a change to the origin Bendis said was specifically meant to bring it closer to that of Moses. It's also revealed that galactic leaders either indifferently allowed it to happen or actively conspired to facilitate it, unwilling even to "make room for Kryptonian refugees,"[72] drawing clear parallels to the Holocaust and the Évian Conference.

Extending the metaphor to the current flaring of Antisemitism around the world, when Superman, Superboy and Supergirl are attacked by several alien races, she asks, "has anti–Kryptonianism been a hidden hate in all of these people?"[73]

The new Superboy is Jon Kent, the son from *Superman: Lois and Clark* who made it through the Rebirth culling, now older. On his father's side he's a first-generation American (technically, since he was born on a different planet in a different

Superman: Leviathan Rising Special #1, July 2019. Written by Brian Michael Bendis and illustrated by Yanick Paquette. DC Comics.

dimension, he's an alien immigrant himself, but it's never addressed and it's likely not canon anymore), and his mixed background is the crux of his character arc. Particularly, when a time-displaced Jor-El appears, disapproving of his son's assimilation and grandson's unfamiliarity with his heritage, Jon becomes conflicted between the clashing cultures and values.[74] Like many children of immigrants, born into one culture with the birthright of another, he seeks to navigate and reconcile them. And like many Jewish children born to immigrants or raised in interfaith homes, he shoulders further responsibility, and choice, as a continuer of an ancient tradition and of survivors of genocide.

These changes add to the Jewish understructure of Superman's mythology, but they work less well as stories. The deliberate destruction of Krypton needlessly complicates the origin and diminishes its potency as a cautionary tale. A catastrophe avoidable if not for hubris and apathy is more relevant and arguably more tragic, and it makes for better motivation for Superman.

The arc's main villain, cosmic cutthroat Rogol Zaar, is surprisingly flat and uninspired, a sharp-toothed, permanently snarling behemoth. Hell-bent on killing any remaining Kryptonians, he turns out to be a genetically-engineered weapon created by Jor-El,[75] a genesis that's derivative of Doomsday's and doesn't adequately explain his motivation. Having Jor-El play a role in Krypton's destruction, however indirectly, sullies the poeticism of Superman's origin, detracts from its moral of collective responsibility and, in the context of the Jewish metaphor, is highly problematic.

Giving Superman a ten-year-old son was a brave development, but it inexorably aged him and it's unlikely being a dad has helped make him cooler in the eyes of kids. And if Jon's backstory wasn't convoluted enough, he was aged into a teenager via yet another parallel dimension, where he was imprisoned and tortured for years by an evil doppelgänger of his father, only to return two weeks later in his own time with full memory but no apparent trauma.[76] Whatever the future has in store for him, it seems likely that he'll follow his father in at least one tradition and have his origin story rewritten.

Bendis boosted Superman's sales, but he hasn't reversed their steady decline. *Superman* Vol. 5 #1 sold nearly 134,000 and *Action Comics* #1001 over 79,000, healthy if disappointing numbers. A year in, *Superman* #12 sold just over 47,000 and *Action Comics* #1012 under 43,000.[77]

The industry, meanwhile, is moving in the opposite direction. Despite the competition from television, streaming, films, video games and social media, and despite the standard comic book price continually rising—from 10¢ to $3.99, while shrinking from 68 pages to 36, though when adjusting for inflation the price has only about doubled since the Golden Age, similar to movie tickets—comics today are arguably the most thriving arm of the publishing field. While U.S. publishing in general shrunk by nearly 5 percent between 2012 and 2018, comics sales grew by nearly 25 percent. In 2018, when print publishing recuperated and grew by 1.3 percent, graphic novel sales shot up by 11.7 percent. Total comic book sales in 2018 reached $1.1 billion, a remarkable rebound from 2000's $255 million.[78]

Comics and superheroes have also moved from marginalia to the mainstream, enjoying long overdue recognition. Millions devotedly attend the movies, think pieces are commonplace and increasingly so are academic studies. Tastemakers like Gabriel García Márquez, Joyce Carol Oates, Salman Rushdie and Umberto Eco have professed reading them and Margaret Atwood, Ta-Nehisi Coates and Doris Lessing have written them.[79] They receive prestigious literary honors, like *Maus*'s 1992 Pulitzer and *March: Book Three*'s 2016 National Book Award.

Some see today as a second Golden Age, like Levitz, who points to the medium's expansion to include new genres, characters, concepts and styles.[80] It's a relatively young art form, still experimenting and pushing boundaries, and still the native format of superheroes. Even with all the advances in special effects, comic books can still do things movies can't, narratively, artistically, budgetarily and daringly.

What movies do best, though, is make money, and there superheroes reign supreme—something that Jack Kirby, ever the visionary, predicted back in the sixties. They routinely reach billion-dollar box office hauls. They account for five of the top ten highest-grossing films of all time, with 2019's *Avengers: Endgame* topping the list at a staggering $2.8 billion.[81] Hundreds of millions of people around the world watch them, making them some of the most popular stories in human history. And it all started with two Jewish teens and one *mashugana* idea.

Superman, and from him the concept of the superhero, were created as a utopian symbol of tomorrow, a promise of unbridled, limitless humanity. The question is whether that promise still stands, or has the idea become obsolete, a sentimental meme and a vacuous form of machismo and pyrotechnics.

When Superman first appeared, the world was undergoing rapid change and facing its gravest threat. He was a shining beacon at a dark time, a Champion of the Oppressed created by the oppressed to first advocate New Deal reform and interventionism, then to rally moral and financial support for the war effort. He and his four-color compatriots reached the youth and adults of America, telling them of the plight of refugees, the poor, the rightless and the persecuted, of victims of war, abuse, and exploitation, of Others. They promoted, in a real sense, a more compassionate, more pluralistic, more peaceful world.

But today there's no unifying threat, no monolithic evil to fight. Challenges are decentralized and more complex, thornier, a very different world for superheroes to tackle. Or so it seems.

Populism, tribalism, nativism and xenophobia are resurgent around the world, giving rise to fantasists and fascists. White nationalism is again an issue in American politics, as is the question of isolationism. Beset by disparity, disinformation and demagoguery, the cultural landscape is balkanized, fractious and indignant.

"Never again" has become all over again as Antisemitism surges worldwide. Violence against Jews has reached levels unseen since the 1940s, doubling in the U.S. between 2015 and 2018 alone. A similar trend across Europe, notably Germany and France, home to Europe's largest Jewish community, has turned Jewish institutions, temples and schools into fortified strongholds guarded by police and even military forces. In New York, a bastion of liberalism with the largest Jewish population in the world after the Tel Aviv conurbation, Antisemitic attacks constituted 60 percent of all hate crimes in 2018—six times the next targeted group and more than all other groups combined.[82]

On October 27, 2018, the worst Antisemitic violence in U.S. history took place at the Tree of Life synagogue in Pittsburgh, Pennsylvania, where eleven people were killed and several more injured in a mass shooting during Shabbat morning services. A second massacre followed five months later in Poway, California, where another neo–Nazi entered a Chabad house on the last day of Passover and shot congregants, including children. More pogroms have followed since.

As a global report finds that "Anti-Semitism is no longer an issue confined to the activity of the far left, far right and radical Islamists triangle—it has mainstreamed and became an integral part of life,"[83] in the U.S. Antisemitic rhetoric, veiled or blatant, can be found on both sides of the congressional aisle.

It's a harsh climate for superheroes, but it's also why they're still relevant, and why they're so popular again. The same cultural forces that gave them rise are again emergent, creating a need for inspiring champions of goodwill and progress. It's a never-ending battle, as fateful as it's ever been, to promote the values of truth, justice and coexistence, and to remind people that they have the power to transform themselves and the world.

Superhero comics have always been morality plays, direct and unabashed about promoting a worldview that has changed remarkably little since their beginning. The duty to protect the weak, the imperative to take action in the face of injustice, society's benefit in accepting the different, otherness as a source of power, social adversity as a crucible of strength, the outsider as benevolent protector, the duality of personal and social identity—are all reflections of the Jewish experience that formed to create a unique American mythology.

The industry has changed a great deal since, now almost entirely owned by multinational corporations. But it has continued to be transgressive, at the vanguard of social justice advocacy. Recent years have also seen it grow to include more women, people of color and LGBTQ readers, creators and characters,[84] demonstrating its continued role as a tool of inclusion.

Comics aren't guiltless of sexism, stereotyping and prejudiced orthodoxies, but their idealization of the human spirit and body (albeit to a specific and impossible standard) has created some of the most powerful and admired minority role models in fiction, often breaking ground for the rest of the entertainment industry. The superhero is by definition a celebration of difference. It's the American dream, dramatized. A metaphor created by Jews now used to represent others, giving superpowers to the powerless.

And Superman started it all. Early on he fought real-world evils, whether obvious Nazi proxies like Nation X or Dukalia (or in *Look* magazine, Hitler and Stalin themselves) or Depression ills like inequality, exploitation and corruption, and later, mostly in other media, bigotry. But he became a company man, and to the most part has since shied away from current events and preoccupations. There was no mention of 9/11 in his comics, no terrorist cells to stop or foreign wars to win. For a journalist he's had remarkably little to say about the world.

Sociopolitical commentary, beyond generalities, is a tricky minefield with a character who's a paragon and a Rorschach test. And he's powerful enough to change these realities, a can of worms that's almost always been opened in the safety of uncanonical works like *Superman: Peace on Earth* ('98), *Superman: Red Son* ('03) and *Injustice: Gods Among Us* ('13) and usually resolved, seldom satisfyingly, with an argument of man's free will and moral responsibility over Superman's providence.

Recently, the *Lois Lane* limited series allowed him to address real-life issues vicariously. Subtitled "Enemy of the People," a reference to president Donald Trump's repeated calumny of the press, it features Lois doggedly exposing the unnamed administration's illicit profiteering from the separation and internment of refugee children while it wages a campaign of misinformation, discrediting and incitement against her, paralleling accusations leveled against the real White House.[85] Though it's handled with a light hand, the story glaringly omits what should be its most interesting point: Superman's commentary, or action, as a child immigrant himself.

On the small screen the Super-oeuvre is more daring. *Supergirl* ('15–), starring the plucky and charming Melissa Benoist, has an unequivocal and unapologetic liberal standpoint. Following a bright and breezy first season it became progressively political, an instrument of social crusading in the original spirit of Superman and with a similar sense of urgency.

The show has engaged with topical issues of sexism, lobbyism, corporate and political malfeasance, freedom and duty of the press, and particularly racism and xenophobia. A major theme has been the question of illegal aliens, cleverly literalized as refugees from other planets.

The show has also featured various interspecies, interracial and same-sex romances. It introduced new characters to the mythology like Alex Danvers (Chyler Leigh), Supergirl's gay adoptive sister, and Dreamer, a fellow alien superheroine named after DREAMers, immigrants who entered the U.S. illegally as minors and seek residency. She's also transgender, played by real-life transgender Nicole Maines, who was the teenage plaintiff in *Doe. v. Regional School Unit 26*, a landmark antidiscrimination case that resulted in a Maine Supreme Court ruling allowing school bathrooms to be used in accordance with gender identity.[86] She's the culmination of the superhero as outsider motif, the ultimate Other—one who's born a strange visitor in their own body.

Siegel and Shuster's stories often lacked subtlety or profundity, but they were always fun and upbeat, something the show, for all its boldness, has largely lost sight of. Its didacticism is often onerous, with story metaphors that come across as tokenism for soapbox preaching. It illustrates that, while engagement with the real world is a source of strength for superheroes, getting too close can become a burden. It's truths and values greater than the reality of the moment that are important.

In 2016 the show introduced a new Superman, played by the likable, slightly lupine Tyler Hoechlin. Though only a guest character appearing in a handful of episodes, his portrayal has struck the right tone, straightforward and warm, if not quite commanding. A *Superman & Lois* series is set to air in 2020, starring Hoechlin and Elizabeth Tulloch as Lois,[87] hopefully bringing the Man of Steel back into the limelight.

Krypton, lasting only two seasons on the Syfy channel ('18–'19), also heavily involved social themes, but was less advocative. Taking place two hundred years before the planet's destruction, it featured Jor-El's father, Seg-El (Cameron Cuffe)—originally Seyg-El in the comics, a nod to Jerry Siegel—and made Zod his son, thus Superman's uncle.[88] It also changed Kryptonian society from scientific to theocratic, based on a rigid caste system answerable to the pope-like Voice of Rao. A world divided by religiopolitical and socioeconomic oppression, dogmatism and groupthink, militarized law enforcement and hostile climate, it's a chronicle of a death foretold and a warning for our own.

When Stan Lee passed away on November 12, 2018, the *Forward* called it "the end of an era not only for American pop culture, but for modern Jews' influence upon it."[89] After nearly a century of evolution, with countless influences added along the way, comics and superheroes aren't as Jewish as they once were. But Jewish creators continue to be prominent and Jewish themes have become more explicit, if still rare. (The subject of Antisemitism has been conspicuously absent, given that comics regularly tackle other bigotries.)

In indie comics in particular, Jewish subject matter has been explored by the likes of Trina Robbins, Art Spiegelman, Ben Katchor and Alison Bechdel. Israeli works likes Rutu Modan's *Exit Wounds* ('08) and *The Property* ('14) and Asaf Hanuka's *The Realist* ('16) have won Eisner Awards, while Joann Sfar's French graphic novel series *The Rabbi's Cat* is an Eisner laureate, international bestseller and 2011 animated film.[90]

In mainstream comics, established voices like Peter David, Adam and Andy Kubert, Brad Meltzer and Brian Michael Bendis and newer entrants like Matt Fraction, Matthew Rosenberg and Tom King continue to bring, to varying degrees, a Jewish sensibility to their work.

Jewish signification can be found in recent works like *Mister Miracle* (October '17–January '19), a continuation of Kirby's Superman branch-off, the Fourth World. It introduced Miracle and Barda's newborn son, Jacob, named after "Jacob's Ladder," an Apokoliptian means of salvation reaching from the hellish Fire Pits to a figurative "heaven," a name borrowed from the famous dream sequence in Gen. 28:10–19. And just as the biblical patriarch fled the fratricidal Esau over a rivalry for their father Isaac's blessing and birthright, *Mister Miracle*'s theme, and to a large extent that of the Fourth World saga overall, is family dysfunction and wrestling with destiny, the conflict between self-actualization, familial obligation and social expectation. Jacob is ostensibly named after Kirby, and so is Oberon—yet another short, stocky, gruff avatar of Kirby's—given here the surname Kurtzberg, Kirby's real name.[91]

Explicit Jewish representation has also increased in recent years. Marvel's Vance Astro, Songbird, Wiccan and Roz Solomon and DC's Kamandi, Felicity Smoak and Swamp Kid are at least partly Jewish. Batwoman, named Kate Kane after Batman co-creator Bob Kane, has been shown celebrating Hanukkah and reading Jewish esoterica like *Sefer Yetzirah*.[92] Her current TV show marks a first for a Jewish superhero, unassumingly showcasing her Jewishness through bat mitzvah references and family gravestones.

The Fantastic Four's Thing, the most autobiographical of Kirby's creations—a gruff, cigar-chomping brawler from the Lower East Side named after himself and his father, Benjamin Jacob Grimm—has been increasingly reconnecting with his faith. First shown pulling a Star of David from behind his "4" insignia (a perfect symbolism) and reciting the *Shema* prayer, he later received an adult bar mitzvah and recently got married in a Jewish ceremony.[93]

The most prominent overtly Jewish character is villain-turned-antihero Harley Quinn, who's half catholic and half Jewish (what New Yorkers affectionately call a "cashew"). Debuting in 1992's *Batman: The Animated Series*, she was based on and voiced by Jewish actress and comedian Arleen Sorkin, imbued with her Borscht Belt humor and verve and given to Yiddish exclamations like *oy* and *plotz* in a stereotypical Brooklyn accent. Quinn grew to become DC's most popular character after Superman, Batman and Wonder Woman, according to co-publisher and CCO Jim Lee, appearing in several comic book series and graphic novels, coleading the *Suicide Squad* film ('16, played by Margot Robbie) and headlining its spinoff *Birds of Prey* ('20) as well as her own animated series (voiced by Kaley Cuoco). It's something the original creators of superheroes could have only dreamed of. Equally significant, her Judaism is apparent but incidental. As Trina Robbins put it, "when you don't make a big deal about your character being Jewish, that's real equality."[94]

The current superhero phenomenon in film and television is almost as Jewish as the Golden Age of comics, tracing back to 1978's *Superman* being produced, directed and mostly written by Jews. *Blade* ('98), the movie that sparked the present trend, was written by David Goyer based on a character created by Marv Wolfman and Jules "Gene" Colan. The *X-Men* films (2000–) are produced by Lauren Shuler Donner (wife of Richard) and several were directed by Bryan Singer. They also centrally feature Jewish themes, two having opening scenes in Auschwitz. The *Spider-Man* trilogy ('02–'07) was produced by Laura Ziskin and directed by Sam Raimi.

The man behind these movies is Israeli-American Avi Arad, a toy designer turned Marvel co-owner and CCO and Chairman and CEO of Marvel Studios (Arad became the co-owner of manufacturer ToyBiz together with fellow Israeli-American Isaac "Ike" Perlmutter, which licensed from Marvel and then became a subsidiary.

They helped recover Marvel from its 1996 bankruptcy, becoming the majority shareholders. Arad has since left to form Arad Productions, producing Marvel films with outside studios like Sony and Fox. Perlmutter remains CEO of Marvel Entertainment). Foreseeing the genre's multimedia appeal, he insisted to skeptical investors that Spider-Man alone was worth a billion dollars. He was wrong. To date, Spider-Man movies have grossed over $7 billion with annual retail sales of $1.3 billion. Following, in August 2009, Marvel, a magazine publisher started during the Depression by a handful of young Jews, sold to the Walt Disney Company for $4.24 billion. Within a decade it made over $18 billion at the box office and became the prime mover of Disney's retail sales, which in 2018 alone totaled $45 billion.[95]

The co-architect of Marvel's revolutionary transformation from licensor to producer of its own movies was Hollywood dealmaker David Maisel, dubbed "Captain Finance" by CNN, who became Marvel Studios' Founding Chairman in 2007.[96] The studio's first film, 2008's *Iron Man*, was directed by Jon Favreau. Taika Waititi directed *Thor: Ragnarok* ('17) and the forthcoming *Thor: Love and Thunder* ('21). Jeph Loeb helmed Marvel Television from 2010 to 2019.

Over at DC, Snyder and Goyer orchestrated the shared movie universe, with *Wonder Woman* ('17) written by Snyder, Allan Heinberg and Jason Fuchs and directed by Patty Jenkins. The "Arrowverse" television shows—*Arrow, Flash, Supergirl, Legends of Tomorrow, Batwoman*—are collaboratively produced by Marc Guggenheim, Andrew Kreisberg, Ali Adler, Sarah Schechter and Phil Klemmer, among others.

People of Jewish background have also played a prominent role in front of the camera. Robert Downey, Jr., headlined the Marvel Cinematic Universe, playing Iron Man in nine films, alongside Gwyneth Paltrow as his love interest Pepper Potts. Scarlet Johansson has costarred as fellow Avenger the Black Widow in seven films, with a forthcoming solo. Michael Douglas and Paul Rudd played two generations of Ant-Man, Rudd bringing his awkward, amiable Jewish charm to the character in four films. Israeli-American Natalie Portman (Neta-Lee Hershlag) has played Thor's paramour Jane Foster in two films and is set to become the new goddess of thunder in the next. Joe Bernthal played the Punisher in two seasons of the Netflix show. Miles Teller was Mister Fantastic in the ill-fated *Fantastic Four* ('15). Andrew Garfield was Spider-Man in two films, and in the animated *Spider-Man: Into the Spider-Verse* ('18) the character can be seen breaking the glass at his wedding.

In DC films, Israeli actress Ayelet Zurer played Lara in *Man of Steel*. Jesse Eisenberg played Luthor in *Batman v Superman* (following Michael Rosenbaum in *Smallville*). Asher Angel was Shazam's alter ego Billy Batson in *Shazam!* (the hero persona was played by Zachary Levi, who isn't Jewish but has still been denied roles for being "too Jewish"). Joaquin Phoenix starred as the Joker in the titular movie. Zoe Kravitz, a Jew of color (an identity so underrepresented in American culture that it might seem an incongruity. Ashkenazi Jews are estimated to comprise only about a third of Israel's population), is the new Catwoman in the upcoming *The Batman* ('21).[97]

On TV, David Mazouz played Bruce Wayne on *Gotham* ('14–'19). A main *Arrow* character, Felicity Smoak, is Jewish, an interesting amalgam of the cerebral, bespectacled neurotic stereotype and a blond bombshell and woman of action, a mix of Clark Kent and Superman. On *Flash* and *Legends of Tomorrow*, Firestorm's co-alter ego Martin Stein was given a rabbinical background and played by Victor Garber—the first Jewish actor to play an openly Jewish superhero, though the hero himself was played by Robbie Amell and later Franz Drameh ('15–'17).

The highest profile character, Israeli actress Gal Gadot has played Wonder Woman in four films, imbuing her with unmistakable Israeli accent, attitude and mannerisms, particularly evident in the adlibbed boat scene in *Wonder Woman* ('17).[98]

Most seminal, though, is *Justice League* costar Ezra Miller's role as the Flash. Although not Jewish in the comics, he's a "very attractive Jewish boy" in the film,[99] marking the first time a superhero and the actor playing them are both Jewish. The portrayal is somewhat retrograde, a fretful, fidgety wisecracker for whom heroism doesn't come naturally, but it's venial given that he's meant to be the everyman character. Miller is set to reprise the role in his own 2022 movie. Finally, Jews get to be superheroes.

Superman, for his part, has been increasingly recognized as Jewish in recent years. The exhibit *From Superman to the Rabbi's Cat: Jewish Comics*, travelling between European museums from 2007 to 2011, examined the parallels between Superman's origin story and that of Moses, as well Jewish refugees. Larry Tye's 2013 hagiography, *Superman: The High-Flying History of America's Most Enduring Hero*, dedicated a chapter to the character's Jewish roots. The American Jewish Historical Society discussed them in their "Comics and the Jews" panel in 2015. In 2018, *CBR* wrote that "the foundations the character was built on were profoundly Judaic," consisting of "Jewish social ideas and…. Jewish lore from the Old Testament." Frank Miller stated in a 2019 interview that "Superman needs to confront his Jewish roots." On *The Simpsons*, Krusty the Clown (Herschel Shmoikel Pinchas Yerucham Krustofsky) exclaimed that the new Superman movie "made a *megillah* of shekels!"[100]

At the same time, what Superman means has increasingly come into question.

George H.W. Bush wore Superman socks with little capes. Barack Obama posed akimbo in front of his statue and another time joked that he was actually born on Krypton and sent to save the Earth. Canadian Prime Minister Justin Trudeau dressed up like him on Halloween. The deputy White House press secretary called Donald Trump "a real-life Superman," spurring several pieces in the press juxtaposing them.[101]

The most powerful men in the world have evoked the most powerful man in fiction, seeking to associate themselves with him, even if facetiously. He's a symbol of might, moral rectitude and purposefulness (and for cynics, hypermasculinity, self-righteousness and institutionalism). But he's more symbol than character, an ideogram, and the world's idea of what he signifies has changed over time. "It may be too difficult to write or draw stories, or versions of the character, that consistently fulfill everyone's heartfelt vision," Bogdanove says. "It may be that the weight of being an American icon is too big a burden."[102]

He continues to struggle with his relevance, or at least the stigma of being irrelevant, with even Warner Bros. reportedly at a loss how to "make Superman relevant to modern audiences." He's a victim of his own success; he's no longer unique, having grandsired a pantheon of superheroes, which now crowd TV and movie screens.

And his great power and unflinching earnestness are a tough sell to an audience accustomed to the likes of brash, snarky Iron Man and homicidal lunatic Deadpool. Still, other bright, optimistic heroes have found recent success, like Shazam, Captain America and Wonder Woman—who even borrowed the tone of *Superman* for her own movie, along with a couple of tribute scenes.[103] It may just be a matter of senescence. After more than eighty years, Superman is one of the most sprawling fictional epics in history. He's the ur-hero, the archetype, the *alter kocker*.

He'll forever be the linchpin of the superhero concept, its *primus inter pares*, with many analogues but no equal. When he first appeared his success was immediate and resounding, and the various media he's appeared in since couldn't contain him any more than chains could. He broke free to become an icon of the American civil religion and part of the world psyche.

What's made him so special wasn't his originality. He had close precursors and immediate successors, and none, even the most popular, have come to be seen as meaningful, as important, as he has. No other modern fictional character has been studied and discussed as he has. There are no Captain America biographies, no essays by world-renowned philosophers about Dorothy Gale. No recurring deliberations in comics or the press about why Thor doesn't create rainstorms in droughty Africa. But virtually everything Superman says, does and undergoes is parsed for meaning. He's understood to embody America's, and more abstractly humanity's, highest ideals, a constantly evolving expression of our idealized self-image.

Superman is the ultimate role model, the best of the good guys. He's a man of great power, and in many ways privilege, who abuses neither and dedicates himself to bettering the lives of others. A man who can do anything, be anything, and chooses to be kind. A man who fights endlessly for the values he believes in, and remembers to do it with a smile and a wink.

Yet he's a conflicted hero, trying to follow simple convictions in a complicated life, to find balance between responsibilities, between personal and social identities, between his past, present and future. For all his powers he's the most human superhero, and the most relatable.

In a genre teeming with heroes that are faster than a speeding bullet, more powerful than a locomotive and able to leap tall buildings in a single bound, the one thing Superman still does better than anyone else is inspire hope. That we can live up to our own potential. That we can make tomorrow better than today. He doesn't need to be made relevant to modern audiences. He needs to inspire them.

So—is Superman Jewish? Depends which one. Not Clark Kent or the Man of Steel; the fictional one or the real one. The fictional one is an alien from planet Krypton who was raised by the Kents in Smallville, Kansas. He's Christian, usually a nonpracticing Protestant or Methodist. But the real one, in the real world, is a comic book character invented by two Jewish teens in the Depression and prewar era. He was created and developed in a distinctly Jewish context and imbued with rich Jewish content, themes and signifiers borrowed from Jewish tradition that continue to manifest today. That Superman is Jewish. And he always will be.

He's evolved since his creation, with his fair share of additions and subtractions, retcons and reboots, versions and variations, but he's still the same as when Siegel and

Shuster created him back in 1934. A hero in red, yellow and blue who represents the best of the red, white and blue, who preaches tolerance for all but the intolerant, and who personifies the indomitable human spirit. A celestial benefactor, a messiah of steel. He's a modern retelling of an ancient myth, of a child saved from catastrophe in a vessel sent to an unknown fate, a helpless survivor who grows to be a mighty savior, a man gifted great power for a greater purpose, a Samson, a Moses, a Jesus. And his story is told and retold, handed down the generations, for the same reason. To make us look up in the sky, and see ourselves.

Where we had thought to be alone, we shall be with all the world.—Joseph Campbell

The New Adventures of Superman, 1966. Warner Bros.

Chapter Notes

Introduction

1. Umberto Eco, "The Myth of Superman," trans. Natalie Chilton for *Diacritics* 2, no. 1 (Spring 1972): 14–22. Originally published as "Il mito di Superman e la dissolozione del tempo" in *Demitizzazione e imagine*, ed. E. Castelli (Padua: Cedam, 1962).

2. Will Eisner, *Comics and Sequential Art: Principles and Practices from the Legendary Cartoonist* (New York: W.W. Norton, 2008), 39.

3. Jonathan Jones, "Comic strips and cubism," *The Guardian*, April 12, 2002: http://www.theguardian.com/books/2002/apr/13/books.guardianreview1

4. Jeet Heer, "Updike: Portrait of the Artist as a Young Fan," *Paris Review*, January 14, 2015, http://www.theparisreview.org/blog/2015/01/14/updike-portrait-of-the-artist-as-a-young-fan/.

Samson, Solomon and Other Supermen

1. Mark Waid, "The Real Truth about Superman: And the Rest of Us, Too," in *Superheroes and Philosophy: Truth, Justice, and the Socratic Way*, ed. Tom Morris and Matt Morris (Chicago: Open Court Publishing Company, 2005), 5.

2. Larry Tye, *Superman: The High-Flying History of America's Most Enduring Hero* (New York: Random House, 2013), 11.

3. Masha Leon, "'Superman at 75' Unmasks the Superhero as a Jew from the Planet Krypton," *Forward*, March 24, 2016, http://forward.com/articles/171301/superman-at-75-unmasks-the-superhero-as-a-jew-from-.

4. Simcha Weinstein, *Up, Up, and Oy Vey: How Jewish History, Culture and Values Shaped the Comic Book Superhero* (Baltimore: Leviathan Press, 2006), 27; Tye, *Superman*, 65; Arie Kaplan, *From Krakow to Krypton: Jews and Comic Books* (Philadelphia: The Jewish Publication Society, 2008), 15. These interpretations were first postulated by Gary Engle in his essay, "What Makes Superman So Darned American?" in the collection *Superman at Fifty: The Persistence of a Legend* (Cleveland: Octavia Press, 1987), 86.

5. Danny Fingeroth, *Disguised as Clark Kent:*

Jews, Comics, and the Creation of the Superhero (New York: Continuum International Publishing Group Inc., 2007), 45; Jerry Siegel unpublished memoir, "Creation of a Superhero," 1979, Los Angeles. Larry Tye Papers, Box 3, Folder 1, Rare Books & Manuscripts Library Collections, Butler Library, Columbia University, New York, NY, 83. Before Superman, Siegel used "Jor-L" as the name of the protagonist of "Federal Men," a 1936 anthology feature he created with Shuster in *New Adventure Comics* #12 about an interplanetary police force in the year 3000.

6. Meir Bar-Ilan, "Angelic Names," *These Are the Names—Studies in Jewish Onomastics*, no. 1 (1997): 33–48 (translated by the author), https://faculty.biu.ac.il/~barilm/angel.html.

7. Grant Morrison, *Supergods: What Masked Vigilantes, Miraculous Mutants, and a Sun God from Smallville Can Teach Us About Being Human* (New York: Spiegel & Grau, 2011), 416; Jerry Siegel unpublished article/outline, "The Life and Times of Jerry Siegel," 1945. Larry Tye Papers, Box 3, Folder 1, Rare Books & Manuscripts Library Collections, Butler Library, Columbia University, New York, NY, 1.

8. Midrash Rabbah 21:5 (online, translated by the author), http://www.daat.ac.il/daat/tanach/raba2/21.htm.

9. Yiddish, observance, Sarah: Tye, *Superman*, 67, 77. Attended: Fingeroth, *Disguised as Clark Kent*, 45. Differ: Brad Ricca, *Super Boys: The Amazing Adventures of Jerry Siegel and Joe Shuster—the Creators of Superman* (New York: St. Martin's Griffin, 2014), 131–2. According to Tye, neither family was observant or attracted to organized Judaism, while Ricca claims they were both orthodox. It's likely a matter of these definitions changing meaning over time.

10. Elliot S. Maggin, *Superman: Last Son of Krypton* (New York: Warner Books, 1978), 13. First appearing in comics in Paul Kupperberg (w), Howard Chaykin (p), Murphy Anderson (i), Jerry Serpe (c), "This Planet is Doomed!" *World of Krypton* #2 (Aug. '79), DC Comics, 13.

11. James K. Brower, "The Hebrew Origins of Superman," *Biblical Archaeology Review* 5, No. 3 (1979): 23–6.

12. Joseph Jacobs and M. Seligsohn, "Solomon, Seal of," *The Jewish Encyclopedia*, V. 11 (1906): 448

(online), http://www.jewishencyclopedia.com/articles/13843-solomon-seal-of.

13. Eric J. Greenberg, "Superhero for the Ages," review of *King David*, by Kyle Baker, *The New York Jewish Week*, March 22, 2002, 3.

14. Daniel Best, "'Jerry and I did a comic book together...': Jerry Siegel & Joe Shuster Interviewed," *20th Century Danny Boy* (blog), August 3, 2012 (6:53 p.m.), http://ohdannyboy.blogspot.com/2012/08/jerry-and-i-did-comic-book-together.html.

15. Portmanteau: David Grossman, *Lion's Honey: The Myth of Samson*, trans. Stuart Schoffman (Edinburgh: Canongate Books, 2007), 35. Exposure: Jerry Siegel (w), Wayne Boring (p), Stan Kaye (i), "Superman's Return to Krypton!" *Superman* #141 (Nov. '60), National Comics Publications [DC Comics].

16. *Superman II*, directed by Richard Lester (1980; Burbank, CA: Warner Home Video, 2006), DVD; *Superman II: The Richard Donner Cut*, directed by Richard Donner (1980/2006; Burbank, CA: Warner Home Video, 2006), DVD.

17. Samsons: Jerry Siegel (w), Joe Shuster (p, i), Paul Lauretta (i), "Superman Joins the Circus," *Action Comics* #7 (Dec. '38), National Comics Publications [DC Comics], 1; Jerry Siegel (w), Joe Shuster (p, i), Paul Cassidy (p), "Superman vs. the Cab Protective League," *Action Comics* #13 (June '39), 1; Jerry Siegel (w), Joe Shuster (p, i), "Superman at the World's Fair," *New York World's Fair Comics* #1 (Apr. '39), 1; Jerry Siegel (w), Joe Shuster (p, i), "Clark Kent Gets a Job," *Superman* #1 (June '39), 2; Jerry Siegel (w), Joe Shuster (p), Paul Cassidy (i), "Superman and the Numbers Racket," *Action Comics* #16 (Sep. '39), 1. Samson: Jerry Siegel (w), Joe Shuster (p), Paul Cassidy (i), "Superman Champions Universal Peace!" *Superman* #2 (Sep. '39), National Comics Publications [DC Comics], 21. First noted in Weinstein, *Up, Up, and Oy Vey*, 27–8. Topples: Jerry Siegel (w), Paul Cassidy (p, i), Joe Shuster (cover), *Superman* #4 (Mar. '40). Acknowledged: Siegel, unpublished memoir, 82.

18. Otto Binder (w), Curt Swan (p), Ray Burnley (i), "The First Two Supermen!" *Adventure Comics* #257 (Feb. '59), National Comics Publications [DC Comics], "Super-men": cover, 1, 7, 13. Leo Dorfman (w), George Papp (p, i), "The Red-Headed Beatle of 1,000 B.C.!" *Superman's Pal, Jimmy Olsen* #79 (Sep. '64), National Periodical Publications [DC Comics], 8–9.

19. Erik Lundegaard, "Truth, justice and (fill in the blank)—Editorials & Commentary—International Herald Tribune," *New York Times* (online), June 30, 2006, http://www.nytimes.com/2006/06/30/opinion/30iht-ederik.2093103.html?_r=1&.

20. Tye, *Superman*, 66; Weinstein, *Up, Up, and Oy Vey*, 28.

Paradigmatic Parallels

1. Danny Fingeroth, *Disguised as Clark Kent: Jews, Comics, and the Creation of the Superhero* (New York: Continuum International Publishing Group Inc., 2007), 50.

2. Joseph Jacobs et al., "Moses," *The Jewish Encyclopedia*, V. 9 (1906): 44–57 (online), http://www.jewishencyclopedia.com/articles/11049-moses.

3. Jerry Siegel (w), Joe Shuster (p, i), "Clark Kent Gets a Job," *Superman* #1 (June '39), National Comics Publications [DC Comics], 1–2.

4. Michael Shapiro, *The Jewish 100: A Ranking of the Most Influential Jews of all Time* (New York: Citadel, 2000). First noted in Arie Kaplan, *From Krakow to Krypton: Jews and Comic Books* (Philadelphia: The Jewish Publication Society, 2008), 9.

5. Simcha Weinstein, *Up, Up, and Oy Vey: How Jewish History, Culture and Values Shaped the Comic Book Superhero* (Baltimore: Leviathan Press, 2006), 26–7; Fingeroth, *Disguised as Clark Kent*, 44–5; Kaplan, *From Krakow to Krypton*, 14; Larry Tye, *Superman: The High-Flying History of America's Most Enduring Hero* (New York: Random House, 2013), 65–6. Jewish Batman films producer and Professor of Practice at the Indiana University Media School, Michael Uslan, was perhaps the first to note the Moses/Superman parallel in the context of critical inquiry, as part of the first-ever accredited college course about comic books, in 1972. (Michael Uslan, *The Boy Who Loved Batman: A Memoir* (San Francisco: Chronicle Books, 2011), 102–3.

6. Jacobs et al., "Moses."

7. *Ibid.*

8. *Superman*, directed by Richard Donner (1978; Burbank, CA: Warner Home Video, 2006), DVD.

9. Mario Puzo et al., *Superman*. Final screenplay, 1976. Online: http://www.supermanhomepage.com/movies/superman_original.txt; Tom Mankiewicz, *Superman: The Movie*. Shooting script. Online; http://bigapricot.org/scripts/superman_I.txt.

10. *Man of Steel*, directed by Zack Snyder (2013; Burbank, CA: Warner Home Video, 2013), DVD.

11. Sigmund Freud, *Moses and Monotheism*, trans. Katherine Jones (Mansfield Centre, CT: Martino Publishing, 2010), 11–25.

12. Jacobs et al., "Moses."

13. "U.S.-Israel Relations: Roots of the U.S.-Israel Relationship," *Jewish Virtual Library* (online), http://www.jewishvirtuallibrary.org/jsource/U.S.-Israel/roots_of_U.S.-Israel.html.

14. Jonathan Mulinix, "Rejected Designs for the Great Seal of the United States," *mental_floss*, last modified June 13, 2012, http://mentalfloss.com/article/30912/rejected-designs-great-seal-united-states.

15. Washington: Bruce Feiler, "Moses vs. Jesus—Who Is America's Prophet?" *Fox News*, Oct. 07, 2009, http://www.foxnews.com/opinion/2009/10/07/bruce-feiler-moses-jesus-americas-prophet.html. Inspired: Bruce Feiler, "It's a Bird! It's a Plane! It's Moses!" *Daily Beast*, Oct. 5, 2009, https://www.thedailybeast.com/its-a-bird-its-a-plane-its-moses.

16. Jerry Siegel (w), Al Plastino (p, i), "How Luthor Met Superboy!" *Adventure Comics* #271 (Apr. '60), National Comics Publications [DC Comics].

17. Siegel & Shuster, *Action Comics* #1, 1.

Sent by His Father

1. Larry Tye, *Superman: The High-Flying History of America's Most Enduring Hero* (New York: Random House, 2013), xiii.

2. Grant Morrison, *Supergods: What Masked Vigilantes, Miraculous Mutants, and a Sun God from Smallville Can Teach Us About Being Human* (New York: Spiegel & Grau, 2011), 416.

3. Based: Thomas Andrae, Geoffrey Blum and Gary Coddington, "Of Superman and Kids with Dreams: A Rare Interview with the Creators of Superman: Jerry Siegel & Joe Shuster," *Nemo, the Classic Comics Library* #2, August 1983, 11. Wordplay: Jerry Siegel unpublished memoir, "Creation of a Superhero," 1979, Los Angeles. Larry Tye Papers, Box 3, Folder 1, Rare Books & Manuscripts Library Collections, Butler Library, Columbia University, New York, NY, 83.

4. Mary: Jerry Siegel (w), Joe Shuster (p, i), "Clark Kent Gets a Job," *Superman* #1 (June '39), National Comics Publications [DC Comics], 1. Ma Kent is first named Martha (spelled Marthe) in *Superboy* #12; William Woolfolk (w), John Sikela (p), Ed Dobrotka (i), "Superboy's Problem Parents!" (Jan. '51), 1. Pa Kent is first named Johnathan in *Adventure Comics* #149; Edmond Hamilton (w), John Sikela (p, i), "Fake Superboy!" (Feb '50), 2. Joseph: Roger Stern (w), Georges Jeanty (p), Dexter Vines (i), Tom McCraw (c), "Clark Kent," *Superman Secret Files and Origins* #1 (Jan. '98), DC Comics, 34. Jerome: *Lois and Clark: The New Adventures of Superman*. Season 2, episode 9, "Season's Greedings," first broadcast Dec. 4, 1994 by ABC. Directed by Randall Zisk and written by Dean Cain.

5. *Superman*, directed by Richard Donner (1978; Burbank, CA: Warner Home Video, 2006), DVD; Mark Waid (w), Leinil Francis Yu (p), Gerry Alanguilan (i), Dave McCaig (c), "A Legacy Reborn," *Superman: Birthright* #3 (Nov. '03), DC Comics, 5.

6. Tye, *Superman*, 70.

7. Mark Waid (w). Alex Ross (p, i, c), "Strange Visitor," *Kingdom Come* #1 (May '96), DC Comics, 1.

8. *Ibid.*, 20.

9. Sacrifices: Dan Jurgens (w, p), Brett Breeding (p, i), Glenn Whitmore (c), "Doomsday!" *Superman* Vol. 2 #75 (Jan. '93), DC Comics. Engineered: Dan Jurgens (w, p) Brett Breeding (i), Gregory Wright (c), "Hunter/Prey," *Superman/Doomsday: Hunter/Prey* #3 (June '94). Sepulcher: Jerry Ordway (w), Tom Grummett (p), Doug Hazlewood (i), Glenn Whitmore (c), "Grave Obsession," *Adventures of Superman* #499 (Feb. '93). Death: Roger Stern (w), Jackson Guice (p), Denis Rodier (i), Glenn Whitmore (c), "Who is the Hero True?," *Action Comics* #689 (July '93). Retrieves: Ordway et al., "Life After Death!" *Adventures of Superman* #500 (June '93).

10. *Superman*, Donner.

11. Dharmesh Chauhan, "The 2006 Tom Mankiewicz Interview," *Superman CINEMA Archives* (*Caped Wonder*), n.d., https://www.capedwonder.com/the-2006-tom-mankiewicz-interview.

12. *Superman II*, directed by Richard Lester (1980; Burbank, CA: Warner Home Video, 2006), DVD. Stamp would go on to play the Devil in 1984's *The Company of Wolves*.

13. *Ibid.*

14. Barry M. Freiman, "One-on-One Interview with Producer Ilya Salkind," *Superman Homepage*, n.d., https://www.supermanhomepage.com/movies/movies.php?topic=interview-salkind; *Superman II: The Richard Donner Cut*, directed by Richard Donner (1980/2006; Burbank, CA: Warner Home Video, 2006), DVD.

15. Eliot S. Maggin, *Miracle Monday* (New York: Warner Books, 1981).

16. Gustav Peebles, "God, Communism and the WB," in *The Man from Krypton: A Closer Look at Superman*, ed. Glenn Yeffeth (Dallas: Benbella Books, 2005), 77–8; *Smallville*. Season 1, episode 1, "Pilot," first broadcast October 16, 2001 by WB. Directed by David Nutter and written by Alfred Gough and Miles Millar.

17. *Smallville*. Season 9, episode 21, "Salvation," first broadcast May 14, 2010 by CW. Directed by Greg Beeman and written by Turi Meyer and Al Septien.

18. *Superman Returns*, directed by Brian Singer (2006; Burbank, CA: Warner Home Video, 2006), DVD.

19. Invited: Rich Goldstein, "Superman Is Jewish: The Hebrew Roots of America's Greatest Superhero," *Daily Beast*, August 16, 2014, http://www.thedailybeast.com/articles/2014/08/16/superman-is-jewish-the-hebrew-roots-of-america-s-greatest-superhero.html. Highlighting: Eric Marrapodi, "Superman: Flying to a church near you," *CNN Belief Blog* (blog), June 14th, 2013 (4:05 PM), http://religion.blogs.cnn.com/2013/06/14/superman-coming-to-a-church-near-you. Site: Pamela McClintock, "The Superman Gospel, According to Warner Bros.," *The Hollywood Reporter*, June 18, 2013, http://www.hollywoodreporter.com/news/superman-gospel-warner-bros-570668.

20. *Ibid.*

21. David Gibson, "Superman: Jesus figure or 'anti-Christ'?" *The Washington Post*, June 27, 2013, https://www.washingtonpost.com/national/on-faith/superman-jesus-figure-or-anti-christ/2013/06/27/3093f5be-df64-11e2-8cf3-35c1113cfcc5_story.html.

22. *Man of Steel*, directed by Zack Snyder (2013; Burbank, CA: Warner Home Video, 2013), DVD.

23. Zimmer: Jennifer Vineyard, "'Man of Steel': Not the familiar Superman (fan)fare," *CNN*, April 5, 2013, http://www.cnn.com/2013/04/05/showbiz/zimmer-man-of-steel. Snyder: Jennifer Vineyard, "'Man of Steel' director Zack Snyder on Superman's Christ-like parallels," *CNN*, June 16, 2013, http://www.cnn.com/2013/06/14/showbiz/zack-snyder-man-of-steel.

24. *Batman v Superman: Dawn of Justice*, directed by Zack Snyder (2016; Burbank, CA: Warner Home Video, 2016), DVD.

World's Finest

1. Grant Morrison, *Supergods: What Masked Vigilantes, Miraculous Mutants, and a Sun God from Smallville Can Teach Us About Being Human* (New York: Spiegel & Grau, 2011), xv.

2. Danny Fingeroth, *Disguised as Clark Kent: Jews, Comics, and the Creation of the Superhero* (New York: Continuum International Publishing Group Inc., 2007), 44.

3. *Ibid.*

4. Snyder: Jennifer Vineyard, "'Man of Steel' director Zack Snyder on Superman's Christ-like parallels," *CNN*, June 16, 2013, http://www.cnn.com/2013/06/14/showbiz/zack-snyder-man-of-steel. 22: Grant Morrison (w), Rags Morales (p), Rick Bryant (i), Brad Anderson (c), "Superman Versus the City of Tomorrow," *Action Comics* Vol. 2 #1 (Nov '11), DC Comics. Obituary: Dan Jurgens (w, p), Brett Breeding (p, i), Glenn Whitmore (c), "Doomsday!" *Superman* Vol. 2 #75 Special Edition (Jan. '93). Counsel: Jeph Loeb (w), Tim Sale (p, i) Bjarne Hansen (c), "Spring," *Superman for All Seasons* #1 (Sep. '98); Brian Azzarello (w), Jim Lee (p), Scott Williams, Richard Friend, Sandra Hope, Matt Banning, Eric Basaldua, Tim Townsend, Joe Weems (i), Alex Sinclair (c), "For Tomorrow" pts. 6–12, *Superman* Vol. 2 #209–215 (Nov. '04–May '05).

5. Snyder & Goyer: Ross McD, "Man of Steel: The top 20 reasons why Superman is Jesus," *Metro*, June 11, 2013, http://metro.co.uk/2013/06/11/man-of-steel-the-top-20-reasons-why-superman-is-jesus-3837465.

6. Geoffrey Dennis, "Why Superman is a Better Jewish Messiah than a Christian Messiah: A Mythic Movie Review of Man of Steel," *Jewish Myth, Magic, and Mysticism* (blog), July 07, 2013 (4:43 PM), http://ejmmm2007.blogspot.com/2013/07/why-superman-is-better-jewish-messiah.html.

7. Mark Waid, Mark Millar, Grant Morrison and Tom Peyer, "SUPERMAN 2000," *Deep Space Transmissions*, n.d., https://sites.google.com/site/deepspacetransmissions/Resources/superman-2000-proposal.

8. Fingeroth, *Disguised as Clark Kent*, 45.

9. Jerry Siegel (w), Joe Shuster (p, i), "Superman, Champion of the Oppressed," *Action Comics* #1 (June '38), National Comics Publications [DC Comics], 1; Jerry Siegel (w), Joe Shuster (p, i), "Clark Kent Gets a Job," *Superman* #1 (June '39), 7; Otto Binder (w), Jim Mooney (p, i), "Supergirl's Greatest Victory!" *Action Comics* #262 (Mar. '60), 5.

10. Masha Leon, "'Superman at 75' Unmasks the Superhero as a Jew from the Planet Krypton," *Forward*, March 24, 2016, http://forward.com/articles/171301/superman-at-75-unmasks-the-superhero-as-a-jew-from. Hillel's quote is from Ethics of the Fathers 1:14.

11. Astronaut: Dennis O'Neil (w), Curt Swan (p), Murphy Anderson (i), "Superman Breaks Loose," *Superman* #233 (Jan. '71), National Periodical Publications [DC Comics], 2. Librarian: John Byrne (w), Mike Mignola (p), Carlos Garzon (i), Petra Scotese

(c), "Family History," *World of Krypton* Vol. 2 #4 (Mar. '88), DC Comics, 10. Cadet: Scott Lobdell, Justin Jordan, Michael Alan Nelson (w), Ed Benes (p, i), Tanya Horie, Richard Horie (c), "Krypton Returns: Part 2" *Superboy* Vol. 6 #25 (Jan. '14), 5.

12. Jerry Siegel (w), Joe Shuster (p, i), "The Origin of Superboy," *More Fun Comics* #101 (Jan. '45), National Comics Publications [DC Comics], 2. In the 2003 graphic novel *The Sandman: Endless Nights* it's insinuated that his survival may not have been coincidental but rather orchestrated by Krypton's sun god Rao. But the book's quasi-allegorical nature, vague setting in DC continuity and obliqueness in the matter make it doubtful as canon, and regardless was likely erased when DC rebooted its continuity in 2011. (Neil Gaiman (w) Miguelanxo Prado (p, i, c) "The Heart of a Star," *The Sandman: Endless Nights* (Nov. '03), Vertigo [DC Comics], 76.)

Hitler, Hollywood and Houdini

1. 1776–1880: "Vital Statistics: Jewish Population in the United States, Nationally (1654—Present)" *Jewish Virtual Library* (online), http://www.jewishvirtuallibrary.org/jsource/U.S.-Israel/usjewpop1.html. 1924: Jonathan D. Sarna and Jonathan Golden, "The American Jewish Experience in the Twentieth Century: Antisemitism and Assimilation," *National Humanities Center*, Revised October 2000, http://nationalhumanitiescenter.org/tserve/twenty/tkeyinfo/jewishexp.htm.

2. Jacob A. Riis. *How the Other Half Lives: Studies Among the Tenements of New York* (New York: Scribner's Books, 1890), X. Jewtown: 2–5.

3. Jacob A. Riis, "The Jews of New York," *The Review of Reviews* 13 (1896): 58–62. Online: https://play.google.com/books/reader?id=ycEGAQAAIAAJ&printsec=frontcover&output=reader&hl=en&pg=GBS.PA58.

4. Larry Tye, *Superman: The High-Flying History of America's Most Enduring Hero* (New York: Random House, 2013), 75–6.

5. Henry Mietkiewicz, "Great Krypton! Superman was the Star's Ace Reporter," *Toronto Star* (Toronto, ON), April 26, 1992, A.10.

6. Irving Bernstein, "Americans in Depression and War," *United States Department of Labor*, accessed Dec. 23, 2015, https://www.dol.gov/oasam/programs/history/chapter5.htm.; James Gregory, "Hoovervilles and Homelessness," *The Great Depression in Washington State Project* (University of Washington), accessed Sep. 8, 2015, http://depts.washington.edu/depress/hooverville.shtml.

7. Eberhard Jäckel and Axel Kuhn, *Hitler: Sämtliche Aufzeichnungen 1905–1294* (Stuttgart: Deutsche Verlags-Anstalt, 1980), 918. Translation from Art Spiegelman's *Maus: My Father Bleeds History* (New York: Pantheon, 1986), 4. In German: "Der Jude ist wohl Rasse, aber nicht Mensch."

8. Malcolm Gladwell, "Getting In: The Social Logic of Ivy League Admissions," *New Yorker*, October 10, 2005, http://www.newyorker.com/

magazine/2005/10/10/getting-in; Geoffrey Kaba-service, "The Birth of a New Institution: How two Yale presidents and their admissions directors tore up the 'old blueprint' to create a modern Yale," *Yale Alumni Magazine*, December 1999, http://archives.yalealumnimagazine.com/issues/99_12/admissions.html.

9. Prominent, Modern Moses: David Cesarani, "FDR and the Jews by Richard Breitman and Allan J Lichtman: This world, the next world and the New Deal," *New Statesman*, June 6, 2013, http://www.newstatesman.com/culture/2013/06/fdr-and-jews-richard-breitman-and-allan-j-lichtman-world-next-world-and-new-deal. Voted: "U.S. Presidential Elections: Jewish Voting Record (1916–Present)," *Jewish Virtual Library* (online), http://www.jewishvirtuallibrary.org/jsource/U.S.-Israel/jewvote.html. Rosenfeld: Matt Lebovic, "How Hitler's 'fake news' assault on America came perilously close to succeeding," *Times of Israel*, Jan. 3, 2019, https://www.timesofisrael.com/how-hitlers-fake-news-assault-on-america-came-perilously-close-to-succeeding.

10. Sarna and Golden, "The American Jewish Experience"; Tara John, "The Battle to Publish Adolf Hitler's *Mein Kampf* in the U.S.," *Time*, Dec. 2, 2015, http://time.com/4132451/adolf-hitler-mein-kampf.

11. Sarna and Golden, "The American Jewish Experience."

12. Frederic Cople Jaher, *The Jews and the Nation: Revolution, Emancipation, State Formation, and the Liberal Paradigm in America and France* (Princeton, NJ: Princeton University Press, 2009), 230; Richard Bernstein, "BOOKS OF THE TIMES; Examining Father Coughlin, Hate Radio Pioneer," *New York Times*, July 10, 1996, http://www.nytimes.com/1996/07/10/books/books-of-the-times-examining-father-coughlin-hate-radio-pioneer.html. First noted in Danny Fingeroth, *Disguised as Clark Kent: Jews, Comics, and the Creation of the Superhero* (New York: Continuum International Publishing Group Inc., 2007), 34, 40.

13. "Des Moines Speech," *PBS*, accessed Jan. 12, 2015, http://www.pbs.org/wgbh/amex/lindbergh/filmmore/reference/primary/desmoinesspeech.html. First noted/mentioned in Fingeroth, *Disguised as Clark Kent*, 40.

14. "Antisemitism in the United States: Henry Ford Invents a Jewish Conspiracy" *Jewish Virtual Library* (online), http://www.jewishvirtuallibrary.org/jsource/Antisemitism/ford1.html; "Antisemitism in the U.S.: "The International Jew" Henry Ford, Sr. (1920)," *Jewish Virtual Library* (online), http://www.jewishvirtuallibrary.org/jsource/Antisemitism/ford.html. First noted in Fingeroth, *Disguised as Clark Kent*, 34, 140.

15. "Henry Ford receiving the Grand Cross of the German Eagle from Nazi officials, 1938," *Rare Historical Photos*, accessed March 3, 2015, http://rarehistoricalphotos.com/henry-ford-receiving-grand-cross-german-eagle-nazi-officials-1938.

16. Frederic Cople Jaher, *The Jews and the Nation: Revolution, Emancipation, State Formation, and the Liberal Paradigm in America and France* (Princeton, NJ: Princeton University Press, 2009), 229–230.

17. "The Immigration Act of 1924 (The Johnson-Reed Act)," *United States Department of State, Office of the Historian*, accessed Jan. 12, 2015, https://history.state.gov/milestones/1921-1936/immigration-act.

18. Clive Irving, "Joe Kennedy's Answer to the 'Jewish Question': Ship Them to Africa," *Daily Beast*, Feb. 1, 2015, http://www.thedailybeast.com/articles/2015/02/01/joe-kennedy-s-answer-to-the-jewish-question-ship-them-to-africa.html.

19. "America and the Holocaust: Breckinridge Long (1881–1958)," *PBS American Experience*, accessed March 3, 2016, http://www.pbs.org/wgbh/amex/holocaust/peopleevents/pandeAMEX90.html.

20. "The Nazi Rally in Madison Square Garden," *American Heroes Channel*, Feb 24, 2015, https://www.youtube.com/watch?v=0gU9op16rjQ.

21. Jerry Siegel unpublished memoir, "Creation of a Superhero," 1979, Los Angeles. Larry Tye Papers, Box 3, Folder 1, Rare Books & Manuscripts Library Collections, Butler Library, Columbia University, New York, NY, 93.

22. Thomas Andrae, Geoffrey Blum and Gary Coddington, "Of Superman and Kids with Dreams: A Rare Interview with the Creators of Superman: Jerry Siegel & Joe Shuster," *Nemo, the Classic Comics Library* #2, August 1983, 9.

23. Andrae et al., *Nemo*, 11.

24. "1938: 'Peace for our time'—Chamberlain," *BBC News on This Day*, Sep. 30, 1938, http://news.bbc.co.uk/onthisday/hi/dates/stories/september/30/newsid_3115000/3115476.stm.

25. "Neville Chamberlain "Peace for Our Time," September 30, 1938," *Britannia*, http://www.britannia.com/history/docs/peacetime.html; "Kristallnacht: A Nationwide Pogrom," *United States Holocaust Memorial Museum*, accessed March 3, 2016, https://www.ushmm.org/wlc/en/article.php?ModuleId=10005201.

26. "Hitler's 'prophecy' speech to the Reichstag, 30 January 1939," *BBC History*, http://www.bbc.co.uk/history/worldwars/genocide/hitler_audio.shtml.

27. "The Farhud," *United States Holocaust Memorial Museum*, accessed March 3, 2016, https://www.ushmm.org/wlc/en/article.php?ModuleId=10007277.

28. Dr. Rafael Medoff, "The American Papers that Praised Hitler," *Daily Beast*, Dec. 20, 2015, http://www.thedailybeast.com/articles/2015/12/20/when-america-s-media-cozied-up-to-hitler.html?source=TDB&via=FB_Page.

29. *Ibid.*; Mark Bulik, "Times Insider: 1922: Hitler in Bavaria," *New York Times*, Feb. 10, 2015, http://www.nytimes.com/times-insider/2015/02/10/1922-hitler-in-bavaria/; "Adolf Hitler: Man of the Year, 1938," *Time*, Jan. 2, 1939 (online), http://content.time.com/time/magazine/article/0,9171,760539,00.html.

30. *Times*: "1,000,000 JEWS SLAIN BY NAZIS,

REPORT SAYS: 'Slaughterhouse' of Europe Under Hitler Described at London," *New York Times*, June 30, 1942, pg. 7 (online), https://www.nytimes.com/1942/06/30/archives/1000000-jews-slain-by-nazis-report-says-slaughterhouse-of-enrope.html. Headlines: "Americans and the Holocaust," *United States Holocaust Memorial Museum*, accessed January 27, 2016, https://exhibitions.ushmm.org/americans-and-the-holocaust/main.

31. Medoff, "The American Papers that Praised Hitler."

32. Danny Fingeroth, *Disguised as Clark Kent: Jews, Comics, and the Creation of the Superhero* (New York: Continuum International Publishing Group Inc., 2007), 19; "Emma Lazarus," National Park Service: Statue of Liberty, https://www.nps.gov/stli/learn/historyculture/emma-lazarus.htm.

33. Lester D. Friedman, *The Jewish Image in American Film* (New York: Citadel Press, 1987), 5.

34. *Ibid.*, 11.

35. Kennedy: Mordecai Richler, "The Man Who Was Hollywood," *New York Times*, March 26, 1989, Section 7; Page 1 (online), https://archive.nytimes.com/www.nytimes.com/books/98/10/18/nnp/berg-goldwyn.html?mcubz=1. Cut: David Denby, "Hitler in Hollywood," *New Yorker*, September 16, 2013, http://www.newyorker.com/magazine/2013/09/16/hitler-in-hollywood. Zola first noted in Simcha Weinstein, *Up, Up, and Oy Vey: How Jewish History, Culture and Values Shaped the Comic Book Superhero* (Baltimore: Leviathan Press, 2006), 53.

36. Joseph Berger, "Jewish Boxers and Wrestlers, and Yiddish Fighting words, at Yivo Institute Exhibition," *New York Times*, April 30, 2015, http://www.nytimes.com/2015/05/01/nyregion/jewish-boxers-and-wrestlers-and-yiddish-fighting-words-at-yivo-institute-exhibition.html?_r=1&referrer.

37. Geoffrey Gray, "BOXING; Jewish Boxers Are Looking to Make a Comeback," *New York Times*, Dec. 27, 2003, https://www.nytimes.com/2003/12/27/sports/boxing-jewish-boxers-are-looking-to-make-a-comeback.html.

38. Berger, "Jewish Boxers and Wrestlers."

39. Allen Bodner, *When Boxing Was a Jewish Sport* (Albany: Excelsior Editions), 2–4.

40. "Yiddish Fight Club." Yivo Institute of Jewish Research at the Center for Jewish History. 15 West 16th Street, New York, NY 10011. Apr. 30–Sep. 30, 2015.

41. *Ibid.*

42. "The Life of Harry Houdini," *The Great Harry Houdini*, accessed Oct. 24, 2015, http://www.thegreatharryhoudini.com.

43. Michael Chabon, *The Amazing Adventures of Kavalier & Clay* (New York: Random House, 2000), 3.

44. "The Life of Harry Houdini."

45. Mel Gordon, "Step Right Up & Meet the World's Mightiest Human—A Jewish Strongman from Poland Who Some Say Inspired the Creation of Superman!!!" *Reform Judaism Magazine*, summer 2011, http://rjmag.org/Articles/index.cfm?id=2822; Thomas Andrae, Mel Gordon, *Siegel and Shuster's*

Funnyman: The First Jewish Superhero, from the Creators of Superman (Los Angeles: Feral House, 2010), 42–7.

46. *Ibid.*

Famous Funnies and Other Firsts

1. Dr. Seymour J. Perlin, "Historical Survey," *Remembrance of Synagogues Past: The Lost Civilization of the Jewish South Bronx*, 2007, http://www.bronxsynagogues.org/ic/bronxsyn/survey.html#I.

2. Arie Kaplan, *From Krakow to Krypton: Jews and Comic Books* (Philadelphia: The Jewish Publication Society, 2008), 28.

3. Art Spiegelman, "Forms Stretched To Their Limits: What Kind of Person Could Have Dreamed Up Plastic Man?," *New Yorker*, April 19, 1999, http://www.newyorker.com/magazine/1999/04/19/forms-stretched-to-their-limits-2.

4. Irish-American: Danny Fingeroth, *Disguised as Clark Kent: Jews, Comics, and the Creation of the Superhero* (New York: Continuum International Publishing Group Inc., 2007), 150. Influenced: Paul Tumey, "Rube Goldberg Butts In," *The Comics Journal*, Feb. 24, 2014, http://www.tcj.com/rube-goldberg-butts-in/.

5. Feiffer: Sage Stossel, "A Conversation With Jules Feiffer," *Atlantic*, March 19, 2010, http://www.theatlantic.com/entertainment/archive/2010/03/a-conversation-with-jules-feiffer/37775. Newspapers: Stan Taylor, "Looking For the Awesome—3. Escape to New York," *The Kirby Effect: The Journal of the Jack Kirby Museum & Research Center*, Dec. 12, 2015, http://kirbymuseum.org/blogs/effect/2015/12.

6. Medium: Fingeroth, *Disguised as Clark Kent*, 28. Literary: Michael Weiss, "Secret Identities: Jewish Comic Book Creators," *Negative Space*, last modified June 13, 1995, https://owl.english.purdue.edu/owl/resource/717/05.

7. Kaplan, *From Krakow to Krypton*, 48, 55.

8. DC: Larry Tye, *Superman: The High-Flying History of America's Most Enduring Hero* (New York: Random House, 2013), 79. Marvel: Fred Van Lente (w), Ryan Dunlavey (p, i), *Comic Book History of Comics* (June '12), IDW Publishing, 46; Fingeroth, *Disguised as Clark Kent*, 57.

9. "Holy $#!%: Where Did The Symbolic Swear Come From?" *Dictionary.com*, http://www.dictionary.com/e/what-the.

10. John Adcock, "Charles W. Saalburg, The Man Who Washed the Kid," *Yesterday's Papers* (blog), Aug. 1, 2016 (2:06 p.m.), http://john-adcock.blogspot.com/2016/08/charles-w-saalburg-man-who-washed-kid.html?m=1; Van Lente & Dunlavey, *Comic Book History of Comics*, 7–8, 11.

11. Jonathan Jones, "Comic Strips and Cubism," *The Guardian* (April 12, 2002): http://www.theguardian.com/books/2002/apr/13/books.guardianreview1.

12. Jules Feiffer, "Jules Feiffer's Comic Relief," *Civilization: the Magazine of the Library of Congress*, June/July, 1998, 45.

13. Jamie Coville, "The Platinum Age 1897–1938," *TheComicsBooks.com—The History of Comic Books*, last modified Feb. 16, 2001, http://www.thecomicbooks.com/old/Platinum.html.

14. Coville, *The History of Comic Books*.

15. Taylor, *The Kirby Effect*.

16. *Famous Funnies*: Coville, *The History of Comic Books*. Some have delineated a slightly different timeline for the various *Funnies* publications, like Kaplan, *From Krakow to Krypton*, 2–3. Rejected: Jerry Siegel unpublished memoir, "Creation of a Superhero," 1979, Los Angeles. Larry Tye Papers, Box 3, Folder 1, Rare Books & Manuscripts Library Collections, Butler Library, Columbia University, New York, NY, 40.

17. 250: "Sweeney Todd, the Demon Barber of Fleet Street in Concert," *PBS*, accessed April 18, 2015, http://www.pbs.org/kqed/demonbarber/penny/index.html. 600k: Mike Ashley, "The Golden Age of Pulp Fiction," *The Pulp Magazines Project*, accessed June 11, 2015, http://www.pulpmags.org/history_page.html.

18. *Ibid.*

19. *Ibid.*

20. Van Lente & Dunlavey, *Comic Book History of Comics*, 17.

21. Jean-Marc Lofficier, "The Wold Newton Universe: Nyctalope," *Cool French Comics*, accessed June 10, 2015, http://www.coolfrenchcomics.com/nyctalope.htm.

22. Waned: Eric P. Nash, *Manga Kamishibai: The Art of Japanese Paper Theater* (New York: Abrams Comicarts, 2009), 13–55, 257–283. Heyday: Oliver Ho, "Manga Kamishibai: The Art of Japanese Paper Theater by Eric P. Nash," *Pop Matters*, Oct. 20, 2009, http://www.popmatters.com/review/112894-manga-kamishibai-the-art-of-japanese-paper-theater-by-eric-p.-nash. Most popular: Zack Davisson, "The First Superhero—The Golden Bat," *Comics Bulletin*, Dec. 19, 2010, http://comicsbulletin.com/first-superhero-golden-bat.

23. Nash, *Manga Kamishibai*, 101–2, 124–147.

24. *Ibid.*, 27–39.

25. Thomas Andrae, Geoffrey Blum and Gary Coddington, "Of Superman and Kids with Dreams: A Rare Interview with the Creators of Superman: Jerry Siegel & Joe Shuster," *Nemo, the Classic Comics Library* #2, August 1983, 10.

26. Siegel unpublished memoir, 28.

27. Credited: Kaplan, *From Krakow to Krypton*, 13, 18; Elaine Woo, "Lee Falk; Created 'The Phantom,' 'Mandrake the Magician' Comics," *Los Angeles Times*, March 16, 1999, http://articles.latimes.com/1999/mar/16/news/mn-17848. Predating: Andrae et al., *Nemo*, 11.

28. *Ibid.*, 10, 15.

29. Van Lente & Dunlavey, *Comic Book History of Comics*, 19; Tye, *Superman*, 10, 33. Gladiator's similarities to Superman also noted in Fingeroth, *Disguised as Clark Kent*, 41 and Van Lente & Dunlavey, *Comic Book History of Comics*, 19.

30. Denied: Hardwicke Benthow, "Superman: The Genesis of a Legend," *The Thoughts and Ramblings of Hardwicke Benthow* (blog), Dec. 28, 2014, https://thoughtsandramblingsofhardwickebenthow.wordpress.com/superman-the-genesis-of-a-legend/. Historians: Gregory Feeley, "When World-views Collide: Philip Wylie in the Twenty-first Century," *Science Fiction Studies* 32, no. 95 (2005), accessed Jan. 2, 2016, http://www.depauw.edu/sfs/review_essays/feeley95.htm. Acknowledge: Siegel unpublished memoir, 83.

31. Evolution: Jerry Siegel (w), Joe Shuster (p, i), "Clark Kent Gets a Job," *Superman* #1 (June '39), National Comics Publications [DC Comics], 7. Possibly also Siegel's 1935 draft, in which Superman is an evolved human from the far future. "a superman": Lester Dent, "Quest of the Spider," *Doc Savage Magazine* #3 (New York: Bantam Books edition, May 1972), 3. Originally published May 1933. "A superman" was also used in an ad promoting the issue a month prior.

32. Spotlighted: Fingeroth, *Disguised as Clark Kent*, 41; Tye, *Superman*, 32–33. Named: Andrae et al., *Nemo*, 15. Fortress: William Woolfolk (w), Al Plastino (p, i), "The Case of the Second Superman," *Superman* #58 (May '49), National Comics Publications [DC Comics]. An earlier version, referred to as "the secret citadel" and located on the outskirts of Metropolis, appeared in *Superman* #17 (July '42). The full concept of the Fortress, including all its similarities to Doc Savage's, appeared in *Action Comics* #241 (June '58).

33. Jerry Siegel, "Lois Lane=Torchy Blane," *Time*, May 30, 1988, 6. Joanne also had aspirations of becoming a reporter herself: Shel Dorf interview, *Siegel and Shuster: Dateline 1930's* #1 (Nov. '84), Eclipse Comics, inside back cover. Amster: Tye, *Superman*, 106.

34. Jerry Siegel, "Happy 45th Anniversary, Superman!" *Action Comics* #544 (June '83), DC Comics, 30–2.

35. Fan mail: Siegel unpublished memoir, 13–14. Teacher: Andrae et al., *Nemo*, 7–8. Shuster was also involved with the student newspaper in his previous school, where ironically he created a humor strip named *Jerry the Journalist*: Shel Dorf, *Siegel and Shuster: Dateline*, 24.

36. *Ibid.*, 9.

37. Jerry Siegel and Joe Shuster, "The Reign of the Superman," originally in *Science Fiction: The Advance Guard of Future Civilization* #3, Jan. 1933, reprinted in Andrae, "Of Superman and Kids," 20–28.

38. Siegel unpublished memoir, 25.

39. In his memoir, Siegel remembers "The Superman" as a comic strip, not book, about twelve panels a page, which he submitted to the Bell Syndicate: *ibid.*, 31. However, in an interview and an essay, both from 1983, he states that it was conceived strictly as a comic book. Surviving cover art, including a 10¢ price tag, supports the latter: Andrae et al., *Nemo*, 10; Siegel, "Happy 45th Anniversary, Superman!" 30–2. Fantastic strength: Siegel unpublished memoir, 28. Consolidated: *ibid.*, 28–9.

40. *Ibid.*, 38, 53, 55; Deborah Friedell, "Krypto-

nomics," *New Yorker*, June 24, 2013, http://www.newyorker.com/magazine/2013/06/24/kryptonomics.

41. 1932: John Kabler, "Up, Up, and Awa-a-y! The Rise of Superman, Inc.," *Saturday Evening Post*, June 21, 1941, 70, http://www.saturdayeveningpost.com/wp-content/uploads/satevepost/rise-of-superman.pdf. Late 1934: Andrae, "Of Superman and Kids," 11. November: Siegel unpublished memoir, 40–3. Recounts: Siegel, "Happy 45th Anniversary, Superman!" 30–2.

42. Siegel unpublished memoir, 42–4.

43. Shuster: Andrae et al., *Nemo*, 11. Suggested, added: *Arena*. "Superman: The Comic Strip Hero," first broadcast April 18, 1981 by BBC Four. Directed by Anthony Wall. Online at https://www.youtube.com/watch?v=eTUrFYU2e_I.

44. Siegel unpublished memoir, 28.

45. Wasn't interested: R.C. Harvey, "Who Discovered Superman," *The Comics Journal*, Jan. 6, 2014, http://www.tcj.com/who-discovered-superman. Recognized: Tye, *Superman*, 28.

46. Siegel unpublished memoir, 51.

47. Siegel unpublished memoir, 58–9.

48. Kabler, "Up, Up, and Awa-a-y!" 73.

49. Siegel, "Happy 45th Anniversary, Superman!" 30–2.

50. Kaplan, *From Krakow to Krypton*, 7.

51. Wallpaper: Siegel, "Happy 45th Anniversary, Superman!" 30–32; Jerry Siegel, "Superman: The Genesis of a Legend," *The Thoughts and Ramblings of Hardwicke Benthow* (blog), n.d., https://thoughtsandramblingsofhardwickebenthow.wordpress.com/the-story-behind-superman-1. Bread board: Shel Dorf, interview with Siegel and Shuster, *Siegel and Shuster: Dateline 1930's* #1 (Nov. 1984), Eclipse Comics, 17. Layers: Andrae, "Of Superman and Kids," 15.

52. *Ibid.*, 11.

53. $174: Siegel unpublished memoir, 58. Syndicates: "Comic Book Superheroes Unmasked," first broadcast June 23, 2003 by The History Channel. Directed by Stephen Kroopnick and written by James Grant Goldin. Online at https://www.youtube.com/watch?v=Ygx_rUJ3XaI.

54. Siegel unpublished memoir, 59–60.

55. Bootlegger: Jay Schwartz, "Cover Story: Jews and the invention of the American comic book," *JWeekly*, Oct. 21, 2005, http://www.jweekly.com/article/full/27413/cover-story-jews-and-the-invention-of-the-american-comic-book/. Costello: Tye, *Superman*, 56. Mags: *Ibid.*, 24–25. Liebowitz: *Ibid.*, 53. Handled: Coville, "The Platinum Age."

56. Harvey, "Who Discovered Superman."

57. Tye, *Superman*, 28.

58. Mayer: Harvey, "Who Discovered Superman." Came around: Arie Kaplan, "How the Jews Created the Comic Book Industry—Part I: The Golden Age (1933–1955)," *Reform Judaism Magazine* 32, no. 1 (Fall 2003), http://reformjudaismmag.net/03fall/comics.shtml. Siegel: Siegel, "Happy 45th Anniversary, Superman!" 30–2.

59. Fingeroth, *Disguised as Clark Kent*, 41; Harvey, "Who Discovered Superman."

60. Mark Seifert, "For Sale at Auction: The Check That Bought Superman," *Bleeding Cool*, March 23, 2012, http://www.bleedingcool.com/2012/03/23/for-sale-at-auction-the-check-that-bought-superman.

61. Liebowitz: Eric P. Nash "Jack Liebowitz, Comics Publisher, Dies at 100," *New York Times*, December 13, 2000, http://www.nytimes.com/2000/12/13/nyregion/jack-liebowitz-comics-publisher-dies-at-100.html. Mayer: Harvey, "Who Discovered Superman."

62. Seifert, "The Check That Bought Superman."

63. "Super Hero Movie Index," https://www.the-numbers.com/movies/creative-type/Super-Hero#tab=year (list incomplete); "Box Office History for Marvel Cinematic Universe Movies," https://www.the-numbers.com/movies/franchise/Marvel-Cinematic-Universe#tab=summary; "Box Office History for DC Extended Universe Movies," https://www.the-numbers.com/movies/franchise/DC-Extended-Universe#tab=summary, *The Numbers*, accessed Oct. 22, 2019.

64. Counsel: Tye, *Superman*, 313. Moore: Joseph Hughes, "Alan Moore on Superman Creators Siegel and Shuster's Plight in 'Occupy Comics' #2 [Essay Excerpt]," *Comics Alliance*, June 14, 2013, http://comicsalliance.com/alan-moore-essay-jerry-siegel-joe-shuster-occupy-comics-creators-rights-superman.

65. Reflect: Jerry Siegel unpublished article/outline, "The Life and Times of Jerry Siegel," 1945. Larry Tye Papers, Box 3, Folder 1, Rare Books & Manuscripts Library Collections, Butler Library, Columbia University, New York, NY, 1. Lamants: Siegel unpublished memoir, 86. Shuster: Andrae et al., *Nemo*, 15.

66. Siegel unpublished memoir, 61–2.

67. Seifert, "The Check That Bought Superman."

68. Tye, *Superman*, 36, 120.

69. Seifert, "The Check That Bought Superman."

70. Siegel unpublished memoir, 75–7, 78, 85–6; Tye, *Superman*, 117–120; Daniel Best, "'A Curse on the Superman Movie!'—A Look Back at Jerry Siegel's 1975 Press Release," *20th Century Danny Boy* (blog), July 8, 2012 (10:35 a.m.), http://ohdannyboy.blogspot.com/2012/07/curse-on-superman-movie-look-back-at.html.

The Big Bang

1. Richard Corliss, "80 Days That Changed the World: Birth of the Superhero," *Time*, March 31, 2003, http://content.time.com/time/specials/packages/article/0,28804,1977881_1977883_1978108,00.html. The article was corrected, originally listing April 18 as the publication date, which is the most commonly cited. Both dates are likely wrong, however. It was in all likelihood later in April or, most probably, May 3, 1938, as detailed in: Brian Cronin, "Comic Legends: Was Action Comics #1 Really Released on April 18th?" *CBR.com*, Apr 23, 2018, https://www.

cbr.com/superman-action-comics-actual-release-date.

2. Clamoring: John Kabler, "Up, Up, and Awa-a-y! The Rise of Superman, Inc.," *Saturday Evening Post*, June 21, 1941, 73, http://www.saturdayeveningpost.com/wp-content/uploads/satevepost/rise-of-superman.pdf. Sales: Eric P. Nash "Jack Liebowitz, Comics Publisher, Dies at 100," *New York Times*, December 13, 2000, http://www.nytimes.com/2000/12/13/nyregion/jack-liebowitz-comics-publisher-dies-at-100.html.

3. Jerry Siegel (w), Joe Shuster (p, i), "Superman, Champion of the Oppressed," *Action Comics #1* (June '38), National Comics Publications [DC Comics], 2.

4. Jerry Siegel, "The Story Behind Superman #1," *The Thoughts and Ramblings of Hardwicke Benthow* (blog), n.d., https://thoughtsandramblingsofhardwickebenthow.wordpress.com/the-story-behind-superman-1.

5. Eric J. Greenberg, "Superman: A Jewish Hero," *Jerusalem Post*, May 1, 1996, 7.

6. Siegel & Shuster, *Action Comics #1*, 1.

7. Kirby: Stan Taylor, "Looking For the Awesome—3. Escape to New York," *The Kirby Effect: The Journal of the Jack Kirby Museum & Research Center*, Dec. 12, 2015, http://kirbymuseum.org/blogs/effect/2015/12. Auction: Michael Cavna, "Rare Superman book draws record $3.2 million top bid: The long, 'cool' journey of a record-setting comic [UPDATED]," August 22, 2014, https://www.washingtonpost.com/news/comic-riffs/wp/2014/08/22/rare-superman-book-draws-record-2-2-million-bid-the-long-journey-of-a-record-setting-comic.

8. Jules Feiffer and Paul Levitz, "Will Eisner's "The Spirit" 75th Anniversary Celebration," panel discussion, School of Visual Arts, New York, November 11, 2015 (online), https://www.youtube.com/watch?v=d8Zg7UUurVk&feature=youtu.be&app=desktop.

9. Shot: Siegel & Shuster, *Action Comics #1*, 3–4. Lois: Jerry Siegel (w), Jack Burnley (p, i), "Superman: The Preston Gambling Racket," *Action Comics #32* (Jan. '41), National Comics Publications [DC Comics], 8–9.

10. Outsold: Fred Van Lente (w), Ryan Dunlavey (p, i), *Comic Book History of Comics* (June '12), IDW Publishing, 32. McClure: Kabler, "Up, Up, and Awa-a-y!" 73.

11. 1.3 million: Tesa Pribitkin, "Superman—The New Deal Symbol of the American Way," *Superman Homepage*, n.d., http://www.supermanhomepage.com/comics/comics.php?topic=articles/new-deal-symbol. *Time*: "The Press: Superman," *Time*, September 11, 1939 (online), http://content.time.com/time/magazine/article/0,9171,711787,00.html. Superman Day: Kabler, "Up, Up, and Awa-a-y!" 15.

12. Larry Tye, *Superman: The High-Flying History of America's Most Enduring Hero* (New York: Random House, 2013), 39.

13. Jerry Siegel unpublished memoir, "Creation of a Superhero," 1979, Los Angeles. Larry Tye

Papers, Box 3, Folder 1, Rare Books & Manuscripts Library Collections, Butler Library, Columbia University, New York, NY, 33, 96.

14. "Nothing less": Siegel & Shuster, *Action Comics #1*, 1. Harmlessly: Jerry Siegel (w), Paul Cassidy (p), "The Phony Pacifists," *Superman #9* (Mar. '41), National Comics Publications [DC Comics], 5.

15. Michael Chabon, "Secret Skin: An Essay in Unitard Theory," *New Yorker*, March 10, 2008, http://www.newyorker.com/magazine/2008/03/10/secret-skin.

16. Umberto Eco, "The Myth of Superman," trans. Natalie Chilton for *Diacritics* 2, no. 1 (Spring 1972): 14–22. Originally published as "Il mito di Superman e la dissolutione del tempo" in *Demitizzazione e imagine*, ed. E. Castelli (Padua: Cedam, 1962). Though not in semiotic terms, Superman's status as the superhero exemplar is also discussed in Danny Fingeroth's *Disguised as Clark Kent: Jews, Comics, and the Creation of the Superhero* (New York: Continuum International Publishing Group Inc., 2007), 50.

17. Benjamin Svetkey, "*The Dark Knight's* Christopher Nolan," *Entertainment Weekly*, July 25, 2008, http://www.ew.com/article/2008/07/25/dark-knights-christopher-nolan.

18. Carmen Nigro, "So, Why Do We Call It Gotham, Anyway?," *New York Public Library* (blog), January 25, 2011, https://www.nypl.org/blog/2011/01/25/so-why-do-we-call-it-gotham-anyway. Batman's city was originally identified as New York in *Detective Comics #33* (Nov. '39), 3.

19. David Hajdu, *The Ten-Cent Plague: The Great Comic-Book Scare and How It Changed America* (New York: Picador, 2008), 50.

20. Fingeroth, *Disguised as Clark Kent*, 64. Fingeroth also describes the Spirit's backdrops as suggestive of Jewish neighborhoods, though he sees stronger correlation to the Jewish Bronx, 62.

21. Fred Van Lente (w), Ryan Dunlavey (p, i), *Comic Book History of Comics* (June '12), IDW Publishing, 37.

22. Jules Feiffer, *The Great Comic Book Heroes* (New York: Bonanza Books, 1965), 50.

23. Robinson: Hajdu, *The Ten-Cent Plague*, 34. Lee: Fingeroth, *Disguised as Clark Kent*, 10.

24. Art Spiegelman, "Forms Stretched To Their Limits: What Kind of Person Could Have Dreamed Up Plastic Man?," *New Yorker*, April 19, 1999, http://www.newyorker.com/magazine/1999/04/19/forms-stretched-to-their-limits-2.

25. Hajdu, *The Ten-Cent Plague*, 34. The figure is most likely inflated: in 1941 *The Post* estimated 108 titles (Kabler 70), and Kaplan (4) and Tye (108) both report 150.

26. Outsold: Arie Kaplan, *From Krakow to Krypton: Jews and Comic Books* (Philadelphia: The Jewish Publication Society, 2008), 4. Crossley: Tye, *Superman*, 38, 42. Adults: Kabler, "Up, Up, and Awa-a-y!" 74.

27. Balloon: Tye, *Superman*, 83, 90. Exhibit: Kurt Andersen, "American Icons: Superman," *Studio 360*, New York, PRI and WNYC, July 6, 2006 (online),

http://www.wnyc.org/story/295935-american-icons-superman. Grossing, 25 million, $1.5 million: Kabler, "Up, Up, and Awa-a-y!" 14–5, 73.

28. *Ibid.*, 76.

29. *Ibid.*, 14–5.

30. *Ibid.*, 14, 76.

31. *Ibid.*, 74.

32. *Ibid.*, 76; Siegel unpublished memoir, 91.

33. Tye, *Superman*, 95. The first installment, "Superman" (aka "The Mad Scientist"), was nominated for the 1942 Academy Award for Short Subject (Cartoon).

34. Van Lente & Dunlavey, *Comic Book History of Comics*, 21; Brian Cronin, "Comic Book Legends Revealed #373," *CBR.com*, http://www.cbr.com/comic-book-legends-revealed-373.

35. Kabler, "Up, Up, and Awa-a-y!" 15. The article erroneously calls it the Superman Club of America.

36. Article: "The Press: Superman's Dilemma," *Time*, April 13, 1942 (online), http://content.time.com/time/magazine/article/0,9171,766523,00.html. Income: Kabler, "Up, Up, and Awa-a-y!" 76. 25 million: Arie Kaplan, "How the Jews Created the Comic Book Industry—Part I: The Golden Age (1933–1955)," *Reform Judaism Magazine* 32, no. 1 (Fall 2003), http://reformjudaismmag.net/03fall/comics.shtml.

37. Siegel unpublished memoir, 90.

38. 39th: Daniel Best, "'Sad Sack and Superman'—Jerry Siegel Goes To War," *20th Century Danny Boy* (blog), August 08, 2012 (4:59 p.m.), http://ohdannyboy.blogspot.com/2012/08/sad-sack-and-superman-jerry-siegel-goes.html. Involvement: Tye, *Superman*, 117. Resumed: Siegel unpublished memoir, 96.

39. Tye, *Superman*, 108. Comics historian Ian Gordon quotes markedly lower, though still impressive, figures; in 1944, 41 percent of men and 28 percent of women ages 18–30 read comics regularly (defined as more than six books a month), as did 16 percent of men and 12 percent of women over 31. The drop is attributed to the reading habits of servicemen. Oddly, Gordon doesn't provide a figure for readers ages 6–17, noting only that girls read 4 to 6 percent fewer comics than boys. *Comic Strips & Consumer Culture, 1890–1945* (Washington: Smithsonian, 2002), 139.

40. Eric P. Nash "Jack Liebowitz, Comics Publisher, Dies at 100," *New York Times*, December 13, 2000, http://www.nytimes.com/2000/12/13/nyregion/jack-liebowitz-comics-publisher-dies-at-100.html.

41. Jerry Siegel, "Happy 45th Anniversary, Superman!" *Action Comics* #544 (June '83), DC Comics, 30–2.

42. Air Force: Kabler, "Up, Up, and Awa-a-y!" 15. Army: Joe Sergi, "The Amazing Adventure of The Man of Steel and the Psychiatric Censor—Superman vs. Doctor Wertham," *CBLDF*, September 19, 2012, http://cbldf.org/2012/09/the-amazing-adventure-of-the-man-of-steel-and-the-psychiatric-censor-superman-vs-doctor-wertham. Navy: "The Press:

Superman's Dilemma." Outselling: John E. Moser, "Madmen, Morons, and Monocles: The Portrayal of the Nazis in Captain America," in *Captain America and the Struggle of the Superhero*, ed. Robert G. Weiner (Jefferson, NC: McFarland & Company, Inc., 2009), 27. The three most popular magazines in the U.S. at the time were *Saturday Evening Post*, *Life* and *Reader's Digest*.

43. Half read: Nancy Lambert, "WWII & Nationalism: 1939–1945," *LIFE Rise of the Superhero: From the Golden Age to the Silver Screen*, Nov. 10, 2017, 29. Billion: Tye, *Superman*, 223.

44. 1939: *Ibid.*, 126. Favored: Van Lente & Dunlavey, *Comic Book History of Comics*, 174. Children: Kabler, "Up, Up, and Awa-a-y!" 15.

45. Joe Simon and Jim Simon, *The Comic Book Makers* (New York: Vanguard, 2003), 42.

46. Stamps: Joe Sergi, "The Amazing Adventure of The Man of Steel." Kirby: Rand Hoppe, "1986/7 Jack Kirby Interview," *The Kirby Effect: The Journal of the Jack Kirby Museum & Research Center*, August 6, 2012, http://kirbymuseum.org/blogs/effect/2012/08/06/19867-kirby-interview.

The Jewish Experience

1. Tom Morris and Matt Morris, "Men in Bright Tights and Wild Fights, Often at Great Heights, and, of Course, Some Amazing Women, Too!" (introduction) in *Superheroes and Philosophy: Truth, Justice, and the Socratic Way*, ed. Tom Morris and Matt Morris (Chicago: Open Court Publishing Company, 2005), x.

2. Art Spiegelman, "Forms Stretched To Their Limits: What Kind of Person Could Have Dreamed Up Plastic Man?," *New Yorker*, April 19, 1999, http://www.newyorker.com/magazine/1999/04/19/forms-stretched-to-their-limits-2.

3. Kane: Michael Weiss, "Secret Identities: Jewish Comic Book Creators," *Negative Space*, last modified June 13, 1995, https://owl.english.purdue.edu/owl/resource/717/05. Spiegelman: Jay Schwartz, "Cover Story: Jews and the invention of the American comic book," *JWeekly*, Oct. 21, 2005, http://www.jweekly.com/article/full/27413/cover-story-jews-and-the-invention-of-the-american-comic-book.

4. Garment workers: Larry Tye, *Superman: The High-Flying History of America's Most Enduring Hero* (New York: Random House, 2013), 14–5; Stan Taylor, "Looking For the Awesome—3. Escape to New York," *The Kirby Effect: The Journal of the Jack Kirby Museum & Research Center*, Dec. 12, 2015, http://kirbymuseum.org/blogs/effect/2015/12; Gary Groth, "The Joe Simon Interview," *The Comics Journal*, July 19, 2011, http://www.tcj.com/the-joe-simon-interview; Marc Tyler Nobleman, *Bill the Boy Wonder: The Secret Co-Creator of Batman* (Watertown: Charlesbridge, 2012), 2; Stan Lee and George Mair, *Excelsior! The Amazing Life of Stan Lee* (New York: Touchstone, 2002), 5. Employed: Howard Sachar, "Jewish Immigrants in the Garment Industry," *My Jewish*

Learning, n.d., http://www.myjewishlearning.com/article/jewish-garment-workers.

5. Eisner: Taylor, "Looking For the Awesome." Award: Julia Goldman, "The King of Comic Books," *The Jewish Week*, May 30, 2002, http://www.thejewishweek.com/arts/arts_guide/king_comic_books.

6. Brought: Grant Morrison, *Supergods: What Masked Vigilantes, Miraculous Mutants, and a Sun God from Smallville Can Teach Us About Being Human* (New York: Spiegel & Grau, 2011), 38. Rooftop: Randolph Hoppe, "Jack Kirby: Superhero Creator of the Lower East Side," *Tenement Museum* (blog), December 8, 2015,https://www.tenement.org/blog/jack-kirby-superhero-creator-of-the-lower-east-side.

7. "Vital Statistics: Jewish Population in the United States, Nationally (1654—Present)," *Jewish Virtual Library* (online), https://www.jewishvirtuallibrary.org/jsource/U.S.-Israel/usjewpop1.html; "Historical National Population Estimates: July 1, 1900 to July 1, 1999," *U.S. Census Bureau* (online), June 28, 2000, https://www.census.gov/popest/data/national/totals/pre-1980/tables/popclockest.txt. Today the figure hovers around 2.25%.

8. Jerry Siegel, "Happy 45th Anniversary, Superman!" *Action Comics* #544 (June '83), DC Comics, 30–2.

9. Lee: Danny Fingeroth, *Disguised as Clark Kent: Jews, Comics, and the Creation of the Superhero* (New York: Continuum International Publishing Group Inc., 2007), 10. Robbins: Schwartz, "Jews and the invention of the American comic book."

10. Simcha Weinstein, *Up, Up, and Oy Vey: How Jewish History, Culture and Values Shaped the Comic Book Superhero* (Baltimore: Leviathan Press, 2006), 18.

11. Mort Weisinger, "Here Comes Superman," *Coronet*, July 1946, 24.

12. Masha Leon, "Comic Book Celebs Discuss Comics and the Jews," *Forward*, October 12, 2015, http://forward.com/the-assimilator/322457/comic-book-celebs-discuss-comics-and-the-jews.

13. Eric J. Greenberg, "Superman: A Jewish Hero," *Jerusalem Post*, May 1, 1996, 7. Also discussed in Kaplan 19, Weinstein 28, Tye 66.

14. Siegel, "Happy 45th Anniversary, Superman!"

15. Jerry Siegel unpublished memoir, "Creation of a Superhero," 1979, Los Angeles. Larry Tye Papers, Box 3, Folder 1, Rare Books & Manuscripts Library Collections, Butler Library, Columbia University, New York, NY, 3–5, 11–2.

16. Tye, *Superman*, 6, 309–10. Despite claims of foul play, Tye found no evidence in his meticulous research.

17. Siegel, unpublished memoir, 17.

18. Donenfeld: David Saunders, "Harry Donenfeld (1893–1965)," *Field Guide to Wild American Pulp Artists*, 2014, http://www.pulpartists.com/Donenfeld.html. Liebowitz: Eric P. Nash "Jack Liebowitz, Comics Publisher, Dies at 100," *New York Times*, December 13, 2000, http://www.nytimes.com/2000/12/13/nyregion/jack-liebowitz-comics-publisher-dies-at-100.html.

19. Wright: "Comic Book Superheroes Unmasked," first broadcast June 23, 2003 by The History Channel. Directed by Stephen Kroopnick and written by James Grant Goldin. Online at https://www.youtube.com/watch?v=Ygx_rUJ3XaI. Tye: Masha Leon, "'Superman at 75' Unmasks the Superhero as a Jew from the Planet Krypton," *Forward*, March 24, 2016, http://forward.com/articles/171301/superman-at-75-unmasks-the-superhero-as-a-jew-from.

20. Liberal: Jerry Siegel unpublished article/outline, "The Life and Times of Jerry Siegel," 1945. Larry Tye Papers, Box 3, Folder 1, Rare Books & Manuscripts Library Collections, Butler Library, Columbia University, New York, NY, 1. Roosevelt: Daniel Best, "'A Curse on the Superman Movie!'—A Look Back at Jerry Siegel's 1975 Press Release," *20th Century Danny Boy* (blog), July 8, 2012 (10:35 a.m.), http://ohdannyboy.blogspot.com/2012/07/curse-on-superman-movie-look-back-at.html.

21. Genesis: Siegel, unpublished memoir, 21. Story: Thomas Andrae, Geoffrey Blum and Gary Coddington, "Of Superman and Kids with Dreams: A Rare Interview with the Creators of Superman: Jerry Siegel & Joe Shuster," *Nemo, the Classic Comics Library* #2, August 1983, 20.

22. Siegel, unpublished memoir, 22.

23. Jerry Siegel (w), Joe Shuster (p, i), "Superman, Champion of the Oppressed," *Action Comics* #1 (June '38), National Comics Publications [DC Comics].

24. Jerry Siegel (w), Joe Shuster (p, i), "Revolution in San Monte Pt. 2," *Action Comics* #2 (July '38), National Comics Publications [DC Comics].

25. Jerry Siegel (w), Joe Shuster (p, i), "The Blakely Mine Disaster," *Action Comics* #3 (Aug. '38), National Comics Publications [DC Comics].

26. Jerry Siegel (w), Joe Shuster (p, i), "Superman in the Slums," *Action Comics* #8 (Jan. '39), National Comics Publications [DC Comics].

27. Jerry Siegel (w), Joe Shuster (p, i), "Superman Goes to Prison," *Action Comics* #10 (Mar. '39), National Comics Publications [DC Comics].

28. Jerry Siegel (w), Joe Shuster (p, i), "Clark Kent Gets a Job," *Superman* #1 (June '39), National Comics Publications [DC Comics], 3–5; Jerry Siegel (w), Paul Cassidy (p, i), "Clark Kent, Police Commissioner," *Action Comics* #37 (June '41).

29. Jerry Siegel (w), Joe Shuster (p), Paul Cassidy (i), "Superman on the High Seas," *Action Comics* #15 (Aug. '39), National Comics Publications [DC Comics]; Jerry Siegel (w), Joe Shuster (p), Dennis Neville (i), "The Orphanage Adventure," *Superman* #3 (Dec. '39).

30. Jerry Siegel (w), Paul Cassidy (p, i), "The Economic Enemy," *Superman* #4 (Mar. '40), National Comics Publications [DC Comics], 2.

31. Jerry Siegel (w), Wayne Boring, Paul Cassidy (p), Paul Cassidy & Paul Lauretta (i), "The Slot Machine Racket," *Superman* #5 (June '40), National Comics Publications [DC Comics], 2; Jerry Siegel

(w), Paul Cassidy, Paul Lauretta (p), Joe Shuster (i), "Professor Cobalt's Quack Clinic," *Action Comics* #26 (Aug. '39), 1, 13.

32. Jerry Siegel (w), Paul Cassidy (p, i), "Mission To San Caluma," *Superman* #6 (Sep. '40), National Comics Publications [DC Comics].

33. Sumptuous: Jerry Siegel (w), Jack Burnley (p, i), "The Preston Gambling Racket," *Action Comics* #32 (Jan. '41), National Comics Publications [DC Comics], 3. Philanthropist: Jerry Siegel (w), Jack Burnley (p, i), "The Lumber Millionaire's Will," *Action Comics* #33 (Feb. '41), 1. Board: Jerry Siegel (w), Leo Nowak (p), "The Plot of Count Bergac," *Superman* #11 (July '41). Hard-pressed: Jerry Siegel (w), John Sikela (p, i), "The Reformation of Nancy Thorgenson," *Action Comics* #40 (Sep. '41), 3.

34. Tye, *Superman*, 49.

35. Bund, La Guardia: Joe Simon and Jim Simon, *The Comic Book Makers* (New York: Vanguard, 2003), 45. Retold in Weinstein, 54 and Van Lente & Dunlavey, 46. Lee: "Comic Book Superheroes Unmasked," first broadcast June 23, 2003 by The History Channel. Directed by Stephen Kroopnick and written by James Grant Goldin. Online at https://www.youtube.com/watch?v=Ygx_rUJ3XaI.

36. Michael J. Ybarra, "The Novelist as Wonder Boy," *Los Angeles Times*, October 9, 2000, http://articles.latimes.com/2000/oct/09/news/cl-33800.

37. *Arena.* "Superman: The Comic Strip Hero," first broadcast April 18, 1981 by BBC Four. Directed by Anthony Wall. Online at https://www.youtube.com/watch?v=Y5oH20iHujo; Siegel, unpublished memoir, 93.

38. Jerry Siegel and Joe Shuster, "How Superman Would End the War," *Look*, February 27, 1940, 16–7.

39. "Jerry Siegel Attacks!" *Das Schwarze Korps*, 25 April 1940, 8. *Trans.* Randall Bytwerk, *German Propaganda Archive* (Calvin College), http://research.calvin.edu/german-propaganda-archive/superman.htm. The article has been referenced often, notably Weinstein 25, Tye 66, 78–9 and Van Lente & Dunlavey 50, though it's never before been reprinted in full.

40. Attribute: Weinstein, *Up, Up, and Oy Vey*, 25; Nancy Lambert, "WWII & Nationalism: 1939–1945," *LIFE Rise of the Superhero: From the Golden Age to the Silver Screen*, Nov. 10, 2017, 32. Conniption: Arie Kaplan, *From Krakow to Krypton: Jews and Comic Books* (Philadelphia: The Jewish Publication Society, 2008), 59; Tye, *Superman*, 79. Reported: John Kabler, "Up, Up, and Awa-a-y! The Rise of Superman, Inc.," *Saturday Evening Post*, June 21, 1941, 15, http://www.saturdayeveningpost.com/wp-content/uploads/satevepost/rise-of-superman.pdf.

41. Tye, *Superman*, 78.

42. Geezer: Jerry Siegel (w), Ira Yarbrough (p, i), "King of the Comic Books," *Superman* #25 (Nov. '43), National Comics Publications [DC Comics]. 101%: *Ibid.*, "The Man Superman Refused to Help."

43. "Hizbullah's Al-Manar TV: Jews Invented Superman In The Service Of Global Jewish Goals," *MEMRI: The Middle East Media Research Institute*, February 20, 2014, https://www.memri.org/reports/hizbullahs-al-manar-tv-jews-invented-superman-service-global-jewish-goals.

44. Jerry Siegel (w), Joe Shuster, Paul Cassidy (p), Paul Cassidy (i), "Europe At War," *Action Comics* #22 (Mar. '40), National Comics Publications [DC Comics]; Jerry Siegel (w), Joe Shuster (p), Paul Cassidy (i), "Europe at War (Part II)," *Action Comics* #23 (Apr. '40).

45. Sara Malm, "Welcome to the Wolf's Lair: Bunker where German army officers tried to assassinate Hitler will open to public as a museum," *Daily Mail*, September 20, 2012, http://www.dailymail.co.uk/news/article-2206073/Welcome-Wolf-s-Lair-Bunker-German-army-officers-tried-assassinate-Hitler-open-public-museum.html.

46. Jerry Siegel (w), Leo Nowak (p), Joe Shuster (i), "The Dukalia Spy Ring," *Superman* #10 (May '41), National Comics Publications [DC Comics].

47. Jerry Siegel (w), Joe Shuster, Wayne Boring (p), Wayne Boring (i), "Fifth Columnists," *Action Comics* #36 (May '41), National Comics Publications [DC Comics].

48. Jerry Siegel (w), Leo Nowak (p), "The Grotak Bund," *Superman* #12 (Sep. '41), National Comics Publications [DC Comics].

49. Cheapen: Fred Van Lente (w), Ryan Dunlavey (p, i), *Comic Book History of Comics* (June '12), IDW Publishing, 50. Reentered: Jerry Siegel (w), Leo Nowak (p, i), "The Oxnalian Revolution," *Superman* #15 (Mar. '42), National Comics Publications [DC Comics].

50. "H-O Superman," *Time*, Feb. 26, 1940, 44.

51. Rabbi: Robert Maxwell, "The Hate Mongers' Organization," *The Adventures of Superman* (radio), April 16–May 20, 1946. Threats: Tye, *Superman*, 82–3, 88.

52. Jerry Siegel (w), Jack Burnley (p, i), "A Summer Snow," *Action Comics* #30 (Nov. '40), National Comics Publications [DC Comics].

53. Jerry Siegel (w), Joe Shuster (p, i), "Every Rising Sun Must Set," *Superman* (newspaper strip), February 15–9, 1942. Erroneously referenced as *Superman* #25 in several sources, but the comic only mentions the occurrence ("I Sustain the Wings!" 3).

54. Daniel Best, "'Sad Sack and Superman'—Jerry Siegel Goes To War," *20th Century Danny Boy* (blog), August 08, 2012 (4:59 p.m.), http://ohdannyboy.blogspot.com/2012/08/sad-sack-and-superman-jerry-siegel-goes.html.

Birthright

1. Alonso Duralde, "How gay is Superman?," *Advocate*, June 2, 2006, http://www.advocate.com/news/2006/06/02/how-gay-superman.

2. John Kabler, "Up, Up, and Awa-a-y! The Rise of Superman, Inc.," *Saturday Evening Post*, June 21, 1941, 15, http://www.saturdayeveningpost.com/wp-content/uploads/satevepost/rise-of-superman.pdf.

3. Spiegelman: Julia Goldman, "The King of Comic Books," *New York Jewish Week*, May 31,

2002, http://jewishweek.timesofisrael.com/the-king-of-comic-books-2. Simon: Danny Fingeroth, *Disguised as Clark Kent: Jews, Comics, and the Creation of the Superhero* (New York: Continuum International Publishing Group Inc., 2007), 24. Kirby: Michael Weiss, "Secret Identities: Jewish Comic Book Creators," *Negative Space*, last modified June 13, 1995, https://owl.english.purdue.edu/owl/resource/717/05.

4. Arie Kaplan, "How the Jews Created the Comic Book Industry—Part I: The Golden Age (1933–1955)," *Reform Judaism Magazine* 32, no. 1 (Fall 2003), http://reformjudaismmag.net/03fall/comics.shtml.

5. Solomon Schechter and Wilhelm Bacher, "Hillel," *The Jewish Encyclopedia*, V. 6 (1906): 397–400 (online), http://jewishencyclopedia.com/articles/7698-hillel.

6. Eisner: Michael Weiss, "Secret Identities." Also quoted in Simcha Weinstein, *Up, Up, and Oy Vey: How Jewish History, Culture and Values Shaped the Comic Book Superhero* (Baltimore: Leviathan Press, 2006), 41. Feiffer: Jules Feiffer, *The Great Comic Book Heroes* (New York: Bonanza Books, 1965), 35. Also quoted in Fingeroth, *Disguised as Clark Kent*, 61.

7. Stan Taylor, "Looking For the Awesome—3. Escape to New York," *The Kirby Effect: The Journal of the Jack Kirby Museum & Research Center*, Dec. 12, 2015, http://kirbymuseum.org/blogs/effect/2015/12.

8. Fingeroth, *Disguised as Clark Kent*, 10–1.

9. Mayrav Saar, "Genetic testing raises an age-old question—are the Jews a people, or a religion?" *New York Post*, June 13, 2010, http://nypost.com/2010/06/13/genetic-testing-raises-an-age-old-question-are-the-jews-a-people-or-a-religion.

10. Borderline: "Superman," *Jew or Not Jew*, Dec. 18, 2006, http://www.jewornotjew.com/profile.jsp?ID=70. Themes: Eric J. Greenberg, "Superman: A Jewish Hero," *Jerusalem Post*, May 1, 1996, 7. Jacobson: Kurt Andersen, "American Icons: Superman," *Studio 360*, New York, PRI and WNYC, July 6, 2006 (online), http://www.wnyc.org/story/295935-american-icons-superman. Birthday: Masha Leon, "'Superman at 75' Unmasks the Superhero as a Jew from the Planet Krypton," *Forward*, March 24, 2016, http://forward.com/articles/171301/superman-at-75-unmasks-the-superhero-as-a-jew-from.

11. Michael Chabon, *The Amazing Adventures of Kavalier & Clay* (New York: Random House, 2000), 585.

12. Carroll Johnson, "The Many Facets of Jules Feiffer," *Library of Congress Information Bulletin*, November 4, 1996, http://www.loc.gov/loc/lcib/9619/feiffer2.html; Jules Feiffer, "Jerry Siegel: the Minsk theory of Krypton," *New York Times Magazine*, Dec. 29, 1996, 15.

13. Harvey Pekar (w) Gary Dumm, Robert Crumb (p, i), "What Superman Means to me," *Snarf* #12 (June '89), Kitchen Sink Press, 27–9.

14. Kabbalah, Buber: Bruce Bachand, "Interview: Elliot S! Maggin," *Fanzing: The DC comics Fan Site*, n.d., http://www.fanzing.com/mag/fanzing09/iview.

shtml. Religions: Elliot S. Maggin, "Is Superman Jewish?" *Quora*, Apr. 1, 2011, https://www.quora.com/Is-Superman-Jewish.

15. *Ibid.*

16. Jerry Siegel unpublished memoir, "Creation of a Superhero," 1979, Los Angeles. Larry Tye Papers, Box 3, Folder 1, Rare Books & Manuscripts Library Collections, Butler Library, Columbia University, New York, NY, 95.

17. Eric J. Greenberg, "Did Superman Have Biblical Roots? Jerry Siegel dies without revealing 'true' origin of the Last Son of Krypton," *New York Jewish Week*, Feb. 9, 1996, 41.

18. Thomas Andrae, Geoffrey Blum and Gary Coddington, "Of Superman and Kids with Dreams: A Rare Interview with the Creators of Superman: Jerry Siegel & Joe Shuster," *Nemo, the Classic Comics Library*, August 1983, 11. Clark Kent may have also been based in part on Wilson Hirschfeld, a Jewish classmate and friend of Siegel and Shuster's who worked with them on the *Torch* and went on to become a bespectacled reporter at the Cleveland *Plain Dealer*. Tye, *Superman*, 106.

19. Fairbanks, amalgam, copies: Andrae et al., *Nemo*, 11, 14. Pose: Tye, *Superman*, 20.

20. Complex: Siegel unpublished memoir, 6, 45. Article: Kabler, "Up, Up, and Awa-a-y!" 14, 76, 70.

21. Jennings Parrott, "Superman to Honor Moral Obligation," *Los Angeles Times*, Nov. 25, 1975, 2; Siegel unpublished memoir, 44, 94.

22. Andrae et al., *Nemo*, 12.

23. Bruce Weber, "Joanne Siegel, the Model for Lois Lane, Dies at 93," *New York Times*, Feb. 15, 2011, http://www.nytimes.com/2011/02/16/arts/16siegel.html?_r=0.

24. *Ibid.* According to Siegel family lore, the costume contest was judged by young newcomer Marlon Brando, who thirty years later would play Superman's father, Jor-El.

25. Feiffer, "Minsk theory of Krypton," 15.

26. Newsboy: Henry Mietkiewicz, "Great Krypton! Superman was the Star's Ace Reporter," *Toronto Star* (Toronto, ON), April 26, 1992, A.10.; Jerry Siegel (w), Joe Shuster (p, i), "Superman, Champion of the Oppressed," *Action Comics* #1 (June '38), National Comics Publications [DC Comics], 4–5; Jerry Siegel (w), Joe Shuster (p, i), "Revolution in San Monte Pt. 2," *Action Comics* #2 (July '38), 7; Jerry Siegel (w), Joe Shuster (p), Paul Cassidy (i), "Europe at War (Part II)," *Action Comics* #23 (Apr. '40), 13.

27. Toronto: Jerry Siegel, "Happy 45th Anniversary, Superman!" *Action Comics* #544 (June '83), DC Comics, 30–2. Film: Andrae et al., *Nemo*, 15. Visit: Michael Minden and Holger Bachmann, *Fritz Lang's Metropolis: Cinematic Visions of Technology and Fear* (Rochester: Camden House, 2002), 4–5. Metropolis is first named in *Action Comics* #16 (Jerry Siegel [w], Joe Shuster [p], Paul Cassidy [i], "Superman and the Numbers Racket," (Sep. '39) National Comics Publications [DC Comics], 3). While it started out as Toronto, it's since become a New York analogue. It's referred to as Manhattan

Island in the 1942 *Superman* serial (Episode No. 7, "Electric Earthquake," first released May 17, 1942 by Fleischer Studios/Paramount Pictures. Directed by Dave Fleischer and written by Seymour Kneitel and Isadore Sparber) and Superman takes Lois flying over the Statue of Liberty in 1978's *Superman*. Following a 1986 comic book revamp the city more obviously resembled New York.

28. Arie Kaplan, *From Krakow to Krypton: Jews and Comic Books* (Philadelphia: The Jewish Publication Society, 2008), 14. Curiously, neither Weinstein nor Fingeroth touch on this.

29. Cognitive: Gregory Cochran, Jason Hardy, Henry Harpending, "Natural History of Ashkenazi Intelligence," *Journal of Biosocial Science* 38 (2006), pp. 659–93 (online), https://web.archive. org/web/20130911054719/http://harpending. humanevo.utah.edu/Documents/ashkiq.webpub. pdf, 4. Herman: David Herman, "Flaunt it, baby!" *Guardian*, June 12, 2003, https://www.theguardian. com/film/2003/jun/12/artsfeatures1.

30. Carl Gustav Jung, *Collected Works of C.G. Jung, Volume 5: Symbols of Transformation*, trans. Gerhard Adler and R.F.C. Hull (Princeton, NJ: Princeton University Press, 1974), 178.

31. *Ibid.*; Siegel unpublished memoir, 43.

32. Established: Paul Kupperberg (w), Howard Chaykin (p) Murphy Anderson (i), "The Jor-El Story," *World of Krypton* #1 (July '79), DC Comics, 2–4. Nobel: Charles Murray, "Jewish Genius," *Commentary*, April 1, 2007, https://www. commentarymagazine.com/articles/jewish-genius.

33. Frontispiece: George Lowther and Joe Shuster, *The Adventures of Superman* (reprint edition) (Bedford: Applewood Books, 1995), ii. Skullcaps: Jerry Siegel (w), Joe Shuster (p, i), "The Origin of Superboy," *More Fun Comics* #101 (Jan. '45), National Comics Publications [DC Comics], 1–3. Enslaved: Elliot Maggin (w), Dave Cockrum (p, i), "The Headband Warriors of Krypton," *Superman* #264 (June '73), National Periodical Publications [DC Comics].

34. Kaplan, *From Krakow to Krypton*, 14; Tye, *Superman*, 66; "Kindertransport, 1938–1940," *United States Holocaust Memorial Museum*, accessed Jan. 27, 2016, https://www.ushmm.org/wlc/en/ article.php?ModuleId=10005260.

35. *Superman*, directed by Richard Donner (1978; Burbank, CA: Warner Home Video, 2006), DVD.

36. Siegel unpublished memoir, 30–43.

37. Hardwicke Benthow, "Man of Tomorrow: Siegel and Keaton's Superman," *The Thoughts and Ramblings of Hardwicke Benthow* (blog), n.d., https://thoughtsandramblingsofhardwickebent how.wordpress.com/man-of-tomorrow-siegel-and-keatons-superman.

38. Jerry Siegel (w), Joe Shuster (p, i), "Clark Kent Gets a Job," *Superman* #1 (June '39), National Comics Publications [DC Comics], 2; Jerry Siegel (w), John Sikela (p), George Roussos (i), "That Old Class of Superboy's!" *Superman* #46 (May '47), 1.

39. *Adventures of Superman* (radio serial), "The Secret Rocket," first broadcast Sep. 29–Oct. 30, 1947;

Ed Herron (w, presumed), Al Wenzel (p, i, cover), *Superboy* #2 (May '49), National Comics Publications [DC Comics], cover; Cary Bates (w), Kurt Schaffenberger (p), Dave Hunt (i), "The Heroic Failures Of Superboy," *The New Adventures of Superboy* (*Superboy* Vol. 2) #22 (Oct. '81), DC Comics, map insert between pages 13–4. Kansas isn't actually mentioned in the film, but a young Clark can be seen racing a Kansas Star train.

40. Otto Binder (w), Al Plastino (p, i), "The Story of Superman's Life!" *Superman* #146 (July '61), National Periodical Publications [DC Comics], 5, 7–8.

41. Recognized: Noelene Clark, "'Man of Steel': Zack Snyder says Superman 'must be taken seriously,'" *Hero Complex*, April 25, 2013, http:// herocomplex.latimes.com/movies/man-of-steel-zack-snyder-says-superman-must-be-taken-seriously/#/0. Chabon: Kurt Andersen, "American Icons: Superman," *Studio 360*, New York, PRI and WNYC, July 6, 2006 (online), http://www.wnyc.org/ story/295935-american-icons-superman.

42. Ron Kaplan, "The truth behind 'Lies': Author blends biblical and comic book legends in latest novel," *NJ Jewish News*, November 13, 2008, http://njjewishnews.com/njjn.com/111308/ ltTruthBehindLies.html. Also mentioned in Tye, *Superman*, x.

43. Pekar, "What Superman Means to me," 27–9.

44. Sigmund Freud, *Moses and Monotheism*, trans. Katherine Jones (Mansfield Centre: Martino Publishing, 2010), 18–9. In fact, Freud sees all heroes as oedipal fantasies of rebelling against the father and killing him in some guise or another. (140)

45. Mark Millar, "Ecosse: Cover story: Is it a bird? Is it a plane? No, it's Superman, but not as we know him," *Sunday Times*, April 27, 2003, http:// www.thesundaytimes.co.uk/sto/news/uk_news/ article228913.ece.

46. Alvin Schwartz, "The Real Secret of Superman's Identity," *Children's Literature* 5 (1976), pp. 117–29 (123–4).

47. Umberto Eco, "The Myth of Superman," trans. Natalie Chilton for *Diacritics* 2, no. 1 (Spring 1972): 14–22. Originally published as "Il mito di Superman e la dissoluzione del tempo" in *Demitizzazione e imagine*, ed. E. Castelli (Padua: Cedam, 1962).

48. Michael Eury, *The Krypton Companion* (Raleigh: TwoMorrows Publishing, 2006), 142.

49. Fingeroth, *Disguised as Clark Kent*, 24–5.

50. Will Murray and Lester Dent (under Kenneth Robeson), *The Wild Adventures of Doc Savage: Flight into Fear* (Boston: Altus Press, 2015), 276.

51. Alvin Schwartz, "The Real Secret of Superman's Identity," 124.

The Secret Identities of Heroes and Hebrews

1. Stan Taylor, "Looking For the Awesome—11. Tales From the Heart," *The Kirby Effect: The Journal*

of the Jack Kirby Museum & Research Center, Feb. 25, 2017, http://kirbymuseum.org/blogs/effect/author/stant.

2. Stan Taylor, "Looking For the Awesome—3. Escape to New York," *The Kirby Effect: The Journal of the Jack Kirby Museum & Research Center*, Dec. 12, 2015, http://kirbymuseum.org/blogs/effect/2015/12.

3. Charles McEvoy, Hugh Langley, Herbert S. Fine: Jerry Siegel unpublished memoir, "Creation of a Superhero," 1979, Los Angeles. Larry Tye Papers, Box 3, Folder 1, Rare Books & Manuscripts Library Collections, Butler Library, Columbia University, New York, NY, 14, 16, 20. All used in *Cosmic Stories*; Leger: Jerry Siegel (w), Joe Shuster (p, i) (as "Leger and Reuths"), "Doctor Occult, the Ghost Detective: The Vampire Master, Part 1," *New Fun Comics* #6 (Oct. '35), National Allied Publications [DC Comics]; 4; Joe Carter: Stan Lee, Jerry Siegel (as "Joe Carter") (w), Dick Ayers (p, i), "The Threat of the Living Bomb!" *Strange Tales* #112 (Sep. '63), Marvel Comics; Jerry Ess: Jerry Siegel (as "Jerry Ess") (w), Paul Reinman (p, i), "Fly Man's Strangest Dilemma," *Fly Man* #36 (Mar. '66), Mighty Comics.

4. Stan Taylor, "Looking For the Awesome—3. Escape to New York."

5. NPR staff, "The 'Amazing Fantastic Incredible' Life Of Stan Lee, Now In Comic Form," *NPR* (online), November 12, 2015, http://www.npr.org/2015/11/12/455639075/the-amazing-fantastic-incredible-life-of-stan-lee-now-in-comic-form.

6. Stated: Michael Weiss, "Secret Identities: Jewish Comic Book Creators," *Negative Space*, last modified June 13, 1995, https://owl.english.purdue.edu/owl/resource/717/05. Simon: Joe Simon and Jim Simon, *The Comic Book Makers* (Lakewood: Vanguard Productions, 2003), 42–3. Anger: Rand Hoppe, "1986/7 Jack Kirby Interview," *The Kirby Effect: The Journal of the Jack Kirby Museum & Research Center*, August 6, 2012, http://kirbymuseum.org/blogs/effect/2012/08/06/19867-kirby-interview.

7. Thomas Andrae, Geoffrey Blum and Gary Coddington, "Of Superman and Kids with Dreams: A Rare Interview with the Creators of Superman: Jerry Siegel & Joe Shuster," *Nemo, the Classic Comics Library* #2, August 1983, 14.

8. Stan Taylor, "Looking For the Awesome—11."

9. Ray Furlong, "Wallenberg family mark centenary with plea for truth," *BBC News Stockholm*, August 4, 2012, http://www.bbc.com/news/world-europe-19101339.

10. *Kill Bill: Vol. 2*, directed by Quentin Tarantino (2004; Santa Monica, CA: Miramax Home Entertainment, 2007), DVD.

11. Jules Feiffer, *The Great Comic Book Heroes* (New York: Bonanza Books, 1965), 18–9.

12. Mario Puzo et al., *Superman*. Final screenplay, 1976. Online: http://www.supermanhomepage.com/movies/superman_original.txt, 77.

13. Benton: Larry Tye, *Superman: The High-Flying History of America's Most Enduring Hero* (New York: Random House, 2013), 192. O'Neil: Michael Eury, *The Krypton Companion* (Raleigh:

TwoMorrows Publishing, 2006), 119. Siegel: Siegel unpublished memoir, 23.

14. Otto Binder (w), Al Plastino (p, i), "The Story of Superman's Life!" *Superman* #146 (July '61), National Periodical Publications [DC Comics], 4–7.

15. "Learn…": Cary Bates, Elliot S. Maggin (w), Curt Swan (p), Bob Oksner, Bob Wiacek (i), "Clark Kent Forever--Superman Never!" *Superman* #297 (Mar. '76), DC Comics, 7–18.

16. Cary Bates, Elliot S. Maggin (w), Curt Swan (p), Bob Oksner (i), "The Double-Or-Nothing Life Of Superman!" *Superman* #299 (May '76), DC Comics, 1, 18.

17. Alvin Schwartz, "The Real Secret of Superman's Identity," *Children's Literature* 5 (1976), pp. 117–29 (125).

18. Danny Fingeroth, *Disguised as Clark Kent: Jews, Comics, and the Creation of the Superhero* (New York: Continuum International Publishing Group Inc., 2007), 47.

19. Guy H. Lillian III, "Cary Bates and Elliot Maggin: The Men Behind the Super-Typewriter," *Superman Through the Ages!* (from *Amazing World of DC Comics* #2, Sep. '74), http://web.archive.org/web/20061005154921/http:/theages.superman.ws/Creators/men-behind-super-typewriter.php.

20. Jodi Picoult, *The Tenth Circle* (London: Allen & Unwin, 2006), 145.

21. Lillian, "Cary Bates and Elliot Maggin: The Men Behind the Super-Typewriter."

22. Feiffer, *The Great Comic Book Heroes*, 19; Jerry Siegel, "Happy 45th Anniversary, Superman!" *Action Comics* #544 (June '83), DC Comics, 30–2.

23. Derrida: Richard Kearney, *Debates in Continental Philosophy: Conversations with Contemporary Thinkers* (New York: Fordham University Press, 2004), 148. Sigmund Freud, *Moses and Monotheism*, trans. Katherine Jones (Mansfield Centre, CT: Martino Publishing, 2010), 146.

24. Friedman: Lester D. Friedman, *The Jewish Image in American Film* (New York: Citadel Press, 1987), 11. Chabon: Michael Chabon, *The Amazing Adventures of Kavalier & Clay* (New York: Random House, 2000), 585. Name: Andrae et al., *Nemo*, 15, 11. Grant: Arie Kaplan, *From Krakow to Krypton: Jews and Comic Books* (Philadelphia: The Jewish Publication Society, 2008), 23. Kaplan is likely misattributing: Christopher Reeve discusses basing his performance on Cary Grant in 1938's *Bringing Up Baby* in his memoir, *Still Me* (New York: Ballantine Books, 1999), 193. Grant didn't play a particularly mild-mannered role in any of his movies predating Superman's creation.

25. *Superman*, directed by Richard Donner (1978; Burbank, CA: Warner Home Video, 2006), DVD; Jules Feiffer, "Jerry Siegel: the Minsk theory of Krypton," *New York Times Magazine*, Dec. 29, 1996, 15.

26. Eury, *The Krypton Companion*, 212.

27. "Jewish Population of Europe in 1933: Population Data by Country," *United States Holocaust Memorial Museum*, accessed May 17, 2016, https://www.ushmm.org/wlc/en/article.php?ModuleId=10005161.

28. Rich Cohen, "Ebb Tide in the Golden Country: All is not as it was for Jews in America," *Tablet*, June 1, 2015, http://www.tabletmag.com/jewish-news-and-politics/191087/ebb-tide-in-the-golden-country.

29. Brigid Alverson, "Graphic Novels Portray Bicultural America," *School Library Journal*, August 9, 2016, http://www.slj.com/2016/08/diversity/graphic-novels-portray-bicultural-america.

30. Friedman, *The Jewish Image in American Film*, 11.

31. Tye, *Superman*, 48.

32. Sage Stossel, "A Conversation With Jules Feiffer," *Atlantic*, March 19, 2010, http://www.theatlantic.com/entertainment/archive/2010/03/a-conversation-with-jules-feiffer/37775.

33. *Lois & Clark: The New Adventures of Superman*. Season 2, episode 18, "Tempus Fugitive," first broadcast March 26, 1995 by WB. Directed by James Bagdonas and written by Jack Weinstein and Lee Hutson. The same line was repeated in *Supergirl* 22 years later, in the suggestively named episode "Exodus." Season 2, episode 15, first broadcast March 6, 2017 by CW. Directed by Michael A. Allowitz and written by Paula Yoo and Eric Carrasco.

34. Don Cameron (w), Joe Shuster (p), John Sikela (i), "Ordeal on Wheels," *More Fun Comics* #107 (Jan. '46), National Comics Publications [DC Comics].

35. Robert Maxwell, "The Meteor from Krypton, part I," *The Adventures of Superman* (radio), June 3, 1943.

36. Mark A. Semich, "At Long Last! Sixty-Five Years in the Making! Jerry Siegel and Joe Shuster's Famous Never-Before-Seen Story from 1940!" *Superman Through the Ages!* n.d. (2005), http://www.superman.nu/k-metal-from-krypton/about-the-story.php.

37. Myrna Oliver, "Jerry Siegel; Co-Creator of Superman," *Los Angeles Times*, January 31, 1996, http://articles.latimes.com/1996-01-31/news/mn-30756_1_jerry-siegel.

38. Elliot S. Maggin, "Is Superman Jewish?" *Quora*, Apr. 1, 2011, https://www.quora.com/Is-Superman-Jewish.

39. Julie A. Sergel, "Silent Holocaust Gets a Voice," *Jewish Post*, n.d., http://www.jewishpost.com/archives/news/Silent-Holocaust-Gets-a-Voice.html.

40. *Superman II*, directed by Richard Lester (1980; Burbank, CA: Warner Home Video, 2006), DVD.

41. *Superman II: The Richard Donner Cut*, directed by Richard Donner (1980/2006; Burbank, CA: Warner Home Video, 2006), DVD.

42. Joseph Jacobs and Judah David Eisenstein, "Sin," *The Jewish Encyclopedia*, V. 11 (1906): 376–379 (online), http://www.jewishencyclopedia.com/articles/13761-sin.

43. Friedman, *The Jewish Image in American Film*, 11.

The Galactic Golem

1. Ludwig Blau, Joseph Jacobs, Judah David Eisenstein, "Golem," *The Jewish Encyclopedia*, V. 6 (1906): 36–7 (online), http://www.jewishencyclopedia.com/articles/6777-golem.

2. "Hebrew: In Ancient Jewish Scriptures," *Jewish Virtual Library*, accessed January 30, 2016, http://www.jewishvirtuallibrary.org/hebrew-in-ancient-jewish-scriptures.

3. Norma Contrada, "Golem and Robot: A Search for Connections," *Journal of the Fantastic in the Arts* 7, no. 2/3 (26/27) (1995): 244 & 251. (pp. 244–54) In a 1935 interview, Čapek disclosed; "R.U.R. is, in fact, my own rendering of the legend of the Golem in modern form ... the Robot is the Golem made flesh by mass production."

4. Golem: Michael Chabon, *The Amazing Adventures of Kavalier & Clay* (New York: Random House, 2000), 86. Ellipses in the original text. The four Hebrew letters referenced are ostensibly either the tetragrammaton יְהֹוָה or an erroneous transliteration of the English spelling emet. Gesture: *ibid.*, 582.

5. Louise Simonson (w), Jon Bogdanove (p), Dennis Janke (i), Glenn Whitmore (c), *Superman: Man of Steel* #82 (Aug. '98), DC Comics, 4.

6. Len Wein (w), Curt Swan (p), Murphy Anderson (i), "The Man Who Murdered the Earth!" *Superman* #248 (Feb. '72), National Periodical Publications [DC Comics], 4.

7. Arie Kaplan (w), Nick Runge (p), Gabe Eltaeb (i), Ulises Arreola (c), "Man of Snow," *DC Universe Holiday Special '09* #1 (Feb. '10), DC Comics.

8. *Superboy*. Season 3, episode 14, "The Golem," first broadcast 19 January 1991 in syndication. Directed by Robert Wiemer and written by Paul Stubenrauch.

9. Otto Binder (w), George Papp (p, i), "The Boy of Steel vs. the Thing of Steel," *Superboy* #68 (Nov. '58), National Comics Publications [DC Comics]. The girl as an influence of *The Golem* on *Frankenstein* is noted in Thomas Andrae, Mel Gordon, *Siegel and Shuster's Funnyman: The First Jewish Superhero, from the Creators of Superman* (Los Angeles: Feral House, 2010), 40–1. Clone: John Byrne (w, p), Dick Giordano (i), Tom Ziuko (c), "The Mirror, Crack'd," *Man of Steel* #5 (Dec. '86), DC Comics.

10. Danny Fingeroth, *Disguised as Clark Kent: Jews, Comics, and the Creation of the Superhero* (New York: Continuum International Publishing Group Inc., 2007), 136; Larry Tye, *Superman: The High-Flying History of America's Most Enduring Hero* (New York: Random House, 2013), 73; Andrae and Gordon, *Siegel and Shuster's Funnyman* & Andrae et al., *Nemo*, 38–41; Simcha Weinstein, *Up, Up, and Oy Vey: How Jewish History, Culture and Values Shaped the Comic Book Superhero* (Baltimore: Leviathan Press, 2006), 31, 50–1, 86–8; Arie Kaplan, *From Krakow to Krypton: Jews and Comic Books* (Philadelphia: The Jewish Publication Society, 2008), 15, 17, 59, 206 (Superman); 109–10 (Hulk); 125 (Ragman); William Moulton Marston (w, as Charles Moulton) Harry G. Peter (p, i), "The Origin

of Wonder Woman," *Wonder Woman* #1 (June '42), All-American Publications [DC Comics], 6.

11. Arie Kaplan, "How the Jews Created the Comic Book Industry—Part I: The Golden Age (1933–1955)," *Reform Judaism Magazine* 32, no. 1 (Fall 2003), http://reformjudaismmag.net/03fall/comics.shtml.

12. Jerry Siegel unpublished memoir, "Creation of a Superhero," 1979, Los Angeles. Larry Tye Papers, Box 3, Folder 1, Rare Books & Manuscripts Library Collections, Butler Library, Columbia University, New York, NY, 12–3.

13. *Ibid.*, 93; Mort Weisinger, "Here Comes Superman," *Coronet*, July 1946, 24; Tye, *Superman*, ix.

14. Marv Wolfman (w), Gil Kane (p, i), Anthony Tollin (c), "If Superman Didn't Exist," *Action Comics* #554 (Apr. '84), DC Comics, 2 & 16. Also mentioned in Kaplan, *From Krakow to Krypton*, 206.

15. "Historical Highlights: The Lend-Lease Act of 1941," *History, Art & Archives of the U.S. House of Representatives*, http://history.house.gov/Historical-Highlights/1901-1950/The-Lend-Lease-Act-of-1941.

16. Refused & rebuffed: David Cesarani, "FDR and the Jews by Richard Breitman and Allan J Lichtman: This world, the next world and the New Deal," *New Statesman*, June 6, 2013, http://www.newstatesman.com/culture/2013/06/fdr-and-jews-richard-breitman-and-allan-j-lichtman-world-next-world-and-new-deal. WRB: "Americans and the Holocaust," *United States Holocaust Memorial Museum*, accessed January 27, 2016, https://exhibitions.ushmm.org/americans-and-the-holocaust/main. Reasons: Michael Berenbaum, "Why wasn't Auschwitz bombed?," *Encyclopedia Britannica*, Feb. 16, 2001 (online), https://www.britannica.com/topic/Why-wasnt-Auschwitz-bombed-717594.

17. "Here's Fortune's Survey on How Americans Viewed Jewish Refugees in 1938," *Fortune*, Nov. 18, 2015, http://fortune.com/2015/11/18/fortune-survey-jewish-refugees; Frank Newport, "Historical Review: Americans' Views on Refugees Coming to U.S.," *Gallup*, Nov. 19, 2015, http://www.gallup.com/opinion/polling-matters/186716/historical-review-americans-views-refugees-coming.aspx.

18. Robert Moses Shapiro, ed., *Why Didn't the Press Shout?: American & International Journalism During the Holocaust* (Jersey City: KTAV Publishing House, Inc., 2003 [Yeshiva University Press]). The book is a collection of thirty papers by journalism and history scholars demonstrating a pattern of denial and concealment by the world press, which almost systematically relegated these stories to the back pages or worse, reported them favorably.

19. Richard Brody, "The Misplaced Nostalgia For Movies Like 'The Graduate,'" *New Yorker*, July 8, 2015, http://www.newyorker.com/culture/cultural-comment/the-misplaced-nostalgia-for-movies-like-the-graduate?. Two years: Germain Lussier, "'Captain America: The Winter Soldier' Sets Up Allegiances For 'The Avengers 2,'" /Film (blog), April 12th, 2013, http://www.slashfilm.com/captain-america-the-winter-soldier-sets-up-allegiances-for-the-avengers-2. Miller: "Comic book hero takes on al-Qaeda," *BBC News*, last updated February 15, 2006, http://news.bbc.co.uk/2/hi/entertainment/4717696.stm.

20. 60%: Frederic Cople Jaher, *The Jews and the Nation: Revolution, Emancipation, State Formation, and the Liberal Paradigm in America and France* (New Jersey: Princeton University Press, 2009), 229–30. 50%: Kaplan, *From Krakow to Krypton*, 4. Lee: Danny Fingeroth, *Disguised as Clark Kent*, 10. Cartoons: Stan Taylor, "Looking For the Awesome—3. Escape to New York," *The Kirby Effect: The Journal of the Jack Kirby Museum & Research Center*, Dec. 12, 2015, http://kirbymuseum.org/blogs/effect/2015/12. Kirby: Kaplan, "How the Jews Created the Comic Book Industry—Part I." Inmates: cover by Alex Schomburg (p, i), *Captain America Comics* #46 (Apr. '45), Timely Comics [Marvel Comics]. Known as "the Holocaust cover" in comic book circles.

21. David Mikics, "Here's Looking at You, Kid," *Tablet*, February 14, 2017, http://www.tabletmag.com/jewish-arts-and-culture/224670/casablanca-isenberg?utm_source=fb&utm_medium=post&utm_term=We.

22. David Hajdu, *The Ten-Cent Plague: The Great Comic-Book Scare and How It Changed America* (New York: Picador, 2008), 40. North is erroneously referred to as columnist.

23. Brian Cronin, "Comic Book Legends Revealed #237," *CBR.com*, Dec. 10, 2009, http://www.cbr.com/comic-book-legends-revealed-237; Philip Willan, "Benito and the Beano," *Guardian*, Nov. 28, 2002, https://www.theguardian.com/artanddesign/2002/nov/28/art.artsfeatures1.

24. Nicholas Yanes, "Graphic Imagery: Jewish American Comic Book Creators' Depictions of Class, Race, Patriotism and the Birth of the Good Captain," in *Captain America and the Struggle of the Superhero*, ed. Robert G. Weiner. (Jefferson: McFarland & Company, Inc., 2009), 61.

25. Weisinger, "Here Comes Superman."

26. Neil Gaiman and Adam Rogers, "The Myth of Superman," *Wired*, June 14, 2006, https://www.wired.com/2006/06/myth.

27. Warren Bernard, *Cartoons for Victory* (Seattle: Fantagraphics, 2015), 182.

The Brave and the Bold

1. John Kabler, "Up, Up, and Awa-a-y! The Rise of Superman, Inc.," *Saturday Evening Post*, June 21, 1941, 15, http://www.saturdayeveningpost.com/wp-content/uploads/satevepost/rise-of-superman.pdf.

2. *Catholic World*: David Hajdu, *The Ten-Cent Plague: The Great Comic-Book Scare and How It Changed America* (New York: Picador, 2008), 81. Article also quoted in Larry Tye, *Superman: The High-Flying History of America's Most Enduring Hero* (New York: Random House, 2013), 128; Fredrick

Wertham, *Seduction of the Innocent* (New York: Rinehart & Company, Inc., 1954,) 15.

3. Fred Van Lente (w), Ryan Dunlavey (p, i), *Comic Book History of Comics* (June '12), IDW Publishing, 20; Arie Kaplan, *From Krakow to Krypton: Jews and Comic Books* (Philadelphia: The Jewish Publication Society, 2008), 11.

4. *Saturday Night Live.* Season 4, Episode 10, "What If Superman grew up in Germany instead of America?" first broadcast January 27, 1979 by NBC. Written by Al Franken.

5. Reversal: Friedrich Nietzsche, *On the Genealogy of Morals*, trans. Carol Diethe (Cambridge: Cambridge University Press, 2006), 145. Degeneration: Nietzsche, *Beyond Good and Evil*, trans. Helen Zimmern. Ebook. (2013, Project Gutenberg), http://www.gutenberg.org/files/4363/4363-h/4363-h.htm, section 62.

6. *Ibid.*, section 251.

7. God is dead: Friedrich Nietzsche, *Thus Spake Zarathustra*, trans. Thomas Common. Ebook. (2016, Project Gutenberg), http://www.gutenberg.org/files/1998/1998-h/1998-h.htm, XXV: The Pitiful. Will to Power: *ibid.*, XV: The Thousand and One Goals.

8. Hermann Rauschning, *Hitler Speaks: A Series Of Political Conversations With Adolf Hitler On His Real Aims* (aka *Voice of Destruction*) (Whitefish: Kessinger Publishing, LLC, 2010), 220. The authenticity of the book has been disputed by some historians.

9. Nietzsche, *Thus Spake Zarathustra*, prologue: section 5.

10. Impoverished: James Hudnall (w), Eduardo Barreto (p, i), Adam Kubert (c), *Lex Luthor: The Unauthorized Biography* ('89), DC Comics. Middle-class: Jerry Siegel (w), Al Plastino (p, i), "How Luthor Met Superboy!" *Adventure Comics* #271 (Apr. '60), National Comics Publications [DC Comics]. Wealthy: Mark Waid (w), Leinil Francis Yu (p), Gerry Alanguilan (i), Dave McCaig (c), "Lex Luthor in Smallville," *Superman: Birthright* #8 (May '04), DC Comics. Following precedent in *Smallville* TV series. Jealousy: Canonical since *Man of Steel* #4 (John Byrne (w, p), Dick Giordano (i), Tom Ziuko (c), "Enemy Mine...," (Nov. '86), et seq.

11. Grant Morrison (w), Jim Lee (p, i), Scott Williams, Sandra Hope, Jonathan Glapion, Mark Irwin (i), Alex Sinclair, Jeromy Cox (c), *The Multiversity: Mastermen* #1 (Apr. '15), DC Comics.

12. Byrne, *Man of Steel* #4, 18.

13. Elliot S. Maggin, *Superman: Miracle Monday* (New York: Warner Books, 1981), 28. Later paraphrased in Mark Waid (w) and Alex Ross' (p, i, c) "Up in the Sky," *Kingdom Come* #3 (July '96), DC Comics. And since elsewhere.

14. *Superman*, directed by Richard Donner (1978; Burbank, CA: Warner Home Video, 2006), DVD; *Man of Steel*, directed by Zack Snyder (2013; Burbank, CA: Warner Home Video, 2013), DVD. Dialogue taken with little alteration from *All-Star Superman* #12 (Grant Morrison (w), Frank Quitely (p), Jamie Grant (i, c), "Superman in Excelsis" (Oct. '08), DC Comics, 6.

15. Grant Morrison (w), Howard Porter (p), John Dell (i), Pat Garrahy (c), "Invaders from Mars," *JLA* #4 (Apr. '97), DC Comics, 12, 18.

Phone Booth, Voting Booth, Confession Booth

1. Kofi Outlaw, "Why *Batman v Superman* Is Smarter Than You Think," *Comicbook.com*, Aug. 01, 2016, http://comicbook.com/dc/2016/07/31/why-batman-v-superman-is-smarter-than-you-think; Ramin Setoodeh, "Why 'Batman v Superman' Is the Donald Trump of Comic-Book Movies," *Variety*, March 28, 2016, http://variety.com/2016/film/news/batman-v-superman-donald-trump-reviews-1201740341.

2. "U.S. Presidential Elections: Jewish Voting Record (1916–Present)," *Jewish Virtual Library* (online), http://www.jewishvirtuallibrary.org/jewish-voting-record-in-u-s-presidential-elections; "Election History: Demographic voting trends," *Pantagraph*, Oct. 17, 2012, http://www.pantagraph.com/news/national/government-and-politics/elections/election-history-demographic-voting-trends/html_2810a66e-1884-11e2-a23c-001a4bcf887a.html; "Jews Vote More Often Than Others," *Jewish Virtual Library* (online), http://www.jewishvirtuallibrary.org/jsource/U.S.-Israel/jewturnout.pdf.

3. Karl Marx, *Critique of the Gotha Program* (Maryland: Wildeside Press, 2008), 27; Ayn Rand, *The Fountainhead* (Centennial Edition) (New York: Sigent, 1996), 23. A popular paraphrasing of "My dear fellow, who will let you?" "That's not the point. The point is, who will stop me?"

4. John Byrne (w, p, i), Petra Scotese (c), "The Price," *Superman* Vol. 2 #22 (Oct. '88), DC Comics.

5. Thomas Whiteside, "Superman is a Liberal" (aka "Up, Up and Awa-a-y!"), *New Republic*, March 3, 1947, 15–7.

6. *Superman Returns*, directed by Brian Singer (2006; Burbank, CA: Warner Home Video, 2006), DVD.

7. Thomas Andrae, Geoffrey Blum and Gary Coddington, "Of Superman and Kids with Dreams: A Rare Interview with the Creators of Superman: Jerry Siegel & Joe Shuster," *Nemo, the Classic Comics Library*, #2 August 1983, 20.

8. Jerry Siegel (w), Paul Cassidy (p, i), Paul Lauretta (i), "The Construction Racket," *Superman* #6 (Sept. '40), National Comics Publications [DC Comics], 10. Jerry Siegel (w), Joe Shuster (p, i), "Superman in the Slums," *Action Comics* #8 (Jan. '39). Jack Schiff (w), Win Mortimer (p, i). "Superman Says: 'Hop on the Welfare Wagon!'" *Action Comics* #187 (June '52).

9. Presidents: Superman met Roosevelt several times, most notably in *Action Comics* #663. Roger Stern (w), Bob McLeod (p, i), Glenn Whitmore (c), "Time and Time Again, Phase Two: Lost in the '40s Tonight" (Mar. '91), DC Comics, 17; He met Truman in *Superman* #48, Jerry Siegel (w), John Sikela

(p, i), "The Man Who Stole the Sun!" (Sep. '47), National Comics Publications [DC Comics], 5; Kennedy also several times, notably in *Superman* #170, a special commemoration issue "authorized by the Kennedy family and the White House." E. Nelson Bridwell (w), Al Plastino (p. i), "Superman's Mission for President Kennedy!" (July '64), National Periodical Publications [DC Comics]; Johnson several times, notably in *Action Comics* #356. Leo Dorfman (w), Wayne Boring (p, i), "The Son of the Annihilator!" (Nov. '67), 9–11; Nixon in *Action Comics* #390, Cary Bates (w), Curt Swan (p), George Roussos (i), "The Self-Destruct Superman!" (July '70), DC Comics, 2; Carter in *Action Comics* #514, Marv Wolfman (w), Gil Kane (p), Joe Giella (i), Gene D'Angelo (c), "World Enough And Time," (Feb. '83), 4 (Carter is seen only in shadow and isn't named); Reagan several times, notably in *Legends* #2, 21–2 (also meeting vice president Bush), #3, 18 & #5, 15. John Ostrander & Len Wein (w), John Byrne (p), Karl Kesel, Dennis Janke (i), Tom Ziuko, Carl Gafford (c) (Nov. '86–Apr. '87); Clinton in *The Spectre* Vol. 3 #22, John Ostrander (w) Tom Mandrake (p, i) Carla Feeny (c), "Spear of Destiny, Part 4: Conclusion," (Sep. '94), 1–2, 17–8; W. Bush in *Justice League* Vol. 2 #6, Geoff Johns (w), Jim Lee (p), Scott Williams, Sandra Hope, Matt Banning, Mark Irwin (i), Alex Sinclair, Tony Aviña (c), "Justice League: Part Six," (Apr. '12), 23–4; Obama in *Superman/Wonder Woman* #20, Peter Tomasi (w), Doug Mahnke (p), Jaime Mendoza, Sean Parsons (i), Wil Quintana (c), "Dark Truth, Part Three: A Matter of Trust," (Oct. '15), 11–21; Washington several times, notably in *Superman* #48, Jerry Siegel (w), John Sikela (p, i), "Autograph, Please!" (Sep. '47), National Comics Publications [DC Comics], 8; and Lincoln, *ibid.*, 9. Becomes president: Roger Stern (w), Tom Grummett (p), Phil Rodier, Doug Hazlewood, Carlos Garzón, Brad Vancata (i), Glenn Whitmore, Matt Hollingsworth (c), "Armageddon 2001: Executive Action," *Action Comics Annual* #3 ('91), DC Comics. Earth-23: Grant Morrison (w), Doug Mahnke (p, i), Tom Nguyen, Drew Geraci, Christian Alamy, Norm Rapmund, Rodney Ramos, Walden Wong (i), Alex Sinclair, Tony Aviña, Pete Pantazis (c), "New Heaven, New Earth," *Final Crisis* #7 (Mar. '09), 1–4. Obama: Beverley Lyons, "Exclusive: Comics writer Grant Morrison turns Barack Obama into Superman," *Daily Record*, January 29, 2009, http://www.dailyrecord.co.uk/entertainment/celebrity/exclusive-comics-writer-grant-morrison-1007392.

10. David S. Goyer (w), Miguel Sepulveda (p, i), Paul Mounts (c), "The Incident," *Action Comics* #900 (June '11), DC Comics, 8; Chuck Dixon and Paul Rivoche, "How Liberalism Became Kryptonite for Superman," *Wall Street Journal*, June 8, 2014, https://www.wsj.com/articles/dixon-and-rivoche-how-liberalism-became-kryptonite-for-superman-1402265792.

11. Bill Willingham, Judd Winick (w), Rick Leonardi (p), Karl Story, Dan Green (i), Alex Bleyaert (c), "Chapter One: The Green Endorsement," *DC Universe: Decisions* #1 (Nov. '08), DC Comics, 13.

12. "Religious composition of adults in Kansas," *Pew Research Center* (Religious Landscape Study), n.d., http://www.pewforum.org/religious-landscape-study/state/kansas; "Vital Statistics: Jewish Population in the United States, by State (1899–Present)," http://www.jewishvirtuallibrary.org/jewish-population-in-the-united-states-by-state.

13. Elliot S. Maggin, "Is Superman Jewish?" *Quora*, Apr. 1, 2011, https://www.quora.com/Is-Superman-Jewish. Mark Millar, "Ecosse: Cover story: Is it a bird? Is it a plane? No, it's superman, but not as we know him," *Sunday Times*, April 27, 2003, http://www.thesundaytimes.co.uk/sto/news/uk_news/article228913.ece. Adheres: Bruce Bachand, "Interview: Elliot S! Maggin," *Fanzing: The DC comics Fan Site*, n.d., http://www.fanzing.com/mag/fanzing09/iview.shtml. Self-evident: Maggin, "Is Superman Jewish?"

14. Cary Bates (w), Curt Swan (p), Joe Giella (i), Tatjana Wood (c), "Superman Takes a Wife!" *Action Comics* #484 (June '78), DC Comics, 14 & 22. In 1999's *Superman: The Last God of Krypton* stand-alone issue he's even revealed to be a direct descendant of Rao, though this was never canonized. (Walter Simonson (w), Greg & Tim Hildebrandt (p, i, c), DC Comics, 33.)

15. *Superman*, directed by Richard Donner (1978; Burbank, CA: Warner Home Video, 2006), DVD; Mario Puzo et al., *Superman*. Final screenplay, 1976. Online: http://www.supermanhomepage.com/movies/superman_original.txt, 40, 44.

16. Elliot S. Maggin, *Superman: Last Son of Krypton* (New York: Warner Books, 1978), 14–33.

17. Church: John Byrne (w), Kurt Schaffenberger (p), Alfredo Alcala (i), Petra Scotese (c), *World of Smallville* #1 (Apr. '88), DC Comics, 1. Puritan: Byrne et al., *World of Smallville* #2 (May '88), 4. Schwartz: *World of Smallville* #1, 15.

18. Dan Jurgens, Karl Kesel, David Michelinie, Louise Simonson, Roger Stern (w), Tom Grummet, Dan Jurgens (p), Denis Rodier, Jerry Ordway (i), Glenn Whitmore (c), *Superman: The Wedding Album* (Dec. '96), DC Comics, 82–91. Chapel named in Special Edition promotional insert "wedding invitation"; *Superman: The Animated Series*. Season 2, episode 22, "The Late. Mr. Kent," first broadcast Nov. 1, 1997 by WB. Directed by Kenji Hachizaki and written by Stan Berkowitz.

19. Jeph Loeb (w), Tim Sale (p, i), Bjarne Hansen (c), "Spring," *Superman for All Seasons* #1 (Sep. '98), DC Comics, 26–7; Joe Kelly (w), German Garcia (p), Joe Rubinstein (i), Glenn Whitmore (c), "For a Thousand Years...," *Action Comics* #761 (Jan. '00), 3; Brian Azzarello (w), Jim Lee (p), Scott Williams (i), Alex Sinclair (c), "For Tomorrow," *Superman* Vol. 2 #204–15 (June '04–May '05); *Man of Steel*, directed by Zack Snyder (2013; Burbank, CA: Warner Home Video, 2013), DVD; *Batman v Superman: Dawn of Justice*, directed by Zack Snyder (2016; Burbank, CA: Warner Home Video, 2016), DVD. Played by Coburn Goss in both films. In the *Man of Steel*'s novelization Leone is a Lutheran pastor in

Metropolis. (Greg Cox, *Man of Steel: The Official Movie Novelization* (London: Titan Books, 2013), chap. 18, Kindle edition.)

20. Fabian Nicieza (w), Allan Goldman (p), Ron Randall (i), Marta Martinez, Pete Pantazis (c), "Redemption (Part II of II)—In Good Faith," *Action Comics* #849 (July '07), DC Comics, 21.

21. James Robinson (w), Ed Benes (p, i), Dinei Ribeiro (c), "The Last Days, Part Two," *Superman* Vol. 4 #41 (Apr. '18), DC Comics, 19.

22. Don Cameron (w), Ira Yarbrough (p), Stan Kaye (i), "Christmas 'Round the World," *Action Comics* #93 (Feb. '46), National Comics Publications [DC Comics]; Jeph Loeb (w) Ed McGuinness, Joe Madureira, Mike Wieringo, Rob Liefeld, Ian Churchill (p), Cam Smith, Norm Rapmund, Wayne Faucher, Art Adams (i), Tanya Horie (c), "Help!" *Superman* Vol. 2 #165 (Feb. '01), DC Comics; *Justice League.* Season 2, episode 23, "Comfort and Joy," first broadcast Dec. 13, 2003 by WB. Directed by Butch Lukic and written by Paul Dini.

23. Jerry Siegel (w) Jack Burnley (p, i), *Superman's Christmas Adventure* (likely Nov./Dec. '40), National Comics Publications [DC Comics]. A promotional giveaway produced for department and chain stores and the first "Christmas special" superhero comic; Jerry Siegel (w), John Sikela (p, i), "The Man Who Hated Christmas," *Action Comics* #105 (Feb. '47); Len Wein (w), Curt Swan (p), Murphy Anderson (i), Gene D'Angelo (c), "Twas the Fright Before Christmas!" *DC Comics Presents* #67 (Mar. '84).

24. Steve Englehart (w), Dick Ayers (p), Alfredo Alcala (i), "An Appointment with Destiny!" *Weird War Tales* #50 (Feb. '77), DC Comics; *Spectre* Vol. 3 #22.

25. Gail Simone (w), John Byrne (p), Nelson DeCastro (i), Guy Major (c), "A Contagion of Madness," *Action Comics* #835 (Mar. '06), DC Comics, 20–2.

Superman vs. the Mad Scientist

1. David Hajdu, *The Ten-Cent Plague: The Great Comic-Book Scare and How It Changed America* (New York: Picador, 2008).

2. Grant Morrison, *Supergods: What Masked Vigilantes, Miraculous Mutants, and a Sun God from Smallville Can Teach Us About Being Human* (New York: Spiegel & Grau, 2011), 52.

3. Fred Van Lente (w), Ryan Dunlavey (p, i), *Comic Book History of Comics* (June '12), IDW Publishing, 58–9, 61.

4. William Moulton Marston, "Why 100,000,000 Americans Read Comics," *American Scholar*, winter 1943–44 (online): https://theamericanscholar.org/wonder-woman/?utm_source=social_media&medium.

5. 1947: Van Lente & Dunlavey, *Comic Book History of Comics*, 61. 1949: Hajdu, *The Ten-Cent Plague*, 151. 1952: *ibid.*, 5.

6. Sold, 1942: "The Press: Superman's Dilemma," *Time*, April 13, 1942 (online), http://content.time.com/time/magazine/article/0,9171,766523,00.html. Sold, 1946: Mort Weisinger, "Here Comes Superman," *Coronet*, July 1946, 24. Membership, 1941: John Kabler, "Up, Up, and Awa-a-y! The Rise of Superman, Inc.," *Saturday Evening Post*, June 21, 1941, 15, http://www.saturdayeveningpost.com/wp-content/uploads/satevepost/rise-of-superman.pdf. Membership, 1946: Weisinger, *Coronet*, 24.

7. Cover by Wayne Boring (p), "The Prankster's Radio Program!" *Superman* #61 (Nov. '49), National Periodical Publications [DC Comics].

8. Jerry Siegel unpublished memoir, "Creation of a Superhero," 1979, Los Angeles. Larry Tye Papers, Box 3, Folder 1, Rare Books & Manuscripts Library Collections, Butler Library, Columbia University, New York, NY, 75.

9. Contract: R.C. Harvey, "Who Discovered Superman," *The Comics Journal*, Jan. 6, 2014, http://www.tcj.com/who-discovered-superman. Liebowitz: Daniel Best, "'A Curse on the Superman Movie!'—A Look Back at Jerry Siegel's 1975 Press Release," *20th Century Danny Boy* (blog), July 8, 2012 (10:35 a.m.), http://ohdannyboy.blogspot.com/2012/07/curse-on-superman-movie-look-back-at.html. $1.5 million: Kabler, "Up, Up, and Awa-a-y!" 76.

10. Scrutinized: Larry Tye, *Superman: The High-Flying History of America's Most Enduring Hero* (New York: Random House, 2013), 49. Forbidden: Best, "A Curse on the Superman Movie!" Expendability: Kabler, "Up, Up, and Awa-a-y!" 73. Refusing: Best, "A Curse on the Superman Movie!"

11. Pitches: *Siegel v. Time Warner Inc.* Case No. 04-8776-SGL(RZx) (C.D. Cal. July 30, 2007), 3–4 (online), https://web.archive.org/web/20071201031013/http://www.trexfiles.com/superboy_0727.pdf. Strip: Kabler, "Up, Up, and Awa-a-y!" 78.

12. Tye, *Superman*, 117.

13. *Ibid.*, 119; Van Lente & Dunlavey, *Comic Book History of Comics*, 153.

14. Confirm: Kabler, "Up, Up, and Awa-a-y!" 73. Contract: Mark Seifert, "For Sale at Auction: The Check That Bought Superman," *Bleeding Cool*, March 23, 2012, http://www.bleedingcool.com/2012/03/23/for-sale-at-auction-the-check-that-bought-superman. Ingrates, Acumen: *ibid.*; Tye, *Superman*, 119.

15. *Ibid.*

16. Recommend: Michael Eury, *The Krypton Companion* (Raleigh, NC: TwoMorrows Publishing, 2006), 20. Contributor: Arie Kaplan, *From Krakow to Krypton: Jews and Comic Books* (Philadelphia: The Jewish Publication Society, 2008), 11. Bumptious: Throughout Eury, *The Krypton Companion*. Talking down: *ibid.*, 40.

17. Joe Simon and Jim Simon, *The Comic Book Makers* (New York: Vanguard, 2003), 12, 15.

18. "Jerry Siegel (1914–1996)," *Superman Super Site*, n.d., http://www.supermansupersite.com/siegel.html; Tye, *Superman*, 186.

19. *Nights of Horror*: Craig Yoe, *Secret Identity:*

The Fetish Art of Superman's Co-Creator Joe Shuster (New York: Harry N. Abrams [Abrams Books], 2009). Janitor: Myrna Oliver, "Jerry Siegel; Co-Creator of Superman," *Los Angeles Times*, January 31, 1996, http://articles.latimes.com/1996-01-31/news/mn-30756_1_jerry-siegel. Delivery boy: Simon, *The Comic Book Makers*, 189.

20. Jerry Siegel (w), Joe Shuster (p, i), "The Medieval Mirthquake," *Funnyman* #4 (May '48), Magazine Enterprises, 4, 13; "The Peculiar Pacifier!" *Funnyman* #5 (July '48).

21. Tye, *Superman*, 78.

22. Louis Menand, "Pulp's Big Moment: How Emily Brontë met Mickey Spillane," *New Yorker*, Jan. 5, 2015, http://www.newyorker.com/magazine/2015/01/05/pulps-big-moment.

23. 200: Hajdu, *The Ten-Cent Plague*, 189. Cover by Johnny Craig (p, i), *Crime SuspenStories* #22 (May '54), EC Comics.

24. Bart Beaty, *Fredric Wertham and the Critique of Mass Culture* (Mississippi: University Press of Mississippi, 2005), 16–21.

25. Treated/clinic: Hajdu, *The Ten-Cent Plague*, 98. Testified: Beaty, *Fredric Wertham*, 16. Delinquents/*Brown v. BoE*: Carol L. Tilley, "Seducing the Innocent: Fredric Wertham and the Falsifications That Helped Condemn Comics," *Information & Culture: A Journal of History* 47, no. 4 (2012); 386, 391.

26. L.E. Stearns, "The Problem of the Comic Supplement," *Wisconsin Library Bulletin* 4 no. 6 (1908): 103; William Wordsworth, "Illustrated Books and Newspapers." In *William Wordsworth: Complete Poetical Works*, London: Macmillan & Co., 1888; Bartleby.com, 1999 (online), https://www.bartleby.com/145/ww994.html; Sterling North, "A National Disgrace and a Challenge to American Parents," *Childhood Education* 17, no. 2 (1940); 56. Originally an op-ed in the *Chicago Daily News*, May 1940.

27. Olive Richard, "Don't Laugh at the Comics," *Family Circle*, October 25, 1940, 10.

28. "The Press: Superman," *Time*, September 11, 1939 (online), http://content.time.com/time/magazine/article/0,9171,711787,00.html; Tye, *Superman*, 127.

29. Interview: Judith Crist, "Horror in the Nursery," *Collier's*, March 27, 1948, 22. Symposium/articles: Joe Sergi, "Tales From the Code: Welcome to Government Comics," *CBLDF*, Dec. 14, 2012, http://cbldf.org/2012/12/tales-from-the-code-welcome-to-government-comics.

30. Fredrick Wertham, *Seduction of the Innocent* (New York: Rinehart & Company, 1954), 16.

31. *Ibid.*, front flap & back flap.

32. Distinguish: *ibid.*, back flap, 14–15. Harmless: 107.

33. *Ibid.*, 25–6.

34. *Macbeth*: *ibid.*, 20, 22. Special: 33.

35. *Ibid.*, 34.

36. *Ibid.*, 189–90.

37. Undermines: *ibid.*, 98. Promotes/engenders: 33–4.

38. Conceit: *ibid.*, 97. Raiment: 32. Thankful: 34.

39. Bestseller/BotM: Van Lente & Dunlavey,

Comic Book History of Comics, 86. BotY/forums: Tilley, "Seducing the Innocent," 384, 389.

40. Andrew Scott Cooper, "Did an Artwork Solve a Decades-Old NYC Crime?" *Observer*, Aug. 19, 2014, http://observer.com/2014/08/did-an-artwork-solve-a-decades-old-nyc-crime.

41. Jenna Weissman Joselit, review of *The Brooklyn Thrill-Kill Gang and the Great Comic Book Scare of the 1950s*, by Mariah Adin, Praeger, 2014. In *American Jewish History* 100, No. 1, Jan. 2016, 155; Yoe, *Secret Identity*.

42. Expert: Mariah Adin, *The Brooklyn Thrill-Kill Gang and the Great Comic Book Scare of the 1950s* (Westport, CT: Praeger, 2014), 112. Officials/Antisemitic: Joselit, review, 155–56. Unearthed: Cooper, *Observer*.

43. Beaty, *Fredric Wertham*, 3–5.

44. Danny Fingeroth, *Disguised as Clark Kent: Jews, Comics, and the Creation of the Superhero* (New York: Continuum International Publishing Group Inc., 2007), 69–72, 76.

45. Arie Kaplan, *From Krakow to Krypton: Jews and Comic Books* (Philadelphia: The Jewish Publication Society, 2008), 74–75; Van Lente & Dunlavey, *Comic Book History of Comics*, 79–80; Hajdu, *The Ten-Cent Plague*, 98–9, 232; "Comic Book Superheroes Unmasked," first broadcast June 23, 2003 by The History Channel. Directed by Stephen Kroopnick and written by James Grant Goldin. Online at https://www.youtube.com/watch?v=Ygx_rUJ3XaI.

46. "Violence in the Media and Entertainment (Position Paper)," *American Academy of Family Physicians* (AAFP), 2016, http://www.aafp.org/about/policies/all/violence-media.html.

47. Crusade: Jerry Siegel (w), Joe Shuster (p, i), Paul Cassidy (p), "Superman Declares War on Reckless Drivers," *Action Comics* #12 (May '39), National Comics Publications [DC Comics]. Throws: *Action Comics* #2, 10. Aircraft: Jerry Siegel (w), Joe Shuster (p, i), "Revolution in San Monte Pt. 2," *Action Comics* #2 (July '38), 11; Jerry Siegel (w), Joe Shuster (p, i), Paul Cassidy (p), "Superman vs. the Cab Protective League," *Action Comics* #13 (June '39), 13; Jerry Siegel (w), Joe Shuster (p), Paul Cassidy (i), "Superman Champions Universal Peace!" *Superman* #2 (Sep. '39), 16.

48. Encountered: Tilley, "Seducing the Innocent," 386, 393, 397 (Edward and Vivian). Claimed: Wertham, *Seduction of the Innocent*, back flap.

49. Michael Chabon, *The Amazing Adventures of Kavalier & Clay* (New York: Random House, 2000), 631; Sigmund Freud, *Moses and Monotheism*, trans. Katherine Jones (Mansfield Centre: Martino Publishing, 2010), 134. For that matter, Freud saw God himself as a father metaphor.

50. Recognized: Tye, *Superman*, 85. Teach: Weisinger, *Coronet*, 24.

51. *Arena*. "Superman: The Comic Strip Hero," first broadcast April 18, 1981 by BBC Four. Directed by Anthony Wall. Online at https://www.youtube.com/watch?v=ViP5sjJflA0.

52. Fingeroth, *Disguised as Clark Kent*, 71.

53. *Ibid.*, 70.

54. "East European Jews in the German-Jewish Imagination from the Ludwig Rosenberger Library of Judaica." The University of Chicago Library, Special Collections Research Center. 1100 E. 57th St., Chicago, IL 60637. Sept. 1, 2008–June 30, 2009. Introduction, online; www.lib.uchicago.edu/collex/exhibits/exeej.

55. Mendelsohn: *ibid.*, Case 1: "'New Jews' vs. 'Old Jews': Emancipation, Assimilation, and the *Ostjuden* as Other," online: https://www.lib.uchicago.edu/e/webexhibits/RosenbergerEastAndWest/NewJewVsOldJew.html. Wasserman: *ibid.*, Case 5, Item 2: "The End of German-Jewish Life: *Ostjuden* as a Metaphor for All Jews," online: https://www.lib.uchicago.edu/e/webexhibits/RosenbergerEastAndWest/TheEndOfGermanJewishLife.html.

56. Edwin J. Kuh, "The Social Disability of the Jew," *Atlantic*, April 1908 (online), https://www.theatlantic.com/magazine/archive/1908/04/the-social-disability-of-the-jew/306261.

57. "East European Jews in the German-Jewish Imagination," introduction.

58. Van Lente & Dunlavey, *Comic Book History of Comics*, 40.

59. Fingeroth, *Disguised as Clark Kent*, 69–71; Kaplan, *From Krakow to Krypton*, 75; Van Lente & Dunlavey, *Comic Book History of Comics*, 80.

60. *Courant*: Arie Kaplan, "How the Jews Created the Comic Book Industry—Part I: The Golden Age (1933–1955)," *Reform Judaism Magazine* 32, no. 1 (Fall 2003), http://reformjudaismmag.net/03fall/comics.shtml. Antisemite: "Letter from Bishop Noll to Cardinal Stritch, April 1, 1946," The Catholic University of America, American Catholic History Research Center and University Archives, http://cuomeka.wrlc.org/exhibits/show/u–s—catholic-bishops—refugee/documents/noll_stritch_apr1946. Parasites: Hajdu, *The Ten-Cent Plague*, 214.3 (photo inserts). Northeastern: *ibid.*, 42.

61. Michael Freedland, "Hunting communists? They were really after Jews," *Jewish Chronicle*, August 6, 2009, https://www.thejc.com/culture/features/hunting-communists-they-were-really-after-jews-1.10702.

62. Lucas Reilly, "What's the Story Behind This Superman Comic?" *Mental Floss*, January 20, 2017, http://mentalfloss.com/article/89914/whats-story-behind-superman-comic.

63. Schwartz/Schiff: *ibid.*. Change: Tye, *Superman*, 62.

64. Hearings: Amy Kiste Nyberg, "Comics Code History: The Seal of Approval," *CBLDF*, n.d., http://cbldf.org/comics-code-history-the-seal-of-approval. News: Hajdu, *The Ten-Cent Plague*, 7.

65. Supporter: "Mortimaer May, Z.O.A. President, Lauded in Senate by Kefauver," *Jewish Telegraph Agency Daily News Bulletin* (J.T.A. News), Dec. 2, 1954, 6, http://pdfs.jta.org/1954/1954-12-02_227.pdf. Committee: United States Senate, "Special Committee on Organized Crime in Interstate Commerce (*The Kefauver Committee*)," https://www.senate.gov/artandhistory/history/common/investigations/Kefauver.htm#Outcome.

66. Testimony of Dr. Frederic Wertham, Hearings before the Subcommittee to Investigate Juvenile Delinquency of the Committee on the Judiciary United States Senate transcripts. Day One, Wednesday April 21, 1954, Afternoon Session. From http://www.thecomicbooks.com/wertham.html.

67. *Ibid.*

68. *Ibid.*

69. Kabler, "Up, Up, and Awa-a-y!" 15.

70. Marston, *American Scholar*.

71. Chairman: "Superman Actor George Reeves 'City Of Hope Little Helper' Membership Card," *Hake's Americana & Collectibles*, https://www.hakes.com/Auction/ItemDetail/204598/superman-actor-george-reeves-city-of-hope-little-helper-membership-card. Parades: George Reeves City of Hope appearance in Wisconsin (ad), *Waukesha Daily Freeman*, March 11, 1955, 14, https://www.newspapers.com/clip/4044837/george_reeves_city_of_hope_appearance. Reeves: Les Daniels, *Superman: The Complete History: The Life and Times of the Man of Steel*, 97. Also in Kaplan, *From Krakow to Krypton*, 85. Daniels doesn't cite the source. Wertham: *Seduction of the Innocent*, 381.

72. Paul Levitz, *75 Years Of DC Comics: The Art Of Modern Mythmaking* (Los Angeles: Taschen America, 2010), 422.

73. Jack Schiff (w), Wayne Boring (p,i), "Help keep your school All American!" (ad, 1949), National Comics Pub., Inc. [DC Comics]; Jack Schiff (w), Al Plastino (p,i), "Superman's Code for Buddies" (ad, 1950), National Comics Pub., Inc. [DC Comics]. Book covers: "Superman Book Cover," *Hake's Americana & Collectibles*, https://www.hakes.com/Auction/ItemDetail/45031/SUPERMAN-BOOK-COVER. Posters: "Superman 'Help Keep Your School All American!' Rare Poster," *Hake's Americana & Collectibles*, https://www.hakes.com/Auction/ItemDetail/204306/SUPERMAN-HELP-KEEP-YOUR-SCHOOL-ALL-AMERICAN-RARE-POSTER.

74. Sergi, "Tales From the Code."

75. Tilley, "Seducing the Innocent," 402.

76. Hajdu, *The Ten-Cent Plague*, 6, 116–26.

77. *New Yorker/Catholic World*: Joe Sergi, "The Amazing Adventure of The Man of Steel and the Psychiatric Censor—Superman vs. Doctor Wertham," *CBLDF*, Sept. 19, 2012, http://cbldf.org/2012/09/the-amazing-adventure-of-the-man-of-steel-and-the-psychiatric-censor-superman-vs-doctor-wertham. *L'Humanité*: "Aux Barricades!" *Time*, Nov. 3, 1947, 30.

78. PTA: Tye, *Superman*, 130. Hoover: J. Edgar Hoover, "January 1960 Law Enforcement Bulletin," United States Department of Justice–Federal Bureau of Investigation, Jan. 1, 1960, 1. In "Federal Bureau of Investigation (FBI) file on the Comics Magazine Association of America, 1960," Feb. 1, 1960, released Sept. 19, 2013, 8. From *Governmentattic.org*, http://www.governmentattic.org/9docs/FBI-ComicsMagazineAssn_1960.pdf.

79. Fredric Wertham, "It's Still Murder," *Saturday Review*, April 9, 1955, 12, 46 and 48, respectively.

80. Legislation: Hajdu, *The Ten-Cent Plague*, 7, 95, 293. Fulton Bill: Rich Johnston, "Canada To Make Crime Comics Legal Again," *Bleeding Cool*, June 8, 2017, https://www.bleedingcool.com/2017/06/08/canada-make-crime-comics-legal.

81. Disfavor: Van Lente & Dunlavey, *Comic Book History of Comics*, 57. Wood: Simon, *The Comic Book Makers*, 151–3.

82. Hajdu, *The Ten-Cent Plague*, 326.

83. "Comic Books and Juvenile Delinquency Interim Report of the Committee on the judiciary," United States Senate, March 14 (legislative Day, March 10), 1955. From http://www.thecomicbooks.com/1955senateinterim.html.

84. Van Lente & Dunlavey, *Comic Book History of Comics*, 103, 191.

85. 1b to 180m: Tye, *Superman*, 129, 223; John Jackson Miller, "Comic Book Sales Figures for 1960," *Comichron*, http://www.comichron.com/yearlycomicssales/postaldata/1960.html. Considering publication delays and bimonthly series, the average is likely even lower. 50 to 15: Joe Queenan, "Drawing on the DARK SIDE," *New York Times Magazine*, April 30, 1989, http://www.nytimes.com/1989/04/30/magazine/drawing-on-the-dark-side.html. According to the Comics Magazine Association of America (CMAA), in 1954 there were about thirty and in 1960 eleven. (Letter from CMAA President John L. Goldwater to FBI Director J. Edgar Hoover, Jan. 25, 1960, 3. In "Federal Bureau of Investigation (FBI) file on the Comics Magazine Association of America, 1960," Feb. 1, 1960, released Sept. 19, 2013, 7. From *Governmentattic. org*, http://www.governmentattic.org/9docs/FBI-ComicsMagazineAssn_1960.pdf.) Marvel: Stan Lee and George Mair, *Excelsior! The Amazing Life of Stan Lee* (New York: Touchstone, 2002), 94.

86. 800: Hajdu, *The Ten-Cent Plague*, 7, 329. Homeless: *Comic Book Superheroes Unmasked*.

87. "The Comics Code of 1954," *CBLDF*, accessed March 30, 2017, http://cbldf.org/the-comics-code-of-1954.

88. "Comics Code Revision of 1971," *CBLDF*, accessed March 30, 2017, http://cbldf.org/comics-code-revision-of-1971.

89. Grant Morrison, *Supergods: What Masked Vigilantes, Miraculous Mutants, and a Sun God from Smallville Can Teach Us About Being Human* (New York: Spiegel & Grau, 2011), 76. Quesada: *Comic Book Superheroes Unmasked*.

90. Wertham, "It's Still Murder," 48.

91. "Exhibit No. 21: National Comics Publications Inc. Editorial Policy for Superman D—C Publications," Hearings before the Subcommittee to Investigate Juvenile Delinquency of the Committee on the Judiciary United States Senate transcripts. Day Two, Thursday April 22, 1954. From http://www.thecomicbooks.com/dybwad.html.

92. John Jackson Miller, *Comichron*.

93. Tye, *Superman*, 151.

94. Eury, *The Krypton Companion*, 5–6.

95. Bill Finger (w), Wayne Boring (p), Stan Kaye (i), "The Man No Prison Could Hold!" *Action Comics* #248 (Jan. '59), National Comics Publications [DC Comics], 2.

96. Robert Kanigher (w), Ross Andru (p), Mike Esposito (i), "I, The Bomb!" *Wonder Woman* #157 (Oct. '65), National Periodical Publications [DC Comics].

97. John Jackson Miller, *Comichron*.

98. Spanking: Otto Binder (w), Kurt Schaffenberger (p, i), "Three Nights in the Fortress of Solitude!" *Superman's Girl Friend, Lois Lane* #14 (Jan. '60), National Comics Publications [DC Comics], 5, 8. Flapjacks/headache: Jerry Siegel (w), Kurt Schaffenberger (p, i), "The Battle Between Super-Lois and Super-Lana!" *Superman's Girl Friend, Lois Lane* #21 (Nov. '60), National Comics Publications [DC Comics], 3, 6, 9.

99. Morrison, *Supergods*, 63.

100. Fingeroth, *Disguised as Clark Kent*, 82.

101. Sigmund Freud, *Moses and Monotheism*, trans. Katherine Jones, 113–5.

102. *Comic Book Superheroes Unmasked*.

103. Bill Finger (w), Wayne Boring (p), Stan Kaye (i), "The Origin of Superman," *Superman* #53 (Aug. '48), National Comics Publications [DC Comics], 1, 3–6.

104. Bill Finger (w), Al Plastino (p, i), "Superman's Return to Krypton" *Superman* #61 (Nov. '49), National Comics Publications [DC Comics], 9.

105. William Woolfolk (w), Wayne Boring (p), Stan Kaye (i), "The Return of Planet Krypton!" *Action Comics* #182 (July '53), National Comics Publications [DC Comics].

106. Otto Binder (w), Dick Sprang (p), Stan Kaye (i), "The Three Magic Wishes," *Superman* #123 (Aug. '58), National Comics Publications [DC Comics]. Otto Binder (w), Wayne Boring (p), Stan Kaye (i), "Superman's Other Life," *Superman* #132 (Oct. '59).

107. Jerry Siegel (w), Wayne Boring (p), Stan Kaye (i), "Superman's Return to Krypton!" *Superman* #141 (Nov. '60), National Comics Publications [DC Comics].

108. Rick Bowers, *Superman versus the Ku Klux Klan: The True Story of How the Iconic Superhero Battled the Men of Hate* (Washington, D.C.: National Geographic Society, 2012), 118–20.

109. Robert Maxwell, "The Atom Man," October–November 1945, and "Atom Man in Metropolis," November–December 1945, *The Adventures of Superman* (radio). Some sources count the saga as 75, 76 or 77 episodes, including the overlapping preceding and subsequent storylines.

110. Robert Maxwell, "The Hate Mongers Organization," *The Adventures of Superman* (radio), April 16, 1946–May 20, 1946.

111. Robert Maxwell, "Clan of the Fiery Cross," *The Adventures of Superman* (radio), June 10, 1946–July 01, 1946.

112. Bowers, *Superman versus the Ku Klux Klan*, 73–5, 145–7, 167–73.

113. *Superman*, "Chapter 1: Superman Comes to Earth," directed by Spencer Bennet (Columbia Film, 1948).

114. *Superman and the Mole Men,* directed by Lee Sholem (Lippert Pictures, 1951).

If I Were a Superman

1. Friend: Michael Eury, *The Krypton Companion* (Raleigh, NC: TwoMorrows Publishing, 2006), 8. Contributed: Arie Kaplan, *From Krakow to Krypton: Jews and Comic Books* (Philadelphia: The Jewish Publication Society, 2008), 11. Agent: Grant Morrison, *Supergods: What Masked Vigilantes, Miraculous Mutants, and a Sun God from Smallville Can Teach Us About Being Human* (New York: Spiegel & Grau, 2011), 81.

2. Danny Fingeroth, *Disguised as Clark Kent: Jews, Comics, and the Creation of the Superhero* (New York: Continuum International Publishing Group Inc., 2007), 78. "Rebuilding the Temple."

3. Brigid Alverson, "Survivors of the First Comic Con Gather at NYCC," *CBR.com,* Oct. 19, 2014, http://www.cbr.com/survivors-of-the-first-comic-con-gather-at-nycc; "About Comic-Con International," Comic-Con International: San Diego, retrieved Oct. 13, 2016, https://www.comic-con.org/about; Calvin Reid, "A Record 250,000 Fans Mob New York Comic Con 2018," *Publishers Weekly,* Oct. 10, 2018, https://www.publishersweekly.com/pw/by-topic/industry-news/comics/article/78281-a-record-250-000-fans-mob-new-york-comic-con-2018.html).

4. Decided: Morrison, *Supergods,* 61. Shooter: Jim Shooter, "How I Spent My Summer Vacation—1965," jimshooter.com (blog), March 10, 2011, http://jimshooter.com/2011/03/how-i-spent-my-summer-vacation-1965.html.

5. Eury, *Krypton Companion,* 26.

6. *Ibid.,* 12–3.

7. Larry Tye, *Superman: The High-Flying History of America's Most Enduring Hero* (New York: Random House, 2013), 162.

8. Eury, *Krypton Companion,* 198.

9. Weisinger: *ibid.,* 13. Schwartz/detested: Tye, *Superman,* 165–166, 227. Freelancer: Jerry Siegel unpublished memoir, "Creation of a Superhero," 1979, Los Angeles. Larry Tye Papers, Box 3, Folder 1, Rare Books & Manuscripts Library Collections, Butler Library, Columbia University, New York, NY, 80.

10. Marvel: Eury, *Krypton Companion,* 49. Lee: Eric J. Greenberg, "Superman: A Jewish Hero," *Jerusalem Post,* May 1, 1996, 7.

11. 1966: Tye, *Superman,* 186. DC likely used scripts Siegel had already written after they fired him, accounting for his 1967 output. Arguing: Fred Van Lente (w), Ryan Dunlavey (p, i), *Comic Book History of Comics* (June '12), IDW Publishing, 152–4. Ruled: Tye, 186. Dropped: Van Lente & Dunlavey, 154–6.

12. Eury, *Krypton Companion,* 14.

13. Translated: Tye, *Superman,* 179. Sales: John Jackson Miller, "Superman Sales Figures," *Comichron,* http://www.comichron.com/

titlespotlights/superman.html. Information isn't available for 1963–1964 but thought to be the same.

14. "The 1960s: The Decade When Everything Changed," *Life,* https://backissues.time.com/storefront/special-editions/life-the-1960s-the-decade-when-everything-changed/prodLITHE1960SBZ.html.

15. Rebecca Lowery, "The Warhol Effect: A Timeline," in *Regarding Warhol: Sixty Artists, Fifty Years,* ed. Elisa Urbanelli (New York: The Metropolitan Museum of Art, 2012), 250; N.a. (likely Robert Bernstein), Kurt Schaffenberger (p, i), "The Super-Surprise!" *Superman's Girl Friend, Lois Lane* #24 (Apr. '61), National Periodical Publications [DC Comics], 5.

16. N.a., "Kryptonite, brainiac, and other Superman language," *Oxford Dictionaries Blog,* Oxford University Press, n.d., http://blog.oxforddictionaries.com/2014/10/superman-language-brainiac-kryptonite.

17. Jerry Ordway (w), Dan Jurgens, Tom Grummett, Curt Swan, Jon Bogdanove, Jim Mooney, Art Thibert, Bob McLeod (p), Brett Breeding, Dennis Janke, Jerry Ordway, Art Thibert, Brett Breeding, Denis Rodier (i), Glenn Whitmore (c), "Dying Breed," *Adventures of Superman* #480 (July '91), DC Comics, 13.

18. Robert Kanigher (w), Ross Andru (p), Mike Esposito (i), "The Soldier of Steel!" *Superman* #216 (May '69), National Periodical Publications [DC Comics].

19. Rightwing: Tye, *Superman,* 165. Admitted: Eury, *Krypton Companion,* 14.

20. Speed: Otto Binder (w) Al Plastino (p, i), "The Story of Superman's Life!" *Superman* #146 (July '61), National Periodical Publications [DC Comics]. Hypnosis: Bill Finger (w), Wayne Boring (p), Stan Kaye (i), "The Man No Prison Could Hold!" *Action Comics* #248 (Jan. '59), National Comics Publications [DC Comics], 8. Ventriloquism: Robert Bernstein (w), Wayne Boring (p), Stan Kaye (i), "The War between Supergirl and the Superman Emergency Squad!" *Action Comics* #276 (May '61), National Periodical Publications [DC Comics], 12. Weaving: Otto Binder (w), Kurt Schaffenberger (p, i), "The Super-Family of Steel!" *Superman's Girl Friend, Lois Lane* #15 (Feb. '60), National Comics Publications [DC Comics], 5. Memory: Edmond Hamilton (w), Curt Swan (p), George Klein (i), "The Last Days of Superman!" *Superman* #156 (Oct. '62), National Periodical Publications [DC Comics], 4. Mathematics: Robert Bernstein (w), Kurt Schaffenberger (p, i), "Baby Lois Lane!" *Superman's Girl Friend, Lois Lane* #10 (July '59), National Comics Publications [DC Comics], 5. Kissing: Robert Bernstein (w), Al Plastino (p, i), "The Great Superman Impersonation!" *Action Comics* #306 (Nov. '63), National Periodical Publications [DC Comics], 2. Sneeze: Jerry Siegel (w), Al Plastino (p, i), "The World of Mr. Mxyzptlk!" *Action Comics* #273 (Feb. '61), National Periodical Publications [DC Comics], 2. Homunculus: Jerry Coleman (w), Kurt Schaffenberger (p,

i), "Superman's New Power!" *Superman* #125 (Nov. '58), National Comics Publications [DC Comics], 3–8.

21. "Reception in America," n.d., retrieved Oct. 13, 2017, *Anne Frank House*, http://www.annefrank.org/en/Anne-Frank/Publication-of-the-diary/Reception-in-America.

22. Eury, *Krypton Companion*, 107. Neil Adams' account of what Shuster told him. According to Julian Voloj and Thomas Campi in *The Artist Behind Superman: The Joe Shuster Story*, Shuster had written in a letter that he was actually the guest of honor at a preview benefit party for the show. (New York: Super Genius, 2018), 180.

23. Rich Cohen, "Ebb Tide in the Golden Country: All is not as it was for Jews in America," *Tablet*, June 1, 2015, http://www.tabletmag.com/jewish-news-and-politics/191087/ebb-tide-in-the-golden-country; Lauren Markoe, "Marilyn Monroe, Liz Taylor were seriously Jewish, exhibit explains," *Washington Post*, Nov. 27, 2015, https://www.washingtonpost.com/national/religion/marilyn-monroe-liz-taylor-were-seriously-jewish-exhibit-explains/2015/11/27/87700262-952c-11e5-befa-99ceebcbb272_story.html?utm_term=.b11695ce2b33.

24. Rachel Shukert, "Jew Pop," *Tablet*, March 23, 2012, http://www.tabletmag.com/jewish-arts-and-culture/94853/jew-pop.

25. N.a., likely Arnold Drake (w), Bob Oksner, Wayne Boring (p, i), "Superman Meets Jerry," *The Adventures of Jerry Lewis* #105 (Apr. '68), National Periodical Publications [DC Comics].

26. Marc Tracy, "Mad Magazine, Irreverent Baby Boomer Humor Bible, Is All but Dead," July 5, 2019, *New York Times*, https://www.nytimes.com/2019/07/05/business/media/mad-magazine-publication-demise.html; Fingeroth, *Disguised as Clark Kent*, 76. Kaplan, a *Mad* writer himself, discusses its Jewish influences at length, *From Krakow to Krypton*, 71–81.

27. Harvey Kurtzman (w), Wally Wood (p, i), "Superduperman," *Mad* #4 (Apr.–May '53), EC comics, 5.

28. "Kirk and Spock bonded over real life anti-Semitism," *Times of Israel*, Feb. 12, 2016, http://www.timesofisrael.com/kirk-and-spock-actors-bonded-over-shared-heritage-of-anti-semitism; Brendan Maher, "Leonard Nimoy, man of many universes," *Baltimore Sun*, March 26, 2000, http://articles.baltimoresun.com/2000-03-26/entertainment/0003270311_1_leonard-nimoy-spock-jewish-activist. "Shaddai" first appears in Genesis 17:1, usually translated as "Almighty." It's found on *Mezuzot* and *Tefillin*.

29. Hoberman: David E. Kaufman, *Jewhooing the Sixties: American Celebrity and Jewish Identity* (New York: Brandeis, 2012), 39. Bestseller: Lester D. Friedman, *The Jewish Image in American Film* (New York: Citadel Press, 1987), 162.

30. Friedman: *ibid.*, 164. Newman was paternally Jewish and identified as Jewish: John Skow, "Paul Newman: Verdict on a Superstar," *Time*, Dec.

06, 1982, http://content.time.com/time/magazine/article/0,9171,923114-5,00.html.

31. Philip Roth, *Reading Myself and Others* (New York: Farrar Straus & Giroux, 1975), 137–8.

32. "Israeli War of Independence: Background & Overview (1947–1949)," *Jewish Virtual Library*, n.d., retrieved May 15, 2016, http://www.jewishvirtuallibrary.org/background-and-overview-israel-war-of-independence.

33. "David Ben-Gurion," *YNet News*, Oct. 19, 2008, https://www.ynetnews.com/articles/0,7340,L-3610688,00.html.

34. Jonathan D. Sarna & Jonathan Golden, "The American Jewish Experience in the Twentieth Century: Antisemitism and Assimilation" part 2, *National Humanities Center*, Oct. 2000, http://nationalhumanitiescenter.org/tserve/twenty/tkeyinfo/jewishexpb.htm.

35. 30%: Howard Sachar, "Jews in the Civil Rights Movement," *My Jewish Learning*, n.d., retrieved March 10, 2017, https://www.myjewishlearning.com/article/jews-in-the-civil-rights-movement. Prinz: Rabbi Evan Moffic, "The Forgotten Speech at the March on Washington," *Huffpost*, Oct. 26, 2013, https://www.huffingtonpost.com/rabbi-evan-moffic/joachim-prinz-march-on-washington-speech_b_3814893.html. Levison: Clarence B. Jones, "On Martin Luther King Day, remembering the first draft of 'I Have a Dream,'" *Washington Post*, Jan. 16, 2011, http://www.washingtonpost.com/wp-dyn/content/article/2011/01/14/AR2011011406266.html.

36. John Jackson Miller, "Comichron's Postal Comics Sales Data Repository," *Comichron*, http://www.comichron.com/yearlycomicssales/postaldata.html.

37. Otto Binder (w), Al Plastino (p, i), "The Super-Duel in Space!" *Action Comics* #242 (July '58), National Comics Publications [DC Comics].

38. Paul Kupperberg (w), Howard Chaykin (p), Murphy Anderson (i), Jerry Serpe (c), "This Planet is Doomed!" *World of Krypton* #2 (Aug. '79), DC Comics, 12.

39. Otto Binder (w), Al Plastino (p, i), "The Story of Superman's Life!" *Superman* #146 (July '61), National Periodical Publications [DC Comics], citizenship 12, childhood 4–5.

40. Eury, *Krypton Companion*, 184, 213. Siegel unpublished memoir, 81.

41. Jerry Siegel (w), Curt Swan (p), George Klein (i), "The Death of Superman!" *Superman* #149 (Nov. '61), National Periodical Publications [DC Comics], Part III p. 5 (killed, tried), Part III p. 7 (Eichmann, deals).

42. Killed & injured: Bruce Robinson, "The Blitz," *BBC History*, March 30, 2011, http://www.bbc.co.uk/history/worldwars/wwtwo/ff3_blitz.shtml. Award: Leon Jaroff, "The Rocket Man's Dark Side," *Time*, March 26, 2002, http://content.time.com/time/health/article/0,8599,220201,00.html.

43. Kaplan, *Krakow to Krypton*, 14.

44. Jim Shooter (w), Wayne Boring (p, i), "The Four Element Enemies!" *Superman* #190 (Oct. '66),

National Periodical Publications [DC Comics]. Zod: Kurt Busiek (w), Rick Leonardi (p), Dan Green (i), Alex Sinclair (c), "The Third Kryptonian Finale: The Stand," *Superman* #670 (Jan. '08), DC Comics, 14–5.

45. Frank Robbins (w), Bob Brown (p), Wally Wood (i), "Superboy's Darkest Secret!" *Superboy* #158 (July '69), National Periodical Publications [DC Comics].

46. Eury, *Krypton Companion*, 212.

47. Cat: *Superman's Girl Friend, Lois Lane* #70. Baby: *Action Comics* #284, *Superman's Girl Friend, Lois Lane* #3, #32, #42, #57, *Superman's Pal, Jimmy Olsen* #18. Old: *Action Comics* #251. Tree-man: *Superman's Girl Friend, Lois Lane* #112. Devil: *Superman's Pal, Jimmy Olsen* #68. Fat: *Superboy* #24, *Action Comics* #270, #298, *Superman* #221. Miniscule: *Superboy* #61, *Action Comics* #242, *Adventure Comics* #270. Giant: *Adventure Comics* #262, #270, *Action Comics* #325, *Superman* #226, #302. Mind-reader: *Action Comics* #283. Split: *Adventure Comics* #255, *Action Comics* #293, #311, *World's Finest Comics* #126, *Superman* #162. Parade balloon: *World's Finest* Comics #131. Sphinx, magnetic, Jesse James double: *Superboy* #103. Kryptonian monster: *Action Comics* #303. Caveman: *World's Finest Comics* #151. Monkey: *Superboy* #142. Giant gorilla: *Superboy* #142. Leper: *Action Comics* #363. Warped shape: *Superman's Girl Friend, Lois Lane* #116. Rainbow glow: *Superman's Girl Friend, Lois Lane* #3. Midas touch: *Action Comics* #193. Lion's head: *Action Comics* #243. Ant's head: *Action Comics* #296. Third eye: *Action Comics* #275. Fire breath: *Action Comics* #283, *Superboy* #115. Diamond-vision: *Adventure Comics* #259. Long hair and fingernails: *Superman* #139. Extra fingers: *Superboy* #105. Face changing colors: *Action Comics* #317. Supporting cast superpowers: *Superman's Girl Friend, Lois Lane* #8, #15, #21, #28, #36, #47, #78, #85, #87, *Superman's Pal, Jimmy Olsen* #2, #15, #16, #37, #39, #62, #68, #76, #93, #96, #99, #111#118, #158, *Action Comics* #253. Insects: *Superman's Girl Friend, Lois Lane* #69, *Superman's Pal, Jimmy Olsen* Jimmy #94.

48. Robert Bernstein (w) Al Plastino (p, i), "The Menace of Metallo," *Action Comics* #252 (May '59), National Comics Publications [DC Comics].

Nazis in Space and Superman on Screen

1. Fred Van Lente (w), Ryan Dunlavey (p, i), *Comic Book History of Comics* (June '12), IDW Publishing, 201–2. The man most responsible was Jewish entrepreneur Phil Seuling, who established Sea Gate Distributions, the first wholesale dealer dedicated to the direct market.

2. Arie Kaplan, "Kings of Comics: How Jews Transformed The Comic Book Industry Part III: The Bronze Age (1979—)," *Reform Judaism Magazine* 32, no. 3 (Spring 2004), http://www.reformjudaismmag.net/04spring/comics.shtml. Requoted in Kaplan's *From Krakow to Krypton: Jews and Comic Books* (Philadelphia: The Jewish Publication Society,

2008), 189. Also paraphrased in Danny Fingeroth's *Disguised as Clark Kent: Jews, Comics, and the Creation of the Superhero* (New York: Continuum International Publishing Group Inc., 2007), 134.

3. Larry Tye, *Superman: The High-Flying History of America's Most Enduring Hero* (New York: Random House, 2013), 188.

4. *Ibid.*

5. Shtetl: Paul Levitz, "Immigration and Comics," *ICv2*, August 17, 2017, https://icv2.com/articles/columns/view/38237/immigration-comics. Megillah: Michael Eury, *The Krypton Companion* (Raleigh: TwoMorrows Publishing, 2006), 136.

6. Prevalent: Kaplan, "Kings of Comics Part III." Attitude: Arlen Schumer, "The 13 Most Influential Jewish Creators and Execs, Part 4," *13th Dimension*, Sep. 22, 2015, https://13thdimension.com/the-13-most-influential-jewish-creators-and-execs-part-4.

7. Jerry Siegel unpublished memoir, "Creation of a Superhero," 1979, Los Angeles. Larry Tye Papers, Box 3, Folder 1, Rare Books & Manuscripts Library Collections, Butler Library, Columbia University, New York, NY, 87; John Jackson Miller, "Superman Sales Figures," *Comichron*, http://www.comichron.com/titlespotlights/superman.html.

8. Maggin: Eury, *The Krypton Companion*, 145. Ross: *ibid.*, 229.

9. Robert Kanigher (w), Werner Roth (p), Vince Colletta (i), "I Am Curious (Black)!" *Superman's Girl Friend, Lois Lane* #106 (Nov. '70), National Periodical Publications [DC Comics], 13.

10. Dennis O'Neil (w), Curt Swan (p), Murphy Anderson (i), "Superman Breaks Loose," *Superman* #233 (Jan. '71), National Periodical Publications [DC Comics], 1.

11. Cary Bates (w), Gray Morrow (p, i), "A Name Is Born," *Superman* #238 (June '71), National Periodical Publications [DC Comics]; E. Nelson Bridwell (w), Curt Swan (p), Frank Chiaramonte (i), Carl Gafford (c), *Krypton Chronicles* #1–3 (Sep.–Nov. '81), DC Comics.

12. *Ibid.*, #3, 10–7.

13. Ludwig Blau et al., "Samael," *The Jewish Encyclopedia*, V. 10 (1906): 665–6 (online), http://www.jewishencyclopedia.com/articles/13055-samael. He's also associated with the serpent of Eden; Zohar 23b, 55a.

14. Elliot S. Maggin (w), Keith Pollard (p), Mike DeCarlo (i), Gene D'Angelo (c), "The Superwoman of Metropolis!" *DC Comics Presents Annual* #2 (July '83), DC Comics, 16.

15. Elliot S. Maggin, *Miracle Monday* (New York: Warner Books, 1981), 35.

16. Elliot S. Maggin (w), Klaus Janson (p, i, c), "The Living Legends of Superman: Chapter Seven," *Superman* #400 (Oct. '84), DC Comics. First noted by Arie Kaplan in conversation with the author.

17. Elliot S. Maggin (w), Curt Swan (p), Murphy Anderson (i), Gene D'Angelo (c), "The Day the Cheering Stopped!" *Superman Annual* #10 ('84), DC Comics, 4–5, 40. This is the second time God talks to Superman, the first being in *DC Comics Presents* #29 (Len Wein (w), Jim Starlin (p), Romeo Tanghal

(i), Jerry Serpe (c), "Where No Superman Has Gone Before!" (Jan. '81), 15–6).

18. Alan Kistler, "SDCC: Remembering the Julius Schwartz Era of Superman," *CBR.com*, Aug. 2, 2013, https://www.cbr.com/sdcc-remembering-the-julius-schwartz-era-of-superman.

19. Elliot S. Maggin (w), Curt Swan (p), Murphy Anderson (i), "Must There Be a Superman?" *Superman* #247 (Jan. '72), National Periodical Publications [DC Comics].

20. Cary Bates (w), Curt Swan (p), Joe Staton (i), Adrienne Roy (c), "The Debut of Superman III!" *Superman* #354 (Dec. '80), National Periodical Publications [DC Comics], 3–7.)

21. Edelstein: Cary Bates (w), Curt Swan (p), Tex Blaisdell (i), "Terra At Nine O'Clock!" *Action Comics* #468 (Feb. '77), National Periodical Publications [DC Comics]. Black: George Pérez (w, p), Jesús Merino (p, i), Brian Buccellato (c), "What Price Tomorrow?" *Superman* Vol. 3 #1 (Nov. '11), DC Comics.

22. Paul Kupperberg(w), Carmine Infantino (p), Bob Oksner (i), Tom Ziuko (c), *Supergirl* Vol. 2 #13–5 (Nov. '83–Jan. '84), DC Comics.

23. E. Nelson Bridwell (w), Ramona Fradon (p), Bob Smith (i), "The Warning of the Wonder Twins!" *Super Friends* #7 (Oct. '77), DC Comics, 6.

24. Eury, *The Krypton Companion*, 226.

25. Levitz: Anthony Ha, Brian Heater, "Celebrating Jack Kirby, the King of Comics, at 100," *TechCrunch*, Aug. 27, 2017, https://techcrunch.com/2017/08/27/100-years-of-jack-kirby/?ncid=mobilenavtrend. Informed: Eury, *The Krypton Companion*, 226.

26. Arie Kaplan, "How Jews Transformed the Comic Book Industry Part II: The Silver Age (1956–1978)," *Reform Judaism Magazine*, 32, no. 2 (Winter 2003), http://www.reformjudaismmag.net/03winter/comics.shtml. Bogdanove is also quoted in Kaplan's *From Krakow to Krypton*, 128–30. Similar points are made by Fingeroth, 99.

27. Jack Kirby (w, p), Vince Colletta (i), "Orion Fights for Earth!" *New Gods* #1 (Mar. '71), National Periodical Publications [DC Comics] 10, 12.

28. Ronin Ro, *Tales to Astonish: Jack Kirby, Stan Lee, and the American Comic Book Revolution* (New York: Bloomsbury USA, 2004), 148.

29. Kazan: *Ibid.*; Rose: Mark Evanier, "The Jack Kirby FAQ," *POV Online* (blog), Dec. 17, 2010, https://web.archive.org/web/20101217041205/http://povonline.com/jackfaq/JackFaq1.htm. Barda first appeared in Jack Kirby (w, p) Vince Colletta (i), "The Closing Jaws of Death!" *Mister Miracle* #4 (Oct. '71), National Periodical Publications [DC Comics].

30. Ronin Ro, *Tales to Astonish*, 48.

31. Dorf: *ibid.*. Letter: Eury, *The Krypton Companion*, 92. Tefillin: Gabriela Geselowitz, "Jewish Artist Jack Kirby Co-Created X-Men and Captain America. But What He Did Next Was Even Better," *Tablet*, Aug. 31, 2017, http://www.tabletmag.com/scroll/244316/jewcy-kirby. Depicted: Jack Kirby (w, p), Mike Royer (i), "Himon!" *Mister Miracle* #9 (Aug. '72), National Periodical Publications [DC Comics], 7.

32. Written word, eternal: Kirby, *New Gods* #1, 7–9. Beyond: Jack Kirby (w, p), Mike Royer (i), "Spawn!" *New Gods* #5 (Nov. '71), National Periodical Publications [DC Comics], 4.

33. Jack Kirby (w, p), Mike Royer (i), "The Pact," *New Gods* #7 (Mar. '72), National Periodical Publications [DC Comics], 19–20.

34. Kirby, *New Gods* #1, 1–2. Highfather's son Orion is also a Moses figure, a child raised in the royal court of his people's enemy only to fight on their behalf upon adulthood.

35. Ro, *Tales to Astonish*, 160.

36. Eury, *The Krypton Companion*, 105–6; Tye, *Superman*, 215. Tye estimates Siegel made $7,000 a year.

37. Living: Eury, *The Krypton Companion*, 105–6. Patrolman: Joe Simon and Jim Simon, *The Comic Book Makers* (New York: Vanguard, 2003), 188.

38. Apoplectic: Van Lente & Dunlavey, *Comic Book History of Comics*, 156. According to Tye, Puzo's payment was actually 5 percent of gross, which would equate to $15 million (Tye, *Superman*, 192). Adams: Eury, *The Krypton Companion*, 105. Interview: Rafael Medoff, "Superman: Saving his Jewish creators," *jns.org* (*Jewish News Service*), June 10, 2013, http://www.jns.org/latest-articles/2013/6/10/superman-saving-his-jewish-creators#.V6Ubk_7dW04=.

39. Daniel Best, "'A Curse on the Superman Movie!'—A Look Back at Jerry Siegel's 1975 Press Release," *20th Century Danny Boy* (blog), July 8, 2012 (10:35 a.m.), http://ohdannyboy.blogspot.com/2012/07/curse-on-superman-movie-look-back-at.html.

40. Eury, *The Krypton Companion*, 105–7; Media: Tye, *Superman*, 216. By other accounts it was Robinson who initiated the campaign: Arie Kaplan, "How the Jews Created the Comic Book Industry—Part I: The Golden Age (1933–1955)," *Reform Judaism Magazine* 32, no. 1 (Fall 2003), http://reformjudaismmag.net/03fall/comics.shtml; and Van Lente & Dunlavey, 156.

41. Medoff, "Superman."

42. Eury, *The Krypton Companion*, 126.

43. Agreement: Tye, *Superman*, 217. By 1988 their annuity was quadrupled to $80,000 (*ibid.*, 242). Fearful: Henry Mietkiewicz, "Great Krypton! Superman was the Star's Ace Reporter," *Toronto Star* (Toronto, ON), April 26, 1992, A.10.

44. Matthew Flamm, "A Demimonde in Twilight," *New York Times*, June 2, 2002, http://www.nytimes.com/2002/06/02/nyregion/a-demimonde-in-twilight.html. Under the penname Mario Cleri.

45. Mario Puzo et al., *Superman*. Final screenplay, 1976. Online: http://www.supermanhomepage.com/movies/superman_original.txt; Tom Mankiewicz, *Superman: The Movie*. Shooting script. Online; http://bigapricot.org/scripts/superman_I.txt. Brando: *You Will Believe: The Cinematic Saga of Superman* (2006; Burbank, CA: Warner Home Video, 2006), DVD.

46. Heston: Tye, *Superman*, 193. Newman & Hoffman: *You Will Believe*.

47. Cost: Tye, *Superman*, 332. Covers: Aljean Harmetz, "The Marketing Of Superman And His Paraphernalia," *New York Times*, June 21, 1981, http://www.nytimes.com/1981/06/21/movies/the-marketing-of-superman-and-his-paraphernalia.html. Grossed: Tye, *Superman*, 203. Accomplished: "Top Lifetime Grosses," *Box Office Mojo*, https://www.boxofficemojo.com/chart/top_lifetime_gross/?area=XWW.

48. "Superman: Blockbuster from Krypton?" *Hollywood Reporter*, 15. In *Supermania78.com*, http://supermania78.com/2014/02/ilyas-big-idea.

49. Peter Sanderson, "Comics in Context," *A Site Called Fred*, July 20, 2006 http://asitecalledfred.com/2006/08/25/comics-in-context-143-san-diego-2006-the-donner-party.

50. Tye, *Superman*, 335.

51. Christopher Reeve, *Still Me* (New York: Ballantine Books, 1999), 193.

52. *You Will Believe*. According to Tye, Siegel said this to Jenette Kahn. (Tye 202) It's entirely possible that several people were present or that Siegel repeated it.

53. Kenneth Plume, "Interview with Director Richard Donner," *IGN*, May 1, 2001 (updated May 20, 2012), https://www.ign.com/articles/2001/05/01/interview-with-director-richard-donner.

54. Pete Hamill, "Watching the Daily News become the Daily Planet," *New York Daily News*, July 7, 2017, http://www.nydailynews.com/new-york/manhattan/pete-hamill-watching-daily-news-daily-planet-article-1.3309200. Originally published July 8, 1977, pg. 40.

55. *You Will Believe*.

56. N.a., "Superman II," *SciFiNow's 80s Sci-Fi Almanac*, July 2014, 42.

57. Mario Puzo, *Superman II* scriptment, 1976, 357–62. Online: https://www.supermanhomepage.com/movies/supermanii_scriptment_2_76.txt. *Superman II* shooting script, 118–26. Online; https://www.supermanhomepage.com/movies/superman_II_shoot.txt. The scene was shot by Donner.

58. Rosenthal: *You Will Believe*. The script was co-written by Lawrence Konner & Mark Rosenthal and directed by Sidney J. Furie, all Jewish. Double: "1987 Domestic Grosses," *Big Office Mojo*, http://www.boxofficemojo.com/yearly/chart/?yr=1987.

59. Inflation: Tim McMahon, "Long Term U.S. Inflation," *InflationData.Com*, April 1, 2014, https://inflationdata.com/Inflation/Inflation_Rate/Long_Term_Inflation.asp. Returned: Chuck Rozanski, "Chuck Goes to New York Part II," *Mile High Comics* (blog), n.d., http://www.milehighcomics.com/tales/cbg105.html.

60. Jim Beard, "Cancelled Comics Cavalcade: 30 Years Later with Paul Kupperberg," *Comics Bulletin*, n.d., https://web.archive.org/web/20140606234133/http://www.comicsbulletin.com/interviews/3621/cancelled-comics-cavalcade-30-years-later-with-paul-kupperberg.

61. Saved: *ibid.*. Sales: John Jackson Miller, *Comichron*, "Star Wars Sales Figures," http://www.comichron.com/titlespotlights/starwars.html; "*Amazing Spider-Man* Sales Figures," http://www.comichron.com/titlespotlights/amazingspiderman.html; "*Superman* Sales Figures," "*Batman* Sales Figures," http://www.comichron.com/titlespotlights/batman.html. Batman sales unavailable for 1977, but likely lower than 1979's 166,000 copies.

62. Market share, Byrne: Jim Shooter, "Superman—First Marvel Issue!" *JimShooter.com* (blog), Aug. 26, 2011, http://jimshooter.com/2011/08/superman-first-marvel-issue.html. Breach: Miller, "*Superman* Sales Figures."

63. Simcha Weinstein, *Up, Up, and Oy Vey: How Jewish History, Culture and Values Shaped the Comic Book Superhero* (Baltimore: Leviathan Press, 2006), 28. The concept's bookend, *tikkun olam*, is mentioned in the context of Krypton's destruction in Tye, 66.

64. Cover by George Pérez (p), Dick Giordano, Jerry Ordway (i), "Beyond the Silent Night," *Crisis on Infinite Earths* #7 (Oct. '85), DC Comics. The issue's title is a corresponding reference to the Christmas song about the birth of Christ.

65. Tye, *Superman*, 227.

66. Eury, *The Krypton Companion*, 64.

Second Coming

1. John Petty, *A Brief History of Comic Books* (Dallas: Heritage Auction Galleries, 2006), 8. https://www.heritagestatic.com/comics/d/history-of-comics.pdf; John Jackson Miller, "Why So Serious? 1984–1989," *LIFE Rise of the Superhero: From the Golden Age to the Silver Screen*, Nov. 10, 2017, 62–70; Arie Kaplan, *From Krakow to Krypton: Jews and Comic Books* (Philadelphia: The Jewish Publication Society, 2008), 161; Paul Levitz, *75 Years of DC Comics: The Art Of Modern Mythmaking* (Los Angeles: Taschen America, 2010), 557–703.

2. Grant Morrison, *Supergods: What Masked Vigilantes, Miraculous Mutants, and a Sun God from Smallville Can Teach Us About Being Human* (New York: Spiegel & Grau, 2011), xvi.

3. Amy Kiste Nyberg, "Comics Code History: The Seal of Approval," *CBLDF*, n.d., http://cbldf.org/comics-code-history-the-seal-of-approval.

4. Midrash: Aaron Sagers, "Exit Sandman: Neil Gaiman Goes In-Depth with Overture, One of 2015's Best Comics," *SYFY Wire*, Dec. 23, 2015, https://www.syfy.com/syfywire/exit-sandman-neil-gaiman-goes-in-depth-with-overture-one-of-2015s-best-comics. E.g., the story of Lilith in *Sandman* Vol. 2 #40 (Aug. '92), from *The Alphabet of Ben Sira* 23a–b. Kabbalah: Jay Babcock, "Magic is Afoot: A Conversation with Alan Moore about the Arts and the Occult," *Arthur*, May 10, 2007 (originally in *Arthur*. No. 4, May 2003), https://arthurmag.com/2007/05/10/1815. Notably, Moore's series *Promethea* ('99–'05), which explores the Tree of Life and its *sefirot*. Surrealism: Morrison, *Supergods*, 167.

5. Pryde's grandparentage: Chris Claremont (w),

John Romita, Jr. (p), Dan Green (i), Glynis Oliver (c), "The Spiral Path," *Uncanny X-Men* #199 (Nov. '85), Marvel Comics, 13. Pryde is the first significant and recurring superhero to be openly Jewish. Unfortunately, her appearance in three X-Men films, played by Ellen Page, omits any sign of Jewishness.

6. Eisenhardt: Greg Pak (w), Carmine Di Giandomenico (p, i), Matt Hollingsworth (c), *X-Men: Magneto Testament* #1 (Nov. '08), Marvel Comics, 2–5. Auschwitz: Chris Claremont (w), Dave Cockrum (p), Josef Rubinstein, Bob Wiacek (i), Glynis Wein (c), *Uncanny X-Men* #150 (Aug. '81), Marvel Comics, 37. Nazi hunter: Chris Claremont (w), John Bolton (p, i), Nel Yomtov (c), "I, Magneto!" *Classic X-Men* #19 (Mar. '88), 5. Israel/Xavier: Chris Claremont (w), Dave Cockrum (p), Bob Wiacek (i), Glynis Wein (c), "Gold Rush!" *Uncanny X-Men* #161 (Sep. '82), Marvel Comics. Legion: Chris Claremont (w), Bill Sienkiewicz (p, i), Glynis Wein (c), "The Only Thing to Fear…," *New Mutants* #25 (Mar. '85), Marvel Comics. While Magneto's background is central to his motivation in the X-Men films, Legion, like Shadowcat, was whitewashed in his titular 2017–19 TV series. The X-Men's Jewish signification, particularly Magneto's, are explored at length in Kaplan, *From Krakow to Krypton*, 111–23; Simcha Weinstein, *Up, Up, and Oy Vey: How Jewish History, Culture and Values Shaped the Comic Book Superhero* (Baltimore: Leviathan Press, 2006), 105–15; and Danny Fingeroth, *Disguised as Clark Kent: Jews, Comics, and the Creation of the Superhero* (New York: Continuum International Publishing Group Inc., 2007), 113–30.

7. Iceman in J.M. DeMatteis (w), Alan Kupperberg (p), Mike Gustovich (i), Bob Sharen (c), "The Fuse!" *Iceman* Vol. 1 #1 (Dec. '84), Marvel Comics, 18. Rosenthal: Roger Stern (w), John Byrne (w, p), Josef Rubinstein (i), George Roussos (c), "By the Dawn's Early Light!" *Captain America* #247 (July '80), Marvel Comics. Roth: J.M. DeMatteis (w), Mike Zeck (p), John Beatty (i), Bob Sharen (c), "Peace on Earth, Good Will to Man," *Captain America* #268. Roth's backstory was used for James Buchanan "Bucky" Barnes in the Captain America films. Sabra: Bill Mantlo (w), Sal Buscema (w), Sal Buscema (i), George Roussos (c), "Monster!" *Incredible Hulk* #250 (Aug. '80), Marvel Comics.

8. Firestorm: Gerry Conway (w), Al Milgrom (w, p) Klaus Janson (i), Adrienne Roy (c), "Make Way for Firestorm!" *Firestorm, the Nuclear Man* #1 (Mar. '78), DC Comics. Raven: Marv Wolfman (w), George Pérez (p), Dick Giordano (i), Adrienne Roy (c), "Where Nightmares Begin!" *DC Comics Presents* #26 (Oct. '80), DC Comics. Nuklon: Roy Thomas (w), Jerry Ordway (p) Mike Machlan (i), Gene D'Angelo (c), "The Infinity Syndrome!" *All-Star Squadron* #25 (Sep. '83), DC Comics. Phantom Stranger as Wandering Jew: Mike W. Barr (w), Jim Aparo (p, i), Tom Ziuko (c), "Tarry Till I Come Again," *Secret Origins* Vol. 2 #10 (Jan. '87), DC Comics.

9. Colossal Boy: Jerry Siegel (w), Jim Mooney (p, i) "The Three Super-Heroes!" *Action Comics* #267 (Aug. '60), National Comics Publications [DC Comics]. The name Gim Allon seems to have first appeared in Jim Shooter (w, p) Curt Swan (p), Jack Abel (i), "The Colossal Failure!" *Adventure Comics* #371 (Aug. '68), National Periodical Publications [DC Comics], 1. Jewish: Paul Levitz (w), José Luis García-López (p), Dick Giordano (i), Adrienne Roy (c), "Star Light, Star Bright… Farthest Star I See Tonight!" *DC Special Series* #21 (aka *Super-Star Holiday Special*) (Apr. '80), DC Comics, 4. First noted in Fingeroth, *Disguised as Clark Kent*, 135 & Kaplan, *From Krakow to Krypton*, 192–3.

10. Michael Cavna, "Why 'Maus' remains 'the greatest graphic novel ever written,' 30 years later," *Washington Post*, Aug. 11, 2016, https://www.washingtonpost.com/news/comic-riffs/wp/2016/08/11/why-maus-remains-the-greatest-graphic-novel-ever-written-30-years-later/?noredirect=on&utm_term=.07a2e478ecae.

11. *Ibid.*

12. Tom Bondurant, "1986: A Guide to Comics' Most Important Year, Ever," *CBR.com*, Nov. 13, 2016, https://www.cbr.com/1986-a-guide-to-comics-most-important-year-ever.

13. Joe Queenan, "Drawing on the DARK SIDE," *New York Times Magazine*, April 30, 1989, http://www.nytimes.com/1989/04/30/magazine/drawing-on-the-dark-side.html.

14. 30 in 1972: Fred Van Lente (w), Ryan Dunlavey (p, i), *Comic Book History of Comics* (June 2012), IDW Publishing, 201. 4000 in 1986: Larry Tye, *Superman: The High-Flying History of America's Most Enduring Hero* (New York: Random House, 2013), 224. 800 in 1979 and 10,000 in 1993: Jonathan V. Last, "The Crash of 1993," *Weekly Standard*, June 13, 2011, https://www.weeklystandard.com/jonathan-v-last/the-crash-of-1993. The latter counts worldwide, though the vast majority were in the U.S. Industry doubled: Queenan, "Drawing on the DARK SIDE." Titles tripled: going by Marvel, which published 40 titles monthly in 1985 and 140 in 1993, Last, "The Crash of 1993." Median price: John Jackson Miller, "Median Comic Book Cover Prices by Year," *Comichron*, https://www.comichron.com/vitalstatistics/mediancoverprices.html.

15. Queenan, "Drawing on the DARK SIDE."

16. Stephen King, "Why I Chose Batman," *Batman* #400 (Oct. '86), DC Comics, back cover flap.

17. Frank Miller (w, p), Klaus Janson (i), Lynn Varley (c), *The Dark Knight Returns* #1–4 (June–Dec. '86), DC Comics. Each issue was originally given a standalone title, before the collected edition was named after the first, *The Dark Knight Returns*, which it's been known as since.

18. Peter Sanderson, "Superman Reborn!" *Amazing Heroes* #96 (June '86), Fantagraphics Books, 29.

19. *Ibid.*, 30.

20. Bible: Rita Kempley, "SUPERMAN," *Washington Post*, Nov. 2, 1985, https://www.washingtonpost.com/archive/lifestyle/1985/11/02/superman/de273fae-da92-4dd7-bf72-e94b9abbcbd0/?utm_term=.bda6e203e8e9. Reaffirmation: John Byrne, *Superman* Vol. 2 #1 (Jan. '87), DC Comics, 24 (afterward/letter column). Elements: JayJay Jackson,

"Marvel issue: SUPERMAN—First Marvel Issue—Byrne's Plot," JimShooter.com (blog), Oct. 25, 2011, http://jimshooter.com/2011/10/superman-first-marvel-issue-byrnes-plo.html. 112 times: Mike Avila, "Behind the Panel: John Byrne on Reinventing Superman and Lois Lane," *SYFY Wire*, April 18, 2018, https://www.syfy.com/syfywire/behind-the-panel-john-byrne-on-reinventing-superman-and-lois-lane.

21. Headlines: Kempley, "SUPERMAN"; Lili Wrightmay, "The Man Who Energizes the Hulk" *New York Times*, May 7, 1989, CN12; Jerry Belcher, "Comic Characters Revised: At 48, Superman Slows a Bit, Kent De-Wimpified," *Los Angeles Times*, June 18, 1986, https://www.latimes.com/archives/la-xpm-1986-06-18-mn-11090-story.html. Marvelized: Byrne, *Superman* Vol. 2 #1, afterword. Sales (Nov. '85): Terry Hoknes, "Historical Comic Book Sales Figures and Charts 1980's and 1990's," *Hoknescomics.com* (blog), n.d., http://www.hoknescomics.com/comicstats.htm. According to the *Times*, *Superman* figures were closer to 80,000. Over one million: Wrightmay, "The Man Who Energizes the Hulk." Forty years: Mort Weisinger, "Here Comes Superman," *Coronet*, July 1946, 24. Even so, sales were barely half of what they reportedly were in 1946.

22. Bauhaus: Jerry Siegel (w), Joe Shuster (p, i), "The Superman Is Born," *Superman* (newspaper strip), January 6, 1939. Heartless: John Byrne (w, p), Dick Giordano (i), Tom Ziuko (c), "From Out the Green Dawn...," *The Man of Steel* #1 (Oct. '86), DC Comics, 4. Also quoted in Tye, *Superman*, 228. Deserved: Sanderson, "Superman Reborn," 34.

23. Byrne, *The Man of Steel* #1, 2–7.

24. 28: Byrne, *Superman* Vol. 2 #1, 17. Reagan: John Ostrander, Len Wein (w), John Byrne (p), Karl Kesel (i), Tom Ziuko (c), "Breach of Faith," *Legends* #2 (Dec. '86), DC Comics, 21–22; "Send for... the Suicide Squad!" #3 (Jan. '87), 18; "...and Let Slip the Dogs of War!" #5 (Mar. '87), 15.

25. Sanderson, "Superman Reborn," 35.

26. *Ibid.*, 36.

27. John Byrne, "Father of LexCorp Tower?" *Byrnerobotics.com* (blog), Aug. 7, 2006, http://www.byrnerobotics.com/forum/forum_posts.asp?TID=13622&mobile=FULL.

28. Jerry Siegel (w), Al Plastino (p, i), "How Luthor Met Superboy!" *Adventure Comics* #271 (Apr. '60), National Comics Publications [DC Comics]. Wolfman reconceived Luthor: John Byrne, "Article: Donald Trump = Lex Luthor" *Byrnerobotics.com* (blog), Aug. 15, 2016, http://m.byrnerobotics.com/forum/forum_posts.asp?TID=50791. Wolfman Quote: Sanderson, "Superman Reborn," 37.

29. Based on: *ibid.*; John Byrne, "FAQ: Questions about Comic Book Projects: Who created the 'new' Lex Luthor for MAN OF STEEL?" *Byrnerobotics.com* (blog), n.d., http://www.byrnerobotics.com/FAQ/listing.asp?ID=2&T1=Questions+about+Comic+Book+Projects#31. Imitating: James D. Hudnall (w), Eduardo Barreto (p, i), Adam Kubert (c), Eric Peterson (cover), *Lex Luthor: The Unauthorized Biography* ('89), DC Comics, 8.

30. As depicted in the "President Lex," "Our Worlds at War" and "Superman/Batman: Public Enemies" (aka "The World's Finest") storylines, running through various titles between Aug. 2000 and March 2004. Cleverly, in 2018 DC reissued the collected *Superman: President Lex* with the cover of *Lex Luthor: The Unauthorized Biography*.

31. John Byrne (w, p), Dick Giordano (i), Tom Ziuko (c), "The Haunting," *The Man of Steel* #6 (Dec. '86), DC Comics, 4.

32. Byrne et al., "Enemy Mine...," *The Man of Steel* #4 (Nov. 1986), DC Comics, 9.

33. Aggressive: Jennings Parrott, "For Clark Kent, Wimpery Is Out," *Los Angeles Times*, May 6, 1986, https://www.latimes.com/archives/la-xpm-1986-05-06-mn-4108-story.html. Republican: Kempley, "SUPERMAN."

34. Patrick Daniel O'neill, "John Byrne: New Tomorrows for the Man of Steel," *Comics Scene* Vol. 2 #1, Jan. '88, 7.

35. Byrne et al., *The Man of Steel* #6, 21–2.

36. Jerry Siegel unpublished memoir, "Creation of a Superhero," 1979, Los Angeles. Larry Tye Papers, Box 3, Folder 1, Rare Books & Manuscripts Library Collections, Butler Library, Columbia University, New York, NY, 23.); Guy H. Lillian III, "Cary Bates and Elliot Maggin: The Men Behind the Super-Typewriter," *Amazing World of DC Comics* no. 2 (Sep. '74), National Periodical Publications [DC Comics], 7.

37. Scheele: J.J. Smith, "Super exhibit opens at the Smithsonian," *UPI*, July 3, 1987 (online), https://www.upi.com/Archives/1987/07/03/Super-exhibit-opens-at-the-Smithsonian/2269552283200. Waid: Tye, *Superman*, 229.

38. Byrne et al., *The Man of Steel* #1, 9–11.

39. Jonathan D. Sarna and Jonathan Golden, "The American Jewish Experience in the Twentieth Century: Antisemitism and Assimilation," *National Humanities Center*, Revised October 2000, http://nationalhumanitiescenter.org/tserve/twenty/tkeyinfo/jewishexp.htm; Sanderson, "Superman Reborn," 34.

40. Reform movement: MJL, "History of the Reform Movement," *My Jewish Learning*, n.d., https://www.myjewishlearning.com/article/reform-judaism. Intermarriage: Valerie S. Thaler, "American Jewish Life, 1980–2000," *My Jewish Learning*, n.d., https://www.myjewishlearning.com/article/american-jewish-life-1980-2000. Cathedral: Dan Jurgens (w, p), George Pérez (i), Glenn Whitmore (c), "Home," *Adventures of Superman* #461 (Dec. '89), DC Comics, 20.

41. Russ Burlingame, "On 'The Death of Superman' and Its Aftermath, Twenty-Five Years Later," *Comicbook.com*, Nov. 19, 2017, https://comicbook.com/dc/2017/11/19/on-the-death-of-superman-twenty-five-years-later.

42. Sanderson, "Superman Reborn," 40.

43. Ignited: John Byrne (w), Mike Mignola (p), Rick Bryant (i), Petra Scotese (c), "Pieces," *World of Krypton* Vol. 2 #1 (Dec. '87), DC Comics, 22. Holocaust: Byrne et al., *The Man of Steel* #6, 20. In this

version Krypton's destruction was possibly man-made: Byrne et al., "History Lesson," *World of Krypton* Vol. 2 #3, 13–6; #4, 15–7.

44. Berkowitz: Byrne et al., *The Man of Steel* #4, 18. Bibbowski: Marv Wolfman (w), Jerry Ordway (p), Mike Machlan (i), Tom Ziuko (c), "Personal Best," *Adventures of Superman* #428 (May '87), DC Comics. Kaminski: Tye, *Superman*, 264.

45. Childhood in Hudnall et al., *Lex Luthor: The Unauthorized Biography*, 16. LES in Eury, *The Krypton Companion*, 226. Jewish in Elliot S. Maggin, "Is Superman Jewish?" *Quora*, Apr. 1, 2011, https://www.quora.com/Is-Superman-Jewish.

46. Byrne et al., "The Mirror, Crack'd," *Man of Steel* #5 (Dec. '86), 12–3.

47. Byrne, *Superman* Vol. 2 #1, 17.

48. Sanderson, "Superman Reborn," 38.

49. Gary Engle, "What Makes Superman So Darned American?" *Superman at Fifty: The Persistence of a Legend* (Cleveland: Octavia Press, 1987), 79–87. The essay, which discusses in part Superman's Jewish signification, was frequently commented on in reviews of the book and widely republished in popular culture anthologies. Scott Raab, "Is Superman Jewish?" 167–8.

50. Otto Friedrich, "Show Business: Up, Up and Awaaay!!!" *Time*, Mar. 14, 1988, 69. The quote was taken from Raab, "Is Superman Jewish?" 167.

51. *Superman 50th Anniversary*. TV special, first broadcast June 5, 1988 by CBS. Directed by Robert Boyd and written by Adam Green, Bruce McCulloch, Rosie Shuster, Robert Smigel. *Superman*: Ben Simon, "Ruby-Spears' Superman: DC Comics Classic Collection," A nimatedviews.com, Nov. 26, 2009, https://animatedviews.com/2009/ruby-spears%E2%80%99-superman-dc-comics-classic-collection. Wolfman served as head story editor and Gil Kane provided character designs based on Byrne's. Uninterrupted: *Superboy* '88–'92; *Lois & Clark: The New Adventures of Superman* '93–'97; *Superman: The Animated Series* '96–'00; *Justice League* '01–'04; *Justice League Unlimited* '04–'06; *Smallville* '01–'11. $1 billion: Friedrich, "Show Business."

52. Declared: Byrne, *Superman* Vol. 2 #1 afterward. Regretting: Mike Avila, "Behind the Panel."

53. Examples: Grant Morrison (w), Frank Quitely (p), Jamie Grant (i, c) "Red Sun Day," *All-Star Superman* #11 (July '08), DC Comics 6; Grant Morrison (w), Rags Morales (p), Mark Propst (i), Brad Anderson (c), "Superman's Mission To Mars," *Action Comics* Vol. 2 #14 (Jan. '13), 17; Joe Keatinge (w), Ming Doyle, Brent Schoonover, David Williams, Tula Lotay, Jason Alexander (p), Ming Doyle, Brent Schoonover, Al Gordon, Tula Lotay, Jason Alexander (i), Jordie Bellaire, Nick Filardi, Jason Wright, Tula Lotay, Lee Loughridge (c), "Strange Visitor," *Adventures of Superman* Vol. 2 #16 (Oct. '14), 2.

54. *The Man of Steel* #1 sold over a million copies, but the ongoing series didn't see nearly as much of an uptick. April 1986's *Action Comics* #587, for example, sold over 61,000 copies, tripling by April 1987's #599 to nearly 182,000. It outsold *Superman*

(renamed *Adventures* with January 1987's #424) for the first time. It dropped to 70,000 with May's #601, once Byrne left and it became a weekly anthology (John Jackson Miller, "Action Comics Sales Figures," Comichron, https://www.comichron.com/titlespotlights/actioncomics.html). *Adventures* saw a smaller and more gradual increase; April 1986's #418 and April 1987's #427 both sold roughly 99,000 copies, but by April 1988's #439 the series was selling nearly 162,000, about 65% more. DC stopped publishing circulation figures in 1988 (John Jackson Miller, "*Superman* Sales Figures," Comichron, http://www.comichron.com/titlespotlights/superman.html).

55. Roger Stern (w), Bob McLeod (p, i), Glenn Whitmore (c), "Secrets in the Night," *Action Comics* #662 (Feb. '91), DC Comics, 19–21; Jerry Ordway (w, p), Dennis Janke (i), Glenn Whitmore (c), "Truth, Justice and the American Way!" *Superman* Vol. 2 #53 (Mar. '91), 1–3.

56. Nuke: Jim Starlin (w), Jim Aparo (p), Mike DeCarlo (i), Adrienne Roy (c), "A Death in the Family: Chapters 1 & 2," *Batman* #426 (Dec. '88), DC Comics. UN: Starlin et al., "A Death in the Family: Chapter 6," *Batman* #429 (Jan. '89), 10–6.

57. Jerry Ordway (w, p), Dennis Janke (i), Glenn Whitmore (c), "Time and Time Again! Phase III: The Warsaw Ghetto," *Superman* Vol. 2 #54 (Apr. '91), DC Comics.

58. David Singer, Ruth R. Seldin, "World Jewish Population, 1991," *American Jewish Year Book 1993* (Philadelphia: Jewish Publication Society, 1994), 427.

59. John Jackson Miller, "1991 Comic Book Sales to Comics Shops," *Comichron*, https://www.comichron.com/monthlycomicsales/1991.html. In fact, DC only published 9 of the top 100 best-sellers that year.

60. Frank Rich, "Term Limit for the Man of Steel: Yes, It's Time for Him to Go," *New York Times*, Nov. 22, 1992 , 4.

61. LA: Friedrich, "Show Business." Cluttered: Tye, *Superman*, 269.

62. Paid: Kevin Melrose, "Shuster estate urges appeals court to reverse Superman ruling," *CBR.com*, May 24, 2013, https://www.cbr.com/shuster-estate-urges-appeals-court-to-reverse-superman-ruling. Last words: Henry Mietkiewicz, "Great Krypton! Superman was the Star's Ace Reporter," *Toronto Star* (Toronto, ON), April 26, 1992, A.10.

63. Isabel Wilkersonnov, "Young Believe Malcolm X Is Still Speaking to Them," *New York Times*, November 18, 1992, A1. The story broke on September 4, when the Long Island-based *Newsday* dedicated its front page article to it (William S. McTernan, "Superman Dead? It's up, up and away for Man of Steel as comics kill him off," A1 & A7). It was picked up by CNN the next day, which dedicated a segment on *Headline News* (https://www.youtube.com/watch?v=ovqnWgRNmZ4).

64. Three million: John Jackson Miller, "1992 Comic Book Sales to Comics Shops," *Comichron*, https://www.comichron.com/monthlycomicsales/

1992.html. Six million: Eric Diaz, "Why We're Still Feeling THE DEATH OF SUPERMAN," *DC Universe*, Sept. 25, 2018, https://www.dcuniverse.com/news/why-were-still-feeling-death-superman. Second highest: Rich Johnston, "25 Years Ago Today, Superman Died At The Hands Of Doomsday—Three Days Later Will He Rise Again In Doomsday Clock?" Bleeding Cool, Nov. 18, 2017, https://www.bleedingcool.com/2017/11/18/25-years-ago-today-superman-died-hands-doomsday-three-days-later-will-rise-doomsday-clock. *X-Men*: John Jackson Miller, "The Best-Selling Comic Book of All Time," *Comichron*, https://www.comichron.com/faq/alltimebestsellingcomicbook.html.

65. Sales: Miller, "*Action Comics* Sales Figures," "*Superman* Sales Figures." By some estimates sales were even higher, with *Action* #687 selling 1.8 million copies and *Adventures* #500 selling 4.2 million: n.a., "Top 10 Best Selling Comic Books Of The Modern Era," *Zap-Kapow Comics*, May 10, 2019, https://www.zapkapowcomics.com/top-10-best-selling-comic-books-of-the-modern-era. Spots: John Jackson Miller, "1993 Comic Book Sales to Comics," *Comichron*, https://www.comichron.com/monthlycomicssales/1993.html. Kahn: Tye, *Superman*, 251. Bestselling: Levitz, *75 Years of DC Comics*, 570.

66. Rich, "Term Limit for the Man of Steel."

67. Mark Potts, "Superman's Last Leap," *Washington Post*, Sep. 5, 1992, https://www.washingtonpost.com/archive/lifestyle/1992/09/05/supermans-last-leap/c1e53279-756f-47f3-b230-07b18c507907.

68. Dan Jurgens (w, p), Rick Burchett (i), Gene D'Angelo (c), "Down for the Count," *Justice League America* #69 (Dec. '92), DC Comics, 22.

69. Vanishes: Jerry Ordway (w), Tom Grummett (p), Doug Hazlewood (i), Glenn Whitmore (c), "Grave Obsession," *Adventures of Superman* #499 (Feb. '93), DC Comics, 5. Appears: Louise Simonson (w), Jon Bogdanove (p), Dennis Janke (i), Glenn Whitmore (c), "The Return!" *Superman: The Man of Steel* #25 (Sep. '93), 21–2.

70. Louise Simonson (w), Jon Bogdanove (p), Dennis Janke (i), Glenn Whitmore (c), "Ghosts," *Superman: The Man of Steel* #21 (Mar. '93), DC Comics, 13.

71. Miller, "1993 Comic Book Sales to Comics Shops," https://www.comichron.com/monthlycomicssales/1993.html.

72. 1974, 1984, 1991: Last, "The Crash of 1993." 1988: Friedrich, "Show Business," 68. 2014: Michael Cavna, "Rare Superman book draws record $3.2 million top bid: The long, 'cool' journey of a record-setting comic [UPDATED]," August 22, 2014, https://www.washingtonpost.com/news/comic-riffs/wp/2014/08/22/rare-superman-book-draws-record-2-2-million-bid-the-long-journey-of-a-record-setting-comic.

73. Bankruptcy: Dan Raviv, *Comic Wars: Marvel's Battle for Survival* (Sea Cliff: Levant Books, 2004). First edition published as *Comic Wars: How Two Tycoons Battled over the Marvel Comics Empire-And Both Lost* (New York: Broadway Books, 2002).

Sales: from the April '93 peak of over 48 million issues to 7 million in "Comic Book Superheroes Unmasked," first broadcast June 23, 2003 by The History Channel. Directed by Stephen Kroopnick and written by James Grant Goldin. Online at https://www.youtube.com/watch?v=Ygx_rUJ3XaI. Other estimates are more conservative; two thirds according to Tye, *Superman*, 267 and similarly 70% according to Last, "The Crash of 1993." Stores: *ibid.*. Here too estimates vary. Tye counts two thirds (267) and Van Lente & Dunlavey count a drop of 9400 to 4500 (52%) between 1993 and 1996 (208). 2000: Shannon O'Leary "Comics Retailers Hope To Rebound in 2018," *Publishers Weekly*, Feb. 09, 2018, https://www.publishersweekly.com/pw/by-topic/industry-news/comics/article/76031-comics-retailers-hope-to-rebound-in-2018.html.

74. 1994: John Jackson Miller, "1994 Comic Book Sales to Comics Shops," *Comichron*, https://www.comichron.com/monthlycomicssales/1994.html. 1996: Miller, "1996 Comic Book Sales to Comics Shops," *Comichron*, https://www.comichron.com/monthlycomicssales/1996.html. 1998: Miller, "1998 Comic Book Sales to Comics Shops," *Comichron*, https://www.comichron.com/monthlycomicssales/1998.html.

75. "Kal": *Seinfeld*. Season 9, episode 20, "The Puerto Rican Day," first broadcast May 7, 1998 by NBC. Directed by Andy Ackerman and written by Alec Berg, Jennifer Crittenden, Spike Feresten, Bruce Eric Kaplan, Gregg Kavet, Steve Koren, David Mandel, Dan O'Keefe, Andy Robin, Jeff Schaffer. Bizzro: Season 8, episode 3, "The Bizarro Jerry," first broadcast Oct. 3, 1996 by NBC. Directed by Andy Ackerman and written by David Mandel. Lois: Season 6, episode 10, "The Race," first broadcast Dec. 15, 1994 by NBC. Directed by Andy Ackerman and written by Tom Gammill, Max Pross, Larry David, Sam Kass.

76. Recognizing: Tye, *Superman*, 67. Seinfeld is a genuine superfan, even naming his son Julian Kal. (Stephen M. Silverman, "Jerry Seinfeld's a Daddy Once More," *People*, March 03, 2003, https://people.com/celebrity/jerry-seinfelds-a-daddy-once-more.) On the show Superman also served as an ironic device, juxtaposed against the characters' petty narcissism and all-too-human shortcomings, a WASPy paragon of propriety contrasted with the Jewish propensity for unreservedness and Talmudic overanalysis. Credits: Ro'i Podim, "The Maestro," *Yedioth Ahronoth*, Dec. 12, 2017 (translated by the author), https://www.yediot.co.il/articles/0,7340,L-5055954,00.html. In fairness, Stan Lee imbued his comics with the same New York Jewish sensibility years earlier, which is the source of the Marvel movies' tone.

77. Michael Rothman, "5 Things You Don't Know About Dean Cain," *ABC News*, Dec. 6, 2014, https://abcnews.go.com/Entertainment/things-dean-cain/story?id=27401545.

78. Klein appeared in 15 episodes in seasons 3 & 4, played by Kenneth Kimmins. Brown in: *Lois & Clark: The New Adventures of Superman*. Season 1, episode 4, "I'm Looking Through You," first

broadcast Oct. 10, 1993 by WB. Directed by Mark Sobel and written by Deborah Joy LeVine and Dan Levine. Murray Brown played by Jack Carter. Season 3, episode 5, "Just Say Noah," first broadcast Oct. 22, 1995 by WB. Directed by David S. Jackson and written by Brad Buckner and Eugenie Ross-Leming.

79. Hilary J. Bader (writer), "A Little Piece of Home" (Bruce Timm commentary track), *Superman: The Complete Animated Series*. DVD. Directed by Toshihiko Masuda. Burbank: Warner Bros. Animation, 2009.

80. Kirby: George Khoury & Pedro Khoury III, "Bruce Timm Interviewed," *The Kirby Collector* no.21, Oct. 1998, 19. Oy: *Superman: The Animated Series*. Season 2, episode 19, "Bizarro's World," first broadcast Oct. 10, 1997 by WB. Directed by Hiroyuki Aoyama and written by Robert Goodman. Funeral: Season 2, episode 26, "Apokolips... Now! Part II," first broadcast Feb. 14, 1998 by WB. Directed by Dan Riba and written by Bruce Timm and Rich Fogel. Rabbi voiced by cantor Joseph Gole.

81. *Superman at Fifty*: Gary Engle, "What Makes Superman So Darned American?" 83–6; Scott Raab, "Is Superman Jewish?" 167–168. Engle bio in "Gary D. Engle" (obituary), *The Plain Dealer*, Apr. 18–21, 2017 (online), https://obits.cleveland.com/obituaries/cleveland/obituary.aspx?n=gary-d-engle&pid=185117660.

82. Eric J. Greenberg, "Did Superman Have Biblical Roots? Jerry Siegel dies without revealing 'true' origin of the Last Son of Krypton," *New York Jewish Week*, Feb. 9, 1996, 41; Greenberg, Eric J. "Superman: A Jewish Hero," *The Jerusalem Post*, May 1, 1996, 7; Jules Feiffer, "Jerry Siegel: the Minsk theory of Krypton," *New York Times Magazine*, Dec. 29, 1996, 15; Michael Chabon, *The Amazing Adventures of Kavalier & Clay* (New York: Random House, 2000); Arie Kaplan, "Kings of Comics: How Jews Transformed the Comic Book Industry" Parts I–III, *Reform Judaism Magazine* 32, no. 1–3 (Fall 2003–Spring 2004), http://www.reformjudaismmag.net/03fall/comics.shtml; Arie Kaplan, *From Krakow to Krypton*; Simcha Weinstein, *Up, Up, and Oy Vey*; Danny Fingeroth, *Disguised as Clark Kent*.

83. Mark Waid (w), Alex Ross (w, p, i, c), *Kingdom Come*, 1–4 (May–Aug. '96), DC Comics.

84. Clark Norman Ross, "Witness to the End," *Absolute Kingdom Come* (Oct. '18), DC Comics, 340. It's actually cowriter Mark Waid who conceived the testamental allegory of the series.

85. Samson: Peter David (w), Dale Keown (p), Sam de la Rosa (i), Glynis Oliver (c), *Incredible Hulk* #373 (Sep. '90), Marvel Comics, 15. David wrote issues #328–467, Feb. '87–Aug. '98. Israeli: Peter David, "Political Correctness and other topics," *PeterDavid.net* (blog), Nov. 19, 2010, https://www.peterdavid.net/2010/11/19/policitical-correctness-and-other-topics. Her father fled Nazi Germany in "PARANOID JEWS?" *PeterDavid.net* (blog), Feb. 27, 2004, https://www.peterdavid.net/2004/02/27/paranoid-jews. Writing: Peter David, "A Super Man," *PeterDavid.net* (blog), Oct. 21, 2011, https://www.peterdavid.net/2011/10/21/a-super-man.

86. Merging: Peter David (w), Gary Frank (p), Cam Smith (i), Gene D'Angelo, Digital Chameleon (c), "Body & Soul," *Supergirl* Vol. 4 #1 (Sep. '96), DC Comics. Devout: Peter David (w), Gary Frank (p), Cam Smith (i), Gene D'Angelo (c), "And No Dawn To Follow The Darkness," #3 (Nov. '96), 16. Demon: Darren Vincenzo (w), Leonard Kirk (p), Cam Smith (i), Gene D'Angelo (c), "Incubus," #13 (Sep. '97). Fire angel: Peter David (w), Leonard Kirk (p), Cam Smith (i), Gene D'Angelo (c), "Teetering On Oblivion," #17 (Jan. '98), 22; "Divine Inspiration" #18 (Feb. '98), 18; "Middle-Aged Crisis," #19 (Mar. '98), 2; "Double-Edged Sword," #23 (July '98), 18; "For Those Who Came in Late," #35 (Aug. '99), 2. Manifestation: Peter David (w), Leonard Kirk (p), Robin Riggs (i), Gene D'Angelo (c), "City of Angels," #38 (Nov. '99), 22.

87. David et al., #1, 2.

88. Remarks: David et al., #23, 12. Nation: *ibid.*, 22. Relics: Peter David (w), Leonard Kirk (p), Prentis Rollins (i), Gene D'Angelo (c), "Comet's Tale," #22 (June '98), 20.

89. Angelology: Peter David (w), Leonard Kirk (p), Prentis Rollins (i), Gene D'Angelo (c), "Through A Fractured Prism," #21 (May '98), DC Comics, 5. Shechina: Peter David (w), Leonard Kirk (p), Robin Riggs (i), Gene D'Angelo (c), "City of Angels," #38 (Nov. '99), 22. Female aspect/Supergirl saves it: David et al., "Through a Mirror Darkly," #49 (Oct. '00), 12.

90. Eden: Peter David (w), Leonard Kirk (p), Robin Riggs (i), Gene D'Angelo (c), "Spiders and Snakes," #72–4 (Sep.–Nov. '02). Tree of Knowledge: David et al., "Desperate Times," #25 (Sep. '98), 18–9. Heaven: David et al., "Wally's Angels," #50 (Nov. '00). Baalzebub: #72, 5 & 8. Plagues: Peter David (w), Todd Nauck (p), Robin Riggs (i), Gene D'Angelo, Digital Chameleon (c), "A Plague on Both Your Houses," #70 (July '02), 18. Metatron: Peter David (w), Jamal Igle (p), José Marzan, Jr. (i), Gene D'Angelo, Digital Chameleon (c), "Pyramid Schemes," #71 (Aug. '02), 4, 10.

91. Peter David (w), Diego Barreto (p), Robin Riggs (i), Gene D'Angelo, Digital Chameleon (c), "Rhyme and Reason," #67 (Apr. '02), 1 (disguised); Peter David (w), Leonard Kirk (p), Robin Riggs (i), Gene D'Angelo, Digital Chameleon (c), "Cashing in Chips," #69 (June '02), 14 (revealed).

92. Claims he's God: David et al., #17, 18. God-Boy: David et al., #50, 36.

93. Mclaughlin, "An Oral History of the Original Death and Return of Superman."

94. Dan Jurgens (w), various artists, *Superman: The Wedding Album* (Dec. '96), DC Comics, 77–91. Metropolis Chapel in Tye, *Superman*, 256.

95. *Lois & Clark: The New Adventures of Superman*. Season 4, Episode 3, "Swear to God, This Time We're Not Kidding," first broadcast Oct. 6, 1996 by WB. Mike played by David Doyle. In an earlier scene, the ceremony is held in nondescript church, under a stained glass window of what looks like a figure in red and blue robes.

Superman Supernal

1. John Petty, *A Brief History of Comic Books* (Dallas: Heritage Auction Galleries, 2006), 8 https://www.heritagestatic.com/comics/d/history-of-comics.pdf; Paul Levitz, *75 Years of DC Comics: The Art of Modern Mythmaking* (Los Angeles: Taschen America, 2010), 633.

2. "Meet Dav Pilkey," *pilkey.com*, n.d., https://pilkey.com/author. Heritage designates the Moder Age from 1980 to date, Levitz from 1998 to 2010.

3. Brigid Alverson, "NYCC Insider Sessions Powered By ICv2: A Demographic Snapshot of Comics Buyers," *ICv2*, Oct. 19, 2017, https://icv2.com/articles/news/view/38709/nycc-insider-sessions-powered-icv2-a-demographic-snapshot-comics-buyers.

4. Levitz, *75 Years of DC Comics*, 702.

5. Metropolis destroyed: "The Fall of Metropolis," May–July '94. Origin altered: "Zero Hour," Sep.–Oct. '94. Faked death: "The Death of Clark Kent," May–July '95. Lost powers: "The Final Night," Nov.–Dec. '96. Married Lois: *The Wedding Album*, Dec. '96. Gained new powers, suit and color: "Electric Superman," Apr. '97–Feb. '98. Split in two: "Superman Red/Superman Blue," Feb.–May '98. 853rd century: "DC One Million," Nov. '98. Metropolis transformed: "Y2K," Feb.–Mar. '00. Interplanetary war: "Our Worlds at War," Aug.–Oct. '00. Krypton's truth: "Return to Krypton," Mar.–Apr. '01, Part II Sep. '02. Joker godlike: "Emperor Joker," Sep.–Oct. '00. Luthor president: "President Lex" et seq., Aug. '00–Mar. '04.

6. Trailer: "Superman/Doomsday," *IMDb*, Sep. 18, 2007, https://www.imdb.com/title/tt0934706. Nadir: John Jackson Miller, "Comic Book Sales by Year," *Comichron*, https://comichron.com/yearlycomicssales.html. Selling: John Jackson Miller, "June 2000 Comic Book Sales to Comics Shops," *Comichron*, https://comichron.com/monthlycomicssales/2000/2000-06.html. *Superman* Vol. 2 # 159 sold under 44,000 copies, *Action Comics* #768 under 41,000 and *Adventures of Superman* #581 under 39,000.

7. J. Correspondent, "Superman Editors Sorry about Omission: Comic Erases Jews from Holocaust," *JWeekly*, July 10, 1998, https://www.jweekly.com/1998/07/10/superman-editors-sorry-about-omission-comic-erases-jews-from-holocaust. First discussed in Simcha Weinstein, *Up, Up, and Oy Vey: How Jewish History, Culture and Values Shaped the Comic Book Superhero* (Baltimore: Leviathan Press, 2006), 30–2; Larry Tye, *Superman: The High-Flying History of America's Most Enduring Hero* (New York: Random House, 2013), 266; and mentioned in Arie Kaplan, *From Krakow to Krypton: Jews and Comic Books* (Philadelphia: The Jewish Publication Society, 2008), 62.

8. *Superman: The Man of Steel* #81, 7–8, 14; #82, 4, 7–8. "Warsaw Ghetto Boy" in #82, 5.

9. First quote: Michael Colton, "Supersensitive 'Superman' Muffs Holocaust Story," *Washington Post*, June 27, 1998, https://www.washingtonpost.com/archive/lifestyle/1998/06/27/supersensitive-superman-muffs-holocaust-story/99dee982-3528-4241-b0e0-9ab689970913. Second quote: J. Correspondent, "Superman Editors Sorry about Omission."

10. Lapse: *ibid.*. Called: J. Correspondent, "Jewish Groups Seek Super Apology from DC Comics," *JWeekly*, July 17, 1998, https://www.jweekly.com/1998/07/17/jewish-groups-seek-super-apology-from-dc-comics.

11. Steven T. Seagle (w), Teddy Kristiansen (p, i, c), *It's a Bird...* (May '04), Vertigo [DC Comics], notably pages 20–2, 41–2, 45, 49, 108–9.

12. 33: Dan Jurgens (w, p), Jerry Ordway (i), Gregory Wright (c), *Zero Hour* #0 (Sep. '94), DC Comics, 29 (foldout). Protestant: Jeph Loeb (w), Tim Sale (p, i), Bjarne Hansen (c), "Spring," *Superman for All Seasons* #1 (Sep. '98), 32–33. Methodist: Fabian Nicieza (w), Allan Goldman (p), Ron Randall (i), Marta Martinez, Pete Pantazis (c), "Redemption (Part II of II)—In Good Faith," *Action Comics* #849 (July '07), 21.

13. "My *sin?*": Brian Azzarello (w), Jim Lee (p), Scott Williams (i), Alex Sinclair (c), "For Tomorrow, Part One," *Superman* Vol. 2 #204 (June '04), DC Comics, 25. "Oh my...": *ibid.*, 7. "that's a *play*": #208 (Oct.), 9. Flash: *ibid.*, 11. Pietà: #210 (Dec.), cover. Delilah: *ibid.*, 7. Pilate: Brian Azzarello (w), Jim Lee (p), Scott Williams, Matt Banning, Eric Basaldua, Sandra Hope, Danny Miki, Tim Townsend, Joe Weems (i), Alex Sinclair (c), #215 (May '05), 6. Zod: #213–15 (Mar.–May '05). *Creation of Adam*: #215, 25–6. "*Kal-El*": #210, 13. Second person: #205 (July '04), 13–4. Trusts Leone: #214, 20–2, #215, 4–5.

14. Kurt Busiek, Fabian Nicieza (w), Carlos Pacheco, Peter Vale (p), Jesús Merino (i), Bruno Hang (c), "Angel," *Superman* #659 (Feb. '07), DC Comics. Cover by Alejandro Barrionuevo.

15. Ludwig Blau and Kaufmann Kohler "Angelology," *The Jewish Encyclopedia*, V. 1 (1906): 583–97 (online), http://www.jewishencyclopedia.com/articles/1521-angelology.

16. Arune Singh, "Super-Stars (Part 1): Mark Waid's "Birthright," The Official Origin," *CBR.com*, Mar. 11, 2004, https://www.cbr.com/super-stars-part-1-mark-waids-birthright-the-official-origin.

17. *Ibid.*

18. Mark Waid (w), Leinil Francis Yu (p), Gerry Alanguilan (i), Dave McCaig (c), "A Legacy Reborn," *Superman: Birthright* #2 (Oct. '03), DC Comics, 4–5; "A Legacy Reborn," #3 (Nov.), 5. *Smallville* was the first to assign the "Mark of El" meaning, though theirs was air.

19. Elements: Geoff Johns (w), Phil Jimenez (p), Andy Lanning, Norm Rapmund, Marlo Alquiza, Lary Stucker (i), Jeromy Cox, Guy Major (c), "The Survivors," *Infinite Crisis* #2 (Jan. '06), DC Comics, 17 (Byrne origin in *Man of Steel* #1); Marv Wolfman (w), Dan Jurgens (p), Jerry Ordway, Cam Smith, Art Thibert, Nelson DeCastro (i), Jeromy Cox, Guy Major (c), "Heaven," *Infinite Crisis Secret Files & Origins 2006* (Apr.), 15 (Legion), 25 (executing the Phantom Zone criminals in *Superman* Vol.2

#22), 41–2 (death of Supergirl in *Crisis on Infinite Earths* #7); Geoff Johns (w), Fernando Pasarin (p, i), Jeromy Cox (c), "The Lightning Saga, Part Two of Five: Dreams and Fire," *Justice Society of America* Vol. 3 #5 (June '07), 17–22 (Legion). Donner: CCM, "Geoff Jones Conquers the Universe," *Comic-Con Magazine*, Winter 2010, 6–10. Krypton: "Last Son, Part I," Geoff Johns, Richard Donner (w), Adam Kubert (p, i), Dave Stewart (c), *Action Comics* #844 (Dec. '06), DC Comics, 1–3 et seq.

20. Geoff Johns (w), Gary Frank (p), Jon Sibal (i), Brad Anderson (c), "Brainiac, Part I: First Contact," *Action Comics* #866 (Aug. '08), DC Comics, 7–13 et seq.

21. Superboy: Geoff Johns (w), Gary Frank (p), Jon Sibal (i), Brad Anderson (c), "Superboy and the Legion of Super-Heroes," *Superman: Secret Origin* #2 (Dec. '09), DC Comics. Lara: "The Boy of Steel," *Superman: Secret Origin* #1 (Nov. '09), 17.

22. Birthday: *ibid.*, 14. Sales: John Jackson Miller, "November 2005 Comic Book Sales to Comics Shops," *Comichron*, https://www.comichron.com/monthlycomicssales/2005/2005-11.html. Eisners (Best New Series 2006, Best Continuing Series 2007 & 2009): n.a., "2006 Eisner Award Winners," *The Beat*, July 22, 2006, https://www.comicsbeat.com/2006-eisner-award-winners; n.a., "2007 Eisner Award Winners," *The Beat*, July 28, 2007, https://www.comicsbeat.com/2007-eisner-award-winners; n.a., "Eisner Award Winners," *The Beat*, July 25, 2009, https://www.comicsbeat.com/eisner-award-winners. *Time*: Lev Grossman, "Top 10 Everything of 2007: Top 10 Graphic Novels," *Time*, Dec. 09, 2007, http://content.time.com/time/specials/2007/article/0,28804,1686204_1686244_1692109,00.html. CBR: Brian Cronin, "The 75 Greatest Superman Stories of All-Time Master List," *CBR.com*, Apr. 20, 2013, https://www.cbr.com/the-75-greatest-superman-stories-of-all-time-master-list/3.

23. Creates: Grant Morrison (w), Frank Quitely (p), Jamie Grant (i, c), "Neverending," *All-Star Superman* #10 (May '08), DC Comics 6. Heals: *ibid.*, 20. Intelligence: "Superman in Excelsis," #12 (Oct. '08), 15. Return: "Funeral in Smallville," #6 (Mar. '07), 21, #12, 19–22.

24. Production: Russ Britt, "'Superman Returns'—with a super budget," *MarketWatch*, June 26, 2006, https://www.marketwatch.com/story/superman-returns-with-a-super-budget-for-warner-bros. Other estimates put it at $276 million: Charles Stockdale and John Harrington, "From 'Transformers' to 'Avatar,' these are the 50 most expensive movies ever made," *USA Today*, July 6, 2018, https://www.usatoday.com/story/life/movies/2018/07/06/transformers-avatar-50-most-expensive-movies-ever-made/762931002. The budget possibly includes the cost of the preceding succession of aborted projects. Disappointing: THR staff, "Bryan Singer: Why 'Superman Returns' Didn't Work," *Hollywood Reporter*, Apr. 17, 2011, https://www.hollywoodreporter.com/heat-vision/bryan-singer-why-superman-returns-179292.

25. Credits: Peter Sanderson, "Comics in Context," *Fred*, Aug. 25, 2006, http://asitecalledfred.com/2006/08/25/comics-in-context-143-san-diego-2006-the-donner-party. Christ: THR staff, "Bryan Singer."

26. International March of the Living, https://motl.org.

27. *Superman*, directed by Richard Donner (1978; Burbank, CA: Warner Home Video, 2006), DVD.

28. Dubbed: Arune Singh, "Super-Stars." Sales: John Jackson Miller, "2004 Comic Book Sales to Comics Shops," *Comichron*, https://www.comichron.com/monthlycomicssales/2004.html; "2005 Comic Book Sales to Comics Shops," https://www.comichron.com/monthlycomicssales/2005.html.

29. September: John Jackson Miller, "2010 Comic Book Sales to Comics Shops," *Comichron*, https://www.comichron.com/monthlycomicssales/2010.html. *Superman* #697: John Jackson Miller, "February 2010 Comic Book Sales to Comics Shops," *Comichron*, https://www.comichron.com/monthlycomicssales/2010/2010-02.html. 1950s: John Jackson Miller, "*Superman* Sales Figures," https://www.comichron.com/titlespotlights/superman.html.

30. Michael Eury, *The Krypton Companion* (Raleigh, NC: TwoMorrows Publishing, 2006), 42.

31. Otto Binder (w), Al Plastino (p, i), "The Story of Superman's Life!" *Superman* #146 (July '61), National Periodical Publications [DC Comics], 12.

32. David S. Goyer (w), Miguel Sepulveda (p, i), Paul Mounts (c), "The Incident," *Action Comics* #900 (June 2011), DC Comics, 8.

33. Vaneta Rogers, "JMS On Leaving Monthly Comics, SUPERMAN's Future," *Newsarama*, Nov. 12, 2010, https://www.newsarama.com/6489-jms-on-leaving-monthly-comics-superman-s-future.html.

34. Vaneta Rogers "Morrison Closes Out ACTION COMICS Run, Teases MULTIVERSITY," *Newsaramy*, Feb. 6, 2013, https://www.newsarama.com/10882-morrison-closes-out-action-comics-run-teases-multiversity.html.

35. Quit: Scott Lobdell (w), Kenneth Rocafort (p, i), Sunny Gho (c), "H'El on Earth, Prelude: They Will Join You in the Sun...," *Superman* Vol. 3 #13 (Dec. '12), DC Comics. CK Dead: *Action Comics* Vol. 2 #10–2 (Aug.–Oct. '12). Outlived: Grant Morrison (w), Rags Morales, Brad Walker (p, i) Rick Bryant (i), Brad Anderson (c), "Superman's New Secret Identity," *Action Comics* Vol. 2 #11 (Sep. '12), 10. Effective tool: Grant Morrison (w), Rags Morales, Brad Walker, Carlos Urbano (p), Rick Bryant, Bob McLeod, Carlos Urbano, Andrew Hennessy (i), Brad Anderson, Gabe Eltaeb (c), "Return of the Forgotten Superman," #12, 28.

36. Changes: Grant Morrison (w), Andy Kubert (p), Jesse Delperdang (i), Brad Anderson (c), "Rocket Song," *Action Comics* Vol. 2 #5 (Mar. '12),

DC Comics, 4. Kents: Grant Morrison (w), Rags Morales, Brad Walker (p), Mark Propst, Andrew Hennessy (i), Brad Anderson, Gabe Eltaeb (c), "Superman and the Fiend from Dimension 5," *Action Comics* Vol. 2 #17 (Apr. '13), 1–3.

37. Grant Morrison (w), Rags Morales (p), Rick Bryant (i), Brad Anderson (c), "Superman Versus the City of Tomorrow," *Action Comics* Vol. 2 #1 (Nov '11), DC Comics, 1–8; Greg Pak (w), Aaron Kuder (p, i), Tomeu Morey, Hi-Fi Design, Blond (c), *Action Comics* Vol. 2 #41–3 (Aug.–Oct. '15).

38. Cameron Bonomolo, "George Perez's Corporate Clash over Superman: 'They Made Me Not Care," *CBR.com*, June 29, 2019, https://comicbook.com/dc/2019/06/29/superman-george-perez-new-52-dc-comics-they-made-me-not-care-corporate-comics.

39. Grant Morrison (w), Rags Morales (w, p), "Inside the Action" (afterward), *Action Comics* Vol. 2 #2 (Dec. '11), DC Comics, 25.

40. Sholly Fisch (w), ChrisCross (p, i), José Villarrubia (c), "Baby Steps," *Action Comics* Vol. 2 #5 (Mar. '12), DC Comics, 1–2, 5–6.

41. Grant Morrison (w), Rags Morales, Brad Walker (p), Rick Bryant, Bob McLeod (i), Brad Anderson, David Curiel (c), "Superman Meets...The Collector of Worlds," *Action Comics* Vol. 2 #8 (June '12), DC Comics, 7.

42. Morrison et al., *Action Comics* Vol. 2 #10.

43. Grant Morrison (w), Rian Hughes (a), "The Map of the Multiverse," *The Multiversity Guidebook* #1 (May '15), DC Comics, 26–7. Tree of Life (particularly as diagrammed by artist Paul Laffoley): Laura Hudson, "*Multiversity* Turns the DC Universe Into a Quantum-Theory Freakfest," *Wired*, Aug. 13, 2014, https://www.wired.com/2014/08/grant-morrison-multiversity-dc.

44. Greg Pak (p), Aaron Kuder (p, i), Arif Prianto (c), "Stormbreaker," *Action Comics* Vol. 2 #25 (Jan. '14), DC Comics, 2. Geoff Johns (w), John Romita, Jr. (p), Klaus Janson (i), Laura Martin (c), "The Men of Tomorrow," *Superman* Vol. 3 #32–8 (Aug. '14–Apr. '15), DC Comics.

45. Heidi MacDonald, "How much did The New 52 really help sales? These charts may hold the answer," *The Beat*, June 4, 2012, https://www.comicsbeat.com/how-much-did-the-new-52-really-help-sales-these-charts-may-hold-the-answer; Pak et al., *Superman* Vol. 3 #38.

46. Exposed: Gene Luen Yang (w), John Romita, Jr. (p), Klaus Janson, Scott Hanna (i), Dean White, Leonardo Olea, Blond (c), "Before Truth, Part 3," *Superman* Vol. 3 #43 (Oct. '15), DC Comics. Look, motorcycle, fight club: *Action Comics* Vol. 2 #41–9 (Aug. '15–Apr. '16); *Superman* Vol. 3 #41–49 (Aug. '15–Apr. '16); *Batman/Superman* #21–7 (Aug. '15–Feb. '16); *Superman/Wonder Woman* #18–26 (Aug. '15–Apr. '16).

47. Dan Jurgens (w), Lee Weeks (p), Scott Hanna (i), Brad Anderson (c), "Arrival, Part 1," *Superman: Lois and Clark* #1 (Dec. '15), DC Comics, 4.

48. Death: Peter Tomasi (w) Mikel Janín (p, i, c) Miguel Sepulveda (p, i), Jeromy Cox (c), "he Final

Days of Superman, Part 8: Do or Die," *Superman* Vol. 3 #52 (July '16), DC Comics, 21. Mxyzptlk: Dan Jurgens (w), Doug Mahnke (p), Jaime Mendoza (i), Wil Quintana (c), *Action Comics* #975–6; Peter Tomasi (w), Patrick Gleason (w, p), Mick Gray (i), John Kalisz (c), *Superman* Vol. 4 #18–9 (all May '17).

49. Marketing: Mark Hughes, "'Man Of Steel' A Solid But Mixed Revival Of Superman Franchise, *Forbes*, June 11, 2013, https://www.forbes.com/sites/markhughes/2013/06/11/man-of-steel-is-a-solid-revival-of-superman-franchise. Grossed: n.a., "Man of Steel," *Box Office Mojo*, https://www.boxofficemojo.com/release/rl4034037249.

50. *Man of Steel*, directed by Zack Snyder (2013; Burbank, CA: Warner Home Video, 2013), DVD.

51. Ali Plumb, "Empire's Man Of Steel Spoiler Podcast Special," *Empire*, June 17, 2013, https://www.empireonline.com/movies/news/empire-man-steel-spoiler-podcast-special.

52. *Batman v Superman: Dawn of Justice*, directed by Zack Snyder (2016; Burbank, CA: Warner Home Video, 2016), DVD.

53. *Justice League*, directed by Zack Snyder (2017; Burbank, CA: Warner Home Video, 2018), DVD.

54. Rob Cain, "Warner Bros. Faces A Possible $50M To $100M Loss On 'Justice League,'" *Forbes*, Nov. 20, 2017, https://www.forbes.com/sites/robcain/2017/11/20/warner-bros-faces-a-possible-50m-to-100m-loss-on-justice-league.

55. Copyright Act of 1976, § 201 & § 304.

56. Tye, *Superman*, 291. Also discussed in Fred Van Lente (w), Ryan Dunlavey (p, i), *Comic Book History of Comics* (June '12), IDW Publishing, 162.

57. Letter: *Larson v. Warner Bros. Entm't Inc.*, Case No. 2:04-cv-08776-ODW(RZx), at *9 (C.D. Cal. Apr. 18, 2013) (online), https://casetext.com/case/larson-v-warner-bros-entmt-inc-4. $277M: Alex Ben Block, "Which Superhero Earns $1.3 Billion a Year?" *Hollywood Reporter*, Nov. 13, 2014, https://www.hollywoodreporter.com/news/superhero-earns-13-billion-a-748281.

58. *Larson v. Warner Bros. Entm't Inc.*

59. *Larson v. Warner Bros. Entm't Inc.*, Case No. 2:04-cv-087400-ODW-RZx (9th Cir. Cal. Feb. 10, 2016). (online), https://cdn.ca9.uscourts.gov/datastore/memoranda/2016/02/10/13-56243.pdf.

60. Kurt Orzeck, "Warner Bros. Again Beats Superman IP Suit In 9th Circ.," *Law360*, Feb. 10, 2016, https://www.law360.com/articles/757942.

61. Dan Jurgens (w), Ian Churchill (p, i), Hi-Fi Design (c), "The New World, Part 1," *Action Comics* #977 (June '17), DC Comics, 7–10, 13–9, cover by Andy Kubert (p), Brad Anderson (i), Hi-Fi Design (c). Dan Jurgens (w), Carlo Barberi (p), Matt Santorelli (i), Hi-Fi Design (c), "The New World, Part 2," *Action Comics* #978 (June '17), 1–7, 10–7.

62. Eric J. Greenberg, "The Comic Book as Resistance," *The New York Jewish Week*, Nov. 28, 2003, 1.

63. Moon: Peter Tomasi (w), Patrick Gleason (w, p), Mick Gray (i), John Kalisz (c), "Son of Superman," *Superman* Vol. 4 #6 (Nov. '16), DC Comics,

12. Hovering: Tomasi et al., "Black Dawn, Chapter 1," *Superman* Vol. 4 #20, cover. Soaring: *ibid.*, 2–3.

64. Darker: Tomasi et al., "Son of Superman, Part One," *Superman* Vol. 4 #1 (Aug. '16), DC Comics. Belt: *Superman* Vol. 4 #20. Trunks: Brian Michael Bendis (w), Jim Lee (p), Scott Williams (i), Alex Sinclair (c), "The Truth," *Action Comics* #1000 (June '18).

65. Sales: Iñigo, "A Look at Superman's Sales," *CBSI*, Feb. 28, 2017, https://comicbookinvest. com/2017/02/28/look-supermans-sales. Bestseller: John Jackson Miller, "2018 Comic Book Sales to Comics Shops," *Comichron*, https:// www.comichron.com/monthlycomicssales/2018. html. *Superman*: Statista Research Department, "Best-selling comic books of all time worldwide as of February 2015," *Statistica*, Aug. 9, 2019, https:// www.statista.com/statistics/583041/best-selling-comic-books. *Comichron* estimates U.S. sales to be around 115 million copies, indicating a significantly lower global number: John Jackson Miller, "75 years of Superman—and a whole mountain of comics sold" (comments), Apr. 18, 2013, https://blog. comichron.com/2013/04/75-years-of-superman-and-whole-mountain.html.

66. E.g., George Gene Gustines, "Brian Michael Bendis Leaves Marvel for DC Comics," *New York Times*, Nov. 7, 2017, https://www.nytimes. com/2017/11/07/books/brian-michael-bendis-marvel-dc-comics.html; Graeme McMillan, "Comic Book Shake-Up: Superstar Brian Michael Bendis Leaves Marvel for DC," Nov. 7, 2017, *Hollywood Reporter*, https://www.hollywoodreporter. com/heat-vision/brian-michael-bendis-leaves-marvel-dc-1055635; David Betancourt, "Here's why it's a big deal that comics star Brian Michael Bendis jumped from Marvel to DC," Nov. 9, 2017, *Washington Post*, https://www.washingtonpost.com/ news/comic-riffs/wp/2017/11/09/heres-why-its-a-big-deal-that-comics-star-brian-michael-bendis-jumped-from-marvel-to-dc.

67. Clark: Brian Michael Bendis (w), Ivan Reis (p), Joe Prado, Oclair Albert (i), Alex Sinclair (c), "The Unity Saga, Part 5," *Superman* Vol. 5 #5 (Jan. '19), DC Comics, 18. Superman: Brian Michael Bendis (w), Ivan Reis (p), Joe Prado (i), Alex Sinclair (c), "Truth," *Superman* Vol. 5 #18 (Feb. '20), 8.

68. *Ibid.*, 20.

69. Torah: Michael Orbach, "Meet Brian Bendis, the man who killed Spiderman," *Jewish Telegraphic Agency*, FEB. 10, 2013, https://www. jta.org/2013/02/10/culture/meet-brian-bendis-the-man-who-killed-spiderman. Oy: Brian Michael Bendis (w), Mark Bagley (p), Art Thibert (i), Transparency Digital (c), "The Letter," *Ultimate Spider-Man* #41 (July '03), Marvel Comics, 22. Mishugas: Bendis et al., "Men of Influence," *Ultimate Spider-Man* #47 (Dec. '03), 14. Fakakta: Bendis (w), Bagley (p), Thibert (i), J.D. Smith (c), "Hollywood: Part 3," *Ultimate Spider-Man* #56 (June '04), 7. Shmendrick: Bendis (w), Bagley (p), Scott Hanna (i), J.D. Smith (c), "Warriors: Part 4," *Ultimate Spider-Man* #82, 5. Shavuos: Brian Michael

Bendis (w), Mike Deodato, Jr. (p, i), Frank Martin, Jr. (c), "The Road to Civil War II," *Invincible Iron Man* Vol. 3 #8 (June '16), 2. Jewish: Susana Polo, "The World's Finest: Batman's Tom King and Superman's Brian Bendis in conversation," *Polygon*, Sep. 25, 2018, https://www.polygon.com/ comics/2018/9/25/17895756/batman-tom-king-superman-brian-bendis-interview.

70. Sawyer: Brian Michael Bendis (w), Patrick Gleason (p, i), Alejandro Sanchez (c), "Seven Crises," *Young Justice* Vol. 3 #1 (Mar. '19), DC Comics, 14. Myand'r: Brian Michael Bendis (w), Brandon Peterson, Ivan Reis (p, i), Joe Prado (i), Alex Sinclair (c), "The Unity Saga: The House of El, Part 7," *Superman* Vol. 5 #13 (Sep. '19), 5. Starfire: Sholly Fisch (w), Lea Hernandez (p, i, c), "Oil's Well," *Teen Titans Go!* Vol. 2 #49 (Dec. '17), 5. White: *Superman: Leviathan Rising Special* #1 (July '19), 10.

71. Mark Hughes, "Exclusive: Bendis To Write Superman, Revive Jinxworld, And Oversee New Custom Imprint At DC Comics," *Forbes*, Feb. 1, 2018, https://www.forbes.com/sites/ markhughes/2018/02/01/exclusive-bendis-to-write-superman-revive-jinxworld-and-oversee-new-custom-imprint-at-dc-comics.

72. Reveal: Brian Michael Bendis (w), Kevin Maguire, Jason Fabok (p, i, pgs. 1–11, 14–22), Adam Hughes (p, i, pgs. 12–3, uncredited), Alex Sinclair (c), "Man of Steel, Part 4," *The Man of Steel* Vol. 2 #4 (Aug. '18), DC Comics 17. Moses: Vaneta Rogers, "BENDIS on MAN OF STEEL: SUPERMAN's Hope, Similarities to SPIDER-MAN and MOSES," *Newsarama*, May 18, 2018, https://www.newsarama. com/39992-bendis-on-man-of-steel-superman-s-hope-similarities-to-spider-man-and-moses.html. Refugees: Bendis et al., *Superman* Vol. 5 #13, 18–9.

73. Marc Andreyko (w), Kevin Maguire (p), Sean Parsons (i), Chris Sotomayor (c), "The House of El: United," *Supergirl* Vol. 7 #31 (Aug. '19), DC Comics, 6.

74. Brian Michael Bendis (w), Adam Hughes (p, i, c), Jason Fabok (p, i), Alex Sinclair (c), "Man of Steel, Part 5," *The Man of Steel* Vol. 2 #5 (Aug. '18), DC Comics, 8–11, et seq.

75. Brian Michael Bendis (w), Ivan Reis (p), Evan Shaner, Brandon Peterson (p,i), Joe Prado, Oclair Albert (i), Alex Sinclair (c), "The Unity Saga: The House of El—The Conclusion: Part Two," *Superman* Vol. 5 #15 (Nov. '19), DC Comics, 15.

76. Bendis et al., *Superman* Vol. 5 #6–10 (Feb.–June '19), DC Comics.

77. John Jackson Miller, "July 2018 Comic Book Sales to Comics Shops," *Comichron*, https:// www.comichron.com/monthlycomicssales/201 8/2018-07.html; "June 2019 Comic Book Sales to Comics Shops," https://www.comichron.com/mont hlycomicssales/2019/2019-06.html.

78. Publishing 2012: Jim Milliot, "Book Sales Dipped in 2013," *Publishers Weekly*, Jun. 27, 2014, https://www.publishersweekly.com/pw/by-topic/ industry-news/publisher-news/article/63131-book-sales-dipped-in-2013.html. Publishing 2018: "Book Publisher Revenue Estimated at $25.8 Billion in

2018," *Association of American Publishers*, June 21, 2019, https://publishers.org/news/book-publisher-revenue-estimated-at-25-8-billion-in-2018. Print vs. graphic novels: Dallas Middaugh, "What We Know About 2018 Graphic Novel Sales," Apr. 17, 2019, https://www.publishersweekly.com/pw/by-topic/industry-news/comics/article/79818-what-we-know-about-2018-graphic-novel-sales.html. Comics 2000: Miller, "Comic Book Sales by Year." Comics 2012, 2018: John Jackson Miller and Milton Griepp, "Comics and graphic novel sales hit new high in 2018," *Comichron*, https://www.comichron.com/yearlycomicssales/industrywide/2018-industrywide.html.

79. Jennifer De Guzman, "Literature's Deep Debt: Ten Literary Luminaries Who Love Comics," *Comics Alliance*, Dec. 14, 2015, https://comicsalliance.com/literary-authors-comic-fans-atwood-rushdie-chabon.

80. Rich Johnston, "The Second Golden Age Of Comics—Paul Levitz's Keynote Closing Speech To #C2Ccon2017," *Bleeding Cool*, Mar. 5, 2017, https://www.bleedingcool.com/2017/03/05/paul-levitzs-keynote-closing-speech-to-c2ccon2017.

81. Mark Evanier, "Kirby at 100," *News From Me* (blog), Aug. 28, 2017, https://www.newsfromme.com/2017/08/28/kirby-at-100; Sarah Whitten, "'Avengers: Endgame' is now the highest-grossing film of all time, dethroning 'Avatar,'" *CNBC*, https://www.cnbc.com/2019/07/21/avengers-endgame-is-the-highest-grossing-film-of-all-time.html.

82. U.S.: "Anti-Semitic Incidents Remained at Near-Historic Levels in 2018; Assaults Against Jews More Than Doubled," *ADL*, Apr. 30, 2019, https://www.adl.org/news/press-releases/anti-semitic-incidents-remained-at-near-historic-levels-in-2018-assaults. EU: Maayan Lubell, "Anti-Semitic attacks rise worldwide in 2018, led by U.S., west Europe: study," *Reuters*, May 1, 2019, https://www.reuters.com/article/us-israel-antisemitism/anti-semitic-attacks-rise-worldwide-in-2018-led-by-us-west-europe-study-idUSKCN1S73M1; Cnaan Liphshiz, "In Europe, synagogues are protected like fortresses. It took decades to get there," *Jewish Telegraphic Agency*, Oct. 29, 2018, https://jta.org/2018/10/29/global/europe-synagogues-protected-like-fortresses-took-decades-get. New York: Tom Winter, "Hate crimes surge in NYC, attacks on Jews almost double," *NBC News*, June 4, 2019, https://www.nbcnews.com/news/crime-courts/hate-crimes-surge-nyc-attacks-jews-nearly-double-n1013781.

83. Lubell, "Anti-Semitic attacks rise worldwide."

84. Shannon O'Leary, "Comics Retailers Hope To Rebound in 2018," *Publishers Weekly*, Feb. 09, 2018, https://www.publishersweekly.com/pw/by-topic/industry-news/comics/article/76031-comics-retailers-hope-to-rebound-in-2018.html.

85. Greg Pak (w), Mike Perkins (p, i), Paul Mounts (c, #1–4, 6), Gabe Eltaeb (c, #5, 7), Andy Troy (c, #9–12), "Enemy of the People," *Lois Lane* Vol. 2 #1–12 (Sep. '19–Sep. '20, DC Comics.

86. Nicole Maines, "I Am Proof That Bathrooms Should Be Gender-Free," *Time*, Nov. 2, 2015, https://time.com/4096413/houston-equal-rights-ordinance-nicole-maines.

87. Nellie Andreeva and Geoff Boucher, "'Superman & Lois' TV Series With Tyler Hoechlin & Elizabeth Tulloch In The Works At The CW," *Deadline*, https://deadline.com/2019/10/superman-lois-tv-series-tyler-hoechlin-elizabeth-tulloch-star-development-the-cw-1202770637.

88. Seyg-El first appeared in *World of Krypton* Vol. 2 #3. John Byrne (w), Mike Mignola (p), Rick Bryant (i), Petra Scotese (c), "History Lesson" (Feb. '88), DC Comics, 7. Uncle Zod: *Krypton*, Season 1, episode 9, "Hope," first broadcast May 16, 2018 by Syfy. Directed by Lukas Ettlin and written by Chad Fiveash, James Stoteraux and David Cob.

89. Andrew Paul, "Stan Lee And The Death Of A Jewish-American Idealism," *Forward*, Nov.13, 2018, https://forward.com/culture/414145/stan-lee-and-the-death-of-a-jewish-american-idealism.

90. *Exit Wounds*: "2008 Eisner Nominations Announced," *CBR.com*, Apr. 14, 2008, https://www.cbr.com/2008-eisner-nominations-announced. *The Property*: Annalee Newitz, "Here Are the Winners of the 2014 Eisner Awards," *Gizmodo*, July 26, 2014, https://io9.gizmodo.com/here-are-the-winners-of-the-2014-eisner-awards-1611453451. *The Realist*: James Whitbrook, "Here Are Your 2016 Eisner Award Winners," *Gizmodo*, July 26, 2016, https://io9.gizmodo.com/here-are-your-2016-eisner-award-winners-1784175893. *The Rabbi's Cat*: *The Beat*, "2006 Eisner Award Winners."

91. Jacob's Ladder: Tom King (w), Mitch Gerads (p, i, c), *Mister Miracle* Vol. 4 #7 (May '18), DC Comics, 15–6, 20. Oberon: King & Gerads, #5 (Feb.), 8.

92. Hanukkah: Geoff Johns, Grant Morrison, Greg Rucka, Mark Waid (w), Keith Giffen, Tom Derenick, Joe Prado (p), Jay Leisten, Rodney Ramos (i), David Baron (c), "The Most Wonderful Time of the Year," *52* #33 (Feb. '07), DC Comics, 10, 13. *Sefer Yetzirah*: "Hydrology Part 4: Estuary," *Batwoman* Vol. 2 # 4 (Feb. '12), 20–21. Kane is Bruce Wayne's maternal cousin, inadvertently (and so far unnoticed) making Batman Jewish.

93. Simcha Weinstein, *Up, Up, and Oy Vey*, 75, 78. Also in Fingeroth, *Disguised as Clark Kent: Jews, Comics, and the Creation of the Superhero* (New York: Continuum International Publishing Group Inc., 2007), 96–7 and Kaplan, *Krakow to Krypton*, 96. Jewish, Star of David: Karl Kesel (w), Stuart Immonen (p), Scott Koblish (i), Liquid! (c), "Remembrance of Things Past," *Fantastic Four* Vol. 3 #56 (Vol. 1 #485, Aug. '02), Marvel Comics, 19–20. bar mitzvah: Dan Slott (w), Kieron Dwyer (p, i), Laura Villari (c), "Last Hand," *The Thing* Vol. 2 #8 (Aug. '06), 15–8. Wedding: Dan Slott (w), Aaron Kuder (p, i), Marte Gracia, Erick Arciniega (c), "4-Minute Warning," *Fantastic Four* Vol. 6 #5 (Vol. 1 #650, Dec. '18).

94. First appearance and Oy: *Batman: The Animated Series*. Season 1, episode 7, "Joker's Favor," first broadcast Sept. 11, 1992 by Fox Kids. Directed by Boyd Kirkland and written by Paul Dini. Plotz:

Season 1, episode 47, "Harley and Ivy," first broadcast Sept. 18, 1993. Directed by Kirkland and written by Dini. Jewish: Paul Dini (w), Bruce Timm (p, i, c), "The Harley and the Ivy," *The Batman Adventures Holiday Special* #1 (Jan. '95), DC Comics, 14. Cashew: Paul Dini (w), Elsa Charretier (p, i), Hi-Fi Design (c), "A Very Harley Holiday!" *DC Rebirth Holiday Special* #1 (Dec. '16), DC Comics, 8. Sorkin: Aaron Couch, "The Story of Harley Quinn: How a '90s Cartoon Character Became an Icon," *Hollywood Reporter*, Aug. 5, 2016, https://www.hollywoodreporter.com/heat-vision/harley-quinn-history-917464. Popularity: Abraham Riesman, "The Harley Quinn Boom Is Just Getting Started," *Vulture*, Aug. 10, 2016, https://www.vulture.com/2016/08/harley-quinn-boom-suicide-squad.html. In the *Batman Adventures Holiday Special* she defines herself as Jewish. In *DC Rebirth* shew specifies her father is Jewish. In the animated series her mother is Jewish, making her fully Jewish by *Halacha* law: *Harley Quinn*. Season 1, episode 10, "Bensonhurst," first broadcast Jan. 31, 2020 by DC Universe. Directed by Cecilia Aranovich Hamilton, Colin Heck and Ben Jones and written by Laura Moran. Robbins: Arie Kaplan, "Kings of Comics: How Jews Transformed The Comic Book Industry Part III: The Bronze Age (1979—)," *Reform Judaism Magazine* 32, no. 3 (Spring 2004), http://reformjudaismmag.net/04spring/comics.shtml.

95. Arad: Dan Raviv, *Comic Wars: Marvel's Battle for Survival* (Sea Cliff: Levant Books, 2004); Geoff Boucher, "Avi Arad: From 'Blade' To 'Morbius,' Three Decades Of Mining Marvel," *Deadline*, Mar. 20, 2019, https://deadline.com/2019/03/avi-arad-marvel-blade-spider-man-morbius-toys-1202576569. Insisted: Raviv, *Comic Wars*, 222. Films: "Box Office History for Spider-Man Movies," *The Numbers*, accessed Oct. 22, 2019, https://www.the-numbers.com/movies/franchise/Spider-Man#tab=summary. Retail: Block, "Which Superhero Earns $1.3 Billion a Year?" Disney: Sarah Whitten, "Disney bought Marvel for $4 billion in 2009, a decade later it's made more than $18 billion at the global box office," *CNBC*, Jul. 22, 2019, https://www.cnbc.com/2019/07/21/disney-has-made-more-than-18-billion-from-marvel-films-since-2012.html; "The Top 150 Global Licensors," *License Global*, Feb. 04, 2020, https://www.licenseglobal.com/magazine-article/top-150-global-licensors-1.

96. Devin Leonard, "Calling all superheroes," *CNN Money*, May 23, 2007, https://money.cnn.com/magazines/fortune/fortune_archive/2007/05/28/100034246/index.htm. Maisel left in 2009 after helping arrange Marvel's sale to Disney.

97. N.a., "Zachary Levi loses work over being 'too Jewish,'" *Daily News*, Jan. 27, 2016, https://www.nydailynews.com/entertainment/gossip/confidential/zachary-levi-loses-work-jewish-article-1.2511750; Noah Lewin-Epstein, Yinon Cohen, "Ethnic origin and identity in the Jewish population of Israel," *Journal of Ethnic and Migration Studies* Volume 45, No. 11 (2018): 8. This equates roughly to 45% of the Jewish population, a figure supported by earlier studies like "Israel: The Sephardi-Ashkenazi Confrontation and Its Implications," *CIA Office of Near East-South Asia Analysis (NESA)*, Apr. 15, 1982 (redacted Jul. 17, 2007), pg. 1 (online), https://www.cia.gov/library/readingroom/docs/CIA-RDP06T00412R000200840001-6.pdf. Estimates vary widely between studies, primarily due to methods of classification. Many Israelis also have mixed ancestry, and the Israeli Central Bureau of Statistics (ICBS) only surveys a generation back.

98. Nicole Sperling, "Gal Gadot: 'Of course' Wonder Woman is a feminist," *Entertainment Weekly*, May 18, 2017, https://ew.com/movies/2017/05/18/gal-gadot-wonder-woman-feminist.

99. *Justice League*, 2018.

100. "From Superman to the Rabbi's Cat: Jewish Comics." Museum of Jewish Art and History (mahJ). Hôtel de Saint-Aignan, 71 rue du Temple, 75003 Paris. Oct. 17, 2007–Jan.27, 2008 (online), https://www.mahj.org/fr/programme/de-superman-au-chat-du-rabbin-15968. It continued on tour to the Jewish Historical Museum in Amsterdam, Mar. 7–June 8, 2008, where it was renamed *Superheroes and Schlemiels: Jewish Memory in Comic Strip Art*; the Jewish Museum Berlin, Apr. 30–Aug. 8, 2010, renamed *Heroes, Freaks, and Super-Rabbis: The Jewish Dimension of Comic Art*; and the Jewish Museum in Stockholm, Apr. 11–Nov. 13, 2011, as *Superheroes and Schlemiels* again. Tye, *Superman*, "A Matter of Faith" 65–80. Masha Leon, "Comic Book Celebs Discuss Comics and the Jews," *Forward*, Oct. 12, 2015, http://forward.com/the-assimilator/322457/comic-book-celebs-discuss-comics-and-the-jews. Jason Cohen, "Bendis Signals a Welcome Return to Superman's Jewish Roots," *CBR.com*, on Feb. 2, 2018, https://www.cbr.com/bendis-dc-superman-jewish-roots. Emily Gaudette, "Frank Miller Wants to Write a Jewish Superman Story Set in WWII," *Inverse*, Oct. 7, 2016, https://www.inverse.com/article/21925-is-superman-jewish-frank-miller-dark-knight-batman-new-york-comic-con. *The Simpsons*. Season 30, episode 18, "Bart vs. Itchy & Scratchy," first broadcast Mar. 24, 2019 by Fox. Directed by Chris Clements and Mike B. Anderson and written by Megan Amram.

101. Bush: The Reliable Source, "You cannot top George H.W. Bush's birthday socks," *Washington Post*, June 12, 2013, https://www.washingtonpost.com/news/reliable-source/wp/2013/06/12/you-cannot-top-george-h-w-bushs-birthday-socks. Obama statue: Karen Dalton-Beninato, "Obama, Lincoln and The Encouraging Double Ds," *HuffPost*, May 19, 2008 (updated Dec. 06, 2017), https://www.huffpost.com/entry/obama-lincoln-and-the-enc_b_101216?guccounter=1. Obama joke: n.a., "McCain, Obama trade jokes, not jabs at dinner," *NBC News*, Oct. 17, 2008, http://www.nbcnews.com/id/27234647/ns/politics-decision_08/t/-mccain-obama-trade-jokes-not-jabs-dinner/#.Xj14wmhKguV. Trudeau: Carly Ledbetter, "Justin Trudeau Dressed As Clark Kent For Halloween

And It Was Super, Man," *HuffPost*, Nov. 1, 2017, https://www.huffpost.com/entry/justin-trudeau-superman-clark-kent-halloween-costume_n_59f9cffde4b046017fb02df7. Trump: Josh Delk, "White House spokesman calls Trump a 'real-life Superman,'" *The Hill*, Jan. 20, 2018, https://thehill.com/blogs/blog-briefing-room/369930-white-house-spokesman-calls-trump-a-real-life-superman.

    102. Eury, *The Krypton Companion*, 232.

    103. Dani Di Placido, "DC Films Still Doesn't Know What To Do With Superman," *Forbes*, Nov. 27, 2019, https://www.forbes.com/sites/danidiplacido/2019/11/27/dc-films-still-doesnt-know-what-to-do-with-superman"; Nicole Sperling, "*Wonder Woman* director on creating a female—and feminine—superhero," June 02, 2017, https://ew.com/movies/2017/06/02/wonder-woman-patty-jenkins-interview. Diana getting stuck in the revolving door and stopping bullets in an alley.

Bibliography

Books

Andrae, Thomas, and Gordon, Mel. *Siegel and Shuster's Funnyman: The First Jewish Superhero, from the Creators of Superman.* Los Angeles: Feral House, 2010.

Chabon, Michael. *The Amazing Adventures of Kavalier & Clay.* New York: Random House, 2000.

Cople Jaher, Frederic. *The Jews and the Nation: Revolution, Emancipation, State Formation, and the Liberal Paradigm in America and France.* Princeton, NJ: Princeton University Press, 2009.

Engle, Gary. "What Makes Superman So Darned American?" In *Superman at Fifty: The Persistence of a Legend,* edited by Dennis Dooley, 79–87. Cleveland: Octavia Press, 1987.

Eury, Michael, ed. *The Krypton Companion.* Raleigh, NC: TwoMorrows Publishing, 2006.

Feiffer, Jules. *The Great Comic Book Heroes.* New York: Bonanza Books, 1965.

Fingeroth, Danny. *Disguised as Clark Kent: Jews, Comics, and the Creation of the Superhero.* New York: Continuum International Publishing Group Inc., 2007.

Freud, Sigmund. *Moses and Monotheism.* Translated by Katherine Jones. Mansfield Centre, CT: Martino Publishing, 2010.

Friedman, Lester D. *The Jewish Image in American Film.* New York: Citadel Press, 1987.

Hajdu, David. *The Ten-Cent Plague: The Great Comic-Book Scare and How It Changed America.* New York: Picador, 2008.

Kaplan, Arie. *From Krakow to Krypton: Jews and Comic Books.* Philadelphia: The Jewish Publication Society, 2008.

Levitz, Paul. *75 Years of DC Comics: The Art Of Modern Mythmaking.* Los Angeles: Taschen America, 2010.

Maggin, Eliot S. *Miracle Monday.* New York: Warner Books, 1981.

_____. *Superman: Last Son of Krypton.* New York: Warner Books, 1978.

Morrison, Grant. *Supergods: What Masked Vigilantes, Miraculous Mutants, and a Sun God from Smallville Can Teach Us About Being Human.* New York: Spiegel & Grau, 2011.

Ro, Ronin. *Tales to Astonish: Jack Kirby, Stan Lee, and the American Comic Book Revolution.* New York: Bloomsbury USA, 2004.

Simon, Joe, and Jim Simon. *The Comic Book Makers.* New York: Vanguard, 2003.

Tye, Larry. *Superman: The High-Flying History of America's Most Enduring Hero.* New York: Random House, 2013.

Van Lente, Fred, and Ryan Dunlavey. *Comic Book History of Comics.* San Diego: 2012.

Weinstein, Simcha. *Up, Up, and Oy Vey: How Jewish History, Culture and Values Shaped the Comic Book Superhero.* Baltimore: Leviathan Press, 2006.

Wertham, Fredrick. *Seduction of the Innocent.* New York: Rinehart & Company, 1954.

Newspapers, Magazines, Journals

Andrae, Thomas, Geoffrey Blum, and Gary Coddington. "Of Superman and Kids with Dreams: A Rare Interview with the Creators of Superman: Jerry Siegel & Joe Shuster." *Nemo, the Classic Comics Library* #2, August 1983.

Eco, Umberto. "The Myth of Superman." Translated by Natalie Chilton. *Diacritics* 2, no/ 1 (Spring 1972): 14–22.

Feiffer, Jules. "Jerry Siegel: The Minsk Theory of Krypton." *New York Times Magazine,* December 29, 1996.

Greenberg, Eric J. "Superman: A Jewish Hero." *Jerusalem Post,* May 1, 1996.

Kabler, John. "Up, Up, and Awa-a-y! The Rise of Superman, Inc." *Saturday Evening Post,* June 21, 1941. http://www.saturdayeveningpost.com/wp-content/uploads/satevepost/rise-of-superman.pdf.

Kaplan, Arie. "How the Jews Created the Comic Book Industry—Part I: The Golden Age (1933–1955)." *Reform Judaism Magazine,* Fall 2003. http://reformjudaismmag.net/03fall/comics.shtml.

_____. "How Jews Transformed the Comic Book Industry Part II: The Silver Age (1956–1978)." *Reform Judaism Magazine*, Winter 2003. http://www.reformjudaismmag.net/03winter/comics.shtml.

_____. "Kings of Comics: How Jews Transformed The Comic Book Industry Part III: The Bronze Age (1979–)." *Reform Judaism Magazine*, Spring 2004. http://www.reformjudaismmag.net/04spring/comics.shtml.

Leon, Masha. ""Superman at 75" Unmasks the Superhero as a Jew from the Planet Krypton." *Forward*, March 24, 2016. http://forward.com/articles/171301/superman-at-75-unmasks-the-superhero-as-a-jew-from.

Mietkiewicz, Henry. "Great Krypton! Superman was the Star's Ace Reporter." *Toronto Star*, April 26, 1992.

Siegel, Jerry. "Happy 45th Anniversary, Superman!" *Action Comics* #544, June 1983.

_____, and Joe Shuster. "How Superman Would End the War." *Look*, February 27, 1940.

Weisinger, Mort. "Here Comes Superman." *Coronet*, July 1946.

Websites and Blogs

Maggin, Elliot S. "Is Superman Jewish?" *Quora*, April 1, 2011. https://www.quora.com/Is-Superman-Jewish.

Sarna, Jonathan D., and Jonathan Golden. "The American Jewish Experience in the Twentieth Century: Antisemitism and Assimilation." National Humanities Center. Revised October 2000. http://nationalhumanitiescenter.org/tserve/twenty/tkeyinfo/jewishexp.htm.

Taylor, Stan. "Looking for the Awesome—3. Escape to New York." *The Kirby Effect: The Journal of the Jack Kirby Museum & Research Center*. December 12, 2015. http://kirbymuseum.org/blogs/effect/2015/12/.

Weiss, Michael. "Secret Identities: Jewish Comic Book Creators." *Negative Space*. Last modified June 13, 1995. https://owl.english.purdue.edu/owl/resource/717/05.

Film, Television, Radio

Donner, Richard, dir. *Superman*. 1978; Burbank, CA: Warner Home Video, 2006. DVD.

_____, dir. *Superman II: The Richard Donner Cut*. 1980/2006; Burbank, CA: Warner Home Video, 2006. DVD.

Kroopnick, Stephen, dir. *Comic Book Superheroes Unmasked*. Aired June 23, 2003. The History Channel. Online at https://www.youtube.com/watch?v=Ygx_rUJ3XaI.

Lester, Richard, dir. *Superman II*. 1980; Burbank, CA: Warner Home Video, 2006. DVD.

Maxwell, Robert. "The Hate Mongers' Organization." *The Adventures of Superman* (radio). Performed by Bud Collyer and Joan Alexander. Aired April 16–May 20, 1946. Broadcast syndication.

Meyer, Turi, and Al Septien, writers. *Smallville*. Season 9, episode 21, "Salvation." Directed by Greg Beeman, featuring Tom Welling, Allison Mack, and Erica Durance. Aired May 14, 2010. CW.

Singer, Brian, dir. *Superman Returns*. 2006; Burbank, CA: Warner Home Video, 2006. DVD.

Snyder, Zack, dir. *Batman vs. Superman: Dawn of Justice*. 2016; Burbank, CA: Warner Home Video, 2016. DVD.

Snyder, Zack, dir. *Man of Steel*. 2013; Burbank, CA: Warner Home Video, 2013. DVD.

Wall, Anthony, dir. *Superman: The Comic Strip Hero*. Aired April 18, 1981. BBC Four. Online at https://www.youtube.com/watch?v=eTUrFYU2e_I.

You Will Believe: The Cinematic Saga of Superman. 2006; Burbank, CA: Warner Home Video, 2006. DVD.

Other Documents

Siegel, Jerry. "Creation of a Superhero." Unpublished manuscript, 1979. Typed. Larry Tye Papers, Box 3, Folder 1, Rare Books & Manuscripts Library Collections, Butler Library, Columbia University, New York.

_____. "The Life and Times of Jerry Siegel." Unpublished manuscript, 1945. Typed. Larry Tye Papers, Box 3, Folder 1, Rare Books & Manuscripts Library Collections, Butler Library, Columbia University, New York.

Index

Numbers in **bold italics** indicate pages with illustrations

www.ingramcontent.com/pod-product-compliance
Lightning Source LLC
Chambersburg PA
CBHW081735270326
41932CB00020B/3278